LAW, PRACTICE AND CONDUCT FOR SOLICITORS

AUSTRALIA
Law Book Co.
Sydney

CANADA and USA
Carswell
Toronto

HONG KONG
Sweet & Maxwell Asia

NEW ZEALAND
Brookers
Wellington

SINGAPORE and MALAYSIA
Sweet & Maxwell Asia
Singapore and Kuala Lumpur

LAW, PRACTICE AND CONDUCT FOR SOLICITORS

Alan Paterson
Director of the Centre for Professional Legal Studies at Strathclyde University

Bruce Ritchie
Director of Professional Practice in the Law Society of Scotland

THOMSON

W. GREEN

Published in 2006 by
W. Green & Son Ltd
21 Alva Street
Edinburgh EH2 4PS

www.wgreen.thomson.com

Typeset by Interactive Sciences Limited, Gloucester
Printed and bound in Great Britain by MPG Books Ltd, Cornwall

No natural forests were destroyed to make this product;
only farmed timber was used and replanted

A CIP catalogue record for this book is available from
the British Library.

ISBN-10 0414 01439 1
ISBN-13 9780 414 01439 8

To our long-suffering families

Alison and Iona

Christopher, Rachel and Michael

FOREWORD

In the Oxford English Dictionary the word "professional" is defined as the declaration or vow made by a person entering an order or any solemn declaration or vow. It is also defined as a vocation, or calling especially one requiring advanced knowledge or training in some branch of learning or science specifically law, theology or medicine. Professionalism is defined as the body of qualities or features such as competence skill etc characteristic of a profession or professional. In the past some professionals actually took an oath. There is, or perhaps some would say was, some sort of moral aspect to being a professional. This is not just a question of standards of competence. Entry to a profession is generally regulated and there may be academic and professional examination and other assessment of standards both of knowledge and of integrity. Nowadays all professions are regulated by a professional body. As far as solicitors in Scotland are concerned that body is the Law Society of Scotland. In the future however, certain aspects of solicitors' conduct will be regulated elsewhere although it is likely that matters which relate strictly to professional conduct or misconduct will still be dealt with by the Law Society. Speaking as someone who is a partner (or should I say member) of a limited liability partnership of solicitors as well as being an academic and who is called upon to provide opinions on professional negligence I think I can say with some certainty that a solicitor nowadays will be extremely fortunate if he or she manages to get through professional life without his or her competence or indeed conduct being called in question at some point in time.

A great deal of a solicitor's time is now taken up with what might be regarded as back-covering exercises. Nowadays it is not enough to act in a competent fashion and in accordance with professional rules and standards. The solicitor's file itself must bear witness to this competence and compliance. A great many solicitors spend time confirming various instructions with clients at some length especially where some risk may be involved in a particular course of action. There are no up-to-date text books which deal fully with all aspects of professional duties and I therefore wholeheartedly welcome this new treatise on law, practice and conduct for solicitors. Professor Alan Paterson, although a full time academic, has wide experience in relation to legal practice and has been very closely involved with legal training for solicitors especially in the diploma in legal practice. He is the Director of the Centre for Professional Legal Studies at Strathclyde University and examiner in Professional Ethics for the Law Society of Scotland. Bruce Ritchie is the Director of Professional Practice in the Law Society of Scotland and over the years has had to deal with a multitude of questions and problems relating to ethics, standards and general professional conduct. Before he took up a position in the Law Society he was a practicing solicitor himself. I can think of no better people to undertake a work of this nature. No firm of solicitors should be without a copy of this book.

Professor Robert Rennie
School of Law
Glasgow University
July 2006

PREFACE

Forty years ago the practise of law/ legal practice in Scotland seemed so much simpler than today. Astonishing to recall, recruitment to the solicitor's branch of the profession was approaching a crisis with fewer than 50 entrants a year. Competition within the profession was strictly contained and the renaissance in Scottish private law was still in embryo. Even then, twenty years before the ethical principles of the profession were enshrined in the Codes of the Faculty of Advocates and the Law Society, the vision of a homogeneous profession with a solid consensus on ethical issues was nearer to an urban myth than a factual reality. Today we have nearly ten times the number of entrants, three times as many practitioners and a largely de-regulated legal market with the concomitant increase in competition and the ethical tensions which this engenders. Put together with the ever more demanding clientele of the consumer society which has insisted on a new professionalism from lawyers, weighted more overtly to the concerns of the client, and inevitably the study and exposition of the law and practise of lawyers becomes an ever more complex subject. A lawyer is a representative of clients, an officer of the court, a member of a firm and of a learned profession, as well as a public citizen. Often there are times when the duties which arise from occupying each of these roles will come in conflict. Indeed many of the most intransigent problems in professional ethics stem from such conflicting demands. Equally it is these conflicts which can and should make a Professional Ethics course one of the most stimulating—and thought-provoking—courses that a student takes while at university. For it is in this field that students and lawyers have to think about the conflicting responsibilities and obligations which they will face in their chosen career. It is not so much a "Conflict of Laws" as a "conflict of obligations"—but the need for a route map is just as strong in the latter as the former. Here the explosion in Scottish private law scholarship and a greater awareness of legal literature in the global market in the last twenty years has been of great assistance for it has underscored the realisation that the issues of personal and professional morality comprising professional ethics should not be examined in isolation from the substantive law (and the law of agency/fiduciary duty in particular) which underpins and provides the context for them.

This book sets out to provide a "route map" for practitioners and students trying to navigate their path through the moral, ethical and legal maze of legal practise in the twenty-first century, by articulating the conflicting obligations confronting lawyers in different contexts and discussing the options for balancing and resolving these conflicts. All authors stand on the shoulders of those who have gone before and our debt to the work of the Websters, Jane Ryder, and Smith and Barton will be obvious from the text. However, our debt to Henderson Begg's pathbreaking work on the *Law of Scotland relating to Law Agents (1883)* is immense. It is a testament to the scale of his achievement that it should have taken over 120 years for the next full length book to be written in the area, and even then our book is less comprehensive in its treatment of the substantive law relating to lawyers than his, because of our greater focus on issues of professional ethics. In a small jurisdiction authors constantly face the difficulty of having to resort to first principles, historical cases and developments in other countries. Our experience has been no different. The relative dearth of decided cases and critical writings on professional ethics in Scotland have encouraged us to extrapolate from the principles of fiduciary duty and the law of agency, and to draw on a wide range of scholarship from around the English speaking world on professional ethics.

Perhaps, inevitably, then this work has had a long gestation period, making the list of those to whom acknowledgement is due for help, support and tolerance, a long one. The origins of the book stem back to the compilation of the Professional Ethics materials for the Diploma in Legal Practice in the late 1980s by one of the authors with input from Jessica Burns and Kenneth Pritchard and others too numerous to mention. It is from these materials, which have been enhanced over the years with the invaluable assistance of the Law Society and the Scottish Solicitors Discipline Tribunal, that the book has been drawn. The book has benefited immensely from discussions over the years with students, colleagues and practitioners in several jurisdictions, with particular acknowledgement being due to Professor Michael Browde of the University of New Mexico, Professor Donald Nicolson of Strathclyde University, Peter Anderson, John Barton, Fiona Raitt and Sheriff William Holligan.

Thanks must also be given to a series of long-suffering and able research assistants (of whom Jan Spy was but the last) without whose help the materials and the book would never have seen the light of day. We would also like to acknowledge the efforts of the support team in the Professional Practice Department (Lisa Hamilton and Sharon McFarlane) and to thank Philip Yelland, the Director of the Client Relations Department of the Law Society for his unfailing support and encouragement with the project over the years. Our debt to the staff of Greens and to Neil McKinnon and Jill Hyslop the commissioning editors, in particular, for their sterling efforts to produce this work, will be obvious. Especial thanks are due to various copyright holders for permission to reproduce material in the book: the Law Society of Scotland, the Law Society of England and Wales, the Scottish Solicitors' Discipline Tribunal, W. Green, Levy and McRae solicitors, MacRoberts solicitors and Professor Robert Black.

Finally, authorship. The principal authors wish to express their profound gratitude to Leslie Cumming and to Ken Baddon who authored the basic text of chapters 9 and 16 respectively, and to Philip Yelland for his revisions to chapter 16. Whilst the principal authors contributed to every chapter, Professor Paterson was primarily responsible for chapters 1, 2, 3, 4, 5, 6, 8, 10 and 14 and Bruce Ritchie for chapters 11, 12, 13 and 15. We would like to thank all those who read and commented on different parts of the text, however, responsibility for any remaining errors must remain with the authors.

Edinburgh, August, 2006.

CONTENTS

Chapter 12—Duties to Third Parties

Chapter 13—Duties to Professional Colleagues

TABLE OF CASES

TABLE OF STATUTES

Statutes are arranged in alphabetical order under each year.

TABLE OF CODES, RULES AND STATUTORY INSTRUMENTS

TABLE OF DISCIPLINE TRIBUNAL DECISIONS
(REFERRED TO AS "DTD")

TABLE OF JOURNAL OF THE LAW SOCIETY OF SCOTLAND REPORTS

TABLE OF FREQUENTLY CITED BOOKS, ARTICLES AND REPORTS

R. Abel, *The Legal Profession in England and Wales.* (Blackwell, Oxford, 1988)

H. Begg, *A Treatise on the Law of Scotland Relating to Law Agents* (2nd edn, Bell and Bradfute, Edinburgh 1883)

R. Billins, *Solicitors' Duties and Liabilities* (Sweet & Maxwell, London, 1999)

R Black, "A Question of Confidence" (1982) J.L.S.S. 299

M. Blake and A. Ashworth, "Ethics and the Criminal Defence Lawyer" 7 (2004) *Legal Ethics* 167

A. Boon and J. Levin, *The Ethics and Conduct of Lawyers in England and Wales* (Hart Publishing, Oxford, 1999)

D Burleigh, "John Francis Bridgwood and Solicitors' Duty to Client and Court" (1989) 26 LSG 11

Clementi Report, *Report of the Review of the Regulatory Framework for Legal Services in England and Wales* (HMSO, London, 2004)

Cordery on *Solicitors* (9th edn) (Butterworths, London, 1995)

G.E. Dal Pont, *Lawyers Professional Responsibility in Australia and New Zealand* (LBC Information Services, Pyrmont, NSW, 2001)

W.G. Dickson, *A Treatise on the Law of Evidence in Scotland* (3rd edn) (Edinburgh, 1887)

R. Dingwall and P. Fenn, "A Respectable Profession" (1987) 7 *International Review of Law and Economics* 51

P. Finn, *Fiduciary Obligations* (The Law Book Co. Ltd, Sydney, 1977)

M. Freedman, *Lawyers' Ethics in an Adversary System* (Bobbs-Merrill, New York, 1975)

M. Freedman, *Understanding Lawyers' Ethics* (Matthew Bender, New York, 1990)

G. Gordon, *Criminal Law* (3rd edn, W Green, Edinburgh, 2001)

J.J. Gow, *The Mercantile and Industrial Law of Scotland* (W. Green, Edinburgh, 1964)

Greens Solicitors Professional Handbook, Part F Parliament House Book (published annually)

J. Griffiths-Baker, *Serving Two Masters* (Hart Publishing, Oxford, 2002)

D. Hayton (ed.), *Laws Future* (Hart Publishing, Oxford, 2000)

J. Ross Harper, *A Practitioner's Guide to the Criminal Courts* (Edinburgh, Law Society of Scotland, 1985)

C. Hollander and S. Salzebo, *Conflicts of Interest and Chinese Walls* (2nd edn) (Sweet & Maxwell, London, 2004)

W.H. Hurlburt, *The Self-Regulation of the Legal Profession in Canada and in England and Wales* (Alberta, Law Society of Alberta and Alberta Law Reform Institute, 2000)

D.A. Ipp, "Lawyers' Duties to the Court" 1998 (114) *Law Quarterly Review* 63

K. Kerner, *Specialism in Private Legal Practice* (CRU, Edinburgh, 1998)

David Luban, *Lawyers and Justice* (Princeton University Press, New Jersey 1988)

G. Maher, "Professional Privilege" 1990 J.L.S.S. 108

I. Macphail, *Evidence* (Law Society of Scotland, Edinburgh, 1987)

I. MacPhail, *Sheriff Court Practice* (W Green, 1998)

D. Nicolson and J. Webb, *Professional Legal Ethics: Critical Interrogations* (Oxford University Press, 2000)

Office of Fair Trading (OFT), *Competition in Professions* (OFT, London, 2001)

V. Ogston and A. Seager, "Legal Professional Privilege" 1987 J. Rev. 38

Ogus, *Regulation: Legal Form and Economic Theory* (Clarendon Press, Oxford, 1994)

A. Paterson, "Self-Regulation and the Future of the Profession" in Hayton (ed.) *Laws Future* (Hart Publishing, Oxford, 2000) 49

A. Paterson, "Professionalism and the Legal Services Market" 1996 *International Journal of the Legal Profession* 137

M. Proulx and D. Layton, *Ethics and Canadian Criminal Law* (Irwin Law Inc, Toronto, 2001)

F. Raitt, *Evidence* (3rd edn) (W. Green, Edinburgh, 2001)

R. Rennie, *Solicitors' Negligence* (Butterworths, Edinburgh, 1997)

F. Reynolds (17th edn) *Bowstead and Reynolds on Agency* (Sweet & Maxwell, 2001)

Y. Ross, *Ethics in Law* (Butterworths, Sydney, 2001)

R. Rotunda and J. Dzienkowski, *Professional Responsibility: A Student's Guide 2005/2006* (ABA, Chicago, 2005).

CHAPTER 1

STANDARDS

Social and Economic Context 1.01

Historically, regulation of the legal profession in Scotland, as in most other jurisdictions, lay in the hands of the courts who had admitted them to practice.[1] Although the supreme courts in many countries retain ultimate control[2] over key aspects of the regulation of the profession (e.g. admission, discipline and professional standard setting), they have long since delegated large aspects of de facto regulation to the profession itself.[3] This ushered in the era of "traditional" self-regulation which reached its height in the years between the 1930s and the 1980s. Since then, the criticism[4] of the restrictive practices associated with traditional self-regulation has led to an ongoing re-negotiation of the "regulatory bargain" implicit in professionalism to achieve a more favourable balance for society and the state between deregulation, self-regulation and independent regulation in the public interest.[5] The broad, multi-layered[6] regulatory framework which has emerged involves the courts, clients,[7] competition authorities, the Legal Services Ombudsmen, the Financial Services Authority, the Department of Trade and Industry,[8] the Immigration Services Commissioner and the Legal Aid Boards.

---

[1] See e.g. *Writers to the Signet v Graham* (1824) 3 S. 237.

[2] See s.56 of the Solicitors (Scotland) Act 1980.

[3] In part this came about as a result of resourcing issues. The courts had neither the staff, nor the time, nor the resources to regulate the profession adequately. This remains the case, and is a potential drawback with respect to those regulatory aspects that the courts have retained. Thus, the Lord President of the Court of Session plays a key role in scrutinising the Practice Rules passed by the Law Society, but has almost no infrastructure to assist him with this task.

[4] See e.g. D. Rhode, "Policing the Professional Monopoly" (1981) 34 *Stanford Law Review* 1, R. Abel, *The Legal Profession in England and Wales* (Blackwell, Oxford, 1988), Ogus, *Regulation: Legal Form and Economic Theory* (Clarendon Press, Oxford, 1994) at p.108, M. Seneviratne, *The Legal Profession: Regulation and the Consumer* (Sweet and Maxwell, London, 1999) at pp.28–9, H.W. Arthurs, "The Dead Parrot: Does Professional Self-Regulation Exhibit Vital Signs?" (1995) 33 *Alberta Law Review* 800, and W.H. Hurlburt, *The Self-Regulation of the Legal Profession in Canada and in England and Wales* (Law Society of Alberta and Alberta Law Reform Institute, Alberta, 2000).

[5] See A. Paterson, "Professionalism and the Legal Services Market", (1996) *International Journal of the Legal Profession* 137. Similarly, in 1997 the President of the GMC called for a new regulatory agreement between his profession, the state and society, to make self-regulation effective, D. Irvine, "The Performance of Doctors" (1997) 314 B.M.J. 1540.

[6] The bewildering array of existing regulators of the legal profession are set out in R. Baldwin, *Regulating Legal Services* (Lord Chancellor's Department, London, 1997).

[7] Clients are rarely thought of as regulators of the profession, but in their increasing ability (at least in the USA) to hold lawyers to account for breach of fiduciary duties, as well as breach of contract, delict, or tort, there can be little doubt that they count as stakeholders in the regulatory process.

[8] On insolvency matters.

The resulting model of self-regulation has been described variously by commentators as "coerced", "mandated", "modulated", "regulated" or "sanctioned",[9] reflecting the fact that self-regulation could better now be described as co-regulation.[10]

While such an approach has many supporters,[11] the solicitors' branch of the profession considers that it has led to them being over-regulated, whilst others point to gaps in the checks on self-regulation[12] and note that the different regulatory layers do not sit comfortably with each other. Thus it is unclear what the respective remits of the Office of Fair Trading and the Scottish Executive are with respect to competition policy and the Scottish legal profession following the passing of the Scotland Act 1998.[13] In England and Wales the "regulatory maze" caused by multiple regulators was one of the factors which lead to the *Report of the Review of the Regulatory Framework for Legal Services in England and Wales* (HMSO, London, 2004) otherwise known as the "Clementi Review" after its chairman, Sir David Clementi. The Review opted for a single, overarching, external regulator for providers of legal services, the Legal Services Board. This is now contained within the provisions of the Legal Services Bill 2006. The Scottish Executive has yet to indicate how they intend to respond to Clementi north of the border, nonetheless it is committed to a more intrusive, independent regulation of the "service" and conduct aspects of the legal profession, as can be seen from the terms of the Legal Profession and Legal Aid (Scotland) Bill 2006.

1.02 Regulating Conduct not Competence

Multiple regulators bring with them a multiplicity of overlapping standards. Interestingly, the great bulk of these standards relate to behaviour and conduct rather than competence or fitness to practice. Thus, despite the fact that entry to the solicitors' profession requires applicants to demonstrate their competence and that they are fit and proper persons to become solicitors, these

---

[9] See A. Paterson, "Self-Regulation and the Future of the Profession" in Hayton (ed.), *Laws Future* (Hart Publishing, Oxford, 2000) at p.49.

[10] At the transnational level also, the norm is multiple deontology and competing national and international regulators. However, there are centripetal forces which push towards fewer or even a single regulator for the legal services market, e.g. the regulatory challenges posed by MDPs or by new players in the legal services market attracted by the growth in conditional fees. In 1999, the President of the English Law Society made a pitch for the Society to be the single regulator for all legal services providers, one year after the President of the English Institute of Chartered Accountants had called for the establishment of a super watchdog to police the regulation of all the professions (Lawtel News Page 30/06/98). At the transnational level, as we have seen, the search is on for a uniform code to govern transnational legal practice akin to a new *lex mercatoria* (see Arthurs, 1999, *op. cit.*).

[11] E.g. A. Boon and J. Levin, *The Ethics and Conduct of Lawyers in England and Wales* (Hart Publishing, Oxford, 1999) p.66, Hurlburt, *op. cit.*, R. Dingwall and P. Fenn, "A Respectable Profession" (1987) 7 *International Review of Law and Economics* 51, D. Nicolson and J. Webb, *Professional Legal Ethics: Critical Interrogations* (Oxford University Press, 2000) p.219; A. Ogus, *Regulation, op. cit.*, Paterson, "Self-Regulation", *op. cit.*, J. Shapland, "Self-Regulation of the Professions", unpublished paper at ESRC Regulatory Policy Seminar Group conference, Strathclyde University 20–21 April 1995, and Seneviratne, *op. cit.* p.219.

[12] E.g. in relation to the education, admission and certification of lawyers.

[13] See *Competition in Professions* (OFT, London, 2001) fn.1 p.2 and paras 2.2–2.5 of the Report by the Research Working Group on the Legal Services Market in Scotland (Scottish Executive, Edinburgh, 2006).

statuses once achieved are rarely thereafter open to scrutiny.[14] In reality, the Law Society of Scotland has quite limited powers[15] to take action against solicitors who through accident, severe illness, substance abuse or even imprisonment, are no longer fit and proper persons to practise as solicitors.[16]

The Principal Standards   1.03

The predominant standards in the everyday lives of most UK lawyers emanate from: (1) the profession and its disciplinary bodies in the guise of standards for professional conduct and service, and (2) courts and clients in their use of contract law,[17] the laws of agency, fiduciary duty, delict and tort to enforce professional obligations. In practice, there is considerable overlap and interdependence between these standards. In this book, therefore, the rules of professional conduct will be considered in juxtaposition with the substantive law which provides the context and framework for legal practice as well as the basis for many of the rules themselves.

The Standards Compared   1.04

If the key standards for lawyers today consist of professional conduct, service and professional negligence, how do they relate to one another?

The test for professional misconduct[18] can be summarised as:

> "behaviour which would be regarded by competent and reputable solicitors as serious and reprehensible"

Unsatisfactory professional conduct[19] is defined as:

> "Conduct by a Solicitor which does not amount to professional misconduct but which involves a failure to meet the standard of conduct observed by competent solicitors of good repute."

---

[14] In 1993, however, Continuing Professional Development was made mandatory for all solicitors in Scotland. See Solicitors (Scotland) (Continuing Professional Development) Regulations. Persistent failure to complete the requisite number of hours may result in a finding of professional misconduct (see para.1.29).

[15] Its limited powers are contained in: (1) s.46 Solicitors (Scotland) Act 1980 which allows the Society to take over the client account of a sole practitioner who has become so debilitated through accident or illness that he/she is incapable of managing their client account, and (2) s.18 of the Solicitors (Scotland) Act 1980 which allows the Society to suspend the practising certificate of solicitors who are detained in a mental hospital, have a curator bonis appointed to their estate, are sequestrated, grant a trust deed for creditors or have a judicial factor appointed to their estate.

[16] Contrast Ontario where ss.37–40 of the Law Society Act (R.S.O. 1990 as amended) allows the regulatory body (the Law Society of Upper Canada) to carry out an investigation involving a medical or psychological examination of a lawyer to see if they are incapacitated "by reason of physical or mental illness, other infirmity or addiction to or excessive use of alcohol or drugs".

[17] Including the Unfair Contract Terms Act 1977 and the Unfair Terms in Consumer Contracts Regulations 1999.

[18] See para.1.05 below.

[19] See para.1.25 below. In NSW and Victoria "unsatisfactory conduct" means conduct that falls short of the standard of competence and diligence that a member of the public is entitled to expect of a reasonably competent legal practitioner. See s.127(2) Legal Profession Act 1987 and s.137 Legal Practice Act 1996.

Or more recently[20] as:

> "professional conduct which is not of the standard which could reason-
> ably be expected of a competent and reputable solicitor but which does
> not amount to professional misconduct and which does not comprise
> merely inadequate professional services."

Inadequate Professional Services[21] consists of:

> "Professional services which are not in any respect of the quality which
> could reasonably be expected of a competent solicitor."

While Negligence[22] is:

> "A failure to meet the standard of care of the reasonably competent
> solicitor."

As can be seen, these tests are fairly similar and somewhat opaque. On their
own they tell us very little. Each requires further amplification if it is to serve
as a consistent basis to guide the conduct of practitioners or the decisions of
disciplinary authorities. Each refers to the objective standards of the "competent solicitor". Perhaps, inevitably, therefore there is considerable scope for
overlap between the competing standards.

While professional misconduct and unsatisfactory conduct cannot overlap
by definition,[23] it is possible for a solicitor's behaviour to fall foul of three of
the four standards (e.g. misconduct, IPS and negligence or unsatisfactory
conduct, IPS and negligence). The overlap between misconduct and negligence was the first to be established.[24] IPS and negligence were conceded to
overlap at the birth of the former in 1988, where the act clearly envisages that
behaviour which leads to a finding of IPS may also amount to negligence
since it contains provisions to prevent double jeopardy from operating in such
a case.[25] It was not until 1993 that the Scottish Solicitors' Discipline Tribunal
established that the Solicitors (Scotland) Act 1980 (as amended) also
envisages that the same behaviour can give rise to both IPS and misconduct.[26]

---

[20] cl.34 of the Legal Profession and Legal Aid (Scotland) Bill 2006.

[21] s.65 Solicitors (Scotland) Act 1980. See also para.2.27 below. With minor variations this
definition is retained in the Legal Profession and Legal Aid Scotland Bill 2006.

[22] See para.1.35 below. There is considerable overlap between professional negligence and
breach of fiduciary duty. See para.1.36 below.

[23] In Scotland at least. In some Australian jurisdictions e.g. NSW, repeated instances of
unprofessional or unsatisfactory conduct can amount to professional misconduct and this is
possibly also the case in Scotland.

[24] In *E. v T.*, 1949 S.L.T. 411 where Lord President Cooper concluded, "there is negligence and
negligence; and I am certainly not prepared to affirm the proposition that according to Scots law
and practice professional negligence cannot amount to professional misconduct." This parallels
the position in England and Australia where it has been held that "mere negligence" cannot be
misconduct but may be unsatisfactory or unprofessional conduct but "gross negligence" or
recklessness may amount to misconduct. See G. Dal Pont, *Lawyers' Professional Responsibility
in Australia and New Zealand* (2nd edn) LBC Information Services, Sydney, 2001 at p.586.

[25] s.56A Solicitors (Scotland) Act 1980.

[26] In *Carpenter*, 1993 J.L.S.S. 117. As the Tribunal noted "The essential feature of the
provisions of s.53A is to enable the tribunal to make orders for the benefit of [the] client without
requiring the client to take a civil action in Court and the whole purpose of section 53A would

Professional Conduct

In regulatory terms, conduct ranges along a continuum from aspirational conduct at one end through good practice, acceptable conduct, unsatisfactory conduct and finally professional misconduct at the other. However, disciplinary measures are restricted to the last two. Historically, activities warranting a finding of professional misconduct have ranged from embezzlement of client funds[27] to failing to register deeds timeously.[28] In recent years the conduct which has come most frequently before the Discipline Tribunal concerns failure to reply to the Law Society, fellow agents[29] and/or clients, breaches of the accounts rules, or misleading the Law Society and/or other parties.[30] Unlike a number of Commonwealth jurisdictions,[31] there has never been an attempt in Scotland to enshrine the definition for "professional misconduct" in a statute. It has been left to a dialogue, reminiscent of a stately dance, between the courts and the discipline tribunals as to who is best suited to the task. In the nineteenth and early twentieth century the Scottish courts took the lead, latterly describing misconduct as behaviour which was dishonourable, improperly motivated or criminal.[32] However, by 1949 the Lord President (Cooper)[33] was to be found observing:

"I shall not attempt to define professional misconduct. But if the statutory tribunal, composed as it always is of professional men of the highest repute and competence, stigmatise a course of professional conduct as misconduct, it seems to me that only strong grounds would justify this court in condoning as innocent that which the Committee have condemned as guilty."

This self-denying ordinance by the ultimate regulator did not last beyond 1984 when Lord President Emslie laid down the test which is followed today both by the Law Society and the Discipline Tribunal. In a case which involved the senior and junior partners of a firm being charged with misconduct in failing to adhere to the solicitors accounts rules, the court quashed the findings of misconduct by the Tribunal against the junior partners on the grounds that they had been excluded from partnership meetings or anything to do with the accounts, and therefore had been unable to prevent the breaches of the rules. Lord President Emslie in absolving the junior partners, observed[34]:

"There are certain standards of conduct to be expected of competent and reputable solicitors. A departure from these standards which would be regarded by competent and reputable solicitors as serious and reprehensible may properly be categorised as professional misconduct. Whether

---

be defeated if it were to be maintained that the tribunal was unable to exercise these powers if professional misconduct was established."

[27] DTD 489/80.

[28] DTD *Goldie* 10/12/97.

[29] See DTD *MacDonald* 18/05/04 where the Tribunal pointed out that it had made it clear on a number of occasions that failure to respond to fellow agents and to the Law Society amounts to professional misconduct.

[30] Scottish Solicitors' Discipline Tribunal Annual Report 2003/2004.

[31] E.g. Ontario, New South Wales, Victoria.

[32] See e.g. *X Insurance Company Ltd v A & B*, 1936 S.L.T. 188.

[33] *E. v T.*, 1949 S.L.T. 411.

[34] *Sharp v Council of the Law Society*, 1984 S.C. 129.

or not the conduct complained of is a breach of rules or some other actings or omissions the same question falls to be asked and answered and in every case it will be essential to consider the whole circumstances and the degree of culpability which ought properly to be attached to the individual against whom the complaint is made."

Although Lord Emslie did not expressly refer to it, this passage resembles in some respects an early English decision in the Court of Appeal on the meaning of misconduct when applied to a doctor, which has been followed in England and the Commonwealth[35] in relation to lawyers. There, Lord Justice Lopes remarked[36]:

"if [a practitioner] in the pursuit of his profession has done something with regard to it which would reasonably be regarded as disgraceful or dishonourable by his professional brethren of good repute and competency, then it is open to the Disciplinary Committee to say that he had been guilty of professional misconduct."

Whether Lord Emslie intended "serious and reprehensible" conduct to be seen as significantly different from "disgraceful and dishonourable" and whether he intended his words to be treated as though they were in a statute, the fact remains that his dictum in *Sharp* is now followed almost like a mantra.[37]

1.06 Professional Misconduct Elaborated

The second part of the *Sharp* dictum indicates that in every case it is necessary to look at the whole circumstances and the degree of culpability of the individual lawyer concerned. It follows that the misconduct of one member of the firm is looked at independently of other lawyers in the firm or the firm itself, even if the partners have held a partnership meeting to agree on the course of conduct.[38] Looking at all the circumstances can entail looking not just at each charge in the case in turn, but also at some or all of the charges *in cumulo*.[39] Sometimes each charge will justify a finding of misconduct, in other cases, while each charge will not sustain such a finding, the aggregate of the charges can amount to misconduct. However, in such cases the Discipline

---

[35] And indeed in Scotland, as the Report of the Clerk to the Discipline Tribunal revealed in 1979/80.

[36] *Allison v General Council of Medical Education and Registration* [1884] 1 Q.B. 750.

[37] This is unfortunate since there is a risk of the test ossifying rather than evolving. In Australia the High Court usefully elaborated on the *Allison* test in *Kennedy v Council of the Incorporated Law Institute of New South Wales* (1939) 13 A.L.J. 563 where Rich J. commented that "misconduct relating to a solicitor . . . need not amount to an offence under the law. It was enough that it amounted to grave impropriety affecting his professional character and was indicative of a failure either to understand or to practise the precepts of honesty or fair dealing in relation to the courts, his clients or the public."

[38] Although a firm can be guilty of a conduct complaint in Victoria (see Legal Practice Act 1996, s.137) the Scottish legislation and the Law Society's practice rules and guidelines clearly do not envisage firmwide responsibility for misconduct despite the possibility of a partnership being convicted of a criminal offence. A further problem stems from the difficulties which Scots law continues to have in attributing *mens rea* to non-natural persons such as partnerships or companies. See e.g. *Transco Plc v HMA*, 2004 S.L.T. 41.

[39] Provided there is an alternative averment of professional misconduct *in cumulo*.

Tribunal has indicated that "by implication, there requires to be some connection or *eiusdem generis* relationship before such charges can be taken together."[40]

If the first leg of the *Sharp* test leaves disciplinary decision-makers with a very wide degree of latitude, the second leg broadens that scope for flexibility even further. In short, as it stands, the test for misconduct in Scotland is characterized by a lack of transparency and a correspondingly large scope for discretion. It follows that if disciplinary decision-makers, lay[41] or legal, are to achieve consistency in this area there is a strong need for authoritative guidance which elaborates on the *Sharp* test.

Guidance on the *Sharp* Test: The Role of Intuition 1.07

Sharp was decided in the 1980s in an era when there were relatively few practice rules, no practice guidelines and no code of conduct. The notion of a tacit consensus amongst the profession on ethical issues had not come under a sustained attack, at least in Scotland, and many still opposed the introduction of a code, as being unnecessary and counter-productive[42] in their reliance on rules and principles rather than the intuitive notions of good practice which had sustained the profession throughout the fifty years of traditional professionalism from the early 1930s.[43] Even some of those who doubted the extent of the tacit consensus argued against a code on the grounds that "it would show the cowboys in the profession how close to the wind they could sail". Leaving aside the mixed metaphor, this was a curious argument for lawyers to support, since they would be the first to criticise any government which chose not to set out the rules of criminal law for similar reasons, as being contrary to the rule of law and democratic freedom.[44]

Barely five years after *Sharp* the Code of Conduct for Scottish Solicitors was promulgated by the Law Society of Scotland.[45] Since then, professional ethics has grown ever more important and ever more complex in the face of a sustained campaign by the government and the consumer movement to remove many of the anti-competitive restrictive practices which the traditional concept of professionalism enshrined.[46] In today's competitive and entrepreneurial environment, professional ethics and a commitment to the core values are the forces which hold the ring between the solicitor's self-interest, the client's interest and the public interest. Further, whatever their merits in the past as guides to ethical conduct, neither intuition nor common sense now offer a reliable guide to ethical conduct in this new challenging environment.

---

[40] 1996 Annual Report of the Scottish Solicitors Discipline Tribunal at p.6. See also Smith and Barton, para.5.02.

[41] Precisely what guidance the tests for misconduct or unsatisfactory conduct offer to lay members of client relations committees is somewhat unclear, since each places a major emphasis on the perceptions and standards of the competent and reputable solicitor.

[42] See e.g. A. Phillips, *Professional Ethics* (Butterworths, 1990). Yet the American legal profession had had an ethical code since the early part of the twentieth century.

[43] See A. Paterson, "Professionalism and the Legal Services Market" 1996 *International Journal of the Legal Profession* 137.

[44] See A. Paterson, Review, 1990 S.L.T. (News) 333.

[45] It was based on the 1988 Code of Conduct for lawyers in the European Community which had been drafted by the CCBE (Conseil des Barreaux de la Communaute Europeenne). The Faculty of Advocates published its Guide to the Professional Conduct of Advocates in 1988.

[46] See A. Paterson, *op. cit.* 1996 and Research Working Group Report, *op. cit.*

While certain issues in professional ethics, for example those touching on honesty, may appear intuitive, there are many ethical questions today where field-testing with successive generations of students reveals that the answer is not intuitively obvious, or where the common sense answer is not that which prevails in professional ethics in Scotland. These include questions such as: the extent of the duty (if any) to blow the whistle on unethical fellow practitioners; whether harm to the client is a necessary part of a finding of misconduct; whether it is permissible to have sex with clients; whether one can circulate all the flats in a local authority district claiming to be a specialist in Housing law, or advertise one's services on beer mats; whether one can breach client confidentiality in order to enforce one's fee; whether a client can give informed consent to a solicitor acting in a situation where there is a conflict of interest; when one can act against a former client on behalf of a new client; whether solicitors can charge a fee and take a commission for the same transaction; the extent of a solicitor's obligations to the other side; and whether one can indirectly mislead the court. It follows, therefore, that intuition or common sense is not a reliable guide in the field of professional misconduct

1.08 Guidance on the *Sharp* Test: The Role of the Court or the Tribunal

The foregoing simply underscores the need for guidance in relation to the test for misconduct amongst Scottish solicitors if consistency is to be achieved. If intuition and common sense are not always to be trusted, where should we look for authoritative guidance? Ultimately the Court of Session, but the dearth of appeals to the court coupled with its frequent preference to leave the application of the test to the Discipline Tribunal,[47] means that in practice the precedents established by the Tribunal are the most obvious source of guidance in this field. They may be the most obvious, however, despite the publication of summarised versions of the most important Tribunal cases between 1961 and 1994.[48] It is still relatively uncommon for these decisions to be cited to Client Relations Committees and other disciplinary committees of the Law Society when deciding conduct cases. However, since Tribunal decisions reflect the social and professional opinions of the day, which may change over time, older decisions of the Tribunal should be cited with the caveat that professional opinions may have changed.

1.09 Guidance on the *Sharp* Test: The Role of the Law Society

The decisions of the Law Society on conduct cases might seem the next best option, however, since these are not published, and the Society has no powers to make findings of misconduct but can only recommend prosecution before the Tribunal, these have not proved a fruitful source of guidance

---

[47] This may change following the Privy Council decision of *Ghosh v G.M.C.* [2001] 1 W.L.R. 1915 which established that the appeal court has only to view the Tribunal Decision in the light of the whole circumstances and the expertise of the Tribunal. The Inner House in *McMahon v Council of the Law Society*, 2002 S.L.T. 363 at p.366K appeared to imply that the court would continue to rely heavily on the expertise of the Tribunal.

[48] I. Smith and J. Barton, *Procedures and Decisions of the Scottish Solicitors' Discipline Tribunal* (T & T Clark, Edinburgh, 1995).

either.[49] However, the Council continues to make a very significant contribution to the articulation of conduct standards in a range of ways e.g. practice rules, codes of conduct, practice guidelines, or guidance from the Professional Practice Committee or its secretariat.

Practice Rules relating to the conduct and discipline of solicitors have a long **1.09.01** pedigree, stemming back to the establishment of the Law Society in 1950, although the power to make such rules (which must be approved by the Lord President of the Court of Session) is now contained in Solicitors (Scotland) Act 1980.[50] It is established that breach of such rules may be professional misconduct,[51] however, it has also been established by the Inner House that the statute means just that. Thus, the breach of even the most central or sacrosanct rule is *never* automatically misconduct, it only *may* be misconduct.[52] The Discipline Tribunal has a discretion in every case as to whether the breach of a practice rule, however flagrant, is misconduct.

Codes of Conduct have a more recent provenance. The 1989 Code emanated **1.09.02** from the work of the CCBE. As its introduction makes clear, the code is a "statement of the basic values and principles which form the foundation of the solicitor profession. It is not intended to be an exhaustive list of all the detailed practice rules (written or unwritten) and detailed obligations of solicitors, but it is the foundation of those rules and may be referred to for guidance in assessing whether or not a solicitor's conduct meets the standard required of a member of the profession." This leads to the somewhat curious position that adherence to the code is not mandatory for solicitors[53] but a breach of them may nonetheless be relevant to a finding of misconduct or unsatisfactory conduct. Whilst this is confusing, it is important to recognise that the Code of Conduct was not an attempt to codify the common law or unwritten rules of professional conduct. This is clear from the introduction to the code and from the decision of the Inner House in *Matthew petitioner*,[54] where the court expressly rejected the suggestion that the code be treated like a practice or discipline rule passed under s.34 of the 1980 Act, adding, "The Code was a document designed . . . for guidance in assessing whether or not a solicitor's conduct met the standard required of a member of the profession . . . [It] cannot easily be read as stating a general proposition which requires enquiry

---

[49] That said, the Council's decisions on what constitutes unsatisfactory conduct, or professional misconduct which does not merit prosecution, could form an instructive database if they were to become available.

[50] s.34. The practice rules which are currently in force can be found in *The Solicitor's Professional Handbook* which is published annually by W. Green & Son, and Division F of the Parliament House Book of which it is an offprint.

[51] s.34(4).

[52] See *Sharp v Council of the Law Society*, 1984 S.L.T. 313 and *Council of the Law Society of Scotland v J*, 1991 S.L.T. 662.

[53] Although, until 2002 solicitor advocates were required under the Code of Conduct (Scotland) Rules 1992 to comply with the provisions of the Code of Conduct and the Supplementary Code of Conduct for solicitor advocates. In January 2003, the Council determined that on its proper construction the code extended to cover the actings of all solicitors on the Roll, not just those with a current practising certificate (2003 J.L.S.S. January at p.9). In 2004, a mandatory Code of Conduct which covers much the same ground as the Scottish Code was promulgated for immigration solicitors.

[54] Unreported Outer House opinion 17.12.97 in a judicial review of a Discipline Tribunal decision.

into the circumstances on every occasion, to see whether there is perhaps a ground for an exception to the prohibition." What mattered was not whether there had been a breach of the code, but whether in the Tribunal's professional judgement following the test established in *Sharp*, professional misconduct had been established. It follows that the growing trend for the Society and its fiscals to rely on provisions in the code rather than precedents of the Discipline Tribunal when framing complaints or prosecuting cases before the Tribunal is one that should be resisted. Finally, the Code of Conduct for Criminal Work,[55] is even more aspirational than the ordinary code.[56] However, breach of it, too, may be taken into account in establishing misconduct or unsatisfactory conduct.[57]

1.09.03 Practice Guidelines, which are promulgated by the Society's Professional Practice Committee, are often quite detailed in nature. They are little more than guides to good practice, nevertheless, their breach also may be taken into account in a conduct complaint. In the past, formal guidance from the committee appeared as announcements which were reported in the Journal of the Law Society, or in the Society's annual report. In recent years, they have appeared as guidelines at the back of the Solicitors Professional Handbook. They are all now contained in the members' information section of the Society's website.[58] Practical guidance from the secretariat to the committee is available on a confidential basis, which provides a considerable measure of protection for perplexed solicitors provided the facts set out to the secretariat are complete and the guidance has been adhered to.

1.09.04 Discretion and the Rule of Law. As we have seen, the written guidance on conduct matters which emanates from the Society varies in its bindingness on the profession. However, disconcertingly, breach of even the strictest practice rule is never automatically misconduct.[59] Instead, breach of the practice rule only *may* amount to professional misconduct.[60] Yet, the breach of the most aspirational practice guideline or of the spirit, of the letter, of an aspirational code provision *may* also be relevant to a conduct finding. This situation is unsatisfactory from the perspective of consistency or the rule of law, since it leaves Client Relations Committees with a very wide measure of discretion in every case.[61] This underlines the need for authoritative guidance from the Discipline Tribunal.

---

[55] See Appendix 2. It was reissued in 2001.

[56] This was the choice of the Law Society, although the Scottish Legal Aid Board requires practitioners who are registered with them to do criminal legal aid to adhere to the Code.

[57] The President in his foreword to the new editions of the Codes in 2002 notes that "a departure from the standards set in the Codes would have to be justified by reference to exceptional circumstances in the particular case".

[58] *www.lawscot.org.uk.*

[59] By contrast, the American Bar Association's Model Rule 8.4 indicates that the knowing breach of the Model Rules constitutes misconduct. Similarly, in Victoria and New South Wales wilful breach of the practice rules constitute misconduct (s.127 Legal Profession Act 1987 and s.137 Legal Practice Act 1996).

[60] This flows directly from the wording of the Solicitors' Scotland Act 1980 (e.g. s.34(4)).

[61] Charles Wolfram in *Modern Legal Ethics* (West Publishing, St Paul, 1986) at p.87 points to similar concerns in relation to the vagueness of some of the American Codes or ethical rules. The resulting discretion opens the way to bias in the application of the rules (e.g. picking on lawyers who represent unpopular clients) and dilutes procedural safeguards.

Guidance on the *Sharp* Test: The Role of Expert Witnesses   **1.10**

The wording of the *Sharp* test with its emphasis on the competent and reputable solicitor and what he/she would regard as "serious and reprehensible", might suggest that, as in professional negligence cases, it would competent to lead expert members of the profession before the Tribunal to provide guidance on the views of the typical or hypothetically reputable solicitor. However, in a case in 1989[62] when an attempt was made to lead evidence to the Tribunal from a former President of the Law Society as an expert witness on ethical considerations, the Tribunal declined to hear his evidence. Their argument was that, at least in standard areas of practice, the members of the Tribunal could be relied on to have the necessary expertise. The Tribunal concluded: "The duty is clearly on the members of this Tribunal to formulate their opinion on the standards of conduct within the profession. The tribunal therefore ordinarily discourages parties [from leading] the evidence of individual practitioners, however experienced they may be, to express their personal opinion regarding the acceptability of a particular course of conduct." If this rationale is adhered to, it would seem that the Tribunal will be equally reluctant to hear evidence from experienced solicitors as to the common practice of the profession.[63]

Applying the *Sharp* Test: The Meaning of "Culpability"   **1.11**

It seems, therefore, that we have to revert to the views of the Discipline Tribunal to give us authoritative guidance on the application of the *Sharp* test. The first point to note is that in assessing whether a course of action amounts to professional misconduct it is not just a question of whether a practice rule or a common law standard has been breached, but also the degree of culpability of the solicitor's acting in all the circumstances. What does "culpability" mean in this context? Although it has been established[64] that for the purposes of the European Convention on Human Rights, professional disciplinary proceedings in the UK are civil in nature,[65] in the minds of many solicitors professional misconduct is a quasi-criminal jurisdiction, perhaps because of the severity of the sanctions which can flow from conviction. Certainly, misconduct must be proved beyond reasonable doubt.[66] It follows that "culpable" should be treated analogously to its use in the criminal law, that is a form of moral blameworthiness which is recognised by the law. As Lord President Emslie observed in *Sharp*, any failure in conduct has to be judged by the "gravity of the failure and consideration of the whole circumstances in which the failure occurred, including the part played by the individual solicitor in question".

---

[62] DTD 761/89.

[63] In any case the Tribunal has asserted that even if a practice is followed by a number of solicitors, it does not in itself sanction conduct which viewed objectively, falls below the standards to be expected of reputable solicitors. DTD *Anderson & Others* 1001/99.

[64] See *R. v Securities and Futures Authority Ltd Ex p. Fleurose* [2001] E.W.H.C. (Admin) 292.

[65] With the result that the privileges against self-incrimination and the right to silence do not apply.

[66] See *S. v B.*, unreported decision of the Court of Session 25/2/81 in Smith and Barton, *op. cit.* 15.

Although it has been little discussed in the context of professional discipline, at least in Scotland, misconduct would seem to require *mens rea* or substitutes such as recklessness or negligence.[67] Thus a solicitor who claimed to clients that the writ in their action had been served timeously on the other side, without checking the file to see if the statement was correct, might still be guilty of misconduct for acting recklessly or in wilful blindness, even if he or she had not consciously lied to the client. Equally, solicitors who negligently let slip privileged or confidential information pertaining to a client can also be guilty of misconduct even if it was not their intention to do so. As in the criminal sphere, ignorance of the law is no excuse. Thus, it was held in *Council of the Law Society v J*,[68] that the fact that the solicitor was ignorant of a new practice rule which had only recently come into force was not a matter that could excuse or reduce the culpability of the solicitor.

The Scottish Solicitors Discipline Tribunal may not have overtly considered the issue of *mens rea*,[69] but they frequently focus on the honesty of the solicitor respondent. Honesty has both subjective and objective elements. As the Privy Council observed in *Royal Brunei Airlines v Tan*[70]:

> "[Honesty] . . . is an objective standard. At first sight this may seem surprising. Honesty has a connotation of subjectivity, as distinct from the objectivity of negligence. Honesty, indeed, does have a strong subjective element in that it is a description of a type of conduct assessed in the light of what a person actually knew at the time, as distinct from what a reasonable person would have known or appreciated. Further, honesty and its counterpart dishonesty are mostly concerned with advertent conduct, not inadvertent conduct. Carelessness is not dishonesty. Thus for the most part dishonesty is to be equated with conscious impropriety. However, these subjective characteristics of honesty do not mean that individuals are free to set their own standards of honesty in particular circumstances. The standard of what constitutes honest conduct is not subjective. Honesty is not an optional scale, with higher or lower values according to the moral standards of each individual. If a person knowingly appropriates another's property, he will not escape a finding of dishonesty simply because he sees nothing wrong in such behaviour."[71]

---

[67] A leading authority in the USA, Charles Wolfram, asserts that it is enough to warrant discipline there if a lawyer knowingly and without coercion commits the relevant acts. It is not necessary, in addition, to show a specific intent to breach the rules. C. Wolfram, *Modern Legal Ethics* (West Publishing, St Paul, 1986) p.89. It is submitted that this could equally well apply in Scotland. In Victoria the Legal Practice Act 1996 s.137 indicates that misconduct must be "wilful or reckless".

[68] 1991 S.L.T. 662.

[69] In the case of *Beaumont petitioner* [2006] CSIH 27 P2412/05, the Inner House might be thought to have ruled, *obiter*, that professional misconduct was a strict liability "offence", indicating that intention or error only went to mitigation and not to culpability. Given that in the criminal law, there are almost no strict liability common law offences (with the possible exception of Breach of the Peace) this is a rather startling proposition, and accordingly it is more likely that the court was simply indicating that ignorance of the law is no excuse.

[70] [1995] 2 A.C. 378 at p.389 *per* Lord Nicholls of Birkenhead.

[71] It follows, as Lord Nicholls added, that reckless behaviour can be dishonest. *ibid.* p.389G.

Defences and Culpability 1.12

There would seem no reason in principle why certain defences known to the criminal law, for example insanity, diminished responsibility by reason of mental handicap, error, duress, necessity, coercion[72] or superior orders[73] could not be used to excuse or justify a solicitor's conduct. Thus, in the unlikely event that the Society chose to prosecute a solicitor who had become insane, before the Tribunal, the latter would be in a position of some difficulty. While illness only goes to mitigation in the eyes of the Tribunal, if the solicitor was so ill as to be incapable of understanding the nature of his or her actions, it is difficult to see the Tribunal being prepared to make a finding of misconduct, however convinced they were as to the need to protect the public from such a solicitor.

Illness, Culpability and Mitigation 1.13

In practice, mental illness is the nearest issue to these to arise with any frequency in the context of professional discipline. The position of the Tribunal has uniformly been to insist that ill health only goes to mitigation and not to culpability.[74] In 1988, a solicitor with ME was informed by the Tribunal that he remained under an obligation to "only accept and continue with such practice as he [could] reasonably undertake".[75] Further, in its Annual Report for 1993 the Tribunal stated that whilst difficulties such as depression and ME and other forms of ill health may operate to mitigate a sentence, they are irrelevant to a finding of misconduct as it is the solicitor's responsibility for as long as he continues to practice, to do so properly. They reiterated their position in the *Frame* case[76] holding that although deteriorating health might affect professional judgement, this did not prevent a finding of misconduct since it was the respondent's duty to recognise his increasing lack of capacity.[77] Similar rulings concerning mental health appear in the Tribunal's Annual Report for 2000[78] and in *Hetherington*.[79] While the Tribunal is prepared to be sympathetic—at least in terms of sanctions—with solicitors who have breached the conduct standards because of illness, they also have to have an eye to public protection. Thus they are less willing to mitigate the penalty for misconduct if the solicitor is still unwell. This is because, as between sympathy for illness and the need to protect the public, not

---

[72] There are several decisions of courts in the USA indicating that duress, if established, would be a complete defence to a misconduct charge. Wolfram, *op. cit.* p.89.

[73] See Gordon and Christie on Criminal Law (3rd edn).

[74] See Smith & Barton, *op. cit.* para.16.02.

[75] DTD 735/88.

[76] 1994 J.L.S.S. 103.

[77] Similarly, in the *Symon* case, 1994 J.L.S.S. 386, the Tribunal declined to treat personal and family circumstances which affected the respondent's health as relevant to the issue of culpability although it did lead them to mitigate the penalty imposed for the respondent's misconduct.

[78] at p.3.

[79] "The Tribunal noted that the Respondent's Psychiatrist had stated that the Respondent's mental illness would diminish his responsibility but not excuse his actions and that his mental illness was not the sole reason for his inability to carry on with his affairs properly. The Tribunal found the Respondent's mental illness a strong mitigatory factor. The Respondent's ill-health had resulted in him lacking personal judgement to rationalise his own affairs in such a manner as to protect the interests of his clients." DTD *Hetherington* 19/09/02 at p.14.

surprisingly, the latter is seen as paramount. Thus, in *Shaw*[80] the Scots Discipline Tribunal imposed a more severe penalty than the offence warranted, an indefinite restriction on the respondent's practising certificate, because the illness was ongoing, in order to protect the public, until such time as the solicitor's health had recovered. Similarly, in *Bogue*[81] the Tribunal took into account the relative size of the transaction and the respondent's ill-health, and that in the light of his age (62) and financial circumstances, any restriction on the respondent's right to practise could have far reaching consequences, but nevertheless concluded that since there had been persistent neglect on the part of the respondent over an extended period, the need for some substantive protection of the public required the Tribunal to restrict the respondent's practising certificate. The Tribunal's concern for public protection contains within it the implicit notion that a solicitor should not just be a "fit and proper person to be a solicitor" when he or she is admitted, but should remain that way. As a policy this makes eminent good sense. Thus, it prevails in the USA,[82] Australia,[83] Ontario,[84] and in the case of Qualified Conveyancers, even in Scotland. Yet, in an unfortunate oversight the governing legislation for Scottish solicitors[85] provides very few powers for taking action against solicitors who have not been guilty of misconduct, who cease to be fit to practise due to illness, alcoholism or substance abuse, as opposed to responding to misconduct.[86]

1.14 Stress and Overwork

While stress in today's pressurised work environments may well be treated by the Council and the Tribunal as akin to illness in terms of mitigating misconduct, being overworked—at least in the case of principals (partners or sole practitioners) will not. Thus in *Drummond*,[87] the Tribunal did not accept the submission that a solicitor has a duty to prioritise his workload on the basis of the resources available to him. The Tribunal held:

> "the basic principle must be that a solicitor should only accept instructions where he has the capacity to conduct the particular work with reasonable diligence, and where circumstances change to the extent that he can no longer cope with his existing workload, the solicitor has the alternative of either arranging that the business giving rise to the excess is entrusted to a suitable person within his practice or alternatively that the client is advised to consult another solicitor. A solicitor's workload is not an acceptable excuse for excessive delay in attending to the affairs of his clients."[88]

---

[80] 1998 J.L.S.S. 9 (April).
[81] 1998 J.L.S.S. 12 (November).
[82] See C. Wolfram, *Modern Legal Ethics* (West Publishing, St Paul, 1986), para.3.3.3.
[83] See G.E. Dal Pont, *Lawyers' Professional Responsibility* (2nd edn, LBC Information Services, Pyrmont, NSW, 2001) at p.641.
[84] See ss.37–40 of the Law Society Act (R.S.O. 1990 as amended).
[85] The Solicitors Scotland Act 1980.
[86] See para.1.02 above.
[87] DTD 884/94.
[88] See also Smith & Barton *op. cit.* p.147 (bottom).

Substance Abuse **1.15**

Substance abuse, whether legal in the case of alcohol or illegal in the case of drugs, does not go to culpability. Nor does it necessarily go to mitigation. Thus in the English case of *Re Howard*[89] an alcoholic solicitor who had been drinking one Saturday evening was called out to a police station nine miles away, as duty agent. The prosecution by the Law Society before the Solicitors' Disciplinary Tribunal alleged that the respondent had been guilty of unbefitting conduct, in that he had been convicted of driving a vehicle after consuming excess alcohol whilst acting in the course of his profession, and had thereby brought the profession into disrepute. The Tribunal was informed that he had accepted the fact that he was an alcoholic, taken appropriate treatment, and, in the opinion of his doctor, successfully given up drinking. Despite being an isolated incident the Tribunal took a very serious view of a solicitor who was intoxicated while carrying out professional duties— especially when acting as a duty solicitor and found him guilty of misconduct and fined him £500 plus costs. It was also recommended that the Law Society should demand that the respondent take a medical examination to ensure his treatment had been successful before granting him a practising certificate. In a comparable Scottish case, *Docherty*,[90] the solicitor stole over £2,000 from a curatory estate. Before the Tribunal, evidence was led to the effect that at the relevant time the solicitor had been suffering from stress, depression and alcohol addiction. The Tribunal accepted that the dishonesty was out of character and the product of the addictive illness which had now been overcome. Further mitigating factors noted by the Tribunal included: that there had been restitution; there had been complete disclosure; and, that there would appear to be little risk of re-offending. The solicitor was not struck off, but suspended from practice as a solicitor for four years. In 2003, a solicitor, *McPherson*,[91] with an admitted alcohol problem and four convictions for drunk driving in 16 years was found guilty of professional misconduct, but the penalty was mitigated, in part, because of his "great efforts to control his illness" and the fact that his professional work had not been adversely affected by his condition. The respondent was allowed to continue to practice but fined £500 plus costs.

Dealing with the Impaired Lawyer **1.16**

Cases involving solicitors suffering from depression, alcoholism or substance abuse bring the role of regulation and discipline for lawyers starkly into focus. The Council or the Tribunal has to weigh in the balance a complex mix of the need to punish, to deter, to protect the good name of the profession, to protect the public, to ensure the fitness of lawyers to practice and to rescue/ rehabilitate lawyers whose ability to practice has been impaired. The tension between these competing objectives is greatest where the impairment is ongoing. Increasingly, the North American jurisdictions and Australia have begun to focus on approaches that effectively prevent future harm to the

---

[89] Decision 4218; Law Society Gazette 14/9/88.
[90] DTD 1047/00.
[91] DTD *McPherson* 1119/03.

public whilst at the same time maximising the chances of rehabilitation. These have included suspension pending treatment, practice under supervision, and rehabilitation programmes.[92] This avenue is only partly open to the Scottish Discipline Tribunal, and even then, only if the Council decides to prosecute the case rather than accept an undertaking not to practice. However, throughout the USA, Canada, Australia, and now the UK, we are seeing the establishment of initiatives to help with lawyers' substance abuse, alcoholism and stress. In all of these jurisdictions there are helplines offering free counselling.[93] As early as 1975, the Law Society of Scotland had established the "Solicitors Advice and Assistance Scheme" for the purpose of helping solicitors who found themselves in difficulties of any kind. It offered guidance and assistance from experienced and independent practitioners on a totally confidential basis. Unfortunately, it foundered through lack of support. Alongside the assistance scheme the Society offered a "locum" service for its members, so that in cases of exceptional pressure of work or staff illness solicitors could turn to the society to help them engage qualified assistants from a register of available solicitors. It too suffered from a lack of resources. The next suggestion was a Law Society "Rescue Service", both as a form of help for solicitors who might otherwise find themselves eventually in disciplinary difficulties with the society, and as a swift and effective means of both resolving some clients' problems and preventing others. Eventually, towards the end of the twentieth century the Society introduced the Practice Advisory Service (PAS), with visits by an expert adviser from the ranks of the profession, triggered by a significant adverse claims record in respect of professional negligence. The visits, therefore, had a regulatory aspect which tended to provoke—at least in the initial stages of the visit—a negative response on the part of the firm being visited. In 2000, it was decided that the PAS should be expanded so that it was no longer simply triggered by the Society in a disciplinary context, but also available at the request of the individual firm. However, this service too withered on the vine, and in 2001 the accounts rules were amended to give the Society power to inspect a practice to ascertain whether the way in which it is conducted puts the public or the profession at risk. In addition, the Professional Practice Department remains available to offer advice to members who wish it. In all of these initiatives, however, the importance of separating the Law Society's guidance function from its disciplining function has been emphasised. Finally, in 2000 the Society reached agreement with its English counterparts to extend its SolCare scheme to Scottish solicitors. This scheme, now called *Law Care*, was established by the English Law Society in 1997 and offers a 24-hour confidential helpline[94] for any solicitor who is suffering stress, depression, or who has an alcohol, drug or other dependency problem.[95] Nonetheless, by keeping the guidance function apart from the discipline function a lacuna is created since, as the Discipline Tribunal observed in *McPherson*,[96] there is no

---

[92] See Wolfram, *op. cit.* p.96 and Y. Ross, *Ethics in Law* (3rd edn, Butterworths, Australia, 2001), pp.172–3.

[93] See Ross, *op. cit.* p.173.

[94] 0800–279-6869; *www.lawcare.org.uk.*

[95] See: *"Easing the Strain"*—Law Society Gazette—100/01 January 9, 2003; *"Finding a Cure"*—Law Society Gazette—100/39 October 16, 2003.

[96] DTD *McPherson* 1119/03.

mechanism to "monitor the sobriety of practising solicitors who admit to having alcohol or drug problems". It seems likely that as pressure for external regulation grows, so too will the focus on "fitness to practice" and with it the need to fill the lacuna.

Inexperience or Junior Status and Supervision   1.17

A close examination of the rulings of the Discipline Tribunal and Inner House decisions also reveals that inexperience or junior status only goes to mitigation and not to culpability. Understandably, the Tribunal has declined to accept inexperience in a sole practitioner as an explanation for failing to have proper accounting procedures.[97] They have been more sympathetic to trainees[98] or new assistants, particularly when acting under the supervision of a more experienced solicitor. Nevertheless, in each case it has been held that youth, inexperience or junior status in the firm does not exculpate a trainee or junior solicitor whose acts or omissions would otherwise merit a finding of professional misconduct, they only mitigate the punishment.[99] It may appear that this is not consistent with the decision on the facts in *Sharp*. However, in that case the junior partners were exculpated from blame in connection with breaches of the accounts rules, not because of their inexperience or junior status, but because of their inability to influence the behaviour of the more senior partners who excluded them from partnership meetings and dealing with accounts.

The reverse side of the coin is that the Tribunal expects a reasonable degree of supervision to be exercised by principals in relation to trainees or unqualified staff. Whilst accepting the propriety of delegating work to such individuals, the Tribunal has indicated that it is essential that the solicitor maintains a high level of supervision to ensure that the standard of work is not less than that which is expected of a qualified solicitor. The amount of supervision necessary in any particular case is a matter for the professional judgement of the solicitor, taking into account the importance and complexity of the work and the reliability and experience of the assistant.[1] The solicitor should also have regard to his/her own experience and the opportunity available to him or her to effect adequate supervision.[2] In *Miller/Morrison*,[3] the Tribunal found Miller guilty of misconduct for her failure to adequately supervise and have regard to the work being carried out by Morrison during the time he was employed by her as an assistant. This was notwithstanding the fact that Miller was placed in a difficult situation as Morrison had previously been a more senior partner than her and was only working as an assistant under her supervision following a period of suspension of his practising certificate.

---

[97] DTD 857/93.

[98] First year trainees are not subject to the disciplinary system of the Law Society since they are not members of the Society or on the Roll.

[99] See DTD 747/89; Smith and Barton para.6.06; DTD 809/90 and Case Study 1 Scottish Legal Services Ombudsman Annual Report 1998 at p.11.

[1] For detailed guidance on supervision for immigration practitioners see the Practice Guidelines for Immigration Practitioners, 2004 J.L.S.S. 49(9), 37.

[2] Discipline Tribunal Annual Report 1988.

[3] DTD 06/01/05.

1.18 Prejudice to the Client

Somewhat surprisingly the Court of Session has ruled that the fact that a solicitor's breach of the practice rule involved no prejudice to the client might be relevant to whether misconduct can be established and not just a point which went to mitigation of sentence.[4] Although it can be argued that this ruling was obiter, it was made after counsel had argued the point and the Inner House were clear in their opinion that professional misconduct is always a matter of circumstances and that it could not be said that "the question of prejudice is entirely irrelevant" to a finding of misconduct as opposed to mitigating the penalty. Frankly, this is a surprising ruling in the light of the *Sharp* test. The reprehensibility of a solicitor's conduct in breaching confidentiality or "borrowing" sums from the client account for short periods of time is not affected by whether the client's interests are compromised.[5] That, at least, is the view of the Discipline Tribunal. In *McRae*,[6] the Tribunal expressly states that "it does not mitigate the gravity of any breach of [a practice rule] merely because none of the clients involved have been prejudiced or that none of the clients are dissatisfied with the solicitor's conduct". Again, in *Goldie*[7] the Tribunal also held that the fact that an unreasonable delay in dealing with correspondence and a failure to record deeds timeously did not in this case cause harm or inconvenience to any party was irrelevant to a finding of misconduct, although they did use the lack of prejudice to mitigate the penalty in the case.[8]

1.19 Mitigation of the Penalty and Public Protection

Mitigation of penalty by the Tribunal can be influenced by a wide variety of circumstances, as we have seen. They include, expressions of contrition, repayment of excessive fees or restitution of funds appropriated, complete disclosure, that the dishonesty was out of character, that the solicitor was suffering from stress, illness or substance addiction (which has now been overcome), that the solicitor had made "great efforts to control his illness", junior status, that the solicitor had experienced difficulties resulting from water damage to his offices,[9] that there was no harm to the client,[10] that there was no personal financial gain,[11] that there was no risk to the public, or the voluntarily winding up of the lawyer's business, etc.[12] Other factors relevant

---

[4] *Council of the Law Society v J.*, 1991 S.L.T. 662.

[5] It has been repeatedly held by the Courts in the USA that the fact that a lawyer's offence did not cause injury to a client or another person does not provide a defence to a misconduct charge. See Wolfram *op. cit.* p.89.

[6] DTD 990/98.

[7] 43(3) J.L.S.S. 127, March 1998.

[8] See also DTD *Murray* 01/03/05 where the Tribunal noted the fact that "the Respondent's client had not been out of pocket" in its determination of the penalty. The court's ruling on the significance of lack of prejudice to the client also seems hard to reconcile with the Tribunal decisions which assert that ill health or substance addiction only go to mitigation and not to culpability.

[9] DTD *McGinley* 06/01/05.

[10] DTD *Hussain* 15/06/04.

[11] DTD *Millar* 09/11/04, DTD *Miller/Morrison* 06/01/05.

[12] See e.g. the *Morrison* case at 1994 J.L.S.S. 264, *Docherty* DTD 1047/00; *Council of the Law Society v J.*, 1991 S.L.T. 662.

to mitigation include: absence of dishonesty,[13] supportive references from other members of the profession and clients[14] and a long unblemished record in the profession.[15] Entering into a Joint Minute of Agreement with the Law Society's fiscal can go towards mitigation of sentence, since to admit the facts as averred, and/or misconduct, saves time and expense for the Tribunal and for witnesses.[16] The Tribunal will also avoid levying a fine where there is little prospect of its payment. In *McMahon v Council of the Law Society*,[17] the Inner House added "the tribunal may be justified in taking a lenient view of an isolated act of misconduct where it is venial in itself, or is explicable, if not excusable, on account of some misfortune or mitigating circumstance. More serious acts of misconduct give less scope for leniency. But where dishonesty with clients' money is involved, there can be few instances, if any where leniency can be shown."[18] However, it is important to note that the Court of Appeal held in *Bolton v Law Society*[19] that since orders by the Tribunal were not primarily punitive, but were directed to ensuring that the offender did not have the opportunity to repeat the offence[20] and to maintaining the reputation of the solicitor's profession and sustaining public confidence in its integrity, considerations which would ordinarily weigh in mitigation of punishment had less effect in misconduct cases than in criminal cases. Thus, suspension might still be ordered even if it would effectively prevent re-establishment of practice. As Lord Bingham MR observed, "The reputation of the profession is more important than the fortunes of any individual member. Membership of a profession brings many benefits, but that is part of the price."[21] Public protection is paramount, but this may also take the form of ensuring access to legal services for the public. Thus in *McCormick*,[22] the Tribunal, "mindful of the scarcity of solicitors in rural areas" declined to impose a restriction on the solicitor's practising certificate, restricting him to acting as an employee rather than a principal (which would have been usual in the circumstances) and opted instead for a censure, a fine and compulsory inspections.

---

[13] See DTD *Hussain* 15/06/04. The tribunal noted that the solicitor's basic integrity was not in question.

[14] DTD *Burkinshaw* 22/04/04, DTD *Oliver* 09/11/04, DTD *Moodie* 20/07/04.

[15] DTD *Malcolm* 23/03/05, DTD *Moodie* 20/07/04.

[16] See Scottish Solicitor's Discipline Tribunal, *Annual Report 2002/2003* at page 2 where it is noted that: "this is much appreciated . . . and is taken into account in imposing sentence."

[17] 2002 S.L.T.363.

[18] Leniency was shown, however, in DTD *Burkinshaw* 22/04/04, which concerned dishonesty with an employer's money. The solicitor had been convicted of embezzlement but the Tribunal "stopped short of striking the Respondent's name from the Roll or imposing a period of suspension which would normally be appropriate for offences involving dishonesty" due to various mitigating circumstances including the sums involved, the fact that he was not sentenced to imprisonment and numerous supportive references received.

[19] [1994] 1 W.L.R. 512. *Bolton* was endorsed by the Inner House in *McMahon v Council of the Law Society of Scotland*, 2002 S.L.T. 363 at p.367A where it indicates that the Tribunal's decision "should be one that both vindicates the reputation of the profession and protects the public against the risk of repetition".

[20] The introduction of measures to help to prevent a re-ocurrence has been considered in mitigation. See DTD *McCormick* 30/09/04—introduction of a case management system and DTD *MacDonald* 18/05/04—winding up of a branch office.

[21] Endorsed by the Privy Council in *Patel v General Medical Council* [2003] UKPC 16 (27/1/03).

[22] DTD 30/09/04.

1.20 The Limits of Professional Misconduct

In the following pages we shall examine areas which illustrate the limits of professional misconduct and which highlight the problems which arise when misconduct overlaps with other standards.

1.21 Acting Without a Practising Certificate or Insurance

Over the years there has been a steady trickle of practitioners who have omitted to renew their practising certificate which usually means that they have also failed to pay their Master Policy insurance premium in relation to professional negligence or their contribution to the Guarantee Fund. The Tribunal has taken a dim view of such cases.[23] Thus in *Feeley*[24] the Tribunal downplayed Feeley's claims that all he had done was two conveyances which he had undertaken without a direct or indirect fee. The Tribunal observed that "by failing to take out a practising certificate, the respondent avoided his various obligations [to the Master Policy, the Guarantee Fund and to the running costs of the Law Society] . . . and would have been without the protection of the Master Policy which itself would have serious consequences in the event of any claim arising." Mr. Feeley was found guilty of professional misconduct and was suspended for five years. (In *McNeil*,[25] the solicitor in question continued to appear for clients in court and to practise generally, despite having had his practising certificate suspended by the Tribunal. This too was held to be misconduct.) Even practising without insurance has been enough to attract the concern of the Tribunal.[26] Understandably, the Tribunal has been concerned by the likelihood that the solicitor would be unable to meet any claim for loss. Thus in the *Gillespie case*[27] the Tribunal commented:

> "It is a solicitor's duty that there are sufficient funds available to finance a practice and the only acceptable alternative is for the solicitor immediately to withdraw from practice. In continuing to practise without indemnity insurance, the respondent exposed herself to possible claims from clients which she would have been unable to meet from her own resources. This could have had very serious consequences"

However, the Tribunal has indicated that lack of insurance cover is still misconduct even if there is a reduced risk of loss to the client. Thus in *Currie*[28] it was held that it is not an excuse to a charge of practising as a solicitor without professional indemnity insurance that the solicitor confines his practice to criminal proceedings, employs no staff and does not hold client's funds.

---

[23] However, there have been several recent cases where the Law Society has chosen not to prosecute a solicitor who has practised without a practising certificate, because of illness on the part of the solicitor, settling instead for an undertaking from the solicitor not to practise. Since the latter may not be easy to enforce, it is not clear that such an approach sufficiently protects the public interest.

[24] 1993 J.L.S.S. 242.

[25] DTD 1010/99; 44(2) J.L.S.S. February 11, 1999.

[26] See, for example, *Lynch* 1995 J.L.S.S. 287.

[27] 1994 J.L.S.S. 224.

[28] 1997 J.L.S.S. 422.

Private and Commercial Life **1.22**

One particularly interesting aspect to professional misconduct is the extent to which a solicitor's private or non-professional life can give rise to discipline for misconduct. In Scotland, it has been established in a series of cases that what a solicitor does in his or her personal or private life can give rise to a finding of professional misconduct. The basis for the decisions has been somewhat less clear.

In 1989 a complaint[29] arose against a Scottish solicitor who was not practising as a solicitor, although designating himself as such. He was the sole director of an English company which was compulsorily wound up following a decision of the Court of Appeal in which the respondent was severely criticised in a number of respects, including seriously misleading investors in the company. The Tribunal accepted that the respondent did not carry on a conventional legal practice, nevertheless they concluded that the respondent by using the designation "solicitor" must accept the responsibilities that are expected of a person bearing that description:

> " . . . a solicitor is expected to conduct himself in a manner consistent with his membership of an honourable profession and this responsibility is concisely set out by Lord Donaldson in *United Bank of Kuwait v Hammoud and Others* [1988] 1 W.L.R. 1051 at 430: 'The great, and perhaps unique, value of the professional advice of solicitors is to be found in a combination of factors which those who consult them are entitled to expect, and usually get: total independence, total integrity, total confidentiality, total dedication to the interests of the client, competent legal advice and competent other more general advice based on a wide experience of people and their problems, both in a personal and a business context. The need to maintain this enviable situation is, of course, the reason and the justification for the unforgiving attitude adopted by the profession towards those of their number, and there will inevitably be a few, who fall below the standards required by them.' In the opinion of this Tribunal, the solicitor is required to maintain the same standard of propriety in his private life and in relation to any commercial ventures as are expected of him in his professional practice; and it is on this basis that the Tribunal considers the actings and conduct of the Company in the same light as if they had been the actings of the respondent in the course of his professional practice."

Unfortunately, it is unclear whether the Tribunal took action because they felt that the solicitor's actions had "brought the profession into disrepute" or whether they were drawing on a kind of "fitness to practice" argument, namely, that to be a practising solicitor requires certain inherent qualities e.g. independence, integrity, honesty, loyalty to the client etc. On the latter analysis, where a solicitor demonstrates in his or her private life a significant lack of these fundamental qualities, the Tribunal may consider this to merit disciplinary action.[30] Indeed, it is possible that the Tribunal was running both arguments or an amalgam of the two.

---

[29] DTD 768/89.
[30] In Australia, the disciplinary authorities appear to be willing to take action in two types of situation involving the lawyer's private life. Firstly, where the lawyer's acts are sufficiently

In the next case, *Jacob*,[31] a Scottish solicitor, designing himself as such, set up a limited company carrying on business throughout the UK as dealers in securities and investment advisers. He was sole director and owned all the shares but one. The company was compulsorily wound up and in the course of the proceedings the Court of Appeal held that the company was preying on unsuspecting members of the public using seriously misleading documents to persuade members of the public to invest in highly speculative investments. The solicitor was brought before the Discipline Tribunal which again quoted Lord Donaldson in *United Bank of Kuwait v Hammoud*[32] and observed that a solicitor is required to maintain the same standards of propriety in private life and in relation to any commercial ventures as are expected in professional practice. The Tribunal directed that the respondent should be struck-off the Roll, observing that the respondent had behaved in a manner wholly unbecoming a solicitor and that "where a solicitor communicates with the public, especially involving the investment of funds, he must act with *uberrima fides* . . . in using the designation "solicitor" the respondent tarnished the reputation of the profession." Here the rationale leans much more closely to "bringing the profession into disrepute" rather than any "fitness" type of argument. However, the argument could equally have been couched as a "fitness" one, as was seen a year later in *Mitchell*[33] where a solicitor was suspended for 10 years by the Tribunal for obstructing receivers of an insolvent company in which she was a director. The solicitor's firm had also provided services to the company and her behaviour in relation to the company was deemed to constitute a failure "to maintain the high standards of propriety to be expected of a solicitor".

This use of the "fitness" argument was repeated two years later in the *Hodson* case.[34] There, an enrolled, but non-practising, solicitor abused his position as Postmaster in a Highland Post office by "borrowing" £2000 of Post Office money in order to meet an unexpected shortfall in funds required to purchase a property. The Tribunal held that although the events were unrelated to his professional qualification, he was guilty of professional misconduct in that he had failed to act with the utmost regard for funds held in trust.

Given that it is clearly established in Scotland that solicitors may be disciplined for acts done in their private life, why should we be concerned whether the ground for discipline is "bringing the profession into disrepute" or a "fitness to practice" one? Each of them is open to the criticism of Wolfram, that they can be used to punish deviant behaviour which has little

---

closely connected with actual practice, even though they do not actually occur in the lawyer's professional life, e.g. where the lawyer has an affair with a client. The second type of case is where the lawyer's conduct outside practice "may manifest the presence or absence of qualities which are incompatible with, or essential for, the conduct of practice". This is essentially a "fitness" type argument. See *New South Wales Bar Association v Cummins* [2001] NSWCA 284 (where the barrister had failed to file a tax return in any of the 38 years in which he had been in practice). In the USA acts which are remote from law practice can found disciplinary action "to the extent that they furnish proof of seriously deficient qualities of relevance to law practice". Wolfram, *op. cit.* p.97. This is clearly a "fitness" type argument.

[31] 1994 J.L.S.S. 304.
[32] [1988] 1 W.L.R. 1051.
[33] 1995 J.L.S.S. 486.
[34] *Hodson* DTD 953/97.

objective relevance to professional practice.[35] However, one difference is that in cases where the acts are not identified in the media or by observers as being done by a solicitor, it is less easy for it to be said that the acts "bring the profession into disrepute".[36] Another is that "bringing the profession into disrepute" as a ground for misconduct is semi-tautologous and as such offers little guidance to interested parties over and above the *Sharp* test. "Fitness to practise", on the other hand, is an explanation that is perhaps more in keeping with the general changes on the regulatory front with respect to the legal profession in the UK in recent years,[37] and the increasing focus on protecting the public interest rather than the reputation of the profession.

Criminal Convictions

1.23

One significant area of a lawyer's private life which can lead to discipline relates to criminal convictions.[38] Understandably, there will always be a certain degree of overlap between behaviour which merits discipline on conduct grounds and that which leads to a criminal conviction.[39] Most serious convictions would merit action under either the "bringing the profession into disrepute" or the "fitness to practice" tests which are applied in relation to a solicitor's private life. However, not every criminal conviction will give rise to a conduct finding.[40] As the Tribunal noted in 1984,[41] "In the English case, *Re a Solicitor* [1960] 2 Q.B. 212, Lord Parker refuted the suggestion that the mere conviction of any criminal offence is evidence of conduct unbefitting a solicitor. The nature of the offence and the frequency were matters to be taken into consideration in determining whether there had been professional misconduct." On the other hand, the Discipline Tribunal is entitled under the Solicitors (Scotland) Act 1980[42] to treat any conviction "by any court of an act involving dishonesty" or which led to a sentence of "imprisonment of not less than two years" as misconduct warranting sanction. One factor which is likely to influence the Tribunal in considering whether a conviction should also be misconduct is whether it involves an abuse of a position of trust. Thus, in May 2002 *Danskin* was found guilty of misconduct by the Tribunal. The finding followed his imprisonment for 18 months in respect of his behaviour towards young boys which involved shameless indecency and lewd, libidinous and indecent practices. The offence was exacerbated in the eyes of the

---

[35] *op. cit.* p.98.

[36] In DTD *Maguire* 1069/01 the Tribunal ruled that the amount of publicity in the media did not increase the extent to which a criminal conviction "brought the profession into disrepute". However, this does not address the argument that where the media fails to note that the accused is a solicitor at all, the profession cannot be brought into disrepute, except in the eyes of his or her professional acquaintances and clients.

[37] See para.1.1 above.

[38] Of course, criminal convictions can also stem from actings in one's professional practice.

[39] The overlap, however, is not a ground for arguments about double jeopardy since the functions of the criminal process and professional discipline are different. See DTD *Maguire* 1069/01. Nor is it open to the solicitor to use the disciplinary process as an opportunity to assert his/her innocence or to appeal from the criminal conviction. The same situation pertains in Australia, see Dal Pont *op. cit.* p.641.

[40] See DTD *Maguire* 1069/01.

[41] DTD 636/84. The Tribunal in an earlier case (DTD 289/67) had argued that a criminal conviction gives rise to a rebuttable presumption of misconduct. This is probably an area where the content of the *Sharp* test has changed over the years. Certainly it is hard to see why an isolated speeding conviction should raise a presumption of misconduct.

[42] s.53(1)(b).

Tribunal in that the behaviour occurred while he held the position of trust to the boys as their Boy's Brigade Captain.[43]

A wide range of offences have led to misconduct findings. Amongst the most spectacular are firearms offences. In *Wright*,[44] the solicitor was found to have a pistol with five rounds of ammunition in the magazine and a "sawn-off" shotgun at his home. Upon being cautioned and charged, the respondent replied inter alia "My life is in danger. I got them from the underworld . . . " The respondent subsequently stated to police officers that he had acquired the shotgun through a Glasgow "heavy" who delivered it to him at a meeting on the platform of Dumbarton Station where the respondent handed over, in exchange, £100 in £10 notes. He was convicted of possessing firearms without a certificate. He was then charged with misconduct and the Tribunal concluded "that any action by a solicitor falling below the standards expected of him by his professional brethren must be open to a finding of professional misconduct even although the particular actings are entirely unrelated to that solicitor's practice, his clients or other members if the profession.". Accordingly he was found guilty of misconduct, but merely censured with a finding for expenses in the light of extenuating circumstances. However, at least in relation to penalty, it may be worth noting that gun control is more of an issue today than it was 20 or so years ago.

Sixteen years later in the *McIntyre* case[45] another solicitor was convicted of possession of two .22 pistols and ammunition without holding a current firearms certificate. He was sentenced to three years imprisonment. Section 53(1)(b) was invoked before the Tribunal. He was censured by the Tribunal, but this was appealed to the Inner House by the Law Society on the basis that censure was an insufficient penalty for the offence. The Inner House found that the original Tribunal had taken its decision on an insufficient and unsatisfactory basis of fact and the case was referred back for a rehearing. At the rehearing the Tribunal took account of certain comments made by the trial judge, namely his concern at the fact the solicitor had been seen in a public street with a firearm which was later found to be loaded, and the fact that ammunition was found in a car used by the solicitor. The Tribunal also observed that events such as the shootings in Dunblane had raised the public awareness of offences involving a breach of the Firearms Acts. It was noted that the public expects members of the solicitors' profession to maintain a high standard both in connection with their behaviour as a solicitor and in their private life. The Tribunal were of the opinion that, if a solicitor convicted of such an offence was seen to be allowed to remain on the roll, public perception of the profession would be diminished and other members of the profession would find it difficult to establish the trust and respect required for the close working relationship among solicitors. The Tribunal held that the respondent was "no longer a fit and proper person to remain on the Roll", his name was struck off and publicity was given to the decision.[46]

---

[43] 2002 J.L.S.S. August at p.9.

[44] DTD 575/83.

[45] DTD 1002/99.

[46] The solicitor's explanation of how he came to be in possession of the firearms was that they have been given to him by a client with instructions that he should pass them over to the police. He stated that it was his intention to hand them over but he had taken them home in the meantime and that they have been in his garage for only a couple of hours. The jury did not believe the respondent.

There have been several attempts to pervert the course of justice. In a 1984 case, the solicitor having given a blood sample when accused of drunken driving, then endeavoured to dispose of the sample down the toilet.[47] He was convicted and a finding of misconduct duly followed. In another case[48] the respondent, who was a passenger in the car involved in a road accident, had initially claimed to have been driving in order to prevent a friend from being prosecuted for drunken driving. Although the deception was maintained only for a few minutes he was convicted and fined £200 in the sheriff court and this too led to a misconduct finding.

Other offences which have lead to a misconduct finding include: reset,[49] possession of a "soft drug",[50] embezzlement,[51] and repeated motoring offences.[52] It is submitted that two or more convictions for drinking and driving would also be misconduct in Scotland either on "fitness" grounds or for "bringing the profession into disrepute." Thus in the case of *McPherson*,[53] the respondent was found guilty of professional misconduct as he had been convicted of drunk driving on four occasions over a period of around 16 years. The Tribunal held:

> "One of the essential qualities of a solicitor is integrity which extends to the personal as well as the professional conduct of a solicitor. The Tribunal were particularly concerned that the Respondent had four convictions for drunk driving, conduct which is regrettably disgraceful and dishonourable and brings the profession into disrepute."

Seriously assaulting a client or a former employee or indeed a fellow reveller at a New Year Party irrespective of provocation, has been held sufficient to constitute professional misconduct because the profession has been brought into disrepute. In the *Jethwa* case,[54] the respondent was convicted of committing a breach of the peace, an assault and resisting lawful arrest in connection with an incident in which he and an associate had repeatedly kicked a publican on the ground outside his pub. Even though the respondent at that stage was on the Roll but not in practice, the Tribunal noted that he was a solicitor and that his conviction had been the subject of adverse press publicity which might have damaged the reputation of the profession. Again, even if a conviction is a trivial one, if it comes after several previous more serious ones, it may lead to a misconduct finding. Thus in the *Diggle* case[55] in England, the solicitor was convicted of the attempted rape of a female solicitor after a ball, in 1993. He was suspended from practice for a year by the Law Society since the conviction constituted misconduct. Subsequently,

---

[47] DTD 591/84.

[48] DTD 782/89.

[49] DTD 544/82.

[50] DTD 287/67.

[51] DTD 489/80, DTD *Burkinshaw* 22/04/04.

[52] DTD 636/84 *Corrigan* (Driving without insurance). The respondent was charged with criminal conduct which was seriously detrimental to and inconsistent with the good name and dignity of the profession. It was further stated that the respondent's conduct was calculated to bring the profession into disrepute.

[53] DTD *McPherson* 1119/03.

[54] DTD 1040 /00. The respondent admitted professional misconduct and was suspended from practice for a year.

[55] *The Scotsman*—16/1/98.

he was convicted on another occasion of being drunk and disorderly and then of another minor offence. The Discipline Tribunal whilst noting the triviality of the latest conviction, nevertheless deemed the combination of convictions to constitute a bad criminal record which merited being struck off the Roll of Solicitors.

In this case, as in the others, it can be seen that in finding misconduct following a criminal conviction the Tribunal has been motivated either by a concern that the "profession has been brought into disrepute" or that the solicitor be "fit to practice"[56] or a combination of the two. In one of the most recent assault cases to reach the Tribunal, *Maguire*,[57] the Tribunal held that a solicitor who had been convicted of assaulting his mother-in-law, causing her to fall down a set of steps, striking her head in the process, and repeatedly kicking her on the body as well as punching his wife and injuring her, was guilty of professional misconduct. The solicitor tried to argue that the assault, while disgraceful, did not demonstrate a lack of fitness (since it did not affect his honesty, truthfulness or integrity) and that it had not been serious enough to "bring the profession as a whole into disrepute", thus neatly refuting the alternate bases on which a finding of misconduct could be founded. The Tribunal, however, reiterated that a solicitor "cannot separate his personal conduct from his membership of the profession" before going on to re-establish both bases. First they indicated that his fitness *was* in question because: "One of the essential qualities of a solicitor is integrity which extends to the personal as well as professional conduct of a solicitor". Secondly, they asserted that the very fact of the conviction for assault was enough to establish damage "to the reputation of the profession", something which was not exacerbated by the extent to which the matter had been featured in the Press.[58] While the dividing line between which criminal convictions will constitute misconduct and which will not, remains partially obscure, the Maguire case supports the use of both the "fitness" test, as well as the "bringing the profession into disrepute". It also, rightly, establishes that domestic violence or abuse may well be misconduct, as Ryder had predicted.[59]

1.24 Misleading Behaviour

Whatever else is contained in the concept of "fitness to practice" for a solicitor, honesty and integrity must surely be amongst the key components. Hardly surprising then that the Code of Conduct, being a statement of core principles on which the profession is founded, should place such a premium

---

[56] The ABA Model Rule MR 8.4(b) indicates that the crimes for which a lawyer may be disciplined are those "that reflect adversely on the lawyer's honesty, trustworthiness or fitness as a lawyer in other respects."

[57] DTD 1069/01.

[58] The rejection of the suggestion that greater press publicity causes greater harm to the profession and thus increases culpability, is in contrast with the Tribunal's hint that in reaching a finding of misconduct they had been particularly influenced by the severity of the assault on the mother-in-law and that the assault on his wife had caused injury. The latter observation is the more curious in the light of the Tribunal's stance that the absence of harm to the client is irrelevant to a finding of misconduct.

[59] J. Ryder, *Professional Conduct for Scottish Solicitors* (Butterworths, Edinburgh, 1995), p.30.

on these attributes. Article 7 of the Code of Conduct states that solicitors must act honestly and in such a way as to put their personal integrity beyond question. Again, arts.8 and 9 respectively require a solicitor not to knowingly mislead the court or a professional colleague. It follows that where a client, the Law Society, the court or a professional colleague is knowingly and deliberately deceived by a solicitor, this will amount to misconduct.[60] There are many precedents in this area. Over the years, there have been a steady stream of solicitors who through pressure of work, incompetence, illness or the like have omitted to take action timeously and then sought to cover up by lying to their clients. Lawyers who have been instructed to lodge a claim with the Criminal Injuries Compensation Board, or a tribunal, or to raise a personal injury action or a divorce in the Sheriff Court have found themselves resorting to deceit by pretending that things are on track, that the action has been raised or the proof fixed and then discharged. In one or two extreme cases the deceit has been taken as far as a claim that a settlement has been reached in the case and the lawyer has then produced "the winnings" from his own pocket.[61] One solicitor even went as far as to print a forged divorce certificate, in a case where he informed the client that he was divorced when, in reality, no action had ever been risen.[62]

The Tribunal has made it clear, however, that misleading statements come in a variety of forms. On the one hand there is an out and out lie, which one knows to be a falsehood. Deliberate lies to a client like this, especially if they are repeated to the Law Society are clear examples of misconduct.[63] Curiously, the Tribunal has taken the view that where a solicitor gives answers to a client about what action he has undertaken for the client, which he knows to be false, this is more likely to be misleading than dishonest behaviour. However, in the case in question it did not make much difference since the Tribunal nevertheless found "a pattern of deceit" which they held particularly serious, as clients and their representatives are entitled to rely on the truthfulness of statements made by solicitors.[64] Next, there is the situation where the solicitor states an untruth without checking whether it is in fact truthful or not. This can amount to recklessness, which will give rise to a misconduct finding, even although there is no intentional dishonesty. Finally, there is the negligent statement which is neither a deliberate nor a reckless falsehood. Provided that this is innocent or inadvertent, this will not be seen as misconduct by the Society or the Tribunal. An interesting illustration of these distinctions can be found in *Nelson*[65] where the respondent had admitted misleading the Law Society. She had written to the Society indicating that she

---

[60] See e.g. DTD *Wilkie* 981/98 and DTD *Carmichael* 991/98.

[61] See DTD *McCulloch* 1142/03. The respondent informed his client that he had won his case when, in reality, it had never even been raised in court. He paid the "winnings", to the sum of £6480, from his own funds by staggered payments spread over several months. See also DTD *McAnulty* 03/12/03 where the solicitor misappropriated funds belonging to other clients to pay the "winnings".

[62] DTD *Anderson* 982/98. See also DTD *Millar* 09/11/04 where the solicitor produced fake court documentation to maintain the pretence that an action had been raised, when in fact it had not.

[63] See *Murray*, 1996 J.L.S.S. 35, DTD *McNeil* 1010/99 and DTD *Malcolm* 23/03/05.

[64] DTD 788/89.

[65] DTD *Nelson* 1134/03.

had made arrangements for a cheque to be paid to a third party. However, no payment was received by the third party because subsequent to writing to the Society the respondent had received a tax demand which she was required to prioritise over the payment to the third party. In the circumstances, the Tribunal held that the letter to the Law Society whilst misleading was not intentionally so, nor was it reckless. Rather, it was innocent since she genuinely intended to send the funds, but had been prevented from so doing by a development that she had not anticipated. Her behaviour was held to be "unprofessional"[66] but not amounting to professional misconduct. It may be the case in the future, however, that this would be regarded simply as an excellent plea in mitigation, since the ruling potentially opens the door to misleading behaviour on a wider scale.

An illustration of intentional or reckless misleading came in the same year.[67] Here the respondent repeatedly misled clients and others over a number of years. For example, he lead two clients to believe that he was prosecuting their divorce actions, when he had, in reality, done nothing; also telling another client that he had raised several actions on his behalf, that they had been unsuccessful and that an appeal hearing had taken place, when again none of these things had actually happened; and finally pretending to the other side's agents and the sheriff clerk in one case that he was unable to obtain his client's instructions when, in fact, he had repeatedly refused to answer increasingly frantic communications from his client. The Tribunal had little hesitation in holding this persistent conduct was professional misconduct.

A further example of intentional misleading came before the Tribunal in 2004.[68] The solicitor had misplaced a set of deeds belonging to a client and required to purchase copies. He then attempted to pass the cost for the copies on to the client by telling her the money was required for the recording of her title, which it was not. An internal memo written by the solicitor stating "I'm not sure how much of this we can lose in Mrs A's fee . . . but I shall try to be as creative as possible", convinced the Tribunal that the solicitor had misled his client. The Tribunal found that a solicitor has a professional duty not to mis-state the factual position to his client, but declined to describe the behaviour as dishonest.

Another recent case[69] tested the boundaries of misleading behaviour and was found to fall just short of misconduct. A solicitor purchased a property as a nominee on behalf of a client. In this case, however, the nominee clause was used to disguise the identity of the purchaser, as it was known that an offer in the name of the purchaser would not have been accepted. The seller formed the impression that she was selling to the solicitor on his own behalf, a presumption which he did not rebut. This impression was added to by three instances of personal contact initiated by the seller. The seller felt deceived when the nominee provision was exercised. It was accepted that the solicitor could not have disclosed that he was acting for the purchaser without

---

[66] Although this is equivalent to "unsatisfactory conduct", this terminology has yet to be endorsed by the Tribunal.

[67] DTD *Craig* 1115/03.

[68] DTD *Moodie* 20/07/04.

[69] DTD *Burd* 06/01/05, see also "Nominee clauses . . . are they deception or smart tactics?", *The Scotsman*, 10/05/05.

breaching client confidentiality, however the Tribunal pointed out that "solicitors must act honestly at all times and in such a way as to put their personal integrity beyond question". In this instance the solicitor's actings had "led to the misleading" of the seller and to the solicitor having to take a position with the seller that was not open with her in order to protect confidentiality. It was important to the finding that the seller was legally represented and that she considered that if she had fully understood the implications of the nominee clause when her own solicitor had explained it to her, she would not have felt deceived. The Tribunal found the conduct to be unprofessional.

Failure to Comply with Proper Forms of Execution 1.25

In several cases, the Discipline Tribunal has held that intentional failure to comply with the proper form of execution of a document amounts to misconduct. In *Oliver*[70] the solicitor, acting in his capacity as a Notary Public, failed to ensure that a Power of Attorney was properly executed, as it was written in Spanish with no translation provided and was signed outwith his presence.[71] The Tribunal held that "The public and the profession are entitled to the protection that documents, signed on oath before a Notary Public, have a status greater than ordinary documents, by virtue of notarisation ... A solicitor must respect the formalities and not take shortcuts." The Tribunal was also concerned by the fact that public confidence in the process may be undermined. This point arose again in *Macadam*[72] which concerned a solicitor who had presented a blank C1 form, for the purpose of obtaining confirmation, to an executor for signature. The Tribunal was very concerned by the solicitor's actions and held, "It is imperative, if the public are to have faith in the legal profession, that solicitors deal with these important forms in a proper and honest manner."

Delay, Carelessness and Incompetence 1.26

For many years the regulatory and disciplinary authorities in the U.K, like their counterparts in a wide variety of other jurisdictions, have been confronted with complaints which raise issues of delay, neglect or incompetence on the part of the practitioner rather than clear cut issues of conduct. Such service complaints arose and continue to arise more frequently than conduct complaints. Most of these cases had to be rejected in the past since they were not seen as raising issues of misconduct.[73] However, after much soul searching the Society, the Tribunal and the court each reached the conclusion that provided the failure was egregious enough, negligence,[74]

---

[70] DTD 09/11/04.
[71] See also DTD *McAnulty* 03/12/03 where the Tribunal found the solicitor had been dishonest regarding the notarising of documents outwith the presence of the deponing witness and signing dockets which he knew to be false.
[72] DTD 16/12/04.
[73] Thus Lord Morrison in *X Insurance Company v A & B*, 1936 S.C. 255 at 250 states "the cases show that some dishonourable act or improper motive is essential in an act of professional misconduct."
[74] *E v T* 1949 SLT 411.

delay,[75] carelessness[76] or incompetence[77] could each amount to misconduct. Of course, each of them could also be unsatisfactory conduct, inadequate professional service or negligence. Indeed, the very same careless or negligent act or period of delay as we saw earlier[78] can at one and the same time constitute misconduct/unsatisfactory conduct, IPS and negligence. In practice, however, the advent of IPS has meant that there is now a remedy in service complaints that was not previously available, and inevitably, the great bulk of service complaints are dealt with under the rubric of IPS. The move away from the traditional concept of professionalism in the last twenty years[79] which we identified earlier has brought with it a greater emphasis on ethical codes, the protection of the public and the enhancement of competence amongst the profession. The arrival of IPS was a clear indication of the way professional regulation was changing, but in some ways even more striking has been the growth in the importance of competence. Competence[80] has long been another of the core elements in "fitness to practice" and not surprisingly features in the Code of Conduct.[81] But it also lay behind the introduction of mandatory Continuing Professional Development in 1993,[82] the recognition of incompetent legal assistance as a ground of appeal in the High Court,[83] the

---

[75] DTD 687/86(a) (failure to reply to a letter of enquiry from the Law Society for over two months), DTD 470/80 (a failure to take any steps in a six year period to wind up an estate. The tribunal relied on Begg on *The Law of Scotland Relating to Law Agents* (2nd edn, p.233): "By the mere acceptance of employment, a Law Agent undertakes to perform, with due diligence and the requisite skill, the business committed to his charge"), DTD 753/89 ("gravely neglecting the affairs of five clients in a relatively short period"), *Gray* 1994 J.L.S.S. 424 and *Marr/Law* 1995 J.L.S.S. 365.

[76] DTD 367/75(a) (misconduct in the light of his failure "in relation to the charge of attempted murder brought against his client, to precognosce witnesses, to arrange a consultation with Counsel prior to the trial, to represent his client at the Pleading Diet and to timeously lodge a special defence", leading to the conviction of his client. During the hearing the fiscal cited the decision in *Writers to the Signet v Mackersy*, 1924 S.C. 776. In that case the solicitor was found guilty of professional misconduct "in respect of his reckless disregard of the duty which was incumbent upon him to take ordinary and recognised measures in order to satisfy himself that a claim for damages which he was instrumental in presenting to the Court of trial was . . . genuine.").

[77] See J.Ryder, *Professional Conduct for Scottish Solicitors* (Butterworths, 1995), pp.40–44. See also DTD *Owens* 471/80 (Gross incompetence by the solicitor in failing to record a disposition and standard security immediately after settlement. When they were presented a year later they contained a number of unauthenticated alterations which led to their rejection by the Keeper of the Registers).

[78] See para.1.04 above.

[79] See A. Paterson, "Professionalism and the Legal Services Market" 1996 *International Journal of the Legal Profession* 137.

[80] For a general discussion of the nature of competence and its links to negligence, see A. Paterson, "Professional Competence" 1983 J.L.S.S. 385.

[81] Arts 5(b) (competence); 5(c) (acting with due expedition); 5(d) (exercising the appropriate level of skill); 5(e) (communicating effectively). There is a close parallel between the code provisions and the elements of competence which were identified by the Law Society's Competence report in 1987. These elements, in turn, were derived from the 1982 American Law Institute—American Bar Association report on Competence, namely: (i) deals with business with appropriate speed; (ii) is specifically knowledgeable about the fields of law in which he or she practises; (iii) exercises an appropriate level of skill in these fields of law; (iv) exercises reasonable care; (v) maintains effective office systems; (vi) communicates effectively with clients; (vii) identifies and avoids the areas of practice in which he or she does not have the knowledge or skill to deal with effectively."

[82] Solicitors (Scotland)(Continuing Professional Development) Regulations.

[83] See *Anderson v HM Advocate*, 1996 J.C. 29 where, in a historic five judge decision of the High Court of Justiciary, it was held that if the conduct of an accused's counsel or solicitor was

accreditation of specialists and the introduction of peer review quality assurance measures in relation to civil legal aid work. Moreover, as the profession grows more specialised,[84] so the requirement of art.5(b) of the code—only acting in those matters where the solicitor is competent to do so—will become more of a hurdle. However, despite its terms, art.5(b) does not require a solicitor to be competent in an area before taking on a case in it, provided he or she takes the necessary steps to make themselves competent or the service which they offer to the client a competent one e.g. by bringing in counsel or a specialist solicitor.[85]

Is there an Ethical Duty to Report another Lawyer's Misconduct? 1.27

In other words, is there a duty to be a "whistleblower" in Scotland? There is nothing in the Practice Rules, Codes of Conduct, Practice Guidelines or decisions of the Discipline Tribunal on this. The rules are similarly silent in Australia, although there are rules in most Australian jurisdictions which require lawyers to report dishonesty or breaches of the Australian Accounts rules.[86] In the USA such a duty exists under the Model Rules where the alleged misconduct raises a "substantial question as to that lawyer's honesty, trustworthiness or fitness as a lawyer."[87] It has also been stated in the USA that where reporting the misconduct would require the disclosure of a client's confidential information, informed consent must be obtained or the report should not be made.[88] Similarly, in England, Principle 19.04 of *The Guide to the Professional Conduct of Solicitors*[89] establishes that "a solicitor is under a duty to report . . . any serious misconduct." The annotation indicates that this would include situations where the solicitor's integrity was in question or he or she was in financial difficulties, or where someone in their office had committed theft. There seems little reason why the same general approach should not apply in Scotland. It follows that there is a common law ethical duty in Scotland to report serious misconduct by another solicitor.[90] Whether it is misconduct to breach this obligation must be a moot point. It is certainly unsatisfactory conduct, and, if the matter relates to the theft of a client's money, extremely unwise, if not misconduct not to report the matter to the Law Society.

---

so incompetent as to deprive him of his or her right to a fair trial, this could be grounds for setting aside the conviction on appeal.

[84] See K. Kerner, *Specialism in Private Legal Practice* (CRU, Edinburgh, 1998). Kerner's survey found that 64% of principals considered themselves to be specialists and 76% reported being consulted as specialists by fellow solicitors.

[85] This solution does not absolve the solicitor from monitoring the quality of the work being done by the specialist.

[86] See Y. Ross, *Ethics in Law* (Butterworths, Sydney, 2001) at p.180.

[87] MR 8.3. In a recent opinion (Formal Opinion 04–433 [2004]) the ABA Standing Committee on Ethics and Professional Responsibility stated that this obligation extends to professional misconduct by non-practising lawyers and to misconduct, even where the activity involved is completely removed from the practice of law.

[88] ABA Standing Committee on Ethics and Professional Responsibility, Formal Opinion 04–433 (2004). It is likely that Scotland would follow the USA in holding that any duty to blow the whistle is trumped by the obligation to protect clients' confidential information.

[89] 8th edn, 1999.

[90] In Australia it has been argued that as officers of the court, solicitors owe an ethical duty to uphold the rule of law and therefore to report lawyers who are known to be breaking the law. Ross, *op. cit.* p.179.

1.28 Unprofessional or Unsatisfactory Professional Conduct

Neither this standard nor its definition has been set out up till now in the legislation which governs Scottish solicitors.[91] Unsatisfactory professional conduct is however defined in the Legal Profession and Legal Aid (Scotland) Bill.[92] Nevertheless, as a logical construct, if it had not existed, as a matter of practice it would have been necessary to invent it. It is, quite simply, behaviour which, while falling just short of professional misconduct, is nonetheless unacceptable and worthy of public condemnation. Unlike misconduct, the test for it is only on the balance of probabilities.[93] Indeed, amongst the clearest examples of unprofessional conduct are the cases where there is insufficient evidence to establish the behaviour beyond reasonable doubt but enough to establish it on the balance of probabilities. In cases where unprofessional conduct is established, the Tribunal takes the view that the "solicitor has no one but himself to blame for having been charged with the offence" and accordingly resolves that there be no liability for expenses on either party.[94] Other examples of unprofessional conduct have included a case where carelessly two Legal Aid claims were made for the same solicitor for different clients at the same time of day. Because it was a mistake rather than deliberate it was deemed to be unprofessional conduct as opposed to professional misconduct.[95] Similarly, in another case[96] where the solicitor had signed blank legal aid forms and persuaded his clients to sign blank and incomplete legal aid forms, the Tribunal took the lenient view that that is was a breach of duty[97] but not misconduct because the solicitor had been motivated solely by expediency rather than anything more venal.

One of the most controversial findings of unprofessional conduct related to a case[98] where the clients, a husband and wife, for whom the solicitor respondent had acted when buying a dwellinghouse, had not paid the lawyer's fee. At a social function in a hotel it was proved beyond reasonable doubt that the solicitor had deliberately run his hands up and down the bare back of the wife above the neckline of her dress. Although considering the behaviour to be improper, because the act was not indecent and was an isolated incident out of business hours and in a social setting, it did not amount to misconduct. In the fracas that followed, the respondent referred to the unpaid bill, in the presence of other parties, in response to being shouted at by the incensed husband. The Tribunal took the view that the respondent had not deliberately breached the client's confidentiality, and treated the reference to the outstanding account as "understandable" in the provoking circumstances in which he found himself. Accordingly there was no misconduct by the respondent. Given the solicitor's behaviour to the wife this was a remarkably

---

[91] However, it is to be found in the relevant legislation of almost all of the Australian States.

[92] Clause 34.

[93] After a disagreement between the Scottish Legal Services Ombudsman and the Law Society (S.L.S.O.: Annual Report 1997, para.3.35) the Society accepted the Ombudsman's argument that it should be proved on the balance of probabilities.

[94] DTD 493/81.

[95] DTD 532/82.

[96] DTD *Anderson & Others* 1001/99.

[97] Because it involved a false declaration that the information in the form was true and complete.

[98] DTD 658/85.

lenient approach from the Tribunal. However, it is worth noting that this decision is twenty years old, and views on sexual harassment have changed in that time. Certainly, the Tribunal in recent years has shown itself sensitive to such gender issues.[99]

Unsatisfactory Conduct Today

1.29

By the end of the Twentieth century, unprofessional conduct was coming under increasing critical attack, in part because it was confusing to public and profession alike, and in part because it was seen as akin to the "not proven" verdict. In addition, it was discovered following a scrutiny of the relevant legislation that the council did not have the power to find a solicitor "guilty" of unprofessional conduct. Accordingly, in May 2000 the Law Society Council replaced "unprofessional conduct" with the concept of "unsatisfactory conduct". The latter was a concept to be found in a variety of Australian states, which it was felt would be less confusing to the public and the profession. Instead of unprofessional conduct, there is now a finding that the conduct of the solicitor did "not amount to professional misconduct but did involve a failure to meet the standard of conduct observed by competent solicitors of good repute".[1] Where unsatisfactory conduct is established, the complainer is told that the complaint has been upheld and that the solicitor has been advised that the conduct is considered to be unsatisfactory. Since 2000, findings of unsatisfactory (or unprofessional) conduct have included: breaching r.5(1) of the 1986 Solicitors (Scotland) Practice Rules by acting for both parties in a transaction in a potential conflict of interest situation on the pretext that both are established clients when this was not the case; breaches of r.5(2) of the 1986 Solicitors (Scotland) Practice Rules; misleading the other side as to developments in a case; repeated failing to complete the required number of Continuing Professional Development hours[2]; breach of the practice guidelines on Closing Dates; failure to respond to letters from the Law Society; failure to obtemper a mandate; a minor breach of confidentiality; sending blank forms to a third party to sign without telling them to take independent legal advice; and repeated failure to respond to a client.

Well intentioned as the change to unsatisfactory conduct undoubtedly was, it is far from clear that it reduced any confusion that may have existed in the minds of the profession and the public.[3] Equally, the reform did not at first clarify whether[4] repeated acts of unsatisfactory conduct can amount to misconduct. However, the Council decided that any findings of unsatisfactory

---

[99] See e.g. DTD *Maguire* 1069/01.

[1] In NSW and Victoria "unsatisfactory conduct" means conduct that falls short of the standard of competence and diligence that a member of the public is entitled to expect of a reasonably competent legal practitioner. See s.127(2) Legal Profession Act 1987 and s.137 Legal Practice Act 1996.

[2] In extreme cases, this may even constitute misconduct. Thus in DTD *McNiven* 1136/03 a solicitor had failed to complete his continuing professional development hours for four years in a row. In finding him guilty of professional misconduct the Tribunal observed that: "It is imperative, if the public is to have confidence in the profession, that solicitors undertake the necessary continuing professional development and keep a record of the continuing professional development undertaken."

[3] The fact that the reform was introduced without any significant consultation with the profession or the public leaves the matter moot.

[4] As in Victoria s.137 Legal Practice Act 1996.

conduct arrived at after January 1, 2003 against a solicitor would be kept on his or her record and might be taken into account in subsequent proceedings, including an *in cummulo* charge of misconduct.[5] This made sense both in terms of deterrence and public protection. Unfortunately, as the Council was aware, there was no more statutory basis for findings of "unsatisfactory conduct" than there had been for "unprofessional conduct". Thus when such findings began to be challenged by way of judicial review in 2006, the Society was advised that they should no longer note such findings on the disciplinary records of solicitors. However, they were also advised that Council and its committees could still express a view that a solicitor's behavior had been unsatisfactory. Fortunately, the difficulties over the status of such findings should be rectified by the provisions of the Legal Profession and Legal Aid (Scotland) Act.

There is one final concern relating to unsatisfactory conduct: its presence offers a temptation to those who place an erroneous emphasis on the term "culpability" in the *Sharp* test, to allow mitigating circumstances to down-grade the finding from misconduct to unsatisfactory conduct rather than to make a finding of misconduct but mitigate the sanction. So long as the sanction associated with unsatisfactory conduct was restricted to noting the finding[6] this was a serious concern. However, if the range of sanctions is extended as the Legal Profession and Legal Aid (Scotland) Bill 2006 provides to include a censure, a fine, an order that the practitioner undertake a specified course of education, or an order to pay compensation to the client of up to £5,000, this would be much less problematic.

1.30 Inadequate Professional Services—The Context

Inadequate professional services (IPS) are a phenomenon that the layperson finds easy to grasp. Yet it is one that most jurisdictions have struggled to address as the tacit agreement between the profession and the wider community enshrined in the traditional concept of professionalism has been "re-negotiated" in favour of clients and consumers in the past twenty years.[7] Today's professionalism has a greater emphasis on client care and better service to clients than that of the 1950s. As we saw earlier, in the past the regulatory or disciplinary authorities were unable to address the great bulk of such service complaints, leaving the complainer with a negligence claim, at best. In the USA, the response has been to expand the grounds of civil suit from negligence to breach of contract and latterly to breach of fiduciary duty.[8] In Australia a "dispute" jurisdiction was introduced. Disputes were defined to include not only disagreements over legal fees but those in relation to pecuniary loss and "any other genuine dispute arising out of the provision of legal services".[9] In the UK the response has been IPS. It emerged as a part of

---

[5] 2002 J.L.S.S. 9.

[6] The terms of the Solicitors (Scotland) Act 1980 do not allow the Law Society to attach any sanctions to such a finding.

[7] See A. Paterson, "Professionalism and the Legal Services Market" 1996 *International Journal of the Legal Profession* 137.

[8] See Third Restatement of the law governing lawyers (American Law Institute, St Paul, 2000).

[9] See e.g. s.122 Legal Practice Act 1996, Victoria. Such disputes are handled separately from and more expeditiously than complaints.

professional discipline and regulation in the Solicitors (Scotland) Act 1988.[10] It was defined as "professional services which are in any respect not of the quality which could reasonably be expected of a competent solicitor".[11] This short but somewhat opaque definition has given rise to a number of keenly contested debates.

Inadequate Professional Services and Negligence 1.31

First, there was the issue as to what to do where the solicitor's behaviour which gave rise to the complaint was potentially negligent. Did that mean that it could not also be IPS? Such a conclusion would have largely defeated the purpose of introducing IPS in the first place. Accordingly it is not surprising to find that the relevant legislation[12] treats IPS as a separate standard from negligence and that the same behaviour can fall foul of the two standards. Secondly, however, it was argued that even if the two standards were different, it would be unfair to the solicitor to investigate the IPS complaint first, since any admission or fact found by the Law Society in examining the file could be used against the solicitor in a subsequent negligence claim. Although this line of thinking prevailed in the Law Society from the inception of IPS, it was finally abandoned in 2001 after years of complaint by successive legal services ombudsmen, because a close scrutiny of the legislation revealed that Parliament clearly envisaged that there would be cases in which the IPS complaint was determined by the Society before the negligence claim had been settled or gone to proof.[13] Today, the Society gives the option to the client as to whether he or she wishes the IPS inquiry to continue while the negligence issue is being resolved, but it is anticipated that in most cases the inquiry will not be suspended.

Inadequate Professional Services—The Limits 1.32

In the decade following the inception of IPS the Law Society also tended to take the view that IPS did not cover the giving of advice or the exercise of professional judgement. However, there was nothing in the statute to justify such a narrow interpretation of "professional services". Moreover, the Discipline Tribunal ruled in several cases that IPS covered advice.[14] Similarly, just as a solicitor exercising his or her "professional judgement" is not thereby exempt from a finding of negligence if no reasonable solicitor would have exercised his or her judgement in that way,[15] so too "professional judgement"

---

[10] See now s.42A–C of the Solicitors (Scotland) Act 1980.

[11] See s.65(1) Solicitors (Scotland) Act 1980. It is sometimes also known as "shoddy work". As Ryder has noted, *op. cit.* p.34, services provided *pro bono* can still give rise to finding of IPS.

[12] s.56A Solicitors (Scotland) Act 1980. The Legal Profession and Legal Aid (Scotland) Bill 2006 expressly provides that IPS can include elements of negligence.

[13] In such cases, the court is permitted to take any award in respect of IPS into account in assessing damages for negligence, in order to prevent double counting. See s.56A(2) Solicitors (Scotland) Act 1980.

[14] E.g. Case 835/92 ("failure to advise the client adequately" about the procedure for buying and selling property in Scotland) and Case 860/93 ("Not advising the client properly" as to what was included in a fee quotation).

[15] *Hunter v Hanley*, 1955 S.C. 200.

will not exempt from a finding of IPS if no "adequately performing" solicitor would have exercised his or her judgement in that way. In 2001, the Law Society Council accepted that IPS could cover advice and the exercise of professional judgement.

The Law Society was also dubious, initially, as to whether behaviour that was a conduct offence could also be IPS.[16] However, in 1993 the Scottish Solicitors' Discipline Tribunal established that the Solicitors (Scotland) Act 1980 (as amended) envisages that the same behaviour can give rise to both IPS and misconduct.[17] Indeed, there is now a strong argument that many acts which constitute a conduct offence will also be examples of IPS.[18]

The next issue is whether IPS should be assessed by looking at each aspect of the service or rather at the overall performance of the solicitor in the case, determining whether, taking it as a whole, it was inadequate. The latter approach has superficial attractions, however, to adopt it would greatly undermine the impact and effect of IPS. In any event, the matter is settled by the fact that the "holistic" approach cannot be reconciled with the words of the statute—which states that IPS exists if the services "are in any respect" not of the appropriate quality.

Finally, when do professional services begin and end? It is tempting to say that professional services cannot begin until the contract for services begins. While normally this will be the case, the wording of the statute would appear to allow a client who has instructed a solicitor, to complain about the adequacy of the service which he or she received from the solicitor while he or she was only a potential client, provided it was in connection with the same matter, because potential clients in such situations can qualify as "any person having an interest", even if they would not be eligible for compensation for the period when they were only potential clients.[19] As for when they end, in 1994 senior counsel advised the Law Society that the service ends on the issue of the fee note. This advice seems highly questionable. While the rendering of a fee note is probably not a professional service, the production of a detailed account at the client's request after the rendering of the fee note, almost certainly is. Again, if firm has a client relations partner, his or her actings in relation to a complaining client would seem to constitute professional services for a client, the more so since it has been held that the mere fact that a client has complained about a solicitor is not sufficient to imply that the contract of services has thereby been terminated.[20] Certainly, in 2001 the Law Society Council accepted that what a solicitor did after the rendering the fee note and

---

[16] Solicitors (Scotland) Act 1980, s.56A.

[17] In *Carpenter*, 1993 J.L.S.S. 117. As the Tribunal noted "The essential feature of the provisions of s.53A is to enable the tribunal to make orders for the benefit of [the] client without requiring the client to take a civil action in Court and the whole purpose of s.53A would be defeated if it were to be maintained that the tribunal was unable to exercise these powers if professional misconduct was established."

[18] This is relevant to the question whether we should separate the investigation and handling of service cases from conduct cases, with different procedures for each, as in Australia. The argument against this is that such is the overlap between conduct and service that to separate them will lead to considerable duplication of investigation and consideration. This, indeed, is one of the fears thrown up by the provisions of the Legal Profession and Legal Aid (Scotland) Bill 2006, which provide for just such a separation.

[19] s.42A Solicitors (Scotland) Act 1980.

[20] 1989 J.L.S.S. 389.

taking it to taxation could constitute IPS. Again, a solicitor's duty to retain case files[21] at the end of a transaction would also seem to constitute a professional service.

Inadequate Professional Services—The Participants 1.33

Any person with an interest can raise an IPS complaint, and this includes beneficiaries and third parties.[22] However, anomalously, only clients are entitled to compensation for IPS.[23] On the other hand, an inadequate professional service can be offered by an individual solicitor or a firm.[24] Despite this, the policy of the Council since 1989 has been to make determinations of IPS against firms rather than individuals, except in unusual circumstances.[25] The rationale behind this approach is that it is the firm rather than the solicitor that receives the fee, just as it has been argued that the primary contract is between the client and the firm rather than the solicitor. It follows that if the partner rendering the inadequate service dies the client remains a client of the firm who continue to be liable for the original IPS.[26]

Inadequate Professional Services—Further Guidance 1.34

Ever since its inception IPS has suffered from the opacity with which it is defined in the statute. The Law Society has been reluctant to provide guidance as to what might constitute IPS.[27] Thus the Society has always argued that its publications which encourage better client care and risk management[28] set more than the minimal adequacy standard of IPS, and are therefore misleading to the public.[29] This position has not assisted in attaining consistency in findings of IPS as between the regulatory bodies.[30] It is to be hoped that the Complaints Commission will make it an early priority to provide further guidance in this area. Some guidance as to what is likely to be considered IPS can be found in the Code of Conduct, and also in the reported decisions of the Discipline Tribunal.[31] That said, a scrutiny of the Annual Reports of the Law

---

[21] Which can last for several years.

[22] Solicitors (Scotland) Act 1980, s.42A.

[23] *Symon*, 1994 J.L.S.S. 386; *Wernham*, 1996 J.L.S.S. 274.

[24] Solicitors (Scotland) Act 1980, s.42A(8).

[25] E.g. where a solicitor is guilty of IPS in one or more cases and then leaves the firm, the Society will sometimes split the consequences of IPS between the solicitor and the firm. Where the firm or the solicitor becomes bankrupt any award of compensation will come from the Master Insurance Policy.

[26] *Symon*, 1994 J.L.S.S. 386.

[27] Originally, the Society produced guidelines suggesting that instances of IPS would include not dealing with the business with due expedition; displaying adequate knowledge about the relevant areas of the law; exercising an appropriate level of skill; maintaining appropriate systems; communicating effectively with the client(s) and others. These were then withdrawn.

[28] See Law Society, *Better Client Care and Practice Management* (updated annually) and *Ensuring Excellence—Even better Practice in Practice* (1998).

[29] For this reason these publications have been excluded, until recently, from the public section of the Law Society's website and given limited public circulation.

[30] E.g. the Client Relations Committees and other disciplinary committees of the Law Society and the Discipline Tribunal.

[31] See I. Smith and J. Barton, *Procedures and Decisions of the Scottish Solicitors' discipline tribunal* (T & T Clark, Edinburgh, 1995).

Society of Scotland reveals that consistently the most frequent forms of IPS relate to delay, failure to communicate, failure to advise adequately,[32] failure to follow instructions and failure to prepare adequately.[33]

1.35 Negligence

If competence relates to a general capacity to perform certain tasks adequately, negligence refers to a want of due care in performing a specific task.[34] It follows, therefore, that there is no inconsistency in stating that a normally competent practitioner can be capable of the occasional negligent act or a practitioner who is generally incompetent can perform an act in a non-negligent fashion. The modern test for professional negligence in Scotland was established in *Hunter v Hanley*.[35] Essentially, negligence by a professional is only established if the course taken by the professional is one "which no professional man of ordinary skill would have taken if he had been acting with ordinary care". This is broadly akin to requiring a solicitor to exercise the standard of care "of the reasonably competent solicitor acting with due care and attention".[36] The similarity between this test and that for inadequate professional services is obvious. However, the duty of care may vary depending on the specialist skills of the solicitor or the competence of the client. In relation to the latter the Privy Council held in the *Pickersgill* case[37] that the solicitor's duty of care to the client depends on the instructions received but that where these are silent, a person not well versed in business affairs may need commercial advice from his or her solicitor in a way that an experienced businessman would not, (in the absence of any hidden legal points).

1.36 Breach of Fiduciary Duty

The final set of standards, the fiduciary duties of a lawyer or law agent will be discussed in greater depth in subsequent chapters (and Chs 6,7,8 and 10 in particular). Often summarized under the umbrella of the loyalty obligation of the lawyer, these obligations cover safeguarding the client's property and information, disclosing all relevant information, not making secret profits, nor preferring the lawyer's interests or a third party's interests over the client's. In practice, claims against lawyers which are classified as professional negligence could often equally well be described as breaches of fiduciary duty. Indeed in the USA and in England it is not uncommon for both heads to be

---

[32] E.g. as to the clients' legal position, as to legal aid (including liability if the client loses, or as to the operation of the statutory clawback), as to recovery from the other side, or in respect of the solicitor's account.

[33] In *McKenzie v Council of the Law Society of Scotland*, 2000 S.L.T. 836 the Inner House held that professional defalcation or incompetence were not necessary elements in IPS.

[34] In 2002 a Pursuers' Panel was established, specifically to provide solicitors who will act in cases of negligence brought against solicitors. See *"Pursuers' Panel provides public with balanced guidance on professional negligence claims"*—J.L.S.S.—May 2003 Vol.48 No.5, page 42. See also, *"Ask the Panel"*, 2005 J.L.S.S. 43.

[35] 1955, S.C. 200.

[36] See R. Rennie, *Solicitors' Negligence* (Butterworths, Edinburgh, 1997).

[37] *Pickersgill & Another v Riley*, 2004 W.L. 62226; [2004] UKPC 14.

raised in the one action.[38] Pursuing a claim under the head of fiduciary duty may have advantages to the client since it may be that breaches of such duties contain no equivalent to contributory negligence, minimizing one's loss or issues of remoteness of damages.[39]

---

[38] Third Restatement of the Law governing Lawyers, *op. cit.* para 49(c). p.348. Begg, *op. cit.* p.245 quotes an English case of *Barber v Stone* in the Queens Bench division of the High Court in 1881 where Mr Justice Grove observes that: "The action was brought for negligence, breach of duty and misconduct. The terms are almost convertible and may be applied to nearly the same kinds of acts."

[39] See S. Baughen, *Professionals and Fiduciaries* (Gostick Hall Publications, Safron Walden, 2002) at p.16.

CHAPTER 2

OBTAINING AND RETAINING CLIENTS

2.01 Introduction

This is an area of professional responsibility which is now primarily policy driven, rather than derived from substantive law or ethical considerations. The key issues are: the public interest in identifying lawyers who are skilled in the area(s) of law which are relevant to their problem(s) and who are accessible in terms of location, opening hours, cost and availability; being protected against false or misleading advertising or against over-zealous solicitation of their business; in the maintenance of an acceptable level of competition between providers of legal services; and the profession's interest in curbing advertising that brings the profession into disrepute, which leads to excessively aggressive competition or which undermines the mutual trust and confidence within the profession.

Inevitably, these interests do not always coincide and in Scotland the history of the last 20 years has been one in which the balance between them has been consistently moving towards the interests of the public.

2.02 Historical Background

Until the 1930s, advertising by solicitors in Scotland was permitted and quite commonplace in certain areas of practice, although not universally welcomed by the professional elite. In the depression era the temptation increased for some solicitors to acquire clients by methods which a sizeable section of the profession regarded as unacceptable. This could range from employing clerks to go around the country armed with mandates ready for signature by accident victims or studying newspaper files as aids to the discovery of likely personal injury claimants[1] to paying third parties such as policemen, prison warders or hospital workers[2] for referring clients to the paying solicitor. Seizing their opportunity, the elite members of the profession in Scotland and England drove through bans on advertising and touting by solicitors and on the payment of referral fees.[3] At about the same time the

---

[1] See *Scottish Law Agents Society v Lawrence*, 1940 S.C. 196; 1940 S.L.T. 148. Such behaviour was castigated by the Inner House as "likely to result in trumped-up and false claims" which would be "harmful to the administration of justice".

[2] Hence the term "ambulance-chasing". In fact, the most celebrated ambulance chaser of the era was an attorney in the USA named Gatner, who pointed out somewhat dryly that paying ambulance drivers for the accident victim's name was a waste of time since they usually didn't know the name or the address of the victim in the first place. Hospital staff were a better bet.

[3] This ban took the form of a rule which prevented the sharing of fees with unqualified persons.

profession's scale fees became minimum fees as well as maximums—thus discouraging price-cutting. Such was the success of these measures that it was 50 years before the Thatcher Government's deregulation campaign began to erode them significantly. During that period these anti-competitive practices established a concept of professionalism[4] which discouraged entrepreneurial-ism and innovation in the profession.

The Renaissance of Advertising **2.03**

During the 1970s the feeling grew that the ban on advertising hit differentially as between elite and non-elite lawyers, and also that the ban was preventing innovations in the profession that would assist lower income clients in a way that was hard to justify in terms of the public interest. Eventually a combination of pressure from the Office of Fair Trading, the consumer movement, and a significant minority of the profession, coupled with a change of heart by the Thatcher Government combined to overcome the profession's resistance. The final straw was the government's threat that unless the profession relaxed the ban on advertising the government would do it for them. Following a full debate at a general meeting, the profession voted in a referendum to bring in advertising and the 1985 rules were the outcome. They were highly restrictive. For example, whilst they did allow advertising on the television they did not allow cinema or billboard advertising. More significantly they specified very narrowly what could be advertised. Anything which was not specifically allowed was still prohibited. Unsurprisingly, the 1985 rules rapidly proved unworkable. The 1987 rules adopted a more relaxed approach permitting wider forms of advertising although still with certain exceptions. Finally, in 1991 rules were passed allowing solicitors to promote their services as they thought fit, subject to certain very limited restrictions. These were repeated in the 1995 rules (the fourth set within a decade) introduced as a partial response to concerns expressed at the 1995 AGM of the Law Society relating to estate agents and others advertising packages including low cost conveyancing fees. The scope for effective and informative advertising in terms of the 1995 rules can be seen from the following two advertisements:

---

[4] See A. Paterson, "Professionalism and the Legal Services Market" (1996) *International Journal of the Legal Profession*, p.137.

The Tanker Braer

- When faced with a disaster like this it is vital to be able to rely on professional, skilled avice.

- This is what solicitors LEVY & McRAE can offer.

- LEVY & McRAE have a considerable breadth of expertise having been directly involved in the legal aftermath of the Piper Alpha and Lockerbie disasters.

- Our Head of Litigation, Mr Peter Watson, handled international claims both in this country and the USA.

- In a statement Mr Watson said: "Shetlanders who believe they may have a claim must not rush to settle without consulting a solicitor. Bearing in mind the operating country of origin of the tanker *Braer* is the USA these claims may be best pursued in the American courts."

- Whether you have suffered loss directly or indirectly as a result of this tragedy or are simply unsure of your position contact us for our expert advice.

- LEVY & McRAE can assist you by handling all your claims whether relating to agriculture, fishing, crofting, tourism, retail or personal. These claims may include–

1. LOSS OF PROFITS

2. LOSS OF OR DAMAGE TO STOCK

3. DERELICTION OF LAND

4. PROPERTY DAMAGE

- If you are interested please contact us by telephone, letter or fax. Alternatively why not meet Peter Watson free of charge at The Shetland Hotel, Lerwick any time today (Friday) January 8 or tomorrow Saturday before 12 noon.

LEVY & McRAE
266 St Vincent St
Glasgow
G2 5RL
Phone: 041 307 2311
Fax: 041 307 6857/6858

Unlike the early years, the advertising rules have caused relatively few problems since 1995.

2.04 The Current Rules

The essence of the Solicitors (Scotland) (Advertising and Promotion) Practice Rules 2006 is contained in r.3–7:

"3. Subject to rules 4 and 7 hereof, a solicitor shall be entitled to promote his services in any way he thinks fit.
4. A solicitor shall not make a direct or indirect approach whether verbal or written to any person whom he knows or ought reasonably to know to be the client of another solicitor with the intention to solicit business from that person.
5. Rule 4 shall not preclude the general circulation by a solicitor of material promoting that solicitor's services whether or not the persons to whom it is directed are established clients.
6. A solicitor shall not be in breach of these rules by reason only of his claim to be a specialist in any particular field of law or legal practice; provided that:—

    (a) the onus of proof that any such claim is justified shall be on the solicitor making it; and
    (b) an advertisement of or by a solicitor or other material issued by or on behalf of a solicitor making any such claim shall conform otherwise to the requirements of rule 7.

7. An advertisement of or by a solicitor or promotional material issued by or on behalf of a solicitor or any promotional activity by or on behalf of a solicitor shall be decent and shall not:—

    (1) contain any inaccuracy or misleading statement[5]; or
    (2) be of such nature or character or be issued or done by such means as may reasonably be regarded as bringing the profession of solicitors into disrepute; or
    (3) identify any client or item of his business without the prior written consent of the client; or
    (4) be defamatory or illegal."

2.05 Media and Content

As r.3 and r.7 reveal, there are now relatively few restrictions as to the media or content of any promotional material or activities by a solicitor.[6] Almost any media can be used, for example, billboards, the cinema, diaries, TV, business cards, golf balls, websites etc, except one that would bring the profession into disrepute. However, simply because the media used are non-

---

[5] See DTD *Gray* 14/01/04. An advert placed in the Yellow Pages suggesting a firm was competent to provide professional advice on English law was held by the Tribunal to be "deliberately inaccurate and misleading" and amounted to misconduct. Although the solicitor held an English law degree, this was not a recent qualification and he had never held a practising certificate for England and Wales. Moreover, the Master Policy would not cover advice on matters of English law.

[6] In addition to the Solicitors (Scotland) (Advertising and Promotion) Practice Rules 2006, there are also the Solicitors (Scotland) (Associates, Consultants and Employees) Practice Rules 2001 which specify that the only names that can appear on a law firm's stationary are those of partners, consultants, associates or employees. Where the names of such individuals do appear on the notepaper, so too, must their designations.

traditional (e.g. recruitment advertisements for staff or magazine articles about lawyers), will not prevent them from being governed by the rules. Rule 7(1) and r.7(2) are in line with the recommendations of the Royal Commission on Legal Services in Scotland and the Monopolies and Mergers Commission. The principal difference in the current rules from the 1995 Rules is that the latter contained two further prohibitions, namely: (1) claiming superiority for his/her services over those offered by another solicitor and (2) comparing his/her fees with those of any other solicitor. These could be partly circumvented if the claim to be, for example, the largest conveyancing firm in the town, could be shown to be true. Again imaginative claims such as "Second to none" or "We are No.1—No.1 High Street" were held not to be a claim to superiority. Nevertheless, the European Commission, and the Office of Fair Trading in the UK, took the view that any prohibition of comparative advertising was anti-competitive, and in 2005 the Society took independent advice on the rules. As a result, the Law Society Council accepted that the prohibitions in r.8 of the 1995 rules against claiming superiority or comparing fees with other solicitors had to be removed. This has been done in the 2006 Rules which came into force in June 2006. The prohibition on inaccurate or misleading adverts remains in the rules, which the Council feel provides more than adequate protection to the public and the profession in respect of bogus claims. In the absence of any recommended fees, it would be well nigh impossible for a firm to lay claim to be the cheapest for any particular service, and the profession can be relied on to bring any apparently spurious claims to the Society's attention. Equally, the requirement that any promotional material or activities be "decent" and not such as may "reasonably be regarded as bringing the profession of solicitors into disrepute" leaves the Law Society and the Discipline Tribunal some room for manoeuvre where they are dubious as to the acceptability of a proposed promotional initiative.

In short, the Society's rules on content and media are not all that more restrictive than those pertaining in any organisation, namely the Voluntary Code of Advertising Practice of the Advertising Standards Authority and the E.C. Directive on Misleading Advertising. The ASA Code is perhaps best summarised as requiring that advertisements should be legal, decent, honest and truthful. The E.C. Directive (implemented in the U.K. in 1988) defines misleading advertising as any advertising which in any way deceives or is likely to deceive recipients and which by its deceptive nature is likely to affect their economic behaviour or which, for those reasons, injures or is likely to injure, a competitor. Under the Society's rules (r.8) solicitors are held responsible for any promotional material issued by a third party describing the solicitors' services and their cost.[7] Whether this extends to a "planted" article about a lawyer in a legal magazine which compares the lawyer's expertise favourably with those of other solicitors is a moot point which has yet to be tested.[8] In any event, the Society has a power under r.9 to require solicitors to

---

[7] There is also a Professional Practice guideline stipulating that where a solicitor's fees for his/her services are advertised either by the solicitor or by a third party whether or not the solicitor is named in such an advertisement, it must show the full range of fees chargeable for such work and not simply the cheapest end of the range. The advertisement must also include mention of outlays and VAT with no less prominence than the fees.

[8] Rule 9 would seem to apply if a solicitor includes a link on his website to an article in a journal which contains comparative material which he himself could not advertise under the rules.

withdraw offending advertisements and a breach of the rules may be professional misconduct. Because of this, and since the Society has the power to grant a waiver from any of the advertising rules, the moral is obvious: if in any doubt as to the legality of any proposed promotional material (e.g. you want to put your firm's name on beer mats)[9] get in touch with the Professional Practice department at the Society, who will give guidance on specific proposals.

2.06 The Growth of Internet Advertising

Another impetus for reform may come from the growth in lawyer advertising on the internet, either through their own websites or participation in chat rooms or in e-mails. In the main, these will be treated like hard-copy advertisements. However the presence of links to other sites, the interactivity of the medium, and the fact that websites are accessible from any part of the globe, may require the evolution of special rules. The last issue may prove most problematic. Does it mean that a lawyer with a website is practicing law on a global basis?[10] If so, can the lawyer be required to conform to the advertising regulations of every jurisdiction from which his or her website can be accessed? This would clearly seem unreasonable, the more so since a website is not a form of "push technology" but something that has to be actively visited by the reader. The better rule would seem to be that lawyers' advertisements on the web should be regulated by the jurisdictions within which they intend to practice. Prudent lawyers will try to limit the jurisdictions to which they wish their sites to apply, for example, by stating that "this website is for inhabitants of the following countries only". This advice is all the more pertinent for those wishing to advertise by email, which is a form of "push technology" and which is therefore more vulnerable to attack, should it reach another jurisdiction.[11]

2.07 Specialisation

Ideally, members of the public want to know not only whether solicitors are experienced in a particular field of law, but also whether they have an expertise in that field. The profession equally has an interest that its members cannot take advantage of each other and the public by claiming falsely to possess an expertise which they do not. The balance between these objectives has not been easy to draw and has shifted on several occasions in the past 20 years. It was unclear from the 1987 rules whether or not a solicitor could claim to be a specialist without failing foul of the rules. This was clarified in the 1991 rules. The original draft version of the 1991 rules allowed solicitors to claim to be specialists but provided no definition of a specialist. This created the possibility for abuse since solicitors could claim to be specialists (by which they meant that they had very considerable experience in a particular field) without actually possessing any great expertise in the field. Accordingly

---

[9] A Dundee solicitor has done this, including his photograph. The Society accepted that using such mats did not, in itself, bring the profession into disrepute.

[10] On the issue of ethical regulation for trans-national or global law firms, see A Paterson, "Self-regulation and the Future of the Profession" in D. Hayton (ed.) *Laws Futures* (Hart Publishing, Oxford, 2000).

[11] See Jason Krause, "Spam I Am", *ABA Journal*, Jan 2005, 22. For further rules governing email advertising see 2.11.

the final version of the 1991 rules and now the 2006 rules, define a specialist as a "solicitor who possesses knowledge of and expertise in a particular branch or area of law or legal practice significantly greater than that which might reasonably be expected to be possessed by a solicitor who is not a specialist in that branch or area of law or legal practice". Rule 7 allows solicitors to claim to be specialists in their advertisements and promotional material but places the onus on them to prove the claim if challenged.

The self-certification approach to specialisation exemplified by this rule is in marked contrast to the certification schemes prevailing in California or Texas. The latter involve peer assessment, examinations, attendance at continuing legal education seminars and the like. Until the 1990s the Law Societies on both sides of the border in the UK favoured this more objective approach. However, the English amended their rules to permit self-certification in 1991 (in the face of strong criticism by the Lord Chancellor's Department) and the Scots followed suit. Despite the misgivings of the consumer movement, self-certification seems not to have been abused, although it is increasingly frequently used, as can readily be seen from the Yellow Pages phone directories. Despite this, the Society has continued to pursue the objective certification of specialists in a number of particular fields. In the years following the establishment of the first panel in 1991 a total of 22 panels have come into existence, including: Agricultural law, Child law, Commercial Leasing, Construction law, Crofting law, Employment law, Family law, Insolvency law, Intellectual Property law, Liquor Licensing law, Medical Negligence, Pensions law and Planning law.

However, from the public's perspective the most striking aspect is that, after 15 years of accredited specialists, less than 400 of the 7,000 or so solicitors in private practice are so accredited,[12] even though research suggests that a majority of Scottish solicitors now regard themselves as specialists.[13] Even adding the 200 solicitor advocates, who are akin to accredited specialists still means less than 10 per cent of solicitors in private practice have chosen this vehicle. This in turn would suggest that the best vehicle for identifying specialist solicitors for Scottish clients has yet to be developed. The Law Society's Specialism Committee ruled in 1999 that accredited specialists could advertise their specialisms on their firm's notepaper. The requirements for accreditation (which last for five years but can be renewed) are that the solicitor must be able to demonstrate the necessary expertise to the satisfaction of a Society adjudication panel (peer review). This entails spending a substantial proportion of time dealing with that type of law and contributing to the development of that particular area of law.[14]

Touting and Solicitation   2.08

Although touting or solicitation were banned in the 1930s, it took until the 1987 rules for a precise definition of touting to emerge, namely, "a direct approach by or on behalf of a solicitor to a person who is not an established client, with the intention of soliciting business from that person". This

---

[12] They can be found on *www.lawscot.org.uk*.

[13] K. Kerner, "Specialism in Private Legal Practice" (1995) Scottish Office Central Research Unit.

[14] See "Promoting Accredited Specialists" (1999) 44(5) J.L.S.S. It should be noted that neither "substantial proportion" nor "necessary expertise" were defined by the committee.

prevented a wide range of unseemly behaviour in the eyes of competent and reputable members of the profession including tracing accident victims and badgering them to sign a retainer, cold calling clients of other firms and offering to do their legal work for them and offering packets of cigarettes to accused persons in police cells in return for instructions. The fact that the rule equally struck at approaching acquaintances met at a church, golf club or country club in pursuit of business, was not always so clearly recognised. Part of what the Discipline Tribunal objected to was the pressure on the client caused by solicitation, thus in a newspaper advertising case which appears almost bizarre to contemporary eyes, the solicitor's invitation to the readers to "Call Now" followed by a phone number, was deemed to be solicitation amounting to misconduct. Again in a 1986 case, DTD 686/86, the solicitor advertised a list of Scottish houses for sale in an English magazine. Anyone asking for the list of properties received a letter on the solicitor's notepaper stating that they would receive future lists free of charge, provided that when and if they came to buy a Scottish property they used the solicitor's firm to act for them. The Tribunal held that this condition, while not contractually binding, undoubtedly put some pressure on each recipient to employ the solicitor, which in their view constituted touting.

2.09 The Demise of Touting?

In the 1991, 1995 and 2006 Advertising Rules there is no specific reference to touting. However, it would be premature to assume that the ban on touting has thereby been abolished. There is still the possibility that what used to be called solicitation will now be said to be conduct bringing the profession into disrepute. Thus in 1995, an English marketing company, "Legal Marketing Direct", began to sell lists of names and addresses of accident victims to solicitors. The lists were compiled from questionnaires completed by members of the public who had stated that they would welcome legal advice. Despite concerns over "ambulance chasing" raised by this initiative, the Law Society for England and Wales concluded that it would not be professional misconduct for the legal profession to participate in this scheme. However, the Professional Practice Committee of the Law Society of Scotland reached the conclusion that to take part in the scheme might bring the profession into disrepute.[15]

2.10 Rule 4 of the 2006 Rules and the Survival of Touting

More significantly, r.4 of the 2006 rules may in part be said to have replaced "touting" providing as it does that a *"solicitor shall not make a direct or indirect approach whether verbal or written to any person whom he knows or ought reasonably to know to be the client of another solicitor with the intent to solicit business from that person"*. Although this wording repeats what was r.5 in the 1991 and 1995 rules, it is still unclear how broadly this will be interpreted by the Discipline Tribunal. Before the 1991 rules the Tribunal had taken the view that touting could occur whether or not the person approached had an existing solicitor. Thus in DTD 703/87, an Edinburgh firm of solicitors who were selling a property belonging to an employee of a major public company, who was moving to England, wrote to the personnel manager of the

---

[15] Council Report, October 1995.

employers in England detailing the services which they could offer to employees of the company who were moving house to Scotland, and asked to be put in touch with the Scots based personnel manager. They added, however, that if the company already had an arrangement with firm of agents in Scotland then they should ignore the letter. They were sent the details of the Scots based personnel manager and promptly wrote to her. Unfortunately for the firm, the company did indeed have Scottish agents, a large Glasgow firm, who promptly objected to the Law Society when they were sent a copy of the Edinburgh firm's letter, by the Scots based personnel manager. The Edinburgh firm indicated in their defence that they had assumed from the fact that they had been sent the details of the Scots-based personnel manager, that the company did not have Scottish agents. The Tribunal, by implication ruled that the defence was irrelevant, holding that the essence of the offence of touting involved taking an unfair advantage over other members of the profession (their competitors), by making a direct approach to would-be clients, whether or not the person or company approached already had a solicitor.[16]

It seems clear from r.4 that there cannot be a breach of the rule if there is no existing solicitor, or if the accused solicitor could not reasonably be expected to know that the client already had a solicitor. The matter, however, has yet to be tested before the Discipline Tribunal. Moreover, if the offence of touting continues in some half-life under the guise of bringing the profession into disrepute, it may be that the Tribunal will still take the view that touting can occur even where there is no existing solicitor. Even if the Tribunal is prepared to recognise a form of "common law" touting in this way, there is likely to be one subtle difference from DTD 703/87. There the emphasis was clearly on protecting the profession from unfair competition. Now, the Tribunal would be much more likely to be influenced by the need to protect vulnerable clients from importunate in-person solicitation, the more so since it would appear that the 2006 rules do not prohibit direct in-person solicitation of business from a person who has no solicitor.[17]

Nevertheless, the Law Society, if not the Discipline Tribunal, seems prepared to take a more relaxed approach to r.4. A few years ago it was accepted that a solicitor "ought reasonably to know [that someone was] the client of another solicitor" if they owned a house or ran a business. However, the Professional Practice Committee now takes the view that such persons may have had a solicitor in the past but that does not necessarily mean that they still do. Mere ownership of a house or business, therefore, is not *per se* sufficient to require a solicitor to conclude that such as person still has an existing solicitor. Again the Professional Practice Committee ruled in April 1995 that where a client is referred to a solicitor by an intermediary such as a bank or insurance broker, the solicitor is not required to check whether the client has an existing solicitor, despite the terms of the rule. Only if the solicitor knows that the client has an existing solicitor or it should be obvious to anyone who cares to see that they have a solicitor, is there a breach of r.4. Nonetheless, the Professional Practice Committee would probably still hold[18] that an untried prisoner is someone whom one ought reasonably to know to be

---

[16] Viewed from 21st century eyes, the primacy given by the Tribunal, in decisions like these, to anti-competitive practices over the interests of the client, is striking.

[17] Rule 7.3 of the Model Rules and 2002 revision continue to prohibit in-person solicitation.

[18] See 1993 J.L.S.S. 115.

the client of another solicitor. Accordingly, an agent who is preparing defence precognitions and seeking a witness statement from an untried prisoner must request permission to precognose him or her from the prisoner's lawyer.[19] Another clear cut example of a breach of the rule was the case of *McPherson*.[20] Here the respondent (who had moved from one firm to another) had visited the home of a client of the former firm uninvited and obtained a mandate from him transferring the client's business to himself. The Discipline Tribunal concluded that this was a breach of the rule, and were also concerned by the fact that prior to so acting, and while still an employee of his former firm, the solicitor had criticised the professional attitude and competence of his employer and made denigrating remarks about the latter's personal life, to the client from whom he subsequently sought a mandate.

2.11 Circulars

The 1987 rules for the first time permitted general circulars of printed matter[21] to be issued, *provided the circulars were not targeted at specific individuals or classes of individuals*. The latter were deemed to be touting. Some smaller firms argued that this dispensation would favour larger and wealthier firms over "other smaller, and less well-heeled, but no less deserving firms, and sole practitioners." The Society however pointed out[22] that the great majority of applications for a waiver under the previous rules to allow a mail shot had come from small firms. Typically, these had either been to retaliate against nationally based estate agents who were moving into country towns with saturation leafleting, or solicitors in socially deprived areas telling the neighbourhood that they could deal with the kinds of legal problem that those living in the area were most likely to have. The Society also noted that the glossy brochures of the large firms were not aimed at the type of client, or the type of business that would normally go to the small or medium-sized firm. The real objection to the 1987 rules, however, was that they, like similar rules in many of the states in the USA, prevented solicitors from using circulars efficiently and effectively. Anomalously, circulars sent only to people who needed the solicitor's services were struck at for targeting, but scattershot, wasteful circulars which covered all those needing the service and some who did not, were permitted. In the USA this anomaly was removed by the Supreme Court in *Shapero v Kentucky Bar Association*.[23] The 1991 and 1995 Scottish rules, however, only partly tackled the problem. Rule 5 in the 2006 rules indicates that despite the terms of r.4, *general circulation by a solicitor of material promoting that solicitor's services, whether or not the persons to whom it is directed are established clients* is permitted. The 2006 rules adds to this for the first time a definition of "general circulation", namely, *circulation to a group of persons (including bodies corporate) who can be categorised by a common description*.

---

[19] This conclusion stems from a consideration of art.9 of the Code of Conduct (not communicating with the clients of another solicitor except via their solicitor) and r.5 of the Advertising Rules.

[20] DTD *McPherson* 1099/02 (1); 13/3/03.

[21] Circulars, of course, have to comply with general advertising rules as to content (rules 7 and 8).

[22] In the Explanatory Memorandum to the 1987 rules.

[23] 486 U.S. 466 (1988).

The combination of rules 4 and 5 would therefore appear to allow targeted, efficient use of circulars to a group of persons with a common problem. The Professional Practice Committee has also recently ruled that in light of the growing use of telesales in place of paper mail shots by many companies, telesales (i.e. cold-calling members of the public) by solicitors will be permissible as a general circulation. The committee agreed that telesales would neither breach the advertising rules nor bring the profession into disrepute and consumers would still have the choice whether to take up or reject the proposal.[24] Email circulars are governed, however, by EU Regulations[25] which are more restrictive than the advertising rules. These regulations prohibit the sending of unsolicited email to individuals[26] for direct marketing purposes unless the recipient has given their consent to receiving such material, or there is an existing customer relationship (and even then only in respect of similar products and services). Solicitors wishing to advertise to businesses by email should also be careful to contact only businesses within their own jurisdiction, to avoid a charge of offering to practice in a jurisdiction in which they are not qualified.[27]

Possible Future Changes   2.12

How should solicitation be reformed? As we have seen, only a few constraints are now left, for example an approach to someone else's client. The Office of Fair Trading takes the view that any restraint in the Advertising Rules against cold calling potential clients, even those of other solicitors, inhibits competition.[28] The fact that it might be perceived as an invasion of privacy,[29] like double glazing salespersons, or that it might be perceived as unseemly to approach an accident victim or their family in the immediate aftermath of the accident, are not matters which the OFT feel it appropriate to attach any importance. On the one hand there are clearly issues relating to not taking advantage of young, inexperienced or particularly vulnerable persons (e.g., through illness, pain, shock or intoxication),[30] although any protections on this score should apply against approaches from either lawyers or claims adjusters, as in the USA.[31] On the other hand it is equally reasonable to argue that most business persons are perfectly able to look after themselves. It is difficult to see what was so heinous in the re-location case, the more so since

---

[24] Minutes of the Professional Practice Committee, Law Society of Scotland, March 2005.

[25] s.22 Privacy and Electronic Communications (E.C. Directive) Regulations 2003.

[26] The Regulations apply only to personal, not business email addresses. They also apply to advertising by SMS (text) messaging.

[27] See DTD *Gray* 14/01/04.

[28] OFT Competition in Professions, 2001.

[29] An American lawyer has already been suspended for a year for sending "spam"—email unsolicited to thousands of internet newsgroups and thereby invading their privacy and entailing them in expenditure while downloading and viewing it.

[30] Such approaches will almost always constitute, "bringing the profession into disrepute". A grey area concerns leaflets in hospital casualty departments, which caused some concern recently (See "Law firms attacked over 'ambulance chaser' hospital ads", *Mail on Sunday*, 10/05/05 p.49 and 17/05/05 p.39). Nevertheless, such leaflets, if they are merely left lying around the departments, are likely to be acceptable as general circulars under r.6.

[31] See *USA S Crt Florida Bar v Went For It, Inc.*, 515 US 618 (1995). Under 49 USCA para.1136(g)(2) Congress legislated to prohibit unsolicited communications with victims and their families for 30 days after an airplane crash, by either attorneys or insurance carriers/loss adjusters.

the approach was coupled with the message that recipients should ignore the communication if they already have a lawyer, and it is almost certain that such a letter would not find its way to the Tribunal now.

2.13 Referrals and Arrangements

Arrangements between firms of solicitors and third parties who refer them clients have an ancient pedigree. Referrals from a third party where there is no financial arrangement between the solicitor, and the third party related to the referral (e.g. those from a CAB, social work office or the police) raise no special ethical issues,[32] except where the third party is also a client. In the latter situation, for example where the referral comes from a building society, bank or other financial institution who is providing the referred client with an endowment policy and/or mortgage and the firm is doing the standard security for the lender as well as the borrower, there is a potential for conflict of interest between the two clients. It may be, for example, that the endowment policy is not in the buyer's interests, or the repossession terms of the mortgage are particularly draconian. In such situations the solicitor may be tempted to favour the referring client (being the source of "repeat business") over the referred client.[33] Where, on the other hand, the referral comes from a third party with whom the solicitor has a financial arrangement, the ethical situation tends to become more problematic. First, as is the case in many other jurisdictions, there is a rule that lawyers may not share fees or profits with an unqualified person.[34] Secondly, as fiduciary agents solicitors may not retain commissions or payments from third parties without disclosure of the details to the client because of the rule against secret profits.[35] Thirdly, if the referrals become a major source of business for the solicitor then the "core value" of independence[36] may come under threat, and a conflict may arise between the duty to act in the client's best interests[37] and the temptation to favour the solicitor's own commercial interests. Equally, where the solicitor acts for both the referring body (with whom there is an arrangement) and for the person being referred, for example, an insurance company and the insured, a trade union and the union members or the Automobile Association and its members, there is the risk, as before, that the solicitor will favour the "repeating client" if a conflict of interest arises, for example, if there is a dispute over the terms of the policy which entitles the referred client to use the solicitor's services. These forms of arrangement have tended not to be seen as particularly problematic by the Law Society. Again the Society has few concerns about referral arrangements between firms of solicitors, e.g. a country correspondent for an Edinburgh firm for Court of Session work, because these do not raise

---

[32] However, in the past firms and the Law Society would claim that there was unfair attraction of business if, e.g. a CAB were to send all of its referrals to one firm of solicitors rather than giving the clients being referred a choice. With the removal of most of the rules against the unfair attraction of business, the basis for such objections no longer exists.

[33] This, of course, is a form of conflict of interest.

[34] Solicitors (Scotland) Practice Rules 1991. Rule 4 stipulates that "a solicitor shall not share with any unqualified person any profits or fees or fee derived from any business transacted by the solicitor of a kind commonly carried on by solicitors in Scotland". The ban was until 1993 a criminal offence under s.27 of the Solicitors' Scotland Act 1980.

[35] See Ch.9 below on commissions and secret profits.

[36] Art.1 Code of Conduct 1992.

[37] Art.2 Code of Conduct 1992.

particular ethical problems, and it is quite acceptable for the fees in the case to be split between the two firms. However, where the third party is a non-lawyer and a non-client, for example, referrals from estate agents or insurance brokers, and particularly where the clients referred are "tied" to using the lawyer if they want special package price from the referrer, there has been greater concern.

Nevertheless, although the Council has debated arrangements on several occasions in the last 15 years, a lack of consensus on the issue has prevented the formulation of a clear ruling for the profession.[38] This has led to the curious situation that independent qualified conveyancers are prevented from being party to arrangements with third parties referring them clients which contain "tying-in" clauses requiring them to use the IQC's services, but solicitors are not, unless the arrangement can be shown to be so egregious as to bring the profession into disrepute. In the end, arrangements even between solicitors and non-lawyer, non-client, third parties have been left to the operation of the practice rule on advertising,[39] the practice rule on fee sharing with unqualified persons, the ethical rules on secret profits (e.g. hidden commissions), the rules on conflicts of interest and if all else fails, the fundamental ethical rule that behaviour should not bring the profession into disrepute.

Types of Arrangement   2.14

Much will depend on the nature of the arrangement. Agreeing with an estate agent to charge a fixed (low) fee for the conveyancing work of all clients referred to you is unlikely to be struck at. Agreeing that the estate agent can quote the client an overall fee including your fixed fee, whereby you are becoming a form of sub-contractor to the estate agent, and requiring the client to come to you if they want the cheap price, is neither struck at by the advertising rules nor the ban on fee-sharing.[40] If it threatens your ability to act in the best interests of the client (e.g. because you allow estate agents to charge a commission of their own choosing and add it to your low fixed fee, presenting it to the client as single fee) there may be a problem both under the MDP rules and under art.2 of the Code of Conduct depending on how the bill is represented to the client. If the solicitor's fees are included in a bill under the estate agent's name, that would be regarded as a multi-disciplinary practice by being a joint venture or partnership between the solicitors and the estate agents. If the estate agent's commission is hidden in the solicitor's own fee note, that would breach the practice rules of fee sharing. If the estate agent pays you a commission for every 10 cases that you charge at the low fee, that would not be struck at as fee sharing, but it would constitute a secret profit which would have to be disclosed to the client under the law of agency. However, the 1991 Practice Rule against fee sharing with unqualified persons was principally designed to strike at the payment by the solicitor of

---

[38] This is in contradistinction from the English Law Society which has had a detailed "Introduction and Referral Code" since 1990.

[39] Particularly where the adverts for solicitors are published and paid for by the third party (especially r.10).

[40] While solicitors may not share their fees with unqualified persons, the Society has no objection to the latter sharing their fees with solicitors.

commission for the introduction of business on a case by case basis.[41] Thus, if you were to pay an estate agent out of your own fees a set commission for each case referred to you by the estate agent this would constitute the sharing of fees which falls foul of the 1991 practice rule. Nevertheless, firms are entitled to pay for the cost of marketing or promoting their firms. Thus, they may pay a fee to be included on a panel to whom referrals will be made, provided that the fee is not expressed as a specific sum per referral or as a percentage of the fees chargeable for referred business. A flat fee is not in breach of the rules and that may be a fee that is reviewed periodically. A scheme which was recently found to be acceptable in the US concerned a company called LegalMatch.com. Participating solicitors paid a flat fee for annual membership to LegalMatch.com, which bought advertising and access to requests for legal services posted by potential consumers. The annual fee was not linked to the fees charged to the client and crucially, the solicitor/client relationships were established off-line and without the participation of LegalMatch.com. It would seem likely that something similar would be within the rules in Scotland.[42] Again, solicitors in Scotland are entitled to pay for the provision of services to the practice, even where the service is provided by the person who has introduced the client. Thus if an estate agent has rendered a service to the client (e.g. organised a survey) then the Law Society takes the view that the "commission" is a fee for service and therefore not in breach of the 1991 rule. It is under this view that the Society was prepared to hold that the payment of referral fees to claims companies such as Claims Direct was not caught by the 1991 practice rule, but rather a fee for a service rendered to the client, e.g. conducting preliminary investigations or obtaining a medical report. However, the service must be a real service and not simply a reward for introducing the client.[43] Thus the Professional Practice Committee has ruled that an introducer who merely carries out a money laundering check is not providing a service for these purposes, since that is a duty incumbent on all solicitors under the accounts rules. Services which have been held to be acceptable for the purposes of the 1991 rule have included carrying out hearing tests, taking statements from witnesses, obtaining photographs of a locus, and completing a detailed questionnaire relating to the particular matter in which the solicitor is instructed. This exception for "fee for services" makes it more difficult to obtain a successful prosecution under the rule.[44] As for the future, the Law Society of England and Wales, after several narrow votes on Council, eventually introduced a scheme in March 2004 which

---

[41] See B. Ritchie, "Fee sharing: making the rules work" (2004) 49(2) J.L.S.S. 42. The following paragraph draws heavily from the article.

[42] Rhode Island Supreme Court Ethics Advisory Panel, Opinion 2005–01, Request 885, February 24, 2005.

[43] See the recent English case: *Sharratt v London Central Bus Company (The Accident Group Test Cases)* [2004] 3 All E.R. 325, in which it was held that purported "investigation fees" which were standard in all cases and which "far outstripped any reasonable charge for the work done" were actually illegal referral fees and had to be reimbursed to the clients.

[44] Rule 5.4.2 of the Code of Conduct for Lawyers in the European Union, 2002 (contained in the Solicitors' Professional Handbook, *op. cit.*), forbids a solicitor who is providing services in a cross-border context from paying a fee or commission as a consideration for only referring a client to the lawyer. This is to prevent the client's free choice of lawyer or the client's interest in being referred to the best available service from being impaired. The wording of this prohibition suggests that it can be got round provided the solicitor can demonstrate that the referrer provided some minimal service to the client.

whatsoever at the local police station or court. The assistant claimed that the covenant was excessively wide in specifying ten miles and preventing him undertaking any "work" at all in the area. The Court of Appeal, however, held that the contract should not be construed so strictly as to destroy the plain meaning of the parties. Even though the actual words used did indeed prevent the assistant from doing work of any sort, e.g. cleaning, in the ten mile radius, the court was of the opinion that a fair reading of the contract would restrict the covenant to applying only to "work as a solicitor". The appeal was therefore dismissed. The decision is not incompatible with the two earlier cases, but is, of course, only of persuasive authority in Scotland.

Client Retention: The Position of Partners   2.17

Here both professional ethics and the law of contract attempt to balance the interests of clients to instruct the solicitor of their choice, of the departing partner(s) to take "their" clients with them and of the remaining partners representing the original firm, to keep as much of the firm's client base as possible. The easiest way to regulate this is in the partnership agreement or, in the case of an assistant, through the contract of employment. Whilst these may, within the bounds set out in paragraph 2.16 prevent the outgoing lawyers from continuing to act for clients of the original firm even where the solicitors might reasonably regard them as being theirs (e.g. because he/she originally brought them to the firm), the remaining partners cannot stop the clients from leaving the firm and instructing a different lawyer. In the absence of an enforceable restrictive covenant in the partnership agreement or the contract of employment, the position is that departing partners may inform clients whom they personally have acted for,[54] not only that they are leaving the firm but that they are joining another firm and that the client has an entirely free choice whether to stay with the old firm, or to instruct the partner in their new firm (or indeed to go to a completely new firm of solicitors altogether).[55] Thus the Professional Practice Committee of the Society ruled in 1991 that even a solicitor who had been required to resign as a partner by the remaining partners with immediate effect, was entitled to write directly to people for whom he had acted while he was a partner in the firm, offering his continuing services as a solicitor, since there was no restrictive covenant in the partnership agreement.[56] The committee has continued to adhere to this line, even ruling in April 2001 that a departing partner can send one reminder (but only one) with a mandate to his or her former clients without breaching r.5 of the advertising rules.[57] However, partners should be careful which files they take with them when they leave. In a case involving a firm of Glasgow

[54] Unless the client was one for whom they acted indirectly, or at the request of one of the remaining partners.

[55] S. Galt, "Mandates" (1989) J.L.S.S. 54. The Law Society Guidelines on Mandates, *Solicitors Professional Handbook op. cit.*, also deal with the position of partners when moving firms and the terms in which they may write to clients of the firm for whom he/she has acted in the past. The issue is discussed, but not resolved, in *Dallas McMillan*.

[56] The Council Report, May 1991.

[57] In the Guidelines on Mandates it is noted that the right to contact clients applies both while the departing partner is still a partner of the original firm and also for a reasonable time after the partner has left. What is a reasonable time depends on the circumstances, but in one case the Professional Practice Committee has accepted that the departing partner's first letter could be sent up to a year from leaving the original firm without breaching the Advertising Rules.

solicitors, three partners left a firm without giving notice, and set up two new offices, both within the same areas as their old firm. There had been a significant amount of planning, as the new offices opened up within days of them leaving. They took with them up to 1500 files and also some members of staff. Lord Milligan ruled that the three partners had "gained substantial commercial advantage by removing the files",[58] even though they argued that the clients would have followed them anyway. They were ordered to pay £78,000 compensation to their former colleagues. Lord Milligan ruled that they were "clearly in breach of their fiduciary duty not to damage the interests of the partnership which they were leaving, by removing files in which they had no right of ownership."[59]

2.18 Client Retention: The Position of Assistants or Associates

In December 1991, and again more recently when issuing the *Guidelines on Mandates*[60] the Professional Practice Committee considered the position of an assistant seeking to leave his or her firm to work elsewhere. Again, they gave paramountcy to the contract of employment. Where this is silent the committee concluded that the question of whether an assistant could directly approach clients for whom he or she had acted while employed at the former firm would depend on whether the assistant could be regarded as the solicitor for the client. It was established in *McKinstry v Law Society*[61] that the assistant or associate is indeed the solicitor of the client while he or she is the nominated solicitor in terms of legal aid. However, whilst concluding that the client might in some other cases regard the assistant as their solicitor, the committee considered that the client would normally be wrong since the solicitor/client relationship is between the client and the firm. Assistants and associates, they ruled, never act[62] on the instructions of the client but on the instructions of the employing solicitor and should therefore generally not write to former clients of the firm for which he or she have acted. They accepted that this might seem anomalous where the client had been brought to the firm by the assistant and where the client had never dealt with anyone in the firm other than the assistant. The committee concluded that, in such circumstances, the clients would be able to find out that the assistant had moved and the details of the new firm from the original firm. Whilst appreciating the committee's logic, it is respectfully suggested that, in situations where the assistant is effectively in sole charge of a branch office, or has been the only solicitor actively involved with a client, it is unrealistic to treat them differently from partners and arguably IPS to the clients to leave them to find out for themselves when "their" solicitor moves firm and if they are lucky with the original firm, the name of the firm to which the assistant has moved. Certainly, even as early as 1976, before the advertising rules were relaxed the Discipline Tribunal held that in such circumstances it was not professional misconduct or unprofessional conduct (in the guise of the unfair attraction of business) for such an assistant to write to clients whom he alone

---

[58] I. Wilson, "Lawyers who accused Anwar had taken 1500 files of clients", *The Herald*, June 1, 2004. p.1.
[59] Finlayson & Turnbull (No.1) 1997 SLT 613 (OH).
[60] *Op. cit.*
[61] 1997 S.L.T. 191.
[62] Except when nominated solicitors.

had acted for to state that he was moving.[63] Moreover, following *McKinstry*, it is clearly the case that when the assistant or associate is the nominated solicitor in a legal aid case, he or she not only may communicate with their client when they are moving firm, but must do so,[64] since they will remain the nominated solicitor for the client at their new firm, unless the client persuades the Legal Aid Board to transfer the nomination to another solicitor, e.g. at the original firm. Perhaps the easiest solution for the assistant or associate who does not wish to run the risk of discipline is to insert a notice in a local newspaper indicating the move of firm. Outwith the principal cities this is an effective and legitimate form of communicating with erstwhile clients.

---

[63] DTD 407/76.
[64] It might well be IPS not to tell the client that you were moving in this situation.

CHAPTER 3

DECIDING WHETHER TO ACT

3.01 Introduction

Whether influenced by an advertisement or some other cause, the solicitor is now confronted with a prospective client. Before deciding to act for the would-be client, the solicitor is required by law to ascertain that the prospective client is who he/she claims to be, and that he/she has the authority to instruct the solicitor. Indeed, the Money Laundering Regulations 2003 have made it mandatory to verify not only the identity of new clients, but also the source of the clients' funds. Notwithstanding these requirements, solicitors are generally free to decide whether or not to act for a client—however there are instances where the law and professional ethics impose restrictions on a solicitor's ability to act or to refuse to act. Further, when accepting instructions from an intermediary on behalf of a client solicitors are required to communicate directly with the client, to ensure that they are fulfilling their obligation to take proper instructions. A solicitor must also consider the duties that are owed to prospective or would-be clients in order to avoid the possibility of becoming the recipient of a conduct or negligence claim at a later date.

3.02 Identifying the "Client": Money Laundering

The Money Laundering Regulations 2003 and the Solicitors (Scotland) Accounts Rules 2001 place a duty on solicitors to know their clients. This involves a two-stage process—firstly identification of the client and secondly identification of the source of the client's funds. Regulation 4(3) of the Money Laundering Regulations 2003 requires I.D. to be produced "as soon as is reasonably practicable after contact is first made" and where satisfactory evidence of I.D. is not obtained the transaction must not proceed further.[1]

3.02.01 Identification of the Client. The regulations require solicitors to verify the identity of every new client with whom they intend to form a business relationship or carry out a one-off transaction, and to retain a record of this identification for at least five years. This should cover the true name, current permanent address (including postcode) and wherever possible, the date and place of birth of the client. If more than three years has elapsed since a client

---

[1] It must be emphasised that prevention of money laundering is strictly enforced. The price of non-compliance with the regulations is high, as evidenced by the recent imprisonment in England and Wales of a solicitor (Jonathan Duff) for unintentional money laundering ((2002) August J.L.S.S. 7).

has been identified then the basic facts, i.e. change of name or address, should be checked. It is strongly recommended that solicitors should request sight of an official document with a photo, for example, a current valid passport or new style drivers licence. The solicitor should also request to see a recent utility bill. For "corporate" clients such as an unquoted company or a partnership where none of the directors/partners is already known to the solicitor, the latter should verify the identity of one or more of the principal directors/partners and/or shareholders as applicable, in the same way as if they were individual clients.[2] Where the client is at a distance another local solicitor should be used to verify the client's identity, or if the client is abroad then a local notary or British Consulate should be used to obtain an affidavit.

Source of Funds. Solicitors are also required to ascertain the source of their client's funds by discussing the client's plans to fund the transaction. Where funds are provided in cash, bank drafts or third party cheques solicitors should make further enquiries, particularly if this is unexpected. Warning signs which should raise suspicions of money laundering include last minute changes to the source of funds or being asked to hold substantial funds without a clear purpose.[3]   **3.02.02**

Identifying the "Client": Agency Considerations   **3.03**

The second reason for identifying the client is because the law of agency requires that an agent cannot work on behalf of a non-existent principal. Consequently, solicitors should take care when accepting instructions from corporate clients to ensure that the company is not in insolvency and therefore retains the status of principal. Where this is not done the court may hold a solicitor to be in breach of warranty of authority and be personally liable for the other side's expenses.[4] Further, even where the company or partnership exists but the solicitor is instructed to act by only one director or partner, is it necessary to check whether he or she has the authority to instruct on behalf of the company or partnership? The answer is that the solicitor must check,[5] but pragmatically there are dangers in taking this to extremes.[6] If in any doubt, the solicitor should ask for a copy of the minutes of a directors or partners meeting. If the only problem is that the client (who is in existence) has not authorised the solicitor's action then the doctrine of ratification can be brought into play. Thus, the Court of Appeal ruled in 1994 that where a solicitor

---

[2] See the Verification of Client Identity checklist at the end of this chapter and Leslie Cumming, "Anti-Money Laundering Procedures" in *Money Laundering—Best Practice and Latest Developments* Papers from an Update Seminar March 12, 2004 The Law Society of Scotland.

[3] See the Source of Funds Flowchart at the end of the chapter and Leslie Cumming, "Anti-Money Laundering Procedures" *op. cit.*

[4] See *Babury Ltd v London Industrial plc* (1989) 189 N.L.J. 1596. Begg on *Law Agents* (para.23, p.281, ch.xix) asserts that law agents who raise legal proceedings in the name of a client who has not authorised it can be personally liable for the other sides' expenses, even when the lawyer has acted in good faith.

[5] Solicitors can rely on the instructions of an individual director for day to day commercial activities of a company, but for any significant matter should rely on the instructions of a majority of the Board.

[6] See Iain Doran's letter in (1993) J.L.S.S. 428. (See also pages 1.1 and 1.2 of the Law Society's *Better Client Care and Practice Management* guidance manual.)

commenced proceedings in the name of a plaintiff, whether a company or an individual, without authority, the plaintiff could ratify the act of the solicitor and adopt the proceedings thus curing the original defect in the proceedings.[7] Just as the authority of a client to raise an action should be checked, so too should the client's authority to defend an action. In *Davidson v Kilwinning Homing Society*[8] a pursuer raised an action seeking to be allowed to become a member of a homing pigeon society. On appeal to the Inner House, he successfully challenged the authority of the solicitors purporting to act for the society in defence of his action, on the grounds that there was evidence that the society had not authorised the instruction of any firm of solicitors to defend the society. The solicitor had only received instructions from the then office-bearers of the society and it was not clear that the latter had obtained authority in general meeting to instruct the lodging of a defence. However, once again, there would seem no reason why ratification should not operate, provided the defenders can obtain the appropriate authority to defend the action from their organisation.

3.04 Identifying the "Client": Questions of Capacity

A third and closely-related issue is the need to identify in what capacity the client is instructing the solicitor. Usually this will be obvious, however there are instances (e.g. in the case of a small family business where the client combines the role of Managing Director and part-owner of the business), where the solicitor would be wise to ascertain whether the client is representing himself/herself as Managing Director or as shareholder, or alternatively purporting to represent the family as a whole or the business itself. While the last two are agency questions the former two relate to capacity. The idea that the client is the whole family business system—family, owners and the business—may sit uncomfortably with lawyers who are concerned that acting for a large number of people may result in conflicts of interest.[9]

3.05 Identifying the "Client": Singular or Plural?

Occasionally, where a solicitor is instructed by a person or body a question will arise as to whether the solicitor in accepting the instructions is thereby also accepting another client. For example, where a person or body is being sued, and has insurance cover, the instruction to the solicitor's firm to act will often come from the insurance company rather than the insured. In this situation, who is the firm's client? In the USA this issue has been raised on frequent occasions in a professional ethics context and in the great majority of cases the answer has been that both the insured and the insurance company are

---

[7] However, rather surprisingly, the court concluded that the issuing of the writ without authority was not a nullity and accordingly the plaintiff in an action which had been begun by solicitors without authority was entitled to adopt the action notwithstanding the expiration of the limitation period applicable to that cause of action. Since the court also held that if a time was fixed for doing a particular act the doctrine of ratification did not apply if it had the effect of extending that time, it is somewhat difficult to understand the reasoning of the court. *Presentaciones Musicales SA v Secunda* [1994] Ch. 271. Begg, *op. cit.*, p.77, para.12 argues that in Scotland it is open to a party in whose name legal proceedings have been taken without authority to homolgate the lawyer's actings, either expressly or tacitly.

[8] 2003 S.L.T. 268.

[9] See K. McCracken, "Who is the Client?" (2004) 49(1) J.L.S.S. 16–17.

clients, with the insured being the "true" client whom the firm should continue to act for, in the event of a conflict of interest preventing the firm from continuing to represent both clients. In Scotland, on the other hand, the custom and practice of solicitors instructed by insurance companies in this way is usually to assume that the client is insurer. It is submitted that this assumption is unwise and that a proper analysis of the law would suggest that both the insured and the insurer are clients.[10] Nevertheless, the Scottish Solicitors' Discipline Tribunal has opted to endorse the "customary" approach in a recent IPS appeal where the insurance company went into liquidation and the insured sought to transfer the papers in the case from the original firm of solicitors to a new firm.[11] The original firm took the view that their only client was the insurance company (and presumably, therefore, that the insured was unrepresented, even though the insured was the person being sued), and declined to implement the mandate without the insurance companies' consent, which was not forthcoming.[12] The Law Society took the view that the failure to implement the mandate was IPS, arguing that the insured was a client. The Tribunal, however, upheld the original firm's argument that their only client was the insurance company. With the greatest respect to the Tribunal it is difficult to see how this analysis of the case can be correct. At the very least, the original firm should have known that they were acting for two clients, the insurance company and the insured, irrespective of which of them had actually instructed them. The insurance policy provided cover for the insured's legal expenses as well as any damages. However, the logic of the Tribunal's position would appear to be that the insured was unrepresented and therefore had no locus to ask for the papers to be transferred to a new agent. Even in the peculiar circumstances of this case, this must surely be an incorrect assessment of the legal position of the insured. In any event, the Society's Professional Practice Committee subsequently reconsidered the point and came down against the Tribunal's view.

Acceptance of Instructions   3.06

In general terms a solicitor is free to decide whether or not to accept instructions from any particular client.[13] In contradistinction to advocates (and to a lesser extent solicitor-advocates)[14] there is no "cab-rank" rule for solicitors, requiring them to act for "clients" who ask them to act for them having tendered an appropriate fee. This holds true in most jurisdictions, although this is alleged to exacerbate the problem of finding lawyers willing to represent unpopular clients, for example, alleged paedophiles, neo-nazis or terrorists. It follows that a refusal to act for such clients, based on moral

---

[10] The alternative is to conclude that the insured is unrepresented and has no liability for the solicitor's fees should the insurance company go into liquidation. Not only does this fly in the face of the insured's expectations (since his or her premiums are intended to pay for his or her legal representation—not just the insurer's representation), it is also hard to square with common sense.

[11] DTD 1124/03 (Simpson & Marwick).

[12] Curiously, the firm also took the position (backed by senior counsel's opinion) that the insured was liable for their fees and therefore that they had a lien over the papers!

[13] Commentary to art.5(a), Code of Conduct; r.12.01 English Guide (8th edn, 1999).

[14] However, art.1(1) of the Solicitors (Scotland) Rules of Conduct for Solicitor Advocates 2002 enables the society to require a solicitor-advocate to represent any person who desires to be represented by a solicitor-advocate.

repugnance, even where the solicitor is the "last lawyer in town" will never be a disciplinary matter, although it may give rise to criticism.[15] However, a refusal to act must not be based upon the race, colour, ethnic or national origins, sex, creed or disability of the prospective client.[16] On the other hand, there are some cases where the solicitor is simply not permitted to begin acting or to continue to act for a "client":

(1) where the "client's" instructions would involve the solicitor in a breach of the law or in behaviour which would amount to professional misconduct[17];

(2) where the solicitor lacks the competence, knowledge, experience, skill, preparation time,[18] resources or wherewithal to pursue the matter with due diligence[19];

(3) where the solicitor knows or has reasonable grounds for believing that the prospective client lacks the capacity, e.g. through infirmity or non-age/ youth, to instruct him or her[20];

(4) where the solicitor knows or has reasonable grounds for believing that the instructions are affected by duress or undue influence[21];

(5) where there is a conflict of interests between the client or prospective client and either the solicitor, the solicitor's firm or an existing client[22];

(6) where the solicitor has previously acted for, and holds relevant confidential information about, the party on the other side of the case or transaction[23];

(7) where another solicitor (the nominated solicitor) is already acting for the "client" in the same matter in a legal aid case, until and unless the Legal Aid Board has agreed to transfer the Legal Aid Certificate[24];

(8) if it is clear that the solicitor or another member of the firm will be called as a witness in the case, unless the evidence will be purely formal[25];

---

[15] In 1990 a well known firm of London legal aid lawyers who worked closely with organisations which helped battered women was widely criticised for announcing to the media that it would not act for defendants in rape cases where the defence was the alleged consent of the victim. See "Taking Sides" (1990) *New Law Journal*, p.157. On the hazards of dealing with stressed, vulnerable or potentially "difficult" clients, see Russell Lang, "The Informed Client", (2004) 49(7) J.L.S.S. 38

[16] Article 11 Code of Conduct; Commentary, r.12.01 English Guide (1999).

[17] Articles 2 and 5(a) Code of Conduct and r.12.02 English Guide (1999).

[18] An exception is possible in urgent cases to allow the solicitor to apply for an adjournment. See "Law Society Guidelines for Immigration Practitioners" (2004) J.L.S.S. 36.

[19] See Ch.1, para.1.24, and Code of Conduct Articles 5(b), (c), (d); r.12.03, English Guide (1999).

[20] *cf.* Begg, *op. cit.*, p.282.

[21] Rule 12.04, English Guide (1999).

[22] Article 3, Code of Conduct; r.3 Solicitors (Scotland) Practice Rules 1986; r.15.01, English Guide; ABA Model Rules 1.7.

[23] This situation, sometimes known as a "successive conflict", is dealt with in Ch.7.

[24] The English rule is even broader, ruling out a new solicitor beginning to act in any case, until the retainer of the first has been terminated—r.12.07, English Guide (1999).

[25] Rule 21.12, English Guide (1999); ABA Model Rules 3.7.

(9) where to do so would permit his or her independence to be impaired.[26]

Instructions from an Intermediary 3.07

Where instructions are received not from a prospective client, but from a third party purporting to represent that "client", a solicitor should communicate with the "client" and obtain his or her instructions in writing or on the telephone, to the effect that he or she wishes the solicitor to act.[27] If it is a new client the solicitor should ensure that money laundering checks are done as unless the intermediary is in the Regulated Sector as defined in the Money Laundering Regulations 2003, a check done by him will have no validity. In most cases client identification will best be done by meeting with the "client". Situations where you should be particularly on your guard include estate agents or banks seeking to complete missives on behalf of one of their clients[28] or a client seeking to have a will drawn up for a close relative or spouse, or a deed signed by the client's spouse or partner, whom you have not met. Recently, several cases have arisen of anxious relatives seeking to have a power of attorney drawn up for an ailing member of the family, where the solicitor has omitted to confirm the instructions with the granter or to ensure that the granter is capax,[29] in the sense of being able not only to give the necessary instructions, but also of understanding the implications of granting such a deed.[30] The Law Society has made it clear that such omissions, however well intentioned, are a breach of the Code of Conduct for Scottish Solicitors[31] and "the stated duty to take proper instructions", and in a number of instances findings of professional misconduct with a reprimand were reached.[32] Surprisingly, this seems to be an area where the Discipline Tribunal has been willing to take a less strict line than the Law Society. In a series of cases since 1980 the Tribunal has repeatedly declined to hold that solicitors who have taken instructions from a third party and failed to communicate with the actual client to verify his or her instructions were guilty of misconduct.[33]

---

[26] Article 1, Code of Conduct.

[27] While it is prudent also to check that another solicitor is not already acting, this is no longer required as once it was—Professional Practice Committee, (1983) J.L.S.S. 466.

[28] Council of the Law Society, (1988) J.L.S.S. 111. This is all the more the case if you have a referral arrangement with the third party. See para.2.13 above.

[29] A decision which in case of any doubt must be based on the advice of the medical profession. As the Professional Practice Committee stressed in 2002 (J.L.S.S. July at p.51), Solicitors are not the judges of mental capacity. That is a matter for the medical profession from whom advice should be sought if there is any doubt as to the client's capacity.

[30] In addition, under the terms of ss.15 and 16 of the Adults with Incapacity (Scotland) Act 2000, neither a continuing power of attorney, nor a welfare power of attorney can be drawn up by a solicitor unless they are (1) expressed in writing (2) signed by the granter and (3) contain a certificate by the solicitor that he/she has interviewed the granter *immediately before* the power of attorney was signed, that he/she is satisfied that the granter understands the nature and extent of the power of attorney being granted and that he/she has no reason to believe that the granter was acting under undue influence. Solicitors signing such certificates should consult the relevant medical practitioner if it is not clear to the solicitor that the grantor is capable and able to give coherent instructions (2002 J.L.S.S. July at p.51). A failure to comply with the provisions of the Act means that the power of attorney has no effect if the granter becomes *incapax*.

[31] e.g. see the commentary to art.3.

[32] 1996 J.L.S.S. 158; Professional Practice Committee (above), 43(7) J.L.S.S. 43, July 1998.

[33] DTD 481/80, DTD 607/85, DTD 612/85, DTD 701/87 and DTD 883/94. Such behaviour would undoubtedly remain unsatisfactory conduct.

3.08 Instructions from, or on behalf of a Child

When dealing with money claims on behalf of children under the age of 16[34] a solicitor may take instructions from a person entitled to act as the child's legal representative (usually a parent) or from the child him or herself, if satisfied that the child has the capacity to give the instructions. Such capacity to give instructions exists when the child "has a general understanding of what it means to do so". A child is presumed to have such an understanding from age 12, but this may be rebutted by evidence to the contrary. Before taking instructions from a child's legal representative, a solicitor must ensure that that person holds parental rights and responsibilities for the child or has been granted the limited right/responsibility to act as the child's legal representative in relation to particular proceedings.[35] In particular it must be remembered that fathers do not automatically hold parental rights and responsibilities, which may, however, be gained by marriage to the child's mother, by agreement with her[36] or by order of the court. Where two or more persons act as the child's legal representative, any one of them may give instructions without the consent of the other. Accordingly a solicitor need not enquire if any other person has the right to act as legal representative of the child. If, however, the representative was appointed by decree or deed, the solicitor should obtain a copy to ensure there are no restrictions on the powers given.

Accepting and obtaining instructions from children themselves requires particular care.[37] A solicitor representing a child must remember that the best interests of the child are always the paramount consideration. This may prove problematic if the solicitor feels that the instructions being given by the child are not in their best interests. If the solicitor cannot reconcile this with their duty to advocate the instructions of their client, they may have to refuse the instruction or withdraw from acting. The solicitor must also make regular assessments regarding the capacity of the child to give instructions and also whether they in fact wish to continue to give instructions. The rules[38] which make it compulsory for solicitors to provide a written letter of engagement upon receiving instructions from a client provide an exception if the client is a child under the age of 12.

3.09 Legal Duties to the Prospective or Would-be Client

What are the solicitor's obligations to "would-be" clients who are either not yet clients, or subsequently deemed not to be clients or for whom the solicitor has declined to act?[39] At first blush it might be thought that they

---

[34] See Professional Practice Guidance (2004) 49(8) J.L.S.S. 39.

[35] Children (Scotland) Act 1995.

[36] Under s.4 Children (Scotland) Act 1995.

[37] For discussion on the Child Protection and Representation Principles for Children's Lawyers 2004 see Driscoll, "Born to Instruct" (2004) 49(12) J.L.S.S. 22.

[38] Section 4(3) Solicitors (Scotland) (Client Communication) Practice Rules 2005.

[39] "Would-be clients" fall into three categories. Those in the process of consulting a lawyer with a view to becoming a client; those who have been rejected by the lawyer as a client (e.g. due to one of the reasons listed in para.4.02); and those who thought that they had entered into a contract of services with the lawyer only for it to be held subsequently that there had been no consensus in idem or the contract was void due to want of formalities, essential validity or fundamental breach. Only the first of these categories can satisfactorily be labelled a "prospective" client.

would not be particularly extensive. Clearly, there are no contractual obligations since there is no contract for services between them. However, it is conceivable that a *quantum meruit* or unjustified enrichment claim might lie by the lawyer where he or she has rendered professional services to the "client" even where it is subsequently held that no contract existed. In the absence of a principal/agent relationship, rarely will the lawyer owe a potential client any fiduciary obligations.[40] However, a solicitor could be liable to a "would-be" client on the basis of a negligent misstatement, or for negligently given advice to a "would-be" client provided there is sufficient reliance or proximity. A celebrated instance of this occurred in the USA in the case of *Togstad v Vesley,Otto, Miller & Keefe*, 291 N.W.2d 686 (Minn. 1980). Mr Togstad was injured in a hospital due to the negligence of the doctor treating him. His wife subsequently sought advice from an attorney, Mr Miller. Each of them, however, came later to have a different recollection of what was said at their interview. Mrs Togstad claimed that Miller had told her that he did not think that the Togstads had a case against the doctor but that he would discuss the case with his partner, and if the latter took a different view, Mr Miller would come back to Mrs Togstad. Thus far their memories agreed, but Miller claimed that he had *in addition* told her that his firm were not experts in medical malpractice, urged her to take a second opinion from another lawyer, and advised her as to the limitation period for such cases. Miller never called Mrs Togstad back and by the time she consulted another lawyer who informed her, correctly, that she and her husband had a cast iron case against the doctor, the limitation period had expired. The Togstads sued Miller and his firm for professional negligence. The jury concluded that Mrs Togstad was the more credible witness and awarded her damages against Miller and his firm. The Supreme Court of Minnesota held on appeal that the Togstads had a right to sue under either contract or negligence, since the defendant had offered legal advice under circumstances which made it reasonably foreseeable to the attorney that if such advice was rendered negligently, the individual receiving the advice might be injured thereby.[41] Having established that a duty of care was owed, the court further held that in failing to perform the minimal research that a reasonably prudent attorney would do before offering advice and in failing to warn Mrs Togstad that there might be a limitation period for her action, Mr Miller had been negligent.

Togstad is an instructive case on a number of fronts. First, on the duty of care to "would-be" clients. Second, on the issue as to when a person becomes a client (see para.4.01 below), and third on the issue as to best practice when declining to act for a client. It emerged clearly from the *Togstad* case that what Mr Miller should have done was either conducted the minimal research required of an attorney prior to offering advice on an area outwith his specialism or indicated clearly that he was not an expert in the field and would therefore not be willing to take the case on, but that Mrs Togstad should

---

[40] R. Black, "A Question of Confidence" (1982) J.L.S.S. 299 would however argue that obligation of confidentiality could arise between the lawyer and the would-be client, irrespective of any ethical duties.

[41] Presumably a solicitor who is asked for legal advice at a party could argue that there is insufficient proximity to justify a duty of care, although a volunteer solicitor at a legal advice centre might well be found liable for negligent advice to those attending the clinic.

consult another lawyer without delay.[42] It is unclear whether, when confronted with such a case, a lawyer is required to raise the topic of limitation periods, but it would certainly seem advisable to do so, even if you are not precisely sure what the relevant period might be.[43] Thereafter, the lawyer who wishes to avoid any possibility of professional negligence should write forthwith to the would-be client stating that the lawyer will not take the case, that there are important time limits that may well be crucial to the preservation of the case, and that the would-be client should get a second opinion if they wish to take the matter further.[44] It is not necessary to say that you think that the case lacks merit, far less why you take that view.

Similarly, where an expectation, even an unreasonable one, may arise on the part of other parties involved in a transaction, that you are acting for them when you are not (for example on the part of the minority shareholders of a limited company when you are acting only for the majority shareholders), it may be advisable to send a letter of non-engagement to those non-clients to prevent the possibility of future claims.[45]

3.10 Ethical Duties to the Prospective or Would-be Client

What duties does the lawyer owe to the prospective client in terms of professional ethics? It seems probable that many if not most of those owed to actual clients also apply to would-be clients, if only for policy reasons. The duties of competence and diligence[46] clearly apply to would-be clients. Thus the Law Society of Scotland's Client Relations and Complaints Office in 1994 considered a case where a daughter acting on her father's behalf consulted a firm of solicitors. The daughter complained as to the quality of the service that had been offered to her father by the solicitors. The Law Society initially considered that since the complainer had been held to be a non-client (in a court action by the solicitors to recover a fee against complainer) there could be no possibility of an inadequate professional service (IPS) complaint. However, since s.42A(1)(a) of the Solicitors (Scotland) Act 1980 refers to "any person having an interest" being able to lodge an IPS complaint, the Society reached the conclusion that non-clients can complain about IPS. The Society nonetheless noted that the Act does not permit a compensation order for IPS to be paid to a non-client.

Perhaps more importantly it is universally held that the duties of confidentiality and privilege apply to prospective clients seeking advice from a lawyer, despite the fact that one or other ultimately decides not to establish the

---

[42] There is no duty on a "rejecting" lawyer to refer the would-be client to an identified lawyer for a second opinion, but it would be somewhat pointless to refer the client to another lawyer whom you knew not to be knowledgeable in the relevant field. It would certainly seem to be good practice to refer the would-be client to a known specialist in that field, or to the Law Society who may be able to suggest an appropriate name or names.

[43] It is probably the counsel of perfection to insist that the referring lawyer research the limitation period even though he or she is not going to act and is not being paid for the advice. However, Cordery on Solicitors and the US courts have made it clear that the burden of ensuring the protection of the would-be client's rights is placed entirely on the solicitor.

[44] See A. Newbold, "A solicitor's liability to 'potential' clients" (1987) 84(44) L.S.G. 3473; S. Blumberg, "Avoiding Malpractice" (1987) Vol. 7 California Lawyer.

[45] See Russell Lang, "Get engaged" (2005) June J.L.S.S. 33.

[46] See above. Also, ABA Model Rules 2002 1.18.

relationship.[47] If this were not the case, no prospective client could consult a lawyer with any confidence that their secrets would be safeguarded. In the absence of candour from the prospective client the lawyer would not be able to make an informed judgement as to whether or not to act, since some of the key factors might be withheld by the apprehensive prospective client. It follows from this that a lawyer who holds confidential or privileged information as a result of a consultation with a prospective client may not thereafter act against that client in the same or a substantially related matter because of the conflict of interest involved. In common with the recent trends in the USA both the Restatement and the Model Rules 2002 would allow a lawyer with confidential information from a prospective client subsequently to act against that prospective client if both clients consent or if certain safeguards are in place.[48] Curiously, neither of these formulations deal with the scenario which occurred in Toronto when a businessman instructed the leading firm of specialist lawyers in a particular field and thereafter proceeded to consult with the only other five firms in Toronto with expertise in the field, with the intention of conflicting them all from acting for his opponent at a later stage. The ploy failed when it was exposed to the court tasked with considering whether to disqualify the other five firms. This is consistent with the principle that the privilege and the confidence may be used as a shield for the client but not as a weapon.

Finally, it seems likely that rules on fees and on client property which has been entrusted to the lawyer will apply equally to prospective clients.[49]

3.11 MONEY LAUNDERING CHECKLISTS

Identifying the Client

Verification of Client Identity Checklist for client — Name: _____

Evidence not obtained — reasons–

1. Client previously identified in– Month .... Year ....

2. Client identified personally by —

Name _____

Position _____

3. Other — state reason fully

_____

_____

---

[47] See Ch.6 (below), and the Third Re-Statement of the Law Governing Lawyers (2000) para.15(1)(a). ABA Model Rules 2002 1.18(b).

[48] See Third Re-Statement of the Law Governing Lawyers (2000) para.15(2); ABA Model Rules 2002 1.18 (c) and (d).

[49] That at least is the position taken by the Restatement and Model Rules 2002. See Third Re-Statement of the Law Governing Lawyers (2000), para.15(1)(b). ABA Model Rules 2002 1.18.

Evidence obtained to verify name and address

Full national Passport ☐

Full National driving licence ☐
Pension Book ☐
Armed Forces ID Card ☐
Signed ID Card of employer known to you ☐

Young person NI card (under 18 only) ☐
Pensioner's travel pass ☐
Building Society passbook ☐
Credit Reference agency search ☐
National ID Card ☐
Copy Company Certificate of Incorporation ☐

Gas, electricity, telephone bill ☐
Mortgage statement ☐
Council tax demand ☐
Bank/Building Society/credit card statement ☐
Young persons medical card (under 18 only) ☐
Home visit to applicants address* ☐
Check of telephone directory* ☐
Check voters roll* ☐
*Suitable for proof of address only.

Evidence obtained for unquoted company or partnership

Certificate of Incorporation or equivalent ☐
Certificate of Trade or equivalent ☐
Latest report and audited accounts ☐
Principal shareholder/partner ☐
Principal director ☐

I confirm that–

   a) **I have seen the originals of the documents indicated above and have identified the above Customer(s), or**
   b) **In accordance with the Regulations, evidence is not required for the reasons stated.**

Signed ———————————————   **Date** ————————————

3.12 SOURCE OF FUNDS

If you have properly identified the new client, this flow chart should be used to ensure that the appropriate level of checking is applied to the funds.

Question
Have you received funds from the client?

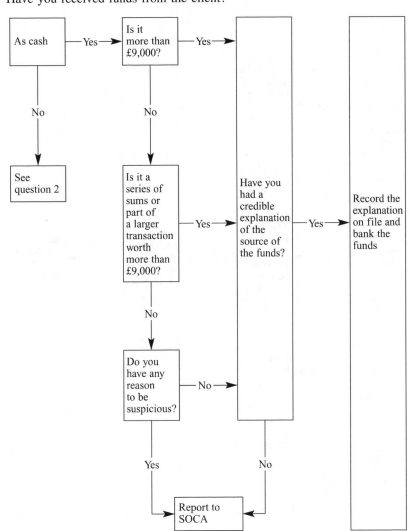

Question 2   Have you received non-cash payment:

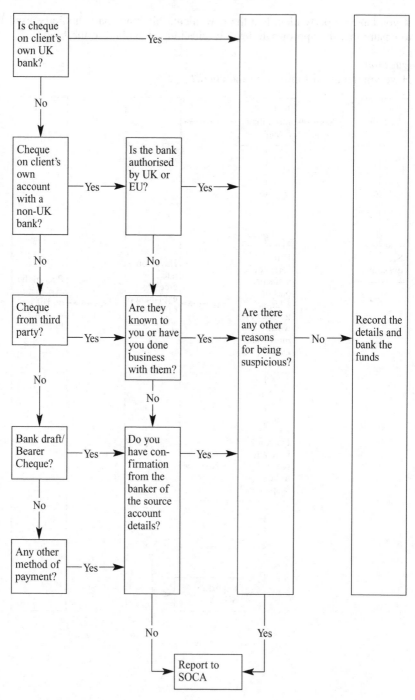

CHAPTER 4

TAKING INSTRUCTIONS

Becoming a Client

How and when do persons become clients? By agreement is the short answer. The relationship has two aspects: ethical and legal. Although the matter has received little attention in the jurisprudence of comparative professional ethics, it would appear that in terms of professional ethics the client/lawyer relationship—which is rooted in trust and often contains strong elements of *delectus personae*—is formed when the lawyer expressly or impliedly agrees to act as the lawyer for the client. The formation of the *legal* relationship between client and lawyer has received rather more attention.[1] In earlier centuries it was classified as a mandate, at least in Scotland, but for more than a century it has been regarded as a contract for services rooted in the law of agency. In the words of Lord Justice Clerk Inglis:

> "The relation of agent and client is in general constituted without any written contract, and without any special contract, either written or verbal. The mere acceptance of employment creates that relation—a relation carrying with it certain well-known consequences, without any necessity for expressing them. The agent, on the one hand, engages that he possesses the requisite skill, and will employ it with all due diligence in the client's service; and the client, on the other hand, becomes bound to supply funds for disbursements, and to pay the agent at the proper time reasonable remuneration for his services. These correlative obligations are all implied, unless any of them be expressly dispensed with."[2]

As Lord Inglis indicates, like most other contracts, the client/lawyer relation can be formed expressly in writing or orally, or implied from actings. The contract begins when the lawyer agrees to act as the lawyer on the client's behalf. Even in the modern era where letters of engagement and written fee charging agreements have become more prevalent, more often than not the initial formation of the relationship is not in writing although, this may well change with the advent of mandatory letters of engagement.[3] Rather it can either be an express oral agreement to act by the lawyer or implied from his or her actings. Such actings are matters of fact which are open to proof in the normal way, including arguments based on personal bar. It might, for example, be argued that once has solicitor has got to the stage of advising the "client" as to the merits of his or her case, and not immediately coupled this with a

---

[1] There is no reason to believe that establishment of the client/solicitor in terms of ethics differs from the position in professional negligence cases or under the law of agency.

[2] *Bell v Ogilvie* (1863) 2 M. 336.

[3] See para.4.02 below.

refusal to take on the case, then the relationship has been established. In the case of *Brady v Neilsons*[4] a professional negligence action was raised against a legal firm alleging a conflict of interest. The key to the case turned on whether the firm who were acting for one party in a property transfer were also acting for pursuer. This led to a consideration of what is required to establish the solicitor/client relationship. It was agreed that the defenders had not advised the pursuer as to his legal position, and that they had neither met him nor written to him about the transaction nor issued a fee-note to him in respect of the transaction. The pursuer, however, pointed to the fact that the transfer was one of a series of related transactions and averred that the defenders had acted for him in obtaining a bank loan as part of the linked transactions; *secondly*, to the fact that the defenders had acted for the pursuer in an unconnected road traffic offence six years before, *thirdly* and most crucially that the defenders had telephoned the pursuer during the property transfer to check that it was all right for the title to be transferred and *lastly* to the fact that the defenders had not told the pursuer to be independently advised at the time of the transfer as they should have done if they were not also acting for him. The Lord Ordinary considered that the pursuer had averred a relevant case and that it could not be inferred from his averments that the defenders had not been his agents in the property transaction. Accordingly he allowed a proof before answer, in part to ascertain whether the telephone conversation could have amounted to the taking of instructions from the pursuer. In the course of his judgment Lord Reed observed:

> "There is no doubt that in certain circumstances the existence of a solicitor-client relationship can be inferred from the conduct of the parties, even if there is no express agreement to that effect. Decisions in earlier cases such as *Bolton v Jameson & MacKay* 1987 SLT 291 or *Tait v Brown & McRae* 1997 SLT (Sh Ct) 63 are therefore of little assistance except as illustrations of particular circumstances in which the inference could or could not be drawn. The circumstances in any particular case will normally have to be ascertained by evidence."

In one English case a person left a writ which had been served on him with other relevant papers with a solicitor who replied that he would "go to the bottom of the matter". Perhaps surprisingly, this was held sufficient to establish the relationship.[5] Again in a Scots case the family solicitor who had acted for the deceased in drafting the original will, discussed the ingathering of the estate with one of the executors on the telephone and asked for an item of the estate held by the executor to be sent to him. This was held by the Client Relations Committee, which subsequently reviewed the case to show that the solicitor had agreed to act in the winding up of the estate, even though there had been no meeting to settle instructions. In a not dissimilar case which came before the Discipline Tribunal in 1986[6] the solicitor denied receiving instructions to wind up an estate. He had received the papers from a distant

---

[4] 1999 G.W.D. 4–209.
[5] *Parnell v Echells* (1839) 3 J.P. 771.
[6] DTD 686/86.

relative with no interest in the estate and the next of kin was *incapax* and thus unable to issue instructions. The Tribunal argued that, in relation to winding up an executry estate, strictly speaking no one can give formal instructions until an executor has been appointed. Nevertheless, from a practical aspect the solicitor's duties commenced, they said, when he accepted responsibility for the deceased's estate. This might be when papers or keys or other property were delivered to him or otherwise when he undertakes to investigate the estate or trace the beneficiaries. It may be some time before the solicitor has identified the next of kin or completed his investigations into the estate, but during this period the solicitor has an ongoing professional responsibility notwithstanding that it was prior to the formal appointment of the executor. In this case the solicitor had settled the deceased's funeral account and accepted responsibility for settling certain other outlays on the deceased's property and made enquiries regarding the status of the next of kin. In such circumstances, the Tribunal held that the solicitor had *de facto* accepted instructions even although the parties who first communicated with the solicitor were not in themselves related to the deceased.

Who is the Agent? 4.02

This is a question which has been somewhat neglected, both as a matter of law and of professional ethics. As we saw in Ch.2, clients are regarded by the Law Society as being clients of the firm rather than the individual lawyers who are advising them. This makes sense from a number of perspectives. Fees are owed to the firm not to the solicitor, and if professional negligence is alleged, it is the firm that is likely to be sued (although the individual lawyer can also be sued). If the individual lawyer handling a case ceases to be employed by the firm or is ill, then normally clients will expect the firm to provide another adviser to handle the case, unless there is a strong element of *delectus personae*. Further, corporate clients deal with teams of lawyers in corporate law firms rather than simply one adviser. This suggests that as a matter of law the contract of services is between client and the law firm rather than with the individual lawyer.

On the other hand, it is also clear that individual lawyers owe ethical, delictual (professional negligence), fiduciary and agency duties to clients. Moreover, especially, where *delectus personae* elements are strong, the client may well see the primary relationship as being with an individual lawyer rather than the firm and if the lawyer becomes unavailable due to illness, incapacity or job transfer then the client may prefer to go elsewhere. This suggests that except where the client is being advised by a sole practitioner, or is a corporate client, there are two contracts of service, not one. The first, and primary contract, is between the client and the firm and the second between the client and the lawyer. These two contracts in turn are influenced by a third contract namely the contract of employment or co-partnery between the solicitor and the firm. This contract may contain restrictive covenants or provision for "gardening leave" as we saw in Ch.2 and have implications for mandates and lien as we will see in Ch.11. The existence of a secondary contract between solicitor and the client is reinforced by the fact that in the UK, unlike some jurisdictions, ethical obligations are only owed by individual lawyers rather than the firm. Even if the conduct complained of stems from a decision of the partnership, only the partners involved in the actual act will be subject to complaint and discipline. There is no concept of corporate responsibility for misconduct in the UK. IPS sanctions, on the other hand, can be levied against either the firm or the individual solicitor or both.

4.03 Letters of Engagement

Whether the legal relationship between client and lawyer is established by actings or orally, it is good practice to write to clients after the initial interview, indicating whether you are taking the case and if so, what steps you are proposing to take, when you will take them, what their consequences will be, what steps the client should take in the meantime, what the client should do if they have a complaint and the basis on which the solicitor's fee charging will be founded.[7] Used properly these letters (termed letters of engagement) can assist solicitors in managing clients' expectations and minimising the risk of claims and client dissatisfaction.[8]

Successive Scottish Legal Service Ombudsmen in their Annual Reports and elsewhere conducted a sustained campaign in support of mandatory letters of engagement for over a decade. The Council of the Law Society considered the matter on several occasions and eventually on the March 18, 2005 the Law Society approved the Draft Solicitors (Scotland) (Client Communications) Practice Rules 2005 which made letters of engagement mandatory in all fields of work undertaken by a solicitor for a client; with a few exceptions:

Provision of Information

    3. *A solicitor shall when tendering for business or at the earliest practical opportunity upon receiving instructions to undertake any work on behalf of a client, provide the following information to the client in writing:*

        a) details of the work to be carried out on behalf of the client;

        b) save where the client is being provided with legal aid or advice and assistance, details of either—

            (i) an estimate of the total fee to be charged for the work, including VAT and outlays which may be incurred in the course of the work;

            (ii) the basis upon which a fee will be charged for the work, including VAT and outlays which may be incurred in the course of the work;

        c) if the client is being provided with advice and assistance or legal aid—

            (i) where advice and assistance or special urgency work is being provided, details of the level of contribution required from the client, and

---

[7] See Guidance Manual p.1.3 and Ryder *op. cit.* Ch.5.

[8] See Sim, "Marking out the Pitch" (2003) 48(12) J.L.S.S. 40 and Allingham, "Terms of Endearment" (2004) 49(4) J.L.S.S. 49.

    (ii) *where civil legal aid, special urgency work or advice and assistance is being provided details of any payment which may be required from property recovered or preserved[9];*

   d) *the identity of the person or persons who will be principally carry out the work on behalf of the client and;*

   e) *the identity of the person whom the client should contact if the client becomes unconcerned in any way with the manner in which the work is being carried out.*

Exceptions

4. (1) *Where a client regularly instructs a solicitor in the same type of work, he need not be provided with the information set out in rule 3 in relation to a new instruction to do that type of work, provided that he has previously been supplied with that information in relation to a previous instruction to do that type of work and is informed of any differences between that information and the information which, if this paragraph (1) did not apply, would have been required to provided to him in terms of rule 3.*

  (2) *Where there is no practical opportunity for a solicitor to provide the information set out in rule 3 to a client before the conclusion of the relevant work for that client then that information need not be provided to that client.*

  (3) *Where a client is a child under the age of 12 years then the information set out in rule 3 need not be provided to that client . . .*

As in the case of all practice rules,[10] breach of these rules may be treated as professional misconduct, but in practice more often than not it will be treated as IPS. Only if there are repeated breaches, or other exceptional circumstances, is it likely that it will be treated as professional misconduct. In addition to the contents required by the new practice rule, it is strongly recommended that solicitors should also insert a clause in their terms of business letter advising the client that the solicitor is required to comply with the Proceeds of Crime Act 2002 and the Money Laundering Regulations 2003. See para.6.22 below. In addition, the Professional Practice Guideline on Terms of Business issued in 1998 provides further advice on good practice in this area.

The Guideline[11] states that as soon as instructions are received from a client or when tendering for business, a solicitor should issue a terms of business letter of engagement, in clear, unambiguous and straightforward terms and

---

  [9] A failure to advise a legally-aided client as to the potential operation of the statutory charge or "clawback" to cover the cost of the client's legal expenses if they win their case, or of the potential liability for the other side's expenses in legal aid cases (as well as the possibility of modification by the court) is likely to be IPS (as the Law Society Council held on four occasions in 2001/2002). A failure to advise an eligible client as to the possibility of being funded by legal aid would not only be unsatisfactory conduct and IPS, it might also lead to a negligence suit. See Websters *op. cit.* para.2.02.

  [10] Solicitor Scotland Act 1980 s.34(4).

  [11] See *Greens Solicitors Professional Handbook, op. cit.*

language. On all occasions the Guideline requires seven items to be addressed as follows:

1. The source of authorisation of the solicitor—the Law Society of Scotland
2. The method by which instructions should be given and received.
3. The authority of the client to instruct.
4. Supervision of client business (i.e. name and status of person responsible for day-to-day conduct of matter and principal responsible for overall supervision if different).
5. Any conflict of interest raised by accepting instructions.
6. The requirement of confidentiality.
7. Procedures for resolving problems.

The Guideline suggests that normally another five items should be listed as follows:

1. Details as to the holding of client money.
2. Fee estimates (except in legal aid cases) to include VAT and prospective outlays.[12]
3. Requirements as to the timing of payment of fees.
4. Responsibility for outlays.
5. Timescale in general.

Finally the Guideline indicates that it is good practice for the following five matters also to be included in the letter:

1. Indemnity/liability for loss.
2. The client's right to taxation.
3. The separate agent and client account in court matters (including legal aid).
4. The lien over titles and papers.
5. The level of service to be provided.

As already indicated a breach of the Guideline on Letters of Engagement by a firm which refuses to use them is unlikely to have any disciplinary consequences—it is largely a matter of good practice.

What is the legal status of a letter of engagement? In most cases they will form part of the letter of engagement will set out the terms of the contract of services which constitutes the client/solicitor relationship either because it contains many of the express terms of the contract or because its terms supersede the implied terms of the contract implied from actings which originally established the client/solicitor relationship. This means that terms can be enforced by either party against the other. Solicitors, therefore should take care to ensure that the terms are accurate, including the statement of fees and outlays e.g. the correct rate of Stamp Duty Land Tax. At the very least,

---

[12] The Code of Conduct for Solicitors 2002 has been amended to indicate that solicitors should advise their clients in writing when it becomes clear that the cost of work will materially exceed any estimate and also when the limit of the original estimate is being approached (see Appendix 1).

breach of a term contained in a letter of engagement, for example failing to inform the client that the costs of an action have substantially exceeded the original estimate, if any, may well amount to IPS. It should also be noted that where a solicitor is asked to do something which departs from the normal standard of care, he or she would be well advised to confirm the instruction in writing.[13]

Implied Terms in the Contract for Services   4.04

Where there is no written contract for services the court will look first to see if there is a contract at all, either oral or based on actings. Thereafter, the court will consider what terms are incorporated into that contract, adjudicated objectively.[14] (Where the court holds that there is no contract, it may nonetheless hold that a claim for remuneration *quantum meruit* lies at the hands of the party rendering services without a contractual basis.)[15] The terms that are likely to be implied once a contract has been established, will depend on the particular task for which the solicitor has been instructed, but will certainly include the duty upon the solicitor to act with the skill and care of the reasonably competent solicitor.[16] Further, the duties probably extend to advising on all relevant matters, protecting the client's interests,[17] consulting with the client on matters outwith the agent's discretion, keeping the client reasonably informed, and carrying out instructions by all proper means.[18] This final duty raises the issue as to whether it is an implied term of the contract that the solicitor or firm will adhere to the ethical rules of the jurisdiction in which the contract is to be carried out. Ryder argues that there is an expectation by the client that the lawyer will not only deliver an adequate professional service, but also comply with the rules for the conduct of his or her profession.[19] This would seem a reasonable expectation on the client's part. Moreover, there is an implied term that the solicitor cannot be asked to implement instructions which would involve a breach of the solicitor's ethical code. There seems no reason why the obligation should not be reciprocal. If that is the case, the question arises whether a client could enforce an ethical obligation through a breach of contract or breach of fiduciary duty action. It is already the case that a breach of Law Society Guidelines or Practice Rules can and has been cited as evidence of a failure by the solicitor to adhere to the required standard of care in an action for professional negligence.[20] Evidence of breaches of the American Bar Association's Model Rules of Professional

---

[13] See R. Rennie, *Solicitors' Negligence* (Butterworths, 1997), p.44.

[14] See Lord MacFadyen in *Robert Barry & Co. v Doyle*, 1998 S.L.T. 1238, a case where the pursuers averred that there was a verbal contract followed by actings which had incorporated their standard terms and conditions into the contract.

[15] *Robert Barry & Co v Doyle* 1998 S.L.T. 1238.

[16] See e.g. *Midland BankTrust Co. Ltd v Hett, Stubbs & Kemp* [1979] Ch. 384.

[17] See e.g. *Bristol & West Building Society v Aitken Nairn, WS,* 1999 S.C. 678.

[18] See R. Rennie, *Solicitors' Negligence*, Butterworths, 1997 at p.25, based on *Tiffin Holdings Ltd v Millican* (1991) 49 DLR(2d) 216.

[19] J. Ryder, *Professional Conduct*, Butterworths, 1995 at p.58.

[20] Whether rooted in delict or contract. See R. Rennie, *op. cit.*, paras 2.18 and 3.05. Curiously, evidence as to what the professional rules are can be led from expert and senior members of the profession. The Discipline Tribunal, however, has made it clear that in cases coming before it, such evidence should ordinarily not be led, since would be to usurp the role of the Tribunal. DTD 761/89.

Conduct are also used in this way.[21] It is unclear whether third parties (e.g. beneficiaries, insurers or the opposing party) could use the ethical rules in the same way. The answer may be that in such cases, the difficulty lies in establishing that the lawyer owes a duty of care to the third party in the first place, rather than evidencing any breach thereof. Although the duties of professional responsibility have a public dimension, there seems no good reason why they should not be directly enforceable by individual clients either through interdict e.g. where privilege or confidentiality are in issue or by damages for breach of contract or fiduciary duty. Certainly, there would seem to be nothing to prevent a client inserting an express term in the contract of services to the effect that the solicitor and his/her firm will abide by the professional rules of the jurisdiction in which the contract is to be carried out.[22]

The contract will contain implied terms as to the extent of the authority of the lawyer to act without instruction from the client (see Ch.5). Again, despite the *delectus personae* element in the client/lawyer relationship, it has become commonplace in these days of increasing specialisation for law firms to delegate aspects of the provision of legal services to other lawyers in the firm and even to non-legally qualified staff. The right to delegate aspects of the client's work in this way is likely to be implied under the contract of service. However, courtesy and good practice makes it advisable to inform the client as to who in the firm is actually handling their work. Telling a client that their work has been handed to another lawyer on even non-lawyer in the firm that they do not know, or worse still that it is proposed to pass it to a solicitor in another firm (e.g. because of a conflict of interest or because that specialism is no longer available in the firm) without first seeking the client's consent, is likely to provoke an IPS complaint or the risk of losing the client. Delegation is another issue which should be raised in a letter of engagement and a further reason for a letter of engagement in the first place. This follows from the case of *Pilbrow v Pearless De Rougemont & Co.*[23] where the Court of Appeal held that where a client asked for the services of a solicitor, but was provided instead with help from an unqualified member of staff, without being informed of this fact, the firm of solicitors could not recover its fees from the client. The court pointed out that the firm:

> "should have trained its receptionist, when faced with a request to see a solicitor, to do one of the following: (i) refer the client to a solicitor; (ii) refer the client to someone who was not a solicitor, but tell the client that

---

[21] See K. Gilliland, "Expanded Use of the Code of Professional Responsibility and the Rules of Professional Conduct: A Basis for Civil Liability?" (1990) 15 J. Legal Prof 355. This is despite the fact that the scope note of the American Bar Association's Model Rules of Professional Conduct makes clear that violation of a rule should not found a cause of action since they are not designed to be a basis for civil liability. Gilliland shows that the courts and litigants are ignoring this homily, urged on by leading writers in the field, e.g. Charles Wolfram, "The Code of Professional Responsibility as a Measure of Attorney Liability in Civil Litigation" (1979) 30 S.C.L. Rev. 290. As a result the scope note of the revised Model Rules Ethics 2000 explains that while violation of a rule should not "itself" give rise to a cause of action but "may be evidence of a breach of the applicable standard of conduct".

[22] This is effectively what the Scottish Legal Aid Board has done in its code for criminal practitioners by insisting that all solicitors doing legal aid work should abide by the voluntary code of conduct for criminal cases.

[23] [1999] 3 All E.R. 355.

this person was not a solicitor; or perhaps, in some circumstances, (iii) refer the client to someone who the receptionist knows is not or may not be a solicitor, refrain from telling him that fact, and alert the referee to the fact that the client had asked for a solicitor. If that last course of action is adopted then it will be the duty of the referee straight away to make clear to the client that she is not a solicitor, it that be the fact."[24]

The courts will also imply a right on the part of both parties to the contract to terminate it under certain conditions, although it will always be easier for the client to terminate the relationship than the lawyer.

Implied Terms in the Contract for Services—Obligations for Clients   4.05

While there are few implied terms imposing obligations on the client, they would normally be expected to pay the lawyer a fair and reasonable fee for services rendered under the contract and to indemnify the lawyer for liability to which the client has exposed the lawyer without the latter's fault.[25] This would extend to reimbursing the lawyer for authorised or impliedly authorised outlays incurred in pursuing the client's case. There is probably an implied term that the client will assist the lawyer in pursuing the client's objectives, however, it is far from clear that there is an implied term that the client will not lie to the lawyer. To imply such a contractual obligation would undermine much of the justification of the privilege, which is designed to encourage clients to tell their lawyers the truth. However, where the lawyer has agreed to take a case on a speculative or conditional fee basis, the onus on the client to be candid with his or her lawyer becomes more clamant. Nevertheless, it is unclear that it would be deemed to be an implied term even in this situation. It follows that lawyers agreeing to act speculatively or on a conditional fee basis would be advised to insert such an obligation into their letter of engagement or written fee charging agreement. Of course, lying to a client breaches the relationship of trust between solicitor and client and justifies termination of relationship ethically and contractually.

Contracting Out of Ethical Obligations   4.06

If the expectation that the solicitor will abide by the ethical rules of the jurisdiction is matched by an expectation that the client may not ask him or her to infringe these rules, can the parties reduce the impact of this mutual restraint by agreeing to reduce the applicability of the rules? Public policy would seem to frown on such a possibility; otherwise it would open the door to corruption or undue pressure from one or other party. While there are some obligations that can be waived by the client e.g. privilege and confidentiality, there is more controversy over permitting clients to consent to conflicts of interest. Some obligations with respect to client property can be by-passed with disclosure, independent advice and consent. However, many more simply cannot be waived.

---

[24] See also the case of *Adrian Alan Ltd v Fuglers (A Firm)* [2002] EWCA Civ 1655 which confirms the Court of Appeal's reasoning in the *Pilbrow* case.

[25] *Restatement of the Law Third, Restatement of the Law Governing Lawyers* (The American Law Institute, St Paul, 2000), p.151, para.17(2).

4.07 Contracting Out of Legal Obligations

There is no Scottish authority on the question whether it is ethically acceptable for a solicitor to include in the contract with the client a term which seeks to exclude the solicitor from any liability to the client for negligence or breach of contract or even only from partial liability to the client.[26] Any attempt by the solicitor to reduce or exclude his or her liability for a breach of the ordinary standard of care and skill, whether in contract or delict, is likely to fall foul of the Unfair Contract Terms Act 1977, unless (perhaps) the client is large business or the restriction on liability can be shown to be "fair and reasonable".[27] Certainly, where the client is an individual or a small business it is most unlikely that the courts will accept any restriction on liability for negligence is reasonable.[28] However, where the firm has become a limited liability partnership, clients are put on notice that there is a limit to the liability of the firm, even when it has been negligent.

---

[26] In England it is unethical to seek to exclude liability altogether, but acceptable to seek to restrict it to the level of the minimum level of cover required by the Solicitors' Indemnity Rules. Any such provision would still be subject to the Unfair Contract Terms Act 1977. See rule 12.11 English Guide (1999). Liability for fraud or breaching professional obligations cannot be limited in this way.

[27] Section 17. The requirement that exclusions or limitations must be fair and reasonable in the circumstances is restricted to consumer contracts or standard form contracts. Most contracts between solicitors and laypersons even in small or medium businesses would fall under one or other of these categories. See Rennie *op. cit.* para.3.08 for a fuller examination of the efficacy of contractual exclusions by solicitors.

[28] Rennie *op. cit.* para.3.08.

CHAPTER 5

EXTENT OF AUTHORITY

Introduction

The authority of solicitors to act on behalf of their clients is governed both by professional ethics and by the law of agency. In Scotland the overlap between these two domains is substantial.[1] As a matter of professional responsibility, in terms of art.5(a) of the Code of Conduct: "Solicitors act as agents of the clients and must have the authority of the clients for their actions". Solicitors who act outside their authority can be guilty of unsatisfactory conduct or even professional misconduct. As a matter of law, the authority of the solicitor to act on behalf of a client[2] is governed by the law of agency. The actual or real authority of solicitors derives either from the instructions of their clients (i.e. express authority) or from their implied authority as a general agent.[3] By custom and practice and in law, the implied authority of solicitors varies with the kind of work that they have been instructed to perform.[4] The extent of a solicitor's actual authority is important because:

(1) it limits his or her ability to bind the client *vis-a-vis* third parties or to recover the cost of his work from the client; and
(2) it opens the solicitor up to potential claims for breach of warranty of authority or for the expenses of any unauthorised proceedings.

Nevertheless, even where solicitors have exceeded their actual authority their clients may still be bound *vis-a-vis* third parties where:

(1) they have subsequently homologated or ratified the solicitor's act; or

---

[1] The same is true in the USA. The relevant Model Rule—1.2(a) (2002 edn) requires that a lawyer "shall abide by a client's decisions concerning the objectives of representation and . . . shall consult with the client as to the means by which they are to be pursued. A lawyer may take such action on behalf of a client as is impliedly authorised to carry out the representation." On the American law of agency on the authority of the lawyer see *Restatement of the Law Third, Restatement of the Law Governing Lawyers* (The American Law Institute, St Paul, 2000), Vol.1, Ch.2 topics 3 and 4.

[2] The scope of the solicitor's authority delimits the sphere in which the solicitor may lawfully bind his or her client.

[3] One who earns his or her livelihood as an agent. By contrast, a special agent is one who is only an agent ad hoc employed, merely to transact a particular piece of business. See Gow, *The Mercantile and Industrial Law of Scotland*, p.522.

[4] See e.g. Begg *on Law Agents* Ch. Viii; D. M. Walker, *The Scottish Legal System* (6th edn), pp.354–55; The Stair Memorial Encyclopaedia, Vol.1, p.253.

(2) the doctrine of apparent or ostensible authority comes into operation.

The latter occurs where the client, by his or her actions has held out the solicitor to have the requisite authority to bind the client despite the act being outwith the solicitor's actual authority. Both these doctrines are a form of personal bar.

5.02 Express Authority

Prima facie, a solicitor is expected to adhere to the scope of authority permitted by the express instructions of the client, which may exceed or fall short of the scope typically afforded to a solicitor undertaking a particular piece of business for a client. In practice, a reasonable latitude will be allowed in construing the terms of the solicitor's retainer or mandate.[5] Nevertheless, as Lord President Inglis observed in *Batchelor v Pattison and Mackersey*[6]:

> "the general rule may be fairly stated to be that the agent must follow the instructions of his client."

5.03 Implied Authority

However, a solicitor need not obtain express and direct authority for every action that is undertaken on behalf of a client, because of his or her implied authority as a general agent.[7] This is because it would be impractical and excessively expensive to consult the client about every small step in a transaction. Similarly, the Discipline Tribunal has held:

> "a solicitor is entitled to the widest discretion in regard to pursuing investigations which he is instructed to carry out and it would place an intolerable burden on the solicitor if he was under a general obligation to seek the consent of his client before making each and every inquiry. . . . although a solicitor has a general duty to keep his client informed, such obligation does not extend to each and every action or item of information which is obtained."[8]

Nevertheless, in order to protect the client from an over-zealous or reckless agent, the solicitor's ability to act without express instructions will be referred to the object of the representation since the extent of the implied authority depends on the nature of the work that the solicitor has been instructed to do.[9] Generally, the international case law establishes that the weightier the legal consequence for the client of the lawyer's action, the more likely it is that the

---

[5] Begg *op. cit.* p.89.

[6] (1876) 3 R. 914. Note also that in legal aid cases the scope of the legal aid certificate must be adhered to.

[7] The solicitor has the implied authority to do all such things that are incidental to the object of the representation.

[8] DTD 567/82. In a similar case, DTD 583/83 the Discipline Tribunal held that "While a solicitor is expected to work closely with his client and keep him fully informed, there is no absolute duty on a solicitor to show every document to his client."

[9] Begg *op. cit.* p.88: D. M. Walker, *The Scottish Legal System* (6th edn), pp.354–55; The Stair Memorial Encyclopaedia, Vol.1, p.253.

court will find that the solicitor exceeded his or her implied authority.[10] Thus, a solicitor engaged to recover a debt will be entitled to raise proceedings, take decree and use diligence to secure payment but not to delay diligence with the effect of giving time or to raise a further debt action to recover the expenses of diligence.[11] Similarly, a solicitor operating for an absent landlord will be able to manage the property and collect rent, but does not have the implied authority to grant a lease.[12]

Implied Authority and Litigation   5.04

One area where the scope of the solicitor's implied authority has frequently been a matter for debate is in relation to litigation and the settlement of disputes. Provided the client's express instructions are not ignored, a solicitor who has been instructed to act in court proceedings has a reasonable measure of discretion in conducting such proceedings,[13] including a wide discretion in deciding which witnesses, if any, should be called to give evidence—a discretion which can only be challenged as misconduct if the solicitor acted maliciously, recklessly or with total disregard for the interests of the client. On the other hand, a solicitor cannot initiate proceedings without express authority (unless it is clearly envisaged by the scope of the client's instructions) nor does he or she have the implied authority to lodge an appeal[14] even if the intention is to protect the interests of the appellant.[15] Similarly, a solicitor has no implied power to refer a matter to arbitration[16] nor, presumably, to mediation. Nor may a solicitor abandon a client's case without the prior consent of the client.[17] Further, it is accepted that neither solicitor nor counsel can enter into an extra-judicial settlement on their client's behalf.[18] The most contentious issue relates to the lawyer's ability to judicially settle or compromise the case without the client's prior consent, for example by accepting a minute of tender. In England it is accepted that a solicitor has the implied authority to settle a case, just as counsel does.[19] In the USA however,

---

[10] See Dal Pont, *Lawyers Professional Responsibility in Australia and New Zealand* (2nd edn) (LBC, NSW, 2001), p.50.

[11] Begg, p.89; Stair Memorial Encyclopaedia, Vol.1, p.253.

[12] *Danish Dairy v Gillespie*, 1922 S.C. 656.

[13] Including incurring necessary and consequential expenses.

[14] *Stephen v Skinner* (1863) 2 M. 287.

[15] *ibid. per* Lord President McNeill at p.290. However, the position might be different if the client was absent or could not be contacted.

[16] *Black v Laidlaw* (1844) 6 D. 1254.

[17] *Urqhart v Grigor* (1857) 19 D. 853 However, counsel may abandon a case without the client's permission, see *Batchelor v Pattison and Mackersy* (1876) 3 R. 918 and *Brodt v King*, 1991 S.L.T. 272. Although it is widely accepted that counsel may abandon a case without the client's consent, following the decision in *Arthur J.S. Hall v Simons* [2002] 1 A.C. 615 (July 20, 2000), Lord Hope of Craighead observed that Lord President Inglis's reference in *Batchelor* to advocates taking on an office, was "no longer in keeping with the modern view" which "places a greater emphasis on the duty owed by the advocate to the client". Lord Hope opined that good faith alone, was no longer sufficient, and that the advocate was required to display the care which an advocate of ordinary skill would take, when exercising his judgement, even when abandoning a client's case.

[18] *Brodt v King*, 1991 S.L.T. 272 at 274 L, *per* L.J.C. Ross and 277 C *per* Lord Dunpark.

[19] *Waugh v Clifford & Sons* [1982] 1 All E.R. 1095. See Cordery on *Solicitors* F [26] F/5. Australia has followed the English cases, although New Zealand has preferred instead to deny solicitors the implied authority to settle cases without having their clients on board. See Dal Pont, *op. cit.* p.52.

the cases and the Model Rules establish, and the Restatement Third asserts, that an attorney has no implied authority to settle an action without first obtaining the client's consent and is open to discipline should he or she attempt to do so.[20] In Scotland counsel clearly can settle a case without the client's consent[21] but the position with relation to solicitors remains unclear. Gow[22] thought that they could, but Begg[23] was uncertain, considering the case law to be equivocal. In the end it may come down to the circumstances. Insurance companies routinely give their solicitors the authority to settle cases up to a financial limit. On the other hand, the Discipline Tribunal held in two cases in 1996 that solicitors who, inter alia, purported to negotiate settlements to their clients' actions without their knowledge or consent were guilty of professional misconduct.[24] On balance, if the general trend internationally is to restrict the agent's implied authority in situations where the implications are most serious for the client, there must be a substantial likelihood that the Scottish courts will reject an implied authority for solicitors to compromise actions without client consent. It would seem that both as a matter of the law of agency and of professional ethics, the wisest course for solicitors in this situation is to obtain instructions from their clients before agreeing to settle.

5.05 Apparent or Ostensible Authority

Even where there is an express instruction from the client restricting the actual authority of the solicitor to less than would normally be afforded by way of implied authority to an agent charged with a particular piece of work, this will have little efficacy if the client has, by word or deed, held out the solicitor to have all the normal authority of a solicitor undertaking that type of task.[25] In other words, any limitation imposed by the client on the lawyer's "normal" authority *vis-a-vis* third parties will only effect third parties who are on notice of that limitation. It follows that in such situations if the solicitor contracts with a third party ostensibly on behalf of his or her principal then the principal will be bound to the third party even if the solicitor lacks the actual authority to enter such a contract.[26] Other cases of ostensible authority include:

(1) those where clients allows a lawyer to behave as his or her agent even where he is not; or

(2) where his agency has been terminated; or

---

[20] See C. Wolfram, *Modern Legal Ethics* (West Publishing, St Paul, 1986) at pp.169–70; Model Rule 1.2(a) and the Commentary (2002 edn) which specifies that the decision to settle a civil action is one for the client, not the lawyer; and *Restatement of the Law Third, Restatement of the Law Governing Lawyers* (The American Law Institute, St Paul, 2000), Vol.1, p.180.

[21] See *Batchelor v Pattison and Mackersy* (1876) 3 R. 918 and *Brodt v King*, 1991 S.L.T. 272.

[22] J.J. Gow, *The Mercantile and Industrial Law of Scotland* (W. Green, Edinburgh, 1964) p.522.

[23] *Op. cit.* p.95.

[24] Moreland 1996 J.L.S.S. 314 and Tulloch 1996 J.L.S.S. 315.

[25] Begg *op. cit.* p.91.

[26] See generally *Freeman and Lockyer v Buckhurst Park Properties (Mangal) Ltd* [1964] 2 Q.B. 480 at p.503.

(3) where the principal allows the solicitor to give the impression that his or her authority is greater than it is.[27]

Ratification or Homologation 5.06

Where a solicitor acts beyond the scope of his or her actual or ostensible authority, the client may still be bound by the solicitor's acts if the client subsequently homologates or ratifies the acts. This will not require an express instruction since a failure to disclaim the solicitor's actions once the client has become aware of them will usually be sufficient to personally bar the client from disclaiming the actions.[28] It is unclear that ratification or homologation necessarily prevents a disciplinary finding against the solicitor, but it probably makes it less likely.[29]

Termination of Authority 5.07

The authority of the solicitor to act on behalf of the client ceases with their agency. To continue to act on behalf of the client once the relationship has been terminated is to risk a "finding" of misconduct or unsatisfactory conduct.[30] If there is any confusion relating to the withdrawal of instructions a meeting should be arranged. Written notice of the withdrawal of instructions should be followed, despite other facts that may direct the solicitor to believe he or she still has authority to act.[31]

Consequences of Acting Outwith Authority 5.08

Solicitors who act outwith the scope of their actual or ostensible authority risk a number of unpleasant consequences:

(1) a "finding" of professional misconduct or unsatisfactory conduct,
(2) that the client will not be bound by such acts but the solicitor will,[32]
(3) that the solicitor will be unable to charge for unauthorised actings,
(4) that the solicitor will be required to cover the expenses of any action which is raised without proper authority,[33] and

---

[27] See B.S. Markesinis and R.J.C. Munday, *An Outline of the Law of Agency* (2nd edn, Butterworths, London, 1986), pp.30–31.

[28] See Begg *op. cit.* p.84.

[29] *Restatement of the Law Third, Restatement of the Law Governing Lawyers* (The American Law Institute, St Paul, 2000) Vol.1 p.178. The possibility of discipline even where there is ratification and the fact that ratification or homologation is not guaranteed, makes the position of a solicitor who has no instructions from his or her client all the more difficult, if a step is required which is outwith his or her authority. For example, if the triennium is about to expire and the solicitor cannot obtain instructions from his or her client, even a decision to raise the action and immediately sist it, may have unpleasant consequences for the unauthorised solicitor.

[30] See e.g. DTD 646/84 and Smith and Barton, *op. cit.* pp.69–70.

[31] DTD 646/84.

[32] E.g. *Thomas v Bain* (1888) 15 R. 613.

[33] *Blyth v Watson*, 1987 S.L.T. 616.

(5) that the solicitor will be liable in damages to the client or third parties for any losses suffered as a result of the unauthorised act.[34]

It is important to note that if a solicitor fails to check the authority of the client or intermediary who is purporting to provide the instructions of a client,[35] the solicitor may incur all of the consequences set out above, including breach of warranty of authority, since the actual client has not authorised the solicitor's acts.[36]

---

[34] This includes a breach of warranty of authority. See generally, Gloag *on Contract* p.155; *Merrick Homes v Duff*, 1994 G.W.D. 29–1731; R. Billins, *Solicitors' Duties and Liabilities* (Sweet & Maxwell, London, 1999) at pp.31 ff.

[35] See para.4.03.

[36] See R. Billins, *Solicitors' Duties and Liabilities* (Sweet & Maxwell, London, 1999).

Chapter 6

CONFIDENTIALITY

Introduction

Of all the duties that are owed by a solicitor to a client, the most paramount are the fiduciary duties or duties of loyalty.[1] These derive from the law of agency, but are mirrored in the common law principles of professional ethics which exist throughout the Anglo-American world. The principal loyalty duties will be dealt with in chapters 7–9. The fiduciary duty of confidentiality is the subject of this chapter. Undoubtedly, the issue of the confidentiality is one of the most important topics in professional relationships today; indeed, the professional obligation for lawyers to hold in confidence certain information relating to clients and their cases is one that is recognised around the world,[2] although the scope of the obligation varies between different jurisdictions.[3] So important is this near universal obligation that it features not just in professional ethics and in agency, but also in the more general law of obligations, in the law of evidence (and solicitor/client privilege in particular), the right to privacy as enshrined in the European Convention on Human Rights and in general community law.[4] Unfortunately, the scope of the protection varies with each area of law as do the exceptions thereto, facts that only add to the complexity of the field. Certainly, in the United States, Australia, Canada and England and Wales it is generally accepted that the ethical obligation of confidentiality and the equitable or contractual obligation of confidentiality imposed on lawyers are roughly co-extensive and that each extends further than that laid down in the law of Evidence. Scots law probably accepts both of these propositions.[5]

The scope of the fiduciary obligation of confidentiality imposed by the law of agency, however, is perhaps more problematic.[6] While the scope of the lawyer and client privilege under the law of evidence has hitherto been less

---

[1] See F. Reynolds (17th edn), *Bowstead and Reynolds on Agency* (Sweet & Maxwell, London, 2001) para.6.032 and the literature referred to therein.

[2] For a discussion of comparative legal privilege see Linklaters *Privileged, Comparative Legal Privilige* (available from *www.linklaters.com*).

[3] See, *A.M. & S Europe Ltd v Commission (Case 155/79)* [1983] Q.B. 878 where the European Court indicates not only that there is a different rationale for lawyer and client privilege in different parts of the EU but that, contrary to the position in the UK, the privilege in EU law is not considered to apply to employed lawyers. Again, it may be that the duty of confidentiality under the law of agency in the USA is more extensive than in the UK. (see below para.6.10).

[4] See Lord Hoffmann in the House of Lords case of *R. v IRC ex parte Morgan Grenfell and Co. Ltd.* [2003] 1 A.C. 563.

[5] See R. Black, *A Question of Confidence* (1982) 27 J.L.S.S. 299 and V. Ogston and A. Seager, *Legal Professional Privilege: An Examination of its Meaning and Application in Scots Law,* 1987 J. Rev. 38.

[6] See below para.6.10.

contentious amongst the common law jurisdictions, its commercial significance in recent times has meant that despite its roots in an adversarial approach to dispute resolution (which has been under attack in the modern era by advocates of ADR as well as a range of legal ethicists on both sides of the Atlantic[7]) there are now persistent calls for the privilege to be extended—first to other methods of dispute processing[8] and secondly to competing providers of professional services e.g. accountants.[9]

6.02 Terminology

Historically, the confidentiality obligation under professional ethics or contract or agency has been known in the Anglo-American world as the duty of client confidentiality and the evidential privilege as legal professional privilege. Scotland, too, recognised the contractual and ethical duties to preserve the clients confidences or "secrets"[10] but took cognisance of two distinct forms of privilege—the privilege of confidentiality or the privilege of solicitor and client communications on the one hand and privilege *post litem motam* (in contemplation of litigation) on the other.[11] Today, notwithstanding the protests by Ogston and Seager[12] against the importation of English concepts, the Scots tend to refer to the duty of confidentiality on the one hand and solicitor and client privilege on the other.[13]

6.03 The Rationale for Confidentiality and Privilege

With confidentiality featuring in so many different normative contexts it might seem unlikely that there should be one rationale for the doctrine which applies to all of the fields. It is difficult to answer this question authoritatively because, with the exception of legal professional privilege, very little has been written about the rationale for the confidentiality in the UK law. In terms of the general obligation of confidentiality—which nowadays relates as much to the nature of the information given as to the relationship between the parties,[14] the law of Scotland is much less developed than in England and Wales.[15] Confidentiality in this sense is a voluntary obligation requiring consent,[16] and

---

[7] E.g. D. Luban, *Lawyers and Justice* (Princeton University Press, New Jersey, 1988), D. Rhode, *In the Interests of Justice* (Oxford University Press, New York, 2000), Nicholson and Webb, *Professional Legal Ethics, op. cit.*

[8] See Scottish Law Commission, *Confidentiality in Family Mediation* 1991, Discussion Paper No. 92 and N. Davidson Q.C. *Confidentiality and Privilege in Commercial Alternative Dispute Resolution* in *Greens' Guide to Alternative Dispute Resolution in Scotland* (edited by S. Moody and R. Mackay) (W. Green, Edinburgh, 1995), p.118.

[9] See OFT, *Competition in Profession, op. cit.*

[10] Begg, *Treatise on Law Agents* (Bell and Bradfute, Edinburgh 1883) pp.235 and 319.

[11] See Ogston and Seager, *op. cit.* and F. Raitt, *Evidence* (3rd edn) (Edinburgh, W. Green, 2001).

[12] *Op. cit.*

[13] Rennie, *Solicitors Negligence* (Edinburgh, Butterworths, 1997) at p.12 para.2.03, refers to actions for breach of confidentiality, Raitt *op. cit.*, p.265 says solicitor and client privilege, as does I. Macphail, *Evidence* (Edinburgh, Law Society of Scotland, 1987) para.18.20.

[14] See *Scotsman Publications v LA* [1990] 1 A.C. 812.

[15] It requires an express or implied contractual obligation or a relationship between the parties in terms of which a confidentiality obligation can be said to arise. See Scottish Law Commission Memorandum No:40 Confidential Information (Edinburgh, SLC, 1977) at para.1–43. It is unclear whether breach of confidence gives rise to a delictual remedy in Scotland. See *ibid.* para.41.

[16] See R. Black, *op. cit.* at p.300.

its rationale would appear to be founded on notions of trust and privacy.[17] The fiduciary duty of confidentiality arising from agency, however, stems from the requirement to act in good faith either by not benefiting from one's knowledge of the clients' secrets[18] or, more broadly, by acting in such a way that safeguards the interests of the client.[19] Curiously, the rationale for the ethical duty of confidentiality has attracted little scholarly attention, other than to assume that its basis must be the same as for the privilege. This seems questionable since, as set out below, the ethical duty of confidentiality extends considerably further than the area covered by professional privilege. Where the two obligations overlap the traditional arguments for the privilege, namely the need to protect the efficient working of the legal system, and the adversarial system in particular, applies equally strongly to confidentiality. However, the greater ambit of confidentiality might suggest that in addition, it is justified by the need to engender trust[20] and to protect client privacy. Finally, legal professional privilege, as we have seen is usually justified on the basis that is essential if the adversarial system is to operate effectively. As Lord Taylor asserted in the *Derby Magistrates*[21] case:

> "The principle which runs through these cases . . . is that a man must be able to consult his lawyer in confidence, since otherwise he might hold back half the truth. The client must be sure what he tells his lawyer in confidence will never be revealed without his consent. Legal professional privilege is thus much more than an ordinary rule of evidence . . . It is a fundamental condition on which the administration of justice as a whole rests."

Similarly Heydon has argued that:

> "The privilege is required to ensure that *all* the relevant facts will be put before . . . [lawyers] . . . , not merely those the client thinks favour him. If lawyers are only told some of the facts, clients will be advised that their cases are better than they actually are, and will litigate instead of compromising and settling. Lawyer-client relations would be full of 'reserve and dissimulation, uneasiness, and suspicion and fear' without the privilege: the confidant might at any time have to betray confidences . . . "

Again the Supreme Court of Canada in *Jones v Smith*[22] observed that:

> "The privilege is essential if sound legal advice is to be given . . . Family secrets, company secrets, personal foibles and indiscretions all must on

---

[17] See A. Boon and J. Levin, *The Ethics and Conduct of Lawyers* (Hart, Oxford, 1999) p.248.

[18] See *Bowstead and Reynolds on Agency op. cit.* para.6.074 and B. Markesinis and R. Munday, *An Outline of the Law of Agency* (2nd edn) (Butterworths, London, 1986) pp.87 ff.

[19] *cf. Liverpool Victoria Friendly Society v Houston* (1900) 3F 42. See also C. Wolfram, *Modern Legal Ethics op. cit.* at p.300.

[20] See art.4 Code of Conduct for Scottish Solicitors (2002).

[21] [1996] 1 A.C. 487.

[22] [1999] 1 S.C.R. 445 at para.46.

occasion be revealed to the lawyer by the client. Without this privilege clients could never be candid and furnish all the relevant information that must be provided to lawyers if they are properly to advise their clients."

6.04 The Nature of Confidentiality and Privilege

The essence of confidentiality and the privilege of confidentiality is that the lawyer is required to refrain from disclosing to the wider world the "secrets" of his or her clients. Moreover, both the privilege and confidentiality belong to the client and only he or she may waive it. However, what has to be protected, and the extent to which it is protected, including the duration of the protection, is controlled not just by the client, but also by the rules of the relevant area of the law.

6.05 Lawyer and Client Privilege

The greatest degree of protection is afforded by the privilege. Thus matters covered by lawyer and client privilege cannot be disclosed by the solicitor even if he or she is put on oath in court. However, the scope of the protection offered to the client by privilege is correspondingly narrower than the other areas of confidentiality:

1. **Only professional communications between the lawyer and the client which are referable to the giving or receiving of advice within the lawyer and client relationship are covered by the privilege.**[23] Although traditionally lawyer and client privilege has been justified by its importance for the proper functioning of the adversarial system,[24] as Wilkinson has observed, "the modern privilege is not . . . confined to communications relating to pending, or contemplated, litigation".[25] While the communications must relate to the giving or receiving of legal advice, if a transaction involves an exchange of communications only some of which feature the giving of legal advice e.g. a Conveyancing transaction, it would seem sensible for the Scottish courts in the absence of contrary authority, to follow the ruling of the Court of Appeal in *Balabel v Air-India*,[26] in focusing on the broad purpose or legal context of the professional communications involved. As Taylor L.J. observed in that case:

---

[23] The fact that the client is in prison does not prevent the communication from being privileged (or confidential). See Websters, *Professional Ethics & Practice for Scottish Solicitors* (Avizandum Publishing Ltd, 2004, 4th edn), para.2.20. and *R. v Sec of State for the Home Dept Ex p. Daly* [2001] 2 A.C. 532.

[24] See para.6.03 above.

[25] A. Wilkinson, *The Scottish Law of Evidence* (Edinburgh, Butterworths, 1986) at p.94. For an account of the early Scottish case law which started by restricting the privilege to cases where litigation was in contemplation, see Dickson, *Evidence* (3rd edn), paras 1670–74 and Ogston and Seager *op. cit.* The modern approach can be traced back to *McCowan v Wright* (1852) 15 D. 229 at 231 and 232 *per* L.J.C. Hope and at 237 *per* Lord Wood.

[26] [1988] Ch 317, now endorsed by the House of Lords in *Three Rivers District Council and Others v Governor and Company of the Bank of England (Appellants)* (2004) [2004] UKHL 48.

"Legal advice is not confined to telling the client the law; it must include advice as to what should prudently and sensibly be done in the relevant legal context . . . "[27]

In that case it was held that in view of the broad range of business and commercial advice provided by lawyers today not all solicitor and client communications should be treated as privileged, but that in a conveyancing transaction communications passing in the handling of that transaction were privileged even though they did not incorporate a specific piece of advice, provided that their broad aim was the obtaining of appropriate legal advice. Similarly, in *NRG v Woodrow*[28] it was held that if in a transaction a lawyer provides not only legal advice but also advice on the commercial wisdom of the transaction then all communications between the solicitor and the client relating to the transaction would be privileged even if they went beyond matters of law, provided they were directly related to the performance by the solicitor of his or her professional duty as a legal adviser to the client. This has now been confirmed by the House of Lords in the culmination of the *Three Rivers* litigation.[29] In a series of cases[30] in 2003 and 2004 involving the Bank of England and the Inquiry into the collapse of the Bank of Credit and Commerce International (BCCI) in 1991, the Court of Appeal appeared to be openly rowing back from the rule laid down in the *Balabel* and *N.R.G.* cases. Thus, they sought to constrain the range of documents covered by the privilege, to insist that the advice given be more closely tied to legal advice and even to suggest that the privilege should be restricted to situations where litigation either existed or was in contemplation. The compatibility of these rulings with the *Balabel* and *N.R.G.* cases was far from clear and when the litigation reached the House of Lords the House unanimously endorsed the line taken in *Balabel* and the dictum quoted above from Lord Justice Taylor, whilst accepting that not all confidential solicitor/client communications would be privileged.[31]

2. **The lawyers must be qualified practitioners acting in their capacity as such, whether they be advocates, solicitors or solicitor advocates.** However, unqualified employees or intermediaries used

---

[27] *ibid.* p.330.

[28] [1995] 1 All E.R. 976.

[29] *Three Rivers District Council and Others v Governor and Company of the Bank of England (Appellants)* (2004) [2004] UKHL 48.

[30] *Three Rivers District Council and Others v Governor and Company of the Bank of England* (No.5) [2003] Q.B. 1556 and *Three Rivers* (No.10) [2003] All E.R. (D) 40 (Nov).

[31] However, the Lords declined to review the decision of the Court of Appeal in the No.5 case, on the definition of "client" and this may yet cause problems. The Court of Appeal employed a restrictive definition of who constituted a client for the purposes of legal professional privilege. On the basis of their decision, it is arguable that where a large corporation instructs a solicitor only communications with specified individuals would qualify for privilege even although, it is unlikely that only one or two individuals will be responsible for instruction. This also means that companies will have to ensure that communications with lawyers are tightly controlled to restrict dissemination within it's own organization to prevent waiving privilege by sharing the information too widely. The House also expressly declined to comment on the usefulness of the US Supreme Court case of *Upjohn Co v United States* (1981) 449 US 383 in this context. (See: *Three Rivers House of Lords Judgement* Winlaw and Watson (available from *www.linklaters.com/ newsanddeals/newdetail.asp?newsid=2125*)).

by the solicitor would also be included.[32] So too are employed or "in-house" lawyers.[33] Foreign lawyers practising in Scotland, for example, under the Lawyers' Establishment Directive (Directive 98/5), would probably also be covered,[34] indeed it is possible that communications between a foreign client and their foreign legal advisers would be regarded as privileged in a Scottish litigation as they currently are in England.[35] Nevertheless, advice given by a qualified lawyer, Scots or otherwise, on a social occasion, for example, at a party or in a pub would normally not be covered unless it is to an existing client about a matter on which the client has already instructed the lawyer. The position of qualified lawyers without a practising certificate e.g. a legal academic advising at a CABx legal clinic is unclear,[36] although the privilege can exist irrespective of whether a fee is charged. Moreover, where a solicitor in private practice advises at a legal clinic, often with the possibility of taking the person advised back to their office as a client, there would seem to be no reason why the original advice is not privileged. In addition, it would appear that if the client bona fide believes that an unqualified person is a qualified lawyer and confides in him or her in consequence, that may still give rise to privilege.[37]

3. **The communications must relate to confidential matters.** Thus details as to matters generally known or knowable e.g. the client's name,[38] address, job and marital status,—even the fact that he or she has retained the lawyer's services, will generally not be covered by the privilege unless the client regards them as secret for some good reason. Nor will the dates and times of meetings with the lawyer be privileged.[39] Details as to the client's whereabouts on the other hand should be regarded as privileged unless they are already in the public

---

[32] See G. Maher, *Professional Privilege* 1990 J.L.S.S. 108 and J. Ryder, *Professional Conduct for Scottish Solicitors* (Law Society of Scotland, Butterworths, 1995) p.56. Intermediaries would only be covered if they have not also received the "confidential" information independently.

[33] Such lawyers are not covered by the privilege under EU law see *AM & S Ltd v EC Commission* [1983] Q.B. 878.

[34] However the scope of the privilege, who is covered by it and who may waive it varies in different parts of Europe, see D.O.A. Edward, *The Professional Secret, Confidentiality and Legal Professional Privilege in the Nine Member States of the European Community* (1978) 23 J.L.S.S. 19, Websters (3rd edn) *op. cit.* p.23 and Ryder, *op. cit.* pp.59–60.

[35] See Maher, *op. cit.* This could apply even if the foreign adviser was a compellable witness in his or her home jurisdiction.

[36] *ibid.*

[37] *ibid.* and A.B. Wilkinson, *The Scottish Law of Evidence* (Butterworths, London, 1986) at p.95 discussing *Gavin v Montgomerie* (1830) 9 S 213 *per* Lord President Hope.

[38] R. Billins, *Solicitors' Duties and Liabilities*, (Sweet & Maxwell, London, 1999) at pp.91–92.

[39] See *R. v Manchester Crown Court, Ex p. Rogers* [1999] 1 W.L.R. 832, and Billins, *op. cit.* p.94. During police investigations into a fatal assault, the police took a statement from a taxi driver that at the relevant time he had picked up a man from the flats where the incident took place and took him to a solicitor's office. The Crown sought to recover documentary records from the solicitor's office showing the time of client's arrival, in order to establish whether the applicant was the man in the taxi. The court considered whether the documents were covered by privilege. It was held that legal professional privilege applied only to communications made for the purpose of seeking or receiving advice. In the instant case the record of time on an attendance note, or on a time sheet or fee record, was not a communication as it recorded nothing which passed between the solicitor and the client and had nothing to do with obtaining legal advice.

domain. Facts that a lawyer knows from observation e.g. the signing of a deed, the handwriting of the client, or the conduct of parties to each other in public, will not be covered by the privilege.[40] More problematic are the lawyers' observations as to his or her client's demeanour, state of mind, sobriety or clothing (e.g. was it dishevelled, bloodstained etc.). In relation to the last two, although it may seem harsh, it is difficult to see why a court should excuse the lawyer from testifying as to these matters on the grounds of privilege.[41] First, they are not communications referable to obtaining advice. Secondly, the privilege is an exceptional protection to clients to encourage candour in the adversarial system. This protection cannot be used to interfere with the course of justice e.g. by passing the murder weapon or a client's business papers which reveal that a fraud has been committed, to the client's lawyer. Similarly, therefore, it is hard to see why the protection of the privilege should be used to exclude the eye witness evidence of the lawyer. On the other hand, the lawyer's assessment of the client's demeanour or state of mind involves complex mixes of observation and communication. It is submitted that the lawyer should be able to claim privilege in relation to his or her assessment on these matters.[42] Further, if the facts seen by the lawyer are clearly referable to the legal advice seeking by the client e.g. "look at my wounds" or being shown round the factory by the client when discussing Health and Safety issues, what the lawyer sees may well be privileged.

The Duties of Confidentiality   6.06

These duties of a lawyer, which arise from professional ethics, from the law of agency and from the general law of obligations, to refrain from disclosing to the wider world the "secrets" of those who confide in him or her, extend more broadly and cover more matters than lawyer and client privilege.[43] While the scope of the privilege has attracted much scholarly attention, much less has been written about the comparative scope of the three duties of confidentiality.[44]

Professional Ethics and Confidentiality   6.07

The duty of confidentiality in terms of professional ethics in Scotland is a matter for common law ethics. However, there are almost no reported decisions of the Discipline Tribunal or Inner House on the topic,[45] so more often than not reference is made to the art.4 of the Code of Conduct for Solicitors 2002 which states that "*The observance of client confidentiality is*

---

[40] Begg, *op. cit.*, pp.314–315 "Counsel and law agents are . . . bound to give evidence as to facts falling under their observation as ordinary witnesses, such, for example, as the commission of a crime, the execution of a deed, the handwriting of their clients, the tenor of documents which they have read, or know of in any other way than through the information of their clients."

[41] This is the view taken by Wilkinson, *op. cit.* p.95, Raitt *op. cit.* p.267. It is rejected by the editor of Walker and Walker, *The Law of Evidence in Scotland* (T&T Clark, Edinburgh, 2000) at para.10.2.3.

[42] See Wolfram, *op. cit.* pp.257–258.

[43] This is accepted in the USA, Canada, Australia, England and Scotland. See e.g. Wolfram *op cit.* p.296, Black *op. cit.* and Ogston & Seager *op. cit.*

[44] Wolfram, *op. cit.* is an honourable exception.

[45] There are, however, a number of conflict of interest cases involving confidentiality.

a fundamental duty of solicitors". Unfortunately the commentary fails to elaborate on the ambit of the duty. Webster[46] and Ryder[47] both take the view that it extends to any confidential information about a client's case or transaction learned during the course of it. It seems clear that, unlike the privilege, it does not matter where the information comes from.[48] Neither need it come in the shape of communications, nor need it be referable to the seeking of legal advice. The duty lies on all enrolled solicitors, although in reality it is rare for lawyers without practising certificates to have clients, to whom the duty is owed.[49] It is sometimes said[50] that the ethical duty of confidentiality extends to professional colleagues and staff of the solicitor. While the former is true the duty cannot extend to the unqualified staff of the solicitor, including first year trainees, since they are not subject to the disciplinary machinery of the Law Society and conduct penalties are not imposed on firms as opposed to individual solicitors. It is, however, true to say that solicitors have an ethical obligation to ensure that their staff respect the confidentiality of clients. It is also the case that unqualified members of staff are covered by the State Protection Act 1998 and may have duties of confidentiality under the law of obligations and/or their contracts of employment.

The information covered by the ethical duty of confidentiality must be regarded as confidential by the client. It is hard to see how, were a client to tell the solicitor casually during an interview what the weather forecast is for the weekend, this could be held to be covered by the ethical duty of confidentiality. Nevertheless, since it will not always be clear to the lawyer what the client wishes to keep out of the public domain, lawyers would be well advised to regard even matters that are generally known or knowable e.g. the client's name, address, job and marital status,—even the fact that he or she has retained the lawyers services, as confidential unless the client advises the solicitor to the contrary. Further, it was noted in *Hilton v Barker Booth and Eastwood*[51] that:

> "It is a solicitor's duty to act in his client's best interests . . . To disclose discreditable facts about a client, and to do so without the client's informed consent is likely to be a breach of duty, even if the facts are in the public domain."

Thus, where a solicitor is asked for the client's address, the solicitor should decline to provide it, unless he or she is aware that the client does not regard their address as confidential. The solicitor may, as a matter of courtesy, offer to send on to the client a letter from the enquirer addressed to the client, care of the solicitor. However, revealing a client's whereabouts to a third party without their permission is a breach of confidentiality and as such may

---

[46] *Op. cit.* pp.30–31.

[47] *Op. cit.* p.52.

[48] See e.g. CCBE Code of Conduct for Lawyers in the EC Principle 2.3.2 and the English *Guide to the Professional Conduct of Solicitors* (8th edn, The Law Society, London, 1999) para.16.01.

[49] If an academic lawyer is professionally qualified but has no practising certificate and advises "clients" at a legal advice clinic, the ethical duty of confidentiality would presumably apply (as well as the duty of confidentiality under the law of obligations).

[50] E.g. in the commentary to art.4 of the Code of Conduct 2002.

[51] [2005] UKHL 8 *per* Lord Walker of Gestingthorpe at para.34.

constitute professional misconduct. Thus a solicitor who revealed his client's movements and air flight details to a third party who in turn passed this to the police leading to the client's arrest was found guilty of misconduct by the Scottish Solicitors Discipline Tribunal. The Tribunal noted that it would have been misconduct even if the client's whereabouts had not been transmitted to the police.[52]

Equally, a solicitor should regard his or her records showing the dates and times of meetings with the client to be confidential, even if they are not privileged.[53] Again facts that a lawyer knows from observation e.g. the signing of a deed, the handwriting of the client, or the conduct of parties to each other in public, should be regarded as confidential even if they are not privileged, as should the lawyer's observations as to his or her client's demeanour, state of mind, sobriety or clothing (e.g. was it dishevelled, bloodstained etc).

Privilege, Ethics and Physical Evidence   6.08

What is the status of physical evidence which is passed to the solicitor by the client or a third party? Even where it is imparted in confidence such evidence is rarely likely to be privileged, both because it is not a communication between the lawyer and client related to the giving of legal advice, and because frequently it will have an independent origin from the lawyer/client relationship. This is equally true where the evidence consists of written matter e.g. a diary, which may be relevant evidence in the case, even if the client were to read sections out to the solicitor. In the same vein, Wilkinson observes that: "it is doubtful if business firms can obtain protection for their business records merely by the device of depositing them . . . . in solicitors' premises".[54] However, where the evidence is a report compiled by the client with a view to litigation it will be privileged.

The evidentiary status of physical evidence entrusted to the solicitor by the client is of particular significance in relation to criminal justice. To allow those accused of crime to suppress physical evidence of an incriminating nature through the simple device of passing it to their lawyers would encourage white collar criminals and murderers alike to safeguard their position by transferring their books or the murder weapon to their lawyers. Unsurprisingly, even where such evidence is prima facie covered by confidentiality, public policy will over-ride the confidence in order to prevent the interests of justice from being thwarted. Thus, in the case of *James McIntyre*[55] the High Court implied that there would be no legal protection for a solicitor where his client gave him illegal guns and ammunition to deliver to the police when there was no gun amnesty in operation. As the judge observed, "it should not be assumed . . . that it is part of a solicitor's function to convey illegally held firearms to the police on behalf of criminals . . . " Certainly, more than one Scottish solicitor who has retained weapons or stolen property from their clients "for safe-keeping" has subsequently been charged with professional misconduct, not to mention reset.

---

[52] DTD 496/81.

[53] See *R. v Manchester Crown Court, ex parte Rogers* [1999] 1 WLR 832, and Billins, *op. cit.* p.94.

[54] *Op. cit.* p.94.

[55] *The Scotsman*—21/1/98.

Solicitors should not agree to keep items which may be the subject of criminal charges or which may be required as evidence in connection with charges brought against their clients. Since lawyers cannot be party to the destruction or even the suppression of evidence in a way that interferes with the interests of justice, their advice may sometimes be that their client should hand the physical evidence to the police. If the client declines to take this advice the solicitor has the option of withdrawing from acting under art.2 of the code of conduct. Furthermore, art.5(a) of the code stresses that a solicitor may not accept improper instructions; for example to assist a client on a matter which the solicitor knows to be criminal or fraudulent—such as the suppression of evidence, but a solicitor may advise on the legal consequences of any proposed course of conduct, or assist a client in determining the validity and scope of application of the law. The dividing line between these two activities is not always easy to draw.[56]

6.09 Privilege, Ethics, and the Police

Where solicitors are approached by the police or the procurator fiscal to make a statement which touches on their clients' confidentiality or privilege, the view of the Law Society's Professional Practice Committee is that they should decline, but offer instead to be precognosced on oath before a sheriff.[57] Where a solicitor answers a question on the direction of the court he or she would be immune from a claim from the client of breach of confidentiality or privilege.[58] Similarly, solicitors should not hand over their files or papers to the police or the fiscal without a warrant from a sheriff, and even then they would be wise to only deliver what is expressly set out in the warrant. Where the solicitor considers that the papers are confidential or privileged or even that the warrant is excessively wide,[59] the documents or evidence should be placed in a sealed envelope and marked accordingly. The solicitor should thereafter seek to be heard by the sheriff as to the admissibility of the evidence or the scope of the warrant.[60]

6.10 Agency and Confidentiality

In Scotland the fiduciary duty of the solicitor as agent in relation to the confidences of the client is an implied term of the contract for services.[61] The only case in point, *Liverpool Victoria Friendly Society v Houston*[62] suggests that it is a positive duty to safeguard the information of the client simply

---

[56] See, "Dealing with a very difficult point of practice" (1998) *The Defender*, p.4.

[57] See Guidance Notes on Confidentiality 2001 para.3 contained in the Solicitors Professional Handbook. If the client (after receiving legal advice) is willing to waive his or her privilege or confidentiality then the solicitor need not insist on being taken before a sheriff. (See Websters, 3rd edn, *op. cit.* para.2.14).

[58] See Guidance Notes *op. cit.*

[59] In a recent case the warrant in seeking to cover the seizing of a client's file had inadvertently allowed the police to take possession of the solicitor's hard drive containing confidential and privileged information on all the solicitor's clients. Such warrants should be challenged as excessive.

[60] See Guidance Notes *op. cit.* Although the Office of Fair Trading has now wide powers under the Competition Act 1998 to conduct "dawn raids" on firms and businesses such inspections do NOT extend to documents covered by privilege or by solicitor/client confidentiality.

[61] *Bowstead and Reynolds on Agency, op. cit.* says not necessarily in England. p.202.

[62] (1900) 3F 42.

because of the fiduciary relationship, which requires the solicitor to refrain from using or disclosing to a third party confidential information acquired in the course of agency in violation of his or her duty to act in good faith.[63] While it has become commonplace for writers in common law countries to endorse such a broad statement of the duty,[64] a closer scrutiny of the case law in England and Wales suggests that the duty is confined to not acting in a way which gives a preference to the interests of another client or the solicitor's own interests over those of the client.[65] The case law also indicates that the fiduciary duty constrains the solicitor's ability to realise a personal profit by the use of the client's confidential information, even where the use in no way disadvantages the client.[66] This may suggest that, despite the broad dicta in the *Liverpool Victoria* case (which are clearly *obiter*), it is far from clear that the fiduciary duty is breached where the disclosure of the information is neither intended to, nor does it, favour the interests of another client or the solicitor over those of the client. If this analysis is correct, then confidentiality as a fiduciary duty is less extensive than confidentiality as a matter of professional ethics.

The Law of Obligations and Confidentiality   6.11

The duty of confidentiality under the law of obligations is akin to the popular notion of confidentiality and is an express or implied condition of many relationships. However, the Scottish cases in the area are sufficiently sparse as to leave it unclear as to exactly when the courts will hold the obligation to arise.[67] It is clear, nonetheless, that the duty can arise from an express or implied contractual stipulation, and also in certain non-contractual relationships where a condition can be implied that any information communicated by one party to the other should be kept confidential.[68] Applied to lawyers, the obligation can be said to arise in circumstances where any reasonable lawyer would realise that the information was being imparted in confidence and expected to be kept so and the lawyer consents expressly or impliedly to safeguard that confidence. As Black has argued,[69] such a voluntary obligation under Scots law requires the consent of the obligor, however, in the case of a client talking to a lawyer, even in a social context, such consent will readily be inferred from the fact that the lawyer has listened to the confidence without demur. For a lawyer to argue successfully that he or she had not agreed to keep the confidence would entail showing that the "confidence" was blurted out without warning, giving the solicitor no opportunity to prevent its revelation, and that the lawyer immediately made it clear that the "confidence" would not be protected. Unlike the duty of

---

[63] See *Liverpool Victoria Friendly Society v Houston* (1900) 3 F 42 and J. Pearson, "Agency" in A.D.M. Forte (ed.), *Scots Commercial Law* (Butterworths, Edinburgh, 1997) at p.284.

[64] e.g. Wolfram, *op. cit.* at p.300 and Pearson *op. cit.*

[65] See *Bowstead and Reynolds on Agency op. cit.* para.6.074, B. Markesinis and R.Munday, *op. cit.* pp.87 ff and the *Second Restatement of the Law of Agency* (St Paul, American Law Institute, 1958) para.395.

[66] *ibid.* para.388 and Wolfram, *op. cit.* p.304.

[67] The duty has been the subject of more case law and scholarly discussion in England. See Scottish Law Commission, Memorandum 40, *Confidential Information* (Edinburgh, S.L.C., 1977) and *Coco v Clark* [1969] R.P.C. 41 at 48.

[68] See Scottish Law Commission, Memorandum 40, *op. cit.*

[69] R. Black, *op. cit.* at p.300.

confidentiality under professional ethics, there seems no reason why a voluntary obligation of confidentiality could not be enforced against the firm as well as the lawyer, thus covering the acts of the unqualified staff of the lawyer.

6.12 Confidentiality and Data Protection

As a solicitor will have access to sensitive personal information regarding their clients it is essential to ensure compliance with the Data Protection Act 1998.[70]

Due to the sensitivity of information held by solicitors, the nature of a solicitor's relationship with their client and, in particular, the potential harm that could result from unauthorised disclosure it is unsurprising that stringent measures have to be taken. Under the act, solicitors have to ensure appropriate technical and organisational measures are taken against unauthorised or unlawful access or use of client's personal information. In addition measures must also be taken to prevent accidental loss, destruction, or damage to, personal information.

This requires consideration of[71]:

1. controlling access to the information (for example: is access to the building or room controlled or can anybody walk in?)
2. ensuring business continuity (for example: are the precautions against burglary, fire or natural disaster adequate?)
3. staff selection and training (for example: is proper weight given to the discretion and integrity of staff when they are being considered for employment?)
4. how breaches of security will be detected and dealt with (for example do systems keep audit trails so that access to personal data is logged and can be attributed to a particular person?)

Under the legislation it is an offence to knowingly or recklessly disclose personal information without the consent of the subject.[72]

6.13 The Commencement of Privilege and Confidentiality: Prospective Clients

The question as to when the duties of privilege and confidentiality commence, still gives rise to debate, at least in Scotland. Thus the only Scottish case on whether prospective clients[73] are protected by privilege, concluded that they were not.[74] However in recent times this single judge case has been almost universally condemned by the commentators[75] since it largely

---

[70] As an in-depth discussion of this area is outwith the scope of this book, it is important to note the additional considerations in relation to a solicitor's duty of confidentiality. Full guidance is available from *www.informationcommissioner.gov.uk/*.

[71] For full information see *www.informationcommissioner.gov.uk/cms/DocumentUploads/Data %20Protection%20Act%201998%20Legal%20Guidance.pdf*.

[72] Data Protection Act 1998 s.55.

[73] i.e. one who has provided the salient facts in his or her case to a lawyer in search of advice and assistance, only to be rejected by the lawyer in question.

[74] *HM Advocate v Davie* (1881) 4 Coup 450.

[75] See e.g. Black, *op. cit.* p.299, Maher, *op. cit.* p.109, Macphail, *op. cit.* para.18–21, Wilkinson, *op. cit.* p.96.

undermines the principal rationale for the privilege and for confidentiality, namely, that it is necessary to encourage trust and candour in clients and prospective clients. The better view would appear to be that provided that the prospective client consulted the solicitor to seek legal advice and in contemplation of the formation of a solicitor-client relationship, that is enough to bring the privilege into operation. Certainly this is the position in England,[76] Australia[77] and the United States.[78] There is even less Scottish authority in relation to the position of the prospective client and the ethical, agency and contractual duties of confidentiality. However, it is submitted that as with the privilege, prospective clients should be covered by all three duties of confidentiality. This is the position in England[79] and the United States.[80]

It would seem to follow from this that a lawyer who holds confidential or privileged information as a result of a consultation with a prospective client may not thereafter act against that client in the same or a substantially related matter because of the conflict of interest involved. In common with the recent trends in the USA both the Restatement and Ethics 2000 would allow a lawyer with confidential information from a prospective client subsequently to act against that prospective client if both clients consent or if certain safeguards are in place.[81]

Child Clients   6.14

It is important to remember that the duty to maintain client confidentiality can be owed equally to child as it can be to an adult. Where a solicitor represents a child who is *capax* the solicitor will owe the duty of confidentiality to the child. As such, the solicitor cannot disclose any confidential information to the child's legal representative or guardian without the child's expressly written and informed consent to do so. It follows that the solicitor should check with the child who is providing instructions as to the child's preferred means of communication, especially where the child lives with an adult who has easy access to the child's correspondence.

If a solicitor takes instruction from the legal representative or guardian the duty of confidentiality will be owed to both the child and their representative. Where the child reaches 16 years of age, or otherwise attains legal capacity to instruct a separate solicitor, the child has the right to have the contents of the original solicitor's file disclosed to their new solicitor so far as it relates to him or her. The child may exercise this right irrespective of whether or not the legal representative or guardian consents even although the representative initially instructed the original solicitor.[82]

---

[76] See *Minter v Priest* [1930] A.C. 558 where the Housel of Lords (including two Scots law lords—Viscount Dunedin and Lord Thankerton) upheld this proposition.

[77] See G.E. Dal Pont, *Lawyers Professional Responsibility* (2nd edn) (NSW, LBC Information Services, 2001) at p.286.

[78] See *Third Re-Statement of the Law Governing Lawyers* (2000) paras 70 and 72 and the Revised Uniform Rules of Evidence.

[79] See *The Guide to the Professional Conduct of Solicitors* (8th edn) (London, The Law Society, 1999) 16.01 (p.324) Comment 4.

[80] See *Third Re-Statement of the Law Governing Lawyers* (2000) para.15(1)(a). ABA Model Rules 2002 1.18(b).

[81] See *Third Re-Statement of the Law Governing Lawyers* (2000) para.15(2); ABA Model Rules 2002 1.18(c) and (d).

[82] See: "Professional Practice" (2004) August J.L.S.S. 42.

6.15 Duration of Privilege and Confidentiality

Here there is a considerable measure of consensus between the courts and commentators, at least in common law countries. The privilege and confidentiality belong to the client and continue in perpetuity unless terminated by waiver by the client, the client's representatives or by the operation of the law. This means that confidential communications between a party and his or her legal adviser remain privileged and confidential notwithstanding the dissolution of the relation of agent and client.[83] This remains the case even after the death of the client or the lawyer. However, here the consensus ends, in the absence of much by way of case law, since there is a debate as to whether the client's personal representatives[84] or executors can waive the client's privilege or confidentiality. Begg is silent on the issue,[85] but Wilkinson considers that:

> "In relation to proprietorial matters in which executors have an interest the privilege passes on the death of the client to his executors. It has been suggested that after the death of the client the privilege cannot be waived because death has removed the only person entitled to waive it. But that can be true only of matters (such as, in most cases, a confession of crime) in which executors have no interest. Where the executors have no interest the alternative and better view seems to be that the privilege cannot be invoked because the interest to invoke it rested solely with the deceased and has lapsed on his death."[86]

Raitt in *Evidence*,[87] appears to agree with Wilkinson's position but Ross in *The Law of Evidence in Scotland*[88] takes the view that the client's personal successors are not only entitled to uphold privilege and confidentiality but should do so unless it has previously been waived by the client. Finally, Black, after a detailed analysis of such case law as exists, concludes that the privilege (and presumably any confidentiality) does not automatically cease on the death of the client but can be waived by the deceased's relatives even where, as in a confession of a crime, they have no interest.[89] Since the interests that privilege and the obligation of confidentiality are designed to protect may conceivably extend beyond the client and the client's lifetime there is logic in the argument that the privilege and the obligation of confidentiality should not be automatically extinguished by the death of the client or, indeed, the lawyer.

---

[83] See the authorities quoted in Black, *op. cit.* and Begg *op. cit.* p.319.

[84] There would seem no reason in principle why an agent with an enduring power of attorney for a client who is now *incapax* should be in a different position from an executor in relation to this issue.

[85] *Op. cit.* p.319, although he takes the view that "when the client dies, his representatives appear to be entitled to plead confidentiality in disputes between them and strangers, but not in disputes inter se. Trustees are not allowed, in questions between them and beneficiaries, to plead confidentiality between themselves and the agent of the trust."

[86] *Op. cit.* p.96. Wilkinson relies on *Mackenzie v Mackenzie's Trustees* (1916) 1 S.L.T. 271 for this proposition. He considers that the case also supports Begg's argument in the foregoing footnote.

[87] (3rd edn, W. Green, Edinburgh, 2001) para.12.11 p.266.

[88] Walker and Walker, *op. cit.* para.10.2.2.

[89] *Op. cit.* p.301.

However, there seems no reason why, as Black argues, the client's personal representatives should not be able to waive either obligation. Moreover, if we accept the argument that the duty of confidentiality, if not the privilege, can be rendered unenforceable if not a nullity by the "public policy" defence,[90] during the client's lifetime, there would seem no reason why the same defence could not be upheld by the court after the client's death, whatever the stance taken by the personal representatives.[91]

Waiver of the Privilege and the Confidentiality 6.16

Only the client or (probably) his or her personal representatives can waive the privilege or the confidence, since they belong to the client alone. They may, however, be waived implicitly or explicitly. The latter is relatively straightforward, in that the client, with or without the advice of the lawyer agrees that his or her privileged or confidential information may be revealed to the wider world, for example where a litigant or an acquitted accused reveals details of their ordeal in order to assist other parties.[92] The former takes a variety of forms: (1) where the client is in dispute with his or her lawyer; (2) where the client agrees to his or her solicitor taking the witness stand (3) where the information has come into a third party's possession by mistake or through interception and (4) where two or more clients are instructing the same lawyer in relation to the same matter.

Waiver: Where the Lawyer and Client are in Dispute 6.17

In a number of jurisdictions e.g. the USA,[93] England and Australia,[94] it has been accepted by the courts and the professional bodies that where clients choose to attack or criticise or come into dispute with their lawyers then they are deemed to have waived their right to insist on the privilege and confidentiality to the extent necessary for the lawyers to defend themselves or to represent their own interests. This is seen by some commentators as an issue of fairness since the client has voluntarily placed aspects of the professional relationship in issue and that it would thereby be unfair to prevent or hamstring the lawyer's attempt to mount a defence in the relevant forum by preventing him or her from relying on the privileged and confidential information which is central to that relationship.[95] Another way of putting the

---

[90] See Black, *op. cit.* and Scottish Law Commission Memorandum No.40, *op. cit.* paras 34–37 and 89.

[91] For the exceptions to the privilege and the confidence, including the public policy defence, see paras 6.16–6.24 below.

[92] This situation is to be distinguished from where the lawyer gives interviews to the media during a trial. While this may be at the client's request or from a belief that this is the best way to present the client's case to the wider world, there is an inherent risk that the lawyer's self-interest in publicity may come into conflict with his or her duty to safeguard the client's confidentiality or with his or her duty to the court and other professional colleagues (See Ryder *op. cit.* p.53).

[93] See Wolfram, *op. cit.* 307 and r.64 and r.83 of the *Third Restatement of the Law Governing Lawyers* (St Paul, American Law Institute, 2000) at pp.486 and 624.

[94] See Jonathan Auburn, *Legal Professional Privilege: Law and Theory* (Hart Publishing, Oxford, 2000) at p.219.

[95] *ibid.*

same argument derives from the USA, namely, that the client should not be permitted to use the privilege and confidentiality—which are designed as a shield to protect the client—to be used by the client as a weapon against his or her own lawyer.[96] Typical examples of this kind of waiver include cases where the client is suing the client for breach of contract or professional negligence. Thus in *Lillicrap v Nalder & Son*[97] it was held by the English Court of Appeal that where a client institutes civil proceedings against his solicitor such an action constitutes an implied waiver of professional privilege in respect of all documents relevant to that particular suit to the extent necessary to allow the court to decide the issue fully and fairly. However, the court also noted that such a waiver should be limited to those matters relevant and directly concerned with the proceedings and as such it could not be utilised as a "roving search" into any other matters in which the solicitor may have acted for the client. Similarly, the same Court held in *Paragon Finance plc (formerly National Home Loans Corporation plc) & Ors v Freshfields (a Firm)*[98] that where a client brought proceedings against his former solicitors for negligence in the handling of a commercial transaction between himself and a third party, the client's waiver of legal professional privilege, implied from his bringing the proceedings, did not extend to confidential communications between himself and different solicitors instructed to pursue and settle his claim against the third party. In relation to confidentiality, as a matter of professional ethics the relevant English authority is to be found in the *Guide to the Professional Conduct of Solicitors* in the commentary to principle 16.02 which states that a solicitor "may reveal confidential information concerning a client to the extent that it is reasonably necessary to establish a defence to a criminal charge or civil claim by the client against the solicitor," or where there is a conduct or service investigation by the Law Society against the solicitor following a complaint by the client.[99] In the absence of any Scottish authority on either the privilege or confidentiality it is submitted that the English position would be adopted here. However, it is less clear what the position would be in two other classes of case which have arisen in North America. There, the courts of the USA and Canada have put aside the privilege where the client has plead "ineffective assistance of counsel" in a criminal or civil case.[1] More controversially, in the USA it has been established by the courts and in the Commentary to the Model Rules[2] that an attorney may breach confidentiality and the privilege to the extent necessary to enforce his or her fee.[3] The same rule exists in New Zealand[4] and allegedly

---

[96] The Model Rules 2002—para.11 Commentary to MR 1.6(b)(5)—rather more felicitously describes this as an illustration of the principle that the beneficiary of a fiduciary relationship may not exploit it to the detriment of the fiduciary.

[97] [1993] 1 W.L.R. 94.

[98] [1999] 1 W.L.R. 1183 (CA).

[99] See note 12, principle 16.02 *Guide to the Professional Conduct of Solicitors* (8th edn), (London, Law Society of England and Wales, 1999). A similar provision can be found in ABA Model Rules 1.6(b)(2).

[1] See Auburn, *op. cit.* p.218.

[2] See Wolfram *op. cit.* p.308 and M.R 1.6(5) Commentary para.11. See also r.64 and r.83 of the *Third Restatement op. cit.*

[3] Wolfram, *op. cit.* refers to one case where the lawyer was able to attach the client property making use of the client's confidential information.

[4] Rules of Professional Conduct for Barristers and Solicitors, r.1.08(ii).

in Australia.[5] There is no UK support for this final approach either in relation to the privilege or confidentiality and any attempt to introduce it by a professional body would run the risk of appearing self-serving.

Waiver: where the client agrees to put the solicitor on the witness   **6.18**
stand or makes a statement through the solicitor whilst insisting on the
"right to silence"

As Begg[6] asserts: "A party adducing his agent as a witness is not entitled to object on the ground of confidentiality to any question proposed to be put on matter pertinent to the issue." Thus the pursuer in *Wylie v Wylie*[7] who had founded in his pleadings on a letter from his solicitor to himself in respect of the subject-matter of the action was held to have waived his legal professional privilege in respect of all relevant correspondence. Lord Fraser noted (at p.9);

> "It would, in my opinion, be contrary to all ordinary conceptions of fairness that the pursuer should be entitled to support his case by reference to one letter passing between himself and his solicitor, while, at the same time, pleading confidentiality of other letters passing between him and his solicitor about the same time and dealing with the questions at issue in this action."

Furthermore, s.1 of the Evidence (Scotland) Act 1852 provides that "where any person who is or has been an agent shall be adduced and examined as a witness for his client, touching any matter or thing, to prove which he could not competently have been adduced and examined according to the existing law and practice of Scotland, it shall not be competent to the party adducing such witness to object, on the grounds of confidentiality, to any question proposed to be put to such witness on matter pertinent to the issue." This section was applied in the case of *Whitbread Group Plc v Goldapple Ltd.*[8] There the defenders sought to recover documents from the pursuers including ones containing legal advice from their legal adviser. The defenders relied on s.1 of the Evidence (Scotland) Act 1852 since the pursuers intended to lead evidence from their legal adviser but the pursuers argued that the evidence led from their adviser would only relate to matters of fact (namely the dates and times of certain agreements), which were therefore not covered by the privilege. Lord Drummond Young in the Outer House held, however, that the adviser's evidence was clearly intended to cover the origins and purposes of the agreements which not mere issues of fact, but confidential matters, and therefore s.1 of the 1852 Act would apply. The pursuers also argued that the fact that a solicitor witness was adduced on one issue did not permit questioning on other issues in the case. The judge accepted (obiter) that in a case raising two or more clearly discrete issues, the statutory waiver of confidentiality on one issue might not extend to the other(s). However, he held that the present case involved a single, complex issue, not several distinct issues.

---

[5] See Dal Pont *op. cit.* p.272.
[6] *Op. cit.* p.319.
[7] 1967 S.L.T. (Notes) 9.
[8] 2003 S.L.T. 256.

6.19 Waiver: where the information has come into a third party's possession by mistake or through interception

Although the area is not devoid of uncertainty, there is authority in Scotland and England to the effect that where privileged or confidential communications between legal advisers and their clients go astray or are intercepted by a third party then their privileged or confidential status will be deemed to have been lost or waived. This is perhaps understandable where the client has intentionally or negligently passed the communications to a third party, on the grounds of implied waiver. It is less understandable if the fault lies elsewhere. However, in 2002 the Professional Practice Committee[9] considered the situation of inadvertent disclosure of papers and emails by a client's legal advisers. Regarding the former, they concurred with the English approach in *Al-fayed v Metropolitan Police Commissioner*[10] where it was held that the disclosing party was only entitled to an order requiring the receiving party to return the documents where a reasonable solicitor would have realised that a mistake had been made regarding the delivery of the documents to them. Otherwise, the receiving party was entitled to make use of the documents as they were no longer privileged.

In relation to emails, the Professional Practice Committee stated that where the contents of an email had to be read in order to realise its confidential status, then privilege was lost and the receiving party was not under a duty to delete the email or return it or to cease acting and could inform his or her own client about the contents. However, if a request to delete the email was received before it had been read, then that request should be complied with.

Even less understandable is the suggestion that if a privileged or confidential communication is stolen or improperly intercepted by a third party it still can be admissible. This is an area with considerable English authority, but not all of which is mutually consistent, the focus being on whether the communication was obtained by the third party improperly. In Scotland, the situation is similarly unsettled. The focus in Scotland appears to involve the balancing of such factors as, the need to have relevant evidence, the excuse for the irregularity and the protection of confidentiality.[11] The case of *Rattray v Rattray*[12] is often referred to as authority for the proposition that improperly obtained communications can be admissible as evidence. In this case, a letter by a defender to a co-defender was illegally intercepted by the pursuer at a post office. Two out of the four judges considered the letter to be admissible but, on different grounds, and neither judge stated that they were laying down a rule of law. It is hardly surprising therefore, that subsequent cases have questioned the soundness of the *Rattray* decision, although it has yet to be overruled. The writers have been similarly sceptical as to the soundness of the reasoning in this case,[13] arguing that the court should be entitled to exclude evidence obtained by illegal or irregular means.

---

[9] 2002 J.L.S.S. November p.43.
[10] [2002] EWCA Civ 780.
[11] *Duke of Argyll v Duchess of Argyll*, 1963 S.L.T. (Notes) 42.
[12] (1897) 25 R 315.
[13] See e.g. Macphail, *op. cit.* para.21.14 and Walker and Walker, *op. cit.* p.148.

More recently in *R v Nottingham Magistrates' Court Ex p. Theobald*[14] Kennedy L.J. offered guidance on the procedure to be followed if a prosecutor comes into possession of material in respect of which the defence can justifiably claim that it is subject to legal professional privilege.

> "The defence may contend that the way in which the material came into the possession of the prosecutor needs to be investigated, and/or that the disclosure of that material had so prejudiced the conduct of the defence that the case should not proceed. If such a contention is raised, there is then a duty on the prosecutor [to] explain to the court, so far as he is able to do so, either by calling evidence or by uncontested statements of fact, how he came into possession of the material and what, if any, use he has made of it, failing which the court may infer—
>
> a) that he has obtained it by proper means, and/or
> b) that his use of it will unfairly prejudice the defendant in his conduct of the proceedings."

Were this to be followed in Scotland it might hopefully serve to limit opportunistic or unlawful interceptions of privileged information.

Waiver: where two or more clients are instructing the same lawyer in relation to the same matter   6.20

As Begg observes: "when a law agent acts for two parties in the same transaction, neither of them is entitled to plead confidentiality in a question with the other, except as regards such communications as may have been made by each party to the agent as is his own exclusive legal adviser."[15] The rationale for this doctrine is that where two or more parties to the same transaction use the same lawyer, then they are deemed to have waived the obligation of confidentiality *vis-a-vis* each other, in keeping with the goal of encouraging candour with their joint adviser. The doctrine does not apply to confidences entrusted to the adviser by one or more of the parties in separate transactions. Whatever the merits of the doctrine, it has clear dangers should a conflict of interest subsequently arise and the lawyer chooses to retain one of the clients but not the other(s). This is because the client(s) who are passed on will not appreciate being told that nothing which they have entrusted to their adviser in the joint representation will be privileged or confidential with respect to the client whom the lawyer has retained. It follows that solicitors who choose to represent two or more clients in a case e.g. a husband and wife, the partners in a partnership or the directors of a company, should stress the implications of the doctrine should a conflict of interest arise at a later stage. Better still, the solicitor should undertake not retain any of the parties should a conflict arise.

The doctrine has been endorsed in two Court of Appeal cases,[16] with the court holding that in the event of a subsequent dispute between the parties the waiver of privilege implied from the joint retainer continues until the

---

[14] [2004] EWHC 1922.
[15] *Op. cit.* p.319.
[16] *Brown v Guardian Royal Exchange* [1994] 2 Lloyd's Rep. 325 and *TSB Bank v Robertt Irving & Burns* [2000] 2 All E.R. 826.

emergence of a conflict of interest between them. Only communications after that date would be privileged and confidential as between the parties. There has been very little modern case law in Scotland on the point although the issue did arise in a Scottish Solicitors' Discipline Tribunal decision in 1982.[17] The respondent in the case (the lawyer complained about), had acted for a husband and a wife jointly in a series of transactions. Upon the breakdown of their marriage, he accepted instructions to act for the wife in the divorce proceedings and to claim financial sums on her behalf. In pursuit of this claim the solicitor used information from an earlier representation of the husband relating to certain life policies. The husband, not surprisingly, objected to what he regarded as a breach of privilege and confidentiality. The Tribunal did not rely on the implied waiver from a joint acting in part because the information about the life policies appears to have come from a separate, earlier representation of the husband. Instead, the Tribunal argued that the duty of the parties to a divorce to make full disclosure of their financial affairs to the court protected the solicitor from a complaint of breach of confidentiality and a finding of professional misconduct. If the Tribunal was in effect relying on a public policy exception to the ethical duty of confidentiality, their decision is probably justifiable. If, however, the Tribunal was implying that they could also override any obligation of privilege, it is not so obvious that it reached the right answer.

6.21 Exceptions to the Privilege and the Confidence

There is a high degree of consensus amongst Scottish writers on legal professional privilege as to the exceptions to the rule.[18] Rather less, however, has been written as to the exceptions to the legal obligation of confidentiality or its counterpart in professional ethics.[19] As to the privilege the principal exceptions are: where the existence of the lawyer/client relationship is in dispute; where the essence of the dispute is whether the communication was made at all; where Parliament has expressly created an exception; and where the communication was in furtherance of a fraudulent or illegal purpose.[20]

6.22 Exceptions to the Privilege: where the existence of the lawyer/client relationship is in dispute

The authorities are agreed that there is an exception where the point at issue is whether a solicitor/client relationship existed at all, or where there is a dispute as to the extent of the authority of the former to act on a client's behalf. The basis of this exception appears to be that it does not undermine the policy behind privilege, namely, the facilitation of the adversarial system.[21] Examples include allowing the recovery by a third party of correspondence between a solicitor and his client to show whether the solicitor had acted

---

[17] DTD 557/82.

[18] See Dickson, *op. cit.* paras 1676–1681; Maher, *op. cit.* p.108; Macphail *op. cit.* s.18.20; Raitt, *op. cit.* paras 12.12–13; Walker & Walker *op. cit.* 10.2.4; Wilkinson, *op. cit.* pp.97–98.

[19] Black, *op. cit.* is a partial exception to this proposition.

[20] As to the suggestion that there might be a public interest exception to the privilege see para 6.24 below.

[21] See Dickson *op. cit.* para 1677.

without instructions for that client,[22] and recovery by a co-defendant of letters between the other co-defendant and his solicitor in order to cast light on the authority of the latter to settle the action.

Exceptions to the Privilege: where the essence of the dispute is whether the communication was made at all 6.23

Statements made by solicitors to their clients or by clients to their solicitors are not privileged if the sole purpose of the inquiry in court is whether the communication was made or not. Thus defenders in an action, who had accused the pursuer of delay in raising his claim, were ordered to reveal correspondence between them and their solicitors at an earlier stage to prove intimation of the claim to the defenders and their knowledge of it.[23]

Exceptions to the Privilege: where Parliament has expressly created an exception 6.24

The common law nature of the privilege and of confidentiality as an aspect of agency or voluntary obligations entails that it is open to Parliament to make exceptions to them in statutes. However, the repeated assertions by courts in recent times of the fundamental nature of the right to privilege, has led them to conclude that they will only hold that a statutory exception to the privilege exists when Parliament has used the clearest and most unambiguous language. Thus in *General Mediterranean Holdings SA v Patel and another*[24] the court held that "the common law recognises the right to [privilege] which arises as between a person and his legal adviser . . . as a right of great constitutional importance, because it is seen as a necessary bulwark of the citizen's right of access to justice whether as a claimant or as a defendant. Legal professional privilege . . . .is also, as Lord Taylor C.J. said in *R v Derby Magistrates' Court, ex p B*,[25] much more than an ordinary rule of evidence, being considered a fundamental condition on which the administration of justice rests." The court went on to hold that the right to [lawyer client privilege] could not be overridden by general or ambiguous words in statue. The court noted the existence of a presumption that even the most general words were intended to be subject to basic rights of the individual and that, although such presumption could be rebutted by express language or necessary implication to the contrary, it could be not be rebutted in this case. Similarly in *R. v IRC ex parte Morgan Grenfell and Co. Ltd*[26] the House of Lords declined to allow tax avoidance legislation to override solicitor client privilege unless it expressly so stated in terms which the House would regard as compatible with the human rights legislation.

A clear statutory exception is s.47(3) of the Bankruptcy (Scotland) Act 1985 which provides that a bankrupt person must answer all questions posed during his or her public examination even if the information is confidential or privileged. However, he or she is not required to disclose communications with a third party (including his or her legal adviser) unless the latter is also

---

[22] *Fraser v Malloch* (1895) 3 S.L.T. 211.
[23] *Anderson v Lord Elgin's Trustees* (1859) 21 D. 654.
[24] [2000] 1 W.L.R. 272.
[25] [1996] A.C. 487.
[26] [2003] 1 A.C. 563.

called for examination.[27] Again, it should be noted that the European Commission under EEC Council Regulation No. 17/62 has very wide investigative powers which contain no protection for legal professional privilege.[28] Maher has also argued that statutory exceptions to the legal professional privilege may include s.168(2) of the Road Traffic Act 1972 and the Prevention of Terrorism Act 1989 and Brown has argued that the Money Laundering legislation in Scotland has restricted the scope of legal professional privilege to a greater extent than the common law.[29] However, there are many other areas where it might be thought that the public interest in transparency might outweigh the "access to justice" justification of the privilege, yet Parliament has expressly chosen not to override the privilege.[30]

6.24.01 Proceeds of Crime Act. Legal Professional Privilege has been further eroded by the enactment of the Proceeds of Crime Act 2002 (POCA) which requires lawyers to report the activities of their client to the Serious Organised Crime Agency (SOCA, *www.soca.gov.uk*) as successors to the National Criminal Intelligence Service (NCIS) if the lawyer knows or even merely suspects that the client is involved in an arrangement which facilitates the acquisition, retention or use of criminal property. The POCA marks the "culmination of increasing international concern over money laundering as a practice"[31] and goes further than previous legislation in that it applies regardless of the specific criminal offence from which the funds being laundered are derived.

The Act sets out a range of offences each of which is punishable by up to 14 years imprisonment on indictment.

6.24.02 POCA s.327. Section 327 provides that it is an offence for a person to "conceal, disguise, convert or transfer criminal property or remove it from the UK". Property is defined as criminal property if a) it constitutes a person's benefit from criminal conduct or it represents such a benefit (in whole or part and whether directly or indirectly) and b) the alleged offender knows or suspects that it constitutes or represents such a benefit. Criminal conduct is conduct which constitutes an offence in any part of the UK or would if it occurred there. Does this mean that if a client confesses to his solicitor that he or a third party has committed a crime and the proceeds are in an offshore bank account, the solicitor would be guilty of "concealing" the property under this section, if the solicitor chose not to pass on the information to the authorities? While there is some ambiguity as to the scope of the word

---

[27] See Macphail *op. cit.* s.18.20 and Raitt *op. cit.* p.267.

[28] As Macphail *op. cit.* notes: "cases have occurred where a document containing the advice of a lawyer to his client was used by the European Commission as evidence of intentional infringement of arts 85 and 86 of the Treaty of Rome". See also *AM & S Europe Ltd v Commission of the European Communities* [1983] Q.B. 878.

[29] See G. Maher, *Professional Privilege* 1990 J.L.S.S. 138 and A. Brown, *Money Laundering and Scottish Solicitors* 1994 J.L.S.S. 132. See also E. Hiley and A. Crawley, "Insolvency, DTI investigations: confidentiality and privilege" (1991) *Law Society's Gazette* 21.

[30] E.g. the Fair Trading Act 1973, s.85(3); the Restrictive Trade Practices Act 1976, s.37(6); the Consumer Safety Act 1978 s 4; the Competition Act 1980, s.3(7); and the Data Protection Act 1998 s.35.

[31] R. Stokes and Professor A. Arora, *The Duty to Report under the Money Laundering Legislation within the United Kingdom*, 2004 J.B.L. 340.

"conceal" it is thought unlikely that it extends to a solicitor who does no more than simply failing to pass on information to the authorities in such a situation.

POCA s.328. Under s.328 of the Act it is an offence where a person "enters **6.24.03** into or becomes concerned in an arrangement which he knows or suspects facilitates (by whatever means) the acquisition, retention, use or control of criminal property by or on behalf of another person", which would include client transactions. As with s.327 there are statutory defences, namely that there will be no offence where an authorised disclosure is made, or where there is reasonable excuse for the failure. There is however no exception for legal privilege. This was confirmed in the case of *P v P*[32] in the English High Court where Dame Butler-Sloss held that there was no legal privilege exemption for matters arising under s.328. The case concerned proceedings in the Family Courts where the wife in divorce proceedings had applied for ancillary relief including financial provision. The lawyers acting for the wife had obtained a forensic accountant's report on the husband's assets and became suspicious that part of his assets were criminal property from tax evasion. Concerned that in negotiating a financial outcome for their client this would be regarded as an "arrangement" falling foul of s.328 the lawyers made a suspicious activity report to NCIS in respect of the husbands suspected tax evasion.[33]

Dame Butler-Sloss held that the act of negotiating an arrangement itself amounts to being concerned in the arrangement and that the offence is not merely committed at the point of execution of the arrangement and accordingly an authorised disclosure had to be made.[34]

P v P confirmed that POCA has far reaching implications. Not only can lawyers not rely on legal professional privilege to prevent disclosure of fraudulent activity falling foul of the Act but it also imposes an obligation on lawyers to make an authorised disclosure of even the most minor criminal activity involving criminal property about which they have become aware or have suspicions, where they are involved in an arrangement concerning that property.[35] This would include matters relating to tax evasion or benefit fraud. There is no lower financial limit or *de minimis* rule in the legislation and the level set for money laundering has no application. The effect of *P v P* was that the number of "suspicious activity reports" made to NCIS by English solicitors alone climb to 12,000 within 12 months of the decision, leading to a delay in court proceedings.[36] The Act may therefore mean that clients will become less willing to disclose information to their lawyers if they believe that their confidential information will be disclosed without their knowledge when even the most minor infringement is suspected.

---

[32] [2003] EWHC Fam 2260.

[33] Bruce Ritchie, *Money Laundering and the Proceeds of Crime Act: Professional Practice Issues and Practical Tips* Guidance note (available from the Law Society of Scotland website: *www.lawscot.org.uk/mlg/SimpleGuideMarch05.pdf*).

[34] Bruce Ritchie, *ibid.*

[35] Janice Jones, "Divorce Lawyers and Proceeds of Crime Disclosure" (2003) 48(11) J.L.S.S. 34.

[36] "Welcome for Money Laundering Decision", *The Herald*, March 14, 2005.

The subsequent decision of *Bowman v Fels*[37] has done something to ameliorate matters. In this case the solicitors for a cohabitee, who sought a share of the value of the house the parties had lived in for 10 years, suspected the other party had included the cost of works on the property in his business accounts and VAT returns even though the work was unconnected with his business. In the light of *P v P* the solicitors made a disclosure to NCIS, suspecting a violation of s.328, without informing their client or the other party and, as NCIS stated that they would be unable to provide authorisation prior to the trial date, applied without notice to adjourn the trial. The defendants appealed but before the appeal could be heard NCIS gave its consent to proceed.

The principal issue in question was identified as whether s.328 was intended to apply to the ordinary conduct of legal proceedings including settlement negotiations. As to the former, the Court of Appeal was unanimous in deciding, for both linguistic and policy reasons, that the section did not apply:

> "The proper interpretation of s.328 is that it is not intended to cover or affect the ordinary conduct of litigation by legal professionals. That includes any step taken by them in litigation from the issue of proceedings and securing of injunctive relief or a freezing order up to its final disposal by judgment. We do not consider that any of these ordinary activities could fall within the concept of 'becoming concerned in an arrangement which ... facilitates the acquisition, retention, use or control of criminal property.' ... In summary, legal proceedings are a state provided mechanism for the resolution of issues according to law. Everyone has the right to a fair and public trial in the determination of his civil rights and duties, which is secured by art.6 of the European Convention on Human Rights. Parliament cannot have intended that proceedings or steps taken by lawyers in order to determine or secure legal rights and remedies for their clients should involve them in 'becoming concerned in an arrangement which ... facilitates the acquisition, retention, use or control of criminal property' even if they suspected that the outcome of such proceedings might have such an effect."[38]

The court also held that, as there was no express exception to legal privilege in s.328 it could not be implied.

Secondly, the court held that settlement negotiations did not constitute an "arrangement" in terms of s.328 but drew a distinction between negotiations in existing or contemplated legal proceedings and negotiations that are independent of litigation which, they felt did fall within the directive and POCA. Whether litigation is in existence is a matter of fact and should not give rise to any difficulty. However, due to the potential difficulties in establishing when proceedings are contemplated (e.g. mere intimation of an accident claim may not amount to contemplated proceedings) it would make sense to record in the client's file whether proceedings are in contemplation. The issue of a letter advising that if payment not made within a time limit an

---

[37] 2005 WL 513404 The following account of the *Bowman* case draws heavily on Bruce Ritchie's Guidance, *op. cit.*

[38] *Bowman v Fels* [2005] EWCA Civ 226 at para.83.

action will be raised without further intimation would clearly demonstrate that proceedings are contemplated. It is also clear that "sham" litigation raised to facilitate money laundering will not be excluded from POCA and litigation lawyers should still disclose where they know their client is seeking advice for money laundering purposes.[39] In addition, the courts retain the ability to refer matters to the authorities where they become aware of irregularities.

In sum, then, examples of "arrangements" under s.328 would include:

a) Where a claim not being part of actual or contemplated legal proceedings is made against a client for repayment of money which is "criminal property"—unless all of the criminal property is repaid to the rightful owner (i.e. none is retained).

b) Executries where there are reasonable grounds to suspect that part of the estate represents monies derived from tax evasion or benefit fraud.

c) Acquisition of property—particularly heritable property—with proceeds of crime, including crime committed by someone other than the client. An example might be a council house purchase where a deposit is being paid by a relative with a conviction or outstanding charges for drug trafficking; or a substantial deposit is paid by a person on benefit.

d) Recovery of fictional debt—if instructed to recover a debt the solicitor may suspect that the alleged debt is a fiction designed to launder criminal property—for example there is little or no supporting documentation for the alleged debt; the instructions are unusual for the client; the "defender" pays the alleged debt direct to the claimants solicitor without protest.

e) Company funds used to meet a personal debt of a director/shareholder.[40]

POCA s.329. Section 329 of the Act concerns "acquiring, using or having **6.24.04** possession of criminal property". However a solicitor would only breach s.329 if he or she knew or suspected that the property in question "constitutes benefit from criminal conduct". In other words innocent possession of property which turns out to be criminal property is not an offence under s.329. Section 330 POCA makes it an offence punishable by up to five years imprisonment on indictment and an unlimited fine to fail to disclose where a person a) knows or suspects; or b) has reasonable grounds for knowing or suspecting that another person is engaged in money laundering and the information comes in the course of business of the regulated sector. Not all solicitors' practices will be in the regulated sector for the purpose of this section as it concerns the dealing in investments as principal or agent, arranging deals in investments, managing investments, safeguarding or administering investments and advising on investments. The Money Laundering Regulations 2003 however go further and encompass a wide range of solicitor's activities including tax advice, conveyancing, estate agency, insolvency practice and the formation, operation or management of a company or a trust.

---

[39] *Inside Claims Lawyers' Liability* RPC May 2005 (available from *www.rpc.co.uk*).
[40] Bruce Ritchie, *ibid.*

In both cases however, there is an exception for professional legal privilege.[41] The privilege exception in s.330 of POCA and in the regulations is defined as information communicated by a client or his representatives in connection with the giving of legal advice or in connection with the seeking of legal advice or in connection with legal proceedings or contemplated proceedings. However information which is communicated with the intention of furthering a criminal purpose is not subject to legal privilege.[42] This means that the defence of legal privilege is not available where the transaction itself is for the purposes of Money Laundering, irrespective of any guilt on the part of the solicitor.[43] The client cannot use the solicitor unwittingly to assist the client in committing a crime.

The two further offences created by the act are those of "tipping-off" under s.333 where a person knows or suspects that a protected or authorised disclosure has been made and that person makes a different disclosure which is likely to prejudice any investigation which might be conducted and s.342 which makes it an offence for a person to make a disclosure likely to prejudice an investigation.

It is a defence if the discloser did not know or suspect that the disclosure was likely to prejudice any investigation or the disclosure was made by a legal adviser a) to a client or to a representative of the client in connection with the giving of legal advice to the client, or b) to any person in connection with legal proceedings or any contemplated proceedings provided that the disclosure was not made with the intention of furthering a criminal purpose.

The case of *P v P*[44] considered the question of "intent" in the context of the offence of "tipping off" under POCA s.333. Dame Butler-Sloss concluded that the requisite "improper intention" was that of the solicitor otherwise the legal privilege exception "would be rendered meaningless". Solicitors are therefore entitled to notify their clients of a SOCA report provided that they themselves have no intention of furthering a criminal purpose. However communication of such information to the client can only be done after the authorised disclosure and Dame Butler-Sloss thought it appropriate to allow seven working days to pass before informing the client.

Two other issues arise in relation to "tipping off". Once a solicitor has made a SOCA report, is he/she required to withdraw from acting, and could that constitute "tipping off". In our view withdrawal is optional and will not constitute "tipping off" unless the solicitor in explaining the cause of withdrawal makes a disclosure. Secondly, we are of the view that giving general advice to clients at the outset of a matter that solicitors require to comply with the Proceeds of Crime Act 2002 and the Money Laundering Regulations is not "tipping off" because at that stage no disclosure has been made. Solicitors should therefore insert a suitable clause in their Terms of Business letter,[45] or put up a notice in the office advising clients that they can

---

[41] s.330(10).

[42] This corresponds with the common law exception to the privilege where the communication was made in furtherance of a fraudulent or illegal purpose. See para.6.23.

[43] R. Stokes and Professor A. Arora, "The Duty to Report under the Money Laundering Legislation within the United Kingdom" (2004) J.B.L. 349.

[44] [2003] EWHC Fam 2260.

[45] See para.4.02.

no longer rely on the duty of privilege or confidentiality where the solicitor knows or suspects that criminal property is involved which would include tax evasion or benefit fraud.[46]

Exceptions to the Privilege: where the communication was in furtherance of a fraudulent or illegal purpose

6.25

Perhaps the most celebrated exception to the privilege relates to communications between the client and the lawyer which are made in furtherance of a criminal or illegal purpose. Since the rationale for the privilege is the furtherance of the administration of justice and access to justice this exception is not difficult to understand. To allow clients who involve their lawyers in carrying out a fraudulent or illegal purpose, to conceal this fact by relying on legal professional privilege would not only undermine the administration of justice but permit clients to have their cake and to eat it. The exception has long been established in the common law,[47] but its limits are still evolving at the present day. The ruling Scottish authority today is *Micosta SA v Shetland Islands Council.*[48] In that case the pursuers (ship owners) brought an action for damages against a local authority whom they accused of abusing their statutory powers relating to the management of a harbour for an improper motive, namely, to punish the pursuers for having allegedly caused oil pollution outwith the waters within the defenders' jurisdiction. Part of the documentation sought to be discovered by the pursuers related to advice to defenders given to them by their solicitors. The pursuers argued that there was an exception to the privilege where the subject-matter of an action was an alleged illegal act on the part of a defender and where the communications are directly relevant to the intention or state of mind of the defender at the relevant time. Lord President Emslie in the Opinion of the court observed:

"*So far as we can discover from the authorities the only circumstances in which the general rule will be superseded are where fraud or some other illegal act is alleged against a party and where his law agent has been directly concerned in the carrying out of the very transaction which is the subject-matter of inquiry.* In this case it is not suggested that the defenders' solicitors were involved at all in the intimation of the alleged threat by the harbour master and [the defenders] were quite entitled to seek advice confidentially... There is no trace in authority of any relaxation of the general rule where the law agent of the party accused of an illegal act has played no part in the act itself, to permit examination of correspondence between that party and his law agent in order to discover that party's state of mind or intention at the relevant time."

However, the *Micosta* test[49] requires to be further unpacked. First, it is clear that the communication itself has to be part of the illegal or fraudulent act. It follows that communications between the client and the lawyer made after a

---

[46] Bruce Ritchie, *ibid.*

[47] It was the basis of several Scottish cases in the nineteenth century e.g. *McCowan v Wright* (1852) 15 D. 494; *Millar v Small* (1856) 19 D. 142 and *Morrison v Sommerville* (1860) 23 D. 232. See also Begg *op. cit.* p.320 and Dickson *op. cit.* para.1678.

[48] 1983 S.L.T. 483.

[49] The passage in italics.

crime has been committed which are made for a legal purpose e.g. seeking advice on how to defend the case, are not covered by the exception and remain privileged. Secondly, as Maher argues, "the privilege also attaches in respect of legal advice on a proposed course of conduct by the client. Thus a client may claim privilege in respect of communications made by her with a view to obtaining advice on the legality of her proposals to break a contract, not declare income to the Inland Revenue or to poison her husband. Of course, in these situations the lawyer's advice must be "legal" not only in the sense of being about the law, but not being against the law."[50] In certain situations, however, there is a thin dividing line between providing advice as to whether a particular course of conduct might be lawful, and unwittingly assisting the client in the planning of a criminal activity. The *Micosta* "test" leaves it unclear as to whether the solicitor has to be aware that he or she is assisting the client in an illegal or fraudulent activity e.g. as an accomplice, before the exception applies, or whether it is enough that the solicitor's advice has unwittingly contributed to the illegal or fraudulent activity. Dickson[51] and Wilkinson[52] took the latter position but the matter was not determined by the courts until the case of *Kelly v Vannet*.[53] This was an appeal to the High Court of Justiciary concerning an MP who was alleged to have used a solicitor's services to further a conspiracy to pervert the course of justice. The Lord Justice Clerk (Cullen) in the Opinion of the Court opted for the position that the solicitor does not have to be aware that he or she is assisting in an illegal or fraudulent activity. As he observed:

> "We do not understand the remarks of the Lord President in *Micosta SA*, as restricting the exemption from privilege to the situation in which a solicitor has himself been a party to the fraud or other illegal act. The advocate depute founded on the following passage in Dickson on *Evidence* (3rd edn), s.1678:
>
>> 'One who consults a legal adviser, with a view to committing a fraud or other crime, makes him either an innocent instrument of his guilt or an accomplice. In neither case will so important a part of the history of the crime be excluded on account of confidentiality; for the ground of policy on which the privilege is founded in ordinary cases must give way, where preserving it would prevent crime from being detected.'
>
> As the advocate depute pointed, out, the common law in England was to the same effect. He referred us to the leading case of *R v Cox and Railton*, a decision of the Court for Crown Cases Reserved. Giving the decision of the court Stephen J at (1884) 14 QBD, pp.166–167 discussed the scope of the privilege in regard to communications between solicitor and client. On the latter page he stated: 'The reason on which the rule is said to rest cannot include the case of communications, criminal in themselves, or intended to further any criminal purpose, for the protection of such communications cannot possibly be otherwise than injurious to the

---

[50] *Op. cit.* 1990 J.L.S.S. 108 at p.111.
[51] *Op. cit.* para.1678.
[52] *Op. cit.* p.98.
[53] 1999 J.C. 109.

interests of justice. Nor do such communications fall within the terms of the rule. A communication in furtherance of a criminal purpose does not "come into the ordinary scope of professional employment". A single illustration will make this plain. It is part of the business of a solicitor to draw wills. Suppose a person, personating someone else, instructs a solicitor to draw a will in the name of the supposed testator, executes it in the name of the supposed testator, gives the solicitor his fee, and takes away the will. It would be monstrous to say that the solicitor was employed in the "ordinary scope of professional employment". He in such case is made an unconscious instrument in the commission of a crime.' "[54]

Relying on the case of *R v Cox and Railton* Lord Justice Thorpe in *C v C (Privilege: Criminal Communications)* [2002] Fam 42 held that communications which are criminal in themselves or intended to further any criminal purpose were not covered by legal professional privilege. As a result an affidavit disclosing evidence of a client's communications in a telephone call to his solicitor was not covered by the privilege as the communications had included an extreme threat to "rip someone's throat out", which as a threat to kill, was criminal.

The fourth aspect of the Micosta test which required clarification was the scope of the words "fraud or some other illegal act". The issue arose in the curious case of *Conoco v The Commercial Law Practice*.[55] Here the Commercial Law Practice had been instructed by a person who had claimed to have information relating to an overpayment of over £1 million mistakenly made by Conoco to a contractor. Their client offered, for a fee, to point Conoco to the root of the mistake and thence to the recovery of overpayment. The client had not been connected with Conoco or the contractor and owed no duty to either. The solicitors who wrote to Conoco on behalf of their client with this proposal did not identify their client in order to preserve the supposed commercial value of the information which he had. The pursuers then petitioned the court under the Administration of Justice Act 1972 seeking an order requiring the solicitors to disclose the identity of the client. Lord MacFadyen (in the Outer House) accepted the defenders' argument that notwithstanding the position in England and the views of several Scottish writers,[56] the identity of a client should normally be privileged as well as confidential. However he went on to hold that fraud, in its broadest sense, was at the root of the situation between the contractor and Conoco. In his view the question for the court was whether that fraud on the part of the contractors tainted the client's position as to deprive the client and the solicitors of the privilege of confidentiality which would otherwise be available to them. Lord

---

[54] However, Lord Cullen's comments should not be read as asserting that the privilege is necessarily waived by dint of the client telling an untruth to his or her lawyer in relation to his or her case, e.g. with respect to an alibi which turns out to be false, which if acted upon might lead to the commission of the crime of perjury. On the other hand where a party and his or her witnesses deliberately engage in deception and or forgery to induce an error from the court the fraud exception will apply. See Lord Goff in *R v Central Criminal Court, Ex p. Francis* [1989] A.C. 346 at 397 and L. J. Longmore in *Kuwait Airways Corp v Iraq Airways Co* [2005] EWCA Civ 286.

[55] 1997 S.L.T. 372.

[56] See Walker and Walker, *op. cit.*, p.147, fn. 47.

MacFadyen could find no direct precedent for the case, accepting that it lay "at the borderline between the rule and exception" and that it was not clearly within the *Micosta* test. Nevertheless, he took the view the balance of competing public policy considerations favoured disclosure rather than confidentiality and ordered that the client's identity should be revealed:

> "I am wary of deciding the issue by an *ad hoc* exploration of public policy consideration. Nevertheless it seems to me that the public policy consideration which underlies the 'fraud exception' may be capable of extension to a situation in which a party and his solicitor, not themselves either guilty of fraud or involved in carrying out a fraudulent transaction, are involved in a transaction, the purpose of which is to derive for the client benefit from his knowledge of a fraud committed by another party."[57]

Conoco is interesting for a variety of reasons. It shows that the limits of solicitor-client privilege continue to pose problems in Scotland despite the seeming clarity of the decision in *Micosta*. Instead, it was the broad approach to the 'fraud' exception taken in an English Court of Appeal case, *Barclays Bank plc and others v Eustice and others*,[58] which seems to have influenced the decision in *Conoco*. In that case, it was ruled that where a client sought legal advice on the structuring of a transaction to be entered into at an undervalue for the purpose of prejudicing the interests of persons making a claim against him under s.423 of the Insolvency Act 1986, that purpose was sufficiently iniquitous for public policy to require that legal professional privilege be overridden to the effect that communications between the client and his solicitors in relation to the setting up of the transaction be discoverable, whether or not either the client or his solicitors believed that the transaction would be set aside under s.423. The case was also followed by Rix J. in *Dubai Aluminium Co Ltd v Al Alawi & Others*,[59] where he refuted the argument that the exception to privilege based on fraud was confined to cases where solicitors had become involved in planning or carrying out iniquitous acts which subsequently became the subject matter of litigation.

However, with the greatest of respect to Lord MacFadyen it is difficult to square the somewhat restrictive approach of *Micosta* which was binding on him, with the much more flexible approach that he took. It may be that the Inner House when next it considers the *Micosta* test will come to the conclusion the *Conoco* was wrongly decided. Certainly, *Conoco's* flexible approach to the use of public policy in relation to client privilege is at variance with one of the latest rulings of the House of Lords in the field, *R. v Derby Magistrates Court Ex p. B*,[60] which is much more in line with the narrow approach of *Micosta*. The case raised the difficult issue of the client who admits to his or her solicitor to having committed a crime for which he or she had been tried (and acquitted) for which a third party is then prosecuted. The efforts of the third party's lawyers to use the public policy arguments to justify

---

[57] At p.380L. For a discussion of the possible implications of the *Conoco* decision, see D. O'Donnell, *A Question of Privilege: Conoco v The Commercial Law Practice* 1997 S.L.P.Q. 163.

[58] [1995] 1 W.L.R. 1238.

[59] [1999] 1 W.L.R. 1964.

[60] [1996] 1 A.C. 487.

breaching the client's privilege were rejected by the House of Lords in a conservative judgment.

The Lord Chief Justice's opinion closed the door firmly on the possibility of any other values being set against confidentiality and the adversarial system:

> "The principle which runs through these cases . . . is that a man must be able to consult with his lawyer in confidence, since otherwise he might hold back half the truth. The client must be sure that what he tells his lawyer in confidence will never be revealed without his consent. Legal professional privilege is thus much more than an ordinary rule of evidence, limited in its application to the facts of the particular case. It is a fundamental condition on which the administration of justice as a whole rests . . . Putting it another way, if a balancing exercise was ever required in the case of legal professional privilege, it was performed once and for all in the 16th century, and since then has applied across the board in every case, irrespective of the client's individual merits . . . it is not for the sake of the appellant alone that the privilege must be upheld. It is in the wider interests of all those hereafter who might otherwise be deterred from telling the whole truth to their solicitors. For this reason I am of the opinion that no exception should be allowed to the absolute nature of legal professional privilege, once established. It follows that *R v Barton* [1973] 1 WLR 115 and *R v Atou* were wrongly decided and ought to be overruled. I therefore consider that these appeals should be allowed on both grounds and the case remitted to the High Court with a direction that the decision of the stipendiary magistrate . . . be quashed."

The rest of their Lordships agreed.

The triumph of legal professional privilege over all other values in the justice arena, including the innocence of a third party which is enshrined in *Derby Magistrates* is not only disquieting, it is also hard to square with the variety of legislative provisions where exceptions have been made to the absolutist doctrine of privilege. To suggest that legal professional privilege is more important than the life imprisonment of an innocent third party (which at the time of the death penalty might have been the life of an innocent third party) appears perverse and bizarre. Moreover, it was quickly to lead the House into the embarrassing situation of reviewing the parameters of the *Derby Magistrates* decision. In *Re L (a minor)*,[61] the House was faced with a conflict between legal professional privilege and the paramountcy of the welfare of the child in care proceedings. The issue concerned an expert's report prepared at the request of the parents in care proceedings. The parents argued that legal professional privilege prevented the report from being made available to other parties, such as the police. The House of Lords (including three of the judges who sat in *Derby Magistrates*) by a 3/2 majority distinguished *Derby Magistrates* and allowed the privilege in the report to be overridden in favour of the welfare of the children. The House sought to save face by drawing a distinction between solicitor-client privilege and the privilege of a report prepared with a view to litigation. The former was

---

[61] [1997] A.C. 16.

absolute, the latter was not, they said. As Lord Jauncey of Tullichettle noted:

"There is . . . a clear distinction between the privilege attaching to communications between solicitor and client and that attaching to reports by third parties on the instructions of a client for the purpose of litigation . . . Whereas a solicitor could not without his client's consent be compelled to express an opinion on the factual or legal merits of the case, a third party who has provided a report to a client can be subpoenaed to give evidence by the other side and cannot decline to answer questions as to his factual findings and opinion thereon."

Moreover, litigation privilege did not apply in this case, said the House, because it was clear from the legislation that care proceedings were non-adversarial and therefore the rationale for the privilege did not exist. Wriggle as they might, the strong dissent and the weakness of the majority's reasoning reveals that there are aspects of *Re L* which are hard to reconcile with *Derby Magistrates*. A further re-think of *Derby Magistrates* may yet be necessary.[62]

6.26 Exceptions to the Obligation of Confidentiality

While much has been written about the exceptions to legal professional privilege, relatively little has been written in Scotland as to the exceptions to the obligation of confidentiality whether based in agency, voluntary obligations, human rights or professional ethics. Given the closeness in rationale for aspects of the duties of confidentiality and legal professional privilege, it seems fair to assume that the exceptions to the latter are likely to be exceptions to the former as well. Certainly, there is no doubt that the third and fourth exceptions (those based on statute and those on allegations of fraud/ illegality) apply. There is, however, a fifth exception which applies to the obligation of confidentiality but which does not, it seems, apply to the duty of legal professional privilege.[63] This is an exception based on a countervailing public policy or public interest. As the Scottish Law Commission Memorandum No.40[64] argues, disclosure of information communicated in confidence may be held to be justified in the public interest. While it is true that the extent of this defence in Scots law is not clear, it probably does, as Black has argued,[65] extend to justifying the disclosure to the authorities of the identity of one who has committed a serious crime, especially if an innocent third party is being accused of the crime. What, however, if the person being

---

[62] For a detailed examination of the criticisms which may be levelled against the hard line approach of the House of Lords in *R v Derby Magistrates*, see Zuckerman *Legal Professional Privilege—The Cost of Absolutism* (1996) 112 L.Q.R. 535. See also Lord Scott in the lead opinion in the *Three Rivers* case [2004] UKHL 48 at para.29 where he notes that the litigation privilege may have to be revisited following *Re L*.

[63] See *B v Auckland District Law Society* [2003] UKPC 38 where the Privy Council held that privilege was a paramount interest and not merely one to be balanced against the public interest. In the *Three Rivers* case Lord Scott in the lead opinion (at para.25) declined to follow the Canadian Supreme Court in *Jones v Smith* [1999] 1 S.C.R. 455 in holding that legal professional privilege can be set aside if a sufficiently compelling public interest for doing so can be shown.

[64] Paras 34–37.

[65] Black, *op. cit.*

identified is your client? In the absence of any guidance from the discipline tribunal or the Law Society it is far from clear that a breach of the ethical (as opposed to the legal) duty of confidentiality will be excused in such circumstances—which was the dilemma which faced Joseph Beltrami in the *Meehan* affair.[66] However, it may well be the case that if your client indicates that he or she intends to commit a serious offence, especially one that is likely to cause serious bodily harm to another, then the Law Society will accept that disclosure is justified.[67] As the Law Society guidance note on confidentiality in 2000 observes:

> "You may receive information from your client about a crime which he is threatening to commit. In those circumstances the client is *not* entitled to the privilege of confidentiality and you would be quite entitled, and some would say obliged to draw the circumstances to the attention of the authorities."

However, if the revelation of the planned offence is part and parcel of the process of seeking legal advice it is less clear that the disclosure could never be privileged, although this is a topic on which there is no consensus. On the other hand there is equally no consensus that there is a duty, ethical or moral, which requires the lawyer to alert the police or the potential victims. At the end of the day the solicitor has to be able to live with his or her choices. Even if the Dunblane killer had revealed to a solicitor in advance of the primary school massacre what he had in mind, as part of a privileged conversation, it is to be hoped that the solicitor would have had the courage to ignore issues of privilege and confidentiality and alerted the authorities even though it opened him or her up to potential suit or discipline for the breach.

Enforcing the Privilege and the Confidence   6.27

Amongst the many interesting issues raised by the extent of the exceptions to confidentiality and legal professional privilege is the question of how these obligations can be enforced. The former can be policed by a complaint to the

---

[66] D. Nicolson and J. Webb, *Professional Legal Ethics* (Oxford University Press, Oxford, 1999) argue on pp.252–253 that the broad exception in relation to the public interest does not apply to the ethical duty of confidentiality in England and Wales. Joe Beltrami, a leading Glasgow criminal lawyer, represented Paddy Meehan, who was convicted erroneously of a murder in 1969. In 1973 and for two years thereafter, Beltrami received a series of visits from another client, "Tank" McGuiness who gradually revealed that he had committed the murder. Beltrami felt bound by the ethical duty of confidentiality to say nothing (although it is clear that what McGuiness had said was not privileged). However, when McGuiness died his relatives wrote to Beltrami to see if he had any written confession from McGuiness. Beltrami did not, but he secured their permission to reveal the oral confession to the authorities. Beltrami thereafter communicated several times with the Law Society with the details of the matter and sending the waivers of confidentiality from McGuiness's next of kin. The Society was unwilling to rule whether disclosure of the confidential information in these circumstances would be considered professional misconduct. Beltrami went to the police but was not prosecuted by the Society. The applicability of the public interest defence in a misconduct case based on breach of confidentiality therefore remains undecided in Scotland. See J. Beltrami, *A Deadly Innocence: the Meehan File* (Mainstream Publishing, 1989).

[67] In England and Wales solicitors are permitted but not required by the Guide to the Professional Conduct of Solicitors 1999 to reveal confidential information (1) to prevent a criminal act being committed which is likely to result in serious bodily harm and (2) to protect children who are being seriously abused. Para.16.02 sub-paras 3 and 4.

Law Society and as a matter of agency by an interdict or damages for breach of fiduciary duty. It is sometimes suggested that the privilege cannot be enforced by the client except by objecting to his or her solicitor giving evidence in court. On this view where the public interest defence permits the breach of the confidence, the solicitor can happily ignore the privilege provided he or she is not actually giving evidence in court. However, increasingly the privilege in the common law world is being seen as a fundamental right as e.g. in *R. v IRC ex parte Morgan Grenfell and Co. Ltd.*,[68] where Lord Hoffman in the House of Lords describes it as "a fundamental human right" which can only be interfered with by the direct words of a statute, and then only in situations which a democratic society would regard as legitimate and necessary.[69] To the extent that this approach is followed in Scotland it would be open to a client to enforce the privilege through an interdict or action for damages, even in a situation in which the public interest defence would apply to a confidence.

6.28 CODA: Exploring the Limits[70]

A Question of Confidence: Communications between solicitor and client
1982 J.L.S.S. 299

The problem

X has been charged with a serious crime. He has been refused bail and remanded in custody. A solicitor, S, has been instructed to represent X in connection with his defence to the crime. S is in no sense X's man of business: he has been consulted only in relation to the particular crime charged. The Crown eventually decides not to proceed against X for that crime. S goes to the prison with the release warrant for X and, having secured his release, offers to drive him home. During the course of the journey X suddenly and unexpectedly blurts out that he, X, committed a particular robbery about which there had recently been a considerable amount of publicity in the press. X does not ask S for advice, nor does S tender any. Is S bound, because of the confidentiality attaching to communications between solicitor and client, not to divulge X's confession, whether in legal proceedings or otherwise? Would it make any difference to S's position if X subsequently died and S then obtained the permission of X's family and personal representatives to disclose X's confession?

Is S under an obligation of confidence?

It seems highly unlikely in the circumstances envisaged that X's statement to S fails within the rule under which communications between solicitor and client are privileged or protected from disclosure in legal proceedings. It is almost certainly no longer the case, as it was once

---

[68] [2003] 1 A.C. 563.

[69] In the *Three Rivers* case in the House of Lords [2004] UKHL 48 Lord Scott in the lead opinion (at para.26) asserted that the privilege is both a procedural and a substantive right.

[70] This article which explores the limits of the public interest exception to the duty of confidentiality is reproduced with the kind permission of the author, Professor Robert Black Q.C., and of the Law Society of Scotland as publishers of the Journal.

thought to be, that only information communicated in connection with litigation either depending or contemplated or apprehended is privileged: *McCowan v Wright* (1852) 15 D 229 at 231–232, 237; *Munro v Fraser* (1858) 21 D 103. But it is clear that in order to be protected from disclosure the information must have been communicated in a professional context. In Burnett, *Criminal Law* (1811), pp 435–436, it is stated:

"It [the privilege attaching to communications to lawyers] does not extend to what their client (or third parties) may have communicated to them, not as his Counsel or Agents, or with a view to their professional advice ... but as friends or acquaintances merely, though they happen at the time to be his professional advisers in other matters."

Kirkpatrick, *Digest of the Scottish Law of Evidence* (1882), para.176, states:

"The privilege applies only to communications of a deliberative or consultative character, with reference to the vindication of the client's rights."

Begg, *Treatise on Law Agents*, 2nd edn, p.314, is to the following effect:

"The privilege is confined to those facts which have come to the knowledge of counsel or law agents, and to advice given by them, during, in the course of, and for the purpose of, their employment."

Similar views are to be found expressed in Dickson on Evidence, 2nd edn, para.1665, and Walkers on Evidence, para.393.

There is very little Scottish authority on the question of the circumstances in which information disclosed to a solicitor will be regarded as privileged. In *HM Advocate v Davie* (1881) 4 Coup 450 the Crown in a trial for perjury sought to lead evidence from a solicitor whom the accused had consulted in connection with the civil action raised against him in which the alleged perjured evidence had been given. The solicitor had refused to act for the accused in that civil action after hearing the nature of the defence which he proposed to put forward. It was held that the solicitor's evidence of his interview with the accused on that occasion was admissible in spite of the accused's objection: since he had declined to act, he had never been the accused's solicitor. The decision is that of a single judge on circuit; no time was taken for consideration; and it is clear from the report that the judge was not convinced that his ruling was correct. It is submitted that the decision is wrong, and that the protection from disclosure applies to information communicated to a solicitor by a person seeking his professional advice or assistance whether or not the solicitor agrees to act on his behalf after hearing what he has to say. That is the position in England: see cases cited in Begg, *Treatise on Law Agents*, 2nd edn, p.314 fn; also *Minter v Priest* [1930] A.C. 558. In the last-mentioned case the House of Lords (including Viscount Dunedin and Lord Thankerton) took the view that communications passing between a solicitor and a person seeking his professional services were privileged even though the solicitor after hearing the prospective client's proposal declined to act. It was sufficient in order for the protection to attach that "the contemplated relationship was that of solicitor and client" (per Viscount Buckmaster at p.568) or that the prospective client "went to see Priest as a solicitor" (per Viscount Dunedin at p.571) or that the communication was made "for the purpose of getting or giving professional advice" (per Lord Atkin at p.581). Lord Atkin went on to say:

"It is further desirable to point out, not by way of exception but as a result of the rule, that communications between solicitor and client which do not pass for the purpose of giving or receiving professional advice are not protected. It follows that client and solicitor may meet for the purpose of legal advice and exchange protected communications, and may yet in the course of the same interview make statements to each other not for the purpose of giving or receiving professional advice but for some other purpose. Such statements are not within the rule."

It is thought, therefore, that the question whether X's statement to S was privileged is not to be answered in the negative, as *HM Advocate v Davie* might suggest, merely because S seems not, at the time when it was made, to have been X's solicitor. The real test seems to be X's purpose in disclosing the information. Did he do so with a view to getting professional advice? If he did not, then his statement was not protected from disclosure in legal proceedings irrespective of whether the relationship of solicitor and client existed, or still existed, or was contemplated, between him and S at that time.

Although, on the facts as stated, it seems fairly clear that X's statement, since not made for the purpose of obtaining legal advice, did not enjoy the privilege attaching to communications between solicitor and client, this may not be the end of the matter. It means that S could have been compelled in legal proceedings to give evidence of X's statement. But it does not necessarily follow that S would have been entitled to disclose the information in any other circumstances. Information communicated to a solicitor may, it is thought, be subject to an obligation of confidentiality even though the solicitor could be required to divulge it in court: *Parry-Jones v The Law Society* [1969] 1 Ch. 1 at 9. The relationship between a solicitor and the person from whom the information is received may be such that the latter would have a remedy if the solicitor voluntarily disclosed the information, even though the situation is not one in which the protection from disclosure in legal proceedings would apply. For example, a client consulting his solicitor in connection with the drawing up of his will may, apropos of nothing and without seeking or requesting the solicitor's advice, divulge that some years previously he had concealed taxable income from the Revenue authorities; that he had committed adultery; that he had bribed a local authority official in order to obtain a business contract; that he had invented a revolutionary new process for reinforcing concrete. Since these items of information were not communicated for the purpose of getting the solicitor's professional advice, it seems that the solicitor could be compelled to give evidence about them in legal proceedings. But it is not a necessary consequence of this that there would be no remedy if the solicitor disclosed (or threatened to disclose) the information to a journalist, to the client's wife or to one of his business competitors.

It is by no means clear in precisely what circumstances the law will accept that an obligation of confidence comes into being when information is disclosed by A to B. In England it has been suggested that:

"if the circumstances are such that any reasonable man standing in the shoes of the recipient of the information would have realised that upon reasonable grounds the information was being given to him in confidence, then this should suffice to impose upon him the equitable obligation of confidence" (per Megarry J., in *Coco v Clark* [1969] RPC 41 at 48).

It is thought that, as far as Scotland is concerned, this may be too broadly expressed in that it seems to envisage that an enforceable obligation to keep information confidential can be forced on the recipient against his will: it is enough that a reasonable man would have realised that the information was being imparted in confidence—the recipient need not, apparently, have accepted that condition or even have been given an opportunity to refuse to receive the information on that basis. In Scotland, it is submitted, an obligation to keep information confidential, like any other voluntary obligation, requires the consent of the obligor. However, particularly where the recipient is a solicitor and the informant his client (or recent ex-client), the consent of the solicitor to receiving the information in confidence would not, it is thought, be difficult to establish and would readily be inferred.

It is thought, therefore, that if S realised that what X was about to tell him was intended to be confidential and if S had an opportunity to prevent the disclosure to him, then S should be held to have consented to receiving the information on a confidential basis. However, S's obligation in these circumstances would be the ordinary obligation of confidentiality that can exist in respect of information communicated by one layman to another (see Scottish Law Commission Memorandum No.40, paras. 13 to 27): there would not exist the special protection from disclosure accorded to information divulged to a solicitor in a professional context for the purpose of obtaining his advice. That being so, it would appear that the obligation would be qualified by the availability of "the public policy defence". Disclosure of information communicated in confidence may be held to be justified in the public interest (see Memorandum No.40, paras. 34 to 37 and 89). The extent of the defence in Scots law is not clear. But in English law, it clearly covers the provision of information about criminal conduct to the police:

"You cannot make me the confidant of a crime or a fraud, and be entitled to close up my lips . . . such a confidence cannot exist" (per Wood, V.C., in *Gartside v Outram* (1856) 26 L.J. Ch. 113 at 114).

"It extends to any misconduct of such a nature that it ought in the public interest to be disclosed to others . . . The exception should extend to crimes, frauds and misdeeds, both those actually committed as well as those in contemplation, provided always—and this is essential—that the disclosure is justified in the public interest" (per Lord Denning, MR, in *Initial Services v Putterill* [1968] 1 Q.B. 396 at 405).

It is thought that whatever the precise limits of the defence of disclosure in the public interest in Scots law, it would certainly cover disclosure to the authorities of evidence of the identity of the person who had committed a serious crime. It may also, strictly speaking, be inaccurate to regard public policy here as operating to provide a defence to a person who has breached an obligation. It may rather be that for reasons of public policy the law will not accept that a legal obligation to keep such information confidential can come into existence at all. In any event, it is thought that X would have had no legal remedy against S had the latter disclosed (or intimated that he was about to disclose) X's statement to the authorities.

The effect of X's death

If, contrary to the view already expressed, X's statement to S was privileged (and not merely subject to an ordinary obligation of confidence) the question arises of the effect of X's death and of any permission to disclose obtained by S from the deceased's family and personal representatives. It is clear that the privilege attaching to communications between solicitor and client is not that of the solicitor but that of the client, who may waive it (Dickson on Evidence, 2nd edn, para.1682; Walkers on Evidence, para.393). It is equally clear that the privilege remains in existence notwithstanding dissolution of the relationship of solicitor and client (e.g. Begg, *Treatise on Law Agents*, pp.318–319; *Hyslop v Staig* (1816) 1 Mur 15 at 17; *Kerr v Duke of Roxburghe* (1822) 3 Mur 126 at 141; *Wight v Ewing* (1828) 4 Mur 584; *Gavin v Montgomerie* (1830) 9 S 213 at 220). In all of the cases cited, however, the dissolution of the relationship was caused otherwise than by death, and the client was still alive at the time when the solicitor's evidence was sought. On the question whether the protection from disclosure survives the client's death there seem to be only two cases, *Executors of Lady Bath v Johnston* 12 Nov 1811 F.C. and *Mackenzie v Mackenzie's Trs* (1916) 1 S.L.T. 271.

In the first case the defender sought to recover correspondence between his deceased predecessor in the barony of Westerhall and the latter's solicitors with a view to discovering with what intention the deceased had expede general service to his late brother. The pursuers (the executors of the deceased's daughter) opposed the defender's application. The court refused to allow recovery, holding the deceased's correspondence 'to come under the general rule regarding confidential correspondence between client and agent' (per Lord President Hope at p.348).

In *Mackenzie* the pursuer sought decree of declarator of marriage against the trustees of a deceased. Defences were also lodged by relations of the deceased who were beneficiaries under his will. Those beneficiaries then moved for a diligence to recover correspondence passing between the deceased and his solicitors around the time when the marriage was alleged to have been contracted, and this was opposed both by the trustees and by the solicitors. Before the First Division the beneficiaries argued:

"[The solicitors] could have a duty of confidentiality only to their client while he lived, and to his representatives in that interest after his death. Here his representatives in that interest were the beneficiaries in the estate, who were anxious to have the matter cleared up and the diligence allowed for that purpose. It was not for the law agents to plead confidentiality when the client's representatives did not insist on it" (1916, 1 S.L.T. 271).

The trustees and solicitors argued:

" . . . they wished for guidance whether the [solicitors] had any further duty of confidentiality in this matter towards their deceased client. They thought they had. It might be true that the representatives of a deceased client could waive the privilege of confidentiality in a question between them and third parties, but here the question was a domestic one, and the fact that it was the comparing beneficiaries . . . that sought the diligence did not seem to his agents to remove the objection to their disclosing, possibly to the prejudice of other members of the family, any confidential information they might have as to his domestic affairs" (1916, 1 S.L.T. at 272).

The opinion of the court was delivered by Lord President Strathclyde in a single sentence:

"In the circumstances of this case, and as a question of status is involved, the diligence will be granted" ((1916) 1 S.L.T. at 272).

Taking these two cases together, it seems clear that the privilege does not automatically cease to exist on the death of the client. But it is not clear from *Mackenzie* whether the decision was that the privilege can be waived by the deceased's representatives, or that the court has the power (perhaps on the grounds of public policy) to require disclosure to be made. If the latter view is the correct one, it is thought that the policy arguments in favour of requiring disclosure of information relating to the identity of the perpetrator of a serious crime are just as weighty (indeed, more so) than those in favour of requiring disclosure of information relevant to determining the status of a litigant as a married woman or not. On either interpretation of *Mackenzie*, therefore, it would seem that, on the facts assumed, S could have been compelled, after X's death, to divulge the statement made to him, even if it had prior thereto been privileged. And if the statement, though not technically privileged, had been made to, and received by, S in confidence, the death of X and the consent of X's family and representatives to disclosure would not, it is submitted, affect S's legal position in any way since even prior thereto disclosure by S would not have entitled X to any remedy against him.

CHAPTER 7

CONFLICT OF INTEREST

A. PRINCIPLES

7.01 Introduction

In the past decade several factors such as the threat of multi-disciplinary partnerships, the attentions of the competition authorities and the fear of the large accounting firms, have led the global legal profession to rediscover the importance of its core values. Integrity, diligence, competence, independence and the preservation of the confidences of their clients are but a few of the positive obligations mentioned in such debates. Yet, curiously, perhaps the paramount ethical obligation in practice for legal professionals in the 21st century, is invariably couched in negative terms, namely, the duty *not* to act when a conflict of interest exists. In truth, underlying this negative duty is a positive obligation which the 21st century legal profession, finds somewhat unfashionable to discuss,[1] namely the fiduciary obligation of loyalty. This fundamental obligation (or set of obligations) dates back to the earliest days of the profession[2] and it is not hard to see why. First, given the information asymmetry[3] which typically pertains between clients and lawyers it is essential that the interests of the former are protected from the self-interest of the latter.[4] This particular form of conflict of interest is discussed in the next two chapters on lawyer/client transactions and lawyers' fees, respectively. Secondly, however, it has long been clear that it is not possible to loyally pursue the interests of, or provide independent advice to, two or more different clients in a matter where those interests are in conflict. This type of conflict—where the lawyer seeks to act for more than one client in the same or a related matter takes two forms—"simultaneous" and "successive" conflicts. The first involves acting for two or more clients at the same time in the same matter. The second arises where a lawyer seeks to act for one client against a former client in the same or a related matter. These separate but

---

[1] At least in the UK, though not in the USA. The UK profession's reluctance to stress the duty of loyalty to the client perhaps reflects the declining loyalty shown to the profession by their clients. Certainly in the UK, as clients have become more willing to shop around for legal services or to put their legal work out to tender, the profession has placed less stress on its fiduciary obligation of loyalty.

[2] The principle enshrined in the loyalty obligation appears in the New Testament, Matthew Ch.6 verse 24: "No man can serve two masters, for either he will hate the one and love the other, or else he will hold to one and despise the other."

[3] See e.g. R. Dingwall and P. Fenn, "A Respectable Profession" (1987) *International Review of Law and Economics* 7 and J. Johnson, *Professions and Power* (Macmillan, London, 1972).

[4] This is, of course, why fiduciary law came into existence.

related forms of conflict will form the subject matter for this chapter. It should be noted, however, that it is not just the conflicting interests of the clients that is the problem. It is the conflict between the underlying ethical and fiduciary duties which the lawyer owes to the different clients which poses the enduring difficulties in this area. Indeed, it might be less confusing if the field was described as conflicts of duty rather than conflicts of interest.[5]

Background 7.02

Given that the loyalty obligation of a fiduciary is largely, though not entirely, a portmanteau or umbrella concept,[6] encapsulating such fundamental values of the profession as safeguarding the client's property and information, disclosing all relevant information, not making secret profits, nor preferring the lawyer's interests or a third party's interests over the client's, and is, moreover, intuitively obvious to laypersons, it may be wondered why conflicts of interest have proved a constant problem for the profession. First, because most lawyers, let alone law firms, have many clients and it is not always easy, particularly where limited companies are concerned, to detect that a lawyer/firm is being asked to act for different clients in the same or a related matter. This is why it is so essential that firms have effective conflict checking systems in place. Secondly, the dividing line between situations where two clients' interests overlap and those where they are adverse to one another can appear less obvious at the time than it does subsequently with hindsight. Thirdly, to insist that all individuals in a multi-party transaction, all partners in a partnership, all directors in a company or married couples entering into transactions require to be separately represented would greatly increase the cost of going to law or dispute resolution and in some cases entail that the parties have to forgo representation.[7] Access problems of another sort constitute a fourth reason, at least in rural communities where lawyers will sometimes act for two clients whose interests potentially conflict rather than insist that one of them (possibly an existing client) travel a considerable distance to find another lawyer. The fifth reason is less altruistic and is one that has become more significant with the raised levels of competition within the profession of the last 20 years.[8] It is the temptation to boost one's fee income or to preserve one's client base in preference to turning away one or both of the clients to a competitor, for what is required by a solicitor's ethical duty may be at odds with the solicitor's economic interest.

---

[5] See e.g. the argument in P.M. Perell, *Conflicts of Interest in the Legal Profession* (Butterworths, Toronto, 1995) pp.5–13. In our view, the duty of loyalty is larger than its constituent elements in the sense that these elements evidence a wider duty on a fiduciary to be loyal to the client.

[6] See P. Finn, *Fiduciary Obligations* (The Law Book Co Ltd, Sydney, 1977) Ch.15 and C. Hollander and S. Salzedo, *Conflicts of Interest and Chinese Walls* (2nd edn) (Sweet & Maxwell, London, 2004) at p.13.

[7] See S. Shapiro, *Conflicting Responsibilities* (American Bar Foundation, Chicago, 1995) at p.46.

[8] Itself the result of consumer pressure and government action to deregulate the legal services market through the removal of perceived anti-competitive elements such as the ban on advertising, the use of scale fees and the professional monopolies. See A. Paterson, "Professionalism and the Legal Services Market" (1996) 3 *International Journal of the Legal Profession* 137.

These five reasons ensured the enduring significance of conflicts of interest late into the 20th century. However, as Janine Griffiths-Baker has argued[9] there are several additional factors which have arisen in the last 20 years which have combined to exacerbate the difficulties experienced by the profession with conflicts of interests associated with acting for two or more clients in the same or a related matter. They are: the increased demand for specialist legal services, the globalisation of commerce, a dramatic growth in the size of the leading law firms and greater mobility within the legal profession. These inter-linked phenomena have indeed had a significant impact on the English legal profession—though rather less of an impact on the Scottish profession. The growth in size of the city law firms and their success in the global marketplace (most commonly through foreign branch offices) has made the multi-office law firm with thousands of transactions annually a commonplace phenomenon. Yet in strict law if one fee-earner in such a firm would be prevented from acting for two clients because of a conflict of interest then this disqualification applies to all other fee-earners in the firm irrespective of where on the globe they are situated and whether the two fee earners had ever met or communicated with each other. To many firms the extension of such imputed disqualifications[10] (as they are called) is highly unrealistic since the London and Hong Kong branches of a firm may have comparatively little to do with each other in real life and therefore the respective branches' (and their lawyers') diligence and commitment is unlikely to be diminished. Moreover, depending on the ITC and Knowledge Management set up within the firm, in practical terms there is little likelihood of confidential information in respect of a London client being spread to the Hong Kong office and vice-versa. It is small wonder that Griffiths-Baker found that many of the large city firms in London routinely ignored or by-passed the rules on conflicts of interest through the use of client consent or Chinese walls.[11] However, she also found that the smaller, national or provincial firms were more likely to be wary of the conflict rules, since they perceived their clients to be less comfortable with them acting in a conflict situation. These differences may help to account for the contradictory outcomes of the attempts on both sides of the Border to reform the ethical rules in relation to conflicts of interest in the last five years. In England and Wales the City of London law firms argued strongly for a relaxation in the rules on conflict of interest there because they were more restrictive than those that existed in mainland Europe and as a result the City firms were being hampered in their efforts to compete with the indigenous firms in countries such as the Netherlands, Germany or Italy.[12] Although the English and Welsh Law Society was persuaded to relax the conflict of interest rules by, *inter alia*, making room for informed consent as far back as 2004, the proposals were not acceptable to the Legal Services Consultative Panel of the Department of Constitutional Affairs and at the time of writing, the changes have still to be implemented. During the same period

---

[9] *Serving Two Masters* (Oxford, Hart publishing 2002) p.vii and Ch.1.

[10] See para.7.08 below.

[11] *Op. cit.* pp.173–178. The mega firms claimed that the number of potential conflicts in the city were so numerous that to enforce the ban on acting in a conflict situation would lead to commerce grinding to a halt or sophisticated corporate clients being forced to use lawyers lacking the necessary expertise.

[12] Given the sizeable market share held by City firms in these countries already, this was not a particularly compelling argument.

the Law Society of Scotland convened its own working party on conflict of interest which contained representatives of several of the large firms. Surprisingly, there was no interest in relaxing the rules on conflict of interest, nor in allowing informed consent by the client to acting where there is a situation of actual conflict.

Identifying a Conflict of Interest 7.03

As will probably be clear from the last paragraph, conflicts are not always easy to identify. It is not unusual for drafters of ethical codes simply not to attempt the task.[13] One view is that a conflict may be hard to define, but you know it when you see it. Unfortunately, as those who deal with complaints to professional bodies can confirm, some solicitors only seem to see a conflict long after it has appeared and when it is too late for avoiding action. Jane Ryder argues[14] that "where facts are disclosed to a solicitor on behalf of one client which may be prejudicial if disclosed to another client without the authority of the first, there is almost certainly a conflict of interest." This is true but it only takes us part of the way. Perhaps the most straightforward answer is that if the ordinary solicitor acting with ordinary care would give different advice to different clients about the same matter, there is a conflict of interest between them.[15] In a similar vein, if either client could reasonably take exception to what the other has asked you to do, you probably have a conflict.[16] On the other hand, it does not matter that the clients are agreed about what they themselves wish to do. Conflict of interest is not a matter for the judgement of the client—it is a matter for the judgement of the solicitor. Only the solicitor has the breadth of experience, training and knowledge to fully advise a client of the nature and extent of his/her interests having regard to the applicable relevant law and to the solicitor's professional judgement.[17]

The Discipline Tribunal has added the further guidance to solicitors who are concerned that they may be in a conflict situation:

"There may ... be occasions when it is not immediately apparent whether a conflict of interest exists and in these circumstances it may be

---

[13] Neither the CCBE Code nor the Code of Conduct for Scottish Solicitors 2002 contains such a definition.

[14] *Professional Conduct for Scottish Solicitors*, (Butterworths/Law Society of Scotland, Edinburgh, 1995) at p.62.

[15] This accords with the ABA Model Rules 2002 r.7.1 which indicates that a conflict of interest exists if the representation of one client "will be directly adverse to another client" or there is a significant risk that the representation "will be materially limited by the lawyer's responsibilities to another client ... ". Similarly, the third restatement of the law governing lawyers (American Law Institute, St Paul, 2000) para.121 indicates that "a conflict of interest is involved if there is a substantial risk that the lawyer's representation of the client would be materially and adversely affected ... by the lawyer's duties to another current client."

[16] See Hollander and Salzedo, *op. cit.* p.3 fn 3.

[17] Of course clients are quite entitled to give instructions which are against their interests in a technical legal sense, as there may well be other dimensions which the client will take into account. For example, a client may instruct a solicitor to agree to an inequitable financial settlement in a divorce action for the sake of maintaining good relations with the other spouse and the children. It is, however, of vital importance to solicitors that they should not expose themselves to a potential claim and/or complaint by having acted for both sides in negotiating the settlement.

necessary to ask the following questions (1) whether the conflict of interest concerns two separate clients of a particular solicitor,[18] (2) is the solicitor continuing to act and advise at least one of the clients and (3) does the representation and advice have a bearing on[19] the subject matter of the particular conflict or dispute."

Conflict of interest is essentially a question of the professional duties owed by a lawyer to his or her clients. These duties arise by virtue of the fiduciary relationship that exists between solicitor and client as a matter of agency law, but also through professional ethics and the law of voluntary obligations.[20] They include: duties of confidentiality, diligence, independence, integrity, competence and loyalty. Where one of these duties cannot be wholly fulfilled without compromising one or more duties that are owed to other client(s), then a conflict of interest exists. When all is said and done the critical test is "whether the solicitor can adequately discharge all duties to his or her respective clients equally".[21]

7.04 Why it matters: the consequences of acting in a conflict

It is important that lawyers avoid acting in a situation of conflict for several reasons. First (and most obviously) because to act in such a situation may involve sacrificing several of the core values. As Webster puts it:

> "A client must at all times be able to look to his solicitor to obtain advice which is independent and impartial and is seen to be so. If the same solicitor acts for both parties, each client is deprived of his right to be independently advised."[22]

Equally, acting in a conflict will prevent the solicitor pursuing the obligation of diligence zealously. It may also put the obligation of confidentiality at risk. As Megarry J. observed in *Spector v Ageda*[23]:

> "A solicitor [is] bound to put at his client's disposal not only his skill but also his knowledge so far as was relevant; and if he is unwilling to reveal his knowledge to his client, he should not act for him. What he cannot do is act for the client and at the same time withhold from him any relevant knowledge that he has."[24]

---

[18] The Tribunal accepted that it was necessary to define a "client" for the purposes of this question and in this connection applied the dictum of Lord Gifford in *Clelland v Morrison*, 1878 6 R 156 at p.169 that "employment of a firm is employment of all the partners of the firm", i.e. that a conflict existed even if it was between the clients of different partners in different branches of a firm.

[19] This formulation would suggest that the Tribunal accepts that it is not necessary for the representation to concern the same subject matter provided the two matters are reasonably related. (See para.7.05 below).

[20] The last is often brought into play through the solicitor's letter of engagement.

[21] Ryder, *op. cit.* p.61.

[22] Webster and Webster, "*Professional Ethics and Practice for Scottish Solicitors*", The Law Society of Scotland, Edinburgh, 1996, para.2.07. See also Janice H. Webster "*Professional Ethics and Practice For Scottish Solicitors*" (4th edn), Avizandum Publishing Ltd, Edinburgh, 2004 for up to date commentary.

[23] [1973] 1 Ch. 30.

[24] *Op. cit. per* Megarry at p.48.

This proposition appears to have been implicitly endorsed by the House of Lords in the case of *Hilton v Barker Booth and Eastwood.*[25] However, as the House also stressed, this duty to disclose information flatly contradicts the duty to the other client not to disclose confidential information. The effect of *Hilton* is that if a solicitor acting for two parties has confidential information regarding one client, which is of relevance to the other, he or she cannot continue to act without first obtaining the consent of the client to whom the information relates to disclose it to the other client. If such consent is not forthcoming, the solicitor must cease acting for one or both of the parties. As Lord Walker noted:

> "If a solicitor put himself in a position of having two irreconcilable duties, it was his own fault . . . As a general rule, a solicitor who had conflicting duties to two clients could not prefer one to the other. He therefore had to perform both as best he could. That might involve performing one duty to the letter of the obligation, and paying compensation for his failure to perform the other. In any case, however, the fact that he had chosen to put himself in an impossible position did not exonerate him from liability."[26]

Unfortunately, the position is more complex than this, since as we saw in Ch.6, Begg is of the view that:

> "when a law agent acts for two parties in the same transaction, neither of them is entitled to plead confidentiality in a question with the other, except as regards such communications as may have been made by each party to the agent as is his own exclusive legal adviser."[27]

This doctrine has clear dangers should a conflict of interest subsequently arise and the lawyer chooses to retain one of the clients but not the other(s). This is because the client(s) who are passed on will not appreciate being told that nothing which they have entrusted to their adviser *in the joint representation*[28] will be privileged or confidential with respect to the client whom the lawyer has retained.[29] Moreover, they are likely to feel that the loyalty obligation is also under threat. It follows that solicitors who choose to represent two or more clients in a case, for example a husband and wife, the partners in a partnership or the directors of a company, should stress the implications of the doctrine should a conflict of interest arise at a later stage. Better still, the solicitor should undertake not retain any of the parties should a conflict arise.

---

[25] [2005] UKHL 8, [2005] 1 All E.R. 651. See para.7.09.03 below.

[26] *Op. cit.* at para.41.

[27] *Op. cit.* p.319. Not only has this view been upheld in the Court of Appeal, it is also expressly endorsed in the explanatory text paras. 30–31 of ABA model rule 1.7 (2002).

[28] Anything imparted to one of the clients in a separate matter will remain confidential, though subject to the principle in *Spector v Ageda.*

[29] The doctrine has recently been endorsed in two Court of Appeal cases, *Brown v Guardian Royal Exchange* [1994] 2 Lloyd's Rep 325 and *TSB Bank v Robertt Irving & Burns* [2000] 2 All E.R. 826 with the Court holding that in the event of a subsequent dispute between the parties the waiver of privilege implied from the joint retainer continues until the emergence of a conflict of interest between them. Only communications after that date would be privileged and confidential as between the parties.

Acting in conflict of interest situations may also give rise to various practical difficulties.[30] As observed by Begg:

"Not only does the agent incur a double liability, but difficulties frequently arise with regard to delivery of deeds so prepared, the right of lien over them, and the respective responsibilities of the parties to the acts of their common agents."[31]

7.05 Sanctions for Acting in a Conflict

A wide range of sanctions can come into play if a lawyer acts in a conflict of interest.[32] Professional misconduct, unsatisfactory conduct and inadequate professional services are but the most obvious. Others include disqualification from continuing to act in a matter or in litigation. Where the conflict of interest has caused damage to a client then IPS, professional negligence,[33] breach of fiduciary duty or breach of contract may be possible.[34] Fee forfeiture is also possible—and not simply through IPS.

7.06 Agency and Fiduciary Duties

The early roots of the prohibition on acting in a conflict situation and its underlying positive obligation of loyalty, stems in significant measure from the law of agency. In 1883, Henderson Begg wrote, "A law agent ought on no account to attempt to act for parties with conflicting interests".[35] This is because the relationship which binds a solicitor to his client is one of fiduciary agency and as Paul Finn has noted, the fiduciary principle "enjoins one party to act in the interests of the other—to act selflessly and with undivided loyalty".[36] Similarly, Millett L.J. (as he then was) observed in *Bristol and West Building Society v Mothew*[37]:

"A fiduciary is someone who has undertaken to act for or on behalf of another in a particular matter in circumstances which give rise to a relationship of trust and confidence. The distinguishing obligation of a fiduciary is the obligation of loyalty. The principal is entitled to the single-minded loyalty of his fiduciary."

---

[30] See e.g. Dal Pont, *op. cit.* pp.188–189.

[31] Begg on *Law Agents* (2nd edn) p.337. In Scotland solicitors will also face the penalty of a double deductable in the hands of the master policy insurers if they are found to have acted in a conflict situation.

[32] See e.g. *Third Restatement on the Law Governing Lawyers, op. cit.* para.122 at pp.255 and 263.

[33] See Rennie, *op. cit.* para.2.18.

[34] Begg, *op. cit.* p.245 cites the modern sounding dictum of Grove J. in an 1881 decision in the Queen's Bench to the effect that an action can be "brought for negligence, breach of duty and misconduct. The terms are almost convertible, and may be applied to nearly the same kind of acts."

[35] Begg on *Law Agents* (2nd edn) p.337.

[36] See "The Fiduciary Principle" in T.G. Youdan (ed.) *Equity, Fiduciaries and Trusts* (Carswell, Toronto, 1989) at p.4. See also P. Finn, "Fiduciary Law and the Modern Commercial World" in Ewan McKendrick (ed.) *Commercial Aspects of Trusts and Fiduciary Obligations* (Clarendon Press, Oxford, 1992) at p.9. Professor Gretton in a recent essay has argued that a trustee is a *fiduciarius*, that is, one who must act in the interests of the beneficiary to the exclusion of his own. See G. Gretton, *Trusts* in K. Reid and R. Zimmermann (eds) *A History of Private Law in Scotland* Vol.1 at p.482.

[37] [1998] Ch. 1.

The loyalty obligation requires a solicitor to discharge with integrity any duties owed to his client. It entails obligations of trust and confidence,[38] and of course, requires solicitors to always act in their clients' best interests, and to represent them to the best of their abilities. The fiduciary also has an obligation to fully disclose any material information which he or she has to the client, even if this information is confidential to another client.[39] As previously discussed, a conflict of interest arises when this obligation of single minded loyalty owed to a client is compromised by a competing interest.

Historically, most of the Scottish case law on conflict of interest dates from the nineteenth century and refers to Agency rather than fiduciary duty.[40] As Begg notes[41] these cases indicate that when a law agent acts for borrower and lender or buyer and seller of heritable property, the lawyer occupies a "very delicate situation, in which more than ordinary care and circumspection are required" and in the double capacity the lawyer is liable to both clients for any failure of professional duty. Thus in *Stewart v McClure Naismith Brodie & Macfarlane*[42] a solicitor was instructed to obtain a loan for his client, and a patent was given for security. The loan was advanced by another client of the solicitor. The patent, however, was invalid. It was proved that the solicitor had known this, but failed to inform the lender. While the House of Lords, on appeal, found that there was no evidence of any wrongdoing of the solicitors,[43] it left intact the reasoning of the Inner House. Lord Shand in the Inner House commented:

> "[W]here, as here, a law agent undertakes double agency—agency for the borrower and also for the lender—he places himself in a very responsible position. I do not say that the position of acting for both parties is one in which the duties are incompatible, but I do say that the responsibility of that position is very considerable with reference to the duty to be discharged to the lender. Should any question arise, such as occurs in this case, I think it is incumbent on the agent to show that he was scrupulously careful in the discharge of his duty to the lender, because an agent who is also acting for the borrower is acting in some respects for an opposing interest, and is liable to the influence or bias which that opposing interest may create."[44]

---

[38] In Scotland the fiduciary duty of the solicitor as agent in relation to the confidences of the client is an implied term of the contract for services. As we argued in para.6.10 above, it may be that the agency/fiduciary duty to safeguard a client's confidences, is confined to not acting in a way which gives a preference to the interests of another client over those of the client. If so, it could be argued that the fiduciary duty of confidence only comes into play in a conflict of interest context where the threatened disclosure of the information favours the interests of another client over those of the client. If this analysis is correct, then confidentiality as a fiduciary duty is less extensive than confidentiality as a matter of professional ethics or confidentiality derived from the law of obligations.

[39] Of course, the fiduciary equally has a duty to the second client to treat his or her information as confidential even although the fiduciary has a duty to disclose the same information to another client with a relevant interest.

[40] Nonetheless, modern day cases are likely to be treated as breach of fiduciary duty.

[41] *Op. cit.* pp.244 and 337.

[42] (1887) 15 R. 1.

[43] This would now be incompatible with cases such as *Hilton* and *Mortgage Express v Bowerman* [1996] 2 All E.R. 836.

[44] (1886) 13 R. 1062 at pp.1092–3.

Although there were the occasional exceptions, e.g. *Oastler v Dill, Smillie & Wilson*[45] the Inner House generally took the line they had adopted in *Stewart*, namely, that it was not, in itself, a failure of professional obligation to represent borrower and lender or seller and purchaser of heritable property.[46] Thus in *Wernham v McLean Baird & Neilson* (a case where one client invested funds which were secured over the property of another client) Lord Anderson observed:

> "I am not prepared to hold that it is an act of professional negligence for a solicitor to act for both borrower and lender in a transaction of this nature. It is a matter of regular practice for solicitors to act for both parties in such a transaction. The duty of suggesting that independent advice should be sought only arises, in my opinion, in a case where there is a real conflict of interests."

This is indeed the modern position. Nevertheless, it was[47] and is accepted that where a solicitor acts for the buyer and seller of heritable property it is impossible to advise both of them as to the price to be offered since the duties involved to each party on this matter, are incompatible. The commentators[48] also agree that the common law prohibits acting for opposing parties in a litigation because their interests necessarily conflict. This is true even where the action proceeds by way of seeking guidance from the court e.g. a multiplepoinding or a special case. Thus in *Dunlop's Trustees v Farquharson*,[49] an action of multiplepoinding where the trustees and the claimants were seeking different outcomes from the court, it was held that the rule that it is improper for the same solicitors to represent parties with conflicting interests applied equally to disputes over matters of fact and to those on law such as multiplepoindings and special cases.[50]

The Scottish case law on conflict of interest leaves a number of key points unresolved.

1. Must the conflict have the potential for a material, adverse effect on one of the clients? The American Third Restatement of the Law Governing Lawyers,[51] considers that it should, for a conflict to arise. Certainly, we believe that if the law is to take account of *potential* conflict (see point 3 below), it must have a material, adverse effect on one of the clients.
2. Is the ban on acting for two parties with opposed interests open ended or is it restricted to representation in the same matter or where the two

---

[45] (1886) 14 R. 12.

[46] See D. Cusine, "Building Societies and Banks", 1986 J.L.S.S. 112.

[47] see Begg, *op. cit.* p.244 and *McPherson's trs v Watt* 5 R (HL) 9. However, Lord Shand in dissenting in the Inner House in that case, opined that it was an everyday occurrence at that time for solicitors to offer the buyer and the seller disinterested advice on the price.

[48] E.g. Begg *op. cit.* p.337; Websters *op. cit.* para.2.08; Ryder *op. cit.* p.61.

[49] 1956 S.L.T. 16.

[50] The court endorsed Begg on not acting for opposing sides in a litigation and his dictum (on p.281) that in such cases the court will set aside the proceedings and order the solicitor to meet the expenses of the abortive proceedings.

[51] *Op. cit.* para.121 at p.248.

matters are reasonably related? Lord Millett in *Bolkiah v KPMG*[52] appeared to favour the former when he stated that:

" . . . a fiduciary cannot act at the same time both for and against the same client, and his firm is in no better position. A man cannot without the consent of both clients act for one client while his partner is acting for another in then opposite interest."

However, Hollander and Salzedo,[53] have argued that this cannot be taken literally and that the approach taken by the Court of Appeal in *Marks & Spencer plc v Freshfields Bruckhaus Deringer*[54] which accepted, *obiter* that the ban on acting referred to two matters which were reasonably related was correct. Certainly, the *Freshfields* case is likely to be followed by Scottish courts. Nevertheless, we do not believe that the loyalty obligation need be so narrowly construed. It is perfectly logical to argue that a strong doctrine of loyalty would not permit a lawyer or his/her firm to act both for and against the same client at the same time, even if the matters were not reasonably related, unless the client gave their informed consent. This was evidenced by a case decided by the Council of the Law Society of Scotland in 2004. In that case a law firm acted for an individual who was suing a large corporation on an employment matter. The law firm noting that the large corporation was putting some of its other legal work out to tender, tendered for the work and was successful with their bid. The large corporation, however, insisted that the law firm withdrew from acting for the individual client who was suing them in the employment case. The Council after a sustained debate concluded that the firm was wrong to accede to this request (against the wishes of the individual client) since to do so was incompatible with their duty of loyalty to the original client.[55]

It might be argued that a strong doctrine of loyalty would be difficult to operate in a small jurisdiction such as Scotland where the number of significant corporate firms is relatively small and it is commonplace for corporate clients to spread their work amongst a number of firms. However, we believe that this is an overly-pessimistic assessment. Some corporate clients make it clear that they do not expect law firms on their panels to act against them in other matters, but others take a more pragmatic view and are prepared to consent to a law firm that is acting for them, or has recently acted for them, in an unrelated matter, to act against them. Our advice to law firms who are asked to act against an existing or recent client in an unrelated matter is as follows:

1) Check that the matter is unrelated and does not obviously entail conflicting obligations to the original and the new client, such as confidentiality. If this is not the case, do not act.

---

[52] [1999] 2 A.C. 222 at p.234.
[53] *Op. cit.* p.29ff.
[54] [2004] 1 W.L.R. 2331 at 2335.
[55] This ruling is in line with the line taken by the courts in the USA. See R. Rotunda and J. Dzienkowski, *Professional Responsibility* (ABA, Chicago, 2005/2006) at p.298.

Law, Practice and Conduct for Solicitors

2) Check that even although the first test has been satisfied, the original client does not object to the firm acting against them in the unrelated matter. This is good commercial sense[56] since the firm will wish to know how much business they are likely to lose if the original client objects to them acting.

3) Ask the original client for a waiver from the loyalty obligation. The ambit of the waiver should be spelt out since it might extend to issues of confidentiality.[57] Such a waiver would require informed consent.

Even if all three steps have been taken, it will still be necessary to be alert to an actual conflict arising from the representation even in an apparently unrelated matter, if steps taken for the new client have an adverse effect on the interests of the original client.

3. Must there be an actual conflict of interest or would (a) a serious possibility of a conflict,[58] (b) a substantial risk of a conflict,[59] (c) a likelihood of conflict,[60] or (d) "a reasonable apprehension of a potential conflict"[61] suffice? This is an important issue effecting the ambit of the ban on acting in a conflict situation. Begg speaks only of "actual conflicts" being struck at and there is little support in the case law for a common law ban on acting where there is only a potential conflict of interest.[62] The debate is whether in situations where there is a substantial or significant risk of a conflict the ban should also operate as a matter of the law of agency or fiduciary duty. Whilst there would appear to be an arguable case for such an extension,[63] not least because the 1986 Practice Rules on conflict of interest implicitly focus mainly on situations where there is a serious potential for conflict, it seems also that at present the existing case law in Scotland (as opposed to that in England) does not cover situations beyond those where an actual conflict exists. If such an extension was to be contemplated, there would seem to be merit in the North American caveat that to take account of the potential conflict it should be likely to have a material, adverse effect on one of the clients (see point one above).

4. Does the doctrine of "informed consent" permitting a solicitor to continue to act in a potential or actual conflict situation exist under the Scottish law of agency/fiduciary duty? There is nothing in Scottish case law to suggest that it does. However, since the leading case in

---

[56] Thus the process has been called checking that there is no "commercial conflict of interest" to prevent one from acting.

[57] In a jurisdiction where the legal and ethical acceptability of "chinese walls" is unsettled, a waiver from issues of confidentiality may be the safer option.

[58] Ryder *op. cit.* p.61.

[59] *Third Restatement of the Law Governing Lawyers op. cit.* para.121 at p.248.

[60] Dal Pont *op. cit.* p.190. Webster para.2.07 refers to "seems at all likely to arise".

[61] *Re Baron Investment (Holdings) Ltd* [2000] B.C.L.C. 272.

[62] Dal Pont *op. cit.* at p.183 however argues that the case law in Australia prevents lawyers from acting in any contentious matter (civil or criminal) where there is only a potential conflict of interest between the two parties' interests.

[63] As we have just seen, both Webster and Ryder indicate that in their view the Scottish common law on conflict of interest already covers situations where there is a substantial or significant risk of a conflict, without pointing to the cases which support such an analysis.

England on informed consent was decided in the Privy Council[64] it is likely to be of persuasive authority here also.[65]

5. What is the ambit of the fiduciary duty of disclosure of information? This is an area in which it has grown increasingly difficult to reconcile the competing UK cases in the last few years.[66]

Professional Ethics and Conflict of Interest 7.07

Until 1986 this area of professional ethics was governed by the common law, namely, decisions of the Court of Session and the Solicitors (Scotland) Discipline Tribunal and its predecessors.[67] It seems clear that the Tribunal was strongly influenced by Begg and by the general principles set out in the cases on conflict of interest enshrined in the law of agency/ fiduciary duty. As the Tribunal observed in 1986[68]:

"The general principle is well established that a solicitor must not represent two clients where a conflict of interest has arisen or is indeed likely to arise. The matter is so fundamental that . . . [it has] never been necessary to have the principle set down in any Practice Rule or other form of regulation and the Fiscal merely referred to the authority of Begg on Law Agents."[69]

The Tribunal endeavoured to set out what the general principle had been in a decision in 1990[70]:

"Put at its simplest, a solicitor cannot serve two masters whose interests conflict and the most obvious case is that solicitor cannot act for opposing parties in any dispute. That example refers to a situation where there are active interests to be pursued, but there are many circumstances where the wider interests of a client require to be protected. A client is entitled to a relationship of mutual trust with his solicitor and within that relationship, the client should have the understanding that he can freely give confidential information to his solicitor on the basis that the information will not be disclosed to any third party, except in relation to that client's business. It is part of the trust that the solicitor will not divulge that information to unconnected third parties or allow it to influence him when advising other clients, and accordingly the mere knowledge of a client's affairs may constitute an 'interest' which will require a solicitor to decline instructions from another client . . . It is the same element of trust that enables a client to expect that the solicitor will maintain an undivided loyalty to that client and that as part of this relationship, the solicitor will not knowingly withhold any information which may be relevant to the interests of that client."

---

[64] *Clark Boyce v Mouat* [1994] 1 A.C. 428.

[65] See para.7.09.01 below.

[66] See para.7.09.03 below.

[67] Some of the latter can be found in I. Smith and J. Barton, *Procedures and Decisions of the Scottish Solicitors' Discipline Tribunal* (T & T Clark, Edinburgh, 1995) Ch.9.

[68] See DTD 689/86.

[69] Ironically, 1986 was the year that the Practice Rule on Conflict of Interest was introduced, but its purpose was to deal with potential as opposed to actual conflicts.

[70] DTD 809/90.

7.07.01 The 1986 Practice Rules. As a result of increasing concern within the council of the Law Society of Scotland and in the profession at large about solicitors acting for different parties, particularly in conveyancing transactions[71] the Law Society determined in 1986 to augment the unwritten rules on conflict of interest with a set of Practice Rules. The Solicitors (Scotland) Practice Rules 1986 came into force on January 1, 1987. The rules are short, straightforward and have stood the test of time.

The basic principle is set out in r.3 which states:

> *"A solicitor shall not act for two or more parties whose interests conflict."*

That statement is entirely unqualified and is the guiding principle which governs the rest of the Practice Rules. While the bulk of the text of the Practice Rules applies specifically to conveyancing transactions,[72] it should be noted that r.3 applies in all areas of law. Although expressed in the singular it has, from the outset, been accepted as including firms as well as individual solicitors.[73]

7.07.02 The Code of Conduct. The r.3 principle was amplified in the Code of Conduct for Scottish Solicitors published by the Council of the Society in October 1989.[74] Article 3 of the code states:

> *"Solicitors (including firms of solicitors) shall not act for two or more clients in matters where there is a conflict of interest between the clients or for any client where there is a conflict between the interests of the client and that of the solicitor or the solicitors firm."*

The text accompanying this article indicates that:

> "In considering whether or not to accept instructions from more than one party and where there is potential for a conflict arising at a later date, solicitors must have regard to any possible risk of breaches of confidentiality and impairment of independence . . . Where a solicitor is requested to act for more than one party in respect of the same matter, the solicitor must be reasonably satisfied that there is no apparent conflict among the interests of all the parties."

---

[71] Acting for both sides in a conveyancing transaction was not uncommon in Scotland, particularly in rural areas, prior to the 1986 Practice Rules. Thus a survey conducted for the Hughes Royal Commission on Legal Services in Scotland (HMSO, 1980, Cmnd 7846. Vol.II p.620) found that the same solicitor acted for the buyer and seller in 18% of conveyancing transactions relating to houses at that time. The society's decision to act was also influenced by a desire to forestall the then Government's interest in eroding the conveyancing monopoly.

[72] See para.7.15 below.

[73] This echoes the common law principle laid down in *Clelland v Morrison* (1878) 6 R. 156 that "Employment of a firm is employment of all the partners of the firm".

[74] The code has been amended from time to time since 1989 but the wording of this fundamental aspect remains unchanged. See Appendix 1.

Potential Conflicts of Interest. Commentators on conflict of interest gen- **7.07.03**
erally draw a distinction between an actual conflict of interest between parties
and a potential conflict of interest. However, the distinction can obscure as
much as it reveals. As the Discipline Tribunal has observed[75]:

> "the phrase 'potential conflict' is habitually used in relation to any
> situation where the two clients have a common interest and consequently
> the use of the word 'potential' can obscure the true situation at any
> particular stage."

In fact the phrase "potential conflict" covers a spectrum of situations from
common interest representations where the potential for conflict may be quite
remote to those where there is a distinct likelihood or very serious risk of a
conflict arising. The former probably occur more frequently than the latter but
a solicitor must remain alert to the risk in any common interest representation
in case the potential conflict turns into an actual conflict. In fact, many
jurisdictions take cognisance of the spectrum which is "potential conflict" and
hold that it is inappropriate for a lawyer to act not only where there is an actual
conflict but also where the potential for conflict is a significant one, i.e. there
is a substantial or significant risk of a conflict arising.[76]

The position in Scotland is not entirely clear. The principal authorities:
Begg on *Law Agents*, r.3 of the 1986 Practice Rules, and art.3 of the Code of
Conduct refer only to situations of actual conflict. However, the Discipline
Tribunal in setting out the basic principle of conflict of interest has included
reference to situations where conflicts "were likely to arise" as well as actual
conflicts.[77] Moreover, the text accompanying art.3 of the Code,[78] seems to
suggest, at least as an aspiration, that a solicitor should not act where the
potential for conflict is one which would pose significant risks to the duties of
confidentiality and independence. Webster and Ryder also take this view. The
position is made more complex by the bulk of the 1986 Practice Rules.
Effectively, what these rules do is to lay down a series of situations, almost all
confined to the field of conveyancing, where no actual conflict need exist, but
where, unless certain exceptions apply, the potential for a conflict arising is
deemed to be so significant that the solicitor is prevented from acting. While
it might be argued that the 1986 Practice Rules have replaced the common law
on conflicts of interest, the fact that the great bulk of the situations of
"vulnerability"[79] or "potential conflict" set out in the rules are restricted to a
relatively narrow area suggests that such an interpretation of the 1986 Practice
Rules should be rejected. Further support for this conclusion comes from the
fact that art.2 of the Code of Conduct for Criminal Work in stating that:

---

[75] Scottish Solicitors' Discipline Tribunal Annual Report 1989, p.3.

[76] See e.g. ABA Model Rules 2002, r.1.7(2); New Zealand Rules of Professional Conduct for
Barristers and Solicitors r.1.07; English Law Society Guide to Professional Conduct para.15.01 "a
significant risk"; Ontario Rules of Professional Conduct 1994, r.5 "likely to be a conflicting
interest".

[77] See e.g. DTD 689/86 and DTD 565/82 "possibility of a conflict".

[78] Which is set out in previous paragraph.

[79] Scottish Solicitors' Discipline Tribunal Annual Report 1995, p.5 "the essential element of
the provision of the 1986 Practice Rules is to ensure that a solicitor does not act in a situation in
which he might be particularly vulnerable".

> *"A solicitor should not accept instructions from more than one accused in the same matter."*[80]

This effectively adopts the same approach as the 1986 Rules by identifying a situation where the potential for conflict was so great that a ban on acting was introduced. In short, although the position cannot be said to be entirely clear cut in Scotland, it is submitted that the better position is that in terms of professional ethics in Scotland, a solicitor should not act, not only in situations of actual conflict but also in situations where there is a substantial or a significant risk of a conflict and breach of duty, arising.[81] Self preservation and self interest also pull towards the same conclusion, especially if consideration is given to the client's perception of matters. If the firm are acting for more than one party in a matter all the affected clients should be advised so that they can make an informed decision on whether to continue instructing that firm. If one of the clients is ultimately less successful in the matter than they had hoped or expected to be, they may well feel that the firm could have done more for them if it had not been acting for the other party as well. Not only could this affect the future flow of business, it could lead to a complaint or a claim. The moral is clear. If in doubt, do not act.

7.08 Imputed Disqualification

In *Clelland v Morrison*,[82] Lord Gifford observed that, *"Employment of a firm is employment of all the partners of the firm"*. The Discipline Tribunal has adopted that dictum in several decisions as reflecting the accepted principle that the clients of one partner in a firm are clients of the firm and that clients of the firm are clients of each and every partner in that firm.[83] In relation to simultaneous conflicts of interest that means that if one solicitor in a firm is prevented from acting due to a conflict of interest, the whole firm is so prevented, both under the law of agency/fiduciary duty and professional ethics. This is what is known as "imputed disqualification" and the doctrine exists in most English speaking jurisdictions.[84] It is based both on principle— that clients "belong" to firms not partners[85] and on pragmatism—the knowledge that lawyers do not practise like hermits, that they frequently brainstorm with one another about difficult cases and that confidentiality of files is remarkably difficult to attain within busy offices, though easier to insist on with respect to the outside world. Literally applied in the modern era of global legal offices the doctrine of imputed disqualification is capable of causing severe problems—especially if the focus shifts to imputed knowledge and the duty of disclosure. The ambit of the fiduciary duty of disclosure is

---

[80] See para.7.17 for further discussion of conflict of interest in criminal matters.

[81] Although we have no doubts as to what the ethical position should be, given the disagreement amongst the authorities, we believe that clarification would be desirable.

[82] 1878 6 R 156.

[83] DTD 689/86.

[84] See e.g. the USA MR 2002 1.10; New Zealand and Australia, Dal Ponte, *op. cit.* pp.181–183.

[85] Although clients may well consider that they have a contract with their lawyer (as well as an ethical relationship) they will also have a principal contract with the firm. In the end of the day it is the firm that receives the fee from the client and which will bear the primary responsibility if the client sues for breach of contract or professional negligence. That said the advent of limited liability partnerships may be changing the respective liabilities of firms and partners.

problematic enough as we have seen, without adding in a doctrine of imputed knowledge which would deem a London partner to have all the knowledge his or her Hong Kong partners. It would be equally problematic if the imputed disqualification of a partner or associate was to be carried with them if they joined another firm—rather like a contagious disease. Fortunately, pragmatic considerations have tempered such excesses, in the interests of lawyer mobility and the business community.[86] However, the ambit of the doctrine in professional ethics in Scotland is unclear. Hitherto, the Discipline Tribunal has been unmoved by the pragmatism argument[87]:

> "It is accepted that in some of the larger firms or in firms where there is more than one place of business, the de facto relationship between individual clients and other partners may be non-existent but nevertheless there remains a communal interest among the partners as a whole in relation to each and every client to the firm."

Although there are no recent Discipline Tribunal cases it is suggested that imputed disqualification should apply in simultaneous conflict cases, but that where a partner or associate moves to a new firm, that firm should only be disqualified from acting in a conflict situation on the basis of the actual knowledge of the partner or associate.

Avoiding or Alleviating Conflicts of Interest—General 7.09

One option might appear to be to simply decline to act for two or more parties in the same matter. However, as indicated in para.7.02 to insist that all directors in a company, all partners in a partnership and all husbands and wives are separately represented in all transactions or that all clients in remote areas must employ different law firms would create substantial access problems. Moreover, such a broad brush approach would still not resolve the problem since it is not always easy, especially in large law firms to detect that one is being asked to act against a second party who is already the client of another solicitor in the firm. For this reason it is vital that all firms, particularly large firms with multiple branches, have thorough systems in place to check for conflict of interest at the earliest possible stage of a matter. Adequate, up to date and accessible records are essential.

Solicitors should remember that the general prohibition in r.3 of the Practice Rules is absolute, and it will not be an adequate defence to a complaint that the individual solicitor did not know that someone else in the firm was acting for the other party. It is far easier to say to a client at the outset that you are unable to act for them because of a conflict of interest with other clients than to inform them after you have commenced acting that they will have to go elsewhere. This will almost certainly incur further, and unnecessary, expense to the clients, while new agents familiarise themselves with the matter. In all probability, in such a situation the firm will have become privy to confidential information, or which the clients regard as confidential,[88] which may mean

---

[86] See e.g. R. Rotunda and J. Dzienkowski, *Professional Responsibility* (ABA, Chicago, 2005) Ch.1.10.

[87] DTD 689/86; the principle was repeated in the Scottish Solicitors' Discipline Tribunal Annual Report 1987.

[88] See para.7.04 above for Begg's argument that confidentiality is limited in situations of joint representation.

that both clients have to be advised to seek separate independent advice. In
many cases, the matter may become the subject of a complaint to the Society
involving the firm in protracted unremunerative correspondence, as well as
possible findings of IPS, unsatisfactory conduct or even professional misconduct. As the saying goes, prevention is better than cure.

7.09.01 **Avoiding or Alleviating Conflicts of Interest—Consent.** In a large part of
the common law world the limitations imposed by the doctrine of conflict of
interest, especially in its broader versions which ban acting if there is a even
a likelihood of a conflict arising, can be partially alleviated through the use of
the concept of "informed consent". This is true both in relation to the law of
agency/fiduciary duty and to professional ethics.[89] As in other areas the
overlap between agency and professional ethics varies between jurisdictions.
Not for the first time the lead has come from courts and commentators in the
USA who have elaborated at some length on the parameters and limitations to
the doctrine of "informed consent". In England and Wales, and possibly
Scotland, the leading authority on the issue in the field of agency/fiduciary
duty is a Privy Council case originating from New Zealand, *Clark Boyce v
Mouat.*[90] The case involved a New Zealand business man who wished to
obtain a loan for his business. Since his own house was already fully
mortgaged, he persuaded his 72 year old mother to mortgage her home in
security for the loan, with the son being responsible for the mortgage.
Unknown to the mother, the son's usual solicitor (who was also a family
friend) had declined to act for both mother and son under the circumstances.
The son then approached the appellant solicitors' firm. The firm indicated to
the mother that she should be independently advised on the matter because she
would be the principal debtor rather than a mere guarantor. As such, she might
lose her home if her son failed to pay. The mother declined and signed a letter
at the firm's request confirming that they had advised her to be independently
advised because of the conflict of interest and she had refused. As the trial
judge subsequently held, she was aware of the financial risk that she ran and
was not seeking advice on the wisdom of the transaction. All she wished from
the lawyers was for them to complete the necessary paperwork to make the
security valid. She was, therefore, akin to an "execution only" client. The
son's business failed and he went bankrupt leaving his mother to pay the
mortgage. She sued the appellants for breach of contract, negligence and
breach of fiduciary duty in failing to refuse to act for her and insufficiently
safeguarding her interests.

   On giving judgement for the solicitor appellants in the Privy Council, Lord
Jauncey stated that:

> "There is no general rule of law to the effect that a solicitor should never
> act for both parties in a transaction where their interests may conflict.
> Rather is the position that he may act provided that he has obtained the
> informed consent of both to his acting. Informed consent means consent
> given in the knowledge that there is a conflict between the parties and

---

[89] See e.g. *The Third Restatement of the Law Governing Lawyers, op. cit.*, para.122; ABA
Model Rules 2002 Rule 1.7(b); Dal Pont, *op. cit.* pp.190–191.
   [90] [1994] 1 A.C. 428 As a Privy Council case, the decision is of persuasive authority in
Scotland.

that as a result the solicitor may be disabled from disclosing to each party the full knowledge which he possesses as to the transaction or may be disabled from giving advice to one party which conflicts with the interests of the other. If the parties are content to proceed upon that basis, the solicitor may properly act."

Lord Jauncey went on to quote the earlier case of *Boulting v Association of Cinematograph Television and Allied Technicians*[91]:

" . . . The client is entitled to the services of his solicitor who . . . must not put himself into a position where he may owe conflicting duties to different clients . . . . But the person entitled to the benefit of the rule may relax it, provided he is of full age and sui juris and fully understands not only what he is doing but also what his legal rights are and that he is in part surrendering them."[92]

In conclusion, Lord Jauncey observed that:

"When a client in full command of his faculties and apparently aware of what he is doing seeks the assistance of a solicitor in the carrying out of a particular transaction, that solicitor is under no duty whether before or after accepting instructions to go beyond those instructions by proffering unsought advice on the wisdom of the transaction."

Clark Boyce left a number of significant issues unresolved. Were there any limitations as to when the doctrine of "informed consent" could be invoked?[93] What steps must the lawyer take to ensure that the client fully understands the situation and the potential consequences of giving consent? What precisely is the client consenting to? To what extent can a client agree to receiving a "limited purpose" service from a lawyer? As to the first, the jurisprudence from the USA and the *Third Restatement of the Law Governing Lawyers*[94] in particular, provides a guide as to potential limitations e.g. informed consent cannot cover opposing parties to a litigation, unfortunately Lord Jauncey's opinion appears to provide something of a blanket imprematur to informed consent without setting limits to its operation. Client understanding is another difficult area. What will suffice for streetwise, sophisticated corporate clients may not be enough for a small businessperson. Thus in *Serving Two Masters*, Janine Griffiths-Baker notes:

"In some cases it may not be easy to establish informed consent. There is a considerable difference between the consent of a large corporate

---

[91] [1963] 2 Q.B. 606.

[92] *ibid.* as *per* Upjohn L.J. at 636. Lord Jauncey also quoted from Richardson J. in *Farrington v Rowe McBride & Partners* [1985] N.Z.L.R. 83 at p.90: "If there is a conflict in [a solicitor's] responsibilities to one or both [clients whose interests conflict] he must ensure that he fully discloses the material facts to both clients and obtains their informed consent to this so acting . . . and there will be some circumstances in which it is impossible, notwithstanding such disclosure, for any solicitor to act fairly and adequately for both."

[93] One limitation to *Clark Boyce* to emerge from subsequent cases is that the rule on informed consent may not apply in a situation where there is a significant risk of undue influence, *Royal Bank of Scotland v Etridge (No.2)* [2002] 2 A.C. 773. It is likely that the findings in *Etridge* will be followed in Scotland. See Ch.11 below for a review of the *Etridge* case.

[94] *Op. cit.* para.122.

client with its own legal department and that of a lay person wishing to set up in business for the first time."[95]

Indeed this argument is sometimes run to justify allowing a differential rule on consent and conflicts as between large businesses (who can be assumed to be able to look after themselves) and individuals (who cannot). However, even in the case of corporate clients, informed consent may not be entirely freely given:

> "I suppose you could say that the firm had fully informed consent as when the conflict was discovered they obviously asked the other acquiring company and us whether we were prepared to accept the conflict. Because we were so far down the line with the deal, neither of us had much choice."[96]

This, in turn, raises further questions about when informed consent must be obtained. Should it be obtained at an early stage when there is only a potential conflict or can it be left until a conflict actually arises? Client protection would seem to argue for the former, whilst case law and practice suggests that sometimes the consent is not sought until there is an actual dispute. Clearly there is less danger in consenting to the lawyer representing more than one client whose interests only potentially conflict than where their interests are in active conflict. It follows that the onus on the lawyer to ensure that the client is fully informed of the risks that he or she is consenting to will be greater in the second situation than the first. Indeed in some jurisdictions informed consent is only effective with potential conflicts but not with actual conflicts, for just this reason.

This brings us to the question of what the client is consenting to. Is it to a watering down of the duties of loyalty, including those of diligence and confidentiality? If so, how far can this go and is it understood that each client will suffer the same degree of reduced protection? We will return to this below when discussing limited purpose representation, however, not the least disconcerting aspect of *Clark Boyce* is that it does not really address such issues. Lord Jauncey implies that what the client is consenting to is a reduction in the duty of disclosure set out in *Spector v Ageda*[97] and that this applies equally to all clients. Similarly each client is agreeing to their lawyer not giving them advice which conflicts with the interests of the other client(s). This amounts to a reduction in the duties of diligence and of loyalty but not the duty of confidentiality.[98] However there is no guarantee that these reductions will impact evenly between each of the clients. Again it is unclear how far the reduction in protection can go. In the USA informed consent only

---

[95] Janine Griffiths-Baker, *Serving Two Masters*, (Hart Publishing, Oxford, 2002), at p.46.

[96] Janine Griffiths-Baker, *ibid.*, p.158. The book contains quotes from clients of solicitors who have acted in conflict of interest situations. This client described what happened when the law firm his company had instructed in respect of a management buy out discovered that the firm was also acting for a rival company.

[97] [1973] 1 Ch. 30. See para.7.04 above.

[98] Ironically, as Begg argued, (see para.6.20 above) joint representation entails the clients by implication agreeing to there being no confidentiality or privilege in matters covered by the joint representation.

operates if the lawyer "reasonably believes that the lawyer will be able to provide competent and diligent representation to each affected client".[99] In quoting with approval from Richardson J. in *Farrington* Lord Jauncey appears to be insisting that despite the informed consent each party must still receive a fair and adequate service. It is submitted that this must be the case, otherwise, informed consent could be used to evade the statutory requirement that a solicitor provides an "adequate professional service".[1]

Finally, how far should the law restrict the client's ability to accept a "limited purpose" service from his or her lawyer? As Ryder argues in relation to *Clark Boyce*:

> "While it might be correct that a solicitor can continue to act with informed consent, it would be most unusual for the parties to agree that the solicitor is disabled from giving advice. Most clients and indeed most solicitors would see it as an essential part of their duty to the client to give advice."[2]

On the one hand the courts have shied away from imposing a duty on solicitors to proffer advice on the wisdom, in business terms, of their clients entering into particular contracts, especially where, as in *Clark Boyce* the client has indicated that she does not wish to receive such advice. This would have the effect of making them unpaid insurers for business risks run by their clients. Moreover, the concept of the "execution-only" client is not unknown in Scotland, for example where the parties have already reached a binding agreement. However, the concept of a lawyer acting as a "mere technician" runs against the notion of the Scottish solicitor as a "general person of business" and undermines the solicitor's status as a professional. Another way of putting this point is that there is an ongoing debate as to the wisdom or ethical propriety of acting as a "limited purpose lawyer". Of course, if the client is a sophisticated business organisation which is happy to restrict its instructions to an "execution only" basis in its letter of retainer, then there may be little harm in accepting that the fiduciary and ethical duties owed to such client may be limited. However, if the client who is to receive the limited service is less streetwise, as Mrs Mouat was, it is imperative that the client is warned at the outset that this is the position, and what it entails. This is particularly important where the lawyer is acting for two clients and treats one as a limited purpose client, since that client's interests will be subordinated to those of the "full" client. Once again, this illustrates the importance of setting out clearly the terms of retainer for the solicitor—client relationship. Where a solicitor is representing more than one client and regards one as the "full" client, then in seeking the informed consent from the "limited purpose" client the solicitor must make it absolutely clear that his or her vigour and diligence will be greater for the full client than the "limited purpose" client and that in

---

[99] Model Rule 1.7(b)(1), 2002 and *Third Restatement of the Law Governing Lawyers, op. cit.* para.122(2)(c).

[1] On the issue of clients contracting out of ethical obligations generally, see para.4.05 above. On IPS see Ch.1 above.

[2] Ryder, *op. cit.* at p.63.

the event of a conflict arising he or she may seek to remain acting for the "full" client.

In an era where professionalism has been re-negotiated with greater empowerment for clients,[3] assessing the limits to informed consent turns on the balance to be drawn between paternalism and client autonomy. Certainly, the courts have been more willing to impose the duty to advise on the business aspect of a transaction where the client is inexperienced or where the solicitor has special expertise on which the client is relying.[4] As we will see in the next chapter, in the realm of professional ethics informed consent without independent advice cannot be used to overcome conflicts between the client and the solicitor. What *Clark Boyce* has left unclear, at least in the field of agency/fiduciary duty, is the limits to the efficacy of informed consent as a defence to inter client conflict.

7.09.02 Ethics and Consent. Whilst it can be argued that informed consent is a way of successfully avoiding certain conflicts of interest under the Scots law of agency, it is important to note that the doctrine of informed consent plays no role in relation to professional ethics in Scotland. Although there are common law countries where consent is a defence in professional ethics as well as agency cases[5] and although England and Wales are seeking to amend their ethical rules to allow a role for "informed consent" in conflict cases,[6] there is nothing in the Code, or, more significantly, in the 1986 Practice Rules which allows informed consent to overcome the ban on acting in an actual conflict of interest.[7] It follows that *Clark Boyce v Mouat*, at least in Scotland, does not extend beyond the law of agency into the realms of professional ethics, which may be no bad thing, given the uncertainties thrown up by that case.

7.09.03 Avoiding or Alleviating Conflicts of Interest—Disclosure. *Clark Boyce v Mouat* raised a further point which has given rise to a considerable amount of litigation both in Scotland and England. It relates to disclosure. Informed consent is predicated on the consent being fully informed. It is not open to a solicitor to withhold key information from a client while at the same time claiming to rely on informed consent as a defence to any conflict of interest. As we saw in para.7.04 above, in *Spector v Ageda*[8] it was held that:

---

[3] See A. Paterson, "Professionalism and the Legal Services Market" 3 (1996) *International Journal of the Legal Profession* 137.

[4] Wilkinson, (1995) N.L.J. October 27, p.1588.

[5] New Zealand, Northern Territory, Queensland, Southern Australia and Western Australia all require the prior informed consent of the parties if a lawyer proposes to represent more than party in matter. See Dal Pont, *op. cit.* at pp.196–7. See also in the USA the ABA Model Rules 2002 r.1.7.

[6] The reforms, however, were held back by the Legal Services Consultative Panel who advised the Lord Chancellor in June 2005 that the proposals lacked (a) a general enough definition of conflict of interest and (b) sufficiently robust safeguards in relation to informed consent. See *www.dca.gov.uk/atoj/lscp*.

[7] It might be argued that in a jurisdiction such as Scotland where the ban on acting stresses actual rather than potential conflicts, there is less need for informed consent to alleviate hardship caused by the ban. Interestingly, r.5 of the 1986 Practice Rules allows consent (though it is not required to be informed) in certain defined circumstances, to permit a solicitor to act in a situation where there is a considerable *potential for conflict*, so long as the solicitor reasonably believes that there is no likelihood of a dispute actually arising between the parties.

[8] [1973] 1 Ch. 30.

"A solicitor [is] bound to put at his client's disposal not only his skill but also his knowledge so far as was relevant; and if he is unwilling to reveal his knowledge to his client, he should not act for him."[9]

Thus in *Mortgage Express Ltd v Bowerman & Partners*,[10] the Court of Appeal held, in distinguishing the *Mouat* case, that a solicitor acting for a lender and the borrower in the purchase of a property who comes into information which might have a material bearing on the potential security (for example, that the valuation of the property obtained for the purpose of the loan is excessive), must pass this information to the lender. Only in this way could the lender reach an informed decision. However, the court observed that if the material information was confidential to the borrower then the solicitor must either obtain the borrower's consent to disclose the information, or decline to act for the lender, or for both parties.

This case was followed by a series of cases[11] placing limits on the duty of disclosure either by the terms of the retainer, or by distinguishing material information on the borrower's creditworthiness (which need not be disclosed) from a threat to the value of the security (the latter could include the impending bankruptcy of the borrower or potential mortgage fraud). These cases, which were mirrored in Scotland, as we will see below, have clouded the issue as to the ambit and application for the fiduciary duty of disclosure. At one extreme is the *Spector v Ageda* argument that a solicitor may not hold back relevant information which he or she has (however and whenever acquired) unless it is confidential (in which case he must get the client's permission to disclose it, or cease to act). At the other is the view that the solicitor's fiduciary duty is tempered by the terms of the retainer which may, possibly by implication, permit the solicitor not to disclose much relevant information that he or she has.[12] Some, but far from all of the inconsistencies between the cases have been resolved by the House of Lords decision in *Hilton v Barker Booth and Eastwood*.[13] There a solicitor had acted for both parties in a transaction to purchase flats which were to be built by the selling party. The solicitors had previously represented the purchaser in criminal proceedings for fraud in which he had been convicted and sentenced to nine months imprisonment. The solicitor held out the purchaser as person of substance by his actings, including paying the £25,000 deposit in the transaction which the seller assumed had come from the purchaser. The purchaser failed to complete the purchase and the seller had to dispose of the flats at a loss. They then sued the solicitors for not revealing the risks which they were running in entering into a contract with the purchaser, because of his criminal conviction. The Court of Appeal concluded that the solicitors should have declined to act for the seller because of a conflict of interest caused by their prior knowledge about the purchaser, but that they had been correct to

---

[9] *Op. cit. per* Megarry J. at 48.
[10] [1996] 2 All E.R. 836.
[11] E.g. *Bristol & West Building Society v May May & Merrimans and Others* [1996] 2 All E.R. 801; Halpern and Peacocke (1997) NLJ June 27, 967; *National Home Loans Corporation plc v Giffen Couch & Archer* 1998 1 W.L.R. 207; *Mortgage Funding Corp plc v Tisdall Nelson Nari & Co* [1998] PNLR 81.
[12] See e.g. *Kelly v Cooper* [1993] A.C. 205.
[13] [2005] UKHL 8; [2005] 1 All E.R. 651.

conclude that they had no duty to communicate what they knew about the purchaser to the seller, because it was confidential information.

The Court of Appeal deduced four propositions from the English cases:

1. A solicitor's duty of disclosure depended on the nature and terms of his retainer;
2. A solicitor was under no obligation (quite the reverse) to disclose to a later client confidential information obtained under an earlier retainer from a former client;
3. If a solicitor acted for more than one party to a transaction then he might be obliged to disclose information obtained in that transaction from one of them to the other;
4. In that event he could not excuse his breach of duty to either of them by reference to the duty he owed to the other.

Although, on appeal, the House of Lords unanimously overruled the Court of Appeal decision, they did not depart from the four propositions of the lower court, determining the matter on other grounds. As they indicated, in this case although the information which the law firm possessed as to the client who had been convicted of fraud was in the public domain and therefore not confidential, their duty to act in his best interests prevented them from sharing their knowledge as to his criminal record with the other client.[14] Where the House really departed from the Court of Appeal was in concluding that the firm's duty to safeguard the fraudster client's interests did not justify them in failing to reveal his record to the selling client as a part of their duty of disclosure and to act in the best interests of the selling client. Thus their breach of duty was not merely in failing to send the seller away to be independently advised (which would have attracted minimal damages) but failing to reveal the fraudster's criminal record which might have saved the selling client from ruin, and thus attracted much greater damages. The equities of the case would appear to account for the House insisting that the firm had to fulfil its duties to both clients even where this was impossible, by upholding one set of duties and paying damages for not upholding the other.

Following *Hilton*, the position on disclosure in England both under the law of agency/fiduciary duty and in terms of professional ethics would appear to be as follows:

1. Where solicitors act for two or more parties and have information regarding one client, which would be of relevance to the other, irrespective of whether it is confidential or discreditable in nature, they are under an obligation to disclose the information to the other client. However, before disclosing such confidential or discreditable information they must get the consent of the client to whom it relates to the disclosure.
2. If the consent to disclosure is not forthcoming, the solicitor must cease acting for the other client, or for both clients.
3. If the client does consent to the disclosure of the information, the solicitor may make the disclosure and continue to act for both

---

[14] In Scotland, at least, as we saw in Ch.6, it is accepted that even although a matter is known to some in the community, the client is entitled to insist that it be treated as confidential as far as those unaware of the matter are concerned.

parties if there is informed consent to his so doing, and the solicitor can act fairly and adequately for both parties.

Lord Walker referred to the dictum of Richardson J in *Farrington v Rowe McBride and Partners*[15]:

> "A solicitor's loyalty to his client must be undivided. He cannot properly discharge his duties to one whose interests are in opposition to those of another client. If there is a conflict in his responsibilities to one or both he must ensure that he fully discloses the material facts to both clients and obtains their informed consent to his so acting ... And there will be some circumstances in which it is impossible, notwithstanding such disclosure, for any solicitor to act fairly and adequately for both."

The agency/fiduciary duty case law in Scotland is less developed than in England, but runs along very similar lines. Thus the points raised by *Mortgage Express Ltd v Bowerman & Partners* appear in the Scottish Inner House decision of *Bank of East Asia Ltd v Shepherd & Wedderburn WS*.[16] The court held that:

> "If a solicitor is instructed by a potential lender simply to prepare a security document for signature by the borrower those instructions do not impose upon him any duty to inquire into and advise about the underlying or future value of the security.[17] On the other hand, if the solicitor is already acting for the potential borrower and by reason of so acting is in possession of information of which the potential lender is ignorant, being information which shows or tends to show the security which has been instructed to prepare is valueless or of significantly less value that the potential lender appears to think, then, if he accepts the potential lender's instructions, he may well, before acting upon the instructions, require to advise the potential lender of the risk of which he is aware. We see no reason, if the circumstances were to give rise to such a duty, to conclude that it would be any less incumbent simply because the potential lender was aware that the solicitor as already acting for the potential borrower."

This case has been followed by *Bristol & West Building Society v Aitken Nairn WS*.[18] Here the pursuers, a building society, advanced a loan to a Mr Newell who was the holder of a barony title. Security for the loan was taken over Freswick Castle. The building society took into account the value of the barony title when evaluating the security, however this information was not passed on to the defenders. The defenders were the solicitors instructed to draft the standard security. Prior to the security being taken the same solicitors had conveyed the barony title to a third party. When Mr Newell failed to

---

[15] [1985] 1 N.Z.L.R. 83 at p.90.

[16] 1995 S.L.T. 1074.

[17] However, it is submitted that the solicitor in this situation might be liable in negligence if he or she failed to inform the lender if an examination of the title revealed that the loan formed part of a "back to back transaction" in which the valuation of the property may have been fraudulently inflated. See *Solicitors Negligence*, 1996 J.L.S.S. 132.

[18] 1999 S.C. 678.

maintain the loan repayments the castle was sold at a loss. The pursuers blamed the defenders for this because the latter had disposed of the barony title and thus reduced the value of the pursuers' security, in breach of their duties to the pursuers under *Bank of East Asia v Shepherd and Wedderburn WS*.

The Temporary Judge (T.G. Coutts Q.C.) held that the action failed. The court considered it crucial to identify what the defenders had been instructed to do. They had not been informed of the unusual features of the transaction involving the barony title and the court held that the defenders' only duty was to obtain good security for the pursuers. In his judgement, the Temporary Judge observed:

> "In my option it is no part of a solicitor's duty towards his client to second guess the knowledge which the client might possess, nor has he any duty to undertake any matter which he is not instructed to do. Instructions require to be express ... There is no general duty on a solicitor to promote the interests of their client outwith the instructions he has been given; see National Home Loans. However, if a solicitor by reason of his acting for the potential borrower is in possession of information of which the potential lender is ignorant, information which shows or tends to show that the security which he has been instructed to prepare was valueless or significantly less valuable than the potential lender appears to think, then there may be a duty to advise the potential lender of the risk."

However, in this case, he concluded that the solicitor's dealings with the barony title were quite reasonable and that if the building society considered that the barony title enhanced the value of the security subjects they should have told the solicitor.

The Inner House, on appeal, agreed with the Temporary Judge's statement of the law but concluded that the pursers and reclaimers (the lenders) had a case for proof that they were unaware of a matter (the transfer of the barony title) which no reasonable solicitor could have believed was of no significance to them.

The *Bank of East Asia* case was also followed in *Leeds & Holbeck Building Society v Alex Morrison & Co.*[19] In it, the Outer House judge (Lady Paton) held that even where facts relevant to the value of the security do come to the solicitor's attention, the decision whether the matter is material or of significance to the lender is for the solicitor, unless the lenders' instructions stipulate otherwise,[20] in the exercise of his professional judgement informed by such commercial expertise as he possesses.

While the ruling in these cases is broadly consistent with the English cases, they have left unresolved the issue of how to act if the information is confidential to the borrower. While it is true, as Begg notes[21] that where a

---

[19] 2001 S.C.L.R. 41.

[20] In *Newcastle Building Society v Paterson, Robertson & Graham*, 2001 S.C. 734 Lord Reed indicated that where a law firm acts for a building society and a borrower, a failure to comply with an express term of the loan conditions by the firm (in this case confirming that the borrowers retained no interest in any additional property) could give rise to an action for breach of duty.

[21] See paras 6.18 and 7.04 above.

lawyer acts for two parties in a transaction there is no confidentiality as between the two clients in relation to that transaction, this does not apply to matters divulged to the lawyer by one client prior to the joint representation or on a separate matter from the joint representation. Nor does it meet the point that disclosure will be seen by the affected client as a betrayal and a breach of the loyalty obligation to that client. It is submitted that the Scottish courts and indeed the Discipline Tribunal should follow the lead from *Hilton* and the related English cases on this matter. This would mean that if a borrower tells the solicitor something material to the transaction e.g. that he intends to breach the terms of the mortgage offer by letting the premises to a tenant, which the solicitor ought to disclose to the lender, a conflict arises if the borrower objects to the confidential information being disclosed. Since the solicitor's duty of disclosure to the lender continues the solicitor must cease to act for the lender or for both parties.[22]

Avoiding or Alleviating Conflicts of Interest: Forewarning the Client. 7.09.04
Where a solicitor opts to represent two or more parties with potentially conflicting interests, but the potential is not so significant as to warrant/require declining to act, the drawbacks which would arise were a conflict subsequently to emerge can be alleviated or mitigated by forewarning the clients at the outset. At a minimum this should include advising the clients at the earliest practicable opportunity that if a dispute arises, the likelihood is that the solicitor will have to cease acting for both or all of the clients. The solicitor may indicate that if this would result in a significant disadvantage to one of the parties, and there would be no concomitant disadvantage to the other client(s) by so acting e.g. a danger of a breach of confidentiality, the solicitor may exceptionally continue to act for one party.[23] In order to avoid misunderstandings or allegations of a breach of the fiduciary duty of loyalty or confidentiality, the solicitor should also advise the clients at the outset that if a conflict arises neither or none of the clients will be entitled to plead confidentiality or privilege in a question with the other, for information imparted to the lawyer in the joint representation before the conflict arises, except for communications made by each party to the solicitor as his or her exclusive lawyer.

Avoiding or alleviating conflicts of interest—Obtaining a Waiver. The 7.09.05
1986 Practice Rules, as is the case with other Practice Rules, allow solicitors to apply for a waiver in respect of particular circumstances covered by the rules. Theoretically, therefore it would be possible for solicitors to apply to the Professional Practice Committee of the Law Society for a waiver of r.3 which bans acting in a conflict of interest situation. Despite this, since the rules came into force the committee has never granted a waiver in respect of r.3. As we will see later, waivers have been sought and granted for other parts of the rules, particularly r.5 which relates to situations where there is a significant or substantial potential for conflict.

---

[22] See also on this F. Silverman, *"The Law Society's Conveyancing Handbook 1994"* (3rd edn.) A.11. Cited with approval in *Halifax Mortgage Services v Stepsky* [1996] Ch 1. For a useful article which reaches broadly similar conclusions on the English and Scots law in this area see R. Rennie, *"Negligence and the Duty to Disclose"* (1997) J.L.S.S. 405.

[23] See the text accompanying art.3 of the Code of Conduct for Scottish Solicitors 2002.

7.09.06 Avoiding or Alleviating Conflicts of Interest—Reaching Agreement. A final method of avoiding conflict is to reach agreement prior to the joint acting. An example can be found in the Practice Guideline on Acting for Separated Spouses.[24] By reaching a binding written agreement on the distribution of the free proceeds of the sale of the matrimonial property, in advance of the sale, the parties tie their hands from trying to require the lawyer to act for one of them against the other.

7.10 What to do if a Conflict Arises

If a conflict of interest emerges in the middle of a matter where the same firm are acting for different parties, the solicitors must take immediate steps to cease acting for at least one of the parties, and normally for both.[25] The departing client(s) must also be advised, preferably in writing, to consult an independent solicitor. Today's competitive climate means that solicitors have to work hard to attract clients in the first place, and then to retain them in the longer term. As such, there is a strong economic incentive to rationalise conflicts, thus avoiding the need to send one or even both clients to a competitor. However, it is always a mistake to rationalise continuing to act in a conflict situation or to attempt to resolve matters and solicitors are generally digging a deeper hole for themselves if they try to do so. It should always be remembered that the Practice Rules are there not only for the protection of clients, but also for the protection of solicitors. It will also be necessary to consider whether the solicitor has confidential information relating to the different clients which would make it impossible to continue acting for any of them.

7.11 Dealing with Unrepresented Parties

In situations where solicitors cannot act for both parties to a transaction, it may be that one of the parties will refuse to instruct another solicitor. No one can be forced to instruct a solicitor against their will, and individuals are always entitled to deal with their legal affairs by themselves. They may take the view that the cost of instructing another solicitor outweighs the benefit to be gained from doing so. Such a view may be misguided, but that is their privilege.

In this situation, the solicitor's duty is to act in the best interests of his or her own client. The other party can be treated as unrepresented. Instructions should be taken from the solicitor's own client after giving advice on what is proposed. If a document is prepared for signature, r.7 of the 1986 Practice Rules should be complied with. The solicitor must advise the unrepresented party, in writing, when issuing the document, that such signature would have legal consequences and they should seek independent legal advice before signing it. Details should not be given as to what the consequences might be, as that would amount to advising them. If the unrepresented party still does not obtain separate advice and signs and returns the document, the solicitor is

---

[24] See *Greens Solicitors Professional Handbook* (2005–2006) F 1220.

[25] See para.7.08.04 above. The Legal Services Consultative Panel for England and Wales recommended strongly to the Law Society in June 2005 that if a conflict arises while the solicitor is acting for two or more clients, then the solicitor should cease acting for both clients. *www.dca.gov.uk/atoj/lscp* This is the predominant position in Australia (Dal Pont, *op. cit.* p.200).

entitled to treat it as delivered on behalf of his or her own client and deal with it accordingly.

The Professional Practice committee of the Law Society of Scotland have held that issuing a document in terms of r.7 includes giving it to the solicitor's own client to be signed by the other party, as well as sending it directly to the other party.

In 1998, the Discipline Tribunal found a solicitor guilty of professional misconduct for failing to comply with r.7. They stated that whatever pressures might be put upon the solicitor, "*where professional obligations arise it is not sufficient for a solicitor merely to follow the instructions of his client*".[26]

Although r.7 deals specifically with transactions involving heritable property, in 1998 the Council issued a Practice Guideline extending the rule to any transaction in relation to which a solicitor issues a document to an unrepresented party. The Council agreed that there was no justification for distinguishing between transactions involving heritable property and other types of transaction.

The notice to the unrepresented party required by r.7 may either be in a separate letter or contained within the document to be signed. It does not require to be acknowledged.

B. Particular Issues

Particular Areas of Practice   **7.12**

The ban on acting in situations of conflict applies to every aspect of a solicitor's practice. Some situations are obvious, for example, solicitors cannot act for pursuer and defender in the same litigation. Others are less obvious. For example, where solicitors are acting for a company and for its directors and/or shareholders, there will be occasions when the interests of the company may conflict with the interests of individual directors or shareholders. As we have seen, since 1986 even certain situations where the potential for conflict is serious or significant have been brought within the scope of Practice Rules. Despite numerous guidance notes from the Professional Practice Committee of Law Society of Scotland, for the reasons set out in para.7.02 above, the complexities of the field mean that getting to grips with conflict of interest entails looking at a wide range of different areas of practice.

Civil Litigation Generally   **7.13**

As we saw at the outset, the duty to avoid acting in a conflict of interest situation is underpinned by three positive duties: loyalty, confidentiality and diligence. It is the last duty which causes particular problems in the litigation field. The duty to pursue the client's interests to the best of the lawyer's ability, known in the USA as "zealous advocacy" involves representation of the client wholly and resolutely. Every issue must be raised, every argument advanced and every question asked in order to advance the client's case, and endeavour to obtain for him or her every legal remedy or defence available.[27]

---

[26] Scottish Solicitors' Discipline Tribunal Annual Report 1998, p.3.

[27] Proulx and Layton, *op. cit.*, p.289. As we shall see in Ch.14 below, the duty of diligence in litigation matters is confined by other duties, particularly those owed to the court.

It follows, as Begg[28] stated, a solicitor cannot be employed on both sides of a law suit. While the 1986 Practice Rules do not specifically prohibit this, it is obvious that such a course of action would be a clear breach of r.3.

That much is obvious, but the matter goes further. When approached by a potential client in relation to civil litigation, it is important to check whether the firm are already acting for the other party to the dispute in relation to any other matter. It is irrelevant that it is an unrelated matter, or even that it is being handled by different partners in a different branch, the prohibition on acting in such circumstances will still apply. In a case considered by the Society's Professional Practice Committee in 1990, one branch of a large firm were acting for the pursuer in litigation while at the same time, a different branch of the firm were acting for the defenders in a totally unrelated conveyancing transaction. Unfortunately this was either not detected, or it was ignored. Not surprisingly though, the defenders complained to the Law Society when they were served with an inhibition on the dependence of the action at the instance of their own solicitors.[29]

This prohibition applies even if the same solicitors are partners in different firms, or firms with branches trading under different names. For example, in 1998 the Society received an enquiry from a partner in one branch of a firm who had been consulted by potential defenders to an action. The claims had already been intimated, and it was known that a solicitor in a different branch of the firm had been consulted by a number of the claimants. It was suggested that a "Chinese Wall" would be established to allow the different branches to act for the pursuers and the defenders. The firm were advised that this would not be sufficient to overcome the difficulty, in what was bound to become a high profile case. Furthermore, neither their own nor their clients' interests would be served if they had to withdraw from acting at a later stage.

A conflict may also arise between different pursuers in the same reparation action if a global offer is made by the defenders to settle the case. Finally, In matrimonial matters the same firm of solicitors should not act for both husband and wife in negotiating a separation agreement—or even in preparing a document that reflects the parties own agreement. The parties have separate interests which will almost certainly conflict. That does not mean that matters cannot be progressed. If one of the parties refuses to seek separate independent advice—and nobody can be forced to see a solicitor against their will—the firm should ensure that they only act for one of the parties in which case the other can be treated as an unrepresented party.[30]

7.14 Conflict of Interest and Representation in Criminal Cases

7.14.01 Acting for co-accused. In 1996 the Council of the Society published a Code of Conduct for Criminal Work. The Code has been revised subsequently and was re-issued in 2002. Article 2 states:

> *"A solicitor should not accept instructions from more than one accused in the same matter"*

---

[28] Begg on *Law Agents* (2nd edn), p.337.

[29] On the other hand there is no conflict of interest if in a procedural matter agreed between the parties, a single agent represents both sides in court to move the matter "of consent".

[30] See para.7.10 above.

The Guidance Note attached to this statement reflects the awareness of the obvious potential conflict of interest when instructions are accepted from more than one accused in the same case, even although such a conflict may not come to the surface. Article 2 applies even were there is a defence common to all accused. Solicitors should not place themselves in a position in which they are given confidential information by one client which may be detrimental to another. A solicitor who accepts instructions and subsequently has to abandon one of the clients is placed in a compromised position and may have to withdraw from acting for all of them. For example if one client pleads guilty he becomes a compellable witness against the other.

In 1995 the Discipline Tribunal found a solicitor guilty of professional misconduct with regard to two separate matters.[31] In the first, the solicitor was acting for two co-accused and the older client had been charged with two matters. His position was that under pressure from the police he had confessed to both whereas in fact he had only committed one of the offences. The younger client's position was that he was innocent of the charge against him, but he had implicated the older client in his replies to the police. The younger client eventually pled guilty and the Crown accepted a plea of not guilty from the older client. The Tribunal took a serious view of this breach of the Conflict of Interest Rules. In the second case, the same solicitor took instructions from two co-accused who were subsequently charged on the same complaint. On two occasions one of the co-accused informed the solicitor's assistant of his intention to incriminate his co-accused, but the firm only withdrew from acting for the co-accused four days before the trial.

Incrimination of the Other Client. In a 1990 case before the Discipline **7.14.02** Tribunal,[32] a solicitor was charged with acting in a conflict of interest situation. He took instructions from two brothers who had been charged with different offences in relation to separate incidents. The first brother, A, was charged with murder, and the second, B, with serious assault. A's defence to the charge of murder was that B had in fact committed the crime. The Tribunal held that it was clearly the solicitor's duty to ensure that B was immediately advised to consult another solicitor.

Crown Witness also a Client. Great care must also be taken where the **7.14.03** solicitor is acting for an accused in one case, who is a witness against another of the solicitor's clients in a different case. This is particularly important if the witness is the complainer, or his credibility is to be challenged. The witness client is entitled to have his confidentiality respected. In situations where the accused is attempting to incriminate or attack the character of the witness client, there will be a conflict of interest between the two and the solicitor should withdraw from acting for the accused client. That message can be difficult to convey to clients, but if a solicitor decides that he cannot act because of a conflict of interest, the Society will always respect that decision if a complaint is received. It is a matter for the solicitor's professional judgement.

---

[31] Scottish Solicitors' Discipline Tribunal Annual Report 1995, p.5.
[32] DTD 809/90.

7.14.04 Relationship Between Legal Representatives. An interesting issue arose in the case of *R v Batt*,[33] when on the second day of the trial, counsel for the prosecution was replaced by another counsel, who, it transpired, cohabited with the defence counsel. The appellant was informed of the development and gave his written consent to the trial proceeding. On appeal against conviction, it was argued that either defence counsel or prosecution counsel should have withdrawn. The appeal was dismissed and it was held that the appellant had made a fully informed choice on the matter. However, giving judgement, Nelson J. observed that it was generally undesirable for husband and wife or other partners living together, to appear on opposite sides in the same criminal matter. Circumstances such as these might give rise to a belief that the case had not been properly conducted. In this case, however, it was held that far from acting improperly, counsel exercised excellent judgement by getting the appellant to sign his consent to the unusual circumstances that had arisen.

7.15 Conveyancing

7.15.01 The 1986 Practice Rules. Acting for both sides in a conveyancing transaction was not uncommon in Scotland, particularly in rural areas, until the 1986 Practice Rules.[34] The danger with the practice is that having started to act for both parties it can be tempting to delay reaching the conclusion that a conflict has arisen, and difficult to tell one or both of the parties to find a new agent. This situation can also arise because at the time of taking instructions there is no apparent conflict, but such a conflict subsequently arises. Doubtless it was these dangers which prompted Henderson Begg and the occasional Court of Session judge to describe acting for the buyer and seller of heritable property as an objectionable practice. The fact remains, as we saw in para.7.06 above, the courts generally took the line that it was not, in itself, a failure of professional obligation to represent borrower and lender or seller and purchaser of heritable property. There was, nonetheless, some dubiety over the propriety of advising both parties on the issue of price and by the 1980s the Tribunal was indicating that whatever may have been the position in the past, it was no longer appropriate for a solicitor to endeavour to advise both the buyer and the seller on the issue of price.[35] However, it was not long before the Law Society—prompted by a desire both to clarify the ethical position and to forestall the then Government's interest in eroding the conveyancing monopoly—determined to tackle the ethical problems thrown up by acting for buyer and seller in a conveyancing transaction. The Society's conclusion was that acting for the buyer and the seller or for the borrower and the lender in a conveyancing transaction was a situation which even if it did not raise an actual conflict of interest almost invariably raised such a significant potential for conflict that it should be subject to regulation if not outright prohibition.[36] The result was the Solicitors (Scotland) Practice Rules 1986:

> "*3. A solicitor shall not act for two or more parties whose interests conflict . . .*

---

[33] TLR, May 30, 1996.

[34] A Survey conducted for the Hughes Royal Commission on Legal Services in Scotland (HMSO, 1980, Cmnd 7846, vol.II, p.620) found that the same solicitor acted for the buyer and seller in 18% of conveyancing transactions relating to houses at that time.

[35] DTD 630/85 and DTD 663/86.

[36] See para.7.07.01 above.

5. *(1) Without prejudice to the generality of rule 3 hereof, a solicitor, or two or more solicitors practicing either as principal or employee in the same firm or in the employment of the same employer, shall not at any stage, act for both seller and purchaser in the sale or purchase or conveyance of heritable property, or for both landlord and tenant, or assignor and assignee in a lease of heritable property for value or for lender and borrower in a loan to be secured over heritable property; provided, however, that where no dispute arises or might reasonably be expected to arise between the parties and that, other than in the case of exception (a) hereto, the seller or landlord of residential property is not a builder or developer, this rules shall not apply if—*

   (a) the parties are associated companies, public authorities, public bodies, or government departments or agencies;
   (b) the parties are connected one with the other within the meaning of section 533 Income and Corporation Taxes Act 1970;
   (c) the parties are related by blood, adoption or marriage, one to the other, or the purchaser, tenant, assignee or borrower is so related to an established client; or
   (d) both parties are established clients or the prospective purchaser, tenant, assignee or borrower is an established client; or
   (e) there is no other solicitor in the vicinity whom the client could reasonably be expected to consult; or
   (f) in the case of a loan to be secured over heritable property, the terms of the loan have been agreed between the parties before the solicitor has been instructed to act for the lender, and the granting of the security is only to give effect to such agreement.

   (2) In all cases falling within exceptions (c), (d) and (e) both parties shall be advised by the solicitor at the earliest practicable opportunity that the solicitor, or his firm, has been requested to act for both parties, and that if a dispute arises, they or one of them will require to consult an independent solicitor or solicitors, which advice shall be confirmed by the solicitor in writing as soon as may be practicable thereafter.

6. *A solicitor shall unless the contrary be proved be presumed for the purposes of rule 4 and rule 5 hereof to be acting for a party for whom he prepares an offer whether complete or not, in connection with a transaction of any kind specified in these rules, for execution by that party.*

7. *A solicitor acting on behalf of a party or prospective party to a transaction of any kind specified in rule 5 hereof shall not issue any deed, writ, missive or other document requiring the signature of another party or prospective party to him without informing that party in writing that;*

   (a) such signature may have certain legal consequences, and
   (b) he should seek independent legal advice before signature.

>   9. *The Council shall have power to waive any of the provisions of
>   these rules in any particular circumstances or case.*
>   10. *Breach of any of these rules may be treated as professional
>   misconduct for the purposes of Part IV of the Act (complaints and
>   disciplinary proceedings)."*

7.15.02 The 1986 Practice Rules explained. Rule 5 is without prejudice to the
general prohibition in r.3. It states, in essence, that the same solicitor or firm
of solicitors shall not *at any stage*[37] act for both seller and purchaser, or
landlord and tenant, or assignor and assignee in a lease of heritable property
for value or for lender and borrower in a loan to be secured over heritable
property.[38] This is because of the significant potential for conflict which can
arise in such situations. However, r.5 goes on to add that provided that (1) no
dispute arises, *or might reasonably be expected to arise*,[39] and (2) the seller of
residential property is not a builder or developer, the prohibition shall not
apply in certain situations. In brief, these situations are when the case
involves: (a) associated companies or public bodies; (b) connected parties
within the meaning of s.839 of the Income and Corporation Taxes Act 1988;
(c) parties related by blood, adoption or marriage; (d) established clients; and
(e) where there is no other solicitor in the vicinity whom the client could
reasonably be expected to consult. There is, however, no unifying theme
which explains this list of exceptions, other than the fact that most of them had
existed for a considerable number of years in England, without causing great
difficulties. In several cases, the exception is justified on the grounds that the
connection between the clients is such that it would not be unreasonable of
them to agree to run the risk of any potential conflict. Again, the final
exception might be justified on the basis of access and client convenience but
the established client exception cannot lay claim to either protection. It is
firmly rooted in pragmatism, if not lawyer self-interest, since it gets round the
potentially awkward problem of which client should be asked to go elsewhere,
and by allowing the lawyer to retain both clients makes the r.5 ban more
palatable to the profession. Nonetheless the exceptions merit some amplification:

>   Category (a)—Associated companies: means companies in the same
>   corporate group, and not simply having directors or
>   shareholders in common.
>   Category (b)—Connected persons: will be strictly defined in accordance
>   with the Court's interpretation of the Income and Cor-
>   poration Taxes Act.
>   Category (c)—Parties related by blood, adoption or marriage: although
>   not restricted to any particular degree of relationship in
>   the wording of the rule, it would be unwise to stray

---

[37] See para.7.19.02.

[38] The lender/borrower situation is dealt with at para.7.16 below.

[39] Of course, parties' interests will always be at odds with each other in relation to the price or
rent to be offered. As such, this is the subject of a specific rule—r.8. It is important to remember
that when dealing with a claim or complaint the circumstances will be looked at with the benefit
of hindsight. It is clear that the disputes that regularly arise in conveyancing transactions are
almost all disputes which could reasonably have been foreseen, such as difficulties with title,
unauthorised alterations, or problems with the purchasers' funding.

beyond the forbidden degrees of marriage. In particular, care should be taken in relation to people described as "cousins". This may be a very tenuous relationship.

Category (d)—Established clients: an established client is defined in the rules as "*A person for whom a solicitor or his firm has acted on at least one previous occasion*". When firms amalgamate, clients for whom solicitors have previously acted will continue to be "established clients" for the purposes of this exemption. The phrase "has acted" does not mean that the solicitor requires to have ceased acting in the previous matter, it can be ongoing. The solicitor must, however, have opened a file with something for which the client could be charged. It does not matter that the client has not yet been charged, or indeed may never be charged. In a 1993 case, a solicitor was charged with acting in violation of r.5. While the sellers were established clients within the meaning of the exception, there was more doubt about the purchasers. The purchasers were introduced to the solicitor by an estate agent with a view to purchasing the property. The solicitor's account was that they had first discussed with him the sale of their existing house, and not until two days later was there any discussion of the proposed purchase. The Discipline Tribunal held that no reasonable solicitor in these circumstances would have regarded the earlier conversation as forming a client relationship in a separate matter from the purchase.[40]

Category (e)—There is no other solicitor in the vicinity—this exception is narrowly interpreted by the Professional Practice Committee. They regard it as restricted to isolated rural and island communities. It is not applicable anywhere in central Scotland, or even relatively populated areas of the Highlands or Borders. For example, in one small Highland town where there was one full time and one part time solicitor's practice, the committee decided that the exemption was not available, even although the nearest town with an alternative firm of solicitors was nine miles away.

Waivers. As is the case with most practice rules, the 1986 Practice Rules allow solicitors to apply for a waiver from its provisions.[41] These requests are considered by the Professional Practice Committee, its convener and secretariat. Requests for a waiver are received on a regular basis but are unlikely to be granted unless justified by evidence of significant hardship or major inconvenience to the client in the particular circumstances of the case. As we have already seen, since the rules came into force, the committee has never granted a waiver in respect of r.3. **7.15.03**

---

[40] *Stewart*, 1993 J.L.S.S. 119.
[41] See r.9.

Waivers are much more commonly sought, and granted in respect of r.5. One case involved a waiver being granted in relation to an excambion of garden ground between neighbouring properties. A plan had already been agreed between the parties, and to save expense the parties all wished to instruct the same firm of solicitors. Only some of the parties were established clients of the firm, hence the need for a waiver. Where the solicitor is acting for the seller and is instructed to act also for joint purchasers (who are not related by blood, marriage, etc.) one of whom is an established client, and the other not, a waiver will, in the absence of special circumstances, be granted to enable the solicitor to act for both parties, provided again of course, that the seller is not a builder or developer of residential property. In fact, builder/developer waivers have turned out to be the most frequently requested, and granted form of waiver. The committee will give sympathetic consideration to a request where there is a close personal connection between the builder and the purchaser, where the sale is from one builder or developer to another, or where the purchaser is a partner or employee in the solicitor's own firm. The fact that a purchaser might be a long established client will not in itself be sufficient to persuade the committee that a waiver should be granted.

In builder/developer cases, the test the committee has applied is whether or not the individual is acting as a builder or a developer in the particular transaction. In one early case a builder had bought a house not for development purposes, but in order to demolish it to provide an access way from another property. In the end, the access was not needed and the builder decided to sell the house. The committee took the view that in the circumstances the developer was not, in the sale, acting as a builder or developer and the same solicitor could act for both parties, the purchaser being his established client.[42]

Again, where a building firm for administrative reasons sold a house to the husband and wife who were its directors and sole shareholders, the committee again felt it reasonable to grant a waiver. On the other hand, the committee decided that in the case where planning permission for residential development was given in principle, this made the owner, whoever he or she might be, a developer within the meaning of the rules.

In the early days of the 1986 Rules, "builder/developer" cases also accounted for the great majority of the applications made for a waiver. Sometimes the committee considered that the conditions imposed by the seller e.g. in private retirement housing or sales by Housing Associations, were such that it was essential that the purchaser should be separately represented. Indeed, in a majority of builder/developer cases which fell within the ambit of the rules, the committee took the view that there was not enough evidence of hardship or major inconvenience to the client to warrant a waiver being granted.[43] The current position is set out in para.7.15.07 below.

7.15.04 **"At any stage".** These words in r.5(1) of the conflict of interest rules are significant. Examples of acting at any stage have included:

> 1. Acting as an estate agent only. Even if all offers are to be submitted to a different firm of solicitors, the firm providing the estate agency

---

[42] See Professional Practice Committee Annual report 1987.
[43] *ibid.*

service would not be entitled to act or give any advice to a prospective purchaser who did not fall within one of the exemptions. However, in 2003 the Professional Practice Committee ruled that waivers will ordinarily be granted from r.5(1) so that a solicitor may act for an established client where the solicitor has provided estate agency services only to a builder/developer if, (1) the property is for a fixed price, (2) a standard missive is negotiated with a different firm of solicitors, (3) there is no actual conflict of interest and (4) the solicitors offer no advice on value or price.[44]

2. Giving advice about a mortgage or finance for a property. If the firm is selling a property, it would only be able to give mortgage advice to a prospective purchaser to whom one of the exemptions applies. This means that care has to be taken about what is included in the property particulars. In 1998 the Professional Practice Committee published a guideline[45] which states that if the firm markets its mortgage advice service in its property particulars, it must include a notice that the firm may not be able to act for the recipient in giving mortgage advice.

Rule 5(2). In cases where solicitors are acting for both parties by virtue of r.5(1) (c), (d) or (e), r.5(2) requires that both parties be advised by the solicitor, at the earliest practical opportunity, that the firm have been requested to act for them both and that if a dispute arises they, or one of them will require to consult an independent solicitor. **7.15.05**

Such advice is necessary to enable the clients to give informed consent to the same firm acting for both. This is not a mere formality but an essential element in ensuring compliance with the r.5.

This advice must be confirmed by the solicitor in writing "*as soon as may be practicable thereafter*". That does not mean when the offer has been submitted or is about to be submitted—far less when missives have been concluded. It means when the solicitor is first instructed by the purchaser in respect of a property that the same firm are selling, or in respect of which the firm knows it is to be instructed by the seller if the sale is being dealt with by an external estate agent.

In a case investigated by the Scottish Legal Services Ombudsman[46] the solicitor had acted for both the seller and the purchaser of a property relying on the r.5(1)(d) exception for established clients. The purchaser was informed that the solicitor was acting for both clients, and that the solicitor would be unable to become involved in determining what price should be offered. However, the seller (the complainer), was not informed of this until after the missives had been concluded. Although the solicitors did not advise the purchaser on the price to be offered, the price of the property had to be substantially reduced due to structural defects. The Complaints Committee held that there had been no IPS, since the complainer would not have received any better price for the property. However, the Ombudsman noted that the complainer was under the impression that he was receiving independent

---

[44] See 2003 J.L.S.S. March at p.9. On waivers generally, see 2002 J.L.S.S. September at p.47.

[45] Journal—April 1998, p.44.

[46] Scottish Legal Services Ombudsman 3rd Annual Report 1993, pp.38–39.

advice from his solicitor. When at such a late stage it became apparent that he was not, he was bound to feel this was inequitable, and that the service he had received was inferior, which indeed he did, considering, with hindsight, that the solicitor had not driven a hard bargain on his side to get a better price. Accordingly the Ombudsman took the view that there was both IPS and unsatisfactory conduct.

Rule 5(2) letters are mandatory. Even if the solicitors are entitled to act and there is no actual conflict of interest, failure to send out such a letter is a breach of the rules. When the Society's inspectors carry out a routine inspection of the firm's accounts, they will ask for files where the firm has acted for both buyer and seller and will report back to the Society where no r.5(2) letters appear in the files. That may, in itself, lead to a complaint of professional misconduct. In practice, it is always regarded as at least unsatisfactory conduct. In 1998, the Scottish Solicitors' Discipline Tribunal highlighted a case where they found a solicitor guilty of misconduct for not complying with r.5(2). The Tribunal said[47]:

> "It does not mitigate the gravity of any breach that none of the clients involved have been prejudiced or were dissatisfied with the solicitors' conduct of a transaction".

7.15.06 Offering for More Than One Party. Rule 8 of the Practice Rules applies to situations where the same firm knowingly intends to act on behalf of two or more prospective purchasers or tenants of heritable property. The clients must be informed of this intention, and a single solicitor shall not give advice about the price or rent to be offered, or any other material condition of the prospective bargain, to more than one client. It is prudent to inform the clients in writing rather than merely verbally. If an offer is prepared for each client in identical terms, except for the price which is left blank, that would be sufficient to comply with r.8.

It is important to note that r.8 operates where the firm knowingly intend to act for two or more prospective purchasers, *irrespective of whether an offer is actually submitted.* Therefore, as soon as the firm is consulted by clients interested in the same property, they must all be advised of this so they have the opportunity to instruct a different firm of solicitors. Solicitors need to proceed with extreme caution if acting under this rule. For example, if one prospective purchaser wishes to submit an early offer there is a clear conflict of interest between him and any other prospective purchaser, and the firm should advise that particular client to instruct a different firm.

7.15.07 Builders and Developers. "Builders Missives" were the subject of particular concern in the 1970s and early 1980s leading up to the introduction of the conflict of interest rules. It was felt that the conditions often imposed by the seller, for example, in private retirement housing, or sales by Housing Associations, were such that it was essential that the purchaser should be separately represented.[48] The 1986 Rules contain a total prohibition on acting

---

[47] Annual Report of the Scottish Solicitors Discipline Tribunal 1998.
[48] Professional Practice Committee Annual Report 1987.

for a purchaser, if the same firm of solicitors is also acting for a builder or developer selling residential property, unless the parties are associated companies or public bodies.[49]

The prohibition only applies to residential property. This is interpreted relatively narrowly, for example, it has been accepted that a university hall of residence was not a residential property for the purpose of the practice rule. The word "developer" has been considered by the Professional Practice Committee on a number of occasions. Some examples include:

1. A housing association
2. A developer selling a building plot, whether serviced or unserviced, with planning permission for residential development, even if the developer client will not be constructing the house to be built.
3. A person who is by trade a builder or developer, and is selling in the course of business, houses or plots which are either part of a larger development or single houses or plots, e.g. a builder selling a house which has been bought as a trade-in, is still a builder for the purpose of r.5.
4. A person who is not by trade a builder or developer but is selling individual plots or houses which are part of a larger development is regarded as having the temporary status of a developer, e.g. a farmer selling more than one residential plot in a field.

However, a person who is not by trade a builder or developer and is selling a single plot or site is not regarded as a developer within the meaning of r.5(1). In these circumstances, a solicitor may consider acting for both parties, provided the parties fall within one of the exemptions, there is no actual conflict of interest and no dispute is reasonably likely to arise. This will remain a matter of judgement of the solicitor. In such transactions there could well be conflicting interests, such as rights of access, services, or maintenance of a private roadway. The safest way to avoid such difficulties would be to decline to accept instructions from both parties in the first place.

The specific prohibition in the rule relates to the situation where the developer is the seller. If the developer is the purchaser, and both purchaser and seller are established clients and wish the firm to act for both, the firm are entitled to consider doing so. However, the firm should exercise extreme caution. There may well be an actual conflict of interest or such a significant potential for conflict that it would be unwise to act for both. If the parties have not reached full agreement on the contract, but one or both of them wishes advice on particular terms, there is a clear conflict and it would be improper to give such advice against the interests of another party for whom the firm is acting.

As we saw earlier, it is possible to seek a waiver under r.9 of the 1986 Rules from the application of r.5(1) and consistently since 1986 the most numerous of such applications have been in relation to builder/developer cases.[50]

---

[49] r.5(1) 1986 Practice Rules.
[50] See para.7.14.03 above.

7.15.08 Sale of the Matrimonial Home. One situation of potential conflict in relation to residential property which arises with some frequency is where a matrimonial home is to be sold as a result of marital breakdown. The Law Society issued practice guidelines on this matter in 1994 and again in 1998.[51] The fundamental principle is that if a jointly owned matrimonial home is being sold by spouses who have separated or are about to separate, a written agreement is required if the firm which is acting for one of the parties in the matrimonial affairs is also to act in the sale. Such an agreement must cover how the free proceeds after sale will be dealt with. This prevents the solicitor being placed in a situation of conflict because one of the spouses has sought to arrest the proceeds in the solicitor's hands or otherwise issued unilateral instructions for their disposal which are inconsistent with acting for both spouses in the sale. If such a legally binding agreement cannot be reached, a different firm of solicitors, independent of the matrimonial dispute, should be instructed in the sale.

Secondly, if a firm is consulted by a married couple to sell their jointly owned property and it transpires that the spouses have separated or are separating, the firm may act in the sale, provided no one in the firm is acting for either of the parties in their matrimonial affairs. The spouses should be advised to seek separate independent advice in relation to their matrimonial position. If they decline to do so and simply wish to sell the property, the same firm may act for both. In the absence of a written agreement determining their distribution the firm should pay over the net free proceeds to each of the spouses in accordance with the title. The net-free proceeds will be the gross proceeds of the sale, less sums required to redeem any secured loans, as well as the expenses of the sale, including conveyancing fees and outlays. It is prudent to advise both spouses, in advance, in writing, what the distribution will be, at least in percentage terms if the actual figures are unknown. A written acknowledgement of this should be obtained from the spouses. If the parties wish some other division, they should be advised that it will need to be agreed in writing, and they should seek separate independent advice before entering into such a written agreement.

If any unsecured loans are to be repaid out of the proceeds of the sale, the solicitors must ensure they have joint written instructions to that effect. If fees are due by one of the parties for other work done on their behalf, these may be deducted from that party's own share of the proceeds.

Where separating spouses, or other joint owners, are selling jointly owned property and one or both of them want the solicitor to act for them in the purchase of a new property in their own name, it will almost certainly be necessary to know what the free proceeds of the sale will be, to ensure that the client will be able to settle the new purchase. A redemption figure will therefore require to be ascertained on the existing mortgage and, if it is an all sums due security, whether the lender will also require other loans to be repaid before granting a discharge. Solicitors will need to know what will be available to each of the couple for their new purchase as soon as possible in case there is a hole in the finances because, for example, a second loan requires to be repaid. This could well give rise to a conflict of interest during the transaction.

---

[51] Professional Practice Guideline: "Acting for separated spouses" (1998) 43(7) J.L.S.S. 43.

Sale of Jointly Owned Property where the Owners are not Spouses or **7.15.09**
civil partners. If such joint owners of property are selling, it may be that there
is a conflict of interest between them over the distribution of the free proceeds
of sale. That will not arise if they wish to apply the proceeds to the purchase
of another property in joint names or, if the proceeds are divided between
them in accordance with the title. It is important to ensure that instructions are
obtained from all joint owners and that those instructions coincide. As with
spouses, if unsecured loans have to be repaid out of the proceeds, the parties
should be advised to get separate independent advice before entering into an
agreement giving instructions to do so. Of course, they may not take such
independent advice and if, after having been given such a warning, joint
written instructions are received those instructions can be accepted.

Transactions with an Element of Gift. Where a property transaction **7.15.10**
includes an element of gift from seller to purchaser there will almost certainly
be a conflict of interest requiring separate representation for purchaser and
seller. This is particularly true of family situations, where a discounted price
may be paid for the property. An example of this, which came to the notice of
the Professional Practice Department involved a company selling a property
to the daughter of its shareholders for a discounted price. Another case arose
when a son bought his parents' property for less than one third of the market
value, having previously been assisting with mortgage payments. In these
situations it may be in the interests of all parties to demonstrate at a later date
that the transaction was at arms length. Separate representation will assist with
that.

Outright Gifts. Where heritable property is to be conveyed for no considera- **7.15.11**
tion there may well also be a conflict of interest between the parties. Gifts
between spouses and gifts from parents to children would not automatically
give rise to a conflict of interest, provided that the donor is clearly capable of
giving instructions and fully understands the nature of the transaction. If the
gift is subject to conditions, there is a conflict of interest and separate agents
should act for both parties. If what is being gifted is more of a liability than
an asset there is also a conflict of interest and, again separate agents should be
instructed.
It will be necessary to take instructions from the donors outwith the
presence of the donee to ensure that they are not being subjected to undue
influence. If they do not agree to being seen on their own, it would be most
unwise to accept instructions, no matter what reasons are given for declining
to do so.

House Purchase Funded by Relatives. A further specific area to be wary of **7.15.12**
is if a house purchase is being funded by other members of the family, for
example, if a council house is to be purchased for an elderly entitled tenant.
There are clearly different interests to be protected in these situations. The
entitled tenant is entitled to the discount as a statutory right. He or she may
also be entitled to security of tenure. The person putting up the money is
entitled to have that investment protected, or at least to be advised on it.
Advice may also be necessary on how the purchase is to be funded, and the
terms of repayment.

It is essential to recognise that these interests may not have been addressed by the parties themselves, and the solicitor needs to make sure that these matters are fully understood by the parties and that there is no dispute between them before he can act for both.

These questions were considered in more detail by Alistair Sim in his Risk Management column in the Journal in July 2002.[52]

7.15.13 Other Examples of Conflict of Interest in Conveyancing. Some other situations which have been referred to the Professional Practice Department in recent years include:

    (a) A partnership leased business premises from the senior partner, who owned the premises. The owner wished to sell, and the new owners wanted to replace the existing lease with a new lease on more onerous terms. Although the new owners had separate agents, the solicitors for the former owner were also acting for the partnership. There was a clear conflict of interest and they were advised they should not act for the existing owner and for the partnership.

    (b) The same firm were acting for purchaser and seller of a property. The purchaser was unwilling to conclude a bargain until loan funding was confirmed. In situations where there was a delay in concluding the bargain, it was held there was a conflict of interest and the firm were advised to refer the purchaser to other agents.

    (c) Solicitors acting for executors selling a property also acted for the prospective purchaser, whose offer was subject to an unduly onerous condition, namely that the purchaser's own property in England was successfully sold. There was a clear conflict of interest, especially as the English transaction was subject to contracts being exchanged, and no bargain would be concluded until the date of entry.

    (d) Where a firm acts for buyer and seller under the established client exemption, if a problem arises with regard to the sale of the purchaser's existing property with the knock on effect that there will be difficulty in setting the other transaction, there is a conflict of interest and the firm should withdraw from acting for at least one party, whether or not the bargain is concluded.

7.16 Financial lender Transactions

7.16.01 Secured Loans. For pragmatic reasons, including keeping costs down, r.5 of the Practice Rules 1986 continued to allow the same solicitor to act for the borrower and the lending institution in house purchase transactions. However, to minimise any conflict of interest r.5(1)(f) requires the terms of the loan to have already been agreed between the parties before the solicitor is instructed by the lender and also requires that the granting of the security only gives effect to that agreement. In its 1988 Annual Report, the Discipline Tribunal stated that acting for both lender and borrower:

    " . . . Requires the solicitor to act with absolute propriety and to protect

---

[52] (2002) 47(7) J.L.S.S. 48.

the interests of the building society with the same degree of care and responsibility as is given to the purchase transaction."[53]

That is, the solicitor must remember that the lender is also a client, to whom certain duties are owed. These duties extend to all communications between the solicitor and the building society.

For example, in one case, a solicitor submitted a mortgage application on behalf of his client. The application was made as though it were for an initial house purchase loan application. However, the client was already the owner of the property which was subject to an existing mortgage. The application was effectively a re-mortgage application. The solicitor was aware of this, and was accordingly found guilty of professional misconduct.[54]

In another case, a solicitor knew or ought to have known that searches in the Register of Sasines and the Register of Inhibitions and Adjudications would have disclosed a number of inhibitions against his client. Nonetheless, he failed to bring this to the attention of the building society. The inhibitions were not effective against the particular purchase, nevertheless, the Tribunal held that the solicitor had an overriding duty to report the matter to the building society and had failed to do so.[55]

A further solicitor was found to be culpable for failing to inform the building society that the loan they advanced was in excess of the true market value of the property. A house had been advertised with availability of 100 per cent loan, together with funds to meet legal fees. In addition, the sellers would give a discount of £2000 to the purchaser. When the solicitor submitted his report on title and requisitioned the loan cheque, he failed to disclose that the notional purchase price was subject to a discount. The Tribunal found that in reality, the discounted price reflected the true market value of the property, and the effect of calculating the loan on the notional price resulted in the society granting a loan in excess of this. While there was no suggestion that the solicitor had been involved in formulating the arrangement, he had a duty to disclose the discrepancy to the building society and in failing to do so he was guilty of professional misconduct.[56]

The lender/borrower rule is still subject to the question of an actual conflict of interest or a dispute which may reasonably be likely to arise. Difficulties have arisen in a number of cases which have been reported and discussed in more detail elsewhere.[57]

A conflict may arise between borrower and lender where there are insufficient funds available to meet stamp duty or recording dues. In 1996 the Discipline Tribunal found a solicitor guilty of professional misconduct where he had neglected to record a number of deeds because there were insufficient funds. The Tribunal said there was a duty to ensure that on cashing the loan cheques sufficient funds were available. If funds are not available and the solicitor has cashed the loan cheque to settle the transaction, the solicitor must

---

[53] Scottish Solicitors' Discipline Tribunal Annual Report 1988 pp.130–131.

[54] *ibid.*

[55] *ibid.*

[56] "House Prices—Duty of Full Disclosure" (1989) 34(5) J.L.S.S. 190.

[57] See para.7.08.03 above and the cases set out therein. See also articles by Professor Robert Rennie in the *Journal*: "The Lender's Need to Know", 1994, p135; "The Expanding Duty of Care", 1995, p.58; and "Certificates of Title", 1995 p.377. There was also a useful item in the caveat column in the Journal of February 1995 at p.71.

fund the stamp duty and recording dues from his own resources to ensure that the lenders' security is recorded timeously.[58] Where the solicitor is not prepared to fund the stamp duty and recording dues personally, he has a duty to withhold settlement and where appropriate, to return the loan monies to the lender.[59]

7.16.02   Commercial Securities. In March 1994, the President of the Society issued a circular advising that in commercial security transactions banks would normally instruct their own solicitor (rather than the borrower's) except in what they regarded as *de minimis* cases. It was accepted that different banks would have different views on what constituted a *de minimis* case. In fact, as reflected in an update from the Professional Practice Committee in 2003, "*de minimis*" can be up to £250,000.[60] A Commercial Security was defined as a, "*transaction* [which] *relates to the secured lending to a customer of a bank or other lending institution where the purpose of the loan is clearly for the customer's business purposes.*" In the Society's view, there is a greater scope for conflict of interest in commercial transactions than in domestic ones.

The genesis of this circular arose from concern over the increasing number and value of claims on the master policy. About 25 per cent of all claims on the master policy arose out of defective security work.[61] The circular followed discussions between the Society's Office Bearers and the Committee of Scottish Clearing Bankers. Other banks may not know of these guidelines. If solicitors are instructed to act for lender and borrower in a commercial security, they should have regard both to the 1986 Practice Rules and to the guidance given in this circular which gives examples of specific problems more likely to arise in a commercial security than in a loan over domestic property. These include the need for disclosure of all relevant circumstances, ongoing negotiations, competing creditors' ranking agreements, leased property as security, and security over property subject to licences or quotas. These are areas where the significant potential for conflict which was the justification of the 1986 Practice Rules, is particularly likely to be present.

A second circular was issued in relation to commercial securities in July 1995, with a view to mitigating the rise in costs entailed by the 1994 guideline. The circular noted that in large commercial security transactions, the lender will often accept representations from the borrower's solicitor as to the title of the property offered as security. These representations are contained in a "Certificate of Title", the requirements of which are prescribed by the lender. By relying on such certificates the lender's solicitor (and thus the lender) is saved the expense of examining the borrower's title. In commending this practice in appropriate circumstances the then President noted that granting such a Certificate of Title is covered by the master policy and does not amount to acting for the lender. As such, there is no breach to the

---

[58] Scottish Solicitors' Discipline Tribunal Annual Report 1996 p.4.
[59] Scottish Solicitors' Discipline Tribunal Annual Report 1988 pp.130–131.
[60] 2003 J.L.S.S. October p.46.
[61] A breach of the conflict of interest rules will lead to a double deductible (excess) if a claim is successful as well as a potential finding of professional misconduct. The current excess is £2,000 per partner up to a maximum of ten partners. The firm could therefore be uninsured for up to £40,000 as well as having to face a loading of up to 250% of the premium over a period of five years. There are only about 1,250 firms of solicitors in Scotland and there is therefore a small insurance pool to fund the master policy.

1986 Practice Rules. However, the solicitor who grants a certificate accepts a duty of care towards the lender, and as such should act carefully[62]:

> "It is absolutely essential that solicitors acting for borrowers consider with the greatest care the nature, requirements and undertakings which are demanded. If it is not possible to meet all the requirements and undertakings or it is necessary to place significant qualifications upon them, then it will be a matter for the lenders and their solicitors to determine whether they require to carry out a full examination for themselves, the increased cost of which will be met by the borrowers."

Borrowers and Guarantors. There is a clear conflict of interest between a **7.16.03** borrower and a guarantor. For example, where a jointly owned home is put up as security for a business loan to only one of the owners, the same firm of solicitors should not act for both of them. The solicitor must make it clear that they are not acting for the owner who is not getting the benefit of the loan. In addition, when issuing the standard security for signature by that person, they must accompany it with a letter in terms of r.7 of the 1986 Practice Rules.[63]

In the case of *Smith v Bank of Scotland*[64] the House of Lords decided that the lender (or their lawyer) has a duty to advise such a joint owner to seek independent advice. The duty to give this advice is imposed where there is a reasonable risk that a potential guarantor's consent might be impaired as a result of a close relationship[65] with a third party (in this case, Mrs Smith acted as guarantor for her husband).

Smith was revisited in the House of Lords in the case of *Royal Bank of Scotland v Etridge (No.2)*[66] where they gave further consideration as to what was meant by "independent legal advice". They held that the solicitor's responsibility to the wife in giving advice is to explain the nature of the documents and the practical consequences of signing them, as well as pointing out the seriousness of risks involved, explain that the decision as to signing the documents is for the wife alone to make, check if the wife is willing to proceed; and to ensure that all explanations are given in non-technical language. However, only in exceptional circumstances would the solicitor have to satisfy "himself of the absence of undue influence". Despite the fact that the *Inner* House declined to apply *Etridge* in Scotland in *Clydesdale Bank plc v Black*[67] it is respectfully submitted that the likelihood must be that *Etridge* will come to be accepted as the law of Scotland.[68]

Notwithstanding the decisions in *Smith* and *Etridge*, in *Forsyth v Royal Bank of Scotland*,[69] Lord Macfadyen held that the lenders' security was valid

---

[62] Circular issued by the President of the Law Society July 25, 1995.

[63] See para.7.10 above.

[64] 1997 S.C. (HL) 111.

[65] See Lord Clyde at p.122 C–D.

[66] [2002] 2 A.C. 773.

[67] 2002 S.L.T. 764.

[68] See, "Good Faith in Contract, Spousal Guarantees and *Smith v Bank of Scotland*", Scott F. Dickson, 1998 S.L.T. 39; G.L. Gretton, "Good News for Bankers—Bad News for Lawyers?", 1999 S.L.T. (News) 53; "Royal Bank of Scotland v Etridge (No.2): The end of a sorry tale?" R. Russell 2002 S.L.T. (News) 55 and R. Rennie "Solicitors' Negligence: Rearguard Action" (2002) 7 *Scottish Law and Practice Quarterly 87*.

[69] 2000 S.L.T. 1295.

even though the same firm acted for lenders, borrowers and guarantor, because the guarantor had instructed solicitors. That may help the lenders, but it does focus attention on the solicitors' conduct in acting for parties with conflicting interests.

7.16.04 Acting for More Than One Lender. In 1998, the Professional Practice Committee concluded that there is a clear conflict of interest between lenders in relation to a Ranking Agreement. As such, the same firm of solicitors should never act for more than one lender, even in *de minimis* cases. The firm should also give careful consideration to potential conflicts of interest before accepting instructions from both borrower and lender in a ranking agreement.[70]

7.17 Family Matters

By the nature of things, joint representations frequently involve different members of a family, close relatives and life partners. Hardly surprising that the Law Society should have recognised that in many legal transactions involving such individuals, for example, house purchase and the associated loan from a financial institution, there will be a community of interest rather than a conflict. In such situations where one party has a solicitor, it will usually be unproblematic for the solicitor to act for the other party or parties. However, in some cases the potential for conflict may be substantial because there is not a complete community of interest between the parties. This may involve wills, welfare powers of attorney, loans, guarantees or additional securities over jointly owned property. If so, separate advice may be necessary, even if there is no outright conflict.

7.17.01 Family Loans. In one case in 1988, a solicitor arranged for his wife to sign a standard security in respect of the loan over the family home which was in joint names. In actual fact, and unbeknown to the wife, the security covered the overdraft for the solicitor's practice, as well as the home loan.[71] The Council considered it to be good professional practice that a spouse in such a position should receive independent advice, so that he or she is fully aware of the implications of signing such a deed. As Ryder notes,[72] it is particularly important that the spouse is made aware of the fact that an "all sums due" clause may mean that further borrowings will create an additional security without further documentation being signed. Similarly, where one part of the "family" lends money to another part in order to assist with the purchase of a house there is always a significant potential for conflict.[73]

Again, as we have seen, the Professional Practice Committee is firmly of the view that there is always a conflict of interest where one spouse is asked to guarantee the loan of another. The same solicitor cannot act for both spouses in such a situation. One spouse must be advised to consult an

---

[70] "Guideline on Conflict of Interest and Ranking Agreements" (1998) 43(4) J.L.S.S. 45.
[71] (1988) J.L.S.S. September "Bulletin".
[72] *Op. cit.* p.69.
[73] See para.7.14.12 above.

independent solicitor. If that spouse or partner refuses to be separately advised, they should be dealt with as an unrepresented party, in accordance with r.7 of the 1986 Practice Rules.[74]

Spouses and Wills. It is not, per se, a conflict of interest where a solicitor **7.17.02** takes instructions from spouses or partners to draft non-mirror wills for them, providing they do not purport to be instructing the solicitor to draw up mirror wills.[75] A will is a private document, requiring authority from the individual for its contents to be disclosed to his or her spouse. A conflict of interest would, however, exist if spouses originally instructed mirror wills to be drafted, then unbeknown to the other, one spouse varied the instructions regarding his or her own will.

Divorce and Mediation. As previously discussed, it is not impermissible for **7.17.03** a solicitor to act for opposing parties in litigation, including a divorce. The problem changes if the lawyer is being asked to act, not as an advocate, but as a mediator in a divorce. This is a developing area of professional ethics, where much has been written in the USA[76] and various other English speaking jurisdictions. However, even with the consent of both parties, such a role cannot be combined with the advocacy role. Nor may a solicitor who has previously acted as a mediator subsequently take on the role of an advocate for either party in the divorce. In a mediation a solicitor mediator is not "acting" for either party.

Separation Agreements. The same firm of solicitors should not act for both **7.17.04** husband and wife in negotiating a separation agreement, or even preparing a document that reflects the parties' own agreement. The parties have separate interests which will almost certainly conflict. If the firm has previously acted for both partners it may not continue to act for one partner in a separation or divorce if it possesses any material information of a confidential nature regarding the other party, which has not arisen from the joint representation. Even where the firm does not have such information the fact that nothing revealed to it in the joint representation is confidential with respect to the other partner may leave the party who has been forced too find a new firm feeling betrayed. There is much to be said for sending both parties to other firms whom you trust. It will certainly represent your best chance of retaining both parties as clients in the future. If the firm does act for one of the parties in a separation, it should not act for the other party in any subsequent divorce or ancillary proceedings.

Sale of the Matrimonial Home after a separation (see also para 7.15.08 **7.17.05** **above).** In many separations or divorces the matrimonial home will require to be sold. As we have seen the Professional Practice Committee has issued guidelines about this, most recently in 1998.[77] That guideline states that:

---

[74] See para.7.10 above.
[75] (2002) 47 J.L.S.S. 43.
[76] See e.g. C. Menkel-Meadow *et al, Dispute Resolution* (Aspen Publishers, New York, 2005) and C. Menkel-Meadow *et al, Mediation* (Aspen Publishers, New York, 2006).
[77] (1998) 43 (7) J.L.S.S. 43. See para.7.14.08 above.

> *"Unless the parties have agreed in writing—i.e. an agreement signed by the parties themselves—how the sale proceeds will be distributed, neither of the solicitors' firms acting for the individual spouses in their matrimonial affairs should act in the sale."*

In these circumstances, a separate third firm should be instructed. The written agreement may be part of a full separation agreement or a stand-alone agreement relating only to the free proceeds of the sale. As stated above, the same firm should not act for both spouses in preparing such an agreement. If the matrimonial home is not in the joint names of the spouses, but in the name of only one of them, there is certainly a conflict of interest, and the non-entitled spouse must be advised to see a separate solicitor.

If the spouses have already reached an agreement dealing with the free proceeds, the solicitors acting for one of them in their matrimonial affairs may also act in the sale of the jointly owned home. Both parties must be accounted to in accordance with the agreement. The solicitor cannot then accept unilateral instructions from one of the spouses to alter or ignore the agreement. Instead, the solicitor would immediately be required to withdraw from acting for the spouse attempting to give unilateral instructions, as there would be a clear conflict of interest.

Both the Discipline Tribunal and the Outer House have held that firms of solicitors acted improperly by not accounting to one of the spouses for their share of the proceeds of a jointly-owned matrimonial home where the solicitors had acted for both parties in the sale.[78]

Occasionally there will be no free proceeds of sale, possibly because the property has only recently been acquired with the aid of a substantial loan, or because of substantial arrears due to the lenders. In these cases it is not necessary to obtain a written agreement about the free proceeds, as there will be none. Indeed, there is a community of interest in proceeding with the sale as speedily as possible, to minimise the cost and delay.

7.17.06 Separation of unmarried couples or where there is no civil partnership. The same principles apply here as in the matrimonial situation. It is unwise to act for both parties in preparing a separation agreement, whether or not that involves the sale of the jointly owned home. Clearly issues of "matrimonial property" will not arise, but there will almost certainly be issues about who contributed what, who brought what into the relationship, and who contributed more during the relationship.

7.17.07 Representation for Children. The Professional Practice Committee is strongly of the opinion that the same firm should not act for both parent and child, or children, in a matter involving residence or contact. The principle of separate representation for children was felt to be of such importance that is should be maintained even where there may not be an obvious conflict of interest between the child and the parent concerned.

The committee were asked for guidance in a case where there was an existing arrangement for residential contact every second weekend and the

---

[78] DTD 462/80 and *Dawson v R Gordon Marshall & Co* 1996, G.W.D. 1243 (Lord Osborne).

father sought a variation to increase that to every weekend. The committee took the view that it would be improper for the same firm to act for the child and his mother in opposing the variation. The child (who was 13) and his mother were both happy to continue with the existing arrangements, but objected to the proposed increase, as they lived in a town some distance away from the child's father and the child would be deprived of the company of his friends every weekend if the variation was successful.

In a 2000 case, a female solicitor accepted instructions to act on behalf of an 11-year-old child. The child's parents were going through an acrimonious matrimonial dispute. A partner in the solicitor's firm was instructed to act on behalf of the husband in the dispute, who was the child's father. The solicitor subsequently formed an intimate personal relationship with the husband. After leaving the first firm, she went on to become a partner in another law firm, which was acting for the wife. However, she continued to accept instructions on behalf of the child. The Tribunal held that it ought to have been apparent to her that continuing to act for the child in this way would inevitably give rise to a reasonable lay apprehension of bias due to a fundamental conflict of interest. The solicitor was censured and fined by the Tribunal.[79]

Partnership Agreements 7.18

Commercial partnerships, like families, frequently give rise to joint representation, for reasons of economy, pragmatism and community of interest. Partners are accorded certain statutory rights under the Partnership Act. For the most part, the legislation gives partners equal rights and obligations to one another. However, where these statutory rights and obligations are to be varied by a separate partnership agreement there will almost certainly be a conflict of interest between the parties thereto.

For example, under the Partnership Act 1890, profits are shared equally and liability for partnership debts is joint and severable. Where the partners are exactly equal, there may be no conflict of interest, and so the same solicitor may act for all the parties. However, if this liability is to be varied, there will be implications for individual partners' liability, which should be spelled out to them, and they should seek independent advice.

In relation to the drawing up of a partnership agreement, unless it is a repetition of the partners' rights and obligations under the Partnership Act 1890 (or any superseding legislation) the same firm should not act for all the partners. The firm can take instructions from one of the partners on the terms of a draft partnership agreement, but should make it clear to the others that they should take separate independent advice on the draft agreement before signing it. Such advice should be communicated to the other partners in writing, even if the document is given to the solicitors' own client to discuss with his fellow partners directly.

Ryder also points to the dangers of a solicitor drawing up a deed of admission for a new partner without being certain that the incoming partner had sought independent advice on the liabilities he was about to assume.[80]

---

[79] Scottish Solicitors' Discipline Tribunal Annual Report 2001.
[80] Ryder p.74.

7.19 Shareholders and Directors

Much of what has been said in relation to partnerships also applies to shareholders who have statutory rights under the Companies Acts as well as rights in terms of the articles of association of the company, or by a separate shareholders' agreement. If shareholders are to be treated differentially in an agreement, they should be separately represented.

Problems may also arise in relation to shareholders, directors and the company, particularly in small private companies, where it may be difficult to differentiate between the interests of the three parties. Solicitors should be clear, from the outset, who they are acting for, be it the company or individual shareholders or directors. If there is a community of interest as there will be on many things if the company is trading profitably, there will often be no difficulty in jointly representing the company, the directors and even the shareholders in a small private company. However, if the directors are giving different personal guarantees, or receiving different share options or there is a ranking agreement for loans to the company from the directors then separate representation will be required. Although the 1986 Practice Rules do not extend to moveable property, where a solicitor is instructed to act for both the seller and the purchaser of shares in a private company, and considers there to be no obvious conflict of interests, because, for example, the parties had each received independent advice as to the valuation of the shares, it may still be prudent for him or her to follow the guidelines contained in the Practice Rules, in order to reduce the risk of conflict arising.

Where the company is in difficulties, the potential for conflict between the company, the directors and the shareholders is quite considerable. Each group, for example, has different interests if a question of wrongful trading arises, and separate representation will be necessary.[81]

7.20 Executries and Trusts

In the administration of an executry or a trust the solicitors' clients are the executors or trustees, not the beneficiaries. A conflict can arise with a beneficiary, even if the will is in clear terms. Any beneficiary, including one who is also an executor or trustee, who seeks advice about their personal interest in the estate should be referred to another firm of solicitors. If a surviving spouse or children are asked to discharge their claim for legal rights they should be advised to seek advice from another firm as there is at least a significant potential conflict of interest in such a decision. There may also be disagreement between the executors themselves, which may require the solicitors to delay implementing the administration of the estate or even withdraw from acting altogether. If there is no majority of the executors or trustees in favour of a course of action the solicitors cannot prefer the instructions of one over those of the other, or progress the matter if the other simply declines to give any instructions. Unless such a stalemate can be resolved in a reasonable time, solicitors should intimate to both sides that they will require to cease acting in the matter if agreement is not reached by a specific date.

Where a solicitor administering the estate is also an executor and a dispute arises with the other executors, the Professional Practice Committee have

---

[81] See generally on conflict of interest and companies, Ryder *op. cit.*, pp.74–75.

made it clear that the solicitor must not use his or her position as executor to ensure that the solicitor's firm continues with the administration. The guidance states that the solicitor should either cease acting or resign as an executor.[82] If the solicitor remains as an executor e.g. because there are other interests in the estate to be protected, he or she must accede to a request of the other executor(s) for another firm to be appointed and obtemper any mandate designed to achieve this, in order to prevent a conflict of interest from arising between the solicitor and the client.

Thus in one case a solicitor and his son were appointed as executors to an estate, along with the deceased's widow. They were then instructed as solicitors in the winding up of the estate. In 1982, following a significant delay in the administration of the estate, the solicitor received a mandate from the deceased's widow demanding the administration be handed over to another firm of solicitors. This mandate was not implemented until 1984. The Tribunal held that the solicitor (and his son) should not have used their position as the majority of the executors to retain control of the administration.[83]

Again, in another case[84] a solicitor was a director of a family company and acted both for the company and the other directors and shareholders. A minority shareholder died leaving her shares to her three daughters and the solicitor was instructed to wind up her estate and transfer her shares to the daughters. Wearing his hat as director the solicitor was opposed to the share transfer but wearing his hat as a solicitor he was obliged to implement it. When he declined to carry through the transfer the Discipline Tribunal held that he was in a conflict of interest of his own making and that what he should have done was either to carry out his duty as solicitor for the estate and transfer the shares or cease acting.

Insurers and the Insured **7.21**

Solicitors frequently receive instructions from an insurer to act for an insured either as a pursuer or a defender. Where the solicitor is acting for the pursuer by way of subrogated rights under an insurance policy, the instructions, and the choice of lawyer may well emanate initially from the insurer. However, the insured may retain an interest for uninsured losses (whether a deductible, an excess, or simply a form of loss that the policy does not cover). In such cases the solicitor may properly act for both clients, provided there is no actual conflict. It makes sense, however, to ensure that the clients are agreed as to their respective liabilities should the action be unsuccessful or what will happen if the two clients cannot agree on a settlement offer.

If however, the solicitor is acting in a case where the insured is the defender the position is more complex. In a challenging decision by the Discipline Tribunal in 2003/4 the conclusion was reached that in such situations there is only one client for whom the solicitor is acting, namely the insurer. While this neatly removes the possibility of a conflict of interest arising between the insured and the insurer, it is respectfully submitted that this analysis must be wrong. To hold otherwise would be to conclude that the insured is unrepresented in the action in which he or she is the defender. Since the insured may

---

[82] The Guideline was originally issued in 1986 and reissued in 1998 J.L.S.S. 42.
[83] DTD 604/85.
[84] DTD 465/80.

be a professional person, even a solicitor insured under the Master Policy, the concept that the insurer has paid premiums to receive cover in a negligence suit, but not representation is a curious one. The sounder view is probably that taken by the Professional Practice Committee who are of the opinion that both the insured and the insurer are clients in this situation.[85] There is clearly a potential for conflict, for example, over good faith and the limits of cover, or over the importance of the insured's reputation and accordingly the willingness of the two clients to accept a settlement offer. To some extent these issues will be dealt with by the terms of the insurance policy, and the solicitor's retainer letter from the insurer, but not always. Should a conflict of interest arise between the insurer and the insured, it has been argued by some that that the solicitor's principal client is the insurer and that the solicitor is only a "limited purpose lawyer" for the insured. Accordingly, where a conflict arises the solicitor would be entitled to stay with the principal client. However, it is unclear that the concept of a "limited purpose lawyer" is recognised in Scotland, either in professional ethics or the law of agency. Even if it is, the solicitor would have to have warned the insured at the outset that if a conflict arose the solicitor would continue to act only for the insurer. Problems might also arise if the solicitor has acquired confidential information from the insured which he or she is obliged to disclose to the insurer. If the information does not arise from the joint representation then the solicitor cannot fulfil both the obligation of disclosure and of confidentiality and must give primacy to the latter but withdraw from acting for the insured. If the information derives from the joint acting the solicitor must share it with the insurer and it will not be confidential since it is information derived from a joint representation. The insured is likely to regard that as a breach of the loyalty obligation— especially if the solicitor has not warned the insured at the outset that there is no confidentiality of information in a joint representation as between the two clients. Perhaps for this reason in the USA the courts take the view that should a conflict arise between the insured and the insurer, which is not dealt with in the retainer letter, the solicitor can only continue to act for the insured—and not for the insurer, with whom he or she may have a closer relationship. Certainly, good practice requires that the solicitor should indicate to both clients *at the outset*, what will happen if a conflict arises and the implications for confidentiality of a joint representation.

7.22   Particular Issues Affecting In-House Lawyers

[The sections under this heading are taken from the Guide for In-House Lawyers on Conflict of Interest with the kind permission of the In-House Law Group of the Law Society of Scotland.]

7.22.01   Conflict of interest at meetings for in-house lawyers. In-house lawyers should be aware that their actions can be scrutinised by the Law Society of Scotland, their employers, the profession at large, the Scottish Executive, the Ombudsman, the general public and the press. It is, therefore, imperative that they act in such a fashion as to be beyond reproach by any of these parties.

One of the most complex issues which needs to be considered is the issue of when to declare an interest in meetings where they may be representing or

---

[85] This is also the view taken in the USA.

advising their employers or be seen or believed to be so representative, or where they are acting in another personal capacity.

If an in-house lawyer has another relevant capacity outside of the work place he or she should so declare before taking part in any meeting or event where confusion may arise. The advice given below should still be considered.

It is vital that decisions at any meeting are taken in a manner which is not only impartial but is seen to be impartial by any party who may have an interest (peripheral or otherwise). Therefore, it is advisable that if an in-house lawyer has an interest in proceedings they should declare it and leave the room. If the interest is so minor as to be incapable of being perceived as having influenced the decision, the in-house lawyer may apply one of the alternative courses of action, detailed below.

There are three main areas where conflict of interest requires to be declared as follows.

- Personal—where the matter before the meeting is one which affects the lawyer, his/her family and friends, or his/her business partners or colleagues.
- Financial/Business—where the lawyer has a direct or indirect financial or other business interest in the matter under discussion. This might be by way of being a partner (salaried or otherwise), employee, shareholder, or owner of the business or organisation under discussion. Similarly, it may arise if the lawyer has previously acted professionally for the person, business or organisation, or expects to so act in the future.
- Organisational—where the lawyer is a member of a professional or trade organisation, club or other body, whether formally constituted or not, which could be affected by the outcome.

If the in-house lawyer has one of the above interests, he or she should consider taking one of the following actions. For meetings at which the lawyer may be required to advise his/her employer:

(a) declare an interest and request another solicitor gives advice on the particular matter. For example, where the lawyer is the applicant or affected neighbour in a disputed planning application or similar situation.
(b) declare an interest and give advice to the employer. For example, where the lawyer has a peripheral interest in a matter, such as where a remote family member may be a member of a club.

For meetings in which the lawyer may take part, outwith the course of his/her employment:

(a) declare an interest and leave the room. Take no part in the discussion. Do not vote. This is the most proper action to take in most cases where a conflict of interest occurs.
(b) declare an interest, remain in the room and take no part in the discussion. Do not vote. This might be in situations where the lawyer's interest is minor, but could still be perceived as influencing his/her decision.

(c) declare an interest and remain in the room in order to give information pertinent to the matter under discussion. Do not vote. This course of action should only be taken where the information the lawyer has to bring to the discussion is so vital that the other persons involved in the meeting could not come to a proper decision without that information being disclosed.

(d) where the lawyer's interest is so minor that no person could possibly perceive it has having influenced his/her decision he/she may declare an interest, remain it the room, take part in the discussion and vote.

It is a matter for each in-house lawyer to decide which of these actions are most appropriate. However, in-house lawyers are advised to discuss matters with their superiors in advance of the meeting at which they believe a potential conflict of interest may arise, whether or not they will be required to give advice or assistance in the matter.

It cannot be overemphasised that all solicitors should walk away from proceedings in the event of a conflict and where a conflict is reasonably foreseeable in the circumstances.

7.22.02 In-house Lawyers and the 1986 Rules. Rule 4 of the 1986 Practice Rules makes specific provision for in-house lawyers. Generally, an in-house lawyer, whose only or principal employer is one of the parties to a transaction, may not act for any other party to that transaction. If no dispute arises or appears likely to arise between the parties to a transaction, the in-house lawyer may act for more than one party thereto if the parties fall into one of the categories in r.4(a) or 4(b). That is, the parties must be associated companies, public authorities or bodies, government departments or agencies; or connected persons within the meaning of s.839 of the Income and Corporation Taxes Act 1988.

Rule 4 is without prejudice to the general principle in r.3, and it is still necessary for in-house lawyers to consider whether or not there is an actual conflict of interest between the respective parties for whom they are asked to act.

On occasion the in-house lawyer may be put under subtle, if not open pressure, to act in a certain way that will lead to a conflict of interest. In such circumstances the lawyer should refer the matter to a superior. Reference can also be made to any of the Committee Members of the In-House Lawyers Group or Bruce Ritchie, Director of the Professional Practice Department of the Law Society.[86]

7.23 Local Government

Individual councillors are not the solicitor's employer and care should be exercised where a councillor asks for advice about non-authority business. Where an authority sets up a company or trust or agrees to be a member of a company or trust, external solicitors should be appointed to advise the company or trust. Where a joint venture is set up with another public body (for example, health, water or transport), each body must continue to receive

---

[86] Tel 0131 476 8124; email bruceritchie@lawscot.org.uk.

separate legal advice. That is, a local authority solicitor cannot advise Health Boards, Scottish Water or Transport Authorities on their statutory functions and vice versa.

PART C. SUCCESSIVE CONFLICTS

Successive Conflicts 7.24

A successive conflict can arise when a lawyer is instructed to act for one client against a former client. This situation clearly involves a potential breach of the loyalty obligation. Usually however, the more serious question in successive conflict situations is whether the lawyer has confidential information with respect to the former client which may be used against them. The legal community has endeavoured to overcome this problem by resort to "chinese walls"—information barriers erected within an organisation to prevent the leakage of information between its different departments.[87] There is no Scottish authority on the matter of successive conflicts, but there have been several important decisions in England, culminating in the House of Lords case of *Bolkiah*.

In *Re a Firm of Solicitors*[88] one of the leading patent lawyers in England 7.24.01 moved from a ten-partner intellectual property department to be the head of the IP department in another firm. While he was still in the original firm, some of his other partners had commenced a major piece of litigation which he discussed with them in a general way. The litigation continued after he left. Subsequently, the patent lawyer and his new firm were instructed to act in a part of the litigation, but for the other side. The original client challenged this development, claiming that the lawyer and his new firm should be disqualified from so acting on the grounds of a successive conflict of interest. The judge ruled that there was no English equivalent to the automatic disqualification which exists in such a situation in the United States. Instead he concluded that a solicitor will only be disqualified from acting against his previous firm's clients if he or she has (or there is a real risk that he or she has) relevant confidential information: that is information which was confidential at the time of communication and which remains both confidential and relevant. The onus of proof is on the solicitor. Although we agree with the judge's basic proposition we are surprised at his conclusion that there was no risk to confidentiality in this particular case. Where a solicitor has general discussions about a case, especially if they relate to its likelihood of success, we are in no doubt that this will constitute relevant confidential information.

In *Prince Jefri Bolkiah v KPMG (A Firm)*,[89] KPMG had been employed by 7.24.02 the prince to act in a private litigation. During this time, the firm provided extensive litigation support, of the sort usually undertaken by solicitors, and were privy to extensive confidential information concerning the prince's assets and financial affairs. The prince had been chairman of the Brunei Investment Agency (BIA) until his removal in 1998. The Brunei government then wished to retain the services of KPMG for the purposes of an

---

[87] See Hollander & Salzedo, *Conflicts of Interest and Chinese Walls, op. cit.* Ch.6, on the use of Chinese Walls in other English speaking jurisdictions.

[88] [1997] Ch. 1.

[89] [1999] 2 A.C. 222.

investigation into the affairs of the BIA. KPMG considered that they could act as it had been two months since they ceased to act for the prince, he was no longer a client, and they had set up an information barrier ("chinese wall") around the relevant department. Lord Millett in the leading judgement held the following:

1. Like a solicitor, an accountant providing litigation support services owed a continuing professional duty to a former client following the termination of the relationship to preserve confidentiality.
2. There is no conflict of interest as the fiduciary relationship ends with the termination of the retainer:

> "The only duty which survives the termination of the client relationship is a continuing duty to preserve the confidentiality of information imparted during its subsidence."[90]

3. The onus is on the plaintiff seeking to restrain his former solicitor from acting for another client to establish:

   (i) That the solicitor was in possession of information which is confidential to him and to the disclosure of which he has not consented; and
   (ii) That the information is or may be relevant to the new matter in which the interest of the other client is or may be adverse to his own.

   > "Although the burden is on the plaintiff, it is not a heavy one. The former may readily be inferred; the latter will often be obvious."

4. "The court should intervene unless it is satisfied that there is no risk of disclosure. It goes without saying that the risk must be a real one, and not merely fanciful or theoretical. But it need not be substantial"
   This is in effect the test formulated by Lightman J in *Re a Firm of Solicitors*.[91]
5. The extent of the solicitor's duty "is a duty to keep the information confidential, not merely to take all reasonable steps to do so".
6. The evidential burden [then] shifts to the defendant firm to show that there is no risk that the information will come into possession of those now acting for the other party. There is no rule of law that Chinese Walls or other arrangements of a similar kind are insufficient to eliminate the risk. But the starting point must be that, unless special

---

[90] This is a very narrow ruling on the ambit of fiduciary duties and of conflict of interest, and goes against the practice in such jurisdictions as USA, Canada, Australia and New Zealand, by denying a continuing loyalty obligation. Hollander and Salzedo, *op. cit.* p.76ff take the view that fiduciary duty can continue after the termination of the retainer. We consider that the loyalty obligation can continue after the termination of the retainer but that, unlike the confidentiality obligation, it diminishes with the passage of time. For our advice to firms asked to act against clients whom they have acted for in the recent past in an unrelated matter, see para.7.06 at p.134 above.

[91] [1997] Ch. 1.

measures are taken, information moves within a firm. In *MacDonald Estate v Martin* Sopinka, J. said[92] that the court should restrain the firm from acting for the second client "unless satisfied on the basis of clear and convincing evidence that all reasonable measures have been taken to ensure that no disclosure will occur". With the substitution of the word "effective" for the words "all reasonable" Lord Millett endorsed Sopinka J.'s reasoning.

> "In my opinion an effective Chinese wall needs to be an established part of the organisation structure of the firm, not created ad hoc and dependent on the acceptance of evidence sworn for the purpose by members of staff engaged on the relevant work."

Bolkiah has been followed in a series of cases touching on various aspects of Lord Millett's tests.

In relation to the argument that the only duty to a former client that subsists after the termination of the retainer is confidentiality there have been two Scottish developments of note: **7.24.03**

(a) The first related to a law firm that was acting for an individual client against a large corporation in an employment case. Noticing that the corporation was putting some of its other work out to tender, the law firm successfully bid to get that work. However, having been requested by the corporation to cease acting for clients in dispute with them, the law firm told their first client that they could no longer act for them. Even although the confidential information held by the firm relating to the individual client was not relevant to the new business and was not under threat, the Law Society Council nevertheless concluded that the law firm was in breach of its duty of loyalty to the individual client, since that duty persisted after the termination of the lawyer/client relationship.

(b) Secondly, in *Connolly and Connolly v Brown*[93] Lord Johnston held that it was an established part of the law of agency that the duty of trust and confidence owed by solicitors to their client could extend after the termination of the relationship.

In relation to the requirement that the information be confidential and relevant to the new matter, there have been three significant English cases. In *Apex International (Ireland) Ltd v IBM UK*[94] a specialist solicitor acted for claimants in an action against IBM concerning allegedly defective chipsets. A settlement was reached in the case which contained a confidentiality clause in relation to confidential information obtained from IBM in the settlement negotiations. In a subsequent case brought by another plaintiff against IBM in relation to very similar allegations over the chipsets, IBM sought to disqualify **7.24.04**

---

[92] (1990) 77 DLR (4th) 249 at 269.
[93] Unreported, May 27, 2004 OH. See Ch.8 for further discussion of this case.
[94] 2000 WL 1918545 (CC).

the specialist solicitor on the grounds of the confidentiality clause in the earlier settlement. Judge Hallgarten Q.C. applied *Bolkiah* and held that there was a real risk of the confidential information being disclosed to the second claimant and upheld IBM's challenge. However, he hinted that in this case, some kind of chinese wall might be appropriate.

Secondly, in *Bodle v Coutts & Co.*,[95] an elite London firm held confidential information about Ms Bodle, a previous client, but was acting for a second client, Coutts & Co., in an action brought by them against the first client. The firm had acted for Ms Bodle in preparing an agreement between herself and her partner and Coutts & Co., whereby Coutts & Co. would lend money to them both. The firm was now acting for Coutts & Co. with regard to non-payment of that debt. Justice Peter Smith held that the firm did indeed hold confidential information in relation to Ms Bodle, including the details of the agreement, but nothing that was relevant to the rather narrow grounds of challenge to the agreement which had been mounted by Ms Bodle in the case. Applying *Bolkiah*, therefore, he dismissed the request that the firm be prevented from acting against Mrs Bodle.

However, in the third case, namely the take over bid by the Philip Green Consortium[96] for Marks and Spencer plc in June 2004, Freshfields, one of the "magic circle" of the top five law firms in the UK, was held by the court to be conflicted out of acting for Philip Green because Marks and Spencer were able to persuade the Court of Appeal that Freshfields had formerly advised them on a key contract which with the confidential information relating to it was highly relevant to the success or otherwise of the hostile take over bid.

7.24.05   In relation to the efficacy of chinese walls, the aftermath of Lord Millett's ruling in *Bolkiah* has been particularly problematic.

In *Koch Shipping Inc v Richards Butler (a Firm)*[97] the Court of Appeal stated, with regard to information barriers, that *Bolkiah* did not establish a rule of law that special measures have to be taken to prevent information from travelling unhindered with in a firm, but rather, that the lack of information barriers meant that information did flow.

In the *Bodle* case the judge offered guidance as to the kinds of measure which might be effective in preventing illicit information flows. Having indicated that in his view the confidential information which the firm held was irrelevant to the case, he further held that even if he had been convinced that the confidential information held by the elite law firm was relevant to Ms Bodle's challenge, he would still have rejected the claim of successive conflict of interest because there was no real risk of disclosure. This was because:

(a) all the principals who acted for Ms Bodle in the past had since left the firm,

---

[95] [2003] EWHC 1865.
[96] See *The Lawyer* (2004) (18) (22) 1 and *Marks & Spencer Plc v Freshfields Bruckhaus Deringer* [2005] P.N.L.R. 4.
[97] [2002] EWCA Civ 1280.

(b) the current staff had no access to Ms Bodle's files as they had been kept in storage and then in a locked cupboard to which only the senior partner had access

(c) all the new staff now dealing with the case were under written instruction not to receive confidential information about Ms Bodle,

(d) the senior partner had also sent a memo to every member of staff, instructing them not to discuss Bodle with any other member of staff, and

(e) the senior partner also personally gave an undertaking to keep the files secure and not to let anyone have access to them, unless Bodle gave permission or the court instructed.

The Judge was particularly impressed by the last three factors in the context of an elite law firm. However, with respect, in the era of Enron and similar scandals it must be questioned whether the convention of "gentlemen" is really a sound basis for ethical guidance. In this respect the Court of Appeal's decision to reject similar undertakings in the Marks and Spencer takeover case appears more realistic and more protective of the public interest. Thus, despite the chinese walls put in place by Freshfields and the repeated undertakings given by the firm and its senior partner, including an averment by all the members of the relevant team in Freshfields that they had not received any confidential information on Marks and Spencer, it was all in vain. The Court of Appeal agreed with the High Court judge below (Mr Justice Collins— formerly a very experienced partner in a city firm) that it must be doubtful that, "*even in a firm the size of Freshfields, that effective barriers can be put in place.*" This decision must surely have cast serious doubt onto the efficacy of chinese walls that are not in place well before a conflict arises.[98]

In conclusion, as was pointed out in the *Koch* case, the issue of successive conflicts is a difficult one. On the one hand, client confidentiality has to be maintained in the current climate of increased professional and client mobility.[99] On the other hand, the "intensity of the adversarial process" could result in the court being persuaded that a risk existed where objectively, that risk was fanciful or theoretical. Nevertheless, despite the clarity of Lord Millett's dictum in *Bolkiah*, the position on chinese walls remains unclear and may require a further ruling from the House of Lords.

One final point. Hitherto it had been thought that imputed disqualification (see para.7.08 above) might also apply to successive conflicts. However, in *Bolkiah*, Lord Millett observed with respect to a successive conflict case:

" . . . There is no cause to impute or attribute the knowledge of one partner to his fellow partners. Whether a particular individual is in

---

[98] For further guidance on what measures may be regarded as appropriate to demonstrate an "information barrier", at least in England, see the Law Society of England and Wales, Draft Solicitors' Practice (Confidentiality and Disclosure) Amendment Rule 2004, Explanatory Note 43.

[99] See "Linklaters denies conflict of interest review", *The Herald*, February 28, 2005.

possession of confidential information is a question of fact which must be proved or inferred from the circumstances of the case".[1]

This observation is based on Lord Millett's belief that there are no successive conflicts of interest, the only duty being that of confidentiality.

Lord Millett gave the leading judgement in *Bolkiah*, however, on the point of imputed disqualification his remarks were *obiter*. Nevertheless, they are likely to be regarded as highly persuasive, even in Scotland. It follows that the ambit of *Clelland* may be restricted to simultaneous conflicts.

---

[1] *Prince Jefri Bolkiah v KPMG (A Firm)* [1992] 2 A.C. 222.

CHAPTER 8

SOLICITOR/CLIENT TRANSACTIONS AND RELATIONSHIPS

Introduction   8.01

This topic raises a special form of conflict of interest, namely that between
the interests of the client and those of the lawyer representing him or her in
any given transaction. Put in a slightly different way, it deals with the tensions
which arise between lawyers' self interest and their duties to their clients.
Such tensions continue to lie at the heart of the regulation of the legal
profession today.[1] As has been recognized in the Commonwealth, an integral
part of being a professional person is to put integrity and duty to clients in
advance of personal interest, a perception shared by the profession and the
public and important to public confidence in the legal system.[2] Sociologists of
the profession,[3] and writers on professional ethics are agreed that the power
differential between the professional adviser and the lay client, coupled with
the latter's inability to assess the competence of the former[4] creates a
vulnerability that needs to be addressed. In extreme cases, there may be undue
influence or dependence allowing the professional to take advantage of the
client,[5] more usually there is a concealment of (or a failure to disclose) the
personal interests of the lawyer leading to a prioritizing of the latter's interests
over those of the client, or a failure to provide a full independent, "zealous"
and loyal representation to the client. Unsurprisingly, these issues have
featured strongly in the many regulatory regimes to which lawyers are subject,
e.g. the law on undue influence, on contracts which are contrary to public
policy, the contractual and delictual duties of care and skill, the fiduciary
duties of agents and in professional ethics. In this chapter we will touch on all
of these, but the principal emphasis will be on the lawyer's fiduciary duties or
duties of loyalty,[6] and on their parallel duties in professional ethics. This is not
to say, however, that these duties are mutually exclusive. Often the one piece

---

[1] In truth, this is not a new phenomenon. Traditional notions of professionalism were designed
to protect clients against their vulnerability and lack of technical expertise as compared with that
of the professional.

[2] See the cases cited in G.E. Dal Pont, *Lawyers' Professional Responsibility in Australia and
New Zealand* (2nd edn, LBC Information Services, NSW, 2001) at p.161.

[3] E.g. I. Illich, *Disabling Professions* and T. Johnson, *Professions and Power*.

[4] See e.g., A. Paterson and A. Sherr, *Quality Legal Services* in F. Regan *et al* (ed.) *The
Transformation of Legal Aid* (Oxford, OUP, 1999).

[5] Not only the client's property may be at risk. In the USA there are a range of reported cases
involving lawyers taking sexual advantage of their clients. See R. Rotunda and J. Dzienkowski,
Professional Responsibility: A Student's Guide 2005/2006 (ABA, Chicago, 2005) pp.392–395,
and ABA Formal Opinion 92–356 (July 6, 1992).

[6] See F. Reynolds (17th edn) *Bowstead and Reynolds on Agency* (Sweet & Maxwell, London,
2001) para.6.032 and the literature referred to therein.

of behaviour by the lawyer will fall foul of several forms of legal standards[7] e.g. the contractual and delictual duties of care and skill as well as fiduciary duty. Pursuing a claim under the latter head rather than the former heads may have advantages because it may be that breach of fiduciary duty contains no equivalent to contributory negligence, minimising one's loss or issues of remoteness of damages.[8]

8.02 Fiduciary Duties in Lawyer/Client Transactions: The General Position

Essentially, fiduciary duties involve obligations of trust and loyalty to another party. Traditionally, these duties are said to require lawyers to subordinate their own interests to those of their clients and to avoid acting in situations where their self-interest might tempt them to compromise their loyalty obligations.[9] For Paul Finn, a leading writer on fiduciary obligations in the common law world, the fiduciary principle "enjoins one party to act in the interests of the other—to act selflessly and with undivided loyalty".[10] As Millett L.J. (as he then was) observed in *Bristol and West Building Society v Mothew*[11]:

"A fiduciary is someone who has undertaken to act for or on behalf of another in a particular matter in circumstances which give rise to a relationship of trust and confidence. The distinguishing obligation of a fiduciary is the obligation of loyalty. The principal is entitled to the single-minded loyalty of his fiduciary. This core liability has several facets. A fiduciary must act in good faith; he must not make a profit out of his trust; he must not place himself in a position where his duty and his interest may conflict; he may not act for his own benefit or the benefit of a third person without the informed consent of his principal ... (In this survey I have left out of account the situation where the fiduciary deals with his principal. In such a case he must prove affirmatively that the transaction is fair and that in the course of negotiations he made full disclosure of all facts material to the transaction. Even inadvertent failure to disclose will entitle the principal to rescind the transaction, the rule is the same whether the fiduciary is acting on his own behalf or on behalf of another ...)"

---

[7] Quite apart from a services or conduct complaint.

[8] See S. Baughen, *Professionals and Fiduciaries* (Gostick Hall Publications, Safron Walden: 2002) at p.16.

[9] Most commonly these duties are discussed in relation to financial transactions in which the lawyer gains at the client's expense. Case law from the USA shows that the duty also applies to sexual relationships between lawyers and clients. See fn 5 above. Taking advantage of a client's vulnerability in this way is sometimes treated as a tort, e.g. in Australia (see Dal Pont, *op. cit.* p.176), but more often it is seen as a breach of fiduciary duty e.g. in Canada, New Zealand (see Dal Pont, *op. cit.* p.176) and the USA (see R. Rotunda and J. Dzienkowski, *op. cit.* pp.392–395). In Scotland an action for breach of fiduciary duty would seem appropriate.

[10] See "The Fiduciary Principle" in T.G. Youdan (ed.) *Equity, Fiduciaries and Trusts* (Carswell, Toronto, 1989) at p.4. See also P. Finn, "Fiduciary Law and the Modern Commercial World" in Ewan McKendrick (ed.) *Commercial Aspects of Trusts and Fiduciary Obligations* (Clarendon Press, Oxford, 1992) at p.9. Professor Gretton in a recent essay has argued that a trustee is a fiduciarius, that is, one who must act in the interests of the beneficiary to the exclusion of his own. See G. Gretton, *Trusts* in K. Reid and R. Zimmermann (ed.) *A History of Private Law in Scotland*, Vol.1, p.482.

[11] [1998] Ch. 1.

Unfortunately, the rhetoric of these fiduciary duties[12]—perhaps the paramount duties of agents—stretches further than the reality of the legal protections which they provide.[13] If lawyers were truly required to place their clients' interests before their own, the law of agency would have:

(a) barred all client gifts to lawyers or transactions between them
(b) made void any transactions which did occur and
(c) required the lawyers to return the gifts and any property acquired from their clients, even if this entailed a financial loss to the lawyers.

In contrast, the actual position in the law of agency is that whether the transaction is gratuitous or onerous there is no absolute ban or nullity in such transactions, they are merely voidable and even then only within the relevant prescriptive period and provided no issue of personal bar can be said to arise. Thus Walker on *Contracts*[14] notes:

> "A solicitor's business is not to make contracts with his client, but to do things for him. A contract between solicitor and client is voidable if the solicitor does not make full disclosure of his personal interest as buyer, seller or otherwise, quite independently of any question of its fairness. Even if the solicitor's interest is fully disclosed the question is whether another, independent, solicitor would have advised the contract. The contract may be upheld if, in all the circumstances existing at the time of the contract it was fair and honest and it is not necessarily voidable because the solicitor ultimately makes a profit from it."

As can be seen, the position is considerably more complex than the rhetoric of the duty of loyalty would suggest. This is because in this context, as in so many others, the law is performing a balancing exercise to take account of a variety of interests. Thus the interest in safeguarding clients from their agents' actions is set against a desire to protect innocent third parties who have acquired the clients' property in good faith and as well as the interests of lawyers who have behaved scrupulously fairly to their clients. As a result, lawyer/client transactions will stand if adequate protections were given to the clients.

What then are these protections and what are their limitations? Despite Finn's comments as to the unhelpfulness of the language in this area, there is

---

[12] Paul Finn has pointed to the unhelpfulness of the language used in this area, ranging as it does from "trust" to "influence" and from "loyalty" to "vulnerability", suggesting that it "tends to overwhelm rather than to illuminate" and that the varied usages in this field are in danger of rendering the term "fiduciary" no more useful than a "chameleon or accordion term". See "The Fiduciary Principle" in T.G. Youdan (ed.) *Equity, Fiduciaries and Trusts* (Carswell, Toronto, 1989) at pp.2 and 26.

[13] Despite this, in a number of common law jurisdictions, principally the USA, a decline in professionalism combined with dissatisfaction with the disciplinary processes has seen a significant rise in the number suits for breach of fiduciary duty. It is perhaps worthy of note that in the case of trustees, fiduciary duties are closer to the rhetoric in that the fairness of the transaction or the reasonableness of the trustees' actions are irrelevant. Scottish Law Commission, *Discussion Paper on Breach of Trust* (The Stationary Office, Edinburgh 2003) p.34.

[14] *The Law of Contracts and related Obligations* (3rd edn, T & T Clark, Edinburgh, 1995), para.15.46.

at least a fair degree of unanimity between common law jurisdictions over the protections. Thus much of Walker's statement would apply in other common law jurisdictions.[15] First, such transactions are voidable at the hands of the client[16] with the onus resting on the solicitor to show why the transaction should not be reduced. Originally this was attributed to a presumption of undue influence or that such contracts were contrary to public policy,[17] however today it is thought to be a product of breach of fiduciary duty alone.[18] The onus of proof arises even if the solicitor is not currently conducting any business for the client, provided a fiduciary relationship still exists[19]; moreover it is still breach of duty even if the solicitor can show that the client would have acted the same way whatever the solicitor had done.

Second, the transaction's voidability can be overcome if the solicitor can prove that: (a) when entered into the transaction was fair and honest,[20] (b) there was no undue influence[21] and (c) the client gave his or her fully informed consent to the transaction following disclosure to the client of all the material facts within the solicitor's knowledge. The importance of the fiduciary obligation of full disclosure was underlined in the case of *Spector v Ageda*.[22] Here a solicitor lent money to her client partly to pay off an earlier loan from a money lender which the solicitor knew to be illegal and therefore unenforceable. In awarding damages for breach of fiduciary duty because she had failed to point this out to the client,[23] Megarry V.C. observed[24]:

> "A solicitor must put at his client's disposal not only his skill but also his knowledge, so far as is relevant; and if he is unwilling to reveal his

---

[15] For England see generally Roger Billins, *Solicitors' Duties and Liabilities* (Sweet & Maxwell, London, 1999), pp.42–44, Cordery *on Solicitors* (9th edn, Butterworths, London, 1995), paras 87–89 and "Solicitors" in *Halsbury's Law Of England* (4th edn), Vol.44 (Butterworths, London, 1995), para.135. For Scotland see Begg, *Treatise on Law Agents* (Bell and Bradfute, Edinburgh, 1883), pp.295–298 and Gloag and Henderson, *The Law of Scotland* (11th edn, W. Green, Edinburgh, 2001). See also for Australia, Dal Pont, *Lawyers' Professional Responsibility* (LBC Information Services, NSW, 2001), Ch.7.

[16] But not of third parties. See e.g. Begg, *op. cit.* p.296.

[17] See e.g. *Macpherson's Trustees v Watt* (1877) 5 R. (HL) 9; *Anstruther v Wilkie* (1856) 18 D. 405.

[18] See para.8.03.

[19] Originally this was since the key issue was whether the solicitor was ever in a position to exert an undue influence the client, but see para.8.03.

[20] Sometimes presented as "fair and reasonable".

[21] In England and Wales commentators accept that the solicitor is required to show that there has been no undue influence on the client (provided the transaction is not one that is readily explicable by the relationship of the parties)—a task that is harder to achieve where the client is young, old, or infirm. In Scotland, recent commentators have denied this, arguing that the pursuer has to prove undue influence in every case, including solicitor/client transactions. This argument has come from an understandable endeavour to keep undue influence separate from breach of fiduciary duty, nevertheless in our view the onus remains on the solicitor to show that there was no undue influence (see para.8.03).

[22] [1973] 1 Ch. 30.

[23] *Spector* was reinforced in a leading New South Wales case on the topic, *Law Society of New South Wales v Harvey* [1976] 2 NSWLR 154 at p.170 where Street C.J. observed: "[There] must be a conscientious disclosure of all material circumstances, and everything known to him relating to the proposed transaction which might influence the conduct of the client or anybody from whom he might seek advice. To disclose less than all that is material may positively mislead. Thus for a solicitor to merely disclose that he has an interest, without identifying the interest, may serve only to mislead the client into an enhanced confidence that the solicitor will be in a position to better protect the client's interests."

[24] At p.48.

knowledge to his client, he should not act for him. What he cannot do is to act for the client and at the same time withhold from him any relevant knowledge that he has."

One area of ambiguity remains. Today's case law in England and Wales[25] and the Antipodes[26] takes it as read that the client must receive independent advice from a solicitor unconnected with his or her own solicitor, who is in full possession of all materials facts known to that solicitor. In Scotland, on the other hand, while this is considered strongly desirable,[27] the courts have been prepared to let certain transactions stand even if there was no independent advice, provided the solicitor can show that another solicitor would have advised it.[28]

The third point is that because the transaction is only voidable, the client may lose his or her ability to reduce the transaction through prescription, through the inability to effect *restitutio in integrum* or the operation of personal bar, for example, ratification or homologation,[29] provided the actings of the client are unequivocal, occur after the solicitor's retainer has been terminated and that the client was fully aware of his or her rights to have the transaction set aside. Moreover if the client wishes to claim damages for breach of fiduciary duty he or she will have to show that the solicitor's breach caused him or her loss.[30]

Nevertheless, the problems associated with transactions between solicitor and client are such that the former would be wise to pay heed to the words of Megarry V.C. in *Spector v Ageda*.[31] Having pointed to the difficulties confronting solicitors who choose to act for clients on both sides of a transaction, he goes on to observe:

"Where, however, one of the parties is the solicitor himself, then the matter seems to me to be entirely different: the solicitor must be remarkable indeed if he can feel assured of holding the scales evenly between himself and his client. Even if in fact he can and does, to demonstrate to conviction that he has done so will usually be beyond possibility in a case where anything to his client's detriment has occurred. Not only must his duty be discharged, but it must manifestly and undoubtedly be seen to have been discharged. I abstain from any categorical negative: the circumstances of life are of such infinite variety. But I can at least say that in all ordinary circumstances a solicitor ought to refuse to act for a person in a transaction to which the solicitor is himself a party with an adverse interest; and even if he is pressed to act after his refusal, he should persist in that refusal. Nobody can insist upon an unwilling solicitor acting for him, at all events when there is a conflict of interests."

---

[25] See e.g. *Longstaff v Birtles* [2001] 1 W.L.R. 470 (CA).

[26] For the relevant Australian and New Zealand cases see Dal Pont, *Lawyers' Professional Responsibility* (LBC Information Services, NSW, 2001) at pp.163–164.

[27] See Begg, *op. cit.* at p.295.

[28] See e.g. *Aitken v Campbell*, 1909 S.C. 1217. It is perhaps of relevance that the Scots cases are of a considerably earlier vintage than the recent Commonwealth authorities in this area.

[29] See e.g. *Clelland v Morrison* (1878) 6 R. 156 and Begg *op. cit.* p.296.

[30] *Swindle v Harrison* [1997] 4 All E.R. 705 where it was shown that the loss was caused not by the breach but by the client's decision to run a known risk.

[31] [1973] 1 Ch. 30 at 48.

In sum, in order to safeguard themselves from an action for breach of fiduciary duty, solicitors confronted with a potential conflict of interest between their personal interests and those of their client should:

    (a) consider very carefully before deciding to continue with the transaction,

    (b) obtain the full, free and informed consent of the client to the transaction having disclosed all the material information that they have, and

    (c) insist that if the client wishes the transaction to go ahead, the client is advised by a fully briefed and independent legal adviser.

8.03 Fiduciary Duties as Contrasted with Undue Influence or Public Policy

In the 100 years from 1850 or so there was a steady stream of Scottish cases[32] in which the voidability of transactions between lawyers and clients was raised because of the special relationship which was deemed to exist between them. However, it cannot be said that it is a particularly satisfactory area of case law. Finn's strictures on the use of language in fiduciary cases apply particularly in these cases, since the terminology used by the judiciary has varied between cases and even within them. Until recent times it has been relatively rare for the judgements to be cast in terms of fiduciary duty, but rather with respect to undue influence, public policy or illegality. It is not disputed by modern scholars that the voidability of such transactions is primarily due to breach of fiduciary duty. However, it is also clear that it remains open to clients and their representatives to plead undue influence in cases involving transactions with their lawyers. Unfortunately, the case law is unclear as to what this amounts to and where the onus lies in such cases, the more so since it has been argued that the law on undue influence varies depending if the transaction relates to a contract, a gift or to a legacy in a will.[33] One area of apparent consensus is that the emergence of undue influence in the 19th century cases derives from English equity cases. Nevertheless, it is frequently asserted today that the law on undue influence in Scotland has not followed the English position that certain relationships e.g. agent and client, raise a presumption of undue influence, (provided the transaction is not one that is readily explicable by the relationship of the parties)[34] and consequently that in every case of alleged undue influence in Scotland the onus is on the pursuer to prove his or her case.[35] With some

---

[32] For example, *Macpherson's Trustees v Watt* (1877) 5 R. (HL) 9; *Anstruther v Wilkie* (1856) 18 D 405; *Grieve v Cunningham* (1869) 8 M. 317. These cases were largely based on English equity cases relating to undue influence.

[33] See e.g. W. McBryde, *The Law of Contract in Scotland* (2nd edn) (W. Green, Edinburgh, 2001) at para.16.33 and W.H.I Wilder *Undue Influence in English and Scots Law* (1940) 56 LQR 97 at p.104.

[34] On this caveat, see Lord Nicholls of Birkenhead in a speech which was endorsed by all his colleagues in *Royal Bank of Scotland v Etridge (No.2)* 2002 2 A.C. 773 at 798–800.

[35] See e.g. W. McBryde, *The Law of Contract in Scotland* (2nd edn, W. Green, Edinburgh, 2001) at para.16–34; D.M. Walker, *Civil Remedies* (W. Green, Edinburgh, 1974), p.155; D.M. Walker, *The Law of Contracts and related Obligations* (3rd edn, T & T Clark, Edinburgh, 1995) at para.15.33 and W.H.I. Wilder *Undue Influence in English and Scots Law* (1940) 56 LQR 97. See also Lord Clyde in *Smith v Bank of Scotland*, 1997 S.C. (H.L.) 111 at 119.

temerity, the authors remain unconvinced, at least in the case of transactions between solicitors and clients where the deed was drafted by the solicitor. A close examination of the case law discussed by the commentators fails to uncover any such case where a solicitor benefited from a gift, legacy or contract with his or her client in which the onus of establishing undue influence was left on the client.[36] The position of legacies drafted by solicitors in their own favour[37] are arguably clear cut. Thus in *Grieve v Cunningham*[38] the Lord President asserted the "well established rule" that the onus was on the solicitor who prepared the will to "show that the settlement in his favour was the free and uninfluenced act of the testatrix", and in *Stewart v MacLaren*[39] the House of Lords ruled that a solicitor who had taken a gift by a will which he had prepared, had to show that the testatrix was not unduly influenced by him. Indeed, D.M. Walker one of the commentators who denies that there is a presumption of undue influence in solicitor/client transactions, in his work on *Civil Remedies*[40] accepts that where a solicitor drafts a will in his or her own favour this "throws on the solicitor the onus of proving that the settlement in his favour was the free and uninfluenced act of the testator". Similarly, in the case of gifts to solicitors from their clients the courts seem happier to place the onus on the solicitor to establish the lack of undue influence rather than the other way round.[41]

In short, it is difficult to see why Scottish clients should be said to be in a less advantageous position than their English counterparts. In addition, therefore, to averring breach of fiduciary duty, clients who feel that their lawyers have benefited to a substantial extent from gifts, wills or contracts drafted by them[42] should expect that the onus will rest on their solicitors to show that no undue influence was exercised by them over the client.

If the position on undue influence is not entirely clear cut, the position on public policy or *pacta illicita* is even less so. Thus, the references to lawyer client transactions being contrary to public policy which are contained in *Begg*[43] and some of the 19th century case law seems to have proved something of a false trail, not least because of the uncertainties associated with that concept in the law of Scotland.[44] It follows that clients wishing to reduce or challenge a transaction which they have entered into with their solicitor would be advised to rely firstly on averments of breach of fiduciary duty,

---

[36] Several cases are discussed by the commentators but either the deed was not drafted by the solicitor mentioned in the deed or the case did not involve a solicitor/client transaction at all. They are therefore arguably not in point. Thus in *Weir v Grace* (1899) 2F (HL) 30 the will was drafted by an independent agent and in *Ross v Gosselin*, 1926 S.C. 325 the offending codicil was penned by the testator herself.

[37] See para.8.09.

[38] (1869) 8M 317.

[39] 1920 S.C. (H.L.) 148 at 153.

[40] (W. Green, Edinburgh, 1974), p.156.

[41] This is arguably what occurred in *Anstruther v Wilkie* (1856) 18 D 405 and in *Logan's Trs v Reid* (1885) 12 R. 1094.

[42] Provided the transactions are not ones which are readily explicable by the relationship of the parties—see Lord Nicholls of Birkenhead in a speech which was endorsed by all his colleagues in *Royal Bank of Scotland v Etridge (No.2)* [2002] 2 A.C. 773 at 798–800. This stipulation is relatively easy to meet with solicitors since, as Walker argued in *Contracts, op. cit.* para.15.46 : "a solicitor's business is not to make contracts with his client, but to do things for him".

[43] *Op. cit.* p.295.

[44] See e.g. W. McBryde, *op. cit.* Ch.19.

secondly and only where it offers an additional advantage, on also pleading undue influence. There would seem little advantage to be obtained from pleading that the transaction was contrary to public policy.

8.04   Ethical Obligations in Lawyer/Client Transactions: The General Position

Originally, these derived from the law of agency but through time they have become enshrined in and further developed through the common law principles of professional ethics which exist throughout the Anglo-American world. Again the rhetoric of loyalty features strongly. Thus, art.2 of the Scottish Code of Conduct states:

> "*Solicitors must always act in the best interests of their clients . . . [and] must not permit their own personal interests . . . to influence their actings on behalf of clients.*"

Similarly, the English Guide to the Professional Conduct of Solicitors asserts[45]:

> "*A solicitor must not act where his or her own interests conflict with the interests of a client or a potential client.*"

The English Guide goes on to indicate that[46]:

> "*In conduct there is a conflict of interest where the solicitor in his or her personal capacity sells to, or purchases from or lends to or borrows from his or her own client.*"

On the surface, therefore, the conduct rules would appear to enforce the rhetoric of loyalty to a greater degree than the fiduciary obligations of agents. In practice, although it can be argued that the conduct rules leave solicitors less room for manoeuvre than the law of agency does,[47] there is relatively little difference between the two regimes. Thus the fact that a solicitor proceeds with a transaction with his or her client does not necessarily mean that the lawyer will be subject to discipline. Such transactions are usually ethically permissible provided the client gives his or her informed consent, in the knowledge of all the material facts and provided that he or she has been independently advised.[48] Informed consent without independent advice will not suffice to protect the solicitor from a conduct charge. If the client declines to be advised by another solicitor who is unconnected with the first lawyer,[49]

---

[45] r.15.04. A similar ban on acting or continuing to act where the client's interests and the practitioner's interests would be or are in conflict, exists in Australia and New Zealand. (Dal Pont, *Lawyers' Professional Responsibility* (LBC Information Services, NSW, 2001) at. pp.162–163).

[46] note 1 to r.15.04.

[47] See J. Griffiths-Baker, *Serving Two Masters* (Hart Publishing, Oxford, 2002) at p.49.

[48] Begg, *Law Agents* (at p.295) and note 1 r.15.04 English Guide.

[49] A solicitor who is in the same firm as the original lawyer, or is connected to that lawyer through blood or marriage will not be considered an independent legal adviser.

then the solicitor must refuse to proceed with the transaction. It will not suffice to show that an independent lawyer would have given the same advice.[50]

While most of the problems which arise in this field can be overcome by a combination of full disclosure, independent advice to the client and client consent, this is not always the case. For example, certain breaches of the Solicitors (Scotland) Accounts Rules cannot be purged by independent advice and consent.[51]

With respect to the closely related issue of taking undue advantage of a client, the conduct rules go less far than those contained in the law of agency. As we have seen,[52] in England and arguably also in Scotland, where a solicitor enters into a transaction with a client there is a presumption of undue influence, which the solicitor must rebut if the transaction is to stand. However, no such presumption arises as a matter of conduct in such transactions. Nevertheless, if it can be shown that the solicitor has abused the fiduciary relationship by taking advantage of the client through, e.g. age, inexperience, ill health, lack of education or emotional vulnerability, it is likely that in Scotland, as in England this will be a conduct offence.[53] One example of such an abuse might include a situation where the solicitor entered into a sexual relationship with a client. This raises issues of undue influence, independence,[54] acting in the best interest of the client[55] and conflict of interest between the lawyer and the client. Nevertheless, contrary to the position with doctors in the UK where it is always misconduct for them to enter such relations with a patient, it will generally only be so for a lawyer in relation to a client where the latter is particularly vulnerable or has become dependent on the lawyer, for example, in a traumatic divorce case. Thus in England, principle 12.09 states that "whilst it would not necessarily be so, it may be an abuse of the solicitor/client relationship for a solicitor to enter into a sexual relationship with a client." In Australia, New Zealand[56] and in America[57] the various states have taken a similarly nuanced stance. However, in the USA following the major overhaul of the ABA Model Rules of Professional Conduct in 2002, a clearer rule has emerged, namely that it is misconduct for a lawyer to have sex with a client unless a consensual sexual relationship existed between them when the lawyer/client relationship was formed.[58] There has been no express ruling on the matter in Scotland, however, we believe that it is likely that the propriety of such a relationship

---

[50] Curiously, in the USA under the Model Rule 1.8 such transactions are ethically permissible even if there is no independent advice provided the transaction is one that is fair and reasonable to the client, there is informed consent, and the client is given an opportunity to consult independent legal advice.

[51] Where the breach involves the dishonest appropriation of the client's property, compensation may be available from the Scottish Solicitors' Guarantee Fund.

[52] See para.8.03.

[53] Principle 12.09.

[54] Article 1 of the Code of Conduct for Scottish Solicitors 2002 stipulates that solicitors must not allow their independence to be impaired or their advice or conduct to be influenced by extraneous considerations or a desire to ingratiate themselves with their clients.

[55] Article 2 of the Code of Conduct requires that solicitors must always act in the best interests of their clients and must not permit their own personal interests to influence their actings on behalf of clients.

[56] Dal Pont, *op. cit.* p.176.

[57] R. Rotunda and J. Dzienkowski, *Professional Responsibility: A Student's Guide 2005/2006* (ABA, Chicago, 2005), pp.392–395.

[58] rule 1.8(j).

will turn on the vulnerability/dependency of the client or whether the sexual relationship had antedated the legal relationship. Clearly informed consent cannot exist here to absolve the practitioner. Moreover, it is not even clear that the conflict of interests thrown up in such cases can be overcome by independent advice, whatever may be the case where the interests of the lawyer and the client are financial in nature.

8.05 General Transactions with Clients

As we saw earlier,[59] where a lawyer[60] enters into a general contract[61] with his or her client that transaction will be voidable for breach of fiduciary duty, although this can be overcome if the solicitor can prove that (a) when entered into the transaction was fair and reasonable[62] (b) that there was no undue influence,[63] (c) the client gave his or her fully informed consent to the transaction following disclosure to the client of all the material facts within the solicitor's knowledge and (d) the bargain was one which an independent agent would have recommended. Thus, Begg asserts[64]:

> "As long as a law agent acts for a party, he ought not to enter into any contracts or transactions with him . . . Where a law agent proposes to enter into a contract with a client or to obtain from him a conveyance or other deed in his own favour, his proper course is, in the first place, to see that the client's interests are committed to the charge of another and independent law agent, and in the second place to supply the new agent with all the information possessed by himself . . . [Such contracts] will be set aside if there has been the slightest impropriety in the agent's conduct, or the least inadequacy in the amount of consideration or cause of granting; that the *onus* of proving the fairness of the transaction lies on the agent; and that he must prove, by other evidence than the deed constituting or embodying the transaction in question, the actual receipt by his client of the money, in consideration of which the deed bears to have been granted."

The fiduciary duty of disclosure bites particularly strongly when the solicitor fails to disclose his or her interest in the transaction e.g. that the property being sold to the client belongs to the solicitor or that the ultimate purchaser of the property that the client is selling is the solicitor. In the leading case of

---

[59] See para.8.02.

[60] The fiduciary constraints imposed on solicitors contracting with their clients extends to close relatives of the solicitor or of other members of his or her firm. This would include a spouse, parent, child, brother or sister or the spouse of any of them.

[61] The list of such contracts could be many and varied. One that has occurred with some frequency in the USA is the literary agreement whereby the lawyer acquires literary or media rights concerning the client's trial or case, including information relating to the representation. Such agreements raise a serious potential conflict of interest between the lawyer and the client.

[62] See *James Gillespie & Sons v James* Gardner, 1909 S.C. 1053. *cf.* the Discipline Tribunal Annual Report 1994 "A solicitor exposes himself to severe criticism where there is a course of contractual dealing with a client or in any transaction where the solicitor has a personal interest, because such action inevitably deprives the client of independent advice and leaves open the question whether the transaction was fair and reasonable in the circumstances."

[63] See para.8.03.

[64] *Op. cit.* pp.295–296.

McPherson's Trustees v Watt[65] Watt, a solicitor in Aberdeen arranged to buy four houses from the Trustees (for whom he acted). Ostensibly, the purchaser was Watt's brother, but in reality the brothers had agreed that Watt would buy two of the houses from his brother without informing the Trustees. This failure to disclose the ultimate purchaser of two of the houses was held to be fatal to the validity of the transaction. As Lord O'Hagan observed[66]:

> " . . . if he becomes the buyer of his client's property, he does so at his peril. He must be prepared to show that he has acted with the most complete faithfulness and fairness; that his advice has been free from all taint of self-interest; that he has not misrepresented anything or concealed anything; that he has given an adequate price, and that his client has had the advantage of the best professional assistance which, if he had been engaged in a transaction with a third party, he could possibly have afforded; and although all these conditions have been fulfilled, though there has been the fullest information, the most disinterested counsel, and the fairest price, if the purchase be made covertly in the name of another without communication of the fact to the vendor, the law condemns and invalidates it utterly. There must be *uberrima fides* between the attorney and the client, and no conflict of duty and interest can be allowed to exist."

Very similar considerations apply to such transactions as a matter of professional conduct. They will be ethically permissible provided the client gives his or her informed consent, in the knowledge of all the material facts and provided that he or she has been independently advised.[67] In 1982 the Scottish Solicitors discipline tribunal[68] had to consider the case of a solicitor who had been instructed to sell a flat for his clients with an asking price of £10,000. At first his efforts met with little success, but after two months he reported that he had received an offer of £8,000. He did not reveal that the offer came from one of his partners. The clients accepted the offer. Three weeks later the partner re-sold the flat for £10,500. A complaint was made to the Law Society in that the solicitor had neither disclosed his partner's interest nor sent the clients to an independent agent for advice. The tribunal relied on the dictum of Lord Gifford in *Clelland v Morrison*[69] that "employment of a

---

[65] (1877) 5 R. (H.L.) 9.

[66] At p.17.

[67] Begg, *Law Agents* (at p.295) and note 1 r.15.04 English Guide. However, it is probable that where the agreement contains a continuing conflict of interest or serious potential conflict of interest, even independent advice and informed consent will not suffice to overcome the ethical problem. Thus if a lawyer was to reach an agreement to acquire the literary or media rights concerning the conduct of the representation by the lawyer of the client in a high profile trial or case, even if the client was independently advised, it would be likely to be regarded as a non-consentable conflict of interest. The temptation to conduct the representation in a way that would enhance the marketability of the story of the case, rather than in the way that is most in the client's interests, is one that has to be avoided. There is no express ethical ruling on this in Scotland. In the USA, ABA Model Rule 1.8(d) bans lawyers from entering into such agreements before the end of the representation of the client, even where the client is independly advised. We believe that this should be position in Scotland also.

[68] DTD 568/82.

[69] (1878) 6 R 156 at 169.

firm is employment of all the partners" with the result that it was as if the respondent had submitted an offer in his own name to his clients. It was observed by the respondent's counsel that there was no evidence that the clients had been prejudiced, that they had received the difference between the respective sale prices together with interest, that there was no charge of conspiracy or dishonesty and that there was no complaint from the clients. However, these matters only went to mitigation at best,[70] and the Tribunal held that the respondent had an absolute duty to disclose his interest to his clients and to direct his clients to seek independent legal advice.[71] He was accordingly found guilty of professional misconduct. Interestingly, in a subsequent case in the Outer House,[72] Lord Johnston held that where an agent is instructed to obtain the best price for a property being sold by his or her client/principal and thereafter discloses to the client that he or she wishes to purchase the property for his or her own benefit, it may not be sufficient to require the client to be independently advised as the obligation of trust and confidence that agent would obtain the best price for the property would also apply to any bid that that agent might make. Thus if the agent then immediately resells the property at a substantial profit he may be held to be in breach of this continuing fiduciary obligation of confidence and trust.

8.06 Loans to and Borrowing from Clients

Loans to and from clients can give rise to particular difficulty. The basic essentials of informed consent and independent advice[73] apply, whether the solicitor is the lender or the borrower. Thus a solicitor who borrowed money from a finance company in his client's name, taking a standard security out over her property, but provided no safeguard or written acknowledgement for the client, was found guilty of misconduct in 1989 for failing to insist that she be independently advised.[74] Again, a solicitor who persuaded a client to lend him £30,000 without independent advice was also found guilty of misconduct,[75] as was the assistant solicitor in 2000 who persuaded several clients to mortgage their property, without independent advice, in order to provide him with a loan so that he could stave off sequestration.[76] At one time it was relatively commonplace for a solicitor to advance clients' funds for the benefit of other clients. That practice stemmed from an era when institutional lending was not generally available and the Tribunal in 1994 reserved its opinion regarding the acceptability of the practice in the present day.[77] In any event, solicitors are required to adhere to the terms of the Solicitors Accounts rules which touch on loans and clients in several respects. Thus r.21 of the 2001

---

[70] See Ch.2.

[71] Consequently where a solicitor, or at least a partner, wishes to offer for a house his firm are selling, the selling client should be referred immediately to another firm of solicitors and the solicitor's agency will be deemed to have terminated. See *Connolly and Connolly v Brown* (Outer House, Court of Session decided on May 27, 2004).

[72] *Connolly and Connolly v Brown* (decided on May 27, 2004).

[73] *Doran v Council of the Law Society of Scotland*, 1992 S.L.T. 456 at 459.

[74] DTD 783/89.

[75] See Discipline Tribunal Annual Report 1994.

[76] See Discipline Tribunal Annual Report 2000.

[77] See Discipline Tribunal Annual Report 1994. Such loans would have to have the prior written permission of the clients under the provisions of the Accounts Rules.

Accounts Rules provides that: "A solicitor shall not borrow money from his client unless his client is in the business of lending money or his client has been independently advised in regard to the making of the loan."[78] Again r.22, in the interests of fraud prevention, prohibits a solicitor acting for a lender where the loan is to the solicitor or a relative. Although, as we shall see later,[79] there is an exception to the need for independent advice in family cases where a legacy to a solicitor is involved, it seems clear that no such exception applies in the case of loans.[80] This emerged from the *Doran* case,[81] where a solicitor borrowed £15,000 from his brother-in-law to purchase his office premises. The brother-in-law obtained the funds by taking out a mortgage secured over his own dwelling-house. The solicitor handled all the legal work in connection with the loan. Although he agreed to be responsible for the loan repayments, nothing in the documentation indicated that the solicitor was the real debtor. The First Division on appeal from the solicitor's conviction for professional misconduct held that in failing (a) to insist that the brother-in-law be separately represented and (b) to create documents to demonstrate the true nature of the transaction the solicitor had indeed been guilty of professional misconduct. In light of the conflict of interest involved in the transaction, the court was not prepared to hold that it was an arrangement between close relatives where separate representation was unnecessary.

It is equally important that clients are safeguarded where they are borrowing from their solicitors and the general requirements of disclosure, informed consent and independent advice will apply wherever the sums and rate of interest involved are significant. In *Newell v Tarrant*[82] a solicitor lent funds to a husband and held deeds to the couple's property on deposit as security, without suggesting to the wife that she seek independent legal advice. There was a clear conflict of interest resulting from the solicitor's position as solicitor to the husband and, in effect, in his position as the couple's banker. The solicitor's failure to consider the wife's interests separately from those of her husband coupled with his own clear position of conflict allowed the court to set aside the transaction on grounds of undue influence.[83]

On the other hand, it is normal for a solicitor to fund a client's outlays in the course of the transaction and some firms will still arrange bridging loans for clients, in their own names, or even make advances to a client in respect of an award of damages which has been made to that client. These arrangements are wholly acceptable provided the accounts rules and the disclosure requirements highlighted in *Spector v Ageda* are adhered to, without the need for independent advice. It should be noted, however, that a law agent is not precluded from taking security for the amount of his or her

---

[78] It will be noted that this rule adds nothing to the common law position. Indeed, it erodes it by introducing an exception in the case of moneylenders.

[79] See para.8.10.

[80] The exception only applies if all members of the family are equal co-beneficiaries. Presumably, if one member of a family was giving similar loans to all other members of the family including the solicitor the exception might apply, but this is not clear.

[81] *Doran v Council of the Law Society of Scotland*, 1992 S.L.T. 456.

[82] [2004] E.W.H.C. 772.

[83] On the meaning of "independent legal advice" see *Royal Bank of Scotland v Etrige (No.2)* [2002] 2 A.C. 773 in Ch.11 below.

fees and cash advances, without the need for independent advice. However, if a standard security is taken for this purpose, the client should be separately advised.

8.07　Joint Venture Contracts

Another area of difficulty relates to contracts entered into between solicitors and clients which are essentially joint ventures rather than transactions which are incidental to the lawyer/client relationship. Lord President Dunedin addressed this situation in *James Gillespie & Sons v James Gardner*[84] where a firm of tradesmen without capital persuaded their law-agent in 1895 to lend them the funds to invest in a joint venture relating to property development. Although the joint venture was successful, in 1908 the sole surviving partner in the firm brought an action of count, reckoning and payment against the law-agent claiming that the law-agent was precluded by his fiduciary relation as law-agent from taking advantage of a transaction entered into with his clients. The Inner House held that you should look to the position of the parties when the transaction was entered into, and to the risks involved, rather than approaching the situation from a position of hindsight. On this basis the bargain was a fair and honest one, and beneficial to the interests of the clients, and the return to the law agent was not excessive. As the Lord President observed:

> " . . . where you have the law-agent and the client entering into a contract about things which do not fall within the matters covered by a law-agent's remuneration, yet in respect of the fiduciary position and in respect of what the law considers the superior position of the law-agent in the matter of knowledge over his client, that bargain will not be supported unless the law-agent can show that the bargain was fair and entered into without concealment of any kind."

It follows that as in other contracts between the lawyer and the client the transaction will be prima facie voidable for breach of fiduciary duty, although this can be overcome if the solicitor can prove that:

(a) when entered into the transaction was fair and reasonable
(b) that there was no undue influence and
(c) the client gave his or her fully informed consent to the transaction following disclosure to the client of all the material facts within the solicitor's knowledge.

Lord Dunedin added that the joint venture would be easier to uphold if the initiative for the joint venture came from the client or if the transaction was not a recent one.

One of the issues about joint ventures is whether the solicitor is acting qua solicitor or merely as a joint adventurer with no responsibility for providing legal or business advice to the co-adventurers. This point arose in another joint venture over property development at about the same time as the *Gillespie* case. In *William Robertson Aitken v The Rev. Thomas MacFarlane Campbell*[85]

---

[84] 1909 S.C. 1053.
[85] 1909 S.C. 1217.

the venture was a success, resulting in a large profit to the law-agent. Thereafter the builder brought an action of reduction of the agreement and for repayment of certain of the profits, on the ground that the law-agent had taken advantage of his position as law-agent to induce the pursuer to enter into an unfair bargain which was to his disadvantage. The law agent pled in defence that the relationship between the parties was that of joint adventurers, and not agent and client. The Inner House considered that even although the transactions were outside the scope of a law-agent's ordinary business, the defender had acted as law-agent in entering into them, and they must therefore be subjected to the closest scrutiny. However, they concluded that, looking to the circumstances of the parties at the time, and to the risks undertaken by the law-agent, the agreements were fair and reasonable, and not liable to reduction. As Lord President Dunedin observed:

> " . . . whenever you come to anything like financing, or purchase and sale, or any bargains of that sort, you are necessarily out of what you may call the ordinary relations of an agent an client. Notwithstanding that, the law . . . is that a contract of any sort between a client and his agent must be scrutinised in a way that a contract between two third parties would not be. Accordingly, I do not think you can solve the question, as the Lord Ordinary seeks to do, by looking at the nature of the transaction, and then saying—'Because this transaction is not an ordinary transaction between a law-agent and his client, therefore the man was not acting as law-agent.' You have to find out whether the general relationship of law-agent and client exists, and then, if you find it does exist, you must apply the strictest scrutiny to the contracts."

The Lord President added that the criterion for deciding the fairness of such a transaction is: "would another law-agent have advised it, or, if the proposition had been made by a third party, would this same law-agent have advised it to his own client?"

Very similar issues arise when joint ventures are examined from the perspective of professional ethics. The first thing the Tribunal has to ask itself is whether the lawyer is acting more as a co-adventurer than as a legal adviser In one 1988 case a solicitor approached an existing client with a proposal that they should jointly purchase some office premises as a speculative venture. The Tribunal held that the main link between the parties was their common interest as prospective purchasers that the clients themselves had direct experience of the marketing of property, and that such solicitor/client relationship as may have existed in relation to this venture was secondary. Regrettably, the solicitor failed to make it clear to the clients that his relationship was strictly commercial and that the clients should look to another solicitor for such legal advice as they might require.

Later, the concept of a joint venture faded and subsequently the solicitor accepted instructions from another client to submit an offer for the same property in competition with the original clients; and the solicitor was charged with having acted in a conflict of interest situation. In view of the actual relationship between the solicitor and the original clients, the conflict of interest charge was not established; but the solicitor's failure to make his position clear had a material bearing on subsequent events and when the original clients attempted to instruct the solicitor to put in an offer for themselves, the solicitor was held culpable in not immediately responding to these clients with an explanation that he could not act for them.[86]

In another case, a client advanced funds in support of a joint venture with the solicitor, who used some of the funds to meet his personal obligations. The Tribunal made a finding of professional misconduct against the solicitor because he had failed to fulfil his obligations at common law, namely, that he failed to repay the loan timeously and a cheque subsequently drawn by the solicitor was dishonoured.[87]

In sum then, in joint venture contracts the first question to be asked is: "Was the solicitor acting as an adviser or simply as a co-adventurer?" The onus is on the solicitor to demonstrate that the position is the latter rather than the former. Where the solicitor is merely acting as a co-adventurer, professional ethics requires that the solicitor fulfil his or her share of the bargain, but it is easier to uphold the transaction as a whole, than if the solicitor was acting as an adviser.

8.08 Gifts

General fiduciary principles prohibit lawyers from retaining a benefit obtained by virtue of a fiduciary position.[88] As Lord President Dunedin made clear in *James Gillespie & Sons v James Gardner*[89] and in *William Robertson Aitken v The Rev. Thomas MacFarlane Campbell*[90] it is widely recognized that a law-agent as a fiduciary is not able to extort from his client as remuneration anything over and above his ordinary professional fees, whether that remuneration is given merely as a gift or as covenanted for. This in part flows from the rule that a solicitor is only entitled to a fair and reasonable remuneration.[91] As Walker asserts[92]:

> "In relation to gifts, a gift by a client is . . . always revocable, without need to prove undue influence, as being other than his proper remuneration. For the law to be otherwise would leave clients open to influence and oppression. A gift to a former solicitor may be unobjectionable and a gift may be ratified after the employment has ended."

The leading case remains *Anstruther v Wilkie*[93] where a client, heavily in debt, agreed to pay his solicitor his full business account and also to gift a further sum of £1000 to him as a reward for the extra trouble which he had had with the client's business as well as for the zealous manner in which he had conducted it. The Lord Justice Clerk observed that there might be onerous

---

[86] Discipline Tribunal Annual Report 1988.

[87] Discipline Tribunal Annual Report 1996 p.3. There was no separate charge under r.9 (now r.21) of the Accounts Rules, whereby a solicitor shall not borrow money from a client unless the client has been independently advised with regard to making the loan, as it was established that the client had been in the practice of lending money for property developments.

[88] Dal Pont, *Lawyers' Professional Responsibility* (LBC Information Services, NSW, 2001). p.163.

[89] 1909 S.C. 1053.

[90] 1909 S.C. 1217.

[91] See Ch.9 above.

[92] D.M. Walker, *The Law of Contracts and related Obligations* (3rd edn, T & T Clark, Edinburgh, 1995) at para.15.46.

[93] (1856) 18 D. 405.

dealings between client and solicitor in the course of which gifts might be made which could not be open to any ground of challenge, but added that in this case:

> "the stipulation for this gift ... I regard as inconsistent with the confidence and trust which the relation of agent implies, and with the protection and defence of the interests of his client, which the relation of agent imposes on the latter. Advantage of the embarrassed condition of the client's affairs the agent shall not take for his own interest, and in order to obtain gifts ... Just as, in various classes of cases (which include medical advisers when their patient is dangerously ill, or in the infirmity of old age, and agent's preparing wills for such parties) an agent undertaking the interests of needy and embarrassed clients, in which any actual benefit is stipulated for and obtained by such adviser, acts in violation of the trust and confidence bestowed in him, and the benefit becomes undue and unfair advantage taken of the infirmities or the embarrassments of the party who is entitled to expect protection in return for that confidence and disinterested assistance in his bodily or pecuniary difficulties: The stipulation in question is, in my opinion, clearly and wholly incompatible with the duty of the agent."[94]

It would be fair to say that the judges in *Anstruther* were not entirely at one as to why the gift was unsustainable, with references to "breach of trust", "*pactum illictum* and "undue influence" appearing in their respective opinions. However they were all agreed that the gift could not stand. It is submitted that what they were feeling for was the notion of breach of fiduciary duty. There was a clear conflict of interest between the lawyer's duty to the client and the lawyer's own interest—hence the outrage of the Lord Justice Clerk at the agent's act: "To talk of it as a gift is absurd, ... preposterous ... I call things by their right names, and therefore I regard this as extortion." The reference to "extra trouble" he regarded as "humbug".[95] In the subsequent case of *Logan's Trustees v Reed*[96] a client assigned the use of a private box in an Edinburgh theatre to his law agent as a free gift. His representatives after his death succeeded in reducing the assignment because personal bar in the shape of acquiescence or delay had not operated. Once more the Inner House uses the phrases "*pactum illicitum*", "contrary to public policy" and "undue influence" but fails to reach a consensus other than as to the reducibility of the assignment. While it is clearly arguable from these cases that a presumption of undue influence arises in relation to gifts from clients to their lawyers,[97] it is submitted that in Scotland *inter vivos* gifts from clients to lawyers[98] constitute a breach of fiduciary duty and are therefore voidable unless the solicitor can show that the gift is "fair and reasonable", (as well as not being the result of undue influence). While there is nothing in the Scottish case law

---

[94] *ibid.* at 416, *per* L.J.C. Hope.

[95] *ibid.* 415.

[96] (1885) 12 R. 1094.

[97] See para.8.03 and W.H.D. Winder, *Undue Influence in English and Scots Law op. cit.* In the common law world the most common form of undue influence in lawyer / client transactions relate to gifts and legacies Dal Pont, *Lawyers' Professional Responsibility* (LBC Information Services, NSW, 2001), p.159.

[98] Other than token gifts or those from close relatives.

on client/ lawyer gifts on the issue of informed consent or the *Aitken* test of "whether an independent lawyer would have advised it",[99] there would seem to be no reason why this should not be the case as in the case of onerous contracts. To offer the client less protection in the case of gratuitous contracts would seem hard to justify. It follows that if a gift to a lawyer from a client is challenged the solicitor will also have to show that either:

(a) the client was separately advised by an independent lawyer who was fully informed of all the circumstances or

(b) that an independent lawyer would have advised the transaction or

(c) that reduction of the gift should be prevented by personal bar, e.g. ratification of the gift after the lawyer/ client relationship has come to an end.[1]

If anything, the position of gifts in terms of professional ethics is even more constrained. Anything more than a token or *de minimis* gift (or one from a close relative) will open the solicitor to discipline unless the client has been independently advised.[2] It is irrelevant whether the gift is in breach of fiduciary duty or subsequently reduced. This strict position is based on three foundations. First, a solicitor is not entitled to more than his or her "fair and reasonable" remuneration for acting on a client's behalf.[3] Secondly, because to allow such gifts to stand in the absence of independent advice would be to give countenance to the perception of undue influence created by such transactions. Thirdly, because to permit clients to make substantial gifts might be to create a perception that the independence of the lawyer was under threat. Thus art.1 of the Code of Conduct for Scottish Solicitors impliedly strikes at receiving substantial gifts from clients when it stresses:

> "Independence is essential to the function of solicitors in their relation-ships with all parties and it is the duty of solicitors that they do not allow their independence to be impaired irrespective of whether or not the matter in which they are acting involves litigation."

---

[99] See para.8.02 above. It is far from clear whether the *Aitken* test or the independent legal advice test really differ substantially in content from the requirement that the gift/ transaction is "fair and reasonable".

[1] Similar protections exist in England and the USA. In the latter, as Wolfram, *op. cit.* p.486 observes, "modern courts . . . place squarely on the lawyer the burden of proof to establish that the gift is fair, equitable, and not the result of undue influence."

[2] Websters (1996), *op. cit.* para.2.11. The same pertains for *inter vivos* gifts in England and Wales under Principle 15.05 of the *Guide to the Professional Conduct of Solicitors, op. cit.* The position is slightly different in the USA and Australia. In the former, M.R.1.8 (a) requires gifts to be "fair and reasonable" and fully informed but not necessarily the subject of independent advice unless (M.R. 1.8(c)) the gift is a substantial one and requires an instrument, in which case independent advice is required, unless the donor is a close relative. In Australia, r.9.2 of the Law Council's Model Rules of Professional Conduct Rule provides that a gift conferring a substantial benefit which requires an instrument, must be the subject of independent advice, Dal Pont, *Lawyers' Professional Responsibility* (LBC Information Services, NSW, 2001), p.159. It is submitted that the UK position is preferable. There seems no good reason why a cash gift of £10,000 from a client is acceptable without independent advice but when the same gift requires an instrument, the client must be independently advised.

[3] See Ch.9 above.

Testamentary Gifts/Legacies and Fiduciary Obligations   **8.09**

Although the client protection issues with respect to testamentary gifts are identical to those for *inter vivos* gifts, the relevant case law for the two areas has evolved sufficiently separately to prevent mutual cross-referencing. In England this was due to differences in probate and equity. In Scotland, the special position of testamentary writings has also played a part. This may help to explain the fact that the courts have stated even more unequivocally than in the "gift" cases, that where a solicitor has drafted a will under which he or she benefits substantially, there is a presumption of undue influence. Thus in *Grieve v Cunningham*[4] the next of kin of an elderly spinster who had died leaving her property to her law agent, sought to challenge the validity of the will (which had been drawn up by the law agent) *inter alia* on the grounds of undue influence. In dismissing the challenge the Lord President observed:

> "I hope the judgment in this case will not be supposed to lend the slightest countenance to the idea that it can in any circumstances be proper for a law-agent to take a deed in his own favour. That is in all circumstances improper. But although that is so, it does not necessarily follow that a deed so taken is null. That is not the law of Scotland. It was the law of Rome, but the rule has not been adopted into our practice. The rule of Scotch law is well stated by the Lord Ordinary, who says that "in many, perhaps in most cases, the presumption against the deed created by the mere circumstance that the party favoured is the law-agent who prepared it, will supply the want of all other elements of fraudulent impetration. It can never be a proper course, in any ordinary circumstances, for a law-agent so to act; and the Lord Ordinary conceives that it will be always upon him to show that the making of the settlement in his favour was the free and uninfluenced act of the testatrix, deliberately entertained and carried through with an entire knowledge of its effect." Judging this case by that rational and well established rule, the question is, whether the defender in this action has discharged himself of the burden laid upon him. I think he has so discharged himself."

The House of Lords reinforced this position in *Forrests v Low's Trustees*[5] and *Stewart v MacLaren*.[6] In the latter Viscount Haldane noted that:

> "when a law-agent takes a gift by will, he has got to show very clearly . . . that the gift is the free and spontaneous gift of the testatrix, knowing what she was doing, and under no influence from him as regards the substance of the disposition. He must show, in other words, that he has confined himself strictly to his business as law-agent, and has not transgressed its very highly binding obligation of confidence."

And Lord Dunedin went on to add:

> "I do not think that there is any conflict of authority as to the position of a law-agent who prepares a will which contains some benefit to

---

[4] (1869) 8 M. 317.
[5] 1909 S.C. (H.L.) 16.
[6] 1920 S.C. (H.L.) 148.

himself . . . It seems to me to stand thus. In the ordinary case a will which is probative proves itself, and a person founding on its provisions need do no more than produce it . . . But when the person who claims is the law-agent who prepared the will, he is bound to do something more; he must clear himself from the idea that the gift in his favour was got by deception or undue influence, or that the testator did not know what he was about when making his will."

Nevertheless, it is submitted that these cases should be read as establishing that the drafting of a will by a solicitor in his or her own favour is *prima facie* a breach of fiduciary duty, allowing the will to be challenged. As in other client property cases, the solicitor should be able to prevent the reduction of the will by demonstrating that the testator was *capax* and that there was no undue influence. In addition, it would seem appropriate to insist that the transaction was "fair and reasonable", and that either:

> (a) the testator was independently advised, or
> (b) an independent solicitor would have advised the transaction or
> (c) that personal bar should prevent the reduction.[7]

8.10 Testamentary Gifts/Legacies and Professional Ethics

In relation to professional conduct, for many years now it has been accepted in Scotland that it is professionally improper for a solicitor to prepare a will in terms of which the solicitor, or his or her family or partners obtains a substantial benefit.[8] It follows that it can never be proper for a solicitor to draft a will under which he or she obtains a share of the residue. He or she must insist that the client instructs an independent solicitor to advise the client (and not simply to attest a will which the original solicitor has drafted). If the client refuses, the solicitor must decline to act. The leading case on this is *Cattanach*[9] where a solicitor drafted a will in which he obtained a legacy worth approximately £65,000. His efforts to bring in an independent solicitor to attest the testamentary writings which he had drafted earlier, were dismissed by the tribunal as being quite inadequate. He was found guilty of professional misconduct and received the maximum fine of £4,000 as well as named publicity. The Tribunal indicated that the penalty might have been less if the legacy had been renounced, but in vain. The solicitor somewhat unwisely appealed the penalty imposed to the Inner House and lost.[10] In its Opinion the Tribunal observed:

> "The procedures to be followed by a solicitor in preparing a will for a client are firstly to take instructions and to advise the client in relation to these instructions, thereafter to prepare the will in accordance with the

---

[7] True, the Scottish case law does not go this far, however, there have been few modern cases in which to put the matter to the test.

[8] See e.g. 1982 J.L.S.S. 27 319, 1983 J.L.S.S. 276 and 1989 J.L.S.S. 389 (DTD 755/89).

[9] DTD 699/87. See I. Smith and J. Barton, *Procedures and Decisions of the Scottish Solicitors Discipline Tribunal* (T & T Clark, Edinburgh, 1995), pp.77–81.

[10] Even taking all the expenses of the matter into account the solicitor would have emerged with a substantial profit. In the circumstances it is not clear that the penalty imposed in this case can be said to have acted as an effective deterrent.

testator's wishes. However, in the event of the solicitor ascertaining that it is the testator's wish to confer a significant benefit on the solicitor or indeed to the solicitor's partner or member of staff or to the families of any of them, then the solicitor has a duty not to proceed further, but to advise his client to be separately represented. It is then for the independent solicitor to take instructions and advise the testator, prepare the testamentary deed and have the same executed. The purpose of this rule is not simply to protect the solicitor in the event of a charge of undue influence . . . the rule is of long standing and is based on the principle that the employment of a solicitor involves a very high degree of trust and influence. As Lord Widgery pointed out, in *Re a Solicitor*[11] the propriety of a solicitor's actings is an entirely separate matter from the validity of the testamentary writing or the particular bequest."

There are only two recognised exceptions to the general principle.[12] The first flows from the reference to "substantial benefit". It is that it is entirely proper for a solicitor to prepare a will in which he or she receives a token legacy of an insubstantial sum of money or a specific legacy of an item of no great value where the purpose of such legacy is to recognise the testator's appreciation of the solicitor's services. What then constitutes a "substantial benefit"? No precise definition has been forthcoming from the Discipline Tribunal. In some jurisdictions it is said to be a relative concept varying with the size of the estate. In Scotland, as in England, it is accepted that it should vary relative to the size of the estate, but also that an amount can be substantial in and of itself.[13] The second exception relates to the solicitor's family. It is accepted that a solicitor may ordinarily make a will for his spouse, his parents or children, or siblings, provided that any potential beneficiary is not materially disadvantaged. For example, it would be in order for a solicitor to make a will for her widowed father dividing the whole residue between herself and her brother who was the only other member of the family; but the making of such a will would not be acceptable if the solicitor had a surviving sister who was not to benefit.[14]

The extent of these exceptions was explored in a Discipline Tribunal in 1989.[15] The solicitor was the senior partner in a small firm. The testator had been employed by that firm throughout her working years and continued to be a close friend of the family even after she retired. In her last will, which was drafted by the solicitor, she left him a one-seventh share of residue. He was subsequently charged with misconduct and in his defence he stated that there had been a special relationship between the testator and the solicitor, and

---

[11] [1975] 1 Q.B. 475.

[12] Exactly the same principle applies in England and Wales. Principle 15.05 of the Guide to the Professional Conduct of Solicitors establishes that "where a client intends to make a gift . . . by will to his or her solicitor, or the solicitor's partner , or a member of staff or to the families of any of them and the gift is of a significant amount, either in itself or having regard to the size of the client's estate and the reasonable expectations of prospective beneficiaries, the solicitor must advise the client to be independently advised as to that gift and if the client declines, must refuse to act." A similar prohibition exists in the USA under Model Rule 1.8(c).

[13] In DTD 780/81 it was held that legacies of £2,000 out of an £80,000 estate and £1,000 out of an estate of £60,000 were substantial both in amount and in proportion to their respective estates and went beyond what would ordinarily be regarded as token amounts.

[14] See 1989 J.L.S.S. 389.

[15] DTD 755/89.

indeed throughout the solicitor's lifetime she had been regarded as part of the family. However, in the absence of an actual relationship, the tribunal was not prepared to accept the close family friendship as an extension to the established exception.[16] The Tribunal also added that: "The essential part of the rule is that the solicitor should neither take instructions nor make such a will, either personally or within his firm, and if *per incuriam* such a will is made outwith the solicitor's knowledge, it is his duty to renounce the bequest at the earliest possible date."

In 1992 the Code of Conduct for Scottish Solicitors was adopted, art.2 of which, on *"The Interests of the client"* provides that[17]:

> "Where solicitors are consulted about matters in which they have a personal or a financial interest the position should be made clear to the clients and where appropriate solicitors should insist that the clients consult other solicitors. For example, neither a solicitor, nor a partner of that solicitor, is generally permitted to prepare a will for a client where the solicitor is to receive a significant legacy or share of the estate."

Given the caveat contained in the introduction of the code[18] it seems most unlikely that this wording was intended to depart from the clarity of the established ethical rules in this area. Thus the reference to "generally" was almost certainly intended to cover the two well known exceptions to the rule that independent advice is required in this field. However, following the adoption of the code, Law Society fiscals have begun to couch complaints before the discipline tribunal in terms of art.2 of the code, rather than by reference to *Cattanach* and its predecessors. This has opened the door to respondents to argue that "generally" can include more exceptions than the two traditional ones. This argument was successful before the Council of the Law Society on one occasion before delegated powers were re-introduced in 2003. However, it is submitted that this is an erroneous approach to the code, which was not intended to codify the common law rules of misconduct. Confirmation of this can be found in a decision of the Discipline Tribunal in 1996 which was confirmed by the Inner House in 1998, before the Tribunal[19] the code of conduct was founded upon in a complaint where it was established that a solicitor had taken instructions and prepared a will on behalf of a client and the will had contained a substantial bequest in favour of that solicitor. The Tribunal found that the solicitor had established a close day-to-day friendship with the testator which extended far beyond the normal solicitor/client relationship. The solicitor had given significant practical help to the testator and the testator had instructed the solicitor to prepare a will containing a bequest to himself of her dwelling-house (valued at approximately £170,000).

---

[16] In the same year the Discipline Tribunal declined to hold that the exception could include "a close family friend as well as a distant relative through marriage, who had stayed with the solicitor and his wife during periods of illness."

[17] In the Commentary section.

[18] The Introduction indicates that while the code contains "a statement of the basic values and principles which form the foundation of the solicitor profession. It is not intended to be an exhaustive list of all the detailed practice rules and detailed obligations of solicitors ... " It is clear, therefore, that the Code of Conduct, despite its title is not a codification of common law misconduct. Indeed, the President of the Law Society in his Introduction to the 1992 Code describes the Code as a "statement of good practice".

[19] Discipline Tribunal Annual Report 1996, p.5.

The Tribunal was referred to the word "generally" in the passage from the code of conduct quoted above, but in the opinion of the tribunal, there was no exception[20] to the established rule as reflected by the code of conduct, where the client was unwilling to consult another agent.[21] The solicitor appealed to the Inner House *inter alia* on the grounds that the Tribunal had failed to take into account relevant considerations including the fact that:

(a) the solicitor and the client had been close friends of long standing
(b) before the execution of the will the petitioner had already been a beneficiary of the testator's testamentary intention and
(c) her fellow executor under the will had wanted her to accept the bequest.

None of these factors were held by the Inner House[22] to constitute an exception to the standard rule.

Conclusion and Proposals for Reform   **8.11**

Given the importance of fiduciary obligations for the regulation of solicitors and the obvious scope for conflicts of interest between those of the client and those of the solicitor in this area it is surprising that it should take twenty or so pages of text to set out the basic fiduciary and conduct rules in the field. One reason is that the protections in this field have derived historically from different parts of the law since they have been perceived as belonging to different legal categories or classifications. However, from a client protection perspective there is little logic to the differing case law on undue influence, breach of fiduciary duty and professional misconduct. To leave the anomalies is to encourage evasion. It surely cannot be acceptable for a solicitor to indicate to his or her client that while he or she may not draft a will for them in terms of which the solicitor receives a substantial benefit, the same result could be achieved by a holograph will or hand written codicil or possibly even an *inter vivos* gifts. To permit this would be to defeat the spirit if not the letter of the rules on drafting deeds or wills. It is therefore to be hoped that the Law Society and the Discipline Tribunal would perceive such an act as in itself professional misconduct. As for the future the answer is surely that solicitor/client transactions[23] should be treated as voidable and potentially open to discipline unless the solicitor can prove that:

(a) when entered into the transaction was fair and reasonable,
(b) that there was no undue influence,

---

[20] Other than the *de minimis* or the familial exceptions.

[21] The same solicitor was also charged at common law in relation to the will of another client who bequeathed property to an unqualified member of the solicitor's staff. While such a course of conduct is specifically prohibited in the corresponding English Code of Conduct, the Tribunal was not prepared to find that the general principle as reflected in the Scottish Code, extended to any will under which a member of the solicitor's staff might benefit.

[22] See *Matthew v Council of the Law Society of Scotland*, 1998 S.C. 306.

[23] Other than *de minimis* or certain familial transactions.

    (c) the client gave his or her fully informed consent to the transaction following disclosure to the client of all the material facts within the solicitor's knowledge, and

    (d) the client was independently advised by another solicitor.

CHAPTER 9

THE ACCOUNTS RULES, CLIENT INTEREST AND MONEY LAUNDERING

Introduction 9.01

This topic also raises issues relating to a form of conflict of interest, and again it is the tension that can arise between the interest of the lawyer and the lawyer's firm on the one hand and their fiduciary and ethical duties to clients on the other. This time the focus is on the most vulnerable of client assets—client money. This has long been an area of concern since lawyers, unlike many other professionals, frequently hold and transact with substantial amounts of client money. In England the profession in the 19th century and earlier, generally held client monies mingled with their own in one account. Even after a spate of serious frauds at the end of 19th century, the profession was slow to react. A special general meeting of the English Law Society in 1907 agreed to a requirement that separate accounts be created for firms and for clients but rejected the suggestion that solicitor's accounts should be inspected annually by an accountant.[1] Subsequently, after the public clamour had died down the resolution was quietly forgotten about. It was not until the Depression that separate accounts and accountants' certificates were introduced in 1934.[2] Although Scottish solicitors were required to pay interest on client money which they held[3] it was not until the Legal Aid and Solicitors (Scotland) Act 1949 that they were required to keep separate accounts which were annually inspected by accountants.

The modern day framework for the rules on handling client money by Scottish solicitors is contained in ss.35–37 of the Solicitors (Scotland) Act 1980 (as amended). The latest version of the rules themselves is the Solicitors (Scotland) Accounts, Accounts Certificate, Professional Practice and Guarantee Fund Rules 2001 (henceforth referred to as the Accounts Rules).

The Accounts Rules 9.02

The purpose of creating rules covering the handling of clients' money is to set parameters for solicitors, and their accountants/advisers and cash room staff as to what is required by way of records when handling client business. The rules also provide a framework to allow for monitoring/supervisory work,

---

[1] H. Kirk, *Portrait of a Profession* (London, Oyez: 1976).

[2] The society's proposals for separate client accounts were rejected at the 1930 AGM, prompting a prominent member of Council (Sir John Withers) to resign and introduce his own Bill on the topic in the House of Commons. It was this provision that eventually prevailed on the statute book.

[3] See Begg, *op. cit.* Ch.XI.

both internal and external. The rules are drawn in general terms and allow for a broad range of systems which would comply with their requirements. They allow solicitors to use simple systems wherever possible. They also allow for sophisticated systems when they are needed to handle larger practices or the more complex types of business. There are a number of suppliers of computer systems who provide accounting solutions which are linked to case management or business systems. Cost/benefit analysis must be carried out if choices are being made in this sector of the market in order to avoid expensive mistakes. If in doubt, take expert advice from an experienced adviser.

9.03   The Key Elements

The key elements of the current Accounts Rules can be divided into 4 sections.

A. Bookkeeping requirements for daybooks and ledgers.
B. Twice yearly reporting to the Law Society.
C. Professional obligations relating to financial dealings for clients. This includes some particularly important elements such as not acting for lenders and anti-money laundering regulations.
D. Making claims against the Scottish Solicitors Guarantee Fund

A. Bookkeeping Requirements

9.03.01   Bookkeeping Rules: Rule 8. The general design of any accounting system needs to meet the requirements set out in r.8. This requires a chronological record of cash receipts and payments separated between clients' monies and the solicitor's own money. Also a set of ledger records should be set up—one for each client. The ledger should record separately the debit, credit and if possible, a running balance for entries in the general client bank account. Separate ledgers or columns should show a record of invested funds held to earn interest for a named client. There should be a separate ledger or column for any overdraft or bridging loan taken for a client.

The solicitor's own section of the accounting should follow the same style—a chronological record of receipts and payments and a set of general ledger cards which group together the business trading accounts. This includes all balance sheet accounts showing assets, liabilities and the capital accounts built up over the years. All accounting records should be retained for at least 10 years. The ultimate purpose of these records is to show clearly the separation of clients' funds and solicitors' funds and the separate record of each individual client. By keeping these accounts the solicitor should be able at all times to demonstrate compliance with r.8 and r.4.

Rule 4—Sum at Credit of Client Bank Account. Rule 4 requires the solicitor to keep in a client bank account or accounts enough money to pay out all balances due to clients at any one time—and thereby avoid the dreaded "shortage on client account". Failure to comply with this aspect of the rules in particular can lead to the appointment of a Judicial Factor to the practice and the solicitor's personal estate and the suspension of the solicitor's practising certificate.

Rule 6—Drawing from Client Account. The next step in understanding the interplay of the various bookkeeping rules is to consider the terms of r.6. This rule deals with the solicitor's entitlement to make payments on behalf of clients without specific instructions being obtained from the client. Payments may only be made from the client's own funds and includes an entitlement to take appropriate fees. In order to take money from the client bank account for or to account of fees, three steps must be taken. Firstly, the legal work which justified the fee must be done. Secondly the fee note must be sent to the client. Finally the fee must be entered into the bookkeeping system and charged to the individual client's ledger. Only then can funds be transferred to the firm's bank account, although the second and third steps can be taken on the same day.[4]

Transfers can be made specifically for the amount of a fee note or a group of fee notes. They can also be done by way of round sums to account of fees debited, leaving the rest of the funds lying in the client bank account until required. This creates a float or surplus funds due to the solicitor within the client bank account. Most solicitors deliberately set up their own float or surplus to cover small inadvertent mistakes on the client account. This is normal, but is a matter for individual judgement.

Rule 6 allows for payments to be made only on the understanding that while there may be enough money in the client bank account to allow a particular payment to be made—there must be sufficient funds held on the individual client's own ledger to cover the payment. If there are not enough funds on the individual ledger payment may be made from the solicitor's own surplus or float. A clear policy must be set to deal with this situation.

What is absolutely forbidden by r.6 is to use one client's monies to finance another client's business without specific authorisation from the "lending" client. Even if this is possible to obtain it is not recommended. Clearly, issues of conflict of interest are bound to arise in such circumstances.

Rule 6 also makes reference to a requirement to enter an individual client name in the payee space when funds are being remitted on their behalf to a bank or other financial institution. This is an important protection to ensure funds are applied to the correct individual. In order to audit this aspect of the rules, all client bank account cheques must be recovered from the bank and be available for inspection. Failure to observe the terms of r.6 can result in individual entries on client ledger being disallowed under the rule. A fee note not rendered to the client or an unauthorised payment on behalf of a client from another client's account can both be set aside.

Depending on the amount involved and whether the solicitor operates a large float or surplus the reversal of such entries can produce a shortage on client account resulting in a breach of r.4. The solicitor is invited to immediately correct the shortage. Failure to do so can lead to serious consequences—a Judicial Factor will be appointed if matters are not corrected.

---

[4] Further details as to the ethics of Fee Charging and the taking of Fees to account under r.6 are contained in Ch.10 below on Fees, Charging and Taxation.

Rule 5—Opening Client Bank Account. The setting up of a client bank account and the introduction of the solicitor's own funds is permitted under r.5. The setting up of a float at the outset of a new practice is an individual decision. If a float is introduced special care should be taken in the early months. Funding client outlays can become very expensive, particularly for new and growing businesses. It is important to decide if it is policy to ask to be put in funds in advance. Setting out the cash expenses including an estimate of fees is useful when dealing with new clients. It also sets out clearly the extent of funding required for the work, and the client's ability/willingness to pay for the work is resolved at an early stage in the process.

Rule 9—Monthly Reconciliation. Once the records have been set up and the transactions have been recorded in the daybooks and ledgers, the next step is to set up some checking systems to prove the accuracy of the accounts. This work is set out in r.9 and r.10. Rule 9 requires a monthly check of client ledger accounts. This is done by making a complete list of debit and credit balances on the client ledgers as at the last day of the month. The total credit balances should always be covered by the amount of money in the client bank account as at the same date. This involves more work than merely checking the balance on the client bank statement at the same date. All entries in the daybook must be matched to the same figure on the bank statement. After allowing for cheques in the pipeline (on the way to being presented against the account) and adjusting for any other differences, this adjusted balance on the bank account should be compared to the total credit balances. This check verifies the surplus or balance position.

All the working papers from this monthly checking must be retained for three years including the summary of the balances/surplus position. The same checking work can be carried out more frequently in busy practices. This is just good practice and not a requirement of the rules. In large practices, computer systems generate such management reports on a daily basis. This is only prudent given the scale and volume of transactions and the need to show a surplus balance at all times. Smaller firms prove their surplus position during the month by running significant floats to deal with the risk of inadvertent errors.

Rule 10—Other Funds. This rule follows the same principle but deals with funds invested in accounts in the solicitors' name for individual clients. The rule only requires the reconciliation work to be done quarterly. If this is done then the whole of the clients funds both general funds and named funds should be checked as at the same date each quarter. Many solicitors check the invested funds more frequently. If the check is being done monthly, then it should coincide with the monthly check of general client funds. This basic control means that all clients' funds are present and accounted for at the same time and date.

Rule 11—Interest to be earned for clients.[5] This rule is intended to secure clients' funds by investing them in an interest bearing account in the solicitors' name in trust for the individual client. The rule requires, where £500 or more is likely to be held for a period of two months, that the funds

---

[5] It has long been recognised that where a solicitor holds a substantial sum of money for a client for a significant period, interest will be due to the client. However, until the 1960s it was

must be invested to earn interest for the client. There is no specific advice or instruction about the type of account.[6] Quite apart from the accounts rules issue, when larger amounts are held for a shorter period, interest should be earned for the client to avoid the risk of a finding of inadequate professional service.

There are a number of schemes operated by the banks which allow for individual accounts to be held in a "bundled" account. Interest is earned on the total sum and is allocated at individual rates to each client based on high street rates interest available for their money. Premium rates may be paid by the solicitor to individual clients. The terms must be set out in the terms of business letter, in order to operate such a scheme, making it clear that the facility earns a higher global rate of interest. The additional interest is for administering the investment facility.

Rule 7—Other entries in the ledger. The other bookkeeping guidance found in the rules is under r.7. This deals with transactions which do not pass through the client bank account. A book entry should be made to keep the accounting records complete and allows the whole transaction to be reviewed on the ledger.

In conclusion, the accounting systems are intended to be easy to keep and easy to check. Any work, whether dealing with the original entries or checking /supervising the work, is best done in small chunks. Looking over a day's work or reconciling work weekly instead of monthly or indeed monthly instead of quarterly may not be required by the rules but is very good practice. Letting work build up until a backlog of accounting work exists is a very dangerous situation. Working without accurate or up to date accounts can result in expensive errors. It can also result in the appointment of a Judicial Factor to the practice in the most serious circumstances.

Rule 12—Designated Cashroom Partner. This introduces the concept of a Designated Cashroom Partner. The concept is based on the partners all being jointly and severally liable for ensuring compliance with the rules, but in addition, partnerships must nominate a person to supervise and generally check the work of the cashroom. A key element is to ensure that individual partners are working within the compliance framework. They will ensure that cashroom staff who have concerns about transactions have a responsible person to handle their concerns. The Designated Cashroom Partner post may

---

commonplace for many firms of solicitors in Scotland to take the view that if the client's money was a relatively small sum or was only being held for a short time, then it was appropriate for the firm to hold on to any interest earned on such sums on the grounds that it would be impractical or uneconomic to allocate the interest to the clients. Some firms even considered the interest to belong to them and could point to a ruling appearing to support this viewpoint from the Law Society of Scotland in 1951. This was a curious reading of the law of agency and of fiduciary duty—and not one which found favour in the USA or in the Commonwealth. In such jurisdictions it has long been commonplace for "unallocatable" amounts of interest on client trust accounts to be taken by the state to fund legal aid cases, or legal education. It was not until *Brown v Inland Revenue*, 1964 S.C. (H.L.) 180 that the issue came before the courts. The Courts were in no doubt that the interest did not belong to the lawyer , but rather to the clients. As Lord Reid observed: "This interest was earned by using clients' money . . . I can therefore find no ground on which it could be held that this interest ever became the property of the [solicitor]." *ibid.* pp.191 and 192.

[6] However, Deposit Receipts are no longer considered a suitable type of investment.

be rotated within the partnership or even be shared by two partners to give cover for holiday/business absences. The person appointed must be able to sign off the twice-yearly Accounts Certificate on behalf of the partnership (see separate paragraph under Accounts Certificate section).

B. Accounts Certificates and the Rules

9.03.02 The Current System. This was introduced in 1998 and replaced the original style of certificate prepared by a professional accountant with a form designed to be submitted by the solicitor. The new form has now been developed into three separate styles:

1. Mainstream practices with client accounts
2. Practices without a client bank account and
3. Practices where the solicitor acts as agent for other solicitors and does not require a client bank account.

All certificates must cover an accounting period of no more than 6 months in duration, and be delivered in one month from the end of the accounting period. Extensions of time may be granted on cause shown, but the certificate must be delivered within 3 months of the due date. Failure to comply with this requirement will result in a process being launched to seek to suspend the solicitor's Practising Certificate under s.40 of the Solicitors' (Scotland) Act 1980 for breach of the rules. It is very rare to proceed to suspension, since delivery of the certificate halts the action. If an Accounts Certificate is delivered after the Practising Certificate has been suspended, the receipt of the late certificate will uplift the suspension, unless the solicitor is subject to a complaint having been made to the Scottish Solicitors Discipline Tribunal. In such circumstances, the supervision would continue until the Tribunal findings are issued. Production of the mainstream style of Accounts Certificates is the responsibility of the Designated Cashroom Partner and in the case of partnerships, one other Partner. They sign on behalf of the partnership and have the responsibility for the accuracy of the figures and information contained in the certificate.

9.03.03 Form of Certificate. Separate certificates must be submitted for each place of business where separate accounting records are held. Conversely, if there is more than one place of business covered by a centralised accounting system then a single certificate listing all branches covered by the accounting system should be prepared. The form of certificate is shown on Sch.1 of the rules. It includes a clear statement of the accounts records being up-to-date and complying with the rules. It refers to checking the reconciliations needed under r.9 and r.10 and includes a list of Powers of Attorney held whether active or dormant. The declaration by the partners who have signed the certificate is an important link in the overall monitoring of compliance with the Accounts Rules and is viewed as such by the Council. Any failure to disclose a breach of rule is considered as two offences—breaching the Rule and misleading the Council of the Law Society. It is not merely an administrative task on the part of the designated cashroom partner.

Figures as at the quarterly reconciliation date are also included on the certificate under "other matters". This shows:

- (a) general client account balances and surplus/deficit every three months,
- (b) totals of invested funds held for named clients as at the same date,
- (c) totals of overdrafts or bridging loans taken for clients as at the same date.

The certificate also asks for information about borrowing levels and how much external finance the firm uses. This covers a wide range of borrowings including hire purchase but excludes the capital value of leasing deals. It is a general indicator of financial gearing and is intended to generate information about figures getting better or worse over a period of time. If an accountant has been asked to help with the work, the extent of help given should be disclosed, as should any rule breach which happened during the period.

The New Certificate System—Some Conclusions. The certificate system **9.03.04** works well and the short timescale allowed to complete the figure work does not affect the majority of firms. In fact late certificates are fewer than when six months was allowed to prepare an annual Accountant's Certificate.

Schedule 2 now deals with practices where no client bank account is operated. The need to notify the council at once if the firm has to open a client bank account is important. So far it has not resulted in a solicitor reporting a change of status.

Finally, there is a separate style of certificate contained at Sch.3 which is for solicitors who restrict their practice to acting as agents for other firms. They do not get paid directly by the client and do not need a client bank account.

Generally, the new Accounts Certificate operates better than the old accountant's certificate form. Accountants may be instructed to help, with the solicitor now able to decide how much help is needed. This allows greater scope for negotiating the accountant's fee compared to the previous arrangements. Having the accountant charge the solicitor for work, which was a Law Society requirement, did create resentment at the time. Now, accountants are instructed on the basis of helping the solicitor and are able to add value to the work. All in all, this is a positive step for the profession to have taken.

C. Professional Practice Section of the Rules

Introduction. This is a very important section. It does not involve book- **9.03.05** keeping systems but contains vital guidance on dealing with clients who are involved in certain types of financial transactions. Many of these rules were created following a set of claims arising from a particular situation. The individual rule was then devised to try to prevent any recurrence. Most of the rules have been highly effective in this regard. Only r.23 (powers of Attorney) has been limited in its impact. The rule about Bridging Loans (r.20) came into play in the late 1980's in response to solicitors becoming involved personally in mortgage fraud based on temporary bridging loans. It was and is highly effective. Temporary bridging in nominee names has ceased to be a problem for the Guarantee Fund. The key element is the exclusion of the solicitor for personal liability. The risk must now remain with the client and the lender.

Rule 21—Borrowing from Clients. This rule prevents the solicitor from borrowing money from a client unless the client is in the business of lending money or has had separate legal advice. Again, this is a practical restriction which seems to have had the appropriate effect.[7]

The Society's monitoring teams routinely check both rules, and lenders who have declined to take separate advice under r.21 are routinely contacted to confirm their position. This has also helped to safeguard the Guarantee Fund.

Rule 22—Secured Loans. The introduction of what is now r.22—prohibiting a solicitor from acting for a lender in specified circumstances—is also very effective. This rule was devised in response to a series of expensive loan frauds initiated by a partner in a firm which was slowly declining in size and reputation. The rule does not prevent a solicitor from buying, selling or negotiating the terms of a loan over a property but does prevent a solicitor from acting on behalf of the lender for the securing, discharging or varying of the standard security for the loan over the property. The rule applies to the solicitor, spouse, partner in business, spouse of the partner, or any separate partnership or company in which the solicitor has a stake. The company restriction does not apply to holdings of less than 5 per cent of a public company quoted on a recognised stock exchange.

The Council has power to waive any of the provisions of the rule in any particular circumstances or case. Any request for a waiver must be submitted at the earliest date in order to avoid delay in obtaining a decision in good time. The circumstances need to relate to the particular transaction—it will not be sufficient to seek a waiver solely on the reputation of the firm.

Rule 23—Powers of Attorney. This part of the rules makes reference to dealing with Powers of Attorney in r.23. The rule specifically requires solicitors acting under continuing powers of attorney to be treated as if they were clients and monies to be recorded in the client ledger as if they were clients' monies. There is a separate and specific reference in r.8(2) to these responsibilities and the need to record any movement of funds handled by an attorney through the books of account.

The rule also imposes an obligation to prepare and submit, as part of the Accounts Certificate, a complete list of Powers of Attorney held by the partners. This list is intended to produce an open record of clients who fall into this vulnerable group. Discussions about this rule have resulted in identifying the particular risks associated with this group of clients. Whilst it is not a condition of the accounts rules, a number of firms have voluntarily created an in-house rule to the effect that the attorney must instruct another partner in the firm in respect of any legal work needed for the client. This is another example of best practice.

---

[7] The converse situation—the lawyer who lends to a client is only problematic from an Accounts Rules perspective if the loans come from other clients' money. However, loans to clients frequently raise conflict of interest concerns as we saw in Ch.8 above.

Rule 24—Moneylaundering.[8] The final rule in this section is r.24—Money Laundering. Anti-money laundering procedures are very important for solicitors as part of their strategy for handling client business as well as being a statutory requirement. The accounts rules are drawn up so as to apply the Money Laundering Regulations 2003 to all clients business. When a solicitor is asked by a client to conduct a piece of business with value attached the solicitor should apply the basic checks required by the Money Laundering Regulations 2003. This involves checking the client's name and address for identification purposes and then checking the source of any funds produced for the proposed transactions. Records of results of these enquiries must be kept. The Law Society has issued a basic form to help with client identification. You may be able to positively identify a client through personal knowledge. If so, make a full note of the circumstances in which they are known to you in the space provided on the form. If the client is not known, evidence must be obtained which would reasonably prove their identity. The form lists a number of standard documents, which would be suitable, but it is not an exhaustive list. Photographic confirmation via a passport or new style driver's licence is recommended, but is not essential if other evidence is available.

Particular problems arise when clients live at a distance or even overseas. Accepting formal confirmation from a person from the regulated sector where money laundering regulations apply to their business is sufficient. Another area of difficulty involves corporate bodies or structures such as trusts. There are many good reasons why such arrangements are needed by clients. Some may need to be set up while others may already be in existence. In such cases, the identification enquiries must continue until you are able to establish a direct link between the person giving instructions and the client. Knowledge of the ownership or control over the vehicle being nominated to conduct the business is essential. Faced with an international/offshore corporate body, the identification must go behind professional nominees to arrive at the person who is the beneficial owner. A variation of "cherchez la femme".

When these enquires are satisfactorily completed, the second stage is to identify the source of the client's funds. This must be discussed at the earliest stage in the business. Using clear terms of business covering the Money Laundering Regulations is an essential protection for the firm or solicitor. The Society has issued a style of letter covering a range of matters, including money laundering. Source of funds most commonly consists of a loan cheque from a regulated lender and a personal cheque drawn on the client's own bank account. Taking a copy for the file is an adequate record of source of funds.

Other funds provided by or on behalf of the client—cash notes, banker's drafts and third party cheques will need further enquiry to be made. There are particular risks associated with these types of payment. Cash because this is associated with the first step in the money laundering chain. Bank drafts are considered to be good in banking risk terms but are only anonymous funds in money laundering terms. Production of a bank draft should be supported by a letter confirming the source bank account for the funds. Such a letter can only be obtained by way of instruction from the client to the banker. Finally, funds

---

[8] See the "Simple Guide to Anti-Money Laundering Regulations" on the Law Society of Scotland website.

from another person brings up the necessity of identifying the person who is providing the funds and may increase suspicion about the source of funds. The last two methods are popular as layering techniques on the road to having clean money. Ask the client why the third party cannot pay the funds over to the client personally and needs to pay them direct to you. Unsatisfactory or evasive answers should be treated as suspicious.

Having discussed the source of funds at an early stage, there is a need to look out for last minute changes in funding arrangements—particularly if the switch involves the use of one of the three payment methods referred to above.

Having a clear picture of the two key checks—client identification and source of funds—is essential. Even more important is the knowledge that these checks are understood and applied by all relevant members of the firm—partners and employees. This is one of the key tasks for the partner nominated as Money Laundering Reporting Officer (MLRO). It should also be supported actively by all partners and a formal system for assessing compliance and reporting to the partners is needed. The report must be done formally on an annual basis. It can and should be done more frequently— particularly if the report indicates any areas of weakness in the firm's performance. The MLRO should carry out reasonable checks to ensure compliance with the firm policy, report on areas for improvement, arrange training for all new staff at an appropriate level of detail and provide a review service for any suspicious activity detected in the firm. Money laundering checks are found to be more effective if linked directly to the firm's systems for opening files and client ledger accounts. If money cannot be handled until the checks are done and logged, money laundering routines get done at the right time. Given the importance of the post, and the risk of urgent action needed if a report is to be made to SOCA, the question of cover for holidays and absence from the office must be considered by the MLRO. A deputy may be needed or good contact arrangements set up.

Training of all staff who deal with clients is recommended and a formal record of all training is needed. One of the first defences open to a member of staff involved in a money laundering investigation is the explanation that they had not been trained to handle the risks, hence the need for training and record keeping. If the suspicious matter has been reported to the MLRO this will also protect the partner/employee who made the report. Such suspicions must be logged and kept separate from the client's own file and the result of the MLRO's consideration also be noted. Suspicions should be reported to SOCA. Current contact details can be got from the website: *www.soca.gov.uk* or on the Society's own website.

If the issue is urgent, fax the full details to SOCA using their form if possible—making clear the grounds for suspicion and the reason for urgent action. Report suspicions at the earliest stage to reduce the risk of disruption to the client's business.

An increasing number of investigations are being carried out by the authorities and production orders or warrants may be served asking for access to clients' files and ledgers. Having records of terms of business, client ID and source of funds for each client will be important at that point. The society's guidance notes to the Accounts Rules and Money Laundering guidance notes on the website are kept up to date and may be a helpful further guide.

D. Guarantee Fund

The Guarantee Fund. The final section of the rules now includes the rules **9.03.06**
dealing with claims made against the Scottish Solicitors' Guarantee Fund.
This part of the rules is the least used and least understood. It would be
reassuring to think that such low usage will continue. It is of relevance to
solicitors who need to intimate a claim arising from the dishonesty on the part
of a Scottish qualified solicitor in practice in the UK or any employee of the
solicitor. In many cases losses arising from dishonesty are dealt with by the
Master Policy insurance scheme which offers protection within the policy to
any innocent partner. Losses arising from the activity of a sole practitioner or
losses in excess of the master policy and top up cover will be directed to the
Guarantee Fund.

The losses, as and when admitted by the Council, are paid from the fund.
The costs of operating the Accounts Certificate system, the monitoring team
and the net expenses of the Judicial Factors, are all paid for via the annual
contribution from all partners/directors in practice. The organisation runs on
a detailed budget including allowances being made for known situations
where losses/claims may arise. Such known cases are restricted to firms where
a Judicial Factor has been appointed.

Applying for a Grant. Any person wishing to apply for a grant from the fund **9.03.07**
must do so as soon as reasonably practicable after the date on which the loss
came to their knowledge. There is a time limit of 12 months on this. In
complex cases it can take a long time to assess the extent of loss from the
point in time when a loss is identified in principle. A lot of work may have to
be done by the Judicial Factor in recreating accounting systems before the
claim can be considered. Grants may include an element to deal with loss of
interest or fees incurred in making the claim. There is a need to exercise
discretion on the part of the Council in this area. The council is also entitled
to consider contributory negligence by the claimant in each claim. The first
hurdle to cross is the question of loss arising from dishonesty on the part of
the solicitor in the conduct of their practice. Failure to demonstrate this clearly
may result in the claim for a grant being rejected.

Applications for a grant must be made on the style of form contained in
Sch.3 of the Accounts Rules. It does not need to be completed by a solicitor,
and in simple cases, the client may deal with the form personally. The form
must be notarised before being submitted. The rules regarding the operation of
the Guarantee Fund are created in terms of s.43 of the Solicitors (Scotland)
Act 1980 and Part I of Sch.3 also applies to this section of the rules.

Conclusion   9.04

The Accounts Rules cover a range of important aspects of a solicitor's
professional responsibilities. Taken individually, they are relatively simple
and are meant to be easily understood and applied. Solicitors are allowed
considerable choice as to how they set up their systems to ensure compliance.
The Society's monitoring team will give new firms some direct advice on how
to set up reliable bookkeeping systems. They may also highlight any instances
where new systems or staff have caused problems and general advice on
corrective action will be given. The changes will have to be handled by the

solicitor, the cash room or their external accountant. The monitoring team resources cannot help with this work.

Finally, an important piece of advice. If, through error or oversight, actions of staff or any other cause, a breach of the Accounts Rules were to occur, solicitors are strongly advised to contact the Chief Accountant or a member of his department to explain the position. Advice will be given and, if helpful, a visit outside the normal inspection cycle may be arranged. A voluntary disclosure and a plan to correct the problem will be considered sympathetically. Contact details can be found on the Society's website, *www.law scot.org.uk.*

CHAPTER 10

FEES, CHARGING AND TAXATION

Introduction

The topic of this chapter—focusing as it does on an aspect of the standard contract between the solicitor and the client—inevitably raises similar issues of fiduciary duty and professional ethics as the previous chapter on lawyer/client transactions. The tensions which can arise between lawyers' own interests and their duties to their client are as likely to appear in the contract of agency/services between them (herein-after the "standard contract"), as in other contracts between lawyers and clients. Indeed, the issue of what to charge the client inevitably creates a tension between the lawyer as business-person and the lawyer as professional. Moreover, as Begg observed, in any contract between solicitors and clients the parties "do not meet on equal terms".[1] Yet, while there is a need to regulate the standard contract in order to protect the interests of the client, there is also a need to balance this against the interests of the lawyer. Thus the solicitor's fiduciary duty to charge no more than a fair and reasonable[2] fee and not to make secret profits (e.g. by retaining an undisclosed commission) has to be balanced against the implied obligation of the client not only to pay that fair and reasonable fee for the services rendered under the contract, but also to reimburse the lawyer for authorised or impliedly authorised outlays incurred on the client's behalf.[3] Moreover, the special character of the solicitor's agency entails wider obligations still. Thus solicitors are not permitted to share fees with unqualified persons[4] and there are situations where a solicitor may be held personally liable to the other side for the expenses of an action raised on behalf of his or her client.

The structure of this chapter will be to examine the following topics: The general agency and ethical principles concerning fees; remuneration issues that arise throughout the transaction; special feeing situations[5]; excessive fees; commissions and secret profits; sharing fees and referral fees.

General Fiduciary Duties and Fees

Balancing the interests of the client and the lawyer under the standard contract of agency/services entails that for pragmatic (if not axiomatic) considerations agency principles are not applied in the same way as in other

---

[1] Begg on *Law Agents* (2nd edn), p.159.

[2] Code of Conduct for Scottish solicitors—art.6.

[3] See para.4.04 above (note that the client can always terminate the contract whenever he wishes without being in breach of contract which is not true of all contracts for the provision of services).

[4] Solicitors (Scotland) Practice Rules 1991.

[5] E.g. written fee charging agreements; speculative fees; contingent fees and equity fees.

contracts between the lawyer and the client. Thus, in contradistinction to general contracts between the lawyer and the client, the standard contract of agency/services between the lawyer and the client is not voidable (for obvious reasons) for breach of fiduciary duty or on public policy grounds. However, in exceptional circumstances, for example, where an independent lawyer would consider that the client has been exploited, it might be reducible on the grounds of undue influence[6] it is hard to see why the standard contract should not be required (as others between solicitors and clients are) to be fair and reasonable in all the circumstances, i.e. one that an independent lawyer would have recommended, and its provisions the subject of informed consent by the client following full disclosure to the client of all the material facts within the solicitor's knowledge and vice versa. Nevertheless, whatever the position may be in relation to other contracts between the lawyer and the client, it seems clear that in relation to the standard contract between the solicitor and the client there is no requirement that the client be independently advised, for the pragmatic reason that to require this would entail an infinite regression.[7] However, perhaps partly in compensation for the reduced protections afforded to clients in the standard contract as compared with other contracts between the lawyer and the client, a number of safeguards have developed over time. Thus, a fee note must clearly advise the client of the fee that they are being charged in relation to a matter and failure to do so can constitute professional misconduct.[8] Again, where a solicitor holds funds on behalf of a client, the fees cannot be taken from the client's account until a fee note has been rendered[9] or issued to the client or the client has given their consent. Further, if the amount of the fee is disputed the client has a common law right to insist that it be submitted on joint remit to a court auditor for taxation,[10] or if the solicitor has raised an action for the fee, a right to insist that the fee note be remitted to a court auditor for taxation.[11]

10.03 Ethical Requirements of Fee Charging

The fundamental ethical rule is contained in art.6 of the Code of Conduct which provides that: *"The fees charged by solicitors shall be fair and reasonable in all the circumstances."*[12] This wording is derived from the fiduciary principles of agency. The Code goes on to provide that:

---

[6] In Scotland historically Courts were very suspicious of any attempts to charge a fee above the recommended rate because it would take advantage of the client.

[7] If the standard contract required independent advice, then that independent advice would require to be independently advised and so on indefinitely.

[8] This was the finding in *McKenzie* S.S.D.T. September 30, 2004 (reported in J.L.S.S. February 2005, p.47) where a solicitor rendered a series of fee notes and associated documents which either confused or misled the client as to the amount of the fee.

[9] Rule 6(1)(d) of the Solicitors (Scotland) Accounts Rules 2001. See also *Murray* S.S.D.T. March 1, 2005 (reported in J.L.S.S. June 2005, p.51).

[10] See Begg, *op. cit.* p.158.

[11] This right has, somewhat unexpectedly come into question by a sidewind in the case *Stronachs Corporate Mountwest 166 Ltd* [2004] Scot SC 101 (October 7, 2004) on *www. bailii.org*. (See para.10.07 below). Until the position is clearer, solicitors should assume that the right remains as it has for over 150 years.

[12] Similar provisions are contained in the Guide to the Professional Conduct of Solicitors (in England and Wales) and the ABA Model Rules of Professional Conduct in the USA, r.1.5.

Factors to be considered in relation to the reasonableness of the fee include:

(a) the importance of the matter to the client;
(b) the amount or value of any money, property or transaction involved;
(c) the complexity of the matter or the difficulty or novelty of the question raised;
(d) the skill, labour, specialised knowledge and responsibility involved on the part of the solicitor;
(e) the time expended;
(f) the length, number and importance of any documents or other papers prepared or perused; and
(g) the place where and the circumstances in which the services or any part thereof are rendered and the degree of urgency involved.

These factors may have a negative weighting on the fee to be charged if for example the work is carried out by an unqualified fee earner in the firm or a very low value is involved. In other words it is inappropriate to start from a base rate value and only apply these factors to increase that.

Normal Fees   **10.04**

In this section we will discuss the ethical aspects of feeing in a normal context, starting with the inception of the lawyer/client relationship.

Quotations and Estimates. After a prolonged debate which lasted the best **10.04.01** part of a decade, the Law Society of Scotland determined to introduce mandatory letters of engagement in 2005.[13] Following the passing of the Client Communications Rules[14] that year, since August 1, 2005 it has been a requirement for solicitors to provide the client or would be client with a quotation or an estimate of the fees that will be charged for the matter. Often it will not be possible to do this with any accuracy, because certain factors will not lie within the control of the solicitor—e.g. in a defended litigation. However if a quotation or an estimate is given it should include VAT and outlays and should be given, or followed up, in writing at the earliest practical opportunity in order to avoid misunderstandings at a later stage. Unlike an estimate, a quotation, if accepted, is binding on the solicitor under normal contract principles. An estimate offers greater leeway, however solicitors should indicate to clients as soon as possible if the final bill is likely to exceed the original estimate and also when the limit of the original estimate is being approached.[15] Failing to adhere to a quotation, or exceeding an estimate significantly without proper warning has been held to be Inadequate Professional Service by the Society in the past as has failing to include VAT or outlays. Failure to include the latter would now be in breach of the Client Communication Rules.[16] When the rules were circulated the Society included

---

[13] See Ch.4 above.
[14] Solicitors (Scotland) (Client Communication) Practice Rules 2005.
[15] See Code of Conduct for Solicitors (2002), art.6.
[16] Rule 3(b).

guidance on the information to be given to comply with them. The guidance on fees is:

> "With the withdrawal of the Society's table of fees, it will not be appropriate to refer to fees recommended by the Society. If, for example in executries, the file is to be feed by an external fee charger such as an auditor or law accountant, the basis on which the external fee charger will be asked to fee up the file needs to be included. If hourly rates are reviewed during the course of the work, the clients will need to be told about any increase or there is a risk that firms will be unable to charge the higher rate.
>
> As well as the hourly rate any commission which will be charged on capital transactions or on the sale of a house would need to be included. In any matter where the account is being rendered on a detailed basis, the charges for letters, drafting papers, etc will need to be expressed as well as the hourly rate. They can be in a separate schedule referred to in the basic letter.
>
> In terms of Section 61A of the Solicitors (Scotland) Act 1980, where a solicitor and client enter into a written fee charging agreement it is not competent for the Court to refer any dispute in the matter to the Auditor for taxation. Where an hourly rate is specified, and that is accepted in writing, the client would still be entitled to seek a taxation, but would not be able to challenge the agreed hourly rate at such a taxation.
>
> It should be made clear at the outset whether the fee quoted is the fee to be charged or only an estimate. If it is not stated as an estimate and the client accepts it in writing that could be regarded as a written fee charging agreement under Section 61A of the 1980 Act. If a client has been given an estimate, they should be advised in writing when it becomes known that the cost of work will materially exceed such an estimate. It is good practice to advise the client when the limit of the original estimate is being approached.
>
> Information should be clear, and terms with which the client may not be familiar such as 'outlays' may need to be briefly explained. If a payment to account is required, that should be clearly stated, as well as the consequences of failing to pay it on time. For example in a Court matter if the client is advised that failure to make a payment to account will lead to the solicitor withdrawing from acting, there is unlikely to be a professional difficulty about withdrawing from acting in compliance with that. However if the consequence is not stated, and the proof is approaching, solicitors could be vulnerable to a complaint if they withdraw at a late stage to the potential prejudice of the client.
>
> If the clients costs are to be paid by a third party such as a Trade Union or Legal Expenses Insurer, specific details of the basis of charging do not need to be set out when writing to the individual client but any part of the fee which that client may be asked to pay should be included—such as a success fee in a speculative action.
>
> While it is not strictly necessary [in order] to comply with the Practice Rule, it is also strongly recommended that any potential liability for other people's costs should be explained. This would include a tenant's liability to meet a landlord's fees as well as the potential liability for expenses in a Court action."

Legal Aid. A solicitor is under a duty to advise clients who may be eligible **10.04.02**
about the existence of the legal aid scheme, including advice and assistance.[17]
Examination of the client's eligibility however depends on the client requesting that and the solicitor being willing to do so. Firms not offering Legal Aid
should inform potential clients of this at the outset and advise them to consult
another firm.[18] Where a case is to be legally aided, the Client Communications
Rules require that the size of the contribution or the factors which will effect
this are to be indicated. Similarly, the rules require that the consequences of
preserving or recovering property should be referred to. Curiously, they do not
require that the letter of engagement should mention the legally aided client's
liability for the expenses of his/her opponent, however, solicitors would be
well advised to do so.[19] Section 32 of the Legal Aid (Scotland) Act 1986
prohibits solicitors from taking any payment for a person in receipt of advice
and assistance or legal aid except for payments which may be made in
accordance with the Act. Solicitors may not therefore charge an additional
private "top up" fee for work covered by Advice and Assistance or by Legal
Aid, whatever they feel as to the adequacy of legal aid fee rates. To do so may
constitute a conduct offence under s.31(3) of the Legal Aid (Scotland) Act
1986 and if detected is likely to trigger the s.31 investigation procedure
established by the Law Society and the Scottish Legal Aid Board in 2005. If,
however, the authorised expenditure under Advice and Assistance has been
used up and an increase has been refused, the solicitor can discuss with the
client the possibility of proceeding privately, but that must be agreed by the
client in advance with terms of business issued in writing at that stage.

Trusts and Executries. Solicitors who are also trustees or executors and wish **10.04.03**
to act professionally for the trust or executry should ensure that they have the
authority in terms of the testator's will to charge fees for services rendered to
the trust or executry.[20] Undertaking work gratuitously does not absolve the
solicitor from observing proper professional conduct or providing an adequate
service.[21]

Rates of Fee: General Issues. Until 1985, the Law Society of Scotland set **10.04.04**
prescribed fees for all work except litigation. Fees for conveyancing and for
executries were according to a set scale depending on the value of the
transaction or of the estate. Scale fees were abolished by the society in 1985.
Between the 1930s and 1985 all forms of advertising by solicitors were
prohibited, and even after advertising was permitted that year, there was still
a prohibition on advertising calculated to attract business unfairly—i.e.

---

[17] A failure to advise an eligible client as to the possibility of being funded by legal aid would
not only be unsatisfactory conduct and IPS, it might also lead to a negligence suit. See Webster,
op. cit. para.2.02.

[18] (2002) J.L.S.S. May, p.46.

[19] A failure to advise a legally aided client as to the potential operation of the statutory charge
or "clawback" to cover the cost of the client's legal expenses if they win their case, or of the
potential liability for the other side's expenses in legal aid cases (as well as the possibility of
modification by the court) is likely to be IPS (as the Council held on four occasions in
2001/2002).

[20] Webster, para.2.22.

[21] *ibid.* Indeed solicitors can be personally liable for the expenses of an action raised on behalf
of clients, at the court's discretion.

advertising fees lower than the norm. The prohibition on such advertising was repealed in 1991.

Fees for litigation were set by the Lord President on the advice of his Advisory Committee whether the fees were to be paid by the solicitor's own client or recovered from another party for the litigation. In 1992 the Lord President accepted that it was no longer appropriate for him to regulate fees between solicitor and client, and he now only regulates fees between party and party.[22]

10.04.05 Rates of Fee: Solicitor/Client—Client Paying. Solicitors and clients are free to agree whatever fees they both think are fair and reasonable for any work the client instructs. Such fees may take the form of a fixed fee which is very common in house purchase and sale, an hourly rate, or some other method. Until recently, the Law Society of Scotland published a recommended Table of Fees for general business, the purpose of which was to recommend charges for professional services except insofar as prescribed by or under statute. However, the table was withdrawn in 2005 after the Society had received advice that it might be challengeable on competition law grounds.[23] A solicitor may charge according to the circumstances of the matter and the fixing of every fee is a balanced judgement rather than an arithmetical calculation.[24] The agreement between solicitor and client does not have to be in writing, although the solicitor must comply with the requirements of the Client Communication Rules as we have seen, but if it is not in writing the client is always entitled to insist upon a taxation before payment.[25]

10.04.06 Rates of Fee: Unit Charges. If the matter is not to be the subject of a fixed fee, solicitors can elect to charge according to a number of units. This was the format set out in the society's former table of fees where time was calculated at 10 units per hour. Solicitors may calculate their own hourly rate and unit value having regard to the costs of the particular firm. A report on these costs can be obtained at no cost by taking part in the Cost of Time Survey carried out annually on behalf of the society by an independent actuary. The survey is organised through the Society and all firms taking part receive an individual report on the average hourly cost rates of solicitors and other fee earners in the participating firm.[26] A report on the average results for all participating firms brought out in the survey is free to those firms.

10.04.07 Written Fee Charging Agreements.[27] These arrangements were made enforceable by a 1990 amendment to the 1980 Act[28] which added s.61A providing as follows:

> (1) "Subject to the provisions of this section, and without prejudice
>   to

---

[22] Act of Sederunt (Rules of the Court of Session amendment no. 3) (Taxation of Accounts) 1992, 1992 S.L.T. (News) 237.

[23] (2005) J.L.S.S. March, pp.7 and 45.

[24] From general regulation 2 in chapter 1 of the Society's former Table of Fees.

[25] Para.10.06 below.

[26] For an explanation of the Cost of Time see the Scottish Law Directory Fees supplement published annually.

[27] See also (1993) J.L.S.S. 395 for an article by Walter Semple.

[28] Law Reform (Miscellaneous Provisions) (Scotland) Act 1990, s.36(3).

(a) Section 32(1)(i) of the Sheriff Courts (Scotland) Act 1971;

(b) Section 5(h) of the Court of Session Act 1988,

where a solicitor and his client have reached an agreement in writing as to the solicitor's fees in respect of any work done or to be done by him for his client it shall not be competent, in any litigation arising out of any dispute as to the amount due to be paid under any such agreement, for the Court to remit the solicitor's account for taxation.

(2) Sub section (1) is without prejudice to the Court's power to remit a solicitor's account for taxation in a case where there has been no written agreement as to the fees to be charged."

[Sub-sections 3 and 4 are dealt with at paragraph 10.05.02]

Section 61A came into force on 4 July 1992. Prior to that, any solicitor's account which was disputed by clients—whether or not the fees had been the subject of a contract in writing before hand—required to be submitted to the auditor for taxation before a solicitor could obtain decree in a court action. Section 61A was introduced to remedy the situation where some corporate clients were thought to have been resorting to taxation even when the basis of feeing should have been clear to them. However, there was no discussion at the time of such agreements becoming the norm for ordinary clients. This is important since with the advent of mandatory letters of engagement in the Client Communications Rules 2005 it is considered by some that any agreement in writing that refers not just to the actual amount of the proposed fee but to the basis of feeing, will be sufficient to exclude taxation for any client. Certainly, the 1990 legislation provided the opportunity for agreements with clients whereby fees are charged on the basis of a pre-existing contract and taxation is excluded. Nevertheless, because, as we saw earlier, the fiduciary protections for clients with respect to contracts between the client and the lawyer are weaker than in the case of other contracts we consider it important that the position regarding the solicitor's fees in a written fee charging agreement is clearly set out in the agreement and that clients are given a full explanation of what is proposed so that they fully understand the implications of what they are being asked to sign. This includes the fact that signing the contract excludes the possibility of taxation. Moreover, there must be no undisclosed advantages to the solicitor in any such agreement. To this end simple language should be used and technical terms avoided. This is part of effective communication.[29]

The crucial words in s.61A are that the agreement refers to "the solicitor's fees in respect of any work done or to be done". Does this mean that the agreement must be for a fixed sum or will it be sufficient to refer to the solicitor's hourly rate? Although some members of the profession take the view that the latter interpretation is to be preferred, such an interpretation offers too little protection to non-corporate clients. Accordingly, the preferred view should be that the written agreement must specify the actual fee to be charged. If it does not, but merely the hourly rate, then it will be open to the client to request taxation over the number of hours charged, even if the hourly

---

[29] Code of Conduct, Article 5(e).

rate cannot be challenged in taxation. The next question is what constitutes a written fee charging agreement? Whilst no set form has been laid down by the Law Society, Walter Semple has suggested that it should include the work to be done; the proposed charge and whether that includes VAT, phone calls, letters and copying; responsibility of outlays; provision for interim fees; and terms of payment.[30] It will be seen that these suggested contents overlap significantly with the fee element in a letter of engagement. Does this mean that whenever there is a letter of engagement which has either been accepted in writing by the client or homologated by his or her actings, there is a written fee charging agreement? Certainly that is the view of some commentators. Moreover it has been argued by some that a written fee charging agreement excludes not only taxation but also the requirement that the fee be fair and reasonable and/or the Law Society's powers to challenge excessive fees under s.39A. Such a draconian result in the case of individual clients would be anomalous and absurd. At any rate, such arguments reinforce the conclusion arrived at earlier that s.61A only applies where a specified total fee is included in the agreement. It is also a reason for suggesting that the client *sign* the written agreement in the full knowledge as to its implications so far as taxation is concerned,[31] rather than constituting the agreement through actings.

Although taxation is excluded in the case of these agreements it should be noted that it is still necessary to resort to court action to enforce the agreement, if the client is unhappy with the bill actually charged. This is because the Council of the Law Society early on determined that resort to the courts could not be excluded by the device of including a warrant for preservation and execution in the agreement.[32] Thus it is still open to the client to challenge a fee note rendered in terms of a written fee charging agreement, either in court or in taxation, on the grounds that the number of hours worked is disputed or excessive or that the work charged for was not instructed or was not done. As noted earlier, some have argued that the existence of a written fee charging agreement excludes the possibility of challenge on the grounds that the fee is not fair and reasonable. With respect there is no statutory basis for such a proposition, since the statute only excludes the client's right to insist on taxation. It says nothing about depriving the client of the ethical and fiduciary requirement that the fees charged must be fair and reasonable in the circumstances.[33] It is also felt to be essential that in every case where a written fee charging arrangement is signed between the solicitor and the client, the client is immediately given a copy of the agreement for his retention. In line with an agent's fiduciary duties, the solicitor must be completely candid and ensure that the client is fully aware of what he is signing. Nevertheless,

---

[30] See W. Semple, "Written Fee Charging Agreements" (1993) J.L.S.S. 395.

[31] It is understood that when written fee charging agreements were introduced, the Law Society Council gave consideration to, but ultimately rejected, a proposal that clients should be independently advised before signing such an agreement. Certainly if some of the extreme consequences being suggested for such agreements are upheld in the courts, the case for such a requirement becomes well nigh irrefutable.

[32] The Solicitors (Scotland) (Written Fee Charging Agreements) Practice Rules 1993.

[33] It seems also to be the case that the Council's powers of scrutiny for grossly excessive fee charging under s.39A of the 1980 Act are not displaced by the existence of a written fee charging agreement since there is no reference to s.39A in s.61A. See Semple *op. cit.*

properly handled, Written Fee Charging Agreements, like letters of engagement can lead to improved relations between solicitors and clients and greater thought will have gone in to the transaction and the relationship between them.[34]

Interim Fees or Fees to Account. There is no reason why a solicitor should **10.04.08** not issue an interim fee or charge fees to account, provided this has been agreed with the client at the outset or subsequently. Indeed it is prudent to include this in a Terms of Business letter to give the client fair warning in advance. The Accounts Rules require that such fees can only be debited to the client account if the client has authorised it or the money is "required for or to account of payment of the solicitor's professional account against a client which has been debited to the ledger account of the client in the solicitor's books *and where a copy of said account has been rendered*".[35]

The italicised words make it clear that an interim fee cannot be charged and the withdrawal from the client account take place, without the client being informed. Even so, it is submitted that it is even better practice to intimate the proposed payment to account to the client in advance, before making the transfer. In addition, the Discipline Tribunal and the courts have also made it clear that the provision only mandates the taking of interim fees which are fair and reasonable in the light of the work actually done for the client to date.[36] It should be noted that if the fee note is shown to be for services between particular dates, the auditor will normally disallow any further fees for work done between these dates in any subsequent fee note unless the original is clearly stated to be an interim fee note. Moreover, where the solicitor is the sole executor it is also good practice to keep the residuary beneficiaries appraised of any interim fees and to submit the final account for taxation or assessment. It is therefore disappointing that in the disquieting case of *Angus*[37] where the solicitor had repeatedly charged grossly excessive interim fees in executries where he was the sole executor (and therefore only *had* to render the fees to himself) the Discipline Tribunal implied that it was professionally acceptable in such situations for the solicitor not to render the interim fee notes to the residuary beneficiaries, provided all the beneficiaries received an accounting in due course. The Tribunal did, however, indicate that in such cases the best course of action is to have the account taxed.

Special Feeing Arrangements **10.05**

Fees Dependent on Success. It is quite acceptable for solicitors and clients **10.05.01** and to agree that fee for a particular piece of work will only be payable in the event that the matter is successfully concluded. That does not just mean litigation; it can apply across a range of commercial work such as tendering for public and private partnerships and can also apply to sales of domestic property. "No sale, no fee" is not uncommon where solicitors advertise their estate agency service. It is perfectly proper for the fee charged in the event of success to reflect the element of risk involved to the solicitor in accepting

---

[34] The commentators view Written Fee Charging Agreements as a positive development. See generally the article by Walter Semple, 1993 J.L.S.S. 395.

[35] See r.6(1)(d) Solicitors (Scotland) Accounts Rules 2001.

[36] See e.g. *Duncan* DTD 17/03/2004.

[37] DTD 19/08/2004.

instructions on such a basis. The fee may be enhanced in the event of success or may be substantially reduced or waived completely if the matter is unsuccessful.

10.05.02 Speculative Actions. It has long been considered to be in the highest traditions of the Scottish profession to assist impecunious pursuers by undertaking certain forms of litigation (primarily personal injury cases) for the normal fee if the case is successful[38] and without fees if the case is lost.[39] However, even the Royal Commission on Legal Services in Scotland[40] was unable to say how frequently such actions arose. Following the introduction of s.61A(3) and (4) of the 1980 Solicitors (Scotland) Act[41] it is now permissible for the solicitor to offer to act on a speculative basis, in three separate ways. First, by agreeing to accept "party and party" expenses from the other side[42] with an uplift (from his or her own client) of up to 100 per cent of the fee element payable by the other side, provided the case is successful.[43] Secondly, by agreeing to litigate for the client on an "agent and client" basis (provided the case is successful), without any proportionate increase. This will cover work done before the start of the litigation as well as any other work the solicitor has carried out that is considered by the auditor to be fair and reasonable in the circumstances. Under this route, the solicitor can rely on the Court of Session and Sheriff Court statutory instruments[44] to persuade the auditor as to the level of expense incurred by the solicitor and that the fee allowable should take account of the responsibility taken by the solicitor.[45] The third option is to reach a written fee charging agreement with the client as to the level of fee recoverable if the case is successful. However, for the reasons stated earlier unless a specified figure is included as opposed to an hourly rate, the client will still be able to challenge the number of hours spent. In addition, a fee set in this way can still be challenged as not being fair and reasonable in the circumstances or grossly excessive in terms of s.39A of the Solicitors (Scotland) Act 1980. Whichever of these three routes is adopted the potential ramifications for the client need to be explained. In Scotland, clients who are eligible for legal aid may well be better off to rely on it rather than

---

[38] See *X Insurance Co. v A and B*, 1936 S.C. 225 *per* Lord President Normand at p.239. "Success" in this context is usually defined as obtaining damages in an action or a settlement in the client's favour.

[39] This still leaves the client liable to pay the outlays and the other side's expenses, if any. The instructing solicitor may include fees to Counsel in his account of expenses, *Sim v Scottish National Heritable Property Co. Ltd* (1889) 16 R 583.

[40] Cmnd. 7846, HMSO, 1980.

[41] Introduced by s.36 of the Law Reform (Miscellaneous Provisions)(Scotland) Act 1990.

[42] This type of account excludes recovery for pre-litigation expenses and any expenses which the auditor regards as not properly chargeable against the other side e.g. excessive consultations with the client or counsel, or late amendments of pleadings, or copying fees and some discretionary additional fees. See W. Semple,"Fees in Speculative Actions" 1994 J.L.S.S. 57.

[43] S.61A (3) and (4) limit the percentage increase allowed on a successful solicitor's fees to that laid down by Act of Sederunt. S.I. 1992/1879 (Sheriff Court) and S.I. 1992/1898 (Court of Session) indicate that the upper limit on the increase should be no more than 100%. Advocates can also agree to act on a speculative basis with a fee uplift limited by Act of Sederunt. If Counsel is instructed, they must agree to accept instructions on a speculative basis if the solicitor is to avoid responsibility for payment. (Scheme for Accounting for Counsel's fees 2002, para.4(2)— Scottish Law Directory Fees Supplement 2005, p.69).

[44] S.I. 1992/1879 (Sheriff Court) and S.I. 1992/1898 (Court of Session).

[45] As Walter Semple has argued, a solicitor may prefer to accept the whole of a satisfactory fee rather than twice what is likely to be an unsatisfactory fee. *Op. cit.*

a speculative fee, especially if there is to be a fee uplift, if for no other reason than the fact that legally aided litigants who lose their cases can often get their liability to pay the other side's expenses modified—sometimes to nothing at all. To compensate for this some solicitors operating on a speculative basis are known to have guaranteed to indemnify clients against such a liability. In addition to the specific legislative requirements of s.61A, the law of agency continues to apply in providing that there must not be undue influence and the solicitor should be candid in disclosing all relevant matters to the client. This will include the fact that neither counsel nor solicitors may agree to act on the basis that the fees will be paid by the client as a percentage of the principal sum recovered in the case. The English equivalent to speculative fees are known as conditional fees and were introduced under the Courts and Legal Services Act 1990. Such fees require to be established by an agreement in accordance with a format established by the English Law Society after consultation with the National Consumer Council. Conditional fees are now far more common in England and Wales than speculative actions are in Scotland because in England and Wales personal injury actions are no longer covered by legal aid.

Speculative Personal Injury Cases. This is an area where much has changed in the last 20 years. Then legal aid fees comprised 90 per cent of fees recoverable in judicial accounts. Now they are less than half the rate in judicial accounts of expenses. Solicitor/client fees are no longer regulated by the Lord President and, as we have seen, both solicitors and counsel are entitled to agree with the client that in a speculative action an uplift or success fee may be charged. Companies such as Quantum Claims are aggressively marketing their services and in 1998 the Inner House in the Court of Session upheld the decision by the Sheriff Principal of Grampian Highlands & Islands that such companies are entitled to enter into a contingency (i.e. percentage) fee agreement with their clients.[46] The public have become familiar with and are attracted by adverts which offer "no win, no fee", although they may not be aware of the drawbacks that can be associated with such a deceptively simple concept. Solicitors, at least are required to discuss the different options for funding a litigation with their client and the ramifications associated with each method. In addition, to assist with the risk of losing and therefore incurring liability for the other side's expenses, after the event insurance has become available. However, this has been less successful in Scotland than in England and Wales.[47] This is partly because south of the border legislation was passed by the Government which made the insurance premiums recoverable as well as the success fee in conditional fee agreements.[48] There have been changes in how trade unions fund their members' cases and there is now strong competition between solicitors firms both in Scotland and England for such union referred business. Indeed some trade unions have ceased to pay their own members' outlays and/or solicitor's fees. Fees recoverable in England and Wales in the event of success are greater than they are in

10.05.03

---

[46] *Quantum Claims Compensation Specialist Limited v Powell*, 1998 S.L.T. 228.

[47] Thus the Compensure Lawsure ATE insurance package which was backed by the Law Society was withdrawn in 2003 because of adverse selection.

[48] This provision in the Access to Justice Act 1990 was an attempt by the Government to encourage the insurance market because they had withdrawn legal aid cover from personal injury cases.

Scotland, and more so since the legislation to allow success fees to be recovered came into force. By the time a case gets to the date of the trial fees in England can be double what they are in Scotland at the same stage. Pre-litigation costs are recoverable to a much greater extent in England and Wales than in Scotland. All in all, conditional fees are a more attractive option for the profession and possibly the public in England and Wales than they are in Scotland. However, this does not lessen the ethical and fiduciary duties of the lawyer in personal injury cases.

Thus, it is essential that solicitors and counsel are satisfied that there are reasonable prospects of success in the case or that the point of principle is so important as to justify proceeding in the face of contrary authority. It is the Society's view that there is no need for solicitors to make any enquiry into the client's means as there are very few people who can readily afford the cost of litigation in the 21st century. No such enquiry is necessary for solicitors or counsel in England and Wales. In speculative actions there is no "cab rank rule" for counsel, as individual counsel in Scotland are free to accept or decline such instructions. When a litigant is receipt of legal aid the existence of the legal aid certificate is made known to both the other side and to the court. A legal aided litigate is referred to as "Assisted Person" and the certificate requires to be lodged in the court process. In England and Wales under the legislation to recover insurance premiums and/or success fees a copy of the arrangement must be given to the other party to the proceedings. It may be that in Scotland a similar change to the rules of court would be appropriate in a speculative action so that the basis upon which the action is proceeding is clear to all parties.

10.05.04 Contingent Fees. These are to be distinguished from speculative fees (with or without an uplift in fees) which they resemble. Contingent fees are contracts for the provision of legal services in which the amount of the lawyer's fees is contingent in whole or in part upon the successful outcome of the matter, either through settlement or litigation, and the fee is expressed as a proportion of the sum obtained in the case. Such fees are commonplace in the USA[49] because civil legal aid coverage is very limited there. However, they are thought to have contributed to two perceived ills in countries where they are permitted: (a) a compensation culture sometimes leading to a litigation explosion and (b) a threat to the lawyer's independence or a conflict of interest between the lawyer and the client because the solicitor has too great a stake in the success of the case. Accordingly, such fees are considered unethical in a wide range of jurisdictions including Scotland, England and Australia.[50] They are also prohibited by the CCBE Code of Conduct, although not by any practice rule or guideline in Scotland.[51] In addition such agreements are treated as *pacta de quota litis* in Scotland and unenforceable in the UK on

---

[49] For a study of the history of contingent fees in USA see *Contingent Fees for Legal Legal Services* by F.B. MacKinnon (a report of the American Bar Foundation) published by Aldine Publishing Company, Chicago in 1964.

[50] See Dal Pont *op. cit.* 400.

[51] In 1995 the Law Society established a Contingency Fees working party. After careful consideration, it concluded that there was no demonstrable evidence of a demand from the profession or the public for contingency fees as such, although "no win—no fee" arrangements could be of attraction to both, and that for this reason as well as their ethical drawbacks, contingency fees were not in the public interest.

public policy grounds. The Inner House have said that such a feeing arrangement would be void and unenforceable if entered into by a solicitor and client.[52] However, a Scottish solicitor can agree to act for a contingent fee in an action raised abroad where such fees are permitted. Equally, a non-solicitor, for example a claims company, can agree to act on a contingent basis on behalf of a Scottish client in Scotland and such a contract would be enforceable. Curiously, a Scottish solicitor who undertakes a speculative action for damages and the settles the case extra-judicially[53] and thus gets a percentage of the winnings, is effectively getting a contingent fee. Even so, such fees have never been treated as unethical or *pacta de quota litis* and therefore unenforceable.[54]

Equity Fees. In the USA, commercial law firms have been accustomed to investing in their corporate clients as an alternative to receiving fees from them. Such arrangements may over a period of time yield a much higher return than the original fee, but may also yield a much lower or even nil return depending on the success of the business. Equity fees raise ethical issues, including whether such investments can compromise the lawyer's independence,[55] and suggest a conflict of interest between the lawyer and the client. It may well be that a new company with limited funds would prefer to pay fees in the form of shares for work done in the initial stages. Solicitors should be wary of taking their entire fee in shares, particularly from a company which is a going concern. If the company cannot afford legal fees it may well be an unsound investment. It is of course important to bear in mind that: **10.05.05**

(a) the fee must still be fair and reasonable in all the circumstances;
(b) the firm will be subject to the same insider dealing regime as ordinary shareholders and;
(c) the firm may not be permitted to sell its shareholding for a certain period of time.

Even if solicitors rely on a blind trust in terms of which they do not make the decisions as to when to buy or sell the shares, they may still be vulnerable to the accusation that their advice to their client is tainted by self interest in safeguarding the value of their own investment rather than pursuing the client's best interests. There is no rule against such an arrangement in Scotland, but solicitors should take great care when discussing such a proposal

---

[52] *Quantum Claims v Powell* cited above. Note that the Court held that the agreement was enforceable in the case before it as the pursuers were a claims company not a firm of solicitors. The Sheriff Principal had considered the old authorities in great detail together with the views of the Institutional Writers and decided that the prohibition against a *pactum de quota litis* applies only to advocates and solicitors. The pursuers were not solicitors and were entitled to decree in terms of their contract. The Sheriff Principal held (1) that there is a general presumption in favour of freedom of contract; (2) the Rule against *pactum de quota litis* restricts that freedom in respect of advocates and solicitors; but (3) no reason had been demonstrated to him for applying that restriction more widely. The Inner House agreed and refused the appeal.

[53] In which case the fee is calculated as a percentage of the amount settled for.

[54] On contingent fees generally see, A. Paterson, "Contingent Fees and their Rivals", 1989 S.L.T. (News) 81.

[55] Baker, *Who wants to be a Millionaire?* ABA Journal February 2000, p.36.

with a client. It would be prudent to insist that the client obtains independent advice from an accountant or other solicitor before coming to an agreement.

10.05.06 Literary Rights as Fees. Occasionally in today's media dominated environment, lawyers in other jurisdictions with impecunious clients involved in a sensationalist criminal case or a high profile litigation have been known to suggest that rather than acting for a fee, they will acquire instead the literary or media rights concerning the conduct of the representation. Although there is no Scottish authority on the matter, we consider that the American answer that this raises a conflict of interest between the client and the lawyer is the correct one.[56] The temptation to conduct the representation in a way that would enhance the marketability of the story of the case, rather than in the way that is most in the client's interests, is one that has to be avoided. Taking fees in this way would constitute a conflict of interest that could not be cured by informed consent.

10.06 Obtaining Payment of Fees; Dealing with Queries and Taxation

In line with the fiduciary duties incumbent upon solicitors, clients should be given adequate information as to the fees which have been charged and solicitors should answer queries that the client or residuary beneficiaries in an estate may have. As previously indicated solicitors are not permitted to withdraw fees from a client account without at the same time issuing a fee note, however, it is common practice for solicitors when a transaction is complete to pass on the balance of any funds held on the client's behalf under deduction of the solicitor's fee. This can cause annoyance to some clients who receive the fee note and the intimation of the deduction at the same time. Whilst the practical sense of not releasing all the clients funds to them without retaining sufficient funds to meet the solicitor's reasonable fee is undoubted, it would obviate the ill feeling in this area if solicitors (a) indicated in their letters of engagement that this was the basis under which they intended to operate and (b) informed the client of the amount of their proposed fee before rendering the fee note, rather than simply making the deduction and dealing with any client dissatisfaction afterwards. Should the client object to the proposed fee, the solicitor may retain sufficient funds to meet what he or she regards as the amount of a reasonable fee and any outlays and remit the balance to the client.[57] It should be remembered that the normal rule has been that a fee cannot be enforced against a client unless the account has first been taxed.[58] (Taxation is the process whereby an independent auditor attached to a court, decides on a reasonable fee based upon the circumstances of each case with the outcome binding upon both solicitors and clients). Thus, in the

---

[56] ABA Model Rule 1.8(d).

[57] Although, in these circumstances it is probably not open to the client to insist that the funds deducted be returned to the client account, if a substantial reduction to the fee charged eventuates. e.g. through taxation, the client would seem to have a case for any lost interest on the sum wrongfully deducted to be paid back into the client account.

[58] See e.g. *Lyall & Wood v Thomson*, 1993 S.L.T. (Sh Ct) 21. The exception is a written fee charging agreement in terms of s.61A The Solicitors (Scotland) Act 1980. For a general discussion on taxation and how it operates today, see the Report of the Scottish Executive's Research Working Group, *op. cit.* 2006 at pp.160–166.

absence of a written fee charging agreement,[59] a solicitor must agree to a request by the client or a party paying an account to submit it for taxation to a mutually agreed and independent auditor,[60] even if the account has already been paid. However, if a client asks for a taxation of a restricted account the solicitor can withdraw the restriction by preparing an itemised account.[61] Moreover, where a client requests a taxation, the client is bound to pay the taxed amount even if it exceeds the original bill.

The fact that a matter can go to taxation is not a justification for failing to give a proper specification to a party. In *Semple Fraser WS v Quayle*,[62] a firm was seeking payment of £11,195.05 outlays " . . . as a reasonable fee . . . for a commercial firm such as the pursuers in all the circumstances of the case given the importance of the matter to the defender".[63] The court found this to be an insufficient specification as neither the number of hours worked nor the hourly rates of the solicitors involved was revealed. The court was of the view that the defender was entitled to a breakdown of how the pursuers arrived at the sum sued for in order to allow the defender to decide whether to incur the cost of taxation. This has been reinforced by a practice guideline[64] in November 2005 which replicates what had been Ch.2 of the former Table of Fees for general business recommended by the Society. Paragraph 1(a) states that the client should be given a narrative, and/or, summary sufficient to indicate the nature and the extent of the work done. If requested the solicitor should give such helpful information as can readily be derived from the records, such as the total recorded time spent, the number and length of meetings, the number of letters and telephone calls. No charge may be made for preparing the fee note or for the provision of such information. However, if the party paying insists on a fully itemised account they should be advised that it will be prepared at their expense.

Limiting the Right to Taxation?   10.07

Although, as we have seen,[65] it has long been thought that a client has the legal right to insist on a taxation in Scotland, a school of thought is emerging that this "fiduciary" protection was watered down by two Acts of Sederunt passed in 1992[66] without any public discussion or consultation on the issue before they were passed. This stems from the fact that the two Acts of Sederunt appear to give the court a discretion as to whether to remit a solicitors' account to taxation or not, once a solicitor has raised an action to enforce his or her fee, i.e. that a client at that stage cannot insist that the account is taxed. The point was highlighted in *Stronachs Corporate v*

---

[59] See para.10.04.07.

[60] Practice guideline on Forms of Account and Taxation, para.2(b)—J.L.S.S. November 2005, p.37.

[61] See *Hamilton v Ferrier* (1868) 6 S.L.R. 151. Webster, *Professional Ethics and Practice* (4th edn, Avizandum Publishing, Edinburgh, 2004), para.2.24 is of the opinion that the solicitor may withdraw a restriction at any time before full settlement of the account provided the position is explained clearly to the client.

[62] 2002 S.L.T. 33.

[63] *ibid.* at 37.

[64] Practice guideline on forms of account and taxation J.L.S.S. November 2005, p.37.

[65] See para.10.02 above, and Begg, *op. cit.* p.158.

[66] Solicitor and Client Accounts in the Sheriff Court (S.I. 1992/1434) and (Rules of the Court of Session Amendment No.3) (Taxation of Accounts) 1992 (S.I. 1992/1433).

Mountwest 166 Limited[67] where the Sheriff Principal of Grampian Highlands & Islands considered whether a remit to the auditor for taxation was an essential pre-requisite for decree to be granted in favour of a solicitor in an undefended action. He reviewed the authorities fully and held that a remit for taxation was not necessary. This decision contrasts with the approach taken some years before by a previous Sheriff Principal in the same Sheriffdom in *Lyall and Wood v Thomson*[68] who took the opposite view. While the point has still to be determined by the Court of Session the matter remains in this somewhat unsatisfactory state. It should be noted that in the *Stronachs* case the Sheriff Principal sought to limit the scope for discretion that his reasoning had led him to by stating that in a defended action where a client sought to assert his/her right to taxation, the sheriff would "require a very cogent reason" for refusing remit the case to taxation. Unfortunately, this cannot disguise the fact that, if the Sheriff Principal is correct, a legal right to insist on taxation which has existed in the Court of Session for 186 years was replaced by a judicial discretion in 1992 without anyone noticing and with no debate or consultation. This contrasts with the provisions of s.61A of the 1980 Act which were part of the 1990 Law Reform Miscellaneous Provisions (Scotland) Act and subject to normal Parliamentary scrutiny. If the Sheriff Principal was correct in the *Stronachs* case the dilution of a fundamental protection for clients in this way is unfortunate and may even call into question the vires of the 1992 Acts of Sederunt. It should be noted that the Society's practice guideline on forms of account and taxation states that a solicitor cannot refuse to agree to taxation unless there is a written fee charging agreement in place.

10.08 Excessive Fees

Submitting a fee note for grossly excessive fees whether knowingly or recklessly can lead to a finding of professional misconduct, with the solicitor's practising certificate being withdrawn by the Council of the Society.[69] In *MacColl v Council of the Law Society of Scotland*[70] a solicitor appealed to the Inner House against a finding of professional misconduct by the Scottish Solicitors Discipline Tribunal. The misconduct was that he had charged grossly excessive fees as well as making improper use of client funds and debiting fee notes to the client's account without her permission or knowledge. The solicitor's defence was that he was not culpable because an unqualified member of staff had prepared the fee notes and charged them to the client's account. The Tribunal ruled that the solicitor must take personal responsibility for the acts of the staff member, which had been done on the solicitor's behalf and which resulted in breaches of the accounts rules then in force. The solicitor may be entitled to delegate work, but cannot delegate responsibility for it as well. The Tribunal was of the view that the solicitor as the principal of his firm "had a duty to supervise all aspects of his practice, including such fees as are rendered and transferred" and, on appeal, the court

---

[67] [2004] Scot SC 101 (October 7, 2004) on *www.bailii.org*.
[68] 1993 S.L.T. (Sh.Ct.) 21.
[69] Section 39A of the 1980 Act.
[70] 1987 S.L.T. 524.

found that the failure of supervision was of a gross order. The court also expressed concern about the solicitor holding a power of attorney for the client who was elderly with the result that the overcharging and illegal debiting represented an unfair advantage taken by the solicitor as attorney over his client.[71]

Another Tribunal decision,[72] illustrates further, the fundamental importance of complying with the accounts rules. In this complaint, a law firm with two solicitors was experiencing cash flow problems. In order to solve the liquidity problems of the firm a practice grew up of the senior solicitor identifying the financial requirements of the firm on a weekly basis and thereafter taking a payment to account from the executries being administered by the firm sufficient to cover these requirements, irrespective of the work done for each of the executry estates during that week. These payments to account were accordingly grossly excessive. The respondent indicated, however, that as each estate was wound up and the fees were taxed, any overpayment of fees was refunded to the estate. The Tribunal accepted that since executry work can often be protracted, payments to account were reasonable, so long as the fees charged were commensurate with the work done and took account of any interim fees already charged. However, the solicitor's conduct was found to be professional misconduct as by taking excessive fees on payment to account, he was indirectly using client money to fund his practice which is contrary to the whole tenor of the accounts rules.[73] The solicitor was suspended from practice for a significant period.

The Tribunal was equally disapproving in *McQuitty*[74] in a case where the fees charged for administering an executry of a farm estate amounted over a 16-month period to £28,808. The auditor of the Court of Session held that the allowable fees should have been only £8,000 plus VAT of £1,400 and outlays, a reduction of £19,404. The Tribunal held that this constituted professional misconduct for grossly overcharging of fees.[75] Although no fabrications were proved against the respondent the Tribunal held that he was sufficiently experienced that he must have known that he was grossly overcharging the estate and therefore they concluded that he had acted dishonestly,[76] adding "It is an essential and absolute quality of a solicitor to be honest, and truthful and to act in such a way that their personal integrity is beyond question. The public expects and is entitled to expect solicitors to be honest and to act in such a way that their personal integrity is beyond question. A solicitor who falls short of this brings the profession into disrepute."

---

[71] In 2003 the Professional Practice Committee decided that "where a solicitor administers clients' funds under a power of attorney or acts in a sole representative capacity he/she should have the fee assessed by an Auditor of Court. Taxation is inappropriate as the client is the solicitor ((2003) J.L.S.S. March, p.9).

[72] DTD 723/87.

[73] Rule 6(1)(d) of the accounts rules does not apply as the fees were unreasonable and grossly excessive. It should be noted that at the time of the *MacColl* case, r.6(1)(d) did not require a fee note to be rendered at the time of the deduction of the interim fee.

[74] DTD August 11, 2002 (*McQuitty*).

[75] Noting that the fee actually charged was over three times the taxed fee.

[76] It is not quite clear whether the Tribunal's approach was to draw an inference of actual knowledge, or rather one of deemed knowledge or simply one of treating recklessness as equivalent to knowledge. It would seem that any of the three are sufficient for the mental element needed for misconduct.

It is not an excuse that the charging of excessive fees in breach of the Accounts Rules is not for the solicitor's own benefit, or for that of the firm's, but rather for the benefit of the clients. Thus, in the *Pirie* case[77] the solicitor on one occasion charged the excessive fee so as to liquidate the assets of a client who was the subject of a claim for compensation for criminal injury, thereby effectively defeating the claim. On another occasion, he charged excessive fees to allow a client to continue claiming income support and on a further occasion, to allow the client to appear entitled to legal aid. The Tribunal found that the assertion for each case that the client had agreed to the particular fees did not legitimise the breach of the Accounts Rules.

Finally, while the charging of grossly excessive fees is clearly misconduct, the Discipline Tribunal has indicated that the gravity of the misconduct is exacerbated where the client is in a vulnerable position e.g. if they are aged and infirm, or where the solicitor has a power of attorney over the client's affairs. In recognition of this, the Professional Practice Committee has ruled that "where a solicitor administers client's funds under a power of attorney or acts in a sole representative capacity he or she should have the fee assessed by an auditor of court.[78] Similarly, both the Law Society and the Discipline Tribunal take a particularly dim view of solicitors who charge excessive fees in executries since there is no client to monitor the charging of fees on an ongoing basis.

10.09 Excessive Fees and the Law Society of Scotland's Powers

Section 39A(2) of the Solicitors (Scotland) Act 1980 gives the Council of the Society power to withdraw a solicitor's practising certificate where the council are satisfied, after enquiry and giving the solicitor an opportunity being heard, that the solicitor has "issued an account for professional fees and outlays of an amount which is grossly excessive (whether or not the account has been paid by or on behalf of the client or debited by the solicitor) to the account held on behalf of the client". The consequence of the withdrawal of the practicing certificate is that the solicitor is suspended from practice.[79] If the solicitor submits the account to the auditor of the Court of Session for taxation with all the supporting papers and refunds to the client whatever sum is taxed off by the auditor, the council must terminate the suspension and restore the practising certificate unless they are of the opinion that the solicitor is liable to disciplinary proceedings. These powers are not curtailed by the existence of a Written Fee Charging Agreement.

10.10 Commissions and Secret Profits

The solicitor/client relationship being rooted in the law of agency is a fiduciary one. As such solicitors are bound to account to their principal for any benefits they receive from their agency, without the principal's knowledge or

---

[77] DTD 930/96 (*Pirie*).

[78] 2003 J.L.S.S. March 9. (Assessment is a less detailed and formal examination of a fee note by an auditor—which is free—as opposed to a full blown taxation which has to be paid for either by the solicitor or the client).

[79] Section 39A(2).

due to some error by the principal.[80] As regards secret commissions, it follows that the basic position is that these must be disclosed to the principal. Gloag, however argued that "where an agent is employed to do work which is not, in the ordinary course of business, done gratuitously, e.g. to effect insurance, and the principal pays nothing for his service, the law will presume that he assented to the agent receiving a commission from the third party, and he can have no claim to recover it from the agent."[81] It is unclear that Gloag's reasoning would be adopted by modern courts or by the Discipline Tribunal and the Law Society no longer endorses the Gloag position.[82] Even if Gloag is correct, his reasoning would not justify the solicitor in not declaring the commission where its amount exceeded anything that could be regarded as a fair and reasonable fee. To seek to retain such a commission without the client's knowledge and consent would probably be a conduct offence and potentially struck at as a breach of fiduciary duty. Moreover, customs of a trade will form no defence to secret commissions where the principal is unaware of them.[83] Certain civil consequences can arise where an agent does receive a secret commission. First, the agent can be dismissed from his employment with the commission being subject to recovery by the principal as a creditor. Secondly, the principal can recover damages from the person who paid the commission irrespective of any recovery from the agent. Thirdly, the agent loses his or her claim to the undisclosed commission.[84] Finally, the principal can rescind the contract.

In contrast to the position in Scotland, the receipt of commissions by solicitors in England is specifically dealt with in a practice rule—the Solicitor's Practice Rules 1990:

Solicitor's Practice Rules 1990, Rule 10: Receipt of commissions from third parties

> *(1) Solicitors shall account to their clients for any commission received of more than £20 unless, having disclosed to their client in writing the amount or basis of calculation of the commission or (if the precise amount or basis cannot be ascertained) an approximation thereof, they have the client's agreement to retain it.*

---

[80] Gloag and Henderson (10th edn, 1995), para.22.6. This duty is akin to that imposed on directors of companies who receive benefits from a promoter even though the company suffers no loss. Another example is provided by Gloag in which an agent employed to sell a ship but unable to find a buyer on the cash terms laid out by the principal, purchased it himself, having received an offer of a higher price although on less advantageous cash terms which was not disclosed to the principal, must account to the principal for the profit made on the transaction. Gloag and Henderson continue by stating that the " . . . agent's liability is measured by the gain he has made, and not by the loss . . . sustained by the principal." *ibid.*, para.22.6. "However, it is not an implied condition in written contracts between agent and principal, that the agent shall not bring his own interests in conflict with those of his principals". *ibid.*, para.22.6.

[81] Gloag, *The Law of Contract* (1921) at p.521. Webster views this as being " . . . in accordance with the general law of agency and secret profit"—para.2.23. Indeed, the principal's implied consent extends to what is the norm in the particular trade, covering, cases where the agent receives two separate commissions of which only one is known to the principal. Gloag and Henderson, *op. cit.* para.22.7.

[82] See Minutes of the Professional Practice Committee 2005.

[83] Gloag and Henderson, *op. cit.*, para.22.7.

[84] See e.g. *Ronaldson & Co. v Drummond & Reid* (1881) 8 R 956.

> *(2) Where the commission actually received is materially in excess of the amount or basis or approximation disclosed to the client the solicitor shall account to the client for the excess.*

Scottish solicitors would do well to regard this as good practice for them also. It is surely better practice where a solicitor receives a commission (for example, for arranging property insurance or from a building society or local authority) that he or she should report as much to their client even although they are not being paid for their work by the client and obtain the client's agreement to the retention of the commission or agree to adjust any fee note to take account of the commission paid to the solicitor. There is nothing wrong with a commission provided it is disclosed and it does not exceed what might be considered a fair and reasonable fee for the work done.

Nowadays, any differences between England and Scotland on this matter are being increasingly eroded as more and more disclosure is being required of solicitors as result of the Financial Services legislation. Thus any pecuniary benefit received from third parties resulting from incidental investment business activities by solicitors must now be disclosed to the client, to whom the benefit belongs, and can only be retained by the solicitors with the client's consent.[85] This will include commission from organising life insurance policies or investment trust business.

10.11 Fee sharing and referral fees

Solicitors cannot share fees or profits with unqualified persons (with certain limited exceptions).[86] The statutory offence of fee sharing was repealed in 1993[87] as part of the measures designed to facilitate the emergence of multi disciplinary practices, although the prohibition persists in the form of the 1991 Practice Rules. Those rules were formally approved by the Secretary of State for Scotland at the time, after consultation with the Director General of Fair Trading, all in accordance with the 1980 Act.[88] In 2004 the Council's Professional Practice Committee published a practice guideline in the form of an article by the Director of Professional Practice[89] which clarified how the 1991 Rules are interpreted by the Council. The Office of Fair Trading has taken a close interest in this area and is aware of the terms of the practice guideline. As is clear from the Scottish Executive's Research Working Party,[90] the OFT remain of the opinion that a ban on fee sharing and referral fees is not in the public interest. In fact, as we saw in Ch.2, there is no prohibition on referral fees being paid to an introducer of business in Scotland provided they are paid by the client as an outlay in the solicitor's fee note and fully disclosed in the Terms of Business letter issued to the client at the outset and in the fee note when it is rendered. Solicitors are entitled to pay for services rendered to the firm, even if those services are rendered by the person who introduces the

---

[85] Solicitors (Scotland) (Incidental Investment Business) Practice Rules 2004 and the guidance to these rules in the Solicitors' Professional Handbook.

[86] Solicitors (Scotland) Practice Rules 1991.

[87] It is very hard to imagine the Crown taking a decision to prosecute a solicitor in the criminal courts for sharing fees with an unqualified person.

[88] Sections 34(3A) and 64A.

[89] J.L.S.S. February 2004, p.42 (also in *Green's Solicitors Professional Handbook, op. cit.*).

[90] *Op. cit.* Chs 5 and 8.

client. In England and Wales the ban on referral fees has been expressly revoked and the Research Working Party concluded that the Scottish position should be reviewed when clearer evidence became available as to how the removal of the ban in England and Wales was working out.[91] It should perhaps be noted that the 1991 Practice Rules contain specific exceptions for retired solicitors; representatives of deceased solicitors; employees of solicitors; public officers either in the course of their duty or where the fees are dealt with in accordance with statutory provisions; law centres; advocates; and lawyers in other jurisdictions.[92]

---

[91] *Op. cit.* para.5.20.
[92] Solicitor (Scotland) Practice Rules 1991, r.4.

CHAPTER 11

TERMINATION OF THE RELATIONSHIP

11.01 Introduction

The vast majority of solicitor/client relationships come to an end when the matter has been successfully concluded, the fee note is rendered without delay and paid within a reasonable time, and both solicitor and client are happy to renew their relationship in future. It is important to render a fee note at the end of a matter and not to delay doing so for months or, as sometimes happens, years. Nothing is more likely to generate ill will towards a solicitor than a fee note arriving unexpectedly after a significant unexplained delay. If there is a problem about preparing the account, it is good practice to tell the client so that he does not think you have simply forgotten about it. In civil litigation there may be a quite understandable delay while judicial expenses are resolved or a legal aid account is prepared and paid by the Scottish Legal Aid Board. However, it is in both the solicitor's and the client's interests that the fee-note or the account of expenses be prepared sooner rather than later.

11.02 Termination by operation of law

Although the termination of the solicitor's agency occurs most frequently through the completion of the task for which the solicitor was engaged, the relationship may also be terminated by operation of law. This will include situations[1] in which either the client or the agent dies, goes bankrupt or insane.[2] In some cases, however, there is an earlier termination, either at the hand of the solicitor or the client.

11.03 Termination by the agent

Solicitors have a wide degree of choice in selecting which clients to act for. However, they have less room for manoeuvre both as a matter of agency and in terms of professional ethics, in relation to ceasing to act for a client. As the Code of Conduct stipulates[3]:

"Solicitors are free to refuse to undertake instructions, but once acting should withdraw from a case or transaction only for good cause and

---

[1] See e.g. Halliday, *Conveyancing Law and Practice*, Vol.1, p.419 or Gow, *The Mercantile and Industrial Law of Scotland* (W. Green & Son, Edinburgh, 1964), p.537.

[2] For the statutory safeguards where a sole solicitor goes bankrupt, becomes incapax or dies, see s.46 Solicitors (Scotland) Act 1980.

[3] Art.5(a). Code of Conduct for Scottish Solicitors 2002.

where possible in such a manner that the client's interests are not adversely affected."

The Code further states[4] that:

"Solicitors shall not. cease to act for clients summarily or without just cause in a manner which would prejudice the course of justice ... a solicitor must have regard to the course of justice in considering whether or not to cease acting on behalf of a client. A solicitor may not simply and suddenly decide that it would no longer be appropriate to act for the client."[5]

Where a solicitor plans to withdraw from acting for a child client the solicitor must follow a more sensitive process than normal as children are more likely to bestow their trust on a much more personal level. Indeed it may be possible that the solicitor represents one of the few trusted adults in a child's life. The solicitor must ensure the child understands matters and give paramount consideration to the child's welfare.[6]

Again in immigration, nationality and asylum work the practice guidelines provide that[7]:

"A solicitor must not withdraw from acting except for good reason and upon reasonable notice, recording the reasons for withdrawing from acting in the file ... Issues of merits, funding and arrangements to provide advocacy must be addressed as soon as reasonably practicable so as to avoid damage either to the client's interests or to the effective operation of the court. Such advice as may be appropriate should be given to the client for alternative representation. Notice of withdrawal from representation must be promptly given to the court in such manner as to minimise prejudice to the client."

Where the solicitor is required to withdraw   11.04

Although, as the Code makes clear, solicitors cannot simply withdraw from acting without good reason, there are a number of situations where it may be necessary to withdraw from acting, and a wider number where it may be appropriate or desirable to do so. As to the former, solicitors require to withdraw from acting if a conflict of interest arises between different clients or between the client and the firm or someone in the firm; if the client wishes the solicitor to mislead the court; or assist in a criminal activity; or if a mandate is received terminating the agency (including intimation of the transfer of a legal aid certificate).

---

[4] Art.5(f).
[5] *cf.* The *Guide to the Professional Conduct of Solicitors* (6th edn): The Law Society of England and Wales. 1993 r.12.17 Termination of Retainer. "A solicitor must not terminate his or her retainer with the client except for good reason and upon reasonable notice."
[6] See the "Professional Practice Guidance" (2004) 49(8) J.L.S.S 42.
[7] See Practice Guidelines for Immigration Practitioners 2004, guideline 6.

11.04.01 Conflict of Interest. The Code of Conduct[8] states that if a conflict should arise solicitors must not continue to act for all of the parties who have conflicting interests, "and in most cases they will require to withdraw from acting for all of the parties". It adds, however, that there may be certain circumstances which would result in a significant disadvantage to one party for the solicitor not to continue to act for that party and there is no danger of any breach of confidentiality in relation to the other party. "In these very special cases, the solicitor may continue to act for one party."

In *Connolly and Connolly v Brown*[9] Lord Johnston held that it is impossible to reconcile somebody acting for himself also being the agent to the other party to a contract which is either being executed or contemplated. If therefore a solicitor wishes to offer for a house his firm are selling, the selling client should be referred immediately to another firm of solicitors.

The question of conflict of interest is dealt with in Ch.8, but it is worth repeating that it is a matter for the judgement of the solicitor and does not merely depend on a dispute arising between the clients. The solicitor may become aware of circumstances where, for reasons of confidentiality, he is unable to tell a client about the reason why there is a conflict of interest but must still cease to act. In these circumstances it is sufficient to explain to the client that a conflict has arisen without going into detail.

It is important to be able to recognise a conflict when it does arise and to cease acting at that stage. Trying to resolve the conflict is likely to lead to a greater difficulty, and to possibly greater prejudice to one or both clients than would have been the case if the solicitor had withdrawn at the correct time.

11.04.02 Duties to the Court. The Code of Conduct states[10] "*Solicitors must never knowingly give false or misleading information to the Court*" and gives the example that it is improper to put forward a statement of events or legal argument which the solicitor knows to be false or misleading. If a client requests a solicitor to do so the solicitor must not only refuse to do so, but must withdraw from acting if the client cannot be persuaded to withdraw the request. Similarly, if having unwittingly put forward on behalf of a client what subsequently transpires to be a false account, the solicitor must withdraw unless the client is willing to make a clean breast of it and allow the solicitor to advise the court of the earlier falsehood even if the client's credibility will be severely dented by that.[11]

11.04.03 Domestic Conveyancing Transactions. After an offer has received a qualified acceptance should the selling client attempt to instruct the solicitor to discontinue negotiations with the purchasing agents in order solely to enter into negotiations with or accept an offer from another party, the solicitor should decline to act further in the sale unless the client reconsiders and adheres to the original instructions. Likewise, where a client has instructed a solicitor to intimate a closing date to other solicitors who have noted their interest, the solicitor should withdraw from acting if the selling client wishes to cancel the closing date and accept an offer submitted in advance of it. Where a solicitor acts for a prospective purchaser he or she will require to

---

[8] Art.3.
[9] (Outer House, Court of Session, May 27, 2004).
[10] Art.8.
[11] Solicitors' duties to the Court are dealt with in more detail in Ch.15 below.

withdraw from acting if the client instructs the solicitor to re-negotiate a successful offer downwards without a valid reason arsing from an unforeseen problem with the title or condition of the property.[12]

Choosing to withdraw from acting 11.05

There are a further range of circumstances where it may be appropriate to withdraw. These include unwillingness to accept advice; failure to make a payment to account; failure to give instructions; unreasonable behaviour by the client; and the need to make a report under the Proceeds of Crime Act 2002 or the Money Laundering Regulations 2003.

Declining to accept advice. It is an unfortunate truth that some clients have **11.05.01** unrealistic expectations of the strength of their case or of the way in which a matter should be dealt with. If a client is unwilling to accept advice, despite attempts to persuade them to do so, a solicitor should seriously consider ceasing to act. The solicitor/client relationship is based on trust, including trust by the client in the solicitor's judgement. When that trust has gone, the relationship is usually irreparably damaged. Of course there may be circumstances where it is appropriate to continue acting. Particularly in litigation, matters are rarely so clear cut that there is not room for a difference of opinion. For example, although there may be a weight of evidence against a client accused of a crime, he is still entitled to require the Crown to prove his guilt beyond reasonable doubt. Similarly a parent is always entitled to seek to maintain contact with children even if there is a considerable body of evidence militating against that. If a solicitor advises a client to settle a case, the solicitor may nonetheless be fully committed to continuing the fight if the client feels the offer is too low. However, there may come a time when advice about the way the matter is conducted is being questioned, leading to a loss of confidence for the client in the solicitor's interest in the matter. If the solicitor carries on in the face of such criticism from the client, it may well be the precursor of a complaint of inadequate service or even a negligence claim. Ceasing to act may be the more appropriate course of action.

Payments to Account. Unless the solicitor has agreed to accept instructions **11.05.02** on a speculative basis, or has agreed that the fee for the whole matter will be paid on conclusion, it will frequently be prudent to ask the private fee paying client to put the solicitor in funds to meet anticipated outlays and fees in advance of the conclusion of a matter, particularly in litigation. Failure to do so will usually be sufficient reason to withdraw from acting. However, it is important that this decision is not taken too late in the day. Clients should be given reasonable deadlines to make payments to account, and some may need a reminder when the deadline arrives. To continue putting off the evil day of ceasing to act is likely to leave the solicitor between the devil and the deep blue sea. It is most unwise to withdraw from acting when a hearing is imminent. That is likely to lead to a complaint of inadequate service if not misconduct. Respect is also an important part of the solicitor/client relationship, and the client's respect will evaporate if deadlines continually come and go with no sanction.

---

[12] Professional Practice Committee Guidelines: *House Purchase and Sale* 2005.

11.05.03 Failure to give instructions. Just as some clients are regularly in communication and may indeed need constant reassurance by the solicitor, there are some who seem to forget that they have instructed a solicitor at all. If instructions cannot be obtained, it is necessary to consider withdrawing from acting and will usually be appropriate to do so. Allowing matters to drift on in the hope that the client will eventually turn up is rarely sensible. Some clients move without communicating their new address. The onus is on the client to keep the solicitor advised of the address at which they can be contacted, and if the client fails to do so there is no obligation on a solicitor to take proactive steps to find the client, even if the solicitor is holding funds for him or her. That does not mean that there will never be a need to make any enquiries, and contacting the family or friends, if known, or in appropriate circumstances the doctor, may be appropriate and may lead to the resumption of the relationship.

If the client is simply burying his or her head in the sand and refusing to give instructions, it will normally be appropriate to terminate the relationship. In these circumstances, it is sensible risk management to advise the client in writing of any time limit that may apply to the matter in which the solicitor has been instructed, even if that time limit is years ahead. Similarly if a date has been fixed for a court hearing and the solicitor withdraws before that hearing has taken place, the letter intimating withdrawal should remind the client of the date of the hearing.

11.05.04 Unreasonable Behaviour. Clients who shout and/or swear abusively at a solicitor or office staff should be warned that a repetition of such behaviour will lead to the solicitor ceasing to act. In particular, staff should not have to tolerate such antisocial behaviour. Similarly, threats of violence are unacceptable and entitle a solicitor to withdraw.

11.05.05 Proceeds of Crime Act. Where solicitors become suspicious or gain actual knowledge of money laundering requiring a report to be made to the Serious Organised Crime Agency (SOCA) in terms of the Proceeds of Crime Act or Money Laundering Regulations 2003, it will not always be necessary to withdraw from acting but it may sometimes be appropriate to do so. In these circumstances, great care needs to be taken about the reason given for withdrawing to avoid being accused of tipping off the client which is itself a criminal offence.[13]

11.05.06 Withdrawal in Court Cases. As we saw earlier,[14] although a solicitor may withdraw from acting in a court case, the solicitor may not do so unless he or she has good cause,[15] has given reasonable notice and has had regard to not prejudicing the course of justice.[16] Occasionally, an accused client who, possibly under pressure from his peers or his family, has instructed a different

---

[13] The implications of the Proceeds of Crime Act are dealt with more fully in Ch.6 and Ch.9 above.

[14] See para.11.03 above.

[15] In *Corrigan* DTD 636/84(b) the Discipline Tribunal indicated that where appropriate the solicitor should also obtain the consent of the court, but that what constitutes "good cause" may be largely subjective on the part of the solicitor.

[16] See the Code of Conduct for Scottish Solicitors 2002, art.5(f). Where a solicitor abandons an action without informing the client, an action for damages may lie. See Begg on *Law Agents op. cit.* p.111.

solicitor will have his or her request for a transfer of the legal aid certificate refused. In those circumstances, the nominated solicitor continues as agent and is responsible for the future conduct of the case.[17] However, if the client refuses to give instructions the solicitor should consider advising the Scottish Legal Aid Board in terms of reg.17(2) of the Criminal Legal Aid Regulations that he requires to withdraw from acting leaving the board responsible for dealing with the legal aid certificate.

Some insights as to when and how a lawyer may properly withdraw from acting in a court case are contained in the cases of *G v Scanlon*[18] and *Venters v H. M. Advocate*.[19] In *G v Scanlon* the Inner House indicated that it would not generally be appropriate for legal representatives to withdraw from acting at the start of a proof or trial simply because the court has denied a request for an adjournment. The court in its opinion stated:

> " . . . a legal representative who has sought and failed to obtain an adjournment to a future date, even if he is (perhaps through being new to the case or for some other understandable reason) wholly unprepared, will normally owe it to his client and to the court not to return his instructions, but to continue to do his best for his client, and to bring to the procedure adopted by the sheriff the advantages, which exist and are emphasised by the granting of legal aid, of legal representation."

In *Venters* the accused had lost his first two solicitors due to respectively a disagreement over the conduct of the defence (whether the character of the complainer should be attacked), and a conflict of interest. At the start of his trial his counsel tendered the special defences of alibi and incrimination. However, the strength of the crown's evidence after the first day was such as to cause the accused to desire to change his plea to self-defence, a stance that was contradictory to the original defence, against his counsel's advice. In the circumstances his counsel and agents indicated to the trial judge that they would have to withdraw. Counsel offered to advise the accused as to his position. The judge agreed to this and counsel advised the accused to seek a continuation to appoint further counsel or at least to have some time in which the accused could prepare the case in more detail. The High Court in its judgement endorsed the course of conduct adopted by the accused's legal representatives.

It is worth noting that simply because your client has changed his or her story is not grounds of itself for ceasing to act. It depends on the circumstances. The original statement may have been false due to panic or a lack of understanding of the law, e.g. on self-defence. It does not mean that the client is necessarily guilty. The client may consider that his or her story is too far-fetched to be believed, nonetheless your duty is to exhort your client to tell the truth, however hard to believe it may be. On the other hand, if your client changes his or her statement and defence in a way that from your earlier conversations you know to be false then you should withdraw.[20]

---

[17] See *McKinstry v Law Society of Scotland*, 1997 S.L.T. 192.

[18] 1999 S.C. 226.

[19] 1999 S.L.T. 1345.

[20] See J. Ross Harper, *A Practitioner's Guide to the Criminal Courts* (Law Society of Scotland, Edinburgh, 1985), pp.140–141.

11.05.07 Recovery of fees after withdrawing. Following intimation of the decision to withdraw from acting, recovery of fees and outlays may be a problem. It will sometimes—but not always—be appropriate to exercise a lien (see below). If the matter was entered into on a speculative basis, and the solicitor withdraws before it is successfully concluded, it will only be possible to seek payment at that stage if there is a contractual basis for doing so—i.e. if there is provision in the terms of business to that effect. It is always worth including a clause in the terms of business letter dealing with payment of fees if the relationship is terminated before its natural conclusion.

If payment is not made voluntarily it may be necessary to sue the former client. As we saw in Ch.6,[21] it is a breach of fiduciary duty to realise a profit by the use of the client's confidential information. Similarly, there is no ruling in professional ethics in the UK (though there is in the USA, Australia and New Zealand) that allows a lawyer to breach confidentiality to the extent necessary to enforce his or her fee.[22] It follows that a solicitor may only use information as to the assets of the former client e.g. for the purposes of doing diligence on the dependence or in execution of a decree, in a way that does not breach the client's confidentiality.

11.06 Termination by client

Both in terms of the law of agency and of professional ethics clients are entitled to terminate the contract with their lawyer whenever they please, without warning and without penalty and, subject to the provisions of the legal aid regulations where relevant, to instruct a new solicitor. Although such termination can be intimated directly by the client, it is normally intimated by a mandate sent by the new solicitor.

11.07 Mandates

If a mandate is received, this terminates the client's instructions to the original solicitor and must be implemented without question and as soon as practicable,[23] unless the original solicitor is entitled to exercise a lien in respect of fees and outlays.[24] If a lien is being exercised that should be stated immediately so that the new solicitor receives a timeous response to the mandate. Even then, the solicitor is under an obligation to get his or her account made up quickly and remitted for taxation, if necessary. Any unreasonable delay in doing this may lead to a finding of professional misconduct.[25]

Just as in other relationships, the unexpected parting may disincline the party who is being left, to let go. This may be for worthy reasons e.g. if there is a risk that the new lawyer is seeking to take advantage of the client. However, more often it is for less altruisitic reasons—namely, that the original

---

[21] See para.6.10 above.

[22] See para.6.17 above.

[23] See DTD 636/84(c) *Corrigan*. The Society's Professional Practice Committee published a guideline on mandates in 1998 which can be found in *Greens Solicitors Professional Handbook*.

[24] See para.11.12 below.

[25] DTD 687/86(b). The Practice Guideline on Mandates makes it clear that only exceptionally would a period in excess of four weeks be regarded as a reasonable time within which to render an account.

solicitor suspects the new solicitor of trying to "acquire" his or her client. Nonetheless the Professional Practice Committee has resolutely given the same advice no matter what the provocation—Act first and ask questions later.

Even if, on receipt of a mandate, the solicitor suspects that there has been an approach to the client in breach of the Society's practice rules, e.g. of the Solicitors' (Scotland) (Advertising and Promotion) practice rules, the mandate must still be implemented. However the solicitor would be entitled to make a complaint about the breach of the rules. It should be stressed that if that complaint is not backed up by evidence, it will almost certainly not be sustainable. The Professional Practice Committee have also expressed the view that solicitors who receive a mandate should not form judgements about or discuss with the client the ethics of the new solicitor—(even if that solicitor would appear to be in breach of the Conflict of Interest Rules by accepting the instructions)—but should implement the mandate. The original solicitor would be entitled to bring the circumstances to the attention of the Law Society either as a professional practice matter or as a formal complaint.

In one case[26] the discipline tribunal found that on receiving a mandate the respondent had written to his former client asking for a meeting to discuss the client's decision to transfer his case to another solicitor and had delayed implementing the mandate pending a reply. The Tribunal held that the respondent's conduct in this regard was quite improper and provided no excuse for failure to implement the mandate. *After* having implemented the mandate the solicitor may write to the former client making a reasonable enquiry as to why the client has instructed a new solicitor. However, while the solicitor may ask for information he or she must not in any way invite the former client to resume the original connection. If the client returns to the original solicitor after having previously signed a mandate, the original solicitor is entitled to resume acting—although not obliged to do so.

Mandates in Executries 11.08

In 1998 the Professional Practice Committee produced a Practice Guideline on Executries[27]:

1. *Where there is a combination of solicitor and non-solicitor executors, a solicitor executor should not use his power as executor to secure the continuity of his acting as solicitor in the winding up of the estate, in which circumstances the solicitor may either cease acting or resign as executor.*

2. *If the solicitor ceases to act but remains as executor, he should bow to the wishes of the other executors on which firm should take over the administration of the estate. Failure to do so gives rise to a conflict between the interests of executors and the interests of the solicitor's practice.*

3. *If the solicitor decides to resign, he should seek a discharge and obtemper any mandate of the remaining executors resolve that another firm should act.*

---

[26] DTD 636/84(c) *Corrigan.*
[27] "Practice Guideline Mandates in Executries" (1998) J.L.S.S. 42.

It is not thought that a clause in a will which has been drawn up by a solicitor and which appoints that solicitor as an executor and the solicitor's firm as the solicitors responsible for winding up the estate, can seek to secure that position by stipulating that the executors cannot request another firm of solicitors to act without the permission of the original firm of solicitors. Such a clause would be likely to be seen as a rather too obvious attempt to obviate the wording of the Practice Guideline.

11.09 Mandates where the solicitor is leaving a firm

One distinct class of mandates occurs where a lawyer, whether a partner or non-partner, leaves the firm and seeks to encourage some of the firm's clients to go with him or her. This situation is covered in the 1998 Law Society Guidelines on Mandates.[28] The guidelines, not entirely convincingly, draw a distinction between the position of partners and non-partners.[29] However, in either case the mandate should be implemented first, and questions asked later.

11.10 Mandates—The Exceptions

There are a few occasions where a mandate does not have to be implemented without delay:

a) First, if the mandate is dated before the solicitor's last meeting with the client or last instructions from him, it is quite proper—although not obligatory—to seek clarification from the client about which solicitor he wishes to act. That may be done in writing, by telephone or in person. If the client confirms the mandate in favour of the new solicitor, that is the end of the matter and the original solicitor cannot pursue it further.

b) Secondly, if the papers contain a confidential social work report or court document which the original solicitor has seen as a officer of the court, but which the client now wishes to see as a party litigant, the solicitor should not pass it to the former client.[30]

c) Thirdly, where the client is receiving legal aid and is seeking to instruct a new solicitor. Here a mandate on its own is insufficient to effect a transfer. Permission must first be obtained from the Scottish Legal Aid Board for the agency to be transferred. Article 7 of the Code of Conduct for Criminal Work lays down the procedure for intimating a change of agency in Criminal Legal Aid. Similar rules apply for civil cases. The procedures were agreed between the Law Society of Scotland and the Scottish Legal Aid Board following the *McKinstry* case.[31] Where there is a nominated solicitor under a legal aid certificate, the certificate must first be transferred to the new solicitor before the mandate is intimated. The original solicitor is not obliged to implement a mandate if the certificate has not been

---

[28] See *Greens Solicitors Professional Handbook*. See also S. Galt, "Mandates" (1989) J.L.S.S. 54.

[29] See Ch.2 above and para.2.17 and 2.18 in particular.

[30] See Professional Practice Committee Decisions, 1986 J.L.S.S. 273.

[31] 1997 S.L.T. 191.

transferred.[32] The form of mandate which was approved by the Scottish Legal Aid Board includes a reason for the request for the transfer. If a certificate has not yet been issued there is no nominated solicitor and a mandate alone is sufficient.

d) Fourthly, where a lien is properly being invoked.[33]
e) Fifthly, where a mandate is received in respect of a client who has been medically certified as incapax, the Law Society's professional practice department takes the view that the solicitor is entitled to regard the mandate as void until satisfied that the client has regained capacity.

Payment of fees on receipt of mandate   11.11

The receipt of a mandate will normally entitle the original solicitor to fee up work in progress and seek payment of the account including outlays. However, the solicitor can only insist on payment of fees at this stage if the contract with the client allows that. Similarly if the agreed feeing arrangement was to reflect an element of success in the matter, that element cannot be charged where the matter has not yet been successful unless there is a contractual basis for doing so. This can be covered in the terms of business letter issued at the outset of the matter.

The former table of fees recommended by the Law Society (which were for guidance only and not mandatory), contained guidance on the charge for implementing a mandate.[34] However the fee was payable when the files and papers were "delivered", and it was therefore not proper to exercise a lien in respect of this delivery fee. The fee is payable by the client and not by the new solicitor, as it is the client's instructions which have been implemented. It is not improper conduct on the part of the new solicitor to fail to pay the fee. If it remains unpaid recovery must be sought through the Small Claims process.

Lien—general   11.12

As mentioned above, in most circumstances it will be appropriate to exercise a lien over the files and papers after termination of the agency if fees and outlays are outstanding, whether those have previously been rendered or are only rendered after the agency has been terminated. The Law Society's Professional Practice Department receives regular calls about the exercise of a lien in these circumstances. The Society will be slow to interfere with a solicitor's exercise of a lien. Lien is fundamentally a matter of law and solicitors will normally be entitled to exercise the remedy in the same way as any other creditor.

Lien—the substantive law. Scots private law recognises a mutuality of **11.12.01** contractual obligations in relation to moveable property such that if one party to a contract has lawful possession of moveable property belonging to the other party to the contract, the first party may retain possession of the property

---

[32] The converse, however, is not true. Thus a nominated solicitor who seeks to break away from a firm taking the legal aid client(s) with him or her, may not take the client's files without permission from the clients or the firm since the files belong not to the solicitor but either to the firm or the client. See *Archibald Finlayson and Ors v Robert Turnbull*, 1997 S.L.T. 613.

[33] See para.11.12.03 below.

[34] Ch.3 Item D3(iii).

in security for that party's claims against the other party. This right of retention or lien, in the case of solicitors is not a mere special lien to cover the monies owed under the existing contract, but by custom and practice constitutes a general lien, which covers all balances due to the solicitor by the client in all transactions between them. Typically, the lien is exercised in relation to papers belonging to the client which are in the lawyer's possession, most commonly, the elements in the case file which are owned by the client.[35] Moreover, the lien will also extend to title deeds,[36] wills[37] or share certificates. However, certain documents are exempt from a lien. It does not cover the register of shareholders in a company since there is a statutory right for the public to inspect this. A lien cannot be exercised over any part of a court process, so that if part of the process has been borrowed it should be returned to the court. It is also improper to exercise a lien over a passport. The passport belongs to the relevant government, not to the client. Finally, deeds and other papers borrowed from a lender or other solicitor must be returned if requested by the sender, and a lien against the solicitor's own client cannot be exercised in the face of such a request.

11.12.02 What a Lien covers. A lien covers the solicitor's business accounts, and advances usually made in the ordinary course of business, such as to counsel or witnesses. It does not cover cash advances to the client,[38] nor, it would appear, the account of an Edinburgh solicitor in Court of Session proceedings, if paid by the country solicitor; nor the account of an English solicitor,[39] unless a Scottish solicitor has paid it, or is liable for it.

11.12.03 Exercising a Lien. A different approach will sometimes need to be adopted depending on whether the agency has been terminated by the solicitor or by the client. If the solicitor has withdrawn from acting for professional reasons—e.g. a conflict of interest has arisen—it may not be appropriate to further inconvenience the client by exercising a lien. Similarly if the solicitors have decided following staff changes that they are no longer able to provide a service in a particular area of practice, they should exercise considerable caution so as not to frustrate the client's ability to instruct new solicitors by exercising a lien.

Whether the agency has been terminated by the solicitor or the client, it is inappropriate to exercise a lien to the client's prejudice. Prejudice is more than mere inconvenience. It means something substantial such as the loss of a right or the risk of decree passing against the client. It does not include a requirement on the client to spend more money—for example to obtain quick copies or extracts from the registers or to take further statements from witnesses. Certainly, obstructing the course of justice by refusing to produce papers entrusted to the lawyer for the purposes of litigation would be considered prejudicial. Thus, if a motion for interim decree has been intimated and the original solicitors hold the very documents which would need to be lodged in court to vouch the client's position, exercising a lien will amount to

---

[35] See para.11.13 below.
[36] See *Ranking of Hamilton of Provenhall's Creditors* (1781) Mor. 6253, perhaps the earliest reported Scottish case of a law agent's lien.
[37] See *Paul v Meikle* (1868) 7 M. 235.
[38] See *Christie v Ruxton* (1862) 24 D. 1182.
[39] See *Liquidator of Grand Empire Theatres Ltd v Snodgrass*, 1932 S. C. (H.L.) 73.

prejudice. Curiously, however, a solicitor may refuse to produce papers required for a professional negligence case which the client is bringing against the lawyer.[40]

If the mandate is received in the middle of a matter, or work has been completed but the fee note hasn't been prepared, the solicitor is entitled to a reasonable time to prepare an account and seek payment. What is a reasonable time will depend on the particular circumstances, but in normal circumstances should not exceed two weeks. If the matter is complicated and requires to be sent to an external Law Accountant for the fee note to be prepared, a reasonable time may extend to a month. It is not proper to exercise a lien for a longer period without rendering a fee note.

It is worth remembering that payment of the original account simply to obtain the files does not prejudice the client's right either to have the account taxed or to make a complaint to the Society about inadequate professional service rendered by the original solicitor. If the Auditor taxes off part of the account the overpayment should be repaid, and the Society's powers under s.42A of the Solicitors (Scotland) Act 1980 include power to determine that the fees and outlays for the service shall be reduced or even cancelled. Failure to implement a determination or direction under s.42A requires to be brought before the Scottish Solicitors Discipline Tribunal in terms of s.53C of the same act.

Where use of a lien is unnecessary. It should be stressed however, that lien is a form of security. Where there is no need to exercise such a security, for example where the client is legally aided or where an estate is being ingathered in an executry and there are more than enough funds to meet even a generous estimate of the lawyer's account, the lien should not be exercised. In the latter situation either the solicitor should retain sufficient funds to cover the likely fee and transmit the rest to the new agent following receipt of a mandate, or the lawyer should consign the whole estate proceeds into a deposit in joint names or finally, the solicitor should simply transfer the executry to the new agent in return from an undertaking from the agent to meet the first solicitor's agreed or taxed account. **11.12.04**

If a matter is covered by Advice and Assistance (rather than legal aid), a lien will not be improper if there is the prospect of recovery. However, the lien should be released if the new solicitor gives an undertaking to inform the original solicitor whether there has been a recovery and—if there has been—to pay the original solicitor's account (at Advice and Assistance rates and subject to any limit on authorised expenditure). Solicitors are not entitled to payment from a client under the Advice and Assistance scheme unless and until there has been a recovery.

Ownership and destruction of files **11.13**

In 1980 and again in 2000 the Law Society of Scotland sought the opinion of the Dean of the Faculty of Advocates on the questions of ownership of files and when they can be destroyed. On both occasions the opinion was that the overwhelming part of the contents of the file is the property of the client and not the solicitor. Interestingly Begg on *Law Agents* in his second edition[41]

---

[40] See *Yau v Ogilvie*, 1985 S.L.T. 91 (OH) Lord McDonald.
[41] *Op. cit.* P110.

refers to an English authority *In re. Wheatcroft*,[42] which held that a solicitor is entitled to retain as his own property letters addressed to him by his client and copies of his own letters to his client even after a change of agency to other solicitors. Following receipt of the Dean's opinion in 2000 the Council of the Society considered the matter further and published Guidelines on the Ownership and Destruction of Files in 2001.[43] It should be stressed that this is guidance and that the onus must always rest with the solicitor as to whether it is safe or prudent to dispose of a file in any particular case.[44] A clause in a terms of business letter advising that a file will be destroyed after a particular period of time would be the most sensible way of demonstrating the client's consent to such destruction. If the file has been retained for longer than the recommended period, it should still be made available to the client if requested even if the stated or suspected purpose is to consider the possibility of a claim or complaint against the original solicitor. *A fortiori*, if such a request is received during the period recommended for retention, it should be implemented.

---

[42] June 8, 1877, Law Reports, 6th Chancery Division, 97.

[43] See *Greens Solicitors Professional Handbook*.

[44] It should also be borne in mind that retention of papers for longer than necessary may raise data protection issues. See Webster *op. cit.* para.2.26 (2004).

CHAPTER 12

DUTIES TO THIRD PARTIES

Introduction

The role of the lawyer today is more complex than in bygone eras. Although the influence of the adversarial system on the role of the lawyer today remains considerable, it is more true than it ever was that the lawyer's duty to safeguard the interests of the client has to be balanced against the lawyer's duties to others. These others include not simply professional colleagues and the courts, who are the subject of the next two chapters, but also a wide range of third parties. It is to these last duties that this chapter is devoted. Principally, they are duties based on contract and agency, those based on negligence and those rooted in professional ethics. The general position in relation to each of these duties will be examined in turn, followed by a specific discussion of the duties relating to: commercial lenders; messengers at arms; other service providers; experts; witnesses; nominees; unrepresented parties; guarantors; other solicitors' clients; undertakings; beneficiaries; references and relations with the Law Society of Scotland.

Contractual and Agency Duties: The General Position

Here the position is essentially as set out in the normal rules of agency. If a solicitor contracts with a third party on behalf of a disclosed client (principal) he/she cannot normally sue or be sued in terms of the contract.[1] The principal exceptions to this general rule are: (a) where the solicitor has instructed another solicitor or possibly an accountant[2] (b) the solicitor expressly agrees to be personally bound (c) the solicitor signs the missives, contract or letter of obligation in his/her own name and in no way qualifies his/her personal liability[3] and (d) where a custom of trade makes the agent personally liable.[4] Where the solicitor reveals the existence but not the identity of the client, the agent can be sued on the contract, especially if the solicitor signed the contract.[5] If, however, the solicitor acts for an undisclosed principal and appears as the principal in the contract then he/she may sue and be sued by the third party in terms of the contract.[6] Finally, if the solicitor

---

[1] See e.g. *A.F. Craig & Co. Ltd v Blackater*, 1923 S.C. 472 and *Stone Rolfe v Kimber Coal Co.*, 1926 S.C. (H.L.) 45.

[2] See para.13.13 below.

[3] See *Johnston v Little*, 1960 S.L.T. 129.

[4] See *Stirling Park v Digby Brown*, 1996 S.L.T. (Sh. Ct) 17 and para.12.06 below.

[5] See *Gibb v Cunningham & Robertson*, 1925 S.L.T. 608.

[6] See e.g. *A.F. Craig & Co. Ltd v Blackater*, 1923 S.C. 472.

contracts for an undisclosed principal who is subsequently disclosed to the third party, the latter has the option of suing either the principal or the agent, but not both.[7]

12.03 Delictual Duties: The General Position

There is insufficient space and time to do justice to this topic within the covers of this work. Those who have a particular interest in the topic will find assistance in the range of books and articles which have been written in the area in the last decade alone.[8] Suffice it to say that historically, Scottish solicitors have been sued for professional negligence by their clients with some considerable frequency in the last 200 years. Often the action has been for breach of contract, negligence and breach of duty all rolled into one.[9] Deliberate wrongdoing by a solicitor can give rise to a delictual remedy by a third party.[10] In those somewhat unusual cases[11] where the solicitor negligently causes personal injury or damage to the property of a client or third party, a duty of care will exist under the standard *Donoghue v Stevenson*[12] test of foreseeability of harm: was the pursuer so closely and directly affected by the solicitor's acts that he/she ought reasonably to have the pursuer in contemplation as being likely to suffer injury. More often the claim against the solicitor will relate to pure economic loss, for example, where a solicitor causes financial loss to his/her client or makes a negligent misrepresentation to a third party. In professional negligence cases relating to pure economic loss the case law in the UK[13] has evolved to a stage that to establish a duty of care some extra element (proximity) in addition to reasonable foreseeability is required.[14] Proximity permeates the case law and divides the commentators[15] but involves an assumption of responsibility and possibly also an element of reliance. Being in a contractual relationship or equivalent thereto will usually be sufficient to establish proximity. Guidance on when the courts are likely to hold that a solicitor has assumed responsibility for a third party can be found in *Midland Bank v Cameron & Others*.[16] There, Lord Jauncey identified four relevant factors when establishing whether a duty of care is owed by a solicitor to a third party:

---

[7] *A.F. Craig & Co. Ltd v Blackater*, 1923 S.C. 472.

[8] See e.g. K. Norrie, "Professional Negligence" in *The Law of Delict*, a forthcoming SULI textbook 2006; R. Rennie, *Solicitors' Negligence* (Butterworths, Edinburgh: 1997); K. Norrie, "Libility of solicitors to third parties", 1988 S.L.T. (News) 309 and 317; R. Rennie, "Solicitors' Negligence: Third Parties join the Queue" (2001) 6 SLPQ 304; R. Rennie, "Widening the Duty of Care", 2004 S.L.T. (News) 245; A.M. Dugdale and K.M. Stanton, *Professional Negligence* (3rd edn, 1998) and R.M. Jackson and J.L. Powell, *Professional Negligence* (5th edn, 2001).

[9] Contractual liability is stricter (in terms of who may sue) and wider (since pure economic loss is always recoverable for breach and because the contract may impose higher or lower standards) than delictual liability. See Norrie, *op. cit.*

[10] See e.g. the cases contained in para.4.02 of R. Rennie, *Solicitors' Negligence, op. cit.*

[11] See e.g. *Haldane v Donaldson* (1840) 1 Rob App 226 and *Al-Kandari v J R Brown & Co (a firm)* [1988] 1 All E.R. 833.

[12] 1932 S.C. (H.L.) 31.

[13] Principally *Hedley Byrne v Heller & Partners* [1964] A.C. 465 and *White v Jones* [1995] 2 A.C. 207.

[14] See K. Norrie, "Professional Negligence", *op. cit.*

[15] *ibid.*

[16] 1988 S.L.T. 611.

1. the solicitor must assume responsibility for advice or information furnished to the third party;
2. the solicitor must let it be known to the third party expressly or impliedly that he claims, by reason of his calling, to have the requisite skill and knowledge to give the advice or furnish the information;
3. the third party must have relied upon that advice or information as matter for which the solicitor had assumed personal responsibility; and
4. the solicitor must have been aware that the third party was likely so to rely.[17]

Norrie, however, considers that *White v Jones*[18] has removed the need to establish factors 3. and 4. Examples of cases where a solicitor has been held to have assumed responsibility in relation to a third party include disappointed beneficiaries under a negligently drafted will,[19] commercial lenders in a domestic conveyance,[20] and banks and others to whom the solicitor has provided an unqualified reference.[21] Whatever the current state of a Scottish solicitor's immunity from negligence suits in respect of court work after the cases of *Arthur Hall and Co. v Simmons*[22] and *Wright v Paton Farrell*,[23] it is probably the case that immunity still exists in relation to court work insofar as third parties interest are concerned.[24]

The standard of care required of a solicitor by the law of negligence was famously established in *Hunter v Hanley.*[25] It is the standard of the reasonable or ordinarily competent solicitor, that is the standard of skill reasonably to be expected of a normally skilled and competent solicitor, acting *in the particular area of law concerned*,[26] in his/her professional capacity. Lord President Clyde, however, described it in the more negative way as "such failure as no [solicitor] of ordinary skill would be guilty of if acting with ordinary care."[27]

Professional Ethics: The General Position   12.04

For much of the twentieth century in the common law world the primary ethical duties of lawyers were owed to their clients, with the partial exception of their duties to the court and to other lawyers. This is reflected to this day

---

[17] At p.616E.

[18] [1995] 2 A.C. 207.

[19] See para.12.13 below.

[20] See para.12.05 below.

[21] See para.12.14 below.

[22] [2002]1 A.C. 615 (July 20, 2000).

[23] 2006 S.L.T. 269. In our view the reasoning of the majority in the House of Lords is to be preferred.

[24] In *Arthur Hall and Co. v Simmons* the House of Lords expressly stated that their decision to remove the immunity of lawyers from negligence suits in respect of court work in England and Wales did not extend to third party suits.

[25] 1955 S.C. 200.

[26] The words in italics are derived from Robert Rennie's argument, with which we agree, as to the impact of specialisation within the profession. See R. Rennie, *Solicitors' Negligence, op. cit.* p.22. We further agree with his argument that a specialist solicitor, holding himself/herself out to be such, is held to a higher standard of care than a generalist.

[27] at pp.204–205. this was to ensure that the law was flexible enough to allow different schools of thought and practice to develop within the professions. See K. Norrie, "Professional Negligence" *op. cit.*

in the Codes of Conduct, Model Rules and ethical guidelines which pervade the common law jurisdictions. However, in the last twenty years a school of thought derived from the psychologist Carol Gilligan,[28] has begun to emerge contrasting the traditional, dichotomous "ethic of justice" which underpins our ethical codes and standards, with an "ethic of care". The latter, favours a diffuse "other centred", responsibility oriented, relational and contextual focus which adds a further level of moral consciousness to traditional legal and ethical reasoning. Practical applications of this and similar lines of argument can be seen in the growing acceptance of mediation as a form of dispute resolution.[29] The "ethic of care" has also had an effect on the teaching of professional ethics, particularly in the USA, and especially when it is taught in conjunction with clinical legal training.[30] It has had rather less impact on content of ethical codes in the common law world. Nonetheless, lawyers in these countries in the 21st century owe more duties to third parties than are sometimes recognised. In terms of the Law Society of Scotland's Code of Conduct solicitors must act honestly at all times and in such a way as to put their personal integrity beyond question.[31] Further, we have little doubt that, as in England and Wales: *"Solicitors must not act, whether in their professional capacity or otherwise, towards anyone in a way which is fraudulent, deceitful, or otherwise contrary to their position as solicitors. Nor must solicitors use their position as solicitors to take unfair advantage either for themselves or another person."*[32] There are specific provisions in the Code of Conduct about not knowingly misleading the courts or other lawyers, but the same duty of honesty applies to any third party.[33] That duty of honesty would prohibit a solicitor from carrying out clients' instructions to do something fraudulent e.g. to ante-date documents with intent to deceive others such as HM Revenue & Customs. Similarly, forging a document and passing it off as genuine is professional misconduct whether or not that is done on the client's instructions. Article 9 of the Code of Conduct requires that solicitors must keep their word to fellow solicitors.[34] We have no doubt that a similar ethical obligation exists with respect to third parties. Again, solicitors must retain their independence from their clients[35] and in their relations with third parties, including the other side to a case, solicitors must not allow their independence to be impaired.[36]

---

[28] See C. Gilligan, *In a Different Voice* (Harvard University Press, 1982), C. Menkel-Meadow, "Portia Redux: Another look at Gender, Feminism and Legal Ethics" in S. Parker and C. Sampford (eds) *Legal Ethics and Legal Practice* (Clarendon Press, Oxford: 1995) 25 and Nicolson and Webb, *op. cit.*, pp.34ff.

[29] *ibid.* at p.51.

[30] See Menkel-Meadow, *op. cit.*, at p.51.

[31] Code of Conduct, art.7.

[32] The Professional Conduct of Solicitors 1996 r.18.01.

[33] See generally on misleading conduct Ch.1 above and para.13.04 below.

[34] See para.13.05 below.

[35] Art.1 Code of Conduct.

[36] This can be seen in the area of debt collecting. In relation to such work the Professional Practice Committee has held that it is improper for solicitors to allow a debt collection agency to send out letters on the solicitors headed paper even if the letters bear the registered office and registered number of the debt collection company. Solicitors accept electronic transfer of data to their own office before such letters are sent but should ensure that they are sent from the solicitors firm not from the debt collection agency. *Journal of the Law Society of Scotland*, May 2002, p.46.

Commercial Lenders **12.05**

Often in domestic conveyancing transactions solicitors will be acting both for the commercial lender and for the purchasing client. In such situations the solicitor will be expected to adhere to the lender's conditions of lending, including not intromitting with the settlement cheque unless the keys and disposition have been received. A failure to do so may lead to a claim based on contract, delict and breach of trust.[37] It may also be considered professional misconduct.[38] However, solicitors can owe delictual[39] and ethical duties to lenders who are not their clients, such as banks who extend them bridging facilities. Thus in one case[40] in 1978 the solicitor bought a dwelling house and cottage. The dwelling house was destroyed by fire before he could take entry, nonetheless he approached a bank for a bridging loan to assist with the purchase, without informing them that the house had been destroyed. He used part of the facility for his own purposes. Further, the solicitor persuaded a friend to pretend to buy the cottage even although there was sitting tenant therein. He again went to the bank for bridging facilities in connection with this "purchase" and used the proceeds for his own purposes. The Discipline Tribunal had little difficulty in holding the solicitor guilty of professional misconduct for (a) misappropriating the bridging loans and (b) in relation to both transactions failing to inform the lender of all relevant circumstances. As they observed:

> "The service of providing bridging loans to Solicitors and their clients is the subject of well established practice and it is clearly understood within the profession that it is the duty of a Solicitor when making an application for a bridging loan to disclose all relevant circumstances to the Bank and thereafter, unless specific arrangements are made to the contrary, to use the monies towards the purchase of the property concerned."

Solicitors' responsibility for accounts of other service providers **12.06**

Here the legal position is clear, as we saw above. An agent for a disclosed principal will not normally be liable for fees of a service provider whom he/she has instructed on behalf of the client. However, there are a growing number of exceptions to this rule. As we will see in ch.13, solicitors have a legal liability to pay the fees of another solicitor they have instructed and this may extend to accountants.[41] Although there is no legal responsibility for solicitors to pay the fees of counsel whom they instruct, there is an ethical obligation so to do. Professional ethics also requires the solicitor to meet the

---

[37] See e.g. *The Mortgage Corporation v Mitchells Roberton*, 1997 S.L.T. 1305.

[38] See e.g. *Banski*, 1988 J.L.S.S. 112.

[39] See again *The Mortgage Corporation v Mitchells Roberton*, 1997 S.L.T. 1305. There solicitors acting for the borrowers but not the lenders in a mortgage transaction undertook not to pass on the funds to the borrower until a standard security was granted and delivered to the lender's agents. They failed to adhere to this undertaking. Lord Johnston in the Outer House held that the borrowers' solicitors were in sufficient proximity to owe a duty of care to the lenders since they knew or ought to have known that the lenders would not have advanced the loan to the borrowers without a security being in place.

[40] DTD 426B/79.

[41] See 1983 J.L.S.S. 466–467.

fees of professional experts such as medical consultants unless the solicitor has expressly disclaimed responsibility at the outset. It is unclear how far this form of professional courtesy extends. The Discipline Tribunal has extended the duty to linguists[42] and to photographers,[43] but would estate agents and hairdressers receive the same treatment? At the Society's Annual General Meeting in 1993 a motion in the following terms was debated. "The Law Society of Scotland resolves that . . . it shall not be professional misconduct for a solicitor to fail to pay the charges for other professional services instructed by him to be carried out on behalf of the disclosed client unless either (a) he has expressly accepted personal responsibility for such charges or (b) he holds funds for the client for the purpose of paying such charges." The motion was defeated by a substantial majority, and the meeting accepted[44] that solicitors should take steps at the outset to ensure that both the client and the other professional instructed understand the position about costs. It is prudent for solicitors to obtain a payment to account from the client in advance to meet the likely cost of a report, and solicitors should ensure that communications from the experts are promptly dealt with. If a solicitor is not prepared to accept personal responsibility for payment of an experts fees, that must be stated when the expert is instructed, so that the expert prepares the report in the knowledge that he must look to the client for payment. Interestingly, in *Stirling Park & Co. v Digby, Brown & Co.*[45] Sheriff Principal MacLeod held that a firm of solicitors who had instructed sheriff officers on behalf of a client were personally liable for their fees. The Sheriff Principal stated that the practice of solicitors accepting personal liability for sheriff officers' fees was so certain, uniform, notorious and reasonable as to give rise to an obligation that was contractually binding upon solicitors through the operation of legally binding custom.[46] It is unclear whether the Discipline Tribunal would feel that there was also an ethical obligation to pay sheriff officers or messengers at arms.

12.06.01 Reporters Appointed by the Court

What is the solicitor's responsibility for the account of a reporter appointed by the court? This question arose in the recent case of *Beaumont petnr.*[47] There a reporter had been appointed by a sheriff to provide a child welfare report. As is usual, the actual instruction of the report came from the representative of one of the parties, namely the petitioner. In law the matter seems to be clear cut. As an agent for a disclosed principal the petitioner would normally have no responsibility for the reporter's fee. Such a conclusion would seem to be reinforced by regulation 10 of the general regulations in the Table of Fees of solicitors in the Sheriff Court[48] which states: "When a remit is made by the Court regarding matters in the record between the parties to an accountant, engineer, or other reporter the solicitors

---

[42] *Mackin*, 1992 J.L.S.S. 327. (Fee for translating a lease from German to English.)

[43] *Hetherington* DTD 19/9/02.

[44] As the Professional Practice Committee had in 1980 and 1983. See 1983 J.L.S.S. 466–467.

[45] 1996 S.L.T. (Sh. Ct) 17.

[46] Support for the Sheriff Principal can be found in McLaren on Court of Session Practice p.1115.

[47] Inner House, [2006] CSIH 27 P2412/05.

[48] (S.I. 1993/3080).

shall not, without special agreement, be personally responsible to the reporter for his remuneration, the parties alone being liable therefore." Further reinforcement would seem to come from rule 33.21(2) of the Ordinary Cause Rules in the Sheriff Court which provides that on making an appointment of a reporter the Sheriff shall direct that the party who sought the appointment or, where the Court makes the appointment of its own motion, the pursuer or minuter as the case may be, shall be responsible in the first instance for the fees and outlays of the reporter.

What then is the position in professional ethics? The conclusion of the Discipline Tribunal and the Inner House was that instructing a court reporter, even if it is one who had been appointed at the request of the court, was the same as instructing a professional expert. It is not entirely clear why this should be so, although in fairness the petitioner only raised the argument based on the regulation before the Inner House and the Ordinary Cause rule appears not to have been raised in either forum.

Duties owed to witnesses **12.07**

Hitherto relatively little has been written in Scotland on the ethical duties which lawyers owe to witnesses. While lawyers may cross examine witnesses vigorously on their clients' behalf this does not entail a licence to demean or humiliate witnesses in a manner which resembles abuse of power. Although witnesses may object to what they see as unnecessary aggression or disparaging remarks by the lawyer, it is unusual for them to make formal complaints in the matter.[49] It follows that solicitors have a duty of courtesy to witnesses. This includes the courtesy of giving witnesses, particularly professional witnesses such as doctors, adequate notice of the date of the hearing to which they will be cited, and not leaving that until the last possible moment. The Society's professional practice department regularly receive calls from witnesses who have been cited without adequate notice, including solicitors themselves. The Discipline Tribunal have noted that "the legal position is that when a solicitor cites a witness to attend court he is personally responsible for his fee and such fee ought to be settled without delay."[50] The responsibility is that of the individual solicitor who signs the citation. In the particular case the Tribunal were dealing with, a chartered surveyor had been cited and had given evidence but his account was not settled for over two years. The solicitor's client had the benefit of legal aid in the case, but the delay in receiving payment from the then Legal Aid Central Committee was held to be no excuse.

In a criminal case where a doctor is a Crown witness, there is no professional duty on a solicitor to meet a fee sought by the doctor unless the doctor has been asked to give an opinion. If the doctor is simply confirming the facts of the matter to the defence agent a fee is not payable as there is a duty on behalf of all Crown witnesses to make their evidence known to the defence if asked. However, it may be necessary to seek the opinion of the doctor on the Crown list on matters such as the severity of a wound (for

---

[49] But see: *The "Librarian" Bites Back as QC Faces Formal Complaint, Scotsman* 21/05/2005. For a further examination of the lawyer's duties to witnesses see paras 14.07.05 and 14.07.06 below.

[50] Procedures and Decisions of the Scottish Solicitors Discipline Tribunal para.16.06 at p.152.

example was the wound life threatening?) or on the prospects for recovery of the complainer. If such an opinion is sought, the doctor may properly charge a fee and the solicitor will have a professional responsibility to meet that (see para.12.06).

The Society has agreed a code of practice for expert witnesses.[51] In 2002, the Professional Practice Committee received a letter from an expert who had been asked for a report. The instructing solicitors had asked that any adverse comments on the client's position be sent under separate cover. The committee felt that seeking a report from an expert in these terms was improper, and that the expert was entitled to seek confirmation in writing that the "good" report would not be used to mislead the other party to the matter or their agents or insurers.[52]

In relation to child witnesses, the Scottish Executive in guidance published in 2003 which was designed to improve the questioning of children it is stated that it is "the duty of every practitioner to ensure that the experience of giving evidence by all children causes as little anxiety and distress to the child as possible in the circumstances".[53] Not only should the party questioning the child confine examination to what is strictly necessary in the interests of justice and the securing of a fair trial, in addition the other parties should remain vigilant to take objection to any inappropriate examination. In particular, there is a need for sensitive awareness towards the child on the day and of the need not to harm the child at any stage of the process, and as such, the tone of questioning should be appropriate to the circumstances and bullying or harassing a child is totally inappropriate.[54] Recent legislation has added further obligations to vulnerable witnesses and to children.[55]

Article 13 of the Society's Code of Conduct for Criminal work—headed Precognition of Witnesses—states "*when carrying out precognition of witnesses, whether personally, through directly-employed staff, or through external precognition agents, the nominated or instructing solicitor has responsibility for the manner in which contact is made by the witnesses and the manner in which the witnesses are actually precognosced. In particular, it is the duty of the solicitor to ensure that any matters associated with the witness of which he is aware which would affect the taking of the precognition or the mode of contact, such as age, disability or other vulnerable status, are taken into account by him and communicated to any precognition agent.*" The Code adds that in cases involving more than one accused there will be separate and different interests but multiple precognitions of civilian witnesses by agents for each accused should be avoided unless it is absolutely essential in the interests of justice and of the accused. Finally, the Code states that every witness should be contacted in writing by the solicitor in advance with effective information about the process of precognition including information

---

[51] see *www.expertwitnessscotland.info*—instructing an expert.

[52] (2002) J.L.S.S. May, p.46.

[53] *Guidance on the Questioning of Children in Court: Sporting Child Witnesses Guidance Pack*, Scottish Executive 2003.

[54] *ibid.*

[55] Vulnerable Witnesses (Scotland) Act 2004 and Protection of Children (Scotland) Act 2003. For fuller information see J.L.S.S. March 2005 at p.14 and December 2005 at p.17 re Vulnerable Witnesses; and May 2005 at p.22 for the Protection of Children. The Scottish Executive Victims and Witnesses Unit website *www.scotland.gov.uk/Topics/Justice/criminal/17416/8451* provides further information about the implementation of the legislation including practitioner guidance.

about to whom a complaint could be made if things are perceived to go wrong. There should be no "cold calling".

Article 10 of the Code of Conduct for Criminal work states that only those witnesses relevant to a case should be cited to attend court and a solicitor must at all times be in a position to justify the citation of all witnesses in a case. Where possible witnesses should be cited prior to the intermediate diet to ascertain whether there is any difficulty about their attendance at court for the trial.

Witness Fees

12.07.01

As we saw in the previous paragraph, solicitors are liable for witnesses' fees. Begg[56] includes "the expenses of witnesses and havers adduced by" solicitors among those fees and charges for which solicitors are personally liable. It is clear and well understood that solicitors are liable to meet the cost of travelling and out of pocket expenses incurred by a witness, but the solicitor may also be personally liable for a fee charged by a professional witness. There is a difference between the liability of the solicitor who cites the witness and what may be recovered from the other side following an award of expenses. The latter is regulated by an Act of Sederunt in the Sheriff Court and by Rules 42.13 and Rule 42.16 (chapter II) in the Court of Session. Begg cites the case of *McDonald v Meldrum*[57] as his authority. Although the report of that case is short, the Inner House (First Division) granted decree against both the party and his solicitor for the witnesses' charges including time. So far as we can see, that case has not been overturned subsequently.

Nominees

12.08

It is not uncommon for solicitors to receive instructions to put in offers in the name of a nominee of the real intended purchaser. There are a number of issues to be considered. Firstly does the nominee really exist? It would be improper to take instructions to submit an offer on behalf of a person from whom the solicitor had no instructions. It is therefore necessary to meet with the nominee before putting such an offer in. Secondly, is there a conflict of interest between the nominee and the real intended purchaser? If missives are concluded, will the real purchaser go through with the transaction or will the nominee be left high and dry? Thirdly, the solicitor must ensure that his/her own personal conduct in the transaction does not deceive the other party. In a case which came before the Discipline Tribunal in 2005 the solicitor put himself forward as the nominee and instructed a different firm of solicitors to put in the offer. However, the role of the nominee solicitor was not merely passive. He viewed the property personally and engaged in conversation with the seller. The client for whom the solicitor had agreed to be nominee was known to the seller and that client's offer had previously been rejected by the seller. Indeed the solicitor was aware that the seller was not willing to sell the property to his client. At a subsequent closing date a separate offer was submitted by the same individual adding to the deception. The Tribunal found that his actings amounted to unprofessional conduct. The Tribunal accepted

---

[56] *Op. cit.* p.289.
[57] (1839) 1 D. 677.

that there is a long established practice of using nominee provisions in missives and that there was nothing wrong with this in principle. In this case it was the solicitor's personal actings that the Tribunal found improper. Given the element of deception involved the solicitor might consider himself fortunate in the disposition of the case.

A company may well instruct that an offer be submitted with a nominee clause and subsequently decide to take title in the name of an associated company. There is no impropriety in that and solicitors are free to take such instructions from company clients.

12.09 Unrepresented Parties

Solicitors may find themselves dealing on behalf of clients with other parties who do not wish to instruct a solicitor. No one can be forced to instruct a solicitor and any party is entitled to deal with their own affairs personally. If the matter is a conveyancing transaction (including a secured loan) r.7 of the Conflict of Interest Rules[58] applies. It states that a solicitor shall not issue any deed, writ, missive or other document requiring the signature of the unrepresented party to him without informing that party *in writing* (our emphasis) that such signature may have legal consequences and he *should* (our emphasis) seek independent legal advice before signature. The Professional Practice Committee have decided that the words "issued to him" in r.7 mean more than just issuing the document directly to the unrepresented party, and include using the solicitor's own client as a means of transmitting a document to an unrepresented party for signature.[59]

In 1998 the Society published a practice guideline extending the provisions of r.7 to other types of transaction. The Society's Professional Practice Committee agreed that there is no justification for distinguishing between transactions involving heritable property and other types of transactions. Solicitors dealing with unrepresented parties in any kind of transaction should not issue to the unrepresented party any document for signature without advising that party in writing that the signature may have legal consequences and he should take independent legal advice before signing it. Such a notice may be in a separate letter or may be contained within the document to be signed and does not require to be acknowledged.[60]

If a purchaser is representing himself/herself in a conveyancing transaction it would be inappropriate for the seller's solicitor to send the titles to the lay purchaser, although it would be proper to allow the titles to be inspected at the solicitor's office.[61]

In exceptional circumstances a solicitor may approach his/her client's opponent (provided they are unrepresented) in an accident case, seeking a statement on the circumstances of the accident. There are obvious downsides to such behaviour and it is not a course of action that should be undertaken lightly.[62]

---

[58] Solicitors (Scotland) Practice Rules 1986.
[59] (2002) J.L.S.S. June, p.49.
[60] (1998) J.L.S.S. October, p.47.
[61] Webster, *op. cit.* (2004), para.5.04.
[62] *ibid.*

Guarantors 12.10

As mentioned in the chapter on conflict of interest[63] there is a clear conflict of interest between a lender or a borrower on the one hand and a guarantor of that loan on the other hand. This includes, but is not restricted to, the joint owner of a house signing a standard security in favour of a bank in respect of a business loan to the other joint owner. In *Barclays Bank v O'Brien*[64] and *Smith v Bank of Scotland*[65] the House of Lords decided that lenders seeking security from a third party must take reasonable steps to make the third party aware of the risks of such a transaction, and of the desirability of taking independent advice prior to entering into the transaction. This new duty to give advice is imposed where there is a reasonable risk that a potential guarantor's consent might be impaired as a result of a close relationship with a third party—in *Smith* the third party was the pursuer's husband. If a lender fails to take such reasonable steps the obligations undertaken by the third party could be set aside by the court provided that the third party can satisfy the court that he entered into the obligation as the result of undue influence, misrepresentation or some other legal wrong perpetrated by the borrower. *Smith* was revisited in the House of Lords in the case of *Royal Bank of Scotland v Etridge (No.2)*[66] where they gave further consideration as to what was meant by "independent legal advice". They held that the solicitor's responsibility to the wife in giving advice is to explain the nature of the documents and the practical consequences of signing them, as well as pointing out the seriousness of risks involved, explain that the decision as to signing the documents is for the wife alone to make, check if the wife is willing to proceed; and to ensure that all explanations are given in non-technical language. Only in exceptional circumstances would the solicitor have to satisfy "himself of the absence of undue influence". Despite the fact that the Inner House declined to apply *Etridge* in Scotland in *Clydesdale Bank plc v Black*[67] it is respectfully submitted that the likelihood must be that *Etridge* will come to be accepted as the law of Scotland.[68]

As a matter of professional ethics, where solicitors are acting for lenders in such transactions, r.7 of the Conflict of Interest Rules 1986 requires them to give notice in writing to the guarantor to seek independent legal advice before signing the security and that is clearly in their own client's interests. If the guarantee is not a standard security the Practice Guideline referred to at para.12.04 above will apply.[69]

---

[63] 7.09.03, 7.15, 7.16.03.
[64] [1994] 1 A.C. 180.
[65] 1997 S.C. (H.L.) 111.
[66] [2002] 2 A.C. 773.
[67] 2002 S.L.T. 764.
[68] For a range of articles on the *Smith* case and its aftermath see e.g. Scott F. Dickson "Good Faith in Contract, Spousal Guarantees and *Smith v Bank of Scotland*", 1998 S.L.T. (News) 39; G.L. Gretton,"Good News for Bankers—Bad News for Lawyers?" 1999 S.L.T. (News) 53; R. Russell,"*Royal Bank of Scotland v Etridge (No.2)*: The end of a sorry tale?" 2002 S.L.T. (News) 55 and R. Rennie, "Solicitors' Negligence: Rearguard Action" (2002) 7 *Scottish Law and Practice Quarterly 87*. For a useful practical checklist to minimise the risk in cases between borrower and spouse, see Sim, *Conflict of interest between borrower and spouse* 1999 J.L.S.S. 44(3) 40.
[69] For a fuller discourse on guarantees between spouses see J.L.S.S. October 2003 pp.34–38.

12.11 Other solicitors' clients

Apart from the general duty of honesty, i.e. not to be fraudulent or deceitful (para.12.04 above) solicitors have no specific duties to other solicitor's clients. From time to time there have been suggestions made to the Society's Professional Practice Committee that it should produce guidelines with specific duties to other parties. The committee has consistently taken the view that a solicitor's duty is to act in the interests of his or her own clients and have declined to produce more guidelines about duties to other parties. For example, a suggestion that a purchaser's solicitor should owe a duty to the seller to ensure that the purchaser will be in funds to settle the transaction was rejected.[70] The committee stated that a solicitor should advise his own client of the risks of concluding a bargain without adequate funding in place. A prudent solicitor should make reasonable enquiries to check that his purchaser client will be in funds to settle the transaction—and pay the solicitors own fees! There is however no duty owed to the other solicitor's client to ensure that the transaction will settle.

In relation to executry work, if solicitors are instructed by executors in terms of the deceased's will, or are themselves such executors, they are entitled to proceed in accordance with the will until ordered not to do so by a court, unless they are aware from their own knowledge that the will is invalid. They are not required to cease dealing with the estate simply because they are advised that another party is seeking to challenge the validity of the will.[71]

12.12 Undertakings given by solicitors to third parties[72]

Solicitors are expected to keep their word to third parties. Closely linked to this is their obligation to honour any undertakings which they have given to third parties. The obligation can exist as a matter of contract as well as in professional ethics. Thus in *United Bank of Kuwait Ltd v Hammoud and others*[73] where an employed solicitor had fraudulently persuaded two banks to advance him money purportedly for firm transactions, but actually for his personal use, through giving undertakings to the banks, the Court of Appeal held that where a solicitor who had actual authority to represent himself as being a practising solicitor with an established firm gave an undertaking which the receiver of the undertaking was entitled to assume was given in the context of an underlying transaction which was part of the usual business of a solicitor, the undertaking would be enforced against the firm as having being given with ostensible authority and therefore binding on the firm. Undertakings are the subject of r.18.02 of the Solicitors Practice Rules in England and Wales. That rule provides that a solicitor who fails to honour an undertaking is *prima facie* guilty of professional misconduct. Rule 18.03 provides that there is no obligation on a solicitor either to give or accept an undertaking but r.18.04 provides that an undertaking is binding even if it is to do something outside the solicitor's control. The matter is not the subject of specific practice rules in Scotland and any complaint about a solicitors

---

[70] J.L.S.S. April 2002, p.45.
[71] J.L.S.S. July 2002, p.5.1.
[72] On honouring undertakings to professional colleagues see para.13.06 below.
[73] [1988] 1 W.L.R. 1051.

conduct in breaching an undertaking to a third party would probably be dealt with under reference to art.7 of the Code of Conduct.[74] Guidance on what constitutes a professional undertaking to third parties can be found in a Discipline Tribunal decision in 1987.[75] There a solicitor's client owed a substantial sum of money to a company. The solicitor in response to letters from the company undertook to inform the company as soon as there were any developments in relation to the sale of the client's business, but repeatedly failed to do so. The fiscal relied on the definition of an undertaking taken from "The Professional Conduct of Solicitors" published by the (English) Law Society[76]:

> *"An undertaking is any unequivocal declaration of intention addressed to someone who reasonably places reliance on it and made by:*
>
> > *(a) a solicitor in the course of his practice, whether personally or by a member of his staff; or*
> >
> > *(b) a solicitor as "solicitor", but not in the course of his practice; whereby the solicitor (or in the case of a member of his staff; his employer) becomes personally bound."*

Counsel for the respondent, however, submitted that "undertaking" was a very special word and that a "professional undertaking" required to contain a strict undertaking, rather as in a formal Letter of Obligation. In finding the solicitor guilty of professional misconduct, the Tribunal came down on the side of the fiscal. They concluded that:

> "there requires to be clear words of intention before a 'professional undertaking' can be inferred, but the undertaking does not require to have the degree of formality as appears in a Letter of Obligation. Indeed it is significant that 'The Professional Conduct of Solicitors' observes that a professional undertaking may be given orally or in writing and that an oral undertaking can have the same effect as a written undertaking. There is no doubt that an unequivocal declaration of intention 'addressed to someone who reasonably places reliance on it' will constitute a professional undertaking, but it is not accepted that this is an exclusive definition. Clearly there requires to be an ongoing relationship between the grantor and the grantee and provided that the grantor intended that the obligation was to be relied upon it may not be necessary to establish actual reliance in order to establish an undertaking."

In a subsequent case in 1993, a solicitor who gave several undertakings to a third party relating to the repayment of loans, despite existing undertakings being unimplemented and the discovery of a forged undertaking on the firm notepaper, was held by the Discipline Tribunal to have acted in a reckless and irresponsible way and found guilty of professional misconduct.[77] It is also clear that solicitors should not give an undertaking to pay money to a third

---

[74] *Solicitors must act honestly at all times and in such a way as to put their personal integrity beyond question.*
[75] DTD 700/87.
[76] (1986) at p.15/1.
[77] 32 DTD 852/93.

party unless they are satisfied that the money is within their control e.g. the redemption of a loan on the sale of a property.

In very unusual circumstances a solicitor can even be held liable in delict to the opposing client in a litigation. *Al-Kandari v J R Brown & Co (a firm)*[78] concerned a bitterly contested divorce in which the plaintiff was the wife of Kuwaiti national. The two children were on the husband's passport which enabled him to abduct them to Kuwait. Eventually they were returned to England and the wife was given care and control of them. The husband obtained access to them by dint of an implied undertaking from his solicitors to retain his passport. The husband tricked them into releasing the passport from their possession to the embassy from whence he was able to recover the passport. He then arranged for his wife to be kidnapped and assaulted while he abducted the children and took them to Kuwait. The plaintiff sued the husband's lawyers for negligence. The Court of Appeal held that although a solicitor would not normally owe a duty of care to his client's opponent in hostile litigation, he would owe such a duty if he stepped outside his role as solicitor for his client and accepted responsibilities towards his client's opponent. In giving an undertaking to keep the passport in their possession, the defendants were acting in an independent capacity in which they owed a duty of care to the plaintiff which they had breached.

On the issue of whether the prosecution owes a duty of care to the accused, see *Daf v Police Commissioner* [1995] 1 All E.R. 833.

12.13 Beneficiaries[79]

The Courts in both England and Scotland have considered whether a prospective beneficiary has a remedy in damages against a solicitor where a testator died before his instructions could be carried out and it was alleged that there had been undue delay in drafting the will. Until recently the case law suggested that the scope for liability for negligence was rather less in Scotland than in England. Thus Scots law, based on the case of *Robertson v Fleming*[80] seemed to indicate that a solicitor owed no liability to a beneficiary for negligently drawing up a will in such a way that defeats the expected legacy. In England liability in such situations was established in *Ross v Caunters*[81] and reiterated by the House of Lords in *White v Jones*[82] where a solicitor was successfully sued by a beneficiary where he had been instructed to prepare a will and delayed to the beneficiary's detriment.[83] However in 2002, in the

---

[78] [1988] 1 All E.R. 833.

[79] See on this topic, Ryder, *Professional Conduct for Scottish Solicitors* (Butterworths, Edinburgh: 1995) pp.92–94.

[80] (1861) 4 Macq 167.

[81] [1980] Ch. 297.

[82] [1995] 2 A.C. 207.

[83] The English position has been further clarified in *Humblestone v Martin Tolhurst Partnership (a Firm)* [2004] WL 229246. In this case the solicitors undertook to draft the testator's will and sent it to him for signature. They checked it when he sent it back but failed to note that the testator had not, in fact, actually signed the will. Their failure to do this was held to constitute a breach of care to the beneficiaries who would have benefited under the will. Mr Justice Mann stated that the defendants owed a consequential duty to the beneficiaries to check that the document had been properly executed. There is, however, no liability in England where a solicitor negligently drafts a document purporting to confer an inter vivos gift in such a way that the gift is unenforceable, *Hemmens v Wilson Browne* [1995] Ch. 23.

Outer House case of *Holmes v Bank of Scotland*,[84] Lord Kingarth inferred that there was no reason to suppose that *White v Jones* would not be followed in Scotland. Further, Lord Kingarth indicated that he did not regard himself as being bound by *Robertson v Fleming*[85] in the light of the 2nd Division decision of *Robertson v Watt & Co.*[86] However, it is likely that in both jurisdictions it will not be actionable for a solicitor who has drafted a will, then in a subsequent transaction for the testator, to adversely affect the value of the legacy.[87]

In an executry, the solicitor's client is the executor and the Court of Session has held that there is no legal obligation to account to beneficiaries.[88] The pursuers were a charity who sued for count reckoning and payment in respect of the defenders' failure to properly apportion liability for capital transfer tax with the result that the accounting for the pursuers' share of residue was less than it should have been. Lord Kirkwood held that the solicitors carried out the work of administering the estate "in their capacity of law agents of the executrix and they had an obligation to account to her for her intromissions." He dismissed the action as irrelevant.

While there may be no legal obligation to account to beneficiaries, there are nonetheless professional duties to beneficiaries owed by solicitors acting for executors. There are several decisions of the Discipline Tribunal where solicitors have been found guilty of professional misconduct in failing to respond truthfully to correspondence from beneficiaries, including one as recently as 2005.[89] In an earlier case the Tribunal said "Notwithstanding the appointment of an executor, a solicitor acting in an estate has a much wider duty than merely to implement the executor's instructions. The solicitor also has an implied duty to the other beneficiaries, particularly . . . where he had already communicated with some of them; and when it became apparent that the executor was unwilling to respond and was thereby inhibiting progress, the respondent ought to have written the other beneficiaries and advised them on the basis of the circumstances then prevailing; and on the death of the executor the solicitor should have taken steps to procure the appointment of a substitute executor. Regrettably the respondent failed to communicate with any of the beneficiaries, even when he became aware that the executor had died." The solicitor was found guilty of professional misconduct.[90] In a case the following year the Tribunal said "a solicitor has a duty to keep all the beneficiaries in an estate reasonably informed of progress and this was especially so when there was a matter of exceptional difficulty might take considerable time to resolve. In such circumstances the respondent ought to have communicated with each of the beneficiaries from time to time in order to seek their continuing approval for his course of action" and found the solicitor guilty of professional misconduct.[91] In this case, there had been a delay of six years although the delay was otherwise justifiable and resulted in the ultimate benefit of the estate.

---

[84] 2002 S.L.T. 544.

[85] (1861) 4 Macq 167.

[86] July 4, 1995, unreported.

[87] See *Clarke v Bruce Lance & Co. (a firm) and others* [1988] 1 All E.R. 365.

[88] *Lorretto School Limited v Macandrew & Jenkins* 1992 S.L.T. 615.

[89] (2005) J.L.S.S. April, p.45—Craig.

[90] Procedures & Decisions of S.S.D.T., pp.138/9 (case 720/88).

[91] Procedures & Decisions of S.S.D.T., p.139 (case 749/89).

In an executry where the solicitor is the sole executor, not only is there a professional duty to correspond with beneficiaries there is also a legal obligation to account to them for the estate. Failure to do so within a reasonable time has led to findings of professional misconduct and in a case in 1985 the Tribunal commented that it was particularly significant that the solicitor complained of was the sole executor.[92] However, the Professional Practice Committee has decided that a solicitor is entitled to take instructions from an executor even if those instructions are to refuse to answer enquiries from beneficiaries. Beneficiaries are not entitled to a service from the solicitor and solicitors should refer beneficiaries to the executor if the executor declines to allow the solicitor to deal with the enquiry.

In an estate where there is a combination of solicitor and non solicitor executors, a solicitor should not use his power as executor to secure the continuity of his acting as solicitor in the winding up of the estate, in terms of a Practice Guideline originally published in 1986 and re-affirmed in 1998.[93] In such circumstances, the solicitor may either cease acting or resign as executor. If he ceases to act, but remains as executor he should bow to the wishes of the other executors on which firm should act in the administration of the estate. If he decides to resign he should obtemper any mandate if the remaining executors decide to instruct another firm. Where the solicitor is the sole executor he is not obliged to conform to the beneficiaries wishes on which firm should act in the administration of the estate, but it might be sensible to do so rather than to be "at war" with the beneficiaries during the administration. It will be a matter for the solicitor's judgement in each case.

Where a beneficiary seeks a copy of the will, the solicitors are entitled to take instructions from the executors. The Professional Practice Committee has agreed that instructions should be taken from the executor on whether someone who has been left a specific or pecuniary legacy can be sent a copy of the will. The committee thought that there is a duty to send a copy of the will to a residuary legatee unless the executor specifically refuses that. Unless it is a small estate, the will should be registered along with the inventory to obtain confirmation of when it will become a public document, and a beneficiary could be directed to the court to inspect the will there. Because a solicitor who is not himself an executor has no legal liability to account to beneficiaries, he has no obligation to advise a party who might be entitled to claim legal rights if the executor instructs him to refrain from doing so, whether or not that would reduce the executor's own share. Webster states "in these circumstances, you have little option but to carry out the executors instructions and handover the executry funds, provided you fulfil your professional duty of advising the executors; but if you have to do this, you should, for your own protection, take a specific discharge from the executors and residuary beneficiaries."[94]

12.14 References

Solicitors should exercise great care when giving references about clients to third parties. Failure to do so may give rise to remedies both in delict and professional ethics. Solicitors should not confirm information unless it is

---

[92] Procedures and Decisions of the S.S.D.T., p.141 (case 625/85).
[93] J.L.S.S. July 1998, p.42.
[94] Webster, para.5.04.

within their own knowledge. For example, the Society's Professional Practice Committee decided in 1997 that solicitors should not countersign applications for shotgun certificates unless they have knowledge of the applicant's background and demeanour over and above simply knowing the applicant as a client and being able to verify the applicant's identity. Solicitors must take care to give references that are true and not misleading. Any facts stated or opinions expressed should either be within the solicitors own personal knowledge or stated to be based on the views of others. In an English case[95] the court found a solicitor liable in damages for giving a third party an unqualified, favourable reference for a client which concealed the fact that the client faced multiple criminal charges of dishonesty in relation to the acquisition of cars, the very matter for which a reference was being sought. Mr. Justice Brooke held that a special relationship exited between the solicitor and the third party in terms of *Hedley Byrne v Heller & Partners*[96] and observed that the solicitor had failed to note that he was governed by three obligations in the case. First, the law relating to legal professional privilege which constrained him from revealing his client's past criminal history,[97] second, the ethical duty to give any reference that was given, with candour and honesty, and third, his legal duty of care to third parties if he gave unqualified references on which they could reasonably be expected to rely." The solicitor, he added, had three courses. He might decline the invitation; he might give an answer with a clear qualification that he accepted no responsibility for it or that it was given without that reflection or inquiry which a careful answer would give; or he might simply answer without any qualification. "If he chose the last course in a case where the requisite special relationship existed, then he would owe a duty to the inquirer to exercise such care as the circumstances required." By not responding with candour and honesty the solicitor was liable in damages to the third party.

Relations with the Law Society of Scotland   **12.15**

At first glance it might appear strange to include a solicitor's duty to the Society in this chapter on duties to third parties. However it is clear from decisions of the Discipline Tribunal down the years that one of the most common reasons for finding solicitors guilty of professional misconduct is their failure to respond to communications from the Society. Indeed it is noteworthy that on many occasions the Tribunal find that the original matter complained of did not amount to misconduct, but that the failure to respond to the society's correspondence on the matter did amount to misconduct leading to a sanction imposed on the solicitor. The Tribunal has continually stressed that failure to respond hampers the Society in the performance of its statutory duty and brings the profession into disrepute. At a time when both the profession and the Society's regulatory function are under scrutiny as never before, it is even more important to deal promptly and efficiently with correspondence from the Society in respect of its regulatory functions, and if solicitors find difficulty in doing that themselves they should consider making use of the facilities afforded by the Legal Defence Union who have considerable experience in dealing with such matters.

---

[95] *Edwards v Lee* (QBD) (1991) N.L.J. 1517; Nov. 1, *The Independent*.
[96] [1964] A.C. 465, 486.
[97] The judge could have added the ethical and contractual duty of confidentiality as well.

CHAPTER 13

DUTIES TO PROFESSIONAL COLLEAGUES[1]

13.01 Introduction

Solicitors play a key role in the justice system. They act as facilitators, the vital cogs which are required to keep the mills of justice turning. Their success in this role owes much to the shared understandings between them as to how the system operates and on their mutual ability to rely on the word of each other—a fact that is underlined every time a represented party is confronted with a party litigant, and no such shared understandings exist. The facilitating role of the lawyer is emphasised in the general heading "Relations between Lawyers" of the Code of Conduct for Scottish Solicitors which states: *"Solicitors shall not knowingly mislead colleagues or where they have given their word go back on it. A solicitor must act with fellow solicitors in a manner consistent with persons having mutual trust and confidence in each other. It is in the public interest and for the benefit of clients and the administration of justice that there be a corporate professional spirit based upon relationships of trust and co-operation between solicitors."*[2]

This has to be read in conjunction with art.2 which provides that solicitors must always act in the best interests of their clients and must not permit the interests of the legal profession to influence their actings on behalf of clients. The different provisions in the Code can give rise to tensions between duties owed to clients and to professional colleagues. The duty in the Code is not a duty of full disclosure, although it can be a very fine line between not disclosing and knowingly misleading, as will be seen in Ch.14.

13.02 Background

Somewhat surprisingly, "Duties to professional colleagues" is not a topic which Begg felt it necessary to address to any significant extent in his book,[3] although that was primarily a treatise on the law relating to law agents. Sir Thomas Lund, Secretary of the Law Society (of England and Wales) is

---

[1] For further reading on this topic see Smith and Barton, *Procedures and Decisions of the Scottish Solicitors' Discipline Tribunal, op. cit.* Ch.10 (Relations Between Solicitors) and para.12.05 (Conditions Attached to a Cheque), para.12.06 (Stoppage of a Cheque) and para.12.07 (Failure to Implement a Letter of Obligation). See also Webster (2004) *op. cit.* Ch.4, and Ryder (1995) *op. cit.* at p.95.

[2] Code of Conduct for Scottish Solicitors Art.9. See also CCBE Code of Conduct for Lawyers in the European Community, 1989 S.L.T. (News) 261.

[3] Henderson Begg, *A treatise on the law of Scotland relating to law agents including the law of costs as between agent and client: with an appendix of relative statutes, acts of sederunt, and all the tables of fees, &c.* (Bell & Bradfute, Edinburgh, 1873).

slightly more forthcoming in his *Guide to the Professional Conduct and Etiquette of Solicitors*[4] where he states: "Do unto others as you would have them do unto you"[5] and suggests that when dealing with another member of the profession there should be "the maximum of frankness and good faith, consistent with our overriding duty to a client in any special case."[6] His view was that it is better to lose a client than to acquire a reputation as being a person whose word cannot be relied upon.

Certainly, it is essential to the practice of law in any jurisdiction that lawyers should be able to trust each other, and to rely on undertakings given by other lawyers. The matter has been considered on a number of occasions by the Scottish Solicitors Discipline Tribunal who have said: "It is an essential feature of negotiations between solicitors that they are conducted in an atmosphere of mutual trust and a solicitor has a professional duty to respect that element of trust in all his dealings . . . The best interests of his clients . . . is not the only consideration. It is essential that at all times a solicitor has regard for his professional relationship with his fellow solicitors . . . The special relationship with mutual trust which subsists between solicitors [is] rightly expected by the public".[7] *Ernst & Young (A Firm) v Butte Mining plc*[8] makes it clear that even in the most hostile litigation, solicitors must be scrupulously fair and should not take advantage of obvious mistakes. This duty is intensified where the solicitor has been a major contributing cause of the mistake. Again, the rules governing the advertising of solicitors' services take into account the need to maintain mutual trust and confidence, while permitting solicitors to market their services effectively and to compete with one another.

Specific Situations   13.03

It follows that the special character of the solicitor's agency carries with it certain obligations to professional colleagues as the Code indicates, for example, not misleading colleagues, keeping your word, honouring undertakings and letters of obligation, honouring cheques, responding to communications from other lawyers, not communicating directly with another solicitor's client and meeting the agreed fees of advocates or corresponding solicitors.

Not Misleading Colleagues   13.04

The opening words of art.9 of the Code of Conduct stipulate that solicitors must not knowingly mislead their colleagues. As we saw in Ch.1, misleading statements come in a variety of forms.[9] First, there is the intentional lie. This is clearly a conduct offence. Thus in one case the Tribunal found "a pattern of deceit" amounted to misconduct since clients and their representatives are entitled to rely on the truthfulness of statements made by solicitors.[10] Next,

---

[4] *Guide to the Professional Conduct and Etiquette of Solicitors* (The Law Society, London, 1960).
[5] *Op. cit.*
[6] *Op. cit.*
[7] DTD Case 726/88.
[8] [1996] 1 W.L.R. 1605.
[9] Para.1.24.
[10] DTD 788/89.

there is the situation where the solicitor states an untruth without checking whether it is in fact truthful or not. This can amount to recklessness, which may give rise to at least an unsatisfactory conduct finding, even although there is no intentional dishonesty. Finally, there is the negligent statement which is neither a deliberate nor a reckless falsehood. Provided that this is innocent or inadvertent, this will not be seen as misconduct by the Society or the Tribunal, although it may amount to unsatisfactory conduct or even professional negligence. Thus stated, the matter seems relatively straightforward. However in the adversarial system, "getting the better" of one's opponent by any fair and legal means is the advocate's objective. In this arena, one person's shrewdness is another's sharp practice, and there are undoubted shades of grey. A solicitor who says "I am not authorised to accept such an offer" or "my client would find that offer quite unacceptable" knowing that both statements are untrue, may consider the lie to be an acceptable form of "gamesmanship" in a negotiation.[11] In truth, if detected, it might still be unsatisfactory conduct. Moreover, with a little effort such statements can be avoided by using ones that convey much the same message, for example, "I'm afraid I couldn't recommend that to my client".

Apart from negotiations there are a number of areas where specific problems can arise with respect to misleading colleagues.

13.04.01 Misleading Colleagues: dealing with two separate offers at the same time. It is not unheard of, particularly in commercial property transactions, for sellers to instruct their solicitors to deal with two separate prospective purchasers at the same time. It would be improper to do so in secret as that would clearly mislead the solicitors acting for the separate prospective purchasers. However, if the selling solicitors are authorised to disclose the true position to the agents acting for each of the prospective purchasers, it would not be improper to continue acting in those circumstances.

13.04.02 Misleading Colleagues: the purchaser's agent. Over the years, cases have arisen where the purchase of a property has fallen through due to the purchaser not being in funds at the date of settlement. The failure of the transaction often brings loss for the seller whose remedy of damages for breach of contract may not be very efficacious against a purchaser whose lack of funds gave rise to the problem in the first place. Perhaps understandably, disgruntled sellers have sometimes taken the view that the purchasers' lawyers were at fault for not alerting them at an earlier date to the likely default. Often the complaint is that the purchaser's agent misled them into believing the purchaser had the means to complete the purchase. Thus, in one case[12] which came before the Discipline Tribunal the purchaser's solicitor was charged with representing to the seller's agent "that funds were available to complete the purchase of the hotel, when he knew or ought to have known that no such funds were available". It was claimed that in the days before the date of settlement the respondent conveyed the impression that the funds would be

---

[11] In the USA the literature on the Ethics of Negotiation is far too voluminous to do justice to in this book. See Menkel-Meadow et al, *Dispute Resolution: Beyond the Adversarial Model* (Aspen, New York, 2005), Ch.4, "Negotiation Law, Ethics and Policy", pp.203–265 and the articles cited therein.

[12] DTD 416/78.

available shortly and subsequently that a cheque was being sent from Amsterdam. Further it was alleged that the purchaser's agent had attended a party at the hotel, with his staff, helping to empty the contents of its cellars when the purchase price had not been paid and "when he knew or ought to have known that the purchase price of the property would not become available and his client would be unable to complete the purchase". The Tribunal observed:

> "Solicitors in practice often have to rely on assurances given by their clients and the Tribunal would not hold a Solicitor as being culpable if he conveyed information to another party which ultimately turned out to be false unless it might be shown that the Solicitor was acting in bad faith. There is nothing in the present Complaint which could be relied upon to establish such *mala fides.*"

With respect to the Tribunal, it may be too restrictive to say that bad faith is required before a conduct offence occurs. If a purchaser's agent makes no enquiries and behaves in a wilfully blind fashion, passing on assurances from the purchaser with blithe enthusiasm in a way that leads the seller into a false sense of security, it seems possible that this might be held to be unsatisfactory conduct, depending on the circumstances. Certainly, the Scottish Legal Services Ombudsman in 2004 and 2005 formed the conclusion that some purchasers' agents were not doing enough to check that the necessary finance is in place for the purchase of a property. However, the Law Society's Professional Practice Committee in 2005 concluded that the duty contained in art.9 of the Code of Conduct not to knowingly mislead other agents was sufficient. This was based on the dual rationale that there would be substantial practical difficulties in conveyancing transactions with such a requirement, especially if a loan was being arranged through an external broker and secondly, that even if there was an indication that finance was in place before missives are concluded, it might fall through prior to completion.

Misleading Colleagues: avoidance of delay in concluding missives. The **13.04.03** robust approach of the Professional Practice Committee in 2005 is slightly at odds with their approach in 1998. Then the committee felt it necessary to publish a guideline to deal with the increasingly common situation of missives being unconcluded until shortly before or even at the date of entry. The guideline[13] refers specifically to the duty not to knowingly mislead professional colleagues set out in art.2 of the Code and states that in residential property transactions solicitors acting on behalf of both purchasers and sellers have a professional duty to conclude missives without undue delay. If the solicitor is instructed to delay concluding, the circumstances should be disclosed to the other solicitor. If the client instructs the solicitor not to disclose such matters, or does not give a reason for such an instruction, the guideline states that the solicitor should withdraw from acting. Experience of calls received in the Society's professional practice department demonstrates that this guideline is frequently not followed, and it is not uncommon for there to be a considerable delay in disclosing a reason why a client is unwilling to

---

[13] See Guidelines on Avoidance of Delay in Concluding Missives in *Greens Solicitors Professional Handbook.*

conclude a bargain. In our view, this is not compatible with the duty to maintain relationships of trust and co-operation. Clearly a solicitor instructed not to conclude a bargain cannot ignore such instructions, but if the conveyancing process in Scotland is not to be brought into disrepute, it is necessary for solicitors to be open with each other about such matters and not to hide behind such phrases as "still awaiting instructions" where that is not in fact the case.

13.05 Keeping One's Word

This obligation follows immediately after the duty not to mislead one's professional colleagues in art.9 of the Code of Conduct and is every bit as important in the canon of legal ethics. Much of the facilitating work done by lawyers to make the justice system work as efficiently and effectively as possible, depends on a lawyer being able to trust another lawyer, who is unknown to him or her, to keep their word. A number of examples can be given.

13.05.01 Keeping One's Word: joint minutes. It may be thought axiomatic that where parties have agreed terms of settlement and their solicitors have signed a joint minute, the joint minute should be lodged in process and decree sought in terms thereof. However in response to a specific situation in 1996 the Professional Practice Committee felt it necessary to issue a Practice Guideline on the matter. In that case, the joint minute provided for a payment of periodical allowance to the defender but the pursuer's solicitor did not move for decree in such terms. The committee felt that by agreeing the terms of a joint minute the pursuer's solicitor had given an implied undertaking that decree would be sought in terms thereof. It should not be necessary for the defender's solicitor to have to check the court process to ensure that this had been done.[14]

13.05.02 Keeping One's Word: not altering documents. Similarly, a Scottish solicitor who altered and lodged in court a joint minute without the knowledge or consent of the party on whose behalf the joint minute had already been signed, was found guilty of misconduct by the Discipline Tribunal in 2001. Although the alteration had not affected the other party's interest, the Tribunal held that the unauthorised alteration was in breach of the implied under-standing from the other party that the document would not be altered and thus constituted a breach of trust.[15] The Tribunal will be equally concerned if the alteration does affect the interests of the other party. Thus in a case in 1968[16] the words "and execution" were omitted from the registration clause of a draft separation agreement, the omission only came to the notice of the respondent solicitor after the deed had been signed by the spouses. The solicitor added the missing words without even seeking the prior approval of the solicitors for the other party, who had noted the omission, but failed to point it out to the respondent. The addition of the words had a material consequence in that the

---

[14] Law Society Guidelines on Duty to Lodge a Joint Minute and move for decree. Re-issued in 1998. See *Greens Solicitors Professional Handbook*.
[15] Discipline Tribunal Annual Report 2000/2001.
[16] DTD 90/68.

addition of the word "and execution" improved the position of the respondent's client in that in the event of a default, registration for preservation and execution would have enabled his client to proceed with diligence without recourse to a court action. The Tribunal indicated that if any significant alterations are to be made the solicitor has a duty to seek the approval of the agents acting for the other parties. The addition of the purported initials of each of the signatories was intended to convey to the third parties that the alteration had the approval of the signatories of the deed and the Tribunal bearing in mind the essence and onus of disproving a probative deed concluded that such action warranted a finding of professional misconduct.

Keeping One's Word: Proceeds of Sale. In a closely related area the **13.05.03** Professional Practice Committee in 2002 dealt with a case involving a separation agreement.[17] The terms of the agreement between the parties set out the division of the proceeds of the sale of the matrimonial home. Following the sale, but before the execution of the separation agreement, the wife's solicitors arrested the proceeds of sale. When the arrestment was lifted the husband's solicitors ignored the terms of the separation agreement and paid all the proceeds to their client. The Professional Practice Committee ruled that this was in breach of art.9 of the Code of Conduct and contrary to the duty to act towards fellow solicitors in a manner consistent with persons having mutual trust and confidence in each other.

Keeping One's Word: Gazumping, Gazundering and Closing Dates (See **13.05.04** **also Duties to Third Parties).** Article 2 of the Code of Conduct refers to solicitors giving their word. When solicitors offer for a property they are not giving their own word but are communicating their clients' instructions, and similarly if the selling solicitors intimate acceptance of such an offer they are not giving their word but communicating their clients' instructions. Nonetheless, in the light of adverse criticism of the system of offer and acceptance for property in Scotland bringing the integrity of that system into disrepute, the Professional Practice Committee published a practice guideline on gazumping and gazundering in early 2005.[18] There had been a guideline on closing dates since 1991. The main thrust of these guidelines is that where the client wishes to go back on prior instructions to offer a particular price, to accept an offer or to fix a closing date, that the solicitor has communicated to the other side, thus putting the solicitor in a position of having to go back on his or her word if he or she accepts the change of instructions, solicitors should withdraw from acting, in order to protect their integrity. Occasionally, there may be exceptional circumstances which can justify continuing to act. Those would include the position where the client has fiduciary duties to others to obtain the best possible price (e.g. a heritable creditor in possession or a trustee). If a purchaser is put on notice that until missives are concluded the property will remain on the market, this would entitle the selling solicitor to continue to act if a subsequent offer is received. The key element is upfront disclosure of the client's position to the solicitor acting for the other party. The same consideration applies to an offer submitted subject to the purchaser obtaining a satisfactory survey and/or valuation. However, the guideline makes clear

---

[17] "Accounting for Proceeds of Sale" (2002) J.L.S.S. October, p.43.
[18] *Greens Solicitors Professional Handbook.*

that if the offer has been submitted "subject to survey" without also being subject to a satisfactory valuation, and the survey does not disclose a problem but the property does not "value up" it would be improper to attempt to re-negotiate the price downwards. It is therefore important to include a reference to a satisfactory valuation to preserve the position in that regard.

13.05.05 **Keeping One's Word: retention of funds.** It is common for funds to be retained at settlement of a conveyancing transaction until outstanding matters are dealt with. It does seem surprising that selling solicitors and their clients are willing to consider doing so for a modest sum, as the additional post-settlement work can be out of all proportion to the benefit gained and many solicitors are reluctant to charge for such post-settlement work. We wonder whether it would not be more sensible to advise the client to accept a lower price at settlement, based on estimates for carrying out the work, and leave the purchaser to deal with the problem. However, if it is agreed that the purchaser can retain funds in this way, it is advisable that the conditions on which the funds are retained should be set out in writing at the time of settlement. The matter should not be left to recollection or file notes of telephone conversations. Each solicitor is entitled to rely both on their opposite number having proper instructions to agree to the terms and that if the conditions are fulfilled the agreement will be implemented and funds released. As the guideline states: "*If funds were retained pending fulfilment of certain conditions by the seller, they should be released when those conditions have been fulfilled in terms of the written agreement. The purchaser's solicitor does not need to seek instructions from his or her client at that stage. Solicitors are entitled to rely upon agreements reached with other solicitors at settlement*".[19] Similarly, where the conditions have not been fulfilled by the seller, but the purchaser's solicitor produces vouching for the actual or estimated expenditure required to do so, the seller's solicitor does not need to obtain further instructions at that time from his client to agree to the release of funds as so vouched. Again, solicitors are entitled to rely on the reciprocity of such agreements.

13.05.06 **Keeping One's Word: "off the record" conversations.** Solicitors act as agents for their clients and are entitled, indeed frequently obliged, to report to their clients communications received from solicitors acting for another party. They may be instructed to disclose such communications to others such as the court or other parties. Where a solicitor wishes to have an "off the record" discussion with another solicitor it is necessary to have this basis agreed in advance. Confidentiality cannot be insisted on after the event. Where a solicitor has agreed to discuss matters "off the record" he or she may only subsequently disclose such matters with the agreement of the other solicitor. Doing so without such agreement would be going back on one's word.

13.06 Honouring Undertakings

Closely linked to "keeping one's word" and indeed overlapping with it, is the obligation of a solicitor to honour his or her undertakings. Again a wide range of examples can be found of this obligation in operation. The obligation

---

[19] Law Society Guidelines on Retention of Funds 1998. See *Greens Solicitors Professional Handbook.*

exists not simply in professional ethics, but also in contract. In one case, a firm of solicitors acted for a client on a particular matter and another firm of solicitors acted for the same client in the sale of a property. When the client failed to meet the fees of the first firm of solicitors the latter obtained (with the client's authority) an undertaking from the second firm that they would retain sufficient funds from the sale of the property as would meet the first firm's fees. The second firm assured the first firm that they would retain the sum "until you have sorted everything out". Despite the first firm requesting the transfer at the due time, the second firm paid the whole property proceeds to their client, who subsequently became bankrupt. The first firm sought to enforce the undertaking in court and the latter held that the second firm had made a clear and unequivocal statement to the first firm that they would retain the sum of money, and that statement constituted an undertaking given by a solicitor, and as officers of the court they were expected to abide by it.[20] In relation to undertakings the Tribunal have indicated[21] that they are prepared to adopt the English Law Society's definition[22] of an undertaking, namely:

> "*An undertaking is any unequivocal declaration of intention addressed to someone who reasonably places reliance on it and made by:*
>
> a) *a solicitor in the course of his practice , whether personally or by a member of his staff; or*
> b) *a solicitor as 'solicitor', but not in the course of his practice; whereby the solicitor (or in the case of a member of his staff, his employer) becomes personally bound.*"

Honouring Undertakings: Accepting Service of a Writ. One example from 13.06.01 professional ethics that reached the Tribunal in 1989 related to a case[23] where a solicitor had agreed to accept service of a court writ on behalf of a client and the pursuer's agents accordingly sent him the principal copy of the Writ. The respondent delayed returning the writ prompting the following observations from the Tribunal:

> "The procedure for the acceptance of service of a court writ is operated for the convenience of parties and their agents, and the arrangement is dependent on the solicitor for the defender obtaining specific instructions and thereafter returning the writ without delay, as the absence of the writ prevents the pursuer's solicitor otherwise serving the writ in the normal way."

The Tribunal further observed that since the respondent had agreed to enter into this procedure he then had a duty to take his client's instructions at the earliest possible date and to return the writ to the pursuer's solicitors. Although the respondent referred to the prospect of reconciliation and was

---

[20] *John Fox (a firm) v Bannister King & Rigbeys (a firm)* [1988] Q.B. 925. Although the case was an English one, there seems little doubt that a Scottish court would reach the same conclusion.
[21] See Smith and Barton, *Procedure and Decisions of the Scottish Solicitors Discipline Tribunal* (T & T Clark, Edinburgh, 1995), p.145.
[22] Now contained in para.18.01, *The Professional Conduct of Solicitors* (1999).
[23] DTD 753/89.

keen to limit the matters in dispute between the parties, this did not effect his overriding duty to the pursuer's solicitors to return the writ as soon as possible, and "his subsequent delay, particularly following letters of reminder, was inexcusable."

13.06.02 Honouring Undertakings: Borrowing Titles. One of the few instances that Begg[24] specifically mentions of a duty to professional colleagues is the duty to return titles which are borrowed from other agents. Begg states "When one agent borrows title deeds or other writs from another, on the usual undertaking to return them on demand, he is not entitled to retain them on any pretext whatever."[25] This long standing duty remains, and it would be improper to attempt to exercise a lien over borrowed titles in respect of some subsequent dispute.

13.06.03 Honouring Undertakings: Client undertaking or firm undertaking. Of course, a firm is only bound by undertakings given that clearly bind the firm as opposed to the firm's client. This distinction can be very important when it comes to undertakings which are required to be given in order that settlement in a conveyancing can take place. It is certainly a trap for the unwary, as the sellers discovered in a case which came to the Professional Practice Committee in 1986.[26] On a sale of licensed premises the purchasers were unable at the date of entry to put up the sum then payable in terms of the missives. The sellers were unwilling to allow the licence to be transferred or to allow the purchasers entry until the purchasers' solicitors undertook that the balance of the price would be paid within 21 days. The purchasers' solicitors wrote to the sellers' solicitors enclosing a payment to account, and saying, amongst other things: "We confirm that the balance will be paid within 21 days of the date hereof, and that interest will run on the outstanding balance at 3 per cent above the basic lending rate." On the strength of the letter entry was given. The purchasers subsequently failed to pay the balance, and the question was asked whether their solicitors were under a professional obligation to pay the money themselves.

The committee considered that in view of the particular terms of the letter, and especially because it was not adopted as holograph, there was no obligation either in law or as a matter of professional ethics for the solicitors to pay the money themselves. The committee concluded that had the undertaking been given more specifically by the solicitors rather than the clients, the decision would have been different. Although the committee may have been correct on the precise facts of the case, the matter was finely balanced—the more so since it was the undertaking that persuaded the sellers to hand over the keys. Barely two years earlier, the Tribunal had interpreted a similar case[27] rather differently. In this complaint, the respondent was charged with failing to honour a professional undertaking, namely, that in exchange for the keys to the shop from the landlord, the sum of £2,600 would be placed on deposit receipt in joint names, and that despite this the

---

[24] *ibid.* Ch.xxiv, para.25.
[25] See *Herbert v Rutherglen* (1858) 20 D. 1164.
[26] "Professional Practice: Undertaking to Meet Balance of Price—Whether Solicitor Personally Bound" (1986) J.L.S.S. 323.
[27] DTD 647/84.

respondent had handed the keys to his client (the tenant) without being put in funds by him and without placing the necessary funds on deposit receipt. It was admitted that the undertaking had been made, initially verbally and then subsequently confirmed in writing, and the Tribunal found that the under-taking had been a material consideration in the settlement being effected and the keys handed over. The Tribunal were not persuaded that the respondent was not bound by the undertaking even though he had been on holiday and therefore did not sign the letter containing the undertaking, nor did they consider it relevant whether the staff member who had given the undertaking was legally qualified or not.[28] The Tribunal noted that a solicitor should avoid giving an undertaking which he is not personally in a position to fulfil but in the event of such obligation being given, held that the solicitor could not rely on the failure of the client to co-operate as an excuse. The Tribunal added: "In such circumstances, it is open to the Solicitor to explain his position to the party to whom the undertaking was given but that if such party insists on compliance with the undertaking then the Solicitor must make the funds available, if necessary from his own monies, in order that the undertaking is fulfilled."

Letters of Obligation[29]   13.07

These are simply a particular form of professional undertaking. Letters of obligation are the oil which allow transactions for the sale and purchase of heritable property in Scotland to settle. Without them the parties would simply be in a standoff. A letter of obligation is a formal undertaking carrying the remedy of specific implement for non performance, despite the normal rules of agency where there is a disclosed principal,[30] but questions of professional conduct may also arise. Not surprisingly, the matter has been considered by the Discipline Tribunal. On a number of occasions the Tribunal has found that failure to implement a letter of obligation amounts to professional misconduct, and in one case decided that it became the solicitors' absolute duty to implement an obligation to deliver a discharge of a security even although the cost of doing so would have to be paid out of the solicitors' own funds.[31] Problems with failure to implement letters of obligation should be less frequent with the establishment of the "Classic" Letter of Obligation by the Society in the mid 1990s.[32]

Letters of Obligation: Some recurring problems   13.08

As a form of professional undertaking, letters of obligation give rise to similar problems as undertakings. First and foremost, the issue of whether the letter binds the firm or merely their client. In 1995, the purchasers of heritable property sought to enforce the terms of a letter of obligation granted at

---

[28] The Tribunal cited with approval *A Guide to the Professional Conduct of Solicitors* 1974 edition at p.67 which stated "that a Solicitor is responsible as a matter of professional conduct for carrying out an undertaking given by a member of his staff, whether admitted or unadmitted".

[29] R. Rennie, "Letters of Obligation" (1993) J.L.S.S. 431; J. Sinclair, *Handbook of Convey-ancing Practice in Scotland* (Butterworths, 1995), para.8.11.

[30] See *Johnston v Little*, 1960 S.L.T. 129.

[31] See, Smith & Barton, *op. cit.* para.12.07 and the cases set out therein. See also the Scottish Solicitors' Discipline Tribunal Annual Report 2002/2003 at p.3.

[32] See the Law Society's Conveyancing Committee "Clarifying the Classic Letter of Obliga-tion" (2003) J.L.S.S. April, p.26.

settlement in the usual way by the sellers' solicitors which stated: "With reference to the settlement of this transaction today we undertake on behalf of our above-named clients to deliver . . . " The court held that the letter only expressed an undertaking on behalf of the sellers, not their solicitors.[33] It is important to check, therefore, when you receive a letter of obligation that it is couched in terms that will bind the sellers' agents as well as the sellers. Failure to do so may give rise to an action for negligence.

Secondly, it is vital to ensure that any undertaking which you give is within your power to implement. Thus particular care should be taken when implementation of an obligation is dependent on a third party. Nor should letters of obligation contain an undertaking to deliver discharges or inhibitions "within a reasonable period".

Thirdly, if an error or a fraud occurs the solicitors granting the letter of obligation may become personally responsible for the loss jointly and severally with the clients.[34] As the clients will rarely have the wherewithal, and the solicitors will be usually be insured, it is the latter who are inevitably selected. On the other hand, a client's fraud will not necessarily vitiate an unconditional undertaking given to the client's solicitors by the other party's solicitors to pay the client's solicitors fees and disbursements.[35]

Fourthly, given the significance of letters of obligation for firms and for the industry the Professional Practice Committee concluded in 1983 that both law and practice dictate that letters of obligation must be signed only by partners.[36] That said, the decision of the Tribunal discussed in para.13.06.03 suggests that if a non-partner does give an undertaking which is relied on to achieve a settlement, this will still bind the firm as a matter of professional ethics.[37]

13.09 Honouring Cheques

As a general rule solicitors are expected to honour cheques drawn on their firm account in favour of a professional colleague. Such cheques should only be stopped in exceptional circumstances. Indeed a solicitor whose car had been retained by a garage under a lien for non payment of the repair bill and who only obtained the release of the car through the issuing of a firm cheque which was then promptly stopped, gave rise to a finding of unsatisfactory conduct by the Council of the Law Society. Where a cheque has been mistakenly made out for too high a figure it would not be improper to substitute a cheque for the correct amount and put a stop on the original cheque but if time is of the essence, as in the settlement date for a transaction, the solicitors must take steps at their own expense to have the correct cheque delivered immediately—preferably by courier—so that it can be banked by the other solicitors without delay. It should be stressed that this does not permit a purchaser's solicitor to reduce the price of a property in response to

---

[33] *Digby Brown & Co. v Lyall*, 1995 S.L.T. 932. See also (1995) J.L.S.S. 323.

[34] *McGillivray v Davidson*, 1993 S.L.T. 693.

[35] *Rooks Rider v Steel* [1993] 4 All E.R. 716.

[36] "Execution of Formal Documents by Non-partner" (1983) J.L.S.S. 279. The committee pointed to the case of *Littlejohn v Mackay*, 1974 S.L.T. (Sh.Ct) 82 and to Bell's *Principles* (10th edn), para.20. They concluded that s.6 of the Partnership Act 1890 in no way alters the general rules of Scots law relating to the execution of a document which purports to be granted by a firm. The profession's attention was also directed to the proviso to s.6.

[37] DTD 647/84.

a request from the client to hold money back to meet additional costs not specified in the missives. There would have to have been a genuine mistake in the original cheque.

Honouring Settlement Cheques. The Code of Conduct states that if a **13.09.01** purchaser's solicitors instruct their bank to stop payment of a settlement cheque, such action could amount to professional misconduct. The Professional Practice Committee and the Discipline Tribunal have taken the view that there may be certain circumstances where it is not improper to stop a settlement cheque, but those circumstances would need to go to the very root of the transaction. For example, if the property has been destroyed (and these circumstances are contrary to the terms of the missives), or in a postal settlement the disposition delivered contains a defect in execution or if a property is sold with vacant possession, and on taking entry the purchaser finds a tenant installed, these are instances that go to the root of the transaction, and provided that the whole settlement is reversed with the deeds and letter of obligation being returned to the sellers' agents, in our view it would not be improper to stop the cheque in those circumstances. If, however, on taking entry the purchaser is unhappy with the state of the property because for example rubbish has been left or doors are missing, that would not go to the root of the transaction—which is the transfer of title to the property with vacant possession—and solicitors would risk a finding of misconduct in accepting the client's instructions to stop the cheque. Again, in our view it would be improper and in breach of trust to stop a cheque simply because the purchasers' own cheque in favour of their solicitors had bounced. You are in the best position to determine the strength of your client's cheque and if you choose to settle the transaction in advance of the cheque being cleared, then you have to take responsibility for that risk. This also is the view of the Tribunal.[38]

Settlement cheque sent to be held as undelivered. One thorny issue relating **13.09.02** to settlement cheques continues to cause problems. While it may be expedient for both parties to a conveyancing transaction to agree that the purchaser can send a cheque in advance of settlement which the seller will hold as undelivered, real problems can arise where the request that the cheque be held as undelivered is imposed unilaterally by the purchaser's agents, usually without warning, on the day of settlement. In 1994 the Professional Practice Committee published a practice guideline[39] on the issue of settlement cheque sent to be held as undelivered. The committee saw no difficulty where the purchaser's solicitors agree with the seller's solicitors in advance that the settlement cheque will be held as undelivered pending confirmation by the purchaser's solicitors that they are in funds. But the guideline makes it clear that it is professionally wrong for an agent to impose such a condition unilaterally, the first intimation of which is in the letter accompanying the cheque received on the morning of settlement.[40] However, the guideline goes on to state that even though it is wrong and improper professional practice to impose such a unilateral condition, that does not entitle the selling solicitor to

---

[38] See DTD 493/81 and Websters (2004) *op. cit.* para.4.02.
[39] See "Professional Practice" (1994) J.L.S.S. 470.
[40] The committee cited with approval, D. Cusine and R. Rennie, *Missives* (Butterworths, 1999), para.6.15 on the matter.

cash the cheque if it is sent "to be held as undelivered". Thus the guideline states "Where money or deeds are sent to be held as undelivered pending purification of a condition, they should be so held if the condition is not purified. Settlement will not take place until they can be treated as delivered, with consequent penalty interest if provided in the missives. The matter is one of practice between agents rather than of law." The words "to be held as undelivered" are therefore invested with an exalted status. In 1998 the committee reaffirmed the guideline, even although the issue continues to divide the profession, stating that it is improper professional practice to impose unilaterally a condition that a cheque in settlement of a transaction be held as undelivered pending confirmation that the solicitor is in funds, but accepting that, while as a matter of law the seller's solicitor might be entitled to encash the cheque and ignore the condition, such action would not be good professional practice as it would destroy the professional trust between agents.[41] Strange though this ruling may appear, and it certainly does where the unilaterally imposed condition seeks to depart from the express terms of the missives (e.g. that the clause in the missives about interest for late settlement will be ignored), in the end of the day to rule otherwise would be to hold that "two wrongs do indeed make a right".

13.09.03 Honouring Cheques: payment to settle a dispute. If on a client's instructions a solicitor makes an offer to settle a dispute, whether court proceedings have been raised or otherwise, and that offer is accompanied by the solicitor's cheque in full or part payment, the solicitor is entitled to stop the cheque if the client changes his mind before the offer is accepted. If the offer is rejected the solicitor is also entitled to accept instructions to stop the cheque. In both of these situations there has been no agreement which the solicitor is instructed to implement, and that distinguishes such a situation from the cheque in settlement of a contract. It would of course be open to the solicitor to send the cheque to be held as undelivered pending the other party's acceptance of the offer, in which case the practice guideline discussed in para.13.09.02 would apply to the solicitor receiving it.

13.10 The duty to reply to correspondence from a fellow solicitor

Failure to implement a Letter of Obligation is frequently linked with a failure to respond to correspondence from the purchaser's solicitor, and that can also give rise to a finding of professional misconduct. In 1994 the Discipline Tribunal stated "It is ordinarily a solicitor's duty to reply to all correspondence relating to a client's affairs which calls for an answer and if exceptionally a solicitor is instructed not to reply to a line of correspondence, the solicitor should convey to the other party in writing that the correspondence is being terminated. In the absence of such intimation, the correspondent (i.e. the other solicitor) is entitled to expect a reply".[42] This case was reinforced by the Tribunal in *McDonald*.[43] Here, a solicitor failed to: implement a mandate, answer corresponding communications, respond to requests for information relating to the mandate, or respond to letters in

---

[41] Professional Practice Committee: "Settlement cheques to be held as undelivered" (1998) 43(10) J.L.S.S. 47.
[42] DTD 884/94.
[43] DTD 18/05/2004.

connection with other title work for a different client. It was held that "failure to respond to fellow agents and to the Law Society amounts to professional misconduct".

However, in the case of *Lewis*[44] a solicitor had acted for a seller in a concluded transaction. The missives required a deed of servitude which had been drafted by the seller's former agents. The purchaser's solicitors contacted the respondent in regard to this and received no reply. The purchaser's solicitors again asked for help and requested that he respond. Eventually the respondent replied and agreed to assist. Despite repeated requests and phone calls the respondent gave the matter little priority, only ever appearing to act when prompted by the purchaser's solicitors and in the end failing to respond at all. Given the broad definition of "undertaking" adopted by the Tribunal[45] this was clearly a breach of a professional undertaking, however the Tribunal held that the respondent's delay and failure to respond related to a matter where he was helping out rather than performing an obligation and as such, although his conduct was unprofessional it was not as serious as to amount to professional misconduct.

The foregoing cases relate to correspondence from professional colleagues. Unsolicited mail from a non-lawyer who is not a client is in a different category. Thus the Professional Practice Committee has stated that there is "no professional obligation to respond to unsolicited circular correspondence, and failure to do so will not land you on the wrong end of a misconduct complaint" where a person sent a circular letter to numerous legal practices asking questions about the firms' knowledge of him and complaining about the 49 firms that failed to respond.[46]

In sum, it seems that there will be no professional obligation to reply to correspondence if it neither relates to work in progress nor relates to an existing duty owed to a client or other party by the recipient. However, it is best to proceed with some care in this area and it remains good practice to respond to correspondence from fellow solicitors to maintain a spirit of co-operation and mutual trust within the profession.

Communicating with other solicitor's client   13.11

Article 9 of the Code of Conduct states specifically: "*It is not permissible for a solicitor to communicate about any item of business with a person whom the solicitor knows to be represented by another solicitor. A solicitor in such circumstances must always communicate with the solicitor acting for that person and not go behind the solicitor's back.*"[47] There is of course nothing to prevent clients communicating directly with each other, and solicitors are free to suggest to clients that they do so. If a solicitor consistently ignores

---

[44] DTD 01/03/2005.

[45] See para.13.06 above.

[46] (2005) J.L.S.S. 36.

[47] As Sir Thomas Lund observed in his *Guide to the Professional Conduct and Etiquette of Solicitors* (The Law Society, London, 1960), p.79, the duty not to communicate with or interview the client of another solicitor applies particularly strongly where proceedings are pending. Webster, *op. cit.* (2004) para.4.07 also notes that: If you have been acting in a case as the agent of another solicitor, you must not subsequently act for that client without the knowledge and consent of the instructing solicitor. If you accept instructions to act for a client who you know to have been previously represented in the matter by another solicitor, you ought to advise the other solicitor of the change.

correspondence from another solicitor, it would also be open to the other solicitor to advise the first solicitor in writing that unless a reply is received by a certain date, the matter will be raised directly with the other solicitor's client. That is not "going behind the other solicitor's back" but is giving the other solicitor fair notice of the consequences of a continued failure to reply.[48] Those are the only circumstances where it would be appropriate to communicate directly with another solicitor's client, apart from the service of formal documents in accordance with the Rules of Court or legislation such as the Agricultural Holdings Act. In those circumstances it is courteous to keep the other solicitor advised of the issue of such formal documents, but there is no professional duty to do so. Care would need to be taken in correspondence with the other solicitor to ensure that correspondence is not misleading. For example, if court proceedings have been raised it would be improper to continue to correspond with the other party's solicitor maintaining the impression (whether by implication or expressly) that proceedings have not been raised.

The Scottish Solicitors Discipline Tribunal has dealt with several cases in which a solicitor has communicated directly with another solicitor's client. In the first, the client and his company had formally been a client of the respondent who had taken his legal business to another solicitor. Despite this, the first solicitor spoke to the former client on the telephone raising a matter which was at issue between the two of them in which the client was being advised by his new solicitor. In the circumstances the Discipline Tribunal had little hesitation in following a similar English Discipline Tribunal decision in concluding that the solicitor had been guilty of "unprofessional conduct".[49] Two years later the Tribunal heard a case where the solicitor acting for a wife in a matrimonial dispute wrote direct to the husband even though he knew that the husband was legally represented. To compound matters the solicitor offensively and scurrilously suggested that the husband should seek some form of psychiatric help. The Tribunal concluded that the respondent's conduct was improper and fell below the standards expected of a reputable solicitor, whilst also determining that in the particular circumstances it was not professional misconduct.[50] It was not until 1986 that we find a case in which the Tribunal was prepared to conclude that a direct approach to the client of another solicitor might be professional misconduct.[51]

13.12 Email sent in error

The Professional Practice Committee have considered this issue.[52] In an English case—*Al-Fayed Metropolitan Police Commissioner*[53] the court held "that if privileged documents were mistakenly disclosed for inspection by one party to litigation in circumstances where it would not have been obvious to

---

[48] In DTD 761/89 it was held that even in the exceptional circumstances where a solicitor may communicate with the clients of another solicitor in relation to court proceedings, it is never acceptable to comment on the merits of the action nor to use intemperate and threatening language.

[49] DTD 428/79.

[50] DTD 510/81.

[51] DTD 660/86.

[52] (2002) J.L.S.S. November, p.43.

[53] [2002] EWCA Civ. 780. For the implications of this decision for legal professional privilege see para.6.19 above.

a reasonable solicitor that a mistake had been made, the disclosing party was not entitled to an injunction ordering the receiving party to return the documents; and the receiving party should be allowed to make proper use of the documents on the basis that they were no longer privileged and no public interest immunity attached to them". The committee agreed with the approach of the English court. In relation to emails, if it is not obvious from the header that the email is not intended for the particular recipient it will only become apparent once the email has been opened and the contents read. The committee agreed that in these specific circumstances there is no duty to delete the email, return it, or to cease acting and the solicitor is entitled to advise his/her own client of the contents. If the email has not yet been opened before a request is received from the sender to delete it, that request should be complied with. It is important to ensure that correspondence and emails are correctly addressed in the first place to avoid such difficulties arising.

Duty to pay agreed fees of Advocates and fellow solicitors   13.13

The Professional Practice Committee has from time to time had to consider the position of solicitors who have, acting on behalf of a client, instructed another solicitor in Scotland or abroad. As far as the correspondent solicitor elsewhere in Scotland is concerned the position is clear[54]:

> "*Where a solicitor, authorised by and acting for a client employs another solicitor, he shall (whether or not he discloses the client) be liable to the other solicitor for that solicitors' fees and outlays, unless at the time of the employment he expressly disclaims any such liability.*"

Similarly, where the other lawyer is an advocate based in Scotland, solicitors are also liable for the agreed fees of advocates as a matter of professional ethics, if not in law. The duty is currently set out in the 2002 Scheme for Accounting and Recovery of Counsel's Fees,[55] and rests with the solicitor who instructs counsel unless the name of the correspondent firm in Scotland from whom the instruction originates is shown in the letter of instruction. The scheme sets out the specific matters to be included in the letter of instruction including, where appropriate, the legal aid reference. If counsel is instructed on a speculative basis, i.e. where the solicitor is only to be paid if the client is successful in the litigation, that must be stated explicitly in every letter of instruction in the case. There is no assumption that because one counsel has agreed to accept speculative instructions another will also agree to do so. As well as the sanctions set out in the scheme failure to pay counsel's fees has been held to be professional misconduct.[56]

---

[54] See 1980 Solicitors (Scotland) Act s.30. and (1983) J.L.S.S. 466–467.

[55] Published in the Members Information Section of the Law Society of Scotland website *www.lawscot.org.uk*. See also (2002) J.L.S.S. April, p.28 for an article by Duncan Murray, then Convener of the Society's Judicial Procedure Committee.

[56] See e.g. DTD 877/93 and *Hetherington* DTD 2003. In this case the Tribunal in commenting on the solicitor's failure to pay the fees of, *inter alia*, three advocates, observed: "The public is entitled to expect that solicitors be fair and honest in their dealings with . . . counsel on behalf of their clients. A solicitor is expected to accept personal responsibility for the expenses incurred by [counsel] on behalf of their clients and the Respondent in failing to make payment has brought the profession into disrepute." Again in DTD 997/98 *(Beaumont)* the solicitor was found guilty of professional misconduct for not paying the fees of a Scottish advocate and an English barrister.

There is a similar obligation to pay for the fees of English barristers. Indeed it seems that the ethical obligation extends to any lawyer who is based abroad who is instructed by a Scottish solicitor on behalf of a client. However, the instructing solicitor may well not incur a legal liability to pay for the foreign lawyer's fees. This was underlined in the case of *Groenius BV v Smith*.[57] In this case, a Dutch partnership of advocates sought to recover payment of invoices from a Scottish firm of solicitors for work done for the latter's client. They claimed that they had been instructed by the Scottish firm and therefore should be paid by them, noting that the cross-border code of conduct practice rules imposed a personal obligation on the instructing solicitor in such circumstances. Although their complaint to the Law Society in relation to the conduct of the solicitor was upheld as misconduct, Lord Clarke in the Outer House dismissed the action. He did so because under the law of agency an agent acting for a disclosed principal is not personally liable for the principal's debts. He further held that the cross-border rules merely laid down proper practice rather than altering the common law of contract. While noting that custom could have made the solicitor personally liable, he concluded that the case of *Livesey v Purdom and Sons*[58] had established that no such custom exists in relation to fees incurred by a lawyer acting in another jurisdiction[59] instructed by a Scots lawyer to act on behalf of his client.

13.14 Duties to former employers and former partners

Where a solicitor moves from one firm to another, and continues to deal with ongoing client matters which were previously dealt with in the original firm, there is a duty to account to the former firm for fees earned in respect of work performed at the former firm unless there has been a specific agreement to the contrary. In particular, in Legal Aid cases where an employed solicitor is the nominated solicitor on the Legal Aid certificate, if Scottish Legal Aid Board are not asked to account directly to the former firm for fees earned while the solicitor was there, it would be improper in the absence of express agreement to retain all the fees for the new firm. Apart from the legal obligation to account there is a professional duty to do so and failure to comply could give rise to a finding of professional misconduct. The question of accounting between former partners will depend on firstly the original partnership agreement (if any) and secondly on what was agreed when the partner left the firm. It is quite in order to agree a clean break with the new firm having the right to retain funds earned while the partner was at the previous firm. It is however sensible to ensure that such an agreement is recorded in writing.

13.15 Crown duties to opposition in criminal cases[60]

In two judgements of the May 11, 2005, the Privy Council considered the duties of disclosure required of the prosecution in criminal cases to ensure a fair trial under art.6 of the European Convention on Human Rights. In these

---

[57] 2003 S.L.T. 80.

[58] (1894) 21 R 911.

[59] In this case the country was England.

[60] The ethics of the prosecutor has attracted a whole literature of its own. See e.g. K. Crispin, "Prosecutorial Ethics" in S. Parker and C. Sampford (eds) *Legal Ethics and Legal Practice* (Clarendon Press, Oxford, 1995) 171, and R. Young and A. Saunders, "The Ethics of Prosecution Lawyers" 7 (2004) *Legal Ethics* 190.

cases, the two Scottish Law Lords (Hope and Rodger) with the concurrence of their colleagues rewrote the duties of the Crown to the defence in Scotland, through their interpretation of the requirements imposed by art.6. In the *Sinclair* case,[61] they held that it is a fundamental aspect of the accused's right to a fair trial that the prosecution is under a duty to disclose to the defence all material evidence in its possession for or against the accused, unless there is some strong public interest which would justify non-disclosure, for example, the need to ensure a witness's safety. This entails that the Crown has a duty to disclose all witness statements to the defence, unless the public interest exception applies. In the *Holland* case, the court further held that the Crown has a duty to disclose a witness's previous convictions to the defence.[62]

---

[61] *Sinclair v HMA* Privy Council DRA No.2 of 2004 (May 11, 2005).

[62] *Holland v HMA* Privy Council DRA No.1 of 2004 (May 11, 2005). For an interesting discussion of the two cases see, P. Duff, "Sinclair and Holland: A revolution in 'disclosure' ", 2005 S.L.T. (News) 10.

CHAPTER 14

DUTIES TO THE COURT

14.01 Introduction

It is in this field, perhaps above all others, that the special character of the solicitor's agency is most apparent. For here we are reminded that the lawyer is a key player in the justice system with obligations not simply to clients, fellow professionals, witnesses and other third parties, but also to the court.[1] Despite the description of solicitors as "officers of the court",[2] it is not the case, as occasional, unguarded, commentators suggest that the lawyer's duty to the court[3] always trumps the lawyer's other duties.[4] In fact, where the lawyers' various obligations conflict, a delicate balancing operation is called for, and in the process the key lodestars will be the needs of the adversarial system of truth finding, the interests of justice, and the human rights requirement of a fair trial or hearing. Numerous articles and even books have been written in the common law world on the appropriate balance to be struck between these competing duties. There is a rich literature in the field, primarily in the United States, but to a lesser extent in Australia, Canada, and England. In these jurisdictions, the balance struck will reflect or in some instances, define, the prevailing conception of the role of the advocate in the adversarial system. Indeed, between and within the jurisdictions there are subtle variations which evolve over time. One view that is gaining considerable currency in most of these jurisdictions is that the appropriate balance will vary depending on the type of case, for example, whether the lawyer is acting

---

[1] See the various duties contained in Code of Conduct for Scottish Solicitors 2002 and art.8 in particular.

[2] It is widely accepted that solicitors in the UK, like lawyers in Australia, Canada and New Zealand, are officers of the court, not least since they are admitted and removed from office by the court. Although barristers in England have been less willing to embrace the description, it seems reasonable to treat advocates in Scotland as officers of the court, since they too are admitted to the public office of advocate by the court.

[3] The lawyer's duty to the court is in fact a bundle of duties just as the duty to the client is a bundle of separate duties. It follows that the when the duties conflict it is a complex balancing of a range of duties which is called for.

[4] See e.g. Dal Pont, *Lawyers' Professional Responsibility* (2nd edn, LBC, Sydney, 2001) at p.444. Even Lord Reid in his famous description of the duties of the defence lawyer in *Rondel v Worsley* refers to the "overriding" duty to the court. In the UK this is no more true than the reverse, namely that the lawyer's duties to the client e.g. to preserve confidences always triumph over the lawyer's duty of candour to the court. The latter is a view famously or infamously espoused by Monroe Freedman for US lawyers in *Understanding Lawyers' Ethics* (Matthew Bender, New York, 1990) and *Lawyers' Ethics in an Adversary System* (Bobbs-Merrill, New York, 1975). In truth, in the UK at least, the tension between the lawyer's duties to the client and to the court will be resolved in different ways depending on the type of case in which it occurs and even on the context in which it occurs.

for a criminal accused or in a civil case against the state, as opposed to a situation in which the parties are more evenly matched or where the values of a liberal democracy are less clearly at stake.[5] Again, there is now a widespread view in the common law world that the role of the family lawyer requires a less adversarial balance between the lawyer's duties.

Historical Background

The historic association between Scottish law agents and the courts stems back to at least the fifteenth century when a professional caste of pleaders began to emerge, in part because legal representation, which had grown up in the canonical courts, subsequently spread to the secular courts.[6] While it is undoubtedly the case that court appearance work was more central to the role of the typical solicitor or procurator two centuries ago than it is now,[7] the association with the courts is not simply a question of rights of audience and Scottish courts having, as courts of justice in many jurisdictions do, an inherent jurisdiction to regulate those who may appear before them. Thus, notaries public, writers to the signet and solicitors in the supreme courts, none of whom historically actually appeared in the Court of Session, were nonetheless admitted to office by that court[8] and subject to professional discipline by the same court.[9] (Provincial law agents on the other hand were admitted to office in, and disciplined by, their sheriff courts). Rather, the link with the courts reflects the importance to the state of regulating entry to the office of solicitor or law agent. Latterly this had both political and fiscal aspects to it. Thus, in the 18th century, Scottish solicitors or procurators were only permitted to act as such after taking the appropriate oaths in court, in an attempt to ensure the loyalty of these solicitors to the Crown after the 1715 and 1745 Jacobite rebellions.[10] Following the 1785 Stamps Act, both admission and annual certification required payment of the appropriate duty.

Prior to the 19th century the WS and the SSC had exclusive rights to act as law agents in the Supreme Courts while in several of the more important sheriff courts[11] the local law agents formed societies whose members attained exclusive rights to practise in these courts. However, following the 1870 Royal Commission into the Courts of Law in Scotland[12] the Law Agents (Scotland) Act 1873 was passed, creating a national and uniform mode of entry for solicitors and notaries and enabling any solicitor to practise in any

---

[5] See e.g. David Luban, *Lawyers and Justice* (New Jersey: Princeton University Press, 1988). These debates have been fought out over many years in the USA but in the last 15 years commentators in most English speaking countries have begun to explore the issues.

[6] See Stair Memorial Encyclopaedia, *Solicitors*, paras 1126–1136; *Advocates*, para.1240; J. Henderson Begg, *A Treatise on the Law of Scotland relating to Law Agents* (hereafter, Begg on *Law Agents* (2nd edn, 1883)), Ch.1 Historical Introduction.

[7] In 2005 the Law Society estimated that about 1,500 of the 9,500 practising solicitors in Scotland (16%) could be classified as court practitioners. (Personal conversation with one of the authors.)

[8] See Begg *op. cit.* Ch.2.

[9] See Begg *op. cit.* Ch.25; *Greens Encyclopaedia of the Laws of Scotland* (W. Green, 1930) Vol.9; *Law Agents*, para.103.

[10] See Stair Memorial Encyclopaedia *Solicitors*, para.1135.

[11] Aberdeen, Glasgow, Edinburgh and Paisley.

[12] C175 (1870).

court. Admission[13] and removal for serious professional misconduct[14] of solicitors were now concentrated in the Court of Session. This reform, as Lord Justice-Clerk Cooper noted in *Solicitors' Discipline (Scotland) Committee v B*.[15] was part of a modernisation process in which Parliament in the latter part of the 19th century transferred the discipline of learned professions from the courts to the professions themselves "subject to the overriding control of the court on appeal".[16] Unfortunately, the 1873 Act in seeking to strengthen the regulatory regime for solicitors from a practical standpoint, inadvertently introduced a conceptual lacuna which has still not been rectified today. Thus the Act provided for the court to handle misconduct whilst expressly leaving the powers of the inferior courts[17] intact "so far as these powers may be necessary for supporting the jurisdiction and maintaining the authority" of those courts.[18] This formulation appears to derive from Erskine[19] and, as Lord Cooper notes,[20] is normally associated with the jurisdiction enjoyed by Scottish courts to deal with contempt of court. Parliament seems to have assumed that the combination of these contempt powers and the misconduct jurisdiction contained in the statute equated to the pre-existing disciplinary powers of the courts over all solicitors. Unfortunately, since the contempt powers refer only to solicitors undertaking court work the statute appears to have created a regulatory vacuum in relation to (1) the discreditable conduct,[21] (falling short of misconduct) of solicitors who do not appear in court and (2) the discreditable conduct (falling short of misconduct) of solicitors who do appear in court, but which is not covered by the contempt of court jurisdiction of the courts. Previously it could have been argued that the courts disciplinary jurisdiction in relation to solicitors covered both of these. Indeed, Lord President Normand and two of his First Division colleagues tried to argue that the common law powers of the courts to deal with discreditable conduct, as distinct from professional misconduct, survived the 1873 Act and its successor, the Solicitors' Scotland Act 1933,[22] in the seven judge case of *Solicitors' Discipline (Scotland) Committee v B*.[23] However, in a fascinating clash between the First and Second Divisions, Lord Justice-Clerk Cooper, with the help of the Second Division and one defector from the First Division, defeated

---

[13] s.7.

[14] s.22.

[15] 1941 S.C. 293 at 296.

[16] at 297.

[17] The Act is silent as to the residual disciplinary powers of the Court of Session, but the position of the latter was drawn into line with that for inferior courts in the Solicitors (Scotland) Act 1933 and again in the Solicitors (Scotland) Act 1980.

[18] s.26.

[19] Institute I, ii, 8.

[20] *Op cit.* p.299.

[21] This equates closely to the modern day concept of unsatisfactory conduct. See Ch.1 above.

[22] Section 25 of the 1933 Act establishes a Discipline Committee to deal with professional misconduct by solicitors although the Court of Session is left as the body responsible for appeals from the Discipline Committee as well as some first instance work and all proposals to strike solicitors from the Roll. Section 35 repeats the formula of s.26 of the 1873 Act by stating that the existing disciplinary powers "of the court or of inferior courts or the judges thereof over solicitors practising before such courts, so far as these powers may be necessary for supporting the jurisdiction and maintaining the authority of [these courts]" are not affected by the Act except in respect to striking solicitors off the roll.

[23] 1941 S.C. 293.

Lord President Normand and the rest of the First Division. Despite Lord Cooper's reputation as a traditionalist, his belief in the modernising intent of Parliament led him[24] to observe: "I can see no escape from the conclusion that any common law powers to deal with discreditable conduct, as distinct from professional misconduct, which may have existed in Scotland prior to 1933, cannot survive the [Solicitors' (Scotland) Act 1933]." Ironically, the actual point of difference between the two camps was ultimately resolved in Lord Normand's favour by the Legal Aid and Solicitors (Scotland) Act 1949 Schedule 7, and the whole of the 1933 Act was subsequently repealed by Sch.7 of the 1980 Solicitors (Scotland) Act. In accordance with the normal canons of statutory construction this did not mean that the common law revived. It follows that the disciplinary powers of the courts over solicitors is now governed by the provisions of the Solicitors (Scotland) Act 1980. Part IV of that Act (as amended)[25] contains the modern day complaints procedures for solicitors and the provisions relating to the Discipline Tribunal. The role of the courts is set out in s.54 (appeals from the Tribunal), s.55 (disposal powers) and s.56 which states: "*Except as otherwise expressly provided, nothing in this Part shall affect the jurisdiction exercisable by the Court, or by any inferior court over solicitors.*" If our reasoning is correct s.56 cannot revive the common law powers of the courts, but must refer to the position as established in *Solicitors' Discipline (Scotland) Committee v B.*,[26] namely, that the courts cannot deal with discreditable behaviour, but only misconduct in accordance with what is now the 1980 Act, but that the courts can still discipline solicitors appearing before them "to the extent necessary for supporting the jurisdiction and maintaining the authority" of the court.[27]

The jurisdiction exercisable by the court: duties to the court   14.03

Even if our analysis is correct with respect to the powers of the courts today in relation to misconduct and discreditable conduct, there remains the issue as to the exact ambit of the courts' residual regulatory and disciplinary powers which are necessary for supporting the jurisdiction and maintaining the authority of the courts. Lord Cooper appears to have thought that the ambit was largely restricted to matters punishable as contempt of court, but with respect, it is clear from the actual practice of the courts, that this is too narrow a reading of the courts' powers, particularly in relation to the award of expenses against solicitors. It is submitted instead that to ask what the residual regulatory powers of the courts are, is simply another way of enquiring as to the scope and enforceability of the duties of solicitors as officers of the courts. These duties to the court are derived from the common law and are owed not to the judges or courts in which a solicitor chooses to practise, as such, but rather to the wider community because of the public interest in the proper administration of justice.[28] It is this wider public interest that the courts are safeguarding by enforcing these duties despite that fact that they are universally referred to as "duties to the court" and partly enforced through the

---

[24] His three supporting colleagues expressly agreed with his analysis on this point.

[25] Primarily by the Law Reform (Miscellaneous Provisions) (Scotland) Act 1990.

[26] 1941 S.C. 293.

[27] s.35, 1933 Solicitors (Scotland) Act.

[28] See Justice D.A. Ipp, "Lawyers' Duties to the Court", 1998 (114) *The Law Quarterly Review* 63 at p.63.

use of the contempt of court powers. The exact scope and ambit of these duties in Scots Law is unclear, because of the dearth of Scottish authority. However, Ipp's account of these duties in Commonwealth jurisdictions seems a worthwhile place to start. For Ipp, the duties cover:

1. a general duty to conduct cases efficiently and expeditiously,
2. a general duty not to abuse the court process,
3. a general duty of disclosure owed to the court, and
4. a general duty not to interfere with the administration of justice.[29]

14.03.01 The duty to conduct cases efficiently and expeditiously—personal liability. From early times it has been recognised that a solicitor whose wrongful conduct has brought about a delay or dislocation of proceedings could exceptionally be penalised either through an award of expenses against the solicitor in person or through a finding of contempt of court. Thus personal liability in expenses may arise from failing to attend court[30] or discharging or adjourning a debate or proof due to the fault of the lawyer. Again it has been held that improperly using the procedure of the court to delay the outcome to which the opponent is entitled can in appropriate circumstances lead to an award of expenses against the lawyer personally. Thus, in a case where the sheriff held that it should have been obvious to the solicitor for the defender at a certain stage that there was no defence to the action, the solicitor was found liable in expenses for failing to withdraw the defences at that stage, and instead allowing the defence to stand for another three months until the action reached the head of the queue of cases awaiting disposal and then consenting to decree.[31]

14.03.02 Disrupting the business of the court—contempt of court. Equally, there have been a few cases where a solicitor or advocate has failed to appear in court at the due time and thereafter been held to be guilty of contempt of court for egregiously wasting the time of the court. Contempt is a *sui generis* offence[32] and has been described as "conduct which challenges or affronts the authority of the court or the supremacy of the law itself".[33] In *Muirhead v Douglas*[34] a solicitor was fined for contempt in being 25 minutes late for court. An appeal to the High Court was unavailing, since Lord Cameron took the view that the solicitor deliberately chose to run the risk of being late and causing "an avoidable and quite possibly serious delay in the due dispatch of the court's business". In more recent times, however, the High Court has shown a reluctance to uphold findings of contempt for failure to appear timeously in court. In *Macara v MacFarlane*[35] a solicitor who was double booked and unable to attend in court to conduct a trial had arranged cover. Unfortunately, the cover arrangements failed and the solicitor was found guilty of contempt for failing to appear on time. His appeal to the High Court

---

[29] *ibid.* p.65.
[30] See *Stewart v Stewart*, 1984 S.L.T. (Sh Ct) 58 at 59.
[31] *ibid.*
[32] See Gerald Gordon, *Criminal Law* (3rd edn, W Green, Edinburgh, 2001) Ch.50.
[33] *H.M. Advocate v Airs*, 1975 J.C. 64 at 69.
[34] 1979 S.L.T. (Notes) 17.
[35] 1980 S.L.T. (Notes) 26.

was successful. Again, in *McKinnon v Douglas*[36] a solicitor was convicted of contempt of court when he failed to appear in the district court as duty agent. However, it was his partner who was the duty agent and because he was ill, the solicitor having tried and failed to find a substitute, chose first to attend to three custody cases in the sheriff court before going to the district court. He was delayed further in attending the district court due to a misunderstanding, and was accordingly one and a half hours late in arriving at the court. Despite offering his profuse apologies he was held liable for contempt on the following day by the district court. The High Court quashed the conviction noting that in the circumstances there was "no neglect of the obligation to support the dignity of the court" nor any "wilful or reckless interference with the administration of justice". Similarly, in *Ferguson v Normand*[37] a solicitor who was double booked for the district and sheriff courts, and through an error of judgement concluded that he could fulfil both obligations, was held by the High Court not to have shown the necessary wilful disregard for the authority or dignity of the court to amount to contempt, although he had acted rashly. In like manner, the High Court in *Murdanaigum v Henderson*[38] suspended a finding of contempt by a sheriff against a solicitor for turning up over an hour late for the start of a trial. The sheriff had twice previously warned the solicitor as to his conduct and regarded the third failure as contempt. The High Court, however, accepted the solicitor's assertion that his lateness stemmed from failing to put the correct entry in his diary and concluded that mere inefficiency could not amount to contempt, and that even given the previous warnings the solicitor's conduct did not amount to a pattern of wilful conduct. Clearly, the climate has changed significantly since *Muirhead*. Now it is evident that negligent or reckless behaviour even, will not constitute contempt. Thus in *McMillan v Carmichael*[39] the accused was found guilty of contempt of court for yawning noisily and stretching his arms above his head at the back of the court and thus distracting the sheriff, without making any attempt to be discreet or stifle his yawn. The High Court overturned the finding on the ground that contempt required a wilful and intentional challenge to the court's authority. While this could in appropriate circumstances be inferred e.g. from the deliberate failure to heed a warning from the judge, recklessness or gross negligence on their own could not give rise to a finding of contempt. Again in *Williams v Clark*,[40] Williams appeared in court late, disrupting another trial, and then his mobile phone started ringing. This was held to be contempt of court, as there were clear signs indicating that phones should be switched off, and the sheriff stated that his behaviour in general amounted to intentional disrespect of the court. However, the conviction was suspended on appeal, as the sheriff was not entitled to take into account other facts, including Williams' lateness, and should have considered only the incident regarding the mobile phone. It was however stated that the ringing of a mobile phone may be regarded as contempt as it causes significant disruption to the court. More recently still was the case of *HMA v Dickie*.[41]

---

[36] 1982 S.L.T. 375.
[37] 1994 S.L.T. 1355.
[38] 1996 S.L.T. 1297.
[39] 1994 S.L.T. 510.
[40] 2001 S.C.C.R. 505.
[41] 2002 S.L.T. 1083.

Here Lord Hardie was confronted with a solicitor who had failed, in his view, to take sufficient steps to find an alternative counsel at relatively short notice to undertake a High Court trial, with the result that the trial had to be postponed. Lord Hardie considered that the solicitor had been cavalier and "grossly reckless resulting in a disregard for the court and the administration of justice". However, in applying *McMillan v Carmichael*,[42] Lord Hardie concluded that gross recklessness could not constitute contempt of court without an intention to challenge or affront the authority of the court or to defy its orders. Lord Hardie considered that the lawyer's behaviour could be viewed in this light, but that equally it was also compatible with sheer incompetence on the part of the solicitor. The solicitor therefore escaped a conviction for contempt of court by the skin of his teeth. The advocate who failed to turn up for a High Court trial before Lord Hardie a year later[43] because he was double booked, was not so fortunate. His conduct in failing to appear was held to be reckless, but not thereby contempt, following *McMillan v Carmichael*.[44] However his attempt to excuse himself by the use of statements which the judge considered to be false, was held by Lord Hardie to constitute contempt of court since he deemed them to have been carefully and deliberately (and not just recklessly) made and therefore in Lord Hardie's opinion displayed the necessary intention to challenge or affront the authority of the court. Lord Hardie's finding was the subject of a successful appeal to the High Court through the medium of the *Nobile Officium*[45] but in allowing the petition the High Court did not object to Lord Hardie's statement of the law. In short, therefore, it is clear that nowadays merely disrupting the business of the courtroom by lateness or failing to appear or by one's general behaviour in court, will not of itself constitute contempt "unless there is wilful defiance of or disrespect to the court, or behaviour which challenges or affronts its authority".[46]

14.03.03 Disrupting the business of the court—professional misconduct.[47] The foregoing cases on contempt and the disruption of the business of the court in no way gainsay the fact that both solicitors and advocates have a duty not to cause delays or dislocations in proceedings before the courts. This duty can in serious cases be enforced through a finding of professional misconduct, not least because, unlike contempt, recklessness or gross neglect can be sufficient to establish professional misconduct. One such case was *Corrigan*.[48] Here the solicitor was found guilty of professional misconduct in respect of his gross failure in his professional duty to take reasonable steps to ensure his timeous attendance or to make other satisfactory arrangements for the representation

---

[42] 1994 S.L.T. 510.

[43] *HM Advocate v Tarbett*, 2003 S.L.T. 1288.

[44] *ibid*. Lord Hardie added that had the failure to appear been a willful act, that would have been contempt.

[45] *John Mayer* 2004, S.C.C.R. 734.

[46] R. McInnes and D. Fairley, *Contempt of Court in Scotland* (C.L.T. Professional Publishing, Hertfordshire, 2000), p.45. See also R. McInnes, "Conflict between Bench and Bar", 2004 S.L.T. (News) 2.

[47] Ryder, *op. cit.* p.82 argues persuasively that delay to court proceedings by a solicitor can also amount to IPS. It is certainly more than arguable that the Court would constitute "any person with an interest" for the purposes of s.33 of the Law Reform (Miscellaneous Provisions) (Scotland) Act 1990. The Law Society to date have given the phrase a narrow interpretation.

[48] See Smith & Barton *op. cit.* at p.134 and DTD 636/84a.

of his clients. Between August 1982 and April 1983 the respondent's conduct in relation to various courts was the subject of adverse comments on five separate occasions. On three of these occasions, the respondent was found guilty of contempt of court, although he was given an absolute discharge on two of them. The Scottish Solicitors Discipline Tribunal looked at the events surrounding the three contempt findings. In relation to the first, they held that the respondent had known that he had two simultaneous trials for some time and should have taken action to resolve the conflict in his diary before the night before, when it was too late. This behaviour was held to be sufficient to constitute professional misconduct. On the second occasion, the respondent failed to attend a trial diet because he had wrongly noted the date in his diary. The Tribunal held that such carelessness did not contain such an element of recklessness or gross neglect that would justify a finding of professional misconduct. On the final occasion, the respondent retained instructions to represent clients in trials in the sheriff court and the district court up to the close of business on the preceding day when it was too late to arrange cover. The respondent was delayed in the sheriff court and was accordingly 35 minutes late for the district court and subsequently held to have been in contempt of court. The circumstances of this case were held by the Tribunal to merit a finding of professional misconduct.

The duty to conduct cases efficiently and expeditiously—the advent of case management. We have seen that solicitors that delay proceedings can be penalised in a variety of ways. It is possible that this may become more of a problem as the culture of judicial case management begins to permeate in the future. Traditionally in Scotland the parties and their legal representatives have effectively been more responsible for the pace of litigation (both civil and criminal), than the judiciary. However in Scotland, as in other parts of the Commonwealth, the increasing cost of litigation has led to a growing recognition that it is inappropriate to leave the progress of proceedings largely to the inclinations of the parties and the work practices of their representatives. In a number of sheriff courts in the last twenty years (principally Dundee and Kilmarnock) the shreival bench has demonstrated that the local legal culture which prevailed amongst the professional participants in courts could be changed. Thus the sheriffs in these courts, by adopting a more restrictive approach to the granting of continuations and adjournments, were able to speed up the pace of litigation in their courts. There have also been a number of procedural reforms, for example the introduction of intermediate diets in summary criminal cases, the Bonomy reforms in solemn cases, and the Coulsfield Rules in personal injury cases in the Court of Session which have encouraged the judiciary to take a more directive/interventionist approach to case management.[49] Further indications of changing times in this area can be found in the dicta of Lord Hardie in the *Dickie*[50] and *Tarbett*[51] cases, which antedated the Bonomy reforms. In the first, Lord Hardie indicated that except in the most unusual of cases adjournments should not be

14.04

---

[49] The most obvious example in England and Wales is the Woolf reforms.
[50] 2002 S.L.T. 1083.
[51] 2003 S.L.T. 1288.

granted simply because the accused wants the services of a particular counsel. He added[52]:

> "Adjournment of cases to later sittings causes problems for witnesses, whose memory may be affected by the passage of time. They may also result in an accused person being detained in custody for a longer period than would otherwise be necessary... Moreover adjournments cause disruption to current and future sittings of the High Court, resulting in unnecessary delays to the determination of cases, additional inconvenience to the public, who are involved as jurors or witnesses and a waste of public expenditure and resources."

In *Tarbett*[53] Lord Hardie was equally trenchant, observing that the practice of seeking numerous adjournments stems from a minority of solicitors not being willing to prioritise High Court work so that cases can proceed to trial at the first opportunity, and a minority of counsel and solicitor advocates seeking adjournments because of inadequate time for preparation, only for the adjourned hearing to be attended by a new counsel or solicitor seeking yet another adjournment for the same reason. He added: "In my opinion such practices are undesirable and are contrary to the interests of justice. They result in unnecessary delays in the commencement of trials, with adverse consequences for the accused, particularly if he is custody, as well as witnesses and prospective jurors. By their actions the minority of practitioners bring the system of justice in Scotland and the legal profession as a whole into disrepute."

14.05 The duty not to abuse the court process[54]

The second set of duties to the court stems from the need to preserve the integrity of the adversarial system. It follows that a lawyer should not seek unreasonably to raise or defend an action for which there is no legal justification. Where the lawyer *knows* that there is no cause for action but raises or continues with it nonetheless, for example, in pursuit of publicity or some other illegitimate motive, he or she will be potentially liable in contempt of court,[55] to a conduct complaint and / or an award of expenses against the lawyer personally.[56] This is true whether the purpose of the lawsuit is to denigrate the other side,[57] to satisfy the client's malice against the opponent[58] or simply to buy time.

---

[52] 2002 S.L.T. 1083 at 1086F.

[53] 2003 S.L.T. 1288 at 1291E.

[54] Ipp, *op. cit.* pp.79–83.

[55] See e.g. *R v Weisz* [1951] 2 K.B. 611 at 617.

[56] Abuse of civil process can also be an actionable wrong. See e.g. D.M. Walker, *Civil Remedies* (W. Green & Son, Edinburgh, 1974), pp.998 *et seq.*

[57] See the New Zealand rule of Professional Conduct r.7.04 "A practitioner must make all reasonable efforts to ensure that legal processes are used for their proper purposes only and that their use is not likely to cause unnecessary embarrassment, distress or inconvenience to another person's reputation, interests or occupation."

[58] E.g. *Re Cooke* (1889) 5 T.L.R. 407 at 408. If, however, the action is well founded, the client's motive is usually irrelevant.

Deliberate and wilful abuse of process[59] through raising or defending a case for which the lawyer is aware that there is no justification is fortunately rare. However, the summary jurisdiction of the court to take action under the common law against wayward officers of the court extends further than this. Although Begg[60] discusses the summary jurisdiction of the courts, he was writing before *Solicitors' Discipline (Scotland) Committee v B.*[61] and its English equivalent—*Myers v Ellman.*[62] *Myers* made it clear that the summary jurisdiction of the English courts was not limited to instances of deliberate wrongdoing or dishonesty. Thus, although a "mere mistake or error of judgement is not generally sufficient ... a gross neglect or inaccuracy in a matter which it is the solicitor's duty to ascertain with accuracy may suffice".[63] Again in *Edwards v Edwards*[64] Sachs J. notes that "anything which can be termed an abuse of the process of the court" is included, adding that "unreasonably to initiate or continue an action when it has no or substantially no chance of success" might be covered. The statutory wasted costs jurisdiction of English courts[65] has now partially superseded the common law inherent jurisdiction of the court with respect to abuse of process, however, it is clear that the earlier case law established that the abuse of process jurisdiction arose if the lawyer knew *or ought reasonably to have known* that the argument was unsustainable. Recklessness is therefore covered as well as intentional actings. What about Scotland? The narrower disciplinary role of the courts,[66] and the dearth of decided cases perhaps requires us to be cautious in reaching a definitive conclusion. In *Manson v Chief Constable of Strathclyde*[67] expenses were awarded against a solicitor who raised an action which was "manifestly incompetent and irrelevant." Moreover, the cases of *Stewart v Stewart*[68] and *Blyth v Watson*[69] strongly suggest that in Scotland also the court can award expenses where the solicitor was reckless or ought reasonably to have known that the argument was unsustainable. In *Blyth* the solicitors for a personal injury victim reached a full and final settlement of the case in 1984 only for them to re-raise the same claim a year later when it looked as though the victim's condition was going to dramatically worsen. Having obtained

---

[59] "It is an abuse of the process of the Court to bring a claim with no genuine belief in its merits but in bad faith and for an ulterior purpose ... A party who makes an exorbitant claim with no genuine belief in its merits, rejecting all reasonable offers of settlement, and exploiting his own inability to satisfy an order for costs in order to bring pressure on the other party to settle for an excessive sum, is abusing the process of the Court", *per* Millett L.J in *Bowring v Corsi* [1994] 2 Lloyd's Law Rep 567 at 580.

[60] Begg on *Law Agents, op. cit.* p.280.

[61] 1941 S.C. 293.

[62] [1940] A.C. 282.

[63] Per Lord Wright in *Myers, op. cit.* at 319.

[64] Per Sachs J. [1958] P 235.

[65] Presently contained in ss.51(1) and (3) of the Supreme Court Act 1981 (as amended). See e.g. *Count Tolstoy-Miloslavsky v Lord Aldington* [1996] 2 All E.R. 556.

[66] A comparison of *Solicitors' Discipline (Scotland) Committee v B.* and *Myers v Ellman* appears to show that the English legislation on solicitors' discipline has expressly reserved more of the common law disciplinary powers of the English courts than the Scottish legislation has for Scottish courts. In practice, the difference is not likely to be that great since Lord Cooper in the former case appears to have underestimated the scope of the summary jurisdiction of Scottish courts, by implying that it was largely confined to the contempt of court power.

[67] *The Scotsman*, Dec 16, 1983 referred to in McPhail, *op. cit.* p.34.

[68] 1984 S.L.T. 58.

[69] 1987 S.L.T. 616.

legal aid they proceeded to raise the action in order to get within the triennium period of limitation. Thereafter, the solicitors accepted that the earlier settlement excluded the subsequent claim. Lord Morrison in the Outer House held that in raising the action the solicitors must have been aware that it was insupportable. In the light of the facts of the case it is respectfully submitted that this need not have been the case, however, it is clear that Lord Morrison was taking the view that the solicitors *ought to have known* that the subsequent claim was insupportable. In *Stewart*, Sheriff Ireland Q.C. took the view that even if the solicitor honestly believed that the defence he had put forward for his client was a tenable one, nevertheless he ought to have known or concluded long before the diet of proof that it was in fact unsustainable, and his failure to do so amounted to an abuse of process. Certainly, it seems undeniable that Webster is right to argue[70] that the lawyer must investigate a case properly before raising an action and should not abuse the process of court by raising an action, out of anger or malice, which is likely to unnecessarily injure the defender.

It should, however, be stressed that in most of the jurisdictions where abuse of process applies, it is clear from the case law that merely because the lawyer chooses to act or to continue to act even when it is obvious that there is little chance of winning, does not necessarily open him or her up to sanction. To hold otherwise would be to severely undermine the effective operation of the adversarial system, for this is an area where the lawyer's duty to pursue the best interests of the client[71] comes in direct conflict with the lawyer's duty to the court. Unpopular clients, or those with weaker cases, would find it even harder than they now do to obtain representation if the two duties were not kept in balance. Thus Lord Esher M.R. observed that[72] where the lawyer knows that the case is "absolutely and certainly hopeless" it is a breach of duty and dishonourable to continue to act. However, he added that it was perfectly acceptable to continue to act if the lawyer is unable to conclude that the case was indeed "absolutely and certainly hopeless". As Sir Thomas Bingham M.R. noted more recently in an analogous situation[73]: "A legal representative is not to be held to have acted improperly, unreasonably or negligently simply because he acts for a party who pursues a claim or defence which is plainly doomed to fail . . . ". As the judge also recognised, it is not always easy to distinguish between a case that is hopeless and one where there is an abuse of process. However, he was surely right to conclude that the benefit of any doubt must be given to the lawyer, i.e. the duty to pursue the best interests of the client.[74]

What more then is required to invoke the jurisdiction? Here it is difficult to be definitive in Scotland, because of the shortage of case law. However one situation where a lawyer who was aware or ought reasonably to have been

---

[70] *Op. cit.* 3.08.

[71] Sometimes know as the duty of "zealous advocacy".

[72] In *Re Cooke* (1889) 5 TLR 407 at 408.

[73] *Ridehalgh v Horsefield* [1994] 3 All E.R. 848 at 863a, although this was a wasted costs order case.

[74] As A. Boon and J. Levin observed in *The Ethics and Conduct of Lawyers in England and Wales* (Hart Publishing, Oxford, 1999) at 218, it would be unfortunate if lawyers who were *bona fide* running test cases in the hope of changing the law were to be penalised by awards of costs against them.

aware that the case or defence was unsustainable will be found liable in expenses is where the lawyer acted from an ulterior or illegitimate motive, thus causing loss to the other side.[75]

Abuse of the court process and defenders—The role of skeleton defences. 14.05.01
It is clear that defenders can be guilty of abuse of process just as pursuers can—and the same range of sanctions exists. Thus courts in a range of jurisdictions have rejected as an abuse of process efforts by lawyers defending civil cases to unnecessarily lengthen the duration of proceedings.[76] Indeed, the case with the lengthiest exposition of the solicitors' liability in expenses in Scotland related to the defence of a case for summary ejection from heritable property, namely, *Stewart v Stewart*.[77] As we saw earlier, the defence solicitor had put forward a frivolous defence although he genuinely believed that it was a tenable argument. However, in finding him liable in expenses Sheriff Ireland Q.C. noted that while he could not be criticised for stating the defence of personal bar as he did, his failure thereafter to apply his mind at any stage prior to the proof to the question whether such a defence could be plausibly be argued, constituted an abuse of process. Sheriff Ireland's exposition of the law is worthy of reproduction *in extenso*:

"It has long been recognised that for certain breaches of duty, such as failing to attend court, a solicitor may be found personally liable in expenses. In my opinion, it is equally a breach of duty if a solicitor improperly uses the procedure of the court to delay the achievement of a result to which a litigant is entitled. When a pursuer asserts a claim by serving a summons or initial writ, he is entitled to the remedy he seeks unless his opponent can show some ground in fact or law why this should not be granted. If no appearance is entered, the pursuer is entitled to decree in absence. If appearance is entered and defences are lodged, the pleadings have to be adjusted and the law debated and the facts ascertained, and it may be months or years before the remedy is achieved. But this delay is not something to which a defender is entitled in order that he may postpone the discharge of his obligations. It arises solely because the time is required to ascertain the truth if there is a genuine dispute about the facts or the law. It seems to me to follow that if a defender who has no defence either in fact or in law uses the procedures not to establish his right but to delay the enforcement of a right which is undeniable, he is guilty of an abuse of process and, if he is a solicitor, ought to pay what his conduct has cost the other party to the litigation . . . [It matters not that] he may honestly have believed that

---

[75] Again, Goldberg J. in *White Industries*, *ibid.* is instructive. As he observed (at p.236): " it involves some deliberate or conscious decision taken by reference to circumstances unrelated to the prospects of success with . . . a recognition that there is no chance of success but an intention to use the proceeding for an ulterior purpose or with disregard of any proper consideration of the prospects of success".

[76] E.g. the USA (see the Model Rules 3.2 "A lawyer shall make reasonable efforts to expedite litigation consistent with the interests of the client"), New Zealand and Australia (see Del Pont *op. cit.* at p.470).

[77] 1984 S.L.T. 58.

there was a defence. A professionally qualified solicitor is in my view required to do more than abstain from dishonesty. It is his positive duty, in the words of Lord Atkin in *Myers* v *Elman*, 'to conduct litigation . . . with due propriety'. I do not intend to suggest that a solicitor acts improperly in all cases by entering appearance and stating a defence which may turn out to be unsubstantial. It may be perfectly proper, if there is initially doubt about the facts or the law, to put in skeleton defences to preserve the position while investigations are made. But as soon as the facts and the law are elucidated, and it appears that there is no defence to the action, the defence should be withdrawn and decree allowed to pass. It is in my opinion improper to allow the defence to stand until the action reaches the head of the queue of cases awaiting disposal, and then to consent to decree. That is to use the intervening time not for the necessary purpose of determining disputed issues of fact or law, but for the improper purpose of delaying the enforcement of a right about which there is no longer any dispute."[78]

Sheriff Ireland's judgement is instructive on a number of fronts. First he recognises (as Lord Esher and Sir Thomas Bingham M.R. did) that the court's summary jurisdiction does not arise simply because the defender has put forward an argument that the court subsequently finds to be unsound, since to do so would undermine the adversarial system. It is submitted therefore that in Scotland, as in England, for so long as we retain the adversarial system substantially in its current guise, then although the lawyer's duty to the client has to be balanced against the duty to the court, the benefit of any doubt should go to the lawyer's duty to safeguard the interests of the client. Secondly, Sheriff Ireland points to the limitations which should attach to the use of skeleton defences. Thus, the Law Society indicated in 1986[79] that except in circumstances of extreme urgency, the lodging of skeleton defences should be avoided, and should not be used simply as a delaying tactic.[80] The Society also added that while bare denials may be relevant they can saddle the

---

[78] For an expression of very similar sentiments in Australia see Goldberg J. in *White Industries Pty Ltd v Flower & Hart* 213 (1998) 156 ALR 169 at 252: "It is perfectly proper for a party and its legal advisers to fight a case and to put an opposing party to proof of its cause, although I question whether it is appropriate to put an opposing party to the proof of an issue, which is not disputed, which will not be a critical issue at trial and which will have the effect of running up costs unnecessarily. Nevertheless, it is not proper, in my view to adopt a positive or assertive obstructionist or delaying strategy which is not in the interests of justice and inhibits the court from achieving an expeditious and timely resolution of a dispute . . . . If a party instructs its legal advisers to adopt such a strategy the legal adviser should inform the party that it is not proper for it to do so and if the party insists, then the legal adviser should withdraw from acting for that party."

[79] (1986) J.L.S.S. 248.

[80] *Ellon Castle Estates v Macdonald*, 1975 S.L.T. (Notes) 66 illustrates the limitations of skeleton defences. Having entered a bare denial the defenders sought to make other averments at a later stage. Since these were held to be incompatible with the bare denial contained in the Process when the case went to the Procedural Roll, the defenders lost the case, thus indicating the dangers of being caught with a straight denial in one's pleadings. (We are indebted to Mike Jones Q.C. for the opportunity to peruse the Process in this case.) Nevertheless, as I. MacPhail, *Sheriff Court Practice* (2nd edn), p.302 indicates, a skeleton defence may be a perfectly fair and relevant defence. See also *Ganley v Scottish Boatowners Mutual Insurance Association*, 1967 S.L.T. (Notes) 45 and *Gray v Boyd*, 1996 S.L.T. 60.

defender with additional and unnecessary expense.[81] Here the lawyer's duty to pursue the best interests of the client is very clearly being tempered by the duty to the court not to commit an abuse of process.[82]

Abuse of the court process and criminal cases. Sheriff Ireland in *Stewart* **14.05.02** referred to an English criminal defence case, *Abraham v Justun*[83] in a way that suggested that criminal cases are no different than civil cases when it comes to the issue of abuse of process. Halsbury,[84] however, suggests that the abuse of power inherent jurisdiction in civil and criminal proceedings has developed along separate lines in England and Wales and that the test is harder to invoke in criminal cases. In our view this should also be the position in Scotland. As Dal Pont[85] argues, the balance between the duty to the client and that to the court should be more in favour of the former than the latter in criminal cases for three reasons: first because the criminal proceedings are initiated by the Crown; second because the prosecution has to prove their case beyond reasonable doubt and the accused is entitled to put the Crown to the test and thirdly that the accused has the sole option as between pleading guilty or not guilty.[86]

Basis of abuse of process jurisdiction. Although the commentators are **14.05.03** agreed that the abuse of process jurisdiction relates to breach of duty to the court, from time to time the question has arisen as to what the basis of the court's jurisdiction is to find the lawyer personally liable in expenses such cases. Lord Wright in *Myers v Ellman*[87] is particularly instructive where he observes that "the underlying principle is that the Court has a right and a duty to supervise the conduct of its solicitors and visit with penalties any conduct of a solicitor which is of such a nature as to tend to defeat justice in the very cause in which he is engaged professionally."[88] For Lord Wright the jurisdiction is compensatory as well as punitive and in this line of thought he is supported by Viscount Maugham.[89] As the cost of litigation rises, the penalty associated with the jurisdiction becomes more severe. Because of this and the court's natural reluctance to undermine the adversarial system, awards of expenses in abuse of process cases are relatively uncommon—in Scotland

---

[81] See *J. C. Forbes Ltd v Duignan* 1974 S.L.T. (Sh Ct) 74 and *Jarvie v Laird* 1974 S.L.T. (Sh Ct) 75. The Society added that solicitors should not use the practice of delaying the revisal of their pleadings until amendment after their opponent has drawn attention to their deficiencies in debate.

[82] In 2002 the Professional Practice Committee ruled that a solicitor who had previously acknowledged a debt and part paid the same, had behaved improperly by subsequently seeking to recall the decree in absence by putting forward a defence of "debt denied". The committee agreed with the sheriff that putting forward such a defence in direct contradiction to a prior admission of the debt was inconsistent with the solicitor's duty as an officer of the court.

[83] [1963] 1 W.L.R. 658.

[84] Laws of England (4th edn, 1995), Vol.44(1), para.168.

[85] *Op. cit.* at p.475. This accords with the view of David Luban that zealous advocacy is more defensible in criminal defence cases than in most civil cases. See D. Luban, *The Good Lawyer* (Rowman & Allanhead, New Jersey, 1984), pp.91–93.

[86] It follows that judges should be slow to seek to emulate Mr Justice Melford Stevenson who sought to dock lawyers' legal aid fees who had attacked the veracity of the police witnesses, because they were not entitled to be mere "loudspeakers for a maladjusted set".

[87] [1940] A.C. 282 at 319.

[88] *Op. cit.* at 319.

[89] *Op. cit.* at 289.

or elsewhere. However, judges and lawyers alike are aware that the jurisdiction exists and the existence of the power to award expenses against lawyers personally influences the behaviour of both the judges and those appearing before them.[90]

14.05.04 The position of counsel. It is widely believed that whatever may be the position concerning the award of expenses against a solicitor for breach of duty to the court through an abuse of process, there is no power in Scotland to award expenses against counsel in the same situation.[91] This is in line with the English position where it was confirmed by the Court of Appeal in *Ridehalgh v Horsfield*[92] that there was no common law power to award costs against a barrister. This situation was said to stem from the fact the common law immunity from suit of barristers and the fact that strictly speaking English barristers are not "officers of the court" on historical grounds and not therefore subject to the court's summary jurisdiction (except with respect to contempt of court). The argument from the barrister's immunity is misconceived, since the policy objectives for the immunity are not the same as those lying behind attempts to make lawyers open to sanction for breaching their duty to the court not to commit an abuse of process.[93] In any event, now that the civil immunity from suit of barristers in litigation has been removed in England and Wales,[94] and arguably also in Scotland,[95] this argument has lost most of its cogency. As for the argument that advocates owe no duties to the court to avoid an abuse of process because they are not strictly officers of the court, this strikes the modern mind as special pleading of a peculiarly unconvincing nature. If barristers or advocates can be punished for contempt, why not for breach of duty to the interests of justice?[96]

While Scottish authority on this point is hard to come by, one of the Institutional Writers, Bankton,[97] states that if "during the dependence of a cause, an advocate discovers that it is unjust or calumnious, he ought to desert it, in consequence of his oath at his admission, and in point of conscience and justice to his character" indicating that a failure to so act was misconduct if not a breach of duty. It is unclear whether Advocates are officers of court. In Scots law, however, they are admitted and removed from the public office of advocate by the Court of Session. Moreover, there is absolutely no doubt from the case law, the Faculty of Advocates' *Guide to the Professional Conduct of Advocates*, and from entry on Advocates in the *Stair Memorial Encyclopaedia*

---

[90] The English experience of wasted costs orders suggests that it is weapon in the judicial armoury which should be used very sparingly. Empirical research suggests that it is not a cost-effective procedure, since it brings less back than the cost of invoking it. See H. Evans, *Lawyers' Liabilities* (Sweet & Maxwell, London, 2002), Ch.7.

[91] See e.g. MacPhail, *op. cit.* at p.628 and *Reid v Edinburgh Acoustics Ltd (No.2)*, 1995 S.L.T. (Notes) 87.

[92] [1994] Ch. 205.

[93] See the judgement of the New Zealand Court of Appeal in *Harley v McDonald* [1999] NZLR 545 at p.558.

[94] See *Arthur J.S. Hall v Simons* [2002] 1 A.C. 615.

[95] But see *Wright v Paton Farrell* 2006 S.L.T. 269 where the First Division, *obiter*, ruled that immunity of suit remains in Scotland for the conduct of legal representatives in criminal trials. However, the justification of the immunity was precisely to enhance the due administration of criminal justice.

[96] See again the reasoning of the New Zealand Court of Appeal in *Harley v McDonald* [1999] NZLR 545.

[97] (IV iii 13).

that members of the Faculty owe extensive duties to the courts and that they can be punished by the court for contempt of court for their conduct in the performance of their professional duties. Finally, Sheriff Ireland in *Stewart* indicates that in his view there was no difference between the duty owed to the court by counsel and by solicitors. It is respectfully submitted that this is the case and that there is no justification for holding that Scottish advocates are not subject to the summary jurisdiction of the court in relation to duties to the court. Accordingly, there would appear to be no reason why a court could not award expenses against an advocate where an abuse of process can be established, even without a statutory intervention.

A general duty of candour owed to the court **14.06**

This duty, which comes into sharpest contrast with the lawyer's duties to pursue his or her client's interests to the best of the lawyer's ability and the duty not to breach the duty of confidentiality to the client, is as longstanding as the duty not to abuse the court process. The strength of the adversarial system in the UK and other common law countries has ensured that it is in this area that curbs on the lawyer's ability to zealously advocate his or her client's cause are most keenly contested.

Candour in matters of law. It has long been established in Scotland, as in **14.06.01** most English speaking countries, that not only must lawyers not deceive the court on matters of law, but also that they are under a positive duty to make full disclosure as to all the law relevant to the case in hand. This means all authorities, statutory or otherwise, which are in point must be brought before the court by each party, *whether they support or undermine the position being argued for by that party.*[98] This requires a lawyer either to keep up to date with changes in the law or to research the field if it is outside the lawyer's normal area of practice. However, the rule does not require the lawyer to present an impartial or disinterested account of the law,[99] and the lawyer is entitled and probably obliged to make all reasonable and good faith efforts to distinguish those authorities which do not support the position for which the lawyer is contending. This obligation of candour applies equally in uncontested as well as contested cases. It has been said that a corollary of the rule is that a lawyer may not advance a legal argument which the lawyer knows to be unsound.[1] As against this the malleability of the common law and the fact that ultimately, to paraphrase Dr Johnson, it is the court's job to determine the soundness of legal propositions rather than the lawyer's, probably entails that the constraints imposed by this injunction may be rather limited.[2] The standard articulation of the principle is to be found by Lord Chancellor Birkenhead in the House of Lords decision in *The Glebe Sugar Refining Company Ltd v The Trustees of the Port and Harbours of Greenock*[3]:

---

[98] See the authorities quoted in M. Blake and A. Ashworth, "Ethics and the Criminal Defence Lawyer" 7 (2004) *Legal Ethics* 167 at p.177.

[99] See e.g. the Commentary to r.3.3 (a)(1) and (3) of the New Model Rules of Professional Conduct in the USA.

[1] See e.g. Webster, *op. cit.* para.3.06.

[2] Doubtless American realists and some post-modern thinkers would argue that this rule imposes almost no constraints on creative counsel.

[3] 1921 S.C. (H.L.) 72.

"It is not, of course, in cases of complication possible for their Lordships to be aware of all the authorities, statutory or otherwise, which may be relevant to the issues which in the particular case require decision. Their Lordships are therefore very much in the hands of counsel, and those who instruct counsel, in these matters, and this House expects, and indeed insists, that authorities which bear one way or the other upon matters under debate shall be brought to the attention of their Lordships by those who are aware of those authorities. This observation is quite irrespective of whether or not the particular authority assists the party which is so aware of it. It is an obligation of confidence between their Lordships and all those who assist in the debates in this house in the capacity of counsel."[4]

The duty of disclosure is not restricted to advocates. Thus the same obligation applies to solicitor advocates[5]:

"*(1)... Where a solicitor advocate is aware of a previous decision binding on the court, or of a statutory provision relevant to a point of law in issue, it is his duty to draw that decision or provision to the attention of the court whether or not it supports his argument and whether or not it has been referred to by his opponent.*"

There is every reason to believe that the rule also applies to solicitors appearing in courts and before tribunals.[6] There have been few reported cases in which the rule has been enforced,[7] but failure to refer to a relevant authority may be reflected in the award of expenses, and could be a conduct offence.

The seeming clarity of the rule hides certain areas of debate. First, the ambit of the rule when applied to a precedent. Does it only apply to precedents which are binding on the court or tribunal before whom the appearance is being made, or does it extend to authorities which are merely persuasive? This is a point that has attracted some attention in Federal jurisdictions such as Australia and the USA where there are many more persuasive than mandatory decisions. There is no definitive ruling on this matter, but it seems likely that Scotland would adopt the position that only decisions which are binding or in point and highly persuasive, for example, they emanate from an English House of Lords Appeal or Privy Council decision not directly binding on a Scots court, need be cited to the court. Thus, despite globalisation and the greater availability of foreign law reports, it would probably be thought unreasonable to expect the rule to apply to foreign case law unless, perhaps, the case is being argued at the level of the House of Lords or the Privy Council.[8] A second area for debate relates to the rationale for the rule. At first blush it seems somewhat curious that the duty of candour extends further in relation to matters of law than it does in relation to matters of fact—when it

---

[4] *ibid.* pp.73–74.
[5] Solicitors (Scotland) Rules of Conduct for Solicitor Advocates 2002, r.6(1).
[6] See e.g. Webster (4th edn) *op. cit.* para.3.06.
[7] However, one such case was *Copeland v Smith* [2000] 1 W.L.R. 1371.
[8] *cf.* the Australian Bar Association's 1995 Code of Conduct, r.25 which abandoned a requirement in the earlier *Code* which referred to the duty to disclose any "binding or persuasive authority" for a simpler reference to "any binding authority" because of the proliferation of law reports. See Dal Pont *op. cit.* p.453.

might be thought that it was easier for the judge to conduct his or her own researches into the former than the latter.[9] Part of the explanation may be that adherence to the rule will usually not involve sacrificing the lawyer's duty to the client, since following it will rarely violate the client's confidentiality and with it the client's trust. The rationale put forward by Lord Birkenhead in *Glebe Sugar Refining*[10] that not to have such rule would entail obtaining a decision based on imperfect knowledge or involve turning the court into a debating assembly upon legal matters, seems less compelling, since such arguments apply equally to questions of fact.

Candour in matters of fact. The basic proposition here is encapsulated in art.8 of the Code of Conduct for Scottish Solicitors: **14.06.02**

> "*Solicitors must never knowingly give false or misleading information to the court*".

Superficially this appears not dissimilar to the lawyer's duty to the court on matters of law. In reality there is a significant difference. While the lawyer must act honestly and non-deceitfully with respect to any evidence which he or she has led in, or information provided to, the court, there is ordinarily no obligation to place all relevant *evidence* before the court. Thus, normally, the lawyer need not disclose the existence and identity of an adverse witness to the other side,[11] nor need the lawyer lead every available witness with relevant information.[12] Indeed, if there is evidence that is actively harmful to the client's case which derives from confidential or privileged discussions with the client, there is a positive ethical obligation not to lay it before the court.

False or fabricated evidence. All but the most ardent supporters of zealous advocacy accept that the adversarial system does not permit lawyers to knowingly put before the court false or fabricated evidence, no matter what the kind of proceeding nor whether the deception causes harm to anyone.[13] The *Young* case[14] involved a solicitor who mislead the court in two separate cases. In the first, the solicitor pretended that his client had died intestate, in order to assist the surviving spouse, even though he was aware that the client had left a holograph will. The solicitor subsequently submitted applications to the court (twice) and to an insurance company (once), indicating that the client had died intestate. In the second case, when the client died, his will was sent to a family member and got lost in the post. The solicitor once more submitted an application to the court stating that the client had died intestate, this time **14.06.03**

---

[9] For this and other critiques of the rule see, C. Wolfram, *Modern Legal Ethics, op. cit.* p.681.

[10] *ibid*. p.74.

[11] Prosecutors are in a special position. The Privy Council ruled in 2005 in *Sinclair v HMA* Privy Council DRA No.2 of 2004 (11/05/2005) that the prosecution must disclose all material evidence in its possession for or against the accused (including witness statements) unless there is some strong public interest which would justify non-disclosure. See para.13.15 above.

[12] See Ipp, *op. cit.* p.68.

[13] But see, M. Freedman, *Lawyers' Ethics in an Adversary System* (Bobbs-Merrill, New York, 1975) and *Understanding Lawyers' Ethics* (Matthew Bender, New York, 1990).

[14] DTD 1089/02.

to save the family the trouble and expense of seeking to prove the tenor of a lost document. The Solicitors (Scotland) Discipline Tribunal held that the solicitor had submitted these applications to the court in the knowledge that they were untrue and dishonest and found him guilty of professional misconduct in that he had knowingly placed before the court information that was not simply misleading but false.

If the *Young* case was straightforward the *Bridgwood* case[15] was rather less so. Mr Bridgwood, a solicitor, found himself in a difficult situation when a longstanding client informed him that she had given the police a false name and address for herself, when arrested. Contrary to his advice, the client refused to disclose her true name to the authorities. Instead, she pled guilty under the false name, thereby avoiding her previous convictions, and Mr Bridgwood spoke in mitigation. He considered it was proper for him to do this, provided that he did not explicitly refer to her using her assumed name, or refer to her character. Unfortunately, the courts did not come to the same conclusion.[16] Mr Bridgwood was convicted for acting in a manner tending and intending to pervert the course of public justice, and was fined £2000 by the Solicitors Disciplinary Tribunal. It was not simply the use of the assumed name that mattered. In the UK a person can call themselves anything they like. Had the change of name been done legally, e.g. by deed poll or marriage, it could not have been a false name. It was the adopting of the assumed name in order to deceive the court over the issue of previous convictions that made it a breach of duty to the court. Similarly, an address is not a false one if it is not the client's principal place of residence, provided it is an address where the client can be contacted. As Burleigh observed:

> "A solicitor takes part in a positive deception of the court when he puts forward to the court himself, or lets his client put forward, information which the solicitor knows to be false, with the intent of misleading the court. The defence solicitor need not correct information given to the court by the prosecution or any other party which the solicitor knows will have the effect of allowing the court to make incorrect assumptions about the client or his case, provided the solicitor does not indicate in any way his agreement with the information."[17]

The English Law Society's criminal law committee considered the case and added that in this situation the following should apply.

1. The solicitor should seek to persuade the client to give the court the correct name and address. If the client refuses the solicitor should withdraw from acting.
2. Where the client gives the correct name but a false address or date of birth, the solicitor should also withdraw, since the false information is relevant to previous convictions or to bail.

---

[15] See D. Burleigh, *John Francis Bridgwood and the solicitors duty to client and court* 1989 LSG 26, 11.

[16] The issue is not a novelty since the Codes of Alberta and British Columbia expressly prohibit misleading the court as to the identity of one's client. See M. Proulx and D. Layton, *Ethics and Canadian Criminal Law* (Toronto, Irwin Law Inc, 2001), p.267.

[17] D. Burleigh, "John Francis Bridgwood and Solicitors, Duty to Client and Court" (1989) 26 LSG 11.

The committee did not deal with the situation of what the lawyer should do if, having withdrawn from acting the client informs the lawyer that they intend to persist in using the false identity and thus pervert the course of justice. The Canadian solution that this "future harm or crime" permits, but does not require the lawyer to breach confidentiality and disclose the deceit[18] may apply in Scotland and England as a public interest exception to the confidence, but would not be effective against an action based on breach of legal professional privilege.

The Bridgwood case is interesting on a number of fronts, not least because of the guidance it might offer in cases of client perjury. It is, after all, a short step from saying that a lawyer who fails to take remedial action where a known falsehood has been put before the court by his or her client, is guilty of assisting in the positive deception of the court, to holding that the lawyer must also take remedial action when the client has given perjured testimony to that court.[19] Equally, while Bridgwood dealt with the situation where the client had misled the court *before* the lawyer became involved in the case, what would be the position if the false evidence had been led in court unwittingly by the lawyer, after he had become involved in the case, e.g. he had not known the client beforehand and therefore happily referred to the client using the false name in ignorance that it was not the client's real name. Clearly, such an innocent error cannot give rise to a conduct offence (unless the lawyer's conduct was negligent or reckless), nonetheless, once the lawyer becomes aware of the deception, it appears that the lawyer must take remedial action. It is unclear however, whether it would be enough to simply withdraw[20]—which might send a coded form of disclosure to the judge and prosecutor, though not a jury—or whether as one or two have argued, the lawyer must correct the error.[21]

The ambit of misleading evidence. In the chapter on standards[22] we noted **14.06.04** that the Scottish Solicitors Discipline Tribunal draws distinctions between (1) intentional and deliberate deceit or lying—which is clearly misconduct, (2) recklessly made statements which are false—which will generally be misconduct and (3) negligent statements which are neither reckless nor intentionally misleading—which will amount to unsatisfactory conduct at most. Similarly, the professional rules of the Faculty of Advocates[23] and the English Bar[24]

---

[18] See M. Proulx and D. Layton, *Ethics and Canadian Criminal Law*, p.269.

[19] On perjury see para.14.06.05ff below.

[20] This is the most common solution in English speaking ethical codes, see para.14.06.05.4 below. In practice this is the solution advised by the Professional Practice Department of the Law Society of Scotland.

[21] See e.g. Stuart-Smith L.J. in *Vernon v Bosley (No.2)* [1999] Q.B. 18; M. Proulx and D. Layton, *Ethics and Canadian Criminal Law*, p.270. Although *Kelly v Vannet*, 1999 J.C. 109 established that the crime/fraud exception to legal professional privilege applied where a Scottish solicitor was unaware that his services were being used to commit a crime, it must be doubtful that a prosecutor could insist that the defence lawyer testify as to his client's confession of perjury, on the grounds that the confession was not privileged because of the crime/ fraud exception. In such a case the confession could hardly be described as a communication in furtherance of a criminal purpose since it occurs after the crime has been committed. See para.6.23 above.

[22] See Ch.1 above.

[23] Guide to Professional Conduct, para.8.1.2.

[24] Code of Conduct, para.302.

refer to the duty not to mislead the court knowingly or recklessly. Commentators on the adversarial system in the anglo-american world have tended, however, to focus on other distinctions when discussing misleading evidence. The first, and basic distinction, as we saw in para.14.06.02 is between putting forward misleading evidence (which is banned) and choosing not to disclose relevant evidence (which is generally permitted). This distinction overlaps extensively with that between actively misleading the court and passively standing by and letting the court fall into error by reason of its failure to ascertain facts which are in the lawyer's knowledge.[25] The latter is acceptable, the former is not. Unfortunately, this is an area of almost infinite shades of grey, as the following excursus on the relevant cases indicates.[26]

Most expositions of the area start with *Tombling v Universal Bulb Co. Ltd*,[27] where a witness appeared in court wearing ordinary clothes, to give evidence at a trial. His lawyer in examining the witness on the stand, elicited the latter's home address, the fact that he had previously been a prison governor, and the nature of his subsequent employment without revealing that the witness was currently imprisoned for a motoring offence. The defence's attempt to persuade the Court of Appeal that this behaviour justified a re-trial failed because the majority of the court took the view (1) that counsel had not set out with the deliberate intention to mislead the court by failing to indicate that witness was currently in prison and (2) because the witness's motoring offence was not relevant to his credibility with respect to a completely unrelated matter. In commenting on whether or not the counsel should have informed the court that his client was appearing from prison, Denning L.J. said:

> "The duty of counsel to his client . . . is to make every honest endeavour to succeed. He must not of course, knowingly mislead the court, either on the facts or on the law, but, short of that he may put such matters in evidence or omit such others as in his discretion he thinks will be most to the advantage of his client . . . The reason is because he is not the judge of the credibility of the witnesses or of the validity of the arguments. He is only the advocate employed by the client to speak for him and present his case, and he must do it to the best of his ability, without making himself the judge of its correctness, but only of its honesty."[28]

A similar issue arises where a lawyer is aware that his client has previous convictions but the judge and the prosecutor are not. The lawyer has no obligation to disclose the convictions and indeed owes a duty of confidentiality to the client not to refer to them. He may therefore stand by silent while

---

[25] See Lord Diplock in *Saif Ali v Sydney Mitchell & Co.* [1980] A.C. 198 at 220.

[26] There are few Scottish cases in this area. However, it is thought that Scottish courts would be likely to adhere to the general lines laid down in the English cases which follow.

[27] (1951) 2 TLR 289.

[28] *ibid.* as *per* Denning L.J. at p.297. Singleton L.J. in dissenting, and Thorpe L.J. in the later case of *Vernon v Bosley (No.2)* [1999] Q.B. 18 at pp.62–63 argued that in leading evidence as to the accused's home address rather than indicating that he was in prison his counsel crossed the line between active and passive misleading.

the court assumes that client is a first offender.[29] However, the lawyer may not describe the client as a first offender, since that would be to actively mislead the court. What if the court asks the lawyer to confirm the client's record? This puts the lawyer into a conflict between the duty of candour and the duty of confidentiality to the client. The lawyer may neither confirm the accuracy of the incorrect record nor breach the client's confidence. An astute lawyer will consult with his or her client as soon as the error is detected and asked for permission to reveal the true position if the lawyer is questioned by the court on the matter, since this is likely to reflect credit on the accused. One Scottish writer has suggested that the lawyer may assert that there are no convictions libelled against the client.[30] It must be doubtful if this would not be seen as actively misleading the court if it was volunteered as an unsolicited submission. But what if it was in response to an enquiry from the court? Given the position of conflict that the judge's question has put the lawyer in, the response might be construed as passively misleading. However, many sheriffs would probably consider it to be actively misleading. The best course of action is to try to avoid the question if one can.

A similar issue arose in an Australian case of *Rumpf*.[31] The lawyer had invited the court to make a reparation order to compensate the victim, against his client, in the hope of attracting a lesser sentence. However, he did not mention that his client was bankrupt and that therefore the order would have been without practical effect. The Full Court of Victoria had little difficulty in holding that by volunteering the proposal of reparation, but not mentioning the bankruptcy, the lawyer had actively misled the court.

The case of *Meek v Fleming*,[32] is often contrasted with the *Tombling* case. Here an action was brought by a press photographer against a Chief Inspector, claiming damages for alleged assault and wrongful imprisonment by him. By the time of the trial the Chief Inspector had been demoted to the rank of station sergeant for being party to a deception in a court of law. His counsel after long and careful reflection decided that he could ethically suppress the evidence of his client's demotion and its cause. Accordingly neither fact was put to the court and indeed steps were taken to keep it from the court in that the defendant appeared in court out of uniform and was repeatedly referred to as "Mr" rather than by rank. The judge and the counsel for the other side frequently referred to the defendant as "Chief Inspector"—with the latter even at the start of the cross-examination confirming with the defendant that he was a Chief Inspector—without correction by the counsel for the defendant. It was held that a new trial should take place as this matter went directly to the credibility of the witness, whose evidence was in conflict with that of the plaintiff. The court took the view that there had been a deliberate deceit by counsel on a matter material to the case with the intent of giving the

---

[29] This remains the prevailing view amongst codes and commentators in the common law world, e.g. the English *Guide to the Professional Conduct of Solicitors* Annex 21F at 405–406, Stuart-Smith L.J. in *Vernon v Bosley (No.2)* [1999] Q.B. 18 and M. Proulx and D. Layton, *Ethics and Canadian Criminal Law*, p.271. However, there are dissenting voices who argue that the lawyer should correct the court's error, feeling that greater candour is now required of today's lawyers. See the discussion of this issue in M. Blake and A. Ashworth, "Ethics and the Criminal Defence Lawyer" 7 (2004) *Legal Ethics* 167 at p.179.

[30] Ross Harper, *op. cit.* (1985).

[31] [1988] VR 466.

[32] [1961] 2 Q.B. 366.

impression that the defendant was still a Chief Inspector. In their view counsel had wrongfully subordinated his duty to the court to his duty to his client.

The distinction between the *Meek* and the *Tombling* cases is that in the former, positive action was taken to deliberately deceive the court, in order to enhance the case of the defendant and concerned matters directly relevant to the case. In the latter case, however, the deception was inadvertent and the information was not thought relevant to the case and was therefore simply omitted. Put another way, in *Meek* the lawyer actively sought to deceive the court on a matter that no reasonable lawyer could consider as immaterial to the case, whereas in *Tombling*, counsel merely omitted to lay certain facts before the court which he considered as non material to the case.

The two contrasting cases offer guidance for other situations. Take the case where a witness or a party is attending in court from prison. Does the lawyer have to reveal this? Sometimes it will be obvious (because of the handcuffs and the attendant policemen) that this is the situation, in which case there is no duty to say anything. It may, nonetheless be good tactics to do so, e.g. where the client appears in court in relation to another offence from the one for which he was imprisoned. By failing to disclose this fact the lawyer may encourage the judge to feel that he or she is being misled and increase the chances that the client will receive a consecutive sentence. Such a course of action should be cleared with the client because of the duty to safeguard privileged and confidential information.[33] However, where it is not obvious that the witness or accused appears from prison, then the lawyer should consider whether the nature of the offence to which the sentence relates is pertinent to the case in hand.

A case raising much the same issues involved a client in Scotland who appeared from custody at a bail hearing. His lawyer was aware, although the sheriff was not, that his client was doubly in custody, since he had been unsuccessful the previous week in obtaining bail in connection with an offence charged in another court. The accused gave his address as care of that of the lawyer's office, when in fact he was in prison. When the sheriff discovered this, he took the view that he had been deliberately deceived. The lawyer's defence was that he genuinely believed that he would be successful with a bail appeal for the earlier offence and that to disclose the prior offence would be to prejudice his client's chances of getting bail for the second offence, even although the offences were completely unrelated. The Law Society of Scotland, applying the *Meek* and *Tombling* cases, concluded that the lawyer had only passively misled the court, since the use of his office address had not been deliberately designed to unfairly advantage the client.

The distinction between actively and passively misleading the court also prompts us to consider what the position would be if the evidence as originally tendered to support the lawyer's case is truthful, but subsequently, because of a change in circumstances, it ceases to be an accurate statement of the position. Is the lawyer guilty of misleading the court if he or she fails to inform the court of the changed circumstances? This issue arose in *Vernon v Bosley (No.2)*.[34] In a somewhat unsatisfactory case, the three judges in the

---

[33] See e.g. J. Ross Harper, *A Practitioner's Guide to the Criminal Courts* (Law Society of Scotland, Edinburgh, 1985), pp.143–144.
[34] [1999] Q.B. 18.

Court of Appeal upheld *Meek* and *Tombling* but disagreed amongst themselves on the fundamentals. The facts concerned a plaintiff who had suffered
from nervous shock following the death of two of his children, before his
eyes, and succeeded in his claim for damages both in the lower court and the
Court of Appeal, having relied heavily on the testimony of his medical experts
to demonstrate the extent of his trauma and his poor prospects of a full
recovery. After seventy days of evidence the proceedings in the personal
injury case had been adjourned. Prior to final submissions being made to the
court in the personal injury case an action was heard in the Family Division
of the High Court, in which the same medical experts reached a more positive
conclusion as to his prognosis than they had in the personal injuries case, thus
enabling the plaintiff to argue that he was well enough to have a residence
order in relation to his remaining children. Counsel for the plaintiff became
aware of the new medical opinion after final submissions had been made in
the tort action, but before the judgement was handed down. He concluded that
he had no ethical obligation to reveal to the personal injury judge that his
client's medical experts had now formed a different conclusion as to his
prognosis, than they had when giving evidence before the judge. Counsel
considered that he was not actively misleading the Court, since the evidence
when originally tendered had been truthful, it was just that circumstances had
changed. Lord Justice Evans agreed with him, but was in the minority. Stuart-
Smith L.J., however, said that counsel had actively misled the court in a
manner akin to what had occurred in *Meek* since in his view counsel's silence
on the changed condition of the plaintiff misled the court as to a material fact
in the case. Curiously, he was prepared to accept that the plaintiff's counsel
did not deliberately intend to deceive the court. Stuart-Smith L.J. considered
that the counsel should therefore have withdrawn[35] from acting unless his
client was willing to reveal the new evidence to the court, although there was
no need for counsel to correct the "error". Thorpe L.J. agreed that the case
was like *Meek* but considered that counsel should have informed the other side
or the court if the client refused to agree to the evidence of his changed
condition being revealed.

The guidance to be derived from this case in Scotland is unclear. A close
reading of the judgements in the Court of Appeal suggests that the outcome
was partially influenced by the English law on discovery and by English
decision of *Re. L*[36] on litigation privilege in Family actions. Secondly, Evans
L.J. in dissent was at pains to argue that this was not a case of evidence being
fabricated, or false evidence having been given originally and not corrected,
or of a witness changing his or her story. Here circumstances had changed. In
the eyes of the plaintiff's counsel he was not actively misleading or deceiving
the court—he was simply not disclosing evidence that he was not required to
proffer to the court. It is difficult not to conclude that, absent a requirement
under the Scottish law of procedure to update the court on any change in the
pursuer's condition after the leading of the evidence and before final
arguments, to follow this case in Scotland would mark a change in the balance

---

[35] In one of the few jurisdictions to have explicitly addressed the point raised in *Vernon*, the
Code of Professional Conduct of the Law Society of Alberta Commentary 15.2 also requires the
counsel to withdraw if the client will not voluntarily disclose the change in circumstances—even
if the change takes place after the case has been judicially determined.

[36] [1997] A.C. 16.

of duties which comprise the adversarial system. Indeed Thorpe L.J. indicated as much when he rejected the dispassionate "role morality" argument of counsel for the plaintiff, advising him to pay more attention to his ordinary moral feelings, and added:

> "In general terms the balance between the advocate's duty to the client and the advocate's duty to the court must reflect evolutionary change within the civil justice system. If evolutionary shifts are necessary to match civil justice reforms they should in my judgement be towards strengthening the duty to the court. Differing practices and procedures in the family justice system, the criminal justice system, and the civil justice system must be reflected in different requirements in, for instance, a criminal trial and a Children Act hearing."

Ipp argues that *Vernon* is an instance of a "growing trend of courts to require cases to be determined in accordance with the objective 'truth' rather than on evidence adduced solely for reasons of perceived tactical advantage."[37] While this may indeed be the case, it is also arguable that what we are witnessing is a recognition that "zealous advocacy in the adversarial system" is more justifiable in criminal law cases or civil cases against the state than in family law or even other civil cases.[38] Thus in *ex parte* applications, which by definition are not adversarial, the lawyer's duty is to make full disclosure of all material facts known to him or her. This might also suggest that it is relevant that *Vernon* was not a criminal case and had family elements. Certainly, Ipp argues that courts in family disputes and disputes involving children impose a duty of frankness and disclosure, stemming from the public interest that overrides the usual rules of the adversarial system.

The acid test for this contextual ethics line of argument would be if there was to be a repetition of the facts of the *Spaulding v Zimmerman*,[39] but this time in Scotland. Here, a minor in the 1950s in Minnesota was injured in a road accident. None of the three doctors examining the teenager for the purposes of supporting his action detected that the accident had begun to produce a life threatening aneurysm in his chest. The neurologist for the defendants, however, noticed it and brought it to attention of the defence lawyer. The plaintiff's lawyer failed to seek discovery of the defendant's medical report as he could have done and the defendant's lawyer settled the case for considerably less than if the aneurysm had been detected. The parties then jointly sought the court's approval of the settlement, since the plaintiff was a minor, which was duly granted. Two years later, the minor had a medical check up for other reasons and the aneurysm was detected. A successful operation then followed. Unsurprisingly, the plaintiff sought to reduce the court's agreement to the settlement. The Supreme Court upheld this application on the basis of the plaintiff's minority and the emergence of "new" evidence, whilst affirming that there was no ethical or legal obligation on the defendant's lawyer to reveal their medical evidence, in the absence of

---

[37] See Ipp, "Lawyers Duties to the Court" 114 (1998) *Law Quarterly Review* 63 at p.69 and Ipp, "Reforms to the Adversarial Process in Civil Litigation" (1995) 69 A.L.J. 705 at pp.712–716.

[38] Support for this argument is contained in D. Luban, D. Rhode, and Ashworth and other post-modern thinkers.

[39] 263 Minn.346, 116 N.W. 2d 704.

a request for discovery from the plaintiff. In Scotland discovery would not be open to the pursuer, and had the injury occurred to an adult, no challenge could have been taken to the settlement or the conduct of the defending lawyer. Moreover, under our adversarial system there would be no obligation in terms of professional ethics on the defendants to disclose their medical evidence to the court or the other side. Nonetheless, if Ipp is correct our courts might equally be tempted to reduce the settlement, on the grounds of his argument that courts in family disputes and disputes involving children impose a duty of frankness and disclosure, stemming from the public interest, that overrides the usual rules of the adversarial system. Even if they did not, the case raises sharply the question of whether the lawyer for the defence should not have allowed his or her conscience as a moral person to override the duty of client confidentiality and disclosed the existence of the aneurysm at the very latest after the settlement had gone through.

Misleading evidence as perjury. A particular variant on the misleading **14.06.05** evidence question which has attracted widespread, and hotly contested, comment in English speaking countries outside the UK, is the issue of client perjury. As Monroe Friedman observed in 1975[40] the problem when perjury arises is that the "lawyer is required to know everything, to keep it in confidence, and to reveal it to the court." This stems from the triple duty of the litigator to diligently elucidate all the relevant facts, to keep such facts confidential and thirdly not to mislead the court. These conflicting duties are exacerbated in the area of criminal defence by the onus on the Crown to prove its case beyond reasonable doubt, the right to a minimally adequate defence,[41] the right to a fair trial,[42] and the right against self-incrimination. As M. Proulx and D. Layton, have observed[43]:

> "The question becomes, how can the profession's ethical standards best accommodate the competing principles of loyalty to the client and solicitude towards the truth-finding function of the criminal justice system?"

Since, as we have seen, even some of the post-modern critics accept the case for neutral partisanship in relation to criminal defence work, it is not difficult to see that when the duty to the client is at its strongest it will sit uneasily with the litigator's duties to the court. It is perhaps for this reason, that the ethical guidance in this area in English speaking jurisdictions is so often unclear or unsatisfactory.[44] Such is the complexity of the field that the lawyer's best course of action can be affected by whether the case is civil or criminal, whether the perjury or proposed perjury arises before, during or after the trial, and whether it involves a client or another witness.

---

[40] "Perjury: The Lawyer's Trilemma" 1 (1975) *Litigation* 26.
[41] Ineffective assistance of counsel (*Strickland v Washington* (1984) 466 US 668) and *Anderson v HMA*, 1996 S.L.T. 155.
[42] See Article 6.1 of the European Convention on Human Rights and *Anderson* at p.158.
[43] *Ethics and Canadian Criminal Law, op. cit.* at p.360.
[44] See *op. cit.* at pp.357–411, Ch.7.

In a difficult area, where there is almost no authority in Scotland and little more in the rest of the UK, there are only a few islands of safety where almost all English language commentators are agreed as to the best options, e.g. the importance of knowledge, the need to seek to dissuade the witness, and the need to take remedial action if persuasion fails.

14.06.05.01 Perjury: the importance of knowledge. As in other areas where the duties to the client and to the court collide to form the parameters of the adversarial system of truth finding, much depends on the state of knowledge of the lawyer. Mere suspicion or even a reasonable belief is not enough. The lawyer must have actual *knowledge*[45] that the version of events that the client proposes to testify to is false or sufficient evidence from the circumstances to reach "an irresistible conclusion of falsity from available information".[46] This may come from a confession from the client or from the latter changing his or her story. However, neither of these in themselves is sufficient to establish knowledge without further probing of the client's story to try to establish its truth or otherwise. The consensus of the commentators extends further. Although it is sometimes suggested the defence lawyers occasionally avoid eliciting from their clients what happened in the case, commentators generally agree that lawyers are not permitted to avoid acquiring knowledge of the client's proposed perjury by wilful blindness or failing to investigate the facts of the case properly. To do so would be to sacrifice the duties of competence and diligence to the client.[47] Equally, it is considered improper to interview an accused client in such a way as to assist the client to construct a version on events that will actually be perjured testimony.[48]

14.06.05.02 Perjury: Persuading the witness to tell the truth. If the lawyer has reached the conclusion that the client has decided to commit perjury or has already committed perjury, almost all of the authorities and commentators suggest that the lawyer must seek to persuade the client or witness not to commit perjury or to correct any perjured testimony that has been offered. Typically, the client/witness should be told that perjury is a crime, that if discovered by the trier of fact it will probably assist in the accused's conviction and if so, to a higher sentence. Next, the lawyer must explain to the client what the options facing him/her are.[49] Most commentators also agree that finally the client should be told that the lawyer may be required to take remedial action. However, there the consensus ends, for although it is probably improper for the lawyer to coerce the accused by threatening a remedial action that he/she has no intention of carrying out; there is little agreement as to what that remedial action might be. Many authorities permit or require withdrawal, but

---

[45] See e.g. The Faculty of Advocates' Guide—"An advocate may not be party to the giving of evidence which he knows to be perjured." Para.9.2.2.3 and ABA Model Rules (2002) 3.3(a)3 and Commentary [8].

[46] *Op. cit.* at p.370.

[47] See *Sankar v State of Trinidad and Tobago* [1995] 1 W.L.R. 194 where the Privy Council required counsel to "investigate the matter fully".

[48] See Blake and Ashworth, "Ethics and the Criminal Defence Lawyer" 7 (2004) *Legal Ethics* 167 at p.176.

[49] See *Sankar v State of Trinidad and Tobago*.

this can be problematic if the trial is part heard.[50] Further the authorities and commentators are sharply divided as to whether disclosure of the perjury to the court is ever permissible.[51]

Perjury: Opting to continue acting. If the client agrees not to commit **14.06.05.03** perjury then the lawyer should continue to act. However, what if the client gives no such undertaking or refuses to correct the perjured testimony? Some authorities consider that the lawyer can continue to act if:

(a) the lawyer does not *know*, but only has a reasonable belief that the client will commit or has committed perjury[52]; or

(b) the lawyer insists that the client does not take the witness stand[53]; or

(c) the client's testimony is restricted to the truthful elements[54]; or

(d) the client either makes an unsworn statement or provides the untruthful parts of the testimony in a narrative format to which the lawyer makes no subsequent reference in the trial[55]; or

(e) the perjury is already complete, the lawyer makes no subsequent reference to the false testimony.[56]

There is one other school of thought of which Monroe Freedman is the most celebrated adherent,[57] namely, that the lawyer having tried and failed to persuade the client to tell the truth, should continue to act as normal and use any testimony, perjured or otherwise in the case. This resolves the conflicts between the duties to the client and to the court, decisively in the former's favour. It is perhaps because it condones active misleading of the court and

---

[50] See para.14.06.05.04 below.

[51] See para.14.06.05.05 below. *Nix v Whiteside* 475 US 157 (1986) is particularly apposite here. There, Chief Justice Burger asserted that counsel's threat to withdraw and disclose the client's perjury to the court if he gave perjured testimony was not a breach of the client's constitutional right to testify on his own behalf. This obiter dictum although supported by a majority of the Supreme Court has attracted much critical comment in the USA and elsewhere. Ironically, the 2002 ABA Model Rules of Professional Conduct 3.3(a)(3) have moved much closer to Burger's position.

[52] See Faculty of Advocates Guide 9.2.2.3 and the ABA Model Rules *op. cit.* 3.3(a)(3). Indeed Commentary [9] of the Model Rules makes it clear that "because of the special protection historically provided criminal defendants" the lawyer cannot refuse to allow such a client to testify if he/she only reasonably believes the testimony to be false as opposed to knowing that it is false. This is the only instance in Model Rule 3.3 where the Rules distinguish between civil and criminal cases.

[53] In some jurisdictions e.g. Canada (see M. Proulx and D. Layton, *op. cit.* p.383) this is probably contrary to the client's constitutional rights to testify on his/her own behalf, although *Nix v Whiteside* did not settle the matter in the USA. It is not clear that art.6.1 of the European Convention enshrines such a right, however, the Privy Council in *Sankar v State of Trinidad and Tobago* (which was subsequently endorsed on the point in *Anderson v HMA*, 1996 S.L.T. 155 at p.163) appeared to accept that the accused's lawyer may not exclude the accused from testifying altogether.

[54] Model Rules 3.3(a)(3) *op. cit.* Commentary [6] and the *Third Restatement, op. cit.* para.120(i).

[55] *Sankar* permits the former approach, the Model Rules *op. cit.* 3.3(a)(3) commentary [7] the latter (if the local state's courts permit this). See also M. Proulx and D. Layton, *op. cit.* p.385.

[56] This approach has few supporters where the lawyers *knows* that perjury has been committed, although Ipp, *op. cit.* appears to indicate that it can be acceptable, at p.87.

[57] See e.g. Freedman, *Lawyers' Ethics in an Adversary System* (Bobbs-Merrill, New York, 1975) and *Understanding Lawyers' Ethics* (Matthew Bender, New York, 1990).

thus fundamentally tips the balance in the adversarial system away from "truth", that this viewpoint has little support in ethical codes or amongst commentators,[58] and we would not support it.

14.06.05.04 **Perjury: Opting to withdraw but not disclosing the perjury.** This approach is perhaps the most widely supported option where the client refuses to agree not to testify falsely or to reveal the completed falsehood to the court. It is supported in England,[59] Canada,[60] Australia[61] and New Zealand[62] and is likely to be followed in Scotland given the persuasive decision of the Privy Council in *Sankar v State of Trinidad and Tobago*. Unfortunately, if the withdrawal requires the permission of the court because the trial is ongoing it may be difficult to get that permission without in effect revealing that perjury has been or is likely to be committed, and thus breaching the duty of confidentiality and loyalty to the client. The use of the formula that the lawyer would be "forensically embarrassed" by continuing certainly reveals the score to the judge and the prosecution, though not necessarily to the jury (if there is one). It is much better for the lawyer to indicate that the relationship with the client has broken down irreparably.[63] Certainly, great care must be taken before withdrawing. Thus in *Tuckiar v The King*[64] counsel was faced with a client in mid trial who confessed to the crime. Counsel announced in open court that he was in the worst predicament of his life and prevented his client from taking the stand. The judge, perhaps irritated by counsel's breach of client privilege and lack of zealousness, commented on the accused's failure to give evidence. The High Court of Australia was not impressed by counsel's way of handling the dilemma he faced, however, they set aside the conviction nonetheless. In another murder trial, *Sankar v State of Trinidad and Tobago*[65] the accused once again informed his counsel in mid-trial of his guilt. Once again counsel told the client to remain silent and thereafter in closing argument made it clear that he was simply putting the prosecution to the test. The Privy Council indicated that in such a situation it was the duty of defence counsel to investigate the matter fully and advise the accused as to his options, if necessary seeking an adjournment for the purpose. It was not appropriate for counsel forthwith to abandon the positive defence originally proposed (e.g. self-defence, provocation or accident) and to refuse to put the accused in the witness box or to allow him to make an unsworn statement from the dock. Instead counsel should have explained the importance of the accused's evidence for the positive defence, and that without it there was in practice no defence. If the accused had persisted in his desire to behave in a manner which was inconsistent with counsel's duty to the court, then counsel could have withdrawn after explaining the options available to the accused.

In Scotland the course of action proposed in *Sankar* poses particular difficulty where the client waits until they are in the witness box before

---

[58] See M. Proulx and D. Layton, *op. cit.* p.388.
[59] See e.g. *Sankar*, English Law Society Guide 1999; Written Standards of the Bar para.12.
[60] See M. Proulx and D. Layton, *op. cit.* pp.362–363.
[61] See Dal Pont, *op. cit.* p.459 and Ross, *Ethics in Law* (3rd edn, Butterworths, Sydney, 1998) pp.431–432.
[62] See Dal Pont, *op. cit.* p.460.
[63] As argued by M. Proulx and D. Layton, *op. cit.* p.379.
[64] (1934) 52 C.L.R. 335.
[65] [1995] 1 W.L.R. 194.

launching into an account of events that is completely inconsistent with the story that he/she has consistently told their lawyer in earlier stages. In the case of solicitor-advocates, under the Solicitors (Scotland) Rules of Conduct for Solicitor Advocates 2002, r.7(4) a solicitor advocate may not be a party to the giving of evidence which he knows to be perjured evidence, or to any other course that would enable a case to be put forward on behalf of a client which the client has informed him is unfounded in fact. Does standing by while your client appears to be perjuring himself/ herself, breach r.7(4)? It is tempting to follow the suggestion in *Sankar* and seek an adjournment in which to have a free and frank discussion with your client. However, under r.7(10) of the Code of Conduct a solicitor-advocate may not, except with consent of his opponent and of the court, communicate with any witness, including his client, once that witness has begun to give evidence until that evidence is concluded. Reconciling this with r.7(4) is not easy. Assuming that you find your client's change of heart unpersuasive and that your client does not wish to change his plea, you can either advise your client that you intend to withdraw, or advise your client that your representation will be limited to questioning whether the prosecution has proved their case. Finally, to complicate matters the Law Society considers that r.7(10) does not apply to ordinary solicitors. Unfortunately, not all the judiciary agrees with them on this point.

Perjury: opting to withdraw but also disclosing the perjury. Although **14.06.05.05** withdrawal without disclosure of the perjury to the court has a wide measure of support, some critics are unconvinced since it merely warns the accused to be less honest with his or her next lawyer. Perhaps for this reason, there has also been a school of thought which favours the opposite of the Freedman argument by ultimately placing the duty of candour before the duty of loyalty and confidentiality. Few commentators have endorsed the lawyer withdrawing and disclosing the proposed perjury *before* it has been committed.[66] However, the threat to do so if the accused persisted with his intention to commit perjury was upheld by the majority of the Supreme Court in the controversial decision in *Nix v Whiteside*.[67] Certainly, the writers have been more willing to advocate the disclosure of a completed client perjury,[68] although relatively few Codes of Conduct clearly support this. One that does, in a considerably stronger form than its earlier version, is the 2002 ABA Model Rules 3.3(a)(3). After more than 40 years of debate amongst American jurists the new Model Rules have come down decisively in favour of disclosure if a perjury has been committed,

---

[66] See, however, M. Proulx and D. Layton, *op. cit.* pp.390ff who consider that the "future-harm" exception to the privilege in Canada would permit, though not require, lawyers in that jurisdiction to disclose future crimes such as the proposed perjury of their clients.

[67] 475 US 175 (1986).

[68] See M. Proulx and D. Layton, *op. cit.* p.401 and the *Third Restatement, op. cit.* para.120 (h) which argues strongly for disclosure in such circumstances. Although *Kelly v Vannet*, 1999 J.C. 109 established that the crime/fraud exception to legal professional privilege applied where a Scottish solicitor was unaware that his services were being used to commit a crime, it must be doubtful that a prosecutor could insist that the defence lawyer testify as to his client's confession of perjury, on the grounds that the confession was not privileged because of the crime/ fraud exception. In such a case the confession could hardly be described as a communication in furtherance of a criminal purpose since it occurs after the crime has been committed. See para.6.23 above.

the client will not correct it and other measures e.g. withdrawal will not cure the perjury.[69] This is a significant shift towards concluding that in the area of perjury, even in criminal cases, ultimately the ABA favoured the duty not to deceive the court or to subvert the truth-finding process[70] over the duties of loyalty and confidentiality to the client.

14.07 A general duty not to interfere with the administration of justice

Ipp's final set of duties to the court relate to the dangers of excessive zeal by a lawyer for his or her client and the need not to overstep the mark.[71] The spectrum of temptation for lawyers ranges from clear cut, criminal interferences with the course of justice such as perjury, tampering with witnesses and forgery to situations where an excess of zeal will constitute a conduct offence at worst such as the permitted limits to defending the guilty, discrediting truthful witnesses, demeaning or denigrating witnesses, taking advantage of obvious mistakes, the lawyer taking the witness stand and finally, acting in a conflict of interest.

14.07.01 Perjury. Perjury is a criminal offence and for a lawyer to encourage a client or witness to commit perjury would not only be criminal act in itself[72] but also a breach of the lawyer's duty to the court, which would not be covered by legal professional privilege. However, there can sometimes be a fine line between refreshing a witness's memory and assisting with perjury.[73]

14.07.02 Tampering with witnesses. It is a breach of the lawyer's duty to the court to put witnesses under pressure to adjust their evidence in particular directions, just as it is impermissible to encourage them to give evidence which the witness does not believe to be true,[74] or to suggest to them that they be forgetful or evasive.[75] While, at least in the USA and England it is permissible to take witnesses through their evidence to refresh their memory the lawyer has to take care that this does not become a process in which witnesses are coached as to the answers to give to possible questions. Equally, while it is acceptable to tell a witness that that you do not propose to call on them to testify, to encourage them to go on a long holiday or in other ways to make it difficult for the opposing side to trace them is to interfere with the course of justice as well as a breach of duty to the court.[76]

---

[69] Model Rules, *op. cit.* 3.3(a)(3) Commentaries [10] and [11].

[70] This argument is ultimately circular since it is the balance between the duties to the court and the duties to the client which delineates the ambit of the truth-finding process in the adversarial system. In other words truth in adversarial system is the product of playing the litigation game according to certain rules—rules which reflect the balance between the lawyer's duties to the client and the court.

[71] *ibid.* pp.87ff.

[72] Namely, Subornation of perjury. See para.47.20 Gordon, *Criminal Law* (3rd edn) W. Green Vol.II.

[73] Ipp, *op. cit.* p.91.

[74] See e.g. Faculty of Advocates Guide, *op. cit.* 9.2.4.4. and Rules of Conduct for Solicitor Advocates, *op. cit.* 7(9).

[75] See generally Dal Pont, *op. cit.* p.462.

[76] See generally, Wolfram, *op. cit.* p.646 and also art.8 of the Code of Conduct for Scottish Solicitors 2002.

Forgery or falsified documentation.[77] It goes without saying that lawyers **14.07.03**
who present false or altered documentation to the court are at risk of criminal
conviction or a finding of misconduct. Thus a solicitor who repeatedly signed
executions of service on summonses although he knew or should have known
that he had not signed the citations on the relevant service copy summonses
was found guilty of misconduct.[78] Again an English solicitor who deliberately
forged his colleague's signature on a witness statement for her own Industrial
Tribunal case received a six month jail sentence for forgery.[79] Even if no one
is harmed by the process it may be misconduct. Thus a Scottish solicitor who
altered and lodged in court a Joint Minute without the knowledge or consent
of the party on whose behalf the Joint Minute had already been signed, was
found guilty of misconduct by the Tribunal. Although the alteration had not
affected the other party's interest, the Tribunal held that the unauthorised
alteration was in breach of the implied understanding from the other party that
the document would not be altered and thus constituted a breach of trust.[80]
Similarly, in a case in 2003[81] the solicitor in question was found guilty of
professional misconduct for notarising documents outwith the presence of the
deponing witness, signing dockets which he knew to be false in respect of the
date and whether the witness was present or not and his tendering of these
documents as evidence in the sheriff court.

The limits to defending the guilty. Occasionally, through an accused's **14.07.04**
confession or otherwise the lawyer for the accused comes to appreciate that
the client is guilty of the offence with which he or she has been charged. This
does not require the lawyer to withdraw from acting or to insist that the client
enters or changes his/her plea to guilty. However, the lawyer's knowledge
coupled with the duty not to mislead the court restricts the scope of the
defence that he or she may run since in the new situation the balance to be
drawn between the lawyer's duties to his or her client[82] and the duties to the
court and the justice system on the other, is subtlety altered. (As such, as was
noted in para.14.01, it reflects that in this situation a slightly different
conception of the role of the advocate in the adversarial system and the scope
for manoeuvre by the lawyer prevails.)

As in the case of perjury, mere reasonable suspicion or belief that the client
is actually guilty will not suffice to restrict the lawyer's scope for action. Nor
is the fact of a confession from the accused sufficient since he or she may be
confused, deluded, exhausted or even trying to shield another person. Where,
however, the lawyer reasonably comes to an "irresistible knowledge"[83] of a
client's guilt based on a thorough investigation of the case then the restriction
on the scope of the defence will apply. Again, as with perjury, commentators
are largely agreed that for lawyers to avoid acquiring knowledge of the
client's guilt by wilful blindness or failing to investigate the facts of the case

---

[77] See also para.14.06.03 above.
[78] DTD 203/61.
[79] The Times, July 17, 1998.
[80] Discipline Tribunal Annual report 2000/2001.
[81] DTD 3/12/2003 (McAnulty).
[82] i.e. to pursue his or her client's interests to the best of the lawyer's ability and not to breach
the duty of confidentiality to the client.
[83] See M. Proulx and D. Layton, *op. cit.*

properly, is to sacrifice the duties of competence and diligence to the client.[84] This is not, however, to suggest that it is part of the lawyer's role set out to form an opinion as to whether his or her client is actually guilty—that would be to usurp the role of the judge and jury. Thus the celebrated Scots defence lawyer, Joseph Beltrami, observed on the matter[85]:

> "When solicitors see a client for the first time they do not—at least, I do not—ask him whether or not he is guilty of the charge. The matter is put this way: How will you be pleading to the charge—Guilty or Not Guilty? If a client says 'Guilty', then steps are taken to act on this instruction. If he replies 'Not Guilty', then the preparation for the defence begins. If, in the course of further dealings with the client, he advises me that he *is* guilty of the charge, then I can take one of two courses. I can send him to a solicitor outside my firm. Or I can continue to defend him—on the clear understanding that, whereas I can put the Crown to the test with regard to proof beyond reasonable doubt, I cannot lead a substantive defence on his part."

Nonetheless, there will be occasions where the client's admission or diligent investigation of the case leaves the lawyer with "irresistible knowledge" of the client's guilt. In these situations the lawyer may not conduct the defence on a basis that is inconsistent with the knowledge, for example, by suggesting to a witness that his or her client is innocent or was elsewhere or that another person committed the crime.[86] Although the lawyer is prevented from running an affirmative defence he or she can and indeed must put the strength of the prosecution's case to the test. This might include[87]:

1) challenging the jurisdiction of the court;
2) challenging the competency or relevancy of the indictment or complaint;
3) challenging the admissibility of evidence;
4) testing the prosecution's evidence in cross-examination—thus even a "truthful" witness can be questioned as to their eyesight or the lighting conditions at the time;
5) leading evidence to support a defence of insanity or self-defence;
6) leading evidence required for a successful plea in mitigation;
7) making submissions as to the sufficiency in law of the evidence to support a verdict of guilty.

14.07.05 The limits to discrediting truthful witnesses. From time to time, particularly where the client has confessed his or her guilt to the lawyer, the latter will be faced with a witness whose testimony the client affirms to be truthful or the lawyer's investigations suggest is truthful, e.g. correctly testifying that the accused was near the scene of the crime at the relevant time and date. Notwithstanding this, the lawyer may cross-examine the witness to test the

---

[84] See M. Proulx and D. Layton, *op. cit.*
[85] J. Beltrami, *The Defender*, (W&K Chambers, Edinburgh, 1980) at p.16.
[86] See e.g. Faculty Guide, *op. cit.*, 9.2.2.6; Rules for Solicitor Advocates, *op. cit.*, 7(12).
[87] See e.g. Faculty Guide, *op. cit.*, 9.2.2.7; Rules for Solicitor Advocates, *op. cit.*, 7(13). See also Blake and Ashworth, "Ethics and the Criminal Defence Lawyer" 7 (2004) *Legal Ethics* 167 at pp.172–174.

witnesses' eyesight, accuracy in estimating distances or height, ability to recall details or to ascertain the lighting conditions. This may not be done in such a way as to suggest an affirmative defence or that the accused was elsewhere or innocent. Indeed, the more vigorous and intensive the cross-examination the more it will appear like an affirmative defence. There are also other difficult areas. Is it legitimate to try to establish in cross-examination that the truthful witness has an animus against the accused, when to do so is not to test the accuracy of the witness's recall or eyesight but rather to suggest that the witness is lying and that the accused is innocent? Similarly, is it permissible to attack the character of the truthful witness? The better answer seems to be in the negative, particularly if it arises in a civil case,[88] but also in criminal defence cases, since both lines of attack are designed to suggest that the witness is lying rather than simply mistaken. It seems then, that when dealing with a truthful witness, it is permissible to seek to establish whether the truthful testimony is more than mere happenstance, but not to go further and to suggest that the witness is lying.[89]

The limits to demeaning or denigrating witnesses and others in court. 14.07.06
Neither an advocate nor a solicitor advocate may suggest to a witness who is testifying that they have been guilty of a crime, fraud or other illegal or improper conduct unless the lawyer has reasonably concluded that there is evidence which could, if necessary, be led in support of the suggestion.[90] It is assumed that this holds true for solicitors also. Harassment of witnesses can distort the truth-finding process as well as amounting to abuse of power. Lawyers who take advantage of their position in examining or cross-examining witnesses to demean, bully, or insult them, risk bringing our system of justice into disrepute as well undermining its long term efficacy.[91] In the USA the federal judiciary has a positive obligation to protect witnesses against harassment. The same obligation should exist in Scotland. This is particularly true in the case of vulnerable witnesses and both in Scotland[92] and England[93] there have been efforts to afford greater protection to such witnesses in recent years. There is little public understanding for the perceived vilification which some victims of rape have been subjected to in the courts in the last twenty years. Apologists for zealous advocacy rightly point to the need for unpopular clients to be provided with effective defence advocacy if the ideals of the adversarial system and the right to a fair trial are to be upheld. However, victim support groups are also correct to claim that vulnerable victims and witnesses also have human rights. It may take a ruling from the European Court of Human Rights to determine how the conflict between these mutually inconsistent human rights should be resolved.[94] Quite apart from the

---

[88] See e.g. Wolfram, *op. cit.* p.651.

[89] For a contrary view see M. Proulx and D. Layton, *op. cit.* pp.66ff.

[90] Faculty Guide, *op. cit.*, 9.2.2.4; Rules for Solicitor Advocates, *op. cit.*, 7(5). See also the English Bar's Code of Conduct para.708(j).

[91] Quite apart from anything else, it difficult to see why honest witnesses who are doing their public duty should volunteer to be abused in this way. Advocates and solicitor advocates who make bullying or offensive remarks to witnesses risk sanction. See Faculty Guide, *op. cit.*, 9.3.2; Rules for Solicitor Advocates, *op. cit.*, 8(2).

[92] Vulnerable Witnesses (Scotland) Act 2004.

[93] See e.g. Blake and Ashworth, *op. cit.* p.185 and Boon and Levin, *op. cit.* p.364.

[94] *ibid.*

law and professional ethics it is perhaps also worth bearing in mind that it is usually unwise tactics to browbeat or demean an elderly, truthful witness or an vulnerable victim since the sympathy of the jury is likely to be with them.

14.07.07 Respecting the court. The duty to avoid excessive zeal for a client and the need not to overstep the mark, requires lawyers as officers of the court to honour any undertakings which they have given to the court.[95] Failure to do so is likely to be a conduct offence. Similarly, a lawyer who defies a clear ruling of the court may either be guilty of contempt of court or of a conduct offence. In *Blair-Wilson, Petnr*[96] a solicitor sought to play a tape-recording to a witness as part of his cross-examination. The sheriff, for reasons which remain unclear, refused to allow this—or at least at that stage of the proceedings. The solicitor's efforts to seek clarification of the sheriff's position lead the latter to regard the solicitor as being in defiance of a court order and therefore guilty of contempt of court. The High Court held that it was established law that if a judge makes a ruling in clear terms which the lawyer then refuses to comply with or obey, this can amount to contempt provided "an intention to challenge or affront the of the court or to defy its order" can be proved.[97] In this case the High Court concluded that the sheriff had not made a clear ruling and that the solicitor had not defied such a ruling and was therefore not guilty of contempt.

14.07.08 The limits to taking advantage of obvious mistakes. Ipp[98] is of the opinion that even in the adversarial system, lawyers, as officers of the court, should not take unfair advantage of obvious mistakes by the other side.[99] As far as mistakes in law are concerned, many English speaking jurisdictions take the view that the lawyer should not take advantage of errors of law (including those by the judge) any more than misleading the court on a point of law.[1] It would seem reasonable to conclude that since acting in this way breaches no duty to the client and conforms to the lawyer's duties to the court to assist with the proper administration of justice, that this should be followed in Scotland also.[2]

However, what about errors of fact? As we saw in relation to misleading the court on matters of fact, a distinction is normally drawn between commission—actively misleading and omission—passively misleading the court. Some have criticised this distinction, arguing that to win by failing to correct a judicial error or an obvious procedural error by the other side, even in a criminal case, is to jeopardise the duty of the lawyer to assist in the proper administration of justice.[3] However, there is good reason to believe that in

---

[95] See Ipp, *op. cit.* pp.86–87.

[96] 1997 S.L.T. 621.

[97] See *McMillan v Carmichael*, 1993 S.C.C.R. 945E and *Ferguson v Normand*, 1994 S.C.C.R. at 814.

[98] *Op. cit.* p.85.

[99] See *Ernst & Young v Butte Mining Plc* [1966] 1 W.L.R. 1605.

[1] See e.g. Blake and Ashworth, *op. cit.* pp.176–177.

[2] On the other hand the Guide to the Professional Conduct of Advocates, *op. cit.* 9.2.2.5 implies that counsel only has a duty to draw a judge's attention to any errors of law that he has inadvertently made where the judge has asked for assistance from counsel on legal matters (in the absence of the jury).

[3] E.g. Blake and Ashworth, *op. cit.* p.188–189 citing David Pannick, *Advocates* (OUP, Oxford, 1992).

Scotland this position does not prevail. When in the past the Crown miscalculated the days before initiating the trial due it being a leap year, and thus miscalculated when the 110th day had arrived, there was no suggestion from any in the profession that the lawyers for the accused had behaved in anything other than impeccable propriety in not revealing this error until after the 111th day was well under way. Joseph Beltrami describes one such case in which he was involved in *The Defender*[4]:

> "There were various editorials in the national Press about this dramatic turn of events, and some writers stated that it was the duty of the defence to advise the prosecution of such a matter, since it was merely a technicality. They went on to argue that the defence should not take advantage of such a situation. My answer to this proposition is that the two accused were acquitted because of the law prevailing in our country at the time. To have advised the prosecution on the Tuesday and so caused them to make application to the Court for an extension would have been betraying the interests of both clients."

The perils of the lawyer taking the witness stand. It is widely accepted that **14.07.09** it is undesirable for a solicitor or an advocate to appear as a witness in a case in which he or she is acting. Thus Webster[5] opines that a lawyer should not act in any proceedings in which he or she is likely to be called as a witness, except to give formal evidence, for example, as to the execution of a deed. Thornton,[6] likewise, indicates that counsel should reject a brief where it can be anticipated that he or she is likely to become a witness. Where a barrister cannot avoid giving evidence, then, he suggests, they are required to withdraw from acting. As so often, this is an area which has attracted considerable commentary in the USA[7] culminating in r.3.7 of the Model Rules 2002. The latter provides that:

> "*A lawyer shall not act as advocate at a trial in which the lawyer is likely to be a necessary witness unless:*
>
> 1) *the testimony relates to an uncontested issue;*
> 2) *the testimony relates to the nature and value of legal services rendered in the case; or*
> 3) *disqualification of the lawyer would work substantial hardship on the client.*"

The rationale for the limits imposed on lawyers acting as witnesses is twofold. First, because there is a potential for misleading the court and secondly because there is a potential for conflict between the lawyer and the client—especially if there is likely to be a conflict between the testimony of the lawyer and that of the client, remembering that the lawyer may be called to testify either by the client or by the other side. The first argument is that the fact finder, particularly if it is a jury, may be confused as to which capacity the

---

[4] J. Beltrami, *The Defender* (Chambers, Edinburgh, 1980) at p.219.
[5] *Op. cit.* para.3.07.
[6] A. Thornton, "Responsibility and Ethics of the English Bar" in R. Cranston (ed.) *Legal Ethics and Professional Responsibility* (The Clarendon Press, Oxford, 1995), p.82.
[7] See e.g. Wolfram, *op. cit.* pp.375–390 and the references contained therein.

lawyer is appearing in, when speaking from the witness box. This is a systemic protection which can be achieved either by the lawyer not testifying or by ceasing to act as advocate.[8]

14.07.10 Avoiding conflicts of interest. As the previous paragraph indicated, the duty to avoid acting in a conflict of interest is another aspect of the lawyer's duty to the court to safeguard the administration of justice. As Ipp argues, the duty to the court "arises from the court's concern that it should have the assistance of independent legal representation for the litigants".[9] While the court will disqualify lawyers where there is a threatened breach of fiduciary duty, it can also do so where continued representation would lead to a breach of duty to the court because the lawyer was no longer able to act with the objectivity and independence required by the court.[10] The Guide to the Professional Conduct of Advocates and the dictum of Lord President Inglis in *Batchelor v Pattison and Mackersey*[11] place a similar emphasis on the importance of the advocate being "entirely independent" in representing a client. Inglis, however, was less clear that a solicitor had the same degree of independence from the client given the contract of employment that exists between the solicitor and the client. It should be said, however, that judges will be understandably reluctant to disqualify a lawyer on this ground if it comes late in the day or it appears like a device for tactical advantage, and when disqualification will be likely to result in undue costs to an innocent party.

---

[8] Another way out of the difficulty is for the lawyer to take another person with him/her to meetings which the lawyer believes might be the subject of litigation, to avoid the lawyer having to be called as a witness.

[9] *Op. cit.* p.93.

[10] Ipp cites case law from New Zealand and Canada to support this proposition, *op. cit.* pp.94–95. See also Dal Pont, *op. cit.* p.446.

[11] (1876) 3 R. 914 at 918.

Chapter 15

FORMS AND REQUIREMENTS OF PRACTICE

Self Regulation 15.01

The legal profession is frequently described as self-regulating, but the reality for the solicitor profession in Scotland is that we are only as self-regulating as the UK Government and the Scottish Executive allow us to be. The profession has not been truly self-regulating since the 1930s, if not longer, and the Law Society of Scotland only exists by virtue of an act of Parliament. The original act was the Legal Aid and Solicitors Scotland Act 1949, and the current act is the Solicitors (Scotland) Act 1980 which has itself been amended many times in the succeeding years. As will be seen in the next chapter, further amendment is on the way in relation to complaints handling, and no doubt there will be more to follow that. The profession does retain power to make Practice Rules through the Council of the Society but they all have to be approved by the Lord President of the Court of Session (another lawyer, of course, though from a different branch of the legal profession). Some rules, notably those prohibiting multi-disciplinary practices and those in respect of solicitor advocates, must also be approved by Scottish Ministers, as successors to the Secretary of State for Scotland, after they have consulted with the Office of Fair Trading. Investment, Business, insolvency work and immigration work done by solicitors are all subject to regulation by other bodies whose reach extends beyond the legal profession, and in recent years solicitors have also been subject to new legislation such as the Proceeds of Crime Act 2002 and subordinate Money Laundering Regulations 2003; the Data Protection Act 1998; the Competition Act 1998; and the Property Misdescriptions Act 1991. Solicitors of earlier generations would find the landscape unrecognisable. The regulatory "bargain" of yesteryear between the profession and the State has been "re-negotiated".[1] In place of self-regulation we now have co-regulation (albeit in a somewhat haphazard and ineffective guise). However, some basics remain relatively untouched, notably the requirements for practising as a solicitor in Scotland which are laid down by s.4 of the Solicitors (Scotland) Act 1980. They are: admission as a solicitor; being on the Roll of Solicitors; and having a current practising certificate. As the Discipline Tribunal has observed these provisions are for the protection of both the public and the profession.[2]

---

[1] See e.g. A. Paterson, "Professionalism and the Legal Services Market" 3 (1996) *International Journal of Legal Studies* 137, A. Paterson, "Self-Regulation and the Future of the Profession" in Hayton (ed.) *Laws Future* (Hart Publishing, Oxford, 2000) and R. Dingwall and P. Fenn, "A respectable profession"? "Sociological and economic perspectives on the regulation of professional services" (1987) 7 *International Review of Law and Economics* 51.

[2] 1993 J.L.S.S. 242—Feeley.

15.02 Admission

15.02.01 The Law Degree. Admission as a solicitor in Scotland is governed by the
Solicitors (Scotland) Act 1980[3] and by regulations passed by the Council of
the Law Society of Scotland, with the concurrence of the Lord President.[4] The
vast majority of newly admitted solicitors possess an LLB Degree from one
of five Scottish universities: Aberdeen, Dundee, Edinburgh, Glasgow and
Strathclyde, which have traditionally offered the LLB for many years. In very
recent years however, five other universities have been accredited by the
society to provide a degree in law in terms of reg.5(a)[5] and some new
solicitors will join the profession from them starting in 2007. The LLB is now
the normal accepted starting point for entering the legal profession in
Scotland. To obtain exemption from the Society's own professional examinations, the degree should contain passes in subjects prescribed by the Council
from time to time. Currently these are: public law and the legal system; Scots
private law; Scots criminal law; Scots commercial; conveyancing; taxation;
and European Community law. However the council, following a review of
the LLB by the Joint Standing Committee on legal education in 2001, has
accepted that passes in subjects equivalent or corresponding to the Society's
examinations will be acceptable.

15.02.02 Pre-Diploma Training Contract. As an alternative to a Law Degree before
taking the Diploma, it is possible to undertake pre-Diploma training for which
a candidate must find full time employment as a pre-Diploma trainee with a
qualified solicitor practising in Scotland.[6] A pre-Diploma training contract
lasts for three years, during which time the trainee must receive training in the
two prescribed areas of conveyancing and litigation, and one of either trusts
and executries or the legal work of a public authority. To be eligible to enter
into a pre-Diploma Training Contract an applicant must have attained certain
educational standards at either SCE Higher Grade or GCE A-Level, although
these qualifications may be relaxed for applicants over 23 years of age with
existing experience of legal work and evidence of some academic attainment.
Certain other prospective entrants such as chartered accountants, commis-
sioned officers in the armed forces, and graduates in a discipline other than
law may also enter pre-diploma training.

15.02.03 Diploma. After either graduating with a degree in law or having completed
the pre-Diploma Training Contract and obtained passes in the Society's
examinations (although a pass in European Community Law can be obtained
during post-Diploma training) would-be entrants are eligible—and are
required unless granted an exemption under reg.28—to undertake the
Diploma in Legal Practice.[7] This is currently available from Aberdeen,
Dundee, Edinburgh and Robert Gordon Universities as well as the Glasgow
Graduate School of Law. The Diploma focuses on the practical knowledge
and skills necessary for the working life of a solicitor including compulsory

---

[3] s.6.
[4] Admission as Solicitor (Scotland) Regulations 2001.
[5] As a result it seems that there are now over 1,000 students a year embarking on LLB degrees
in Scotland.
[6] reg.10.
[7] reg.5(2)(c).

courses in conveyancing, civil court practice, criminal court practice, private client work, financial services and related skills, accountancy, professional ethics, and a choice of either company and commercial or public administration. The Diploma course lasts seven months and much of the teaching is carried out by part-time tutors who are practising solicitors.

Traineeship. After obtaining the Diploma all prospective solicitors are **15.02.04** required to serve a two-year post-Diploma Training Contract with a practising solicitor in Scotland who may be in private practice, the Crown Office, local authority or certain public bodies.[8] There is no requirement to cover all areas of law during the traineeship and much will depend on the type of work which the firm itself undertakes. The Society recommends certain salaries for each of the two years, although these are not obligatory. In recent years, competition among the larger firms has led them to offer more than the recommended rate but some trainees may still be paid less than that rate. It is a matter for agreement between the employer and the trainee.

During the traineeship, all trainees must complete log books which are used by both the training firm and the Society to monitor progress and to address any problems arising. Trainees are required to attend a professional competence course (PCC) during their traineeship. This may be offered in-house by their firm or by universities or other external providers. In the case of external providers the PCC will be a two-week block release, usually taken at the end of the first year of training. The core of the PCC emphasises skills training and generic issues such as practical ethics, but there is provision for specialist electives.

Test of Professional Competence. The 2001 Regulations anticipate a test of **15.02.05** profession competence to be administered by the Society.[9] However, a pilot exercise suggested that it would be very difficult to introduce an examination which would be fair to all trainees. Accordingly, the Test currently consists of the satisfactory completion of the log books. Before obtaining a final discharge, the training firm will also be asked to certify to the Society that the trainee is a fit and proper person to become a solicitor.

Admission as a Solicitor. It is possible, subject to satisfactory progress, for **15.02.06** trainees who have completed the first year of training to seek admission as a solicitor holding a restricted practising certificate.[10] The main purpose of this is to enable the trainee to gain valuable experience of appearing in court, although appearance in court is not compulsory. Before the trainee can seek a full practising certificate, the Test of Professional Competence must be passed and the training contract must be discharged together with the certificate of fitness from the training firm mentioned above. If the trainee fails the test, he cannot practice as a solicitor after the end of the Traineeship.[11]

---

[8] reg.7. It is possible to spend part of the traineeship on secondment outside Scotland or as a "stage" in Brussels.

[9] reg.18.

[10] regs 34–36.

[11] Solicitors (Scotland) (Restriction on Practice) Rules 2001, r.7.

15.03 Qualification from outwith Scotland

15.03.01 England, Wales and Northern Ireland. Those who have already been admitted as solicitors in England and Wales or Northern Ireland may re-qualify in Scotland without obtaining a degree in Scots law, undertaking the Diploma or going through a traineeship. They are required to pass examinations in conveyancing with trusts and succession; Scots criminal law; and civil and criminal evidence and procedure. These examinations are known as the intra-UK transfer test. For those who qualified in England and Wales or Northern Ireland after January 1, 1992 an additional exam on European Community law and Institutions must also be passed. In addition, a certificate of good standing from the Law Society (for England and Wales) or the Law Society of Northern Ireland must be produced certifying that the applicant was admitted by that Society on a particular date; his/her name continues to appear on the Roll of Solicitors; and the applicant has not been struck off or suspended. An entrance fee (currently £250) is also payable.

15.03.02 Other States of the European Union. Lawyers from other member states of the European Union who wish to be admitted as solicitors in Scotland may also bypass a degree in Scots law, the Diploma and a traineeship, but require to pass an aptitude test comprising four examinations: the law of property, including trusts and succession, in family law; the Scottish legal system including evidence and civil and criminal procedure; European Community law and institutions; and professional conduct and the Accounts Rules. They also require to produce a certificate of good standing from their home Bar Association and to pay an admission fee. From 2001, lawyers from other member states of the European Union may also register with The Law Society of Scotland in terms of reg.15 of the European Communities (Lawyers Practice) (Scotland) Regulations 2000, which came into being following the Establishment Directive of the European Union. A registered European lawyer may practice in Scotland using his home professional title, but will be required to obtain a registration certificate from the Society each year. After three years continuous practice as a registered European lawyer, he or she is entitled to practice as a Scottish solicitor, but will be subject to the regulatory powers of the Society, including the requirement to have a practising certificate.[12]

15.03.03 Elsewhere. Qualified lawyers from any other jurisdiction are required to obtain a degree in Scots Law or serve under a pre-Diploma training contract then undertake the Diploma and traineeship as described above.

15.04 The Roll

The Roll of Solicitors is kept by the Council of the Law Society of Scotland and consists of the names of all solicitors who have been admitted[13] and who have paid to the Society the annual fee to remain on the roll.[14] This fee is reviewed from time to time, and at the time of writing it is £55.00.

---

[12] See also para.15.10 below.
[13] s.7.
[14] s.7.

Practising Certificates **15.05**

The Practising Certificate year is November 1 to October 31.[15] Any solicitor **15.05.01**
whose name is on the roll may apply for a practising certificate, although the
Council has discretion in certain circumstances.[16] These circumstances are:
the solicitor has not held a practising certificate for more than 12 months; has
not paid a fine or expenses imposed by the discipline tribunal; a period of
suspension has expired; the solicitor has been sequestrated (whether he or she
has obtained a discharge or not); has delayed in responding to the Council in
relation to a complaint; or he has failed to implement a direction following a
finding of Inadequate Professional Service. In any of these circumstances six
weeks notice of the intention to apply for a practising certificate must be given
(although this can be waived by the council). The Council has discretion over
whether to grant or refuse the application or to issue a certificate subject to
conditions. If any of these circumstances do apply, the Council will frequently
impose a condition that the solicitor may only practise as an employed
solicitor for a period of time and may not undertake legal aid in his or her own
name. If the solicitor is aggrieved at the Council's decision an appeal lies to
the Court of Session.[17] The Act specifically requires consultants to hold
practising certificates.[18]

If a solicitor becomes incapable by reason of mental disorder; is sequestrated **15.05.02**
or signs a trust deed for creditors; or a judicial factor is appointed to the
solicitor's estate, the solicitor's practising certificate is automatically suspended for the duration of such disability.[19] If the suspension arises from
sequestration, signing a trust deed or a judicial factor the solicitor may apply
to the council to have the suspension lifted which the Council may refuse or
grant subject to conditions.[20] Again a right of appeal lies to the court of
session from the Council's decision.[21]

In every case, before the Council can issue a practising certificate the solicitor **15.05.03**
requires to complete an application form containing a number of declara-
tions.[22] These relate to the guarantee fund (to which all solicitors who are
principals in private practice require to contribute); CPD the accounts rules;
professional indemnity insurance; and practising certificates held in other
jurisdictions. If the application form is not correctly completed and not
accompanied by the correct remittance together with evidence of Professional
Indemnity cover under the master policy (if required) the practising certificate
will not be issued until these matters are dealt with. This can cause problems
since practising without a practising certificate is a conduct offence.[23]

---

[15] s.17.
[16] s.15.
[17] s.16.
[18] s.21.
[19] s.18.
[20] s.19.
[21] s.19(8).
[22] Solicitors (Scotland) Practising Certificate Rules 1988.
[23] See para.1.21 above.

15.06 Continuing Professional Development

The professional regulation of the education and training of Scottish solicitors no longer ends with qualification. In keeping with most professions in the 21st century, the solicitors' branch of the profession is committed to the concept of lifelong learning. As a result, all new principals must attend a training course run by the Society, within 12 months of becoming a principal,[24] and the whole profession is now required to undertake 20 hours of continuing professional development a year.[25]

15.07 The Unauthorised Practice of Law

The scope of the lawyers professional monopoly in the United Kingdom is considerably smaller than in many other jurisdictions. In Scotland it is restricted to (1) drawing or preparing for gain[26] (a) any writ[27] relating to heritable or moveable property or (b) any writ relating to any action or proceedings in any court or (c) any papers on which to found or oppose an application for a grant of confirmation in favour of executors and (2) rights of audience in the Higher Courts.[28] It follows that, unlike many other jurisdictions including the United States, Australia, New Zealand[29] and most civilian countries, anyone can give legal advice in Scotland and be paid for it, provided they do not hold themselves out to be lawyers or legally qualified.[30] Perhaps for this reason there has been far less discussion of the unauthorised practice of law, for example, by accountants, than in jurisdictions such as the United States.[31]

15.08 Forms of Practice

Of the 10,000 (approximately) solicitors with practising certificates, about 2,000 practice in the public sector or in commerce and industry. The great majority however are in private practice as principals, consultants, associates or employees.

---

[24] Solicitors (Scotland) (Practice Management Course) Practice Rules 2004 r.4 contains certain limited exemptions and r.5 enables the Council to waive the application of the rules on cause shown.

[25] Solicitors (Scotland) (Continuing Professional Development) Regulations 1993. Five hours must be on management training. Again, the Council has power to waive the application of the regulations.

[26] Unqualified persons who draw up such documents for gain are guilty of an offence under s.32 Solicitors (Scotland) Act.

[27] Writs for these purposes exclude wills, powers of attorney, certain stock transfers and mandates. s.32(3).

[28] Excluding party litigants.

[29] See G. Dal Pont, *Lawyers' Professional Responsibility in Australia and New Zealand* (LBC Information Services, Sydney, 2001), p.5.

[30] It is an offence to pretend to be legally qualified if one is not—s.31 Solicitors (Scotland) Act 1980.

[31] See e.g. C. Wolfram, *Modern Legal Ethics* (West Publishing, 1986), pp.824–849. The limited scope for the unauthorised practice of law in the UK may mean that the Big 5 Accounting firms will feel less of an imperative in the UK to pursue multi-disciplinary partnerships rather than forming affiliated law firms.

Practising as a Principal. A solicitor may practice as a principal in more than **15.08.01**
one practice unit. Private practice as a principal can take one of three forms:
sole practitioners; partner in a firm; or member of an incorporated practice. In
Scotland there are no specific rules about the name a firm can take (unlike
England and Wales) but it should not be misleading or bring the profession
into disrepute or it would breach the advertising rules. As at the time of
writing there are approximately 1,250 practice units in Scotland of which
approximately 550 (44 per cent) are sole practitioners. Only about 70 are
incorporated practices. The others are all firms varying in size from 2 partners
to over 50 partners. The average practice unit has three partners, and although
the number of practising certificates has almost trebled in the last 30 years, the
number of principals in private practice has only gone up by 50 per cent.
Clearly partnership is coming later in a solicitor's career than was the case in
the 1970's, and many solicitors are choosing alternative ways to practise
law.

Before solicitors can set up their own practice they require to have been
employed as solicitors for a cumulative period of three years of which at least
the most recent year must be immediately beforehand.[32] An existing firm may
assume new partners who have not acquired three years experience provided
that at least one of the existing partners has already practised as a principal for
three years, but two or more solicitors wishing to set up a new firm each
require to have accumulated three years experience if they are to be partners.

All principals in private practice require to contribute to the Scottish
solicitors guarantee fund,[33] and require to be insured under the Master Policy
arranged by the Council of the Society with a consortium of insurance
companies.[34] The Master Policy currently provides minimum cover of £1.5
million for each and every claim unless the claims arise out of a single error
or course of conduct, in which case the total cover for all such claims is £1.5
million. The cover is reviewed from time to time. Professional indemnity
insurance is the single most expensive item which principals in private
practice require to meet to comply with the 1980 Act and the Society's
Practice Rules. The annual premium comprises a number of different
components of which the most costly is the per partner element, the others
being a per practice unit element and an additional premium if the ratio of staff
to partners is more than 4 to 1.

If a claim is successful the firm will be required to meet a self-insured
amount or excess which currently amounts to £3,000 per partner. This can be
doubled in particular circumstances such as missing a limitation period (e.g.
a triennium); a breach of the Conflict of Interest rules; or the dishonesty of a
partner or member of staff. For some reason the self insured amount is capped
at 15 partners (£45,000 or £90,000 as the case may be) irrespective of how
many more partners there may be. If the claim (including any expenses on
either side) amounts to more than the self insured amount, the firm's premium
may also be loaded by up to 250 per cent for the following five years, so risk
management to avoid claims arising is increasingly important.

---

[32] Solicitors (Scotland) (Restriction on Practice) Practice Rules 2001.
[33] Sch.3 of the 1980 Act.
[34] Solicitors (Scotland) Professional Indemnity Insurance Rules 2005.

15.08.02 Incorporated Practices. Incorporated Practices have been permitted since 1987 but until this century very little use was made of them. The current rules[35] allow incorporation to take the form of a company (limited or unlimited) or a limited liability partnership. Formal recognition by the Society is needed before a practice can trade as either a company or an LLP. The rules require three months notice to be given, but this is waived regularly. Only qualified solicitors holding a practising certificate free of conditions may be members or directors of an incorporated practice either as individuals, as firms or as other incorporated practices. Limited liability only applies to business debts of the firm (including uninsured damages awards), and does not extend to accounting for clients funds. If a professional negligence claim is made, the LLP like all practice units must have insurance cover to a minimum of £1.5 million per claim. Any uninsured award will run first against the assets of the business. In addition, there is the possibility of personal liability at common law on the part of the individual whose negligence caused the loss, to the extent that it is uninsured, but no personal liability on the other members of the incorporated practice.

Each member is required to give an irrevocable undertaking to the council accepting joint and several unlimited liability to reimburse grants paid by the guarantee fund to persons who have suffered pecuniary loss by reason of dishonesty on the part of the incorporated practice or any director or employee. The memorandum and articles of association of the practice must contain provisions to deal with the situation where, for whatever reason, there is no longer a solicitor exercising day to day management and control of the practice including the operation of the client account and arrangements for making available to clients or to some other solicitor or incorporated practice the clients' papers and client funds. The incorporated practice must copy to the Law Society of Scotland any document which requires to be filed with the registrar of companies or with the accountant in bankruptcy. The need for such disclosure may have been one of the inhibiting factors behind the low take up of the provisions of the Incorporated Practice Rules. There is no minimum number of members of an incorporated practice, so that a company with only one member may seek recognition, although two or more members are required for a limited liability partnership.[36]

15.08.03 Associates, Consultants and Employees. Solicitors may practice as consultants to or associates of a practice unit. In either case the solicitor must hold an unrestricted practising certificate, but does not require to contribute to the guarantee fund. There are no rules restricting the way in which a consultant may be remunerated, but an associate must be in the employment of the practice unit.[37] It follows therefore that an associate cannot be "an associate partner" as the terms are mutually exclusive. Solicitors who are consultants, associates or employees may be named on the practice unit's nameplate or professional stationery provided that their status and designation is unambigu-

---

[35] Solicitors (Scotland) (Incorporated Practice) Practice Rules 2001.

[36] For useful information about becoming an LLP see Article in J.L.S.S. of March 2001 (by Walter Semple at p.28) and November 2001 (by David Bennett at p.23). They can also be found on *www.journalonline.co.uk*

[37] Solicitors (Scotland) (Associates, Consultants & Employees) Practice Rules 2001, r.2.

ously stated in such a manner as to distinguish them clearly from the principals of the practice unit.[38]

Solicitors who have been struck off or suspended   **15.09**

A solicitor who has been struck off the roll or is suspended from practice may not be employed or remunerated in any capacity whatsoever by a practice unit of solicitors without the prior written consent of the council,[39] nor can a solicitor associate in business with or provide facilities for a struck off or suspended solicitor.[40]

European Lawyers   **15.10**

European Lawyers[41] may apply to The Law Society of Scotland for registration but must provide evidence of professional indemnity insurance which is equivalent to that provided by the Master Policy. In addition, they must either contribute to the Scottish solicitors guarantee fund or provide evidence that they are covered by an equivalent guarantee in their home state. Registered European lawyers are subject to the same rules of professional conduct as solicitors in Scotland, including the codes of conduct and the practice guidelines issued by the Council of the Society from time to time. Given the limited market for legal services in Scotland and the large number of Scottish firms competing within that market, not to mention the climate, it is likely that Scotland will become a net exporter of European lawyers rather than a net importer.

Registration certificates issued by the Council to European Lawyers will be suspended in the event of incapacity by reason of mental disorder; sequestration; signing a trust deed for creditors; or the appointment of a judicial factor and—as with solicitors in Scotland—the suspension is ended by termination of the disability and the European lawyer may apply to the council to terminate a suspension arising out of sequestration, signing a trust deed or a judicial factors appointment which may be refused or granted with or without conditions.

As England, Wales and Northern Ireland are not separate member states of the European Union, solicitors from these jurisdictions may not seek registration as European lawyers which might be thought to be an anomaly. As mentioned above however[42] they can re-qualify in Scotland by passing certain examinations. If they have not re-qualified they may work in Scotland as solicitors qualified in their own jurisdiction, but may not use the word "solicitor" on its own to do so, as that would imply that they are qualified in Scotland.

---

[38] Solicitors (Scotland) (Associates, Consultants and Employees) Practice Rules 2001.
[39] Section 47 of the 1980 Act.
[40] Solicitors (Scotland) (Restriction on Association) Practice Rules 2004.
[41] As defined by the European Communities Lawyers Practice (Scotland) Regulations 2000.
[42] Para.1.7 above.

15.11 Multi-National Practices (MNPs)

In 2004 the 1980 Act was amended to allow the Council to register foreign lawyers (RFLs) (i.e. lawyers qualified in any jurisdiction outside Scotland).[43] A series of rules were promulgated to allow foreign lawyers to apply for registration[44] and to allow Scottish solicitors to form MNPs with RFLs[45] and to what extent.[46] The regime may appear complicated but is in fact fairly straightforward. A key feature is that the Society can only register a foreign lawyer for the express purpose of joining an MNP as a partner (or member if it is an Incorporated Practice). This is not a back door method of re-qualifying in Scotland without passing exams. The RFL cannot undertake work in Scotland reserved for Scottish qualified solicitors by s.32 of the 1980 Act. As at the date of writing only two MNP's have been recognised, although others are in the pipeline. With globalisation in the corporate and commercial field now a reality it is almost certain that this will be an expanding area in the coming years.

15.12 Multi-Disciplinary Practices and Alternative Business Structures

MDPs are a totally different creature from MNPs although the similarity of the initials can create confusion.[47] For nearly 20 years there has been an ongoing debate in the UK[48] as to whether solicitors should be allowed to practice law in partnership with advocates or non-lawyers. The former suggestion has always been rejected by the Faculty of Advocates while the latter was prohibited by statute until 1993 and is now covered by two separate practice rules.[49] Nevertheless, the Office of Fair Trading and the large accounting firms have continued to press for the prohibition on such partnerships being lifted. Such partnerships it is said would (a) introduce greater flexibility in business structures, thus allowing external investment in law firms (b) enhance client choice through the provision of a "one-stop" shop for professional services and (c) address the fact that many of today's problems are multidisciplinary in nature. While there is some truth in each of these arguments, it is also the case that many of the alleged advantages of MDPs could be obtained through law firms employing a wide range of professionals in their firms and rewarding them financially at the level of an

---

[43] s.60A of the 1980 Act. In practice most "foreign" lawyers seeking registration will be qualified in England.

[44] Solicitors (Scotland) (Foreign Lawyers) (Registration) Rules 2004.

[45] Solicitors (Scotland) (Multi National Practices) Practice Rules 2005 and Solicitors (Scotland) (MNP Principal Place of Business) Practice Rules 2005.

[46] Solicitors (Scotland) (Registered Foreign Lawyers) Etc. Practice Rules 2005.

[47] For a fuller account of MDPs see A. Paterson, "MDPs—a critique" 8 (2001) *International Journal of the Legal Profession* 155. See also the Review of MDPs contained in Annexe E *Report by the Research Working Group on the Legal Services Market in Scotland* (Scottish Executive, Edinburgh, 2006).

[48] MDPs were considered by both the Royal Commission on Legal Services in England and Wales, and in Scotland in 1979 and 1980, respectively. More recently, they featured strongly in the OFT Report on *Competition in the Professions*, 2002, the Clementi Report on Regulatory Review on Legal Services, 2004 and the DCA White Paper on *The Future of Legal Services* (HMSO, London, 2005).

[49] Solicitors (Scotland) Practice Rules 1991 and Solicitors (Scotland) (Multi-Disciplinary Practices) Practice Rules 1991.

equity partner).[50] The potential dangers for the profession and for society of MDPs controlled by non-lawyers are profound:

1) they may undermine the collegiate nature of the legal profession and its core values, namely, competence, independence, confidentiality, loyalty (in the conflict of interests context), access to justice and a particular commitment to the rule of law[51];

2) they may undermine the protections to clients e.g. in the fields of conflict of interest, confidentiality and independence, or in the shape of the Guarantee Fund;

3) they may actually create conflicts of interest whilst restricting client choice in that lawyer partners will be more likely to refer clients to their accountant/ surveyor/ architect partner, rather than the best independent adviser to do the job;

4) Multi-disciplinary partnerships as a concept create major regulatory challenges which most competition authorities have failed to grapple with effectively. Frequently it is assumed that the solution is for each profession in a multi-disciplinary partnership to regulate its own members. Yet transparency—telling the clients the different standards to which each member of staff dealing with their business will be held—is impractical. It would be a recipe for confusion amongst clients and "buck-passing" by staff and their professional bodies or insurers whenever a complaint arose. The very notion that only some of the personnel in a multi-disciplinary partnership would be covered by legal professional privilege or the guarantee fund serves to show how unrealistic such a proposition is. The public interest clearly requires a single set of standards and a single regulatory framework for all partners in a multi-disciplinary partnership. However, there is no consensus between the professions on issues such as confidentiality and conflict of interest and no obvious mechanism to achieve it, nor is there an overarching regulatory agency which could cover all the different professions which might be represented in an MDP.

The Society remains resolutely opposed to the concept of MDPs notwithstanding proposals by the Lord Chancellor to introduce legislation in England and Wales to permit them and indeed to allow anyone who is not legally qualified to own all or part of the law firm subject only to a test of "fitness to own".[52] It is difficult to see how that test could properly be set up to eliminate

---

[50] Solicitors can share fees with people who are wholly employed by them by virtue of r.4(iii) of the Solicitors (Scotland) Practice Rules 1991 (commonly known as the fee sharing rules).

[51] The Advocate General in his opinion in the *Price Waterhouse v Dutch Bar* case (Case C-309/99) indicated that while the Dutch ban on MDPs between lawyers and accountants is an appreciable restraint on competition, it is one which might be justified in the interests of guaranteeing such core values of the legal profession as independence, confidentiality and conflicts of interest. While an MDP controlled by accountants is very likely to be committed to providing the most cost-effective corporate legal services it is unlikely to have a particular commitment to the rule of law or the independence of the profession.

[52] DCA White Paper on *The Future of Legal Services* (HMSO, London, 2005) and the Legal Services Bill 2006. The *Report by the Research Working Group on the Legal Services Market in Scotland* (Scottish Executive, Edinburgh, 2006) discussed MDPs and alternative business structures in Ch.8 but came to no firm conclusions as to their desirability.

the risk of control by people with dishonest motives as the criteria would need to be objective (e.g. a criminal conviction for dishonesty) and not subjective (e.g. based on unsubstantiated suspicion however genuinely held). It may only be a matter of time before the next Enron comes around.

Chapter 16

COMPLAINTS AND DISCIPLINE

Legislative Background

16.01

The legislative framework within which the Law Society of Scotland is required to operate a system for handling complaints is fragmented; the result of a series of legislative reforms over the twenty-odd years since the principal legislation was last consolidated. The Solicitors (Scotland) Act 1980 conspicuously failed to provide (and, as amended, still fails to provide) a coherent system for handling complaints. As this is being written the Legal Profession and Legal Aid (Scotland) Bill (the Bill) has been introduced into the Scottish Parliament which, if enacted, will set up a Legal Services Complaints Commission. This commission will deal with complaints of inadequate services itself, and will pass on to the society complaints about solicitors' conduct. The Bill will give the Society greater powers to deal with unsatisfactory conduct, including for the first time the power to impose a financial sanction. At present, such a sanction can only be imposed by the Discipline Tribunal. The conduct sanctions proposed include compensation to the "client" of up to £5,000.

The Law Society of Scotland is a statutory body, and has only those powers and functions expressly conferred upon it, although it is to be noted that s.1(3) of the 1980 Act enables the Society to do: "anything that is incidental or conducive to the exercise of these functions or the attainment of those objectives". The functions referred to are "the functions conferred upon it by this Act"[1]; and the "objectives" are the broad objects of the Society defined in subs.(2). It is submitted that the better view of s.1(3) is that it confers powers that are incidental to other powers expressly conferred; rather than that it can be used to confer a power completely separate from any of those specifically mentioned elsewhere in the Act.

The starting point for analysing the powers and duties of the Society in relation to complaints against solicitors is not to be found in the 1980 Act, but in s.33 of the Law Reform (Miscellaneous Provisions) (Scotland) Act 1990. That section requires the Council of the Law Society of Scotland to investigate where:

"a person with an interest has made a complaint . . . that [a solicitor] has—

(a) been guilty of professional misconduct; or

---

[1] s.1(1).

(b)   provided inadequate professional services."

It follows that the Law Society only has power to investigate if it receives a complaint from "a person having an interest" and that complaint alleges facts which are capable of amounting to either professional misconduct or inadequate professional service, if proved.

A significant minority of the complaints received do not satisfy these requirements. These are identified and checked through a sifting process, as discussed in para.16.5 below.

16.02   Interest to Complain

The wording of s.33(1) is somewhat obscure; it refers to the situation "where a person having an interest has made a complaint". It is submitted that "having an interest" must refer to having an interest to make the complaint, but it would have been clearer if the draftsman had included the words "to do so" at the appropriate point. However, that would still beg the question "who has an interest to make a complaint?" The vast majority of complaints received come from the solicitor's own client; clearly, a client has an interest to complain. The more difficult question is "who else might have an interest?".

Others who, it is well established, can have an interest to complain, include:

- Beneficiaries, where concerns are expressed about an executry;
- a Sheriff or Judge;
- the Scottish Legal Aid Board;
- the Keeper of the Registers;
- the Council of the Law Society itself;
- the Scottish Legal Services Ombudsman.

However, a significant number of complaints received by the Law Society's client relations office[2] relate to concerns expressed in relation to the actings of solicitors "on the other side", of either a court action or a transaction. Although it is not difficult to imagine how such a person might have an interest to make a complaint of professional misconduct, there is (on the face of it) an intellectual or semantic difficulty in a person to whom no service was provided making a complaint of inadequate professional service.

Nonetheless, the concept of a person "having an interest", is clearly wider than the word "client"; The Bill defines the phrase as "any person who appears to the commission to have been directly affected by the suggested inadequate professional services" in respect of a services complaint, but there is no definition in respect of a conduct complaint. Guidance as to how "interest to complain" should be interpreted can be taken from the context in which it is used, the "mischief" which the law is seeking to control, and the incidental powers and functions of the Society. It is therefore necessary to consider conduct cases and service cases separately.

---

[2] Hereafter referred to as "CRO".

Interest to Complain in Conduct Cases   **16.03**

All allegations of professional misconduct involve issues of public protection; the Society has a very wide duty to promote the interests of the public in relation to the solicitors' profession,[3] and (it is well established) can act *ex proprio motu* in such matters. It follows that the Society should not adopt an unduly restrictive interpretation of "interest to complain" in this context. Anyone affected by the solicitor's conduct, including an opposing party in a matter, is likely to be held to have a sufficient "interest"; and it might even be, depending on the nature, circumstances and gravity of the allegation, that no greater interest is required than being a concerned member of the public.

The essential test, it is submitted, is not whether or not a person falls into a specified category of potential complainer, but whether he or she has an interest to pursue the specific complaint. On the basis of advice received, the Society would not be required to entertain a complaint from a "mere busybody", such as in the English case of *R. v I.R.C., ex parte Federation of Self-Employed*.[4] However, the Society can investigate a matter on its own initiative if it considers it appropriate.

Interest to Complain in Service Cases   **16.04**

In service cases, the test must still be whether the complainer has an interest to pursue the specific complaint which he or she makes; but the range of people who would have an interest to pursue a complaint about a specific matter will generally be narrower than if the behaviour complained of is apt to raise an issue of professional conduct. It is submitted that the complainer must have "an interest" in the level of service provided; and that it is therefore unlikely that a "concerned member of the public" could ever have an interest to complain about a service issue. Generally, the complainer will be someone who could expect to benefit from the service provided by the solicitor. The word "benefit" includes, in this context, those who would benefit indirectly such as the beneficiaries in an executry, whose position might be improved by a good service (or prejudiced by a poor one) provided to the executor.

However, even in service cases there may be circumstances in which an opponent might have an interest to complain. There are two schools of thought on the issue, but no authoritative statement of the law. On one view, a "service" complaint should only be made by the person receiving the service (or someone claiming through him); however, the new Complaints Commission are likely to adopt the more liberal view, which seems also to represent the balance of opinion, that an opponent can be directly affected by the service. Although a solicitor does not provide a service to his client's opponent, the opponent may be affected or prejudiced if a bad service is provided to the client. Examples, taken in abstract, tend to confuse the issue rather than clarify it; but one simple example will illustrate the point. If a solicitor delays dealing with a matter, the effects of the delay might prejudice the opponent as well as the solicitor's own client.

Each case will turn very much upon its own particular facts, but one of the matters which might assist in resolving the question whether a "third party" complainer has an interest to complain may be whether or not he or she might

---

[3] s.1(2)(b) of the 1980 Act.
[4] [1982] A.C. 617.

be capable of benefiting from any of the remedies which the Society can provide under s.42A(2) of the 1980 Act. Again, examples may confuse the issue, rather than elucidate, but the question of abatement of fees can be used to illustrate the point. An opponent ("A") who is responsible for paying the solicitors' fees of "B" could benefit from an abatement of fees charged by B's solicitor.

16.05 Sifting

The case managers in CRO are responsible for handling the complaints process within the Law Society. Many of them are qualified solicitors and all have some background of legal training. Because the Society has only the powers conferred upon it by statute, it must reject any complaint which it does not have power to investigate. The initial sift is currently carried out by the case manager in the CRO. The Society has no power to refuse to consider frivolous or vexatious complaints. The Bill will, if enacted, give the new commission such a power, but if the commission directs the Society to investigate a complaint the Society will require to do so and could not refuse on the grounds that it is frivolous or vexatious. Until the Bill becomes law, if a case manager feels that a complaint is outwith the Society's power to investigate, the papers are then considered by a "sifting panel" comprising one solicitor and one non-solicitor drawn from the members of the Society's Client Relations Committees. Only if both sifters agree, is a complaint rejected; if either of them considers it to be valid, it proceeds to investigation.

There is a particular difficulty where the complaint contains an allegation of conduct which might be considered to fall short of the standards to be expected of competent and reputable solicitors but could not reasonably be labelled "serious and reprehensible". Without that label, the matter cannot amount to professional misconduct (see Ch.1) and the allegation is outwith the terms of s.33 of the 1990 Act. It follows that such a complaint should be rejected by the sifting panel. Once the proposed new provisions are in force the Society will have power to consider "unsatisfactory conduct."

16.06 The Law Society's Statutory Powers and Duties

It has already been noted[5] that the statutory framework for managing complaints against solicitors is fragmented (and, currently, incomplete). The provisions which do exist generally fall into two distinct categories; those relating to investigation and those concerning disposal of a complaint. The exception is s.33 of the Law Reform (Miscellaneous Provisions) (Scotland) Act 1990, which covers elements of both categories. The effect of that section (which applies also to advocates and conveyancing and executry practitioners) in relation to the Law Society's obligation to investigate complaints against solicitors has been described in para.16.1. As to the disposal of complaints, it requires that, after investigating, the Law Society must make a written report (to the complainer and the solicitor) of:

a) the facts of the matter as found by [the Council]; and

---

[5] See para.16.1 above.

b) what action [the Council] propose to take, or have taken, in the matter.

In addition to specific powers of investigation and disposal, there are certain powers of enforcement (following disposal) which also must considered. Each will be considered at the appropriate point in the remainder of this chapter, the arrangement of which is (so far as is practicable) chronological.

At this point, though, it is worth noting that the Council has made arrangements (under s.3A of the 1980 Act) whereby its statutory functions in relation to complaints are carried out by committees or individuals using delegated powers. At present there is no statutory power to refuse to deal with a complaint on the grounds of time bar. The Society's policy is that it will not investigate a complaint made more than two years after either the end of the service provided or of the matter coming to the attention of the complainer provided the complainer has exercised due diligence. For example, if a problem with the title to a property only emerges when the client tries to sell it, and could not have been reasonably expected to have been discovered earlier, it will be investigated. However, if the client had been made aware of the problem at the time of the purchase but only makes a complaint five years later during a sale, it will be regarded as time barred. The Bill will require the commission to reject a complaint if it is not made timeously in respect of rules to be made by the commission.

Common Causes of Complaint 16.07

The potential causes of complaint are infinitely varied, and (necessarily) depend very much on the nature of the work which is in hand. Certain common themes, though, are clearly discernible. Allegations of "delay" and "failure to communicate" feature to some extent in virtually every complaint which passes through the CRO.

Clients often perceive a conflict of interest (or, at least, a lack of demonstrable impartiality) even where there is no technical conflict such as to justify an allegation of professional misconduct. Solicitors are perhaps not sufficiently alert to the need to see matters from the client's perspective and to identify situations in which it would not be improper to act but would be unwise.

Complaints and Conciliation 16.08

Having encouraged firms for many years to nominate a specific partner to supervise client relations, the Society introduced practice rules[6] in 2005 requiring all firms of two or more partners to nominate a client relations partner with specific responsibility to deal with complaints and advise the society who that is. Sole practitioners are encouraged to set up a "buddy" system for referral of complaints if the client is unhappy about speaking to the person about whom they are aggrieved. The rules require the firm to have a written procedure for handling complaints. Experience shows that many complaints can be resolved without a formal investigation if the parties, with a little encouragement, discuss their difficulties. The Law Society procedure for handling complaints therefore involves an initial informal stage during

---

[6] Solicitors (Scotland) (Client Relations Partner) Practice Rules 2005.

which the case manager will seek to clarify the issues and encourage the solicitor and the complainer to resolve the matters in issue by agreement.[7] This procedure is not applied to allegations of serious professional misconduct, nor to cases in which it is clear that the solicitor's own complaints-handling system has included attempts at conciliation and these have failed to resolve matters.

Conciliation, if it is to work at all, requires to be concluded with reasonable speed; protracted correspondence tends to lead the parties into more entrenched position, so the time allowed for conciliation is limited to 21 days. If the matter has not been resolved within that time, a formal investigation is instituted.

The Bill will give the new commission power to refer a services complaint to the firm complained of in the first place to try and resolve amicably, unless that has already been tried and failed. Even if it is tried and has failed, the commission will still be entitled to offer to mediate itself to see if the matter can be resolved without a formal investigation. Mediation is not compulsory. Both the complainer and the solicitor must agree to it.

16.09 Formal Investigation—Overview

Although the relevant primary legislation provides various powers for the Law Society in relation to investigation and disposal of complaints, it neither prescribes procedures nor (except in the case of procedural rules for the Scottish Solicitors' Discipline Tribunal) confers power to do so by secondary legislation. Although there are specific statutory provisions which can be invoked in support of the investigation, the administrative procedures, whereby a complaint is managed, are approved (and from time to time revised) by the Council, but do not appear in any formal rules or regulations.

The procedures are characterised by the following basis steps:

1. Case Manager clarifies the substance of the complaint and produces a "schedule of issues", which the complainer is invited to approve—the schedule specifies whether each issue is one of conduct, of service or both.

2. The schedule is intimated to the solicitor who is invited to respond and to provide the file of papers within 21 days.

3. If the solicitor delays responding, or does so incompletely or ineffectively, a statutory notice will be served calling upon him to comply.

4. The complainer is send a copy of the solicitor's response and may comment on it.

5. All papers are then forwarded to a reporter to prepare a report and opinion on the matter.

6. Both parties have an opportunity to comment on the report and opinion.

---

[7] For fuller information see "Improving Client Relations" (2001) J.L.S.S. September, p.8.

7. The matter is placed before a client relations committee for decision.[8]

Identifying Issues 16.10

The real issue or issues of concern to a complainer are not always immediately clear from the initial complaint. The case manager may need to seek clarification from the complainer, and that might be provided by letter or by telephone. Even when the complaint appears to be clear, it often emerges later that there are additional issues which the complainer wishes to have considered. In order to focus attention, and to avoid having additional issues raised by the complainer at a later stage, the case manager begins a formal investigation by identifying the issues which appear to require investigation. A copy of the "Schedule of Issues" is then sent to the complainer, who is invited to comment and advised that it will not be possible to add further issues later unless those issues were unknown at the time the schedule was prepared.

The schedule will show, separately, issues of inadequate professional service and issues of professional conduct. Where one fact or set of facts raises issues both of service and of conduct, there will be two separate issues listed. Whereas service issues can be libelled against an individual solicitor, they usually will cite the firm; allegations of professional misconduct must cite a named individual solicitor since our legislation, unlike some other jurisdictions, does not provide for firms to be guilty of professional misconduct.

However, the subsequent procedures for investigation are the same for both types of complaint, up to the point at which a Client Relations Committee considers the matter.

The Solicitor's Response 16.11

By the time the schedule of issues is sent to the solicitor, he/she will usually have been aware of the complaint for some time and probably will have been invited to try to resolve the matter by conciliation. The Law Society therefore expects a prompt and comprehensive response when the formal investigation is begun, and the case manager will ask that the solicitor provide:

- comments on the issues raised, and
- the relevant file of papers,

within 21 days. This time limit can be extended, on request and for cause shown, but otherwise will be strictly applied. If no response is received, the case manager will issue a statutory notice in terms of s.15 and/or s.42C of the 1980 Act, each of which is examined in detail below.[9] At this, as at every other stage, it is in the best interests of both parties that matters are progressed with reasonable speed.

The solicitor's response may be given by the client relations partner, rather than the fee earner who dealt with the subject matter; but it is essential that the

---

[8] If the committee considers that an allegation of professional misconduct is capable of being proved, it makes a recommendation to the professional conduct committee.

[9] See para.6.21 below.

individual complained against has an opportunity to comment on any allegation of professional misconduct. Whoever is responding, it should be noted that the Law Society expects a full and effective response to each allegation. Perfunctory responses such as "denied" obstruct effective investigation, do not (in the long run) assist the solicitor, and might lead to a new and separate allegation of professional misconduct. Similarly, prevarication over disclosure of the original file assists no-one in the long term and can lead to further statutory procedures.

Furthermore, on a practical level, solicitors should have in mind that, when preparing responses, they will have no further opportunity to respond to the complaint before the papers are sent to the reporter.

16.12 Further Investigation

The response provided by the solicitor will be copied to the complainer. This is for information only, although if the complainer does comment the comment will be made available to the reporter. The file will at this stage be placed in the reporter queue. However, the case manager will be expected to identify whether further evidence is required possibly from 3rd parties at this point and seek it urgently.

16.12.01 **Statutory Powers in Aid of Investigation.** It is convenient, at this point, to consider the limited statutory provisions available to the Law Society to ensure an effective investigation. These are s.15(2) and s.42C of the Solicitors (Scotland) Act 1980.

Section 15 of the 1980 Act provides for the Council to have discretion, in certain cases, to refuse a practising certificate or to issue one subject to conditions. It is not, therefore, overtly a tool for the investigation of complaints. However, one of the circumstances in which the discretion applies[10] is in the following terms:

> "when, after a complaint has been made—
>> (i) relating to his conduct[11] of the business of a client his attention has been drawn by the Council to the matter, and he has not replied or has not furnished a reply which would enable the Council to deal with the matter; or
>> (ii) of delay in the disposal of the business of a client and he has not completed that business within such period as the Council may fix as being a reasonable period within which to do so,
>
> and, in either case has been notified in writing by the Council accordingly."

The relevant part is para.(i), and it is important for solicitors to note two points. Firstly, although it is the current practice of the Law Society to warn a solicitor that the provision might be invoked, it is not strictly necessary for a warning to be given. The initial letter to the solicitor (intimating the complaint and calling for his response) is sufficient to draw the matter to his

---

[10] See s.15(2)(i).
[11] Note that "conduct of the business of a client" does not imply that the issue has to be one of professional conduct, it includes "service" complaints.

or her attention. If there is no reply, or an inadequate reply, the conditions in para.(i) are then fulfilled and the council would be entitled (without further warning) to issue the written notification required by the last line.

The second point to note, although this is not as obvious as it perhaps ought to be, is that the invocation of this provision is not an insubstantial matter. The effect is that the solicitor loses his or her right to an unrestricted practising certificate. His or her next application for a certificate may be refused outright, or granted only subject to conditions. In terms of the s.15 notice, the solicitor will need to give six weeks notice of intention to apply for a practising certificate before the start of the next practice year.

Section 42C was not part of the original Act. Under it, the Council (if satisfied that it is necessary for them to do so in order to investigate a complaint of professional misconduct or inadequate professional services) may give written notice to a solicitor or an incorporated practice, requiring:

- production or delivery of specified documents, and
- an explanation regarding matters relevant to the complaint.

The documents which can be specified include[12] all relevant "books, accounts, deeds, securities, papers and other documents in the possession or control of [the] solicitor", including any such documents relating to any trust of which the solicitor is a sole trustee (or trustee jointly only with one or more of his partners or employees). The fact that the papers relate to other matters as well as the relevant ones is not a reason to refuse disclosure,[13] and an application may be made to the court to enforce compliance[14].

The Report Stage   16.13

The reporter will be selected from amongst the members of the client relations committees, or from a panel of reporters, mainly on the basis of availability at the relevant time. Reporters may be either solicitors or non-solicitors; in either case, they have no specific statutory authority, and their involvement is thus part of the administrative arrangements made by the Law Society to enable complaints to be investigated in order for it to fulfil its statutory obligation to investigate. Although the office of reporter has no statutory basis, reporters are protected (as long as they act in good faith) from civil liability for their work by para.11A in sch.1 to the Solicitors (Scotland) Act 1980.

The purpose of the report is two-fold. Firstly, the reporter will review all the available papers (usually comprising the Law Society file and the solicitor's case file) and prepare a summary of the facts and circumstances relevant to the matters in issue. Having done so, he/she will apply the relevant statutory definitions to the facts, and express an opinion as to what action should be taken on the complaint in terms of s.33(1)(ii) of the 1990 Act.

Usually, the report will be completed within 28 days of the papers being sent to the reporter, but it can take longer than this if the matter is complex or

---

[12] s.38(2), applied by s.42C(3).
[13] s.42C(2)(a).
[14] s.42(C)(4), applying Part II of Sch.3.

voluminous, or if the reporter (having started to deal with the matter) is unexpectedly required to divert attention to other matters or needs additional information to complete the report.

16.14 Post-Report Consultation

The completed report will initially be checked by the case manager. It will then be issued simultaneously to both the complainer and the solicitor, and each is invited to comment; each will be asked to respond within 14 days. The comments of each party will not be copied to the other, since they should not raise any new issues; the Society's experience when (under earlier procedures) papers were cross-copied at this stage, was that the result was always more correspondence, but it rarely revealed anything that was not apparent from previous papers. Very exceptionally, if a new matter emerges which could not reasonably have been raised earlier, the case manager may invite further comments from either or both of the parties.

The purpose of the comments on the report is to allow both parties an opportunity to bring to the attention of the Client Relations Committee any matter (of fact or of law) in respect of which a party believes that the reporter may have made a mistake or omission, or any matter which the party believes has been included in the report inappropriately. Depending on the nature of the comments made, the case manager may invite the reporter to provide a supplementary note, but the more usual practice is that the original report, together with the comments of both parties, is placed before a Client Relations Committee as soon as is practicable after expiry of the period allowed for comments. If the case relates to service and the parties both accept the reporter's opinion and recommendations, the matter can be resolved on that basis.

16.15 Decision Making

At this point, the process moves from investigation to decision making. It is therefore convenient to consider here the "action"[15] which it possible for the Council to take in respect of various complaints.

16.16 Disposal of Complaints—Service Cases

The Council, now acting through the relevant committees, has a full decision-making role in relation to "service" complaints, including imposing sanctions when a complaint is upheld. By contrast, when dealing with a complaint alleging professional misconduct, the Council can express an opinion as a result of its investigation but the only positive "action" it can take is to make a complaint to the Scottish Solicitors' Discipline Tribunal.

In service complaints, s.42A(1)(b) of the 1980 Act specifically envisages that the council might "uphold" the complaint. There is no complementary power to 'dismiss' the complaint (although s.3A(5)(a)(i), forbidding delegation of this function to an individual, refers to the power "to uphold or dismiss" a complaint) and the usual practice is to say that the complaint

---

[15] In terms of s.33(1)(ii) of the 1990 Act.

cannot be upheld and/or that no further action will be taken. If the complaint is upheld, the council then has various powers of sanction under s.42A(2), which must now be considered.

Restriction of Fees. Under s.42A(2)(a), the Council may determine that the **16.16.01** fees and outlays to which the solicitor shall be entitled in respect of the professional services provided to the client shall be nil, or such other sum as the council may specify. A restriction of fees will be considered in every case where an IPS complaint is to be upheld. The fee is the payment the solicitor receives for the work he/she does; if the work is of poor quality, the logical sanction is to abate the fee. Where the solicitor has already abated the fee, and the extent of the abatement appears reasonable, the decision might be to formalise the position by restricting the fee to the amount billed.

There is an incidental power, in sub-section (3) to direct the solicitor to take steps to give effect to a determination limiting fees. The solicitor may be directed:

a) to refund, wholly or to a specified extent, fees and outlays already paid by or on behalf of the client; or

b) to waive, wholly or to a specified extent, the right to recover fees and outlays.

It is worth noting that the power to order abatement/refund of fees includes a power to order a refund to someone who has paid fees/outlays on behalf of the client. This could include the Scottish Legal Aid Board, or an employer who has paid solicitors' fees as part of a relocation package. Thus, this power can benefit someone other than the client.

Although these powers relate to fees *and outlays*, it is usually not appropriate to abate outlays. These are sums paid by the solicitor on behalf of the client (such as search fees, stamp duty, and registration fees), which the client would be liable to pay in any event. However, if the inadequacy of service resulted in additional outlays, then it will usually be appropriate to restrict the outlays to those which would have arisen in any event.

Remedial Action. Under s.42A 2(b) the solicitor can be directed "to secure **16.16.02** rectification at his own expense of any such error, omission or other deficiency . . . as the Council may specify". This is a very wide power to order a solicitor to take (at his own expense) action to remedy the consequences of any error or omission comprised in the inadequate service. However, a solicitor should not be ordered to do something which it is beyond his powers to do; compare the following two situations:

a) A solicitor completed a conveyancing transaction without ensuring that a necessary right of way was granted by an adjoining land-owner—he should not be ordered to procure the granting of the right of way, because he cannot do so (the adjoining landowner might refuse to co-operate);

b) A solicitor completed a conveyancing transaction but failed to register the transaction—he can be directed to secure registration, dealing with all necessary paperwork and paying any relevant fees.

This power is capable of benefiting a complainer other than the solicitor's own client. Rectification cannot involve payment of money as compensation is covered under s.42A 2(d).

16.16.03 Other Action "in the interests of the client". Unlike the previous sanctions in terms of s.42A 2(l) this one can only benefit the solicitor's own client. The solicitor can be directed "to take, at his own expense, such other action in the interests of the client as the council may specify". On the face of it, this is a very wide power; it probably is impossible to provide an exhaustive list of possible orders. By way only of example, therefore, it is suggested that a solicitor might be directed:

    a) to instruct (at his own expense) another solicitor to complete the work;

    b) to have an account of fees and outlays taxed; or

    c) to procure a title indemnity insurance policy to cover the effects of a conveyancing error;

    d) (where an error such as failing to lodge defences, has let to decree against the client and consequent credit "blacklisting") to take such steps as he can to have the listing removed;

    e) to provide a detailed accounting of the handling of client's money.

16.16.04 Compensation. The solicitor may be directed "to pay to the client by way of compensation such sum, not exceeding £5000,[16] as the Council may specify" in terms of s.42A 2(d). It should be noted that there is no power to award compensation to anyone other than the client. Thus, if a complaint is made by the beneficiary in an executry, the solicitor cannot be ordered to pay compensation to the complainer—any compensation must be paid to the executors, then distributed amongst the beneficiaries entitled to share in the residuary estate.

It is clear, from the limit of £5000, that this power can only provide limited assistance to a complainer who has suffered significant financial detriment. However, the legislation does not restrict compensation to stress and inconvenience. It is competent to award compensation for financial loss, especially if it is readily quantifiable.

If the complainer also makes a claim for professional negligence, any award of compensation made by the Society under s.42 *may* (our emphasis) be taken into account in computing damages. The Bill repeats this provision but will *require* (our emphasis) the Commission to take into account any damages or compensation awarded by a court for such a claim. There seems to be no logical basis for this difference and the only equitable approach must surely be to require other compensation to be taken into account in both directions.

It will often be appropriate to award compensation *in addition* to all or any of the other sanctions, since compensation is the only order which provides for stress/anxiety/inconvenience; the other remedies deal with the legal and financial implications of IPS.

---

[16] Increased from £1000, with effect from April 1, 2005. The £1,000 limit had been introduced on June 3, 1991.

No Sanction. Occasionally, there may be a rare case in which a service 16.16.05
complaint will be upheld but none of the powers in s.42A(2) will be exercised.
This is permissible, since the statute says that (on upholding a complaint) the
council "*may* take . . . " (rather than "*must* take . . . " or "*shall* take . . . ") any
of the specified steps. However, there is a logical difficulty in saying "the
solicitor provided an inadequate service, but he need not make amends". If the
complainer has already had compensation (through a civil court award, or by
abatement of fees), and the IPS was not serious, it might be appropriate for
there to be "no *further* sanction", but clear reasons should be given for any
such decision.

The fact, if it be a fact, that the complainer suffered no loss, prejudice or
detriment, is not normally, in itself, a reason to award "no sanction". He or
she will have suffered some stress and/or inconvenience, which usually will
merit at least a nominal award of compensation.

New Commission's Powers in Service Complaints 16.17

The new Bill contains a similar variety of powers the commission will be
able to exercise if it upholds a services complaint, apart from the level of
compensation which has been somewhat unexpectedly increased to £20,000.
The Bill gives Scottish Ministers power to increase this figure (or reduce it)
by order without further primary legislation, although they must consult the
relevant professional organisation and consumer interest groups before doing
so.

Disposal of Complaints—Conduct Cases 16.18

When dealing with an allegation of professional misconduct, there is at
present no express statutory power for the Council to take any action other
than to make a complaint to the Scottish Solicitors' Discipline Tribunal in
terms of s.51 of the 1980 Act. There is no power to "uphold" or "dismiss" the
complaint, although the anomalous s.3A(5)(a)(i) applies here as it does in
service cases. That section prevents arrangements being made for an individual to discharge the function "of determining . . . whether to uphold or dismiss
a conduct complaint (within the meaning of the said s.33(1))".

It must immediately be noted that, in s.33(1),[17] "conduct complaint"
includes complaints about both service and conduct, the expression being used
in distinction to "handling complaint".[18] This is most unsatisfactory, since
"the said s.33(1)" does not create a function of upholding or dismissing a
complaint, but merely functions of investigating, finding facts, and determining what (if any) action to take. This will hopefully be resolved if the new Bill
is enacted.

It is submitted that s.3A must be taken to be using the words "uphold" and
"dismiss" in a fairly loose (rather than technical) way. It cannot have the
effect of indirectly authorising the Council to "uphold" a conduct complaint
in the sense of finding a solicitor guilty of professional misconduct, since that
would be to confer upon the Council a power which is conferred[19] on the
Scottish Solicitors' Discipline Tribunal. Such an interpretation would require
clear words of enactment.

---

[17] 1990 Act.
[18] As to which, see para.16.21 below.
[19] By s.53(1).

Thus, in relation to a complaint of professional misconduct, the Council is required to make a report as to the facts it has found,[20] and as to the action it has taken or proposes to take[21] in relation to those facts. In making a report as to the facts, the Council must say what facts it believes have been established beyond reasonable doubt (the evidential standard for proving professional misconduct).

In order to make a transparent decision as to what (if any) action to take, it is necessary to express an opinion as to whether or not those facts amount to professional misconduct. That opinion, in order to demonstrate that the correct factors have been considered, must show whether the facts that have been found involve a departure from the standards of conduct to be expected of a competent and reputable solicitor; and (if so) whether the circumstances are serious and reprehensible, involving significant culpability on the part of the individual solicitor concerned. The Bill contains no definition of misconduct and the "*Sharp*" test will presumably continue to be the appropriate one until the courts decide otherwise. The Bill does contain a definition of "unsatisfactory conduct" which is "professional conduct which is not of the standard which could reasonably be expected of a competent and reputable firm of solicitors, a competent and reputable incorporated practice or, as the case may be, such a competent and reputable limited liability partnership but which does not amount to professional misconduct and which does not comprise merely inadequate professional services."[22]

If the facts are proved, and involve a serious and reprehensible departure from recognised standards of conduct, then a further decision is required. Section 51 of the 1980 Act enables (but does not require) the Council to make a complaint to the Discipline Tribunal. In the ordinary course of events, it is likely to follow logically that there will be a complaint if there has been a serious and reprehensible failure, but there is a discretion and it must be shown that the discretion was exercised and why it was exercised in a particular way. A guidance note setting out the considerations to be taken into account in exercising this discretion is contained in Appendix 3.

In cases where there is a departure from recognised standards of conduct but the circumstances are not thought to be "serious and reprehensible" the council currently records its findings of fact, and its opinion thereon, as required by s.33(1)(i). In these circumstances, there will be insufficient grounds to make a complaint to the Discipline Tribunal and the "action" taken or to be taken is simply to note the result of the investigation and advise the complainer and solicitor of that. In recent years such "findings" of unprofessional or unsatisfactory conduct[23] have occurred with some regularity, but lack of a clear statutory basis has prevented the attachment of effective sanctions to them. This gap in the legislation enabling the Council to sanction conduct which is unsatisfactory but is not sufficiently serious to amount to professional misconduct will be cured by the Bill. Clause 36 of the Bill will insert a new section into the 1980 Act (s.42ZA) giving the Council of the Society power to censure the solicitor; require the solicitor or any of the partners in the firm to undergo appropriate education or training; impose a fine

---

[20] s.33(1)(i) of the 1990 Act.
[21] s.33(1)(ii).
[22] Cl.34.
[23] See paras 1.28–1.29 above.

of up to £2,000; and/or award compensation "to the client" of up to £5,000.

Finally, if the facts established do not involve a departure from the standards of conduct reasonably to be expected of a competent and reputable solicitor, the findings of fact will be reported and the "action" will be "none". For the reasons mentioned above, it is not appropriate to "dismiss" the complaint.

The Committee Stage   **16.19**

At the time of writing there are currently twelve Client Relations Committees. Each of them consists of equal numbers of solicitors and non solicitors with a quorum of two of each. Committees currently have authority, by reason of arrangements made by the Council under s.3A of the 1980 Act:

a) to uphold a complaint alleging inadequate professional services, and determine which (if any) of the Council's powers under s.42A of the 1980 Act should be exercised by way of sanction;

b) to determine that a complaint alleging inadequate professional services should not be upheld;

c) to determine that a complaint of professional misconduct should not be upheld and, if appropriate, to express the opinion that the solicitor's conduct, while not serious and reprehensible, was unsatisfactory;

d) to express the opinion that professional misconduct is capable of being proved beyond reasonable doubt and make a recommendation in respect thereof to the Professional Conduct Committee.

Thus, in the vast majority of cases, it will be one of the Client Relations Committees that discharges the Council's duty (in terms of s.33(1)(i) and (ii) of the 1990 Act) to report to the complainer, and to the solicitor complained against, the facts of the matter and the action to be taken as a result thereof. The sheer number of committees raises the issue of consistency of decision-making. In IPS matters it is hoped that some form of database of past decisions might be compiled and the same could be done for instances of unsatisfactory conduct. In cases of professional misconduct the Council has instituted a further committee—the Professional Conduct Committee—in part to deal with questions of consistency and proof. Thus in those cases where a Client Relations Committee considers that an allegation of professional misconduct is capable of being proved beyond reasonable doubt, the Client Relations Committee will express its opinion and refer the matter (with a recommendation as to the action to be taken) to the Professional Conduct Committee.

The Professional Conduct Committee   **16.20**

This is a Council committee, constituted in terms of art.22 of the society's constitution, charged with responsibility for discharging the council's obligations under s.33(1)(i) and (ii) of the 1990 Act in those cases in which a Client Relations Committee has opined that an allegation of professional misconduct is capable of being proved. The arrangements made by the Council[24] for the

---

[24] Under s.3A of the 1980 Act.

exercise of its functions in this regard enable the PCC to dispose of a complaint in any one of four ways:

a) if satisfied that professional misconduct is capable of being proved, and that it is appropriate to do so, the committee may make a complaint to the Scottish Solicitors' Discipline Tribunal in terms of s.51(1) of the 1980 Act, and appoint a fiscal to prosecute the complaint;

b) if satisfied that professional misconduct is capable of being proved, but of the opinion that it is not appropriate to make a complaint to the Scottish Solicitors' Discipline Tribunal, it may express its opinion to this effect;

c) if it considers that the solicitor's conduct was unsatisfactory but does not amount to professional misconduct, it may express its opinion to this effect;

d) if it considers that neither professional misconduct nor unsatisfactory conduct can be proved, it may determine that no further action should be taken.

In February 2006, the Council approved a guidance note in respect of the tests to be applied by the Professional Conduct Committee when deciding whether a matter should be prosecuted before the tribunal. That guidance note is printed in Appendix 3.

16.21 The Discipline Tribunal

The Scottish Solicitor's Discipline Tribunal (S.S.D.T.) is constituted by s.50 of the 1980 Act; it is an independent tribunal, whose members are appointed by the Lord President of the Court of Session, and comprise both solicitors and members (called "lay members") who are not solicitors. At each hearing, there must be at least four members; at least one must be a lay member and there must be a majority of solicitor members (see Sch.4 of the 1980 Act).

Prior to the introduction of "inadequate professional service", the Tribunal's only function was to exercise original jurisdiction in matters of professional misconduct; now, it also has a limited appellate jurisdiction.[25]

If, after investigation of a complaint, the Law Society concludes that professional misconduct is capable of being proved, it may make a complaint to the S.S.D.T. (s.51(1) of the 1980 Act). If the complaint is upheld, the Tribunal has various powers available to it, under s.53 of the 1980 Act, including the ultimate sanction of striking a solicitor off the roll (the formal name of the register of qualified solicitors). The full powers are:

(a) order that the name of the solicitor be struck off the roll; or

(b) order that the solicitor be suspended from practice as a solicitor for such time as it may determine; or

(ba) order that any right of audience held by the solicitor by virtue of s.25A be suspended or revoked;

(c) subject to sub-s.(3), impose on the solicitor or, as the case may be, the incorporated practice a fine not exceeding £10,000; or

---

[25] The paucity of such appeals has made it difficult for the Tribunal to develop much of feel for such cases.

(d) censure the solicitor or, as the case may be, the incorporated practice; or

(e) impose such fine and censure him or, as the case may be, it; or

(f) order that the recognition under s.34 (1A) of the incorporated practice be revoked; or

(g) order that an investment business certificate issued to a solicitor, a firm of solicitors or an incorporated practice be—

  (i) suspended for such time as they may determine; or

  (ii) subject to such terms and conditions as it may direct; or

  (iii) revoked.

In "service" matters, a solicitor who is dissatisfied with the Law Society's determination to uphold a complaint (or with the action it took by way of sanction) may appeal to the Tribunal. This will cease if the Bill is enacted. Any review of the commission's decision in a services complaint will be undertaken by an appeals committee to be set up by the commission itself. In addition the Tribunal can uphold a complaint about service with powers in line with those given to the society.[26]

Subject to Sch.4 of the 1980 Act, the Tribunal regulates its own procedure by rules made with the concurrence of the Lord President. Up to date details (and notes of past decisions) are available from the Tribunal's website at: *www.ssdt.org.uk*. Appeals from Tribunal decisions are heard by the Court of Session Inner House.[27]

Appeals and Review   16.22

As we have seen, where a complaint of service is upheld by the Council, the solicitor has a right of appeal to the Discipline Tribunal and from there to the Inner House. Findings of unsatisfactory conduct, however, can only be challenged by judicial review. Findings of misconduct by the Tribunal can be appealed to the Inner House. The complainer, however, has no right to appeal the dismissal or upholding of a service or conduct complaint at any stage. Instead the complainer's sole remedy is judicial review or to take their case to the Scottish Legal Services Ombudsman.

The Scottish Legal Services Ombudsman   16.23

The Scottish Legal Services Ombudsman is appointed by the Scottish Ministers, and has powers to investigate the way in which professional bodies (The Law Society of Scotland and the Faculty of Advocates) handle complaints against their members. Its jurisdiction, therefore, is restricted to "handling complaints".

So far as solicitors are concerned, a complainer who is dissatisfied with the way in which the Society has handled (or is handling) a complaint, or with a decision by the Society not to investigate a complaint, may ask the Ombudsman to review the matter. The Ombudsman's main powers are set out in s.34 and s.34A of the 1990 Act. These are powers to investigate, and (if satisfied that there was inadequacy or error in the original handling of the

---

[26] Under s.42A.

[27] The court's decisions are published on *www.scotcourts.gov.uk*

complaint) to recommend remedial action including reinvestigation and the payment of compensation by the professional body to the complainer.

The Ombudsman cannot change the Society's decision, nor order the Society to do so, but it can recommend that a complaint be re-examined and can publish information if her recommendation is not followed. She also prepares an annual report, which is sent to Scottish Ministers and published, summarising her work and highlighting any general concerns arising out of her examination of specific cases.

Up to date details of the Ombudsman's work, and information about contacting her office, are available from the website at: *www.slso.org.uk.*

In view of the changes proposed in the Bill the Office of Scottish Legal Services Ombudsman will come to an end when the Scottish Legal Services Complaints Commission comes into being. The Commission will take on the oversight powers of the Ombudsman in relation to conduct complaints and will have the power to enforce its decisions.

CODE OF CONDUCT FOR SOLICITORS HOLDING PRACTISING CERTIFICATES ISSUED BY THE LAW SOCIETY OF SCOTLAND

I. The function of the lawyer in society

In a society founded on respect for the rule of law lawyers fulfil a special role. Their duties do not begin and end with the faithful performance of what they are instructed to do so far as the law permits. Lawyers must serve the interests of justice as well as those whose rights and liberties they are trusted to assert and defend and it is their duty not only to plead their clients' cause but also to be their adviser.

The function of lawyers therefore imposes on them a variety of legal and moral obligations (sometimes appearing to be in conflict with each other) towards:

    (a) the clients;
    (b) the courts and other authorities before whom the lawyers plead their clients' cause or act on their behalf;
    (c) the public for whom the existence of a free and independent profession, bound together by respect for rules made by the profession itself, is an essential means of safeguarding human rights in face of the power of the state and other interests in society.
    (d) the legal profession in general and each fellow member of it in particular.

II. The nature of rules of professional conduct

Rules of professional conduct are designed to ensure the proper performance by the lawyer of a function which is recognised as essential in all civilised societies. The failure of the lawyer to observe these rules must in the last resort result in disciplinary sanction. The willing acceptance of those rules and of the need for disciplinary sanctions ensures the highest possible standards.

The particular rules of all the Bar Associations and Law Societies in the European Community are based on identical values and in most cases demonstrate a common foundation which is also reflected in Bar Associations and Law Societies throughout the world.

THE CODE

1. Independence

Independence is essential to the function of solicitors in their relationships with all parties and it is the duty of all solicitors that they do not allow their independence to be impaired irrespective of whether or not the matter in which they are acting involves litigation.

Independence means that solicitors must not allow themselves to be restricted in their actings on behalf of or in giving advice to their clients, nor must they allow themselves to be influenced by motives inconsistent with the principles of this code. For example, solicitors must not compromise their professional standards in order to promote their own interests or the interests of parties other than their clients. Advice must not be given simply to ingratiate solicitors with their clients, courts or third parties. Non-independent advice may be worse than useless, in that it may actively encourage someone to undertake a course of action which is not in his or her best interests.

When representing clients in court solicitors appear as agents and speak for their clients, but this does not mean that they are permitted to put forward statements or arguments which they know to be untruthful or misleading. Similarly, in relation to other services solicitors, although acting as agents, must remain independent for their advice and actings to be of value.

2. The interests of the client

Solicitors must always act in the best interests of their clients subject to preserving their independence as solicitors and to the due observance of the law, professional practice rules and the principles of good professional conduct. Solicitors must not permit their own personal interests or those of the legal profession in general to influence their actings on behalf of clients; further, their actings must be free of all political considerations.

Solicitors in advising clients must not allow their advice to be influenced by the fact that a particular course of action would result in the solicitor being able to charge a higher fee. Solicitors are not permitted to buy or pay for business introductions, although commission may be paid to a fellow lawyer.

Solicitors should not allow themselves to be persuaded by clients to pursue matters or courses of action which the solicitor considers not to be in the clients' interests. It may be appropriate for solicitors to refuse to act where clients are not prepared to follow the advice given.

Where solicitors are consulted about matters in which they have a personal or a financial interest the position should be made clear to the clients and where appropriate solicitors should insist that the clients consult other solicitors. For example, neither a solicitor, nor a partner of that solicitor, is generally permitted to prepare a will for a client where the solicitor is to receive a significant legacy or share of the estate.

Solicitors are the agents of their clients and as such are not permitted to conceal any profit deriving from their actings for clients and must make known to their clients the source of any commission so arising.

3. Conflict

Solicitors (including firms of solicitors) shall not act for two or more in matters where there is a conflict of interest between the clients or for any client where there is a conflict between the interest of the client and that of the solicitor or the solicitor's firm.

In considering whether or not to accept instructions from more than one party and where there is potential for a conflict arising at a later date, solicitors must have regard to any possible risk of breaches of confidentiality and impairment of independence. If, having decided to proceed, a conflict should later arise solicitors must not continue to act for all the parties and in most cases they will require to withdraw from acting for all of the parties. There may, however, be certain circumstances which would result in a significant disadvantage to one party were the solicitor not to continue to act for that party and there is no danger of any breach of confidentiality in relation to the other party. In these very special cases, the solicitor may continue to act for one party.

Solicitors must accept instructions only from clients or recognised agents authorised to give instructions on behalf of the clients; for example, persons authorised by a power of attorney or another lawyer. Where a solicitor is requested to act for more than one party in respect of the same matter, the solicitor must be reasonably satisfied that there is no apparent conflict among the interests of all the parties and that each party is indeed authorising the solicitor to act.

4. Confidentiality

The observance of client confidentiality is a fundamental duty of solicitors.

This duty applies not only to the solicitors, but also to their partners and staff, and the obligation is not terminated by the passage of time. This principle is so important that it is recognised by the courts as being essential to the administration of justice and to the relationship of trust which must exist between solicitor and client. However, some legislation and, in special circumstances, the court may require a solicitor to break the obligation of confidentiality particularly if the client is using the solicitor to further a criminal purpose.

5. Provision of a professional service

Solicitors must provide adequate professional services

Solicitors are under a professional obligation to provide adequate professional services to their clients. An adequate professional service requires the legal knowledge, skill, thoroughness and preparation necessary to the matter in hand. Solicitors should not accept instructions unless they can adequately discharge these. This means that as well as being liable for damages assessable by a court of law for any act of negligence in dealing with a client's affairs, a solicitor may face sanctions by the Law Society in respect of a service to a client which is held to be an inadequate professional service.

(a) *Solicitors must act on the basis of their clients' proper instructions or on the instructions of another solicitor who acts for the client.*

Solicitors act as the agents of the clients and must have the authority of the clients for their actions.

A client may withdraw authority at any time by giving due notification to the solicitor. However, such withdrawal cannot act retrospectively.

Solicitors are required to discuss with and advise their clients on the objectives of the work carried out on behalf of the clients and the means by which the objectives are to be pursued. Acceptance of instructions from clients does not constitute an endorsement or approval of the clients' political, social or moral views, activities or motivations. With the agreement of the client a solicitor may restrict the objectives and the steps to be taken consistent with the provision of an adequate professional service. A solicitor may not accept an improper instruction; for example, to assist a client in a matter which the solicitor knows to be criminal or fraudulent, but, subject to any relevant legislation, a solicitor may advise on the legal consequences of any proposed course of conduct or assist a client in determining the validity, scope or application of the law.

Solicitors are free to refuse to undertake instructions, but once acting should withdraw from a case or transaction only for good cause and where possible in such a manner that the clients' interests are not adversely affected. This obligation will not, however, prevent solicitors from exercising their rights at law to recover their justified fees and outlays incurred on behalf of their clients.

> (b) A *solicitor shall act only in those matters where the solicitor is competent to do so.*

Where a solicitor considers that the service to a client would be inadequate owing to the solicitor's lack of knowledge or experience it would be improper for the solicitor to accept instructions and agree to act.

> (c) *Solicitors shall accept instructions only where the matter can be carried out with due expedition and solicitors shall maintain appropriate systems in order to ensure that the matter is dealt with effectively.*

Where a solicitor considers, for example, that the service to a client would be inadequate, owing to pressure of work or the like so that the matter would not be dealt with within a reasonable period of time, it would be improper for the solicitor to accept instructions and agree to act.

> (d) *Solicitors are required to exercise the level of skill appropriate to the matter.*

In deciding whether or not to accept instructions from a client, and in the carrying out of those instructions, a solicitor must have regard to the nature and complexity of the matter in hand and apply to the work the appropriate level of professional skills.

> (e) *Solicitors shall communicate effectively with their clients and others.*

Solicitors shall provide to their clients in writing at the earliest practical opportunity information in relation to the:

(a) work to be carried out by the solicitor

(b) fees and outgoings to be charged by the solicitor or basis upon which such fees and outgoings are to be charged, such as the hourly rate to be charged if the basis is legal Advice and Assistance or Legal Aid, the contribution payable (if any) and the consequences of preserving or recovering property should be referred to, as should a legally-aided clients liability for the expenses of his or her opponent;

(c) identity of the person or persons by whom the work will be carried out;

(d) identity of the person to whom the client should refer in the event of there being any dissatisfaction in relation to the work; unless in exceptional circumstances it is considered inappropriate to do so. Clients who provide a regular flow of instruction of the same type of business and subject matter should receive such a communication whenever the terms previously communicated are amended.

Solicitors are required to try to ensure that their communications with their clients and others on behalf of their clients are effective. This includes providing clients with relevant information regarding the matter in hand and the actions taken on their behalf.

Solicitors should advise their clients of any significant development in relation to their case or transaction and explain matters to the extent reasonably necessary to permit informed decisions by clients regarding the instructions which require to be given by them. Information should be clear and comprehensive and where necessary or appropriate confirmed in writing. In particular solicitors should advise clients in writing when it becomes known that the cost of work will materially exceed any estimate that has been given and should also advise the client when the limit of the original estimate provided is being approached.

The duty to communicate effectively extends to include the obligation on solicitors to account to their clients in respect of all relevant monies passing through the solicitor's hands.

(f) *Solicitors shall not act, nor shall they cease to act for clients summarily or without just cause, in a manner which would prejudice the course of justice.*

Where the matter in issue involves the courts or otherwise involves the administration of justice, a solicitor must have regard to the course of justice in considering whether or not to cease acting on behalf of a client. The solicitor may not simply and suddenly decide that it would no longer be appropriate to act for the client.

(g) *Solicitors shall comply with the specific rules issued from time to time by the Law Society of Scotland*

Subject to the consent of the Lord President of the Court of Session the Law Society is empowered to issue specific practice rules regarding the conduct of solicitors and other matters affecting the affairs of clients. All solicitors must comply with these rules.

6. Professional fees

The fees charged by solicitors shall be fair and reasonable in all the circumstances.

Factors to be considered in relation to the reasonableness of the fee include the:

    (a) importance of the matter to the client;

    (b) amount or value of any money, property or transaction involved;

    (c) complexity of the matter or the difficulty or novelty of the question raised;

    (d) skill, labour, specialised knowledge and responsibility involved on the part of the solicitor;

    (e) time expended;

    (f) length, number and importance of any documents or other papers prepared or perused; and

    (g) place where and the circumstances in which the services or any part thereof are rendered and the degree of urgency involved.

7. Trust and personal integrity

Solicitors must act honestly at all times and in such a way as to put their personal integrity beyond question.

Solicitors' actions and personal behaviour must be consistent with the need for mutual trust and confidence among clients, the courts, the public and fellow lawyers. For example, solicitors must observe the accounts rules which govern the manner in which clients' funds may be held by solicitors and which are designed to ensure that clients' monies are safeguarded. Solicitors who are dishonest in a matter not directly affecting their clients are nonetheless guilty of professional misconduct.

8. Relations with the courts

Solicitors must never knowingly give false or misleading information to the court and must maintain due respect and courtesy towards the court while honourably pursuing the interests of their clients.

For example, it would be improper for a solicitor to put forward on behalf of a client a statement of events or a legal argument which the solicitor knew to be false or misleading. Accordingly, if a client requests a solicitor to put forward a false story the solicitor must refuse to do so.

In the course of investigation a solicitor must not do or say anything which could affect evidence or induce a witness, a party to an action, or an accused person to do otherwise than give in evidence a truthful and honest statement of that person's recollections.

9. Relations between lawyers

Solicitors shall not knowingly mislead colleagues or where they have given their word, go back on it.

A solicitor must act with fellow solicitors in a manner consistent with persons having mutual trust and confidence in each other.

It is in the public interest and for the benefit of clients and the administration of justice that there will be a corporate professional spirit based upon relationships of trust and co-operation between solicitors. For example, the settlement of property transactions in Scotland is facilitated by the underlying trust between solicitors. A specific example of this is the payment of the price by a cheque drawn by the purchaser's solicitor on a joint stock bank in favour of the seller's solicitor. Were the purchaser's solicitor to instruct the bank to stop payment of the cheque such action could amount to professional misconduct.

It is not permissible for a solicitor to communicate about any item of business with a person whom the solicitor knows to be represented by another solicitor. A solicitor in such circumstances must always communicate with the solicitor acting for that person and not go behind the solicitor's back.

The rules governing the advertising of solicitors' services take into account the need to maintain mutual trust and confidence, while permitting solicitors to market their services effectively and to compete with one another.

10. Civic professionalism

Solicitors have a duty not only to act as guardians of national liberties, but also to seek improvements in the law and the legal system.

It is the striving by solicitors for improvement both in general terms and in relation to the individual needs of a particular client that prevents the law and legal services "from degenerating into a trade or mere mechanical act" (Lord Cooper, *Selected Papers*, Edinburgh 1957, p.77). Many solicitors fulfil this obligation through working on the many committees of the Law Society of Scotland, including those not only commenting and advising on proposed legislative changes and areas of law reform but also recommending and promoting new ideas for reform. Others are involved at the highest level with other reforming bodies and many seek public appointment, both locally and at a national level.

This duty extends beyond the issues of freedom and liberty, through the entire system of law, to the day-to-day legal services provided by solicitors.

11. Discrimination

Solicitors must not discriminate on grounds of race, sex, sexual orientation religion or disability in their professional dealings with clients, employees or other lawyers.

Legislation already provides that it is unlawful to discriminate against individuals either directly or indirectly in respect of their race, sex or marital status. However, solicitors should be prepared to observe not only the letter but also the spirit of the anti-discrimination legislation in dealings with clients, employees and others. In particular, solicitors should ensure that within their own firms, there is no discrimination in employment policy and opportunities for promotion and advancement are open on an equal basis to all employees. In addition, solicitors should give active consideration to opportunities for the disabled.

CODE OF CONDUCT FOR CRIMINAL WORK

1. Seeking Business

A solicitor shall seek or accept only those instructions which emanate from the client properly given and should not accept instructions given as a result of an inducement or subject to any improper constraint or condition.

GUIDANCE NOTE

This statement of good practice is a reminder that a solicitor is an officer of the court and as such has obligations and duties to the court. It is a reminder that a solicitor should always act properly when dealing with criminal law work.

It is essential that a solicitor should at all times remain independent of the client and that the solicitor should be free to give appropriate legal advice. Accordingly no instructions should be accepted in circumstances where it could be alleged that inducements have been offered in exchange for instructions. No instructions should be accepted in circumstances where those instructions are subject for whatever reason to restrictions or constraints which compromise the solicitor's freedom to give appropriate independent legal advice. It follows that a client should not be considered as a "friend" and that the solicitor must always remain "at arms length" from the client. This will ensure that both the client and the court can be confident that the advice tendered by the solicitor is impartial and independent.

A solicitor should accept instructions only from the client directly and not from a third party on behalf of the client. There may be circumstances in which a solicitor is asked by the family or a friend of the accused person to visit the accused in custody. It is the duty of every solicitor to check with the police station to ascertain if the person in custody has requested another solicitor or the duty solicitor. If the person in custody has indeed requested the services of another solicitor or the duty solicitor, then the solicitor contacted by the family or friend may not visit the police station.

Moreover, instructions must come directly from the person detained and not by virtue of the police arranging for a specific solicitor to be contacted who is unknown to and has not been requested by the accused.

Any instructions given as a result of an inducement by a third party on the solicitor's behalf must not be accepted. A solicitor will be deemed to be strictly liable for the actions of third parties who contact potential clients and any third party who contacts potential clients shall be deemed to have acted on the instructions of the solicitor whether or not the solicitor is instructed as a result of the third party's approach. If the client's co-accused is instructing a solicitor contact must be made through that solicitor. All reasonable steps must be taken to ascertain the identity of the co-accused's solicitor.

Solicitors are reminded of the terms of s.31 of Legal Aid (Scotland) Act 1986. Any contract of agency between a solicitor and a client which is based upon any inducement may be illegal and may be subject to action in the criminal or civil courts. Such contracts may also form the basis of a complaint of professional misconduct and may lead to disqualification in terms of s.31.

2. Conflict of Interest

A solicitor should not accept instructions from more than one accused in the same matter.

GUIDANCE NOTE

This Statement reflects the awareness which solicitors have always had of the obvious potential conflict of interest that will arise when instructions are accepted from more than one accused person in the same case, even though that conflict may not arise and the defence is common to all accused. Nevertheless, solicitors should not place themselves in the position whereby they may obtain information confidential to the defence of one accused which at the same time may be detrimental to the defence of another.

Accordingly when it becomes apparent to the solicitor that he has received instructions from two or more parties in the same case a solicitor may accept instructions from one of the accused and any others must be told immediately that separate representation must be sought.

Solicitors are also reminded that great care must be taken in situations where one of the solicitor's clients gives evidence against another client of that solicitor. The client, who is acting as a witness, is entitled to have his confidentiality respected as against the interests of the accused. In some situations, such as where the accused is incriminating or attacking the character of the client, who is a witness, there will be a conflict of interest and the solicitor should not act.

A solicitor should not apply for a Legal Aid Certificate for more than one accused person in any matter. However, a duty solicitor should responsibly carry out his duties under the Legal Aid scheme and be aware of the terms of this statement.

A solicitor may suggest that an accused seeks representation from a particular solicitor but that alternative solicitor must be based within the same jurisdiction as the accused. However, the choice of a solicitor always lies with the accused person and a solicitor must always ask an accused if he wishes a particular solicitor to be instructed before a recommendation can be made.

3. Preparation and Conduct of Criminal Cases

A solicitor is under a duty to prepare and conduct criminal legal aid cases by carrying out work which is actually and reasonably necessary and having due regard to economy.

GUIDANCE NOTE

It is essential at each stage of the conduct of a criminal case that the necessary preparation is undertaken timeously. It is essential that a solicitor should use his best endeavours to discover all relevant information and evidence relating both to the Crown case and any substantive case for the defence.

The solicitor must remember that his primary duties are to the client and the court and ensure that the case is properly prepared and there is no prejudice to the client.

Every solicitor should carry out these duties in a responsible and professional manner. With these duties uppermost in mind, the solicitor must not view criminal cases only as a means of financial enrichment.

For the purposes of cases which are legally aided, this statement is declaratory of reg.7(1) of the Criminal Legal Aid (Scotland) (Fees) Regulations 1989. Regulation 7(1) states that "subject to the provisions of regs. 4, 5, 6 and 9 and para.(2) of this Regulation, a solicitor shall be allowed such amount of fees as shall be determined to be reasonable remuneration for work actually and reasonably done, and travel and waiting time actually and reasonably undertaken or incurred, due regard being had to economy".

When requested, files and information should be provided to the Scottish Legal Aid Board.

Abuse of the Legal Aid system may be fraudulent and may be considered as professional misconduct and may lead to disqualification under s.31 of the Legal Aid (Scotland) Act 1986.

Any complaints can be dealt with in terms of s.31 of the Legal Aid (Scotland) Act 1986.

4. Identification of solicitor

A solicitor who seeks access to any party who is in custody should have in his possession an identification card provided by the Law Society of Scotland and should exhibit this upon request.

GUIDANCE NOTE

This statement is designed to prohibit unqualified employees or individuals from attending meetings with persons in custody. It will ensure not only that impersonation of solicitors or trainees is made more difficult, but also that only those persons qualified to provide independent legal advice are granted access.

Acceptable forms of confirmation of identity include the production of a valid identification card issued by the Law Society of Scotland; of a valid CCBE card provided by the Law Society of Scotland or of a valid and current practising certificate together with a form of visual identification.

5. Custody visits

Only a solicitor or trainee solicitor who has been instructed to do so may visit the client in custody.

GUIDANCE NOTE

This statement restricts access to a person in custody in a police office, prison and cell area.

There are occasions when a solicitor has taken instructions from the family or friend of an accused and has then visited a person in custody. It is the duty of every solicitor to check with the Police Station to ascertain if the person in custody has requested another solicitor or duty solicitor. If the person in custody has indeed requested the services of another solicitor or the duty solicitor, then the solicitor contacted by the family or friend may not visit the police station.

Moreover, instructions must come directly from the person detained and not by virtue of the police arranging for a specific solicitor to be contacted who is unknown to and has not been requested by the accused.

6. Property to persons in custody

A business card and legal documents should be the only items given by a solicitor to a person in custody.

GUIDANCE NOTE

It has become apparent that certain solicitors have attended to the so called "needs" of their clients in custody by providing them with cigarettes, newspapers, meals, access to the solicitor's mobile phone and money. Actings of this sort may be a contravention of s.41(1) of the Prisons (Scotland) Act 1989 which forbids certain forms of donation. In addition, this statement shall include the giving to family or friends of the person in custody any items for onward transmission.

7. Legal Aid Mandates

All legal aid mandates requesting the transfer of papers and legal aid relating to a criminal matter shall be completed and executed by the assisted person in the form agreed by the Scottish Legal Aid Board and the Law Society of Scotland.

GUIDANCE NOTE

The matter is governed by the Criminal Legal Aid (Scotland) Regulations 1987, para.17(3), which states "where an assisted person desires that a solicitor, other than the solicitor presently nominated by him shall act for him, he shall apply to the board for authority to nominate another specified solicitor to act for him and shall inform the board of the reason for his application; and the board, if it is satisfied that there is good reason for the application and, in the case of Legal Aid made available under s.24 or s.26 of the Act that it is in the interests of justice or, as the case may be, is reasonable, for him to receive or to continue to receive Criminal Legal Aid, may grant the application".

It seems clear from a plain construction of this regulation that changes of agency where the client is legally aided in a criminal case can only take place if the board gives the client authority to nominate another specified solicitor. Until the board gives its authority the client cannot instruct another solicitor unless he wishes to do so without the benefit of legal aid, which fact should be notified to the board.

Therefore the chronology of transfers of agency in criminal cases should be (1) the client approaches his proposed new solicitor to ascertain if he is willing to act; (2) client applies to board for authority to transfer the agency; (3) board grants authority; (4) client instructs new solicitor; (5) new solicitor serves mandate on previous solicitor. The board's authority to transfer must ante-date any mandate.

This statement would solve many issues including inducements to transfer agency and "mandate wars". Adoption of this interpretation would of course meant that legally aided clients and fee paying clients will not be treated precisely equally. However, that objection has to be seen in the light of the need to comply with the regulations which effectively impose a statutory suspensive condition on any mandate and the requirement that solicitors should inform a transferring client that instructions cannot be accepted until the regulations are complied with.

Any complaints about conduct under this section can be dealt with in terms of s.31 of the Legal Aid (Scotland) Act 1986.

8. Consultations with Clients at Liberty

A solicitor should not consult with a client, who is at liberty unless the consultation takes place in 1) the solicitor's office; 2) a court or 3) a hospital; a solicitor may exceptionally attend the house of a client who is unable to attend the solicitor's office due to illness.

GUIDANCE NOTE

The solicitor should not visit a client within his home unless it is impossible for the client to attend the offices of the solicitor through ill health. A solicitor leaves himself open to various allegations and indeed risks if he should attend at the home of a client. All solicitors should be aware that there is a risk. For example a solicitor could be within a house which contains drugs or stolen goods.

It will not always be possible to consult with an accused within a solicitor's own office. However, such consultations should take place within a similar office environment, such as the interview rooms within a court building. However, it is accepted that there will be occasions when it is not possible or appropriate to interview a client within an office environment, for example when the client is in hospital. The onus is on a solicitor to justify an interview at any other place if called upon to do so. The geography and rural nature of Scotland will be taken into account.

9. Expenses

No payment in money or kind should be made to an accused person, a member of the accused person's family or potential witnesses.

GUIDANCE NOTE

The only payments which a solicitor is entitled to make to an accused person, to members of his family or to witnesses are the legitimate expenses paid to witnesses who were cited to appear at court on behalf of the defence. It is appropriate for a solicitor to advance travel vouchers to a witness who shall be travelling a significant distance.

Any payment of expenses made by a solicitor should be properly recorded and vouched.

10. Defence Witnesses

Only those witnesses relevant to a case should be cited to attend court.

GUIDANCE NOTE

Ideally, a witness should be interviewed before citation. A solicitor must take all reasonable steps to obtain directly from a witness the potential evidence in a case. It is accepted that this is not always possible and indeed a solicitor could leave himself open to criticism and complaint if he should not cite a witness when he has been specifically instructed to do so by an accused person. Nevertheless, a solicitor must at all times be in a position to justify the citation of all witnesses in a case.

Defence witnesses should be cited sufficiently far in advance of the trial date to give them adequate warning of the requirement to attend court. Where possible, witnesses should be cited prior to the intermediate date in order to ascertain at that stage whether there is any difficulty about the defence witnesses' attendance at court for the trial date. Common courtesy demands that defence witnesses should be given adequate notice of their requirement to attend court as witnesses.

In providing a citation, a solicitor should advise the witness of their right to claim legitimate expenses. These include travelling to and from court. Neither witnesses nor indeed an accused person should be transported to court by a solicitor.

In recent times, it had been suggested that some persons with no involvement in a case have been cited to attend court only to provide these persons with expenses. Additionally, it has been asserted that parties have been brought to court from custody, who have no relevance whatsoever to the case but who are cited simply to allow them to meet other prisoners at court. Such actions cannot he tolerated.

Solicitors should make a point of speaking to defence witnesses at court in order, as a matter of courtesy, to advise them of the court procedure and the likely timetabling for the case in respect of which they have been cited. Solicitors should advise their clients that they as professional persons ultimately take the decision as to which defence witnesses require to be cited. Solicitors are the judges of whether or not a particular witness's evidence is relevant. In addition, solicitors should ensure that legitimate expenses claimed by defence witnesses are paid promptly. Witnesses of course require to be advised that any claim for expenses require to be properly vouched.

A solicitor should keep a contemporaneous record of his actings and financial dealings in terms of this code and provide this if so requested by the Law Society of Scotland.

11. Sensitive material and the client

11.1 A solicitor should not show a client sensitive material related to his case at all, other than in circumstances where the solicitor is present and it is possible to exercise adequate supervision to prevent the client retaining possession of the material or making a copy of it.

11.2 A solicitor should not give a client for retention by him, even on a temporary basis, copies of witness precognitions; witness statements; productions or like documents relating to his case, unless there are exceptional circumstances justifying such a course in a particular case. If the solicitor believes that such exceptional circumstances exist he should, when giving the items to the client, explain that the items must be retained securely by the client; must be kept confidential; must not be shown to others, let alone released to others; must not be copied and must be returned to the solicitor by a fixed date, which must be as soon as possible having regard to the circumstances justifying giving the items to the client in the first place.

11.3 *"Sensitive material" for the purposes of article 11.1 above includes:*

    (a) *a precognition or statement of a victim of a sexual offence*

    (b) *a photograph or pseudo-photograph of any such victim or a deceased victim*

    (c) *a medical or other report or statement relating to the physical condition of any such victim or a deceased victim*

    (d) *any document, other than a document served on the client by the Crown or by a co-accused, containing the addresses or telephone numbers of witnesses or their relatives/friends or information from which their addresses and telephone numbers could be deduced.*

GUIDANCE NOTE

From time to time the society has been asked to give its views of the practice of giving to accused persons copies of the precognitions or statements of witnesses and of other documents associated with the accused's case.

In the vast majority of criminal cases the accused is in receipt of Legal Aid and it has been judicially declared that the accused has no proprietorial claim on the case papers. These belong to the solicitor. Where solicitors have sought to justify the practice of giving copies of precognitions and other documents to an accused, they have usually done so by seeking to rely on the duty which a solicitor has to communicate information to a client and thereafter to take instructions in respect of that information.

The view of the society is that a solicitor should not give copies of precognition statements or documents to an accused, unless there are exceptional circumstances justifying a departure from this general practice. Exceptional circumstances might include a case of a particular length or complexity, necessitating giving the accused copies of documents to allow the formulation of a response. Even in this situation, the solicitor should only allow the client limited controlled access on the clear understanding that the client must keep the documents confidential and as to how long they may be kept.

In the view of the society, under no circumstances should a client ever be given possession of sensitive documents such as precognitions and statements of victims in sexual cases, medical or post-mortem reports, explicit photographs, or any documents which might disclose the private address or telephone numbers of witnesses.

There are unfortunate and worrying examples of problems which can arise if these guidelines are not observed: copies of witness statements could be circulated in the public domain, leading to witnesses being intimidated; the statements of victims of sexual crimes could be used is a form of pornography within prison; an extract from a firearms register complete with addresses and types of weapon has been circulated in a prison.

In addition, those solicitors who observe best practice find themselves coming under pressure from clients who indicate that instructions will be withdrawn if they are not provided with copy precognitions.

12. Retention of papers

12.1 *In general terms, the solicitor should be aware of the general guidelines on retention and destruction of papers as issued from time to time by the Law Society of Scotland.*

12.2 *In murder cases and other cases involving life imprisonment, the papers should be retained indefinitely.*

12.3 *In other Solemn and in any Summary case, the papers should be retained for 3 years.*

As a general rule, a solicitor might regard it as good practice in every case to retain indefinitely a copy of the complaint or indictment and a copy of the Legal Aid Certificate.

GUIDANCE NOTE

Another issue associated with case papers is the question of the length of time such papers should be retained once a case has been concluded and how such papers should ultimately be destroyed if at all.

The options for retention are:

(1) indefinitely;
(2) destruction after a fixed period;
(3) destruction at the discretion of the solicitor; or
(4) a combination of the above, depending on the nature of the case and the likelihood or risk that reference to the original case papers will be necessary.

The society is conscious of the consequences of recommending retention of too many papers for too long, having regard to the difficulties of office storage and the expense of "off-site" storage. On the other hand, certain types of cases involve offences of such gravity, complexity or high public profile, that the possibility of issues arising in future years is a real one. Solicitors should be aware of the existence of the Scottish Criminal Cases Review Commission and for the need to retain files where solicitors believe that there is a possibility that it will be of future importance to the client. Other offences may have sentence implications in the short to mid-term, for example, petitions for restoration of a driving licence after disqualification; re-imposing the unexpired portion of a sentence after re-offending. Solemn cases might be expected to throw up more difficulties than summary. In legally-aided cases, solicitors are reminded that in terms of the code of practice in relation to Criminal Legal Assistance, issued by the Scottish Legal Aid Board, records shall be maintained and accessible for a period of three years from the date of payment of the relevant account by the board.

Destruction of Case Papers

Solicitors should note that when case papers are being destroyed it is vital that this is done in a comprehensive, secure and confidential way. If the solicitor does not destroy the papers personally, then they should be destroyed by a suitably qualified commercial firm.

13. Precognition of Witnesses

When carrying out precognition of witnesses, whether personally, through directly employed staff, or through external precognition agents, the nominated solicitor or instructing solicitor is responsible for the manner in which contact is made with the witnesses and the manner in which the witnesses are actually precognosced. In particular, it is the duty of the solicitor to ensure that any matters associated with the witness of which he is aware which would affect the taking of the precognition or the mode of contact, such as age, disability or other vulnerable status, are taken into account by him and communicated to any precognition agent.

GUIDANCE NOTE

When precognoscing witnesses, a solicitor has responsibility to ensure that this is done in a way which is as sympathetic as possible to the needs of the witness. A solicitor does not discharge this responsibility simply by passing to a precognition agent a copy of the list of witnesses and asking the precognition solicitor to commence precognoscing them. Where a solicitor is aware of peculiarities of the witnesses which would affect the way in which they ought to be contacted or the way in which they should be precognosced, such as that they are children, that they are disabled in some way or anything else, the solicitor has a duty to ensure that the precognition agent is equipped with enough information about the case to carry out the precognition work properly. A solicitor who fails to ensure that the precognition agent is aware of such sensitive information which is known to the solicitor does not thereafter avoid responsibility for distress or inconvenience etc. which is caused to the witness by a failure to observe the particular characteristics of the witness.

Every witness should be contacted in writing by the solicitor in advance with effective information about the process of precognition. This should include information about to whom to complain, if things are perceived to go wrong. There should be no "cold calling". Notice should be given as to who will take the precognition and due regard should be had to the venue and timing for the convenience of the witness.

It should be pointed out that the witness may have a friend or supporter present, provided that person is not also a witness in the case under investigation.

Care should be taken with vulnerable witnesses or witnesses who might be subjected to intimidation. The nature of the charge should be considered and it might be appropriate to precognosce the reporting officer with a view to obtaining information about witnesses prior to precognoscing them.

It may be that in certain cases the gender of the precognition taker should be considered. Crimes of indecency may, at least as far as victims are concerned, be better precognosced by precognoscers of the same sex.

Prior to the taking of the precognition, the witness should be able to satisfy himself that the precognition taker is who he says he is. Those instructed by solicitors to obtain precognitions should carry identification and a letter of authority from the instructing solicitor.

In cases involving more than one accused, there will obviously be separate and different interests but liaison between solicitors can very often result in a witness only having to undergo one session rather than a number of separate sessions. Where possible, multiple precognitions of civilian witnesses by each accused should be avoided unless this is absolutely essential in the interests of justice and of the accused.

The witness should be given a copy of these guidelines.

14. Other Rules of Professional Conduct

A solicitor should at all times comply with good professional practice and the ethics of the solicitors' profession as set out in practice rules, other codes of conduct and textbooks on professional ethics.

GUIDANCE NOTE

The essence of professional ethics is such that it cannot be codified. Many texts provide guidance on the professional behaviour expected of solicitors. Solicitors have a duty to inform themselves of these texts and to approach their work in a manner consistent with the principles of good ethical practice. A solicitor acting outwith the terms of this code may be called upon to justify his conduct.

GUIDANCE FOR REGULATORY COMMITTEES IN RESPECT OF THE TESTS TO BE APPLIED BY THE PROFESSIONAL CONDUCT COMMITTEE WHEN DECIDING WHETHER OR NOT A MATTER ALLEGING PROFESSIONAL MISCONDUCT SHOULD BE PROSECUTED BEFORE THE SCOTTISH SOLICITORS' DISCIPLINE TRIBUNAL

Introduction

The Council has decided, through its Professional Conduct Committee that it is important that all those involved in the process—complainers, solicitors, reporters and committee members are fully aware of the transparency of the criteria applied in deciding whether or not the actings of a solicitor may amount to professional misconduct and whether or not to refer that conduct to the independent Scottish Solicitors' Discipline Tribunal.

The definition of professional misconduct is:

"A serious and reprehensible departure from the standard of conduct to be expected of a competent and reputable solicitor"—*Sharp v the Council of the Law Society of Scotland* 1984 S.L.T. 313.

In considering whether the "serious and reprehensible" test is met it is necessary to bear in mind the question of intention on the part of the solicitor. An innocent mistake, for example, would be highly unlikely to meet the test.

There are two basic tests which require to be met for a prosecution to be pursued. These are:

The evidential test

The public interest test.

The Evidential Test

1. The evidential test was set out and confirmed in the case of *Sharp v the Council of the Law Society of Scotland* which was reported in 1984.

   Subsequent to that case, in decisions of the independent Scottish Solicitors' Discipline Tribunal it has been made clear that the evidential test to be passed if professional misconduct is to be proved is that there must be proof beyond reasonable doubt available in order to convict the solicitor.

2. For any committee considering a report on this matter with a view to making a recommendation to the Professional Conduct Committee, it will be enough for the committee to be satisfied on the basis of the report and the evidence available that there appears to be professional misconduct and that that conduct appears to be capable of being

proved beyond reasonable doubt. If the recommendation to prosecute is accepted and a fiscal appointed, then the fiscal has the power to:

a. Review the position and seek such evidence as may be necessary to advance matters.
b. To advise if, in the fiscal's view, on the basis of the evidence available, there are limited prospects of a successful prosecution, in order that the matter may be considered further by the Professional Conduct Committee in the light of the fiscal's advice.
c. Prepare the necessary papers and proceed with the prosecution.

The Public Interest Test

In a case where the evidential test is believed to be capable of being proved then the reporter and committee should carefully consider the public interest case in deciding whether or not the matter should be prosecuted before the tribunal. In most cases where the evidential test is satisfied council believe that it will be in the public interest to prosecute a solicitor for an allegation of misconduct.

There will be circumstances, however, where the public interest does not require that a prosecution is taken.

The following are factors which the council recognises might lead to a decision not to bring a prosecution to the Discipline Tribunal.

1. The solicitor is or was at the time of the misconduct suffering from significant mental or physical ill health supported by the appropriate evidence and there appears to be little prospect of a repetition of the conduct or of further misconduct.
2. There has been a long delay between the misconduct taking place and the date of the determination unless:

   a) The delay either in whole or part has been caused by the solicitor who is the subject of the complaint.
   b) That the misconduct has only recently come to light.
   c) The complexity of the investigation has required an extended investigatory process.
   d) That the delay either in whole or part has been caused by the suspension of the investigation whilst negligence or other "proceedings" have been in progress.

3. The solicitors future intentions regarding practice where a solicitor may have indicated that he is going to retire, has retired, or has provided an irrevocable written undertaking duly witnessed with relevant medical evidence to say that he will not practice again. Provided, always, that the undertaking will not be acceptable if the undertaking is being given purely to avoid disciplinary proceedings.
4. A combination of these factors.

   Where the public interest test for prosecution is not met it remains open for a view to be expressed that the conduct complained of may amount to professional misconduct but in the particular circumstances of the complaint the matter will be noted on the solicitor's record for five years.

INDEX